NETWORK-CENTRIC SERVICE-ORIENTED ENTERPRISE

NETWORK-CENTRIC SERVICE-ORIENTED ENTERPRISE

William Y. Chang
AcuMaestro, Inc. USA

A C.I.P. Catalogue record for this book is available from the Library of Congress.

ISBN 978-90-481-7646-5
ISBN 978-1-4020-6456-2 (e-book)

Published by Springer,
P.O. Box 17, 3300 AA Dordrecht, The Netherlands.

www.springer.com

Printed on acid-free paper

Dedication

To my wife, Kathy, my son, Robert,

and all sentient beings

—William

Contents

Preface

Corporate information is skyrocketing in business values; for enterprise, what is best practice for developing and maintaining goals and standards to enhance information management and business operations?

The growing need to incorporate and exchange information across networks has driven corporations to establish infrastructure for high-distribution communities in a timely and safe manner. ***Service-Oriented Enterprise (SOE)*** is lauded as a mainstream business-information collaboration solution due to its decentralized, loosely coupled, and highly interoperable nature. Through SOE, composite applications can be created, modified, and removed in a dynamic use of services. This allows corporate information to be abstracted from existing applications and data, and creating new possibilities for assets to be either provided by external platforms or provisioned from external sources.

Within a business/commercial paradigm, SOE translates to a set of flexible services and processes that an organization wishes to make available to its customers, partners, and/or associates. From a technical perspective, SOE evolves existing integration concepts into the notion of a contract – a technology-neutral and business-specific representation of the function.

The history of the term network-centricity has represented different perceptions in the realm of enterprise services. In such traditional ***Information Technology (IT)*** domains as the telecommunications industry, networking has comprised a complex and expensive asset-management effort for service carriers. Network operators are consistently challenged to manage technologies and associated procedures that are continually growing and changing. Efficiency of resource management via network-centricity has widely been regarded as a cornerstone of business assurance.

However, as network technologies develop toward increasingly modularized and streamline design, the industry-wide shift is to a more complex paradigm – one in which single providers are no longer capable of providing comprehensive product sets to satisfy every need of their target customers. In turn, this trend has driven service providers and network operators alike from network-centric (*resource-centric*) practice, toward a service-centric business paradigm that resets focus upon ***Quality of Service (QoS)*** and service-level management.

The intent of this movement has been to improve efficiency of value-chain model integration with other service providers. Greater alliance allows service providers to leverage technology for product enrichment (through value-chain implementation), while reducing costs and risks with the relationship of destiny-sharing. In a context of service-provider operations, both network-centric and service-centric practices aim to support horizontal interoperability and efficiency. Some companies, marketing perspective, promote the idea of user-centricity, proclaiming their strategies are proactively driven by their end customer's desires.

This means that, while corporate entities have striven to improve value-chains by creating more "what-users-want" products, rapid advancements in business and technology have indicated that optimal functionality rests with neither service-centric nor user-centric practices. In essence, outcome numbers are still intimately linked to levels of efficiency and effectiveness in corporate operations both vertically and horizontally.

Following the advent of TCP/IP and the Internet, both of which have wielded tremendous socioeconomic impact worldwide, the ***Department of Defense (DoD)*** initiated a new IT revolution. Based upon the ***Global Information Grid (GIG)*** model, and focusing on performance outcomes of organizational adaptation, survival, and competency, ***Network-Centric Operations (NCO)*** was created to address networked information sharing and decision efficiency.

The applications of NCO are used by DoD in next-generation battle applications for mobilized soldiers to obtain and provide thorough warfare awareness in any place at any time. The vision of NCO is to foster an agile, robust, interoperable, and collaborative organization in which martial, commercial, and covert users all share knowledge on a secure and dependable global network.

NCO enables excellent decision-making, effective operations, and efficient process transformation. The concept of network-centricity in this new context is no longer about telecommunications networks or computer networking; rather, it regards an emerging body of organized behaviors pertaining to real-time information management. This unprecedented level of information collaboration allows users and systems to share insights and add values to a sharable knowledge community.

NCO is markedly different from a data-centric paradigm where data is centralized for access – it allows geographically disparate users, units, and organizations to act as a cohesive team. In sharing a common business-operational picture, the process of information position to action (a figure that DoD calls "speed of execution") is optimized.

This invention has informed the direction of enterprises in different ways than in the defense industry. In the commercial arena, adoption of SOE encourages enterprises to employ ***Service-Oriented Architecture (SOA)*** as the supporting technology. Yet, as business operations began moving away from the legacy flow-through process into an SOA-based flat and peer-to-peer framework, some weaknesses of pure SOA surfaced. For instance, some crucial business attributes and relationships were sacrificed for SOA transformation, and the new stateless paradigm requires intricate service designs to compensate for displaced hierarchical relationships. Additionally, while SOA has reached a certain level of maturity in most deployments, it remains in its nascent phase per wireless applications, especially with ad-hoc networking.

Network-centricity in general business operations assists in making any system's business data available to all users at any time, subject to security and access controls. Another notable feature, from an implementation perspective, is that new systems only need to be developed when new information is required.

To differentiate from the military's NCO, the term ***Network-Centric Business Operations (NCBO)*** is used throughout this book to detail illustrations of enriched and generic enterprise applications. In essence, it is this combination of business policies, techniques, and procedures that allows networked resources to create decisive ***Information Superiority (IS)*** in business operations.

A cornerstone of successful NCBO is up its ability to leverage enterprise services and capacities in order to share workforces across departments, organizations, or companies. Such capabilities amount to an optimization of corporate-data management. Supported by reliable, consistent, and predictable communications between services that are deployed across a distributed enterprise, NCBO can reach higher standards in business fulfillment and assurance.

The insights and values of this new concept are critical to an enterprise's success; thus, it should be seen as a general advantage to business operations. Furthermore, exposure of NCBO to the whole enterprise as an integrated framework (work processes, data flows, Web services, network communications, et al.) can impact existing corporate cultures. An example: the on-demand computing feature of NCBO, capable of dynamically shifting work between similar services and routing the results, can help enterprises to identify and leverage similar or redundant resources. This forces an enterprise to reshape its organizations and responsibilities.

Network-Centric Service-Oriented Enterprise (NCSOE) is seen as heralding the next generation of enterprise-level business information collaboration. Using an NCBO framework, NCSOE can enforce information and decision superiority in decentralized, loosely coupled, and highly interoperable service environments. From a standpoint of system integration, this book establishes a system-to-system view of information technologies, offering a synergistic combination of data- and information-processing capacities upon an innovative network-management framework.

Maximizing the advantage of SOA openness, NCBO presents compelling additions to support optimization of corporate performance and investment yield. Although GIG working with SOA is not a new idea (in fact, many government projects such as Federal Enterprise Architecture have comprehensive requirements in project management and interface standards), it is worthwhile to acknowledge that the uniqueness of this book is its practical focus upon tightly integrated business policy, quality-control monitoring and capabilities, and wireless network technology that addresses the entire spectrum of NCBO implementation.

This book begins by examining current service-oriented technologies and their associated service-management aspects, including two detailed models courtesy of DoD and ***TeleManagement Forum (TMF)***. Subsequently, these subjects are extended to cater to wireless-networking technologies in transport services, concentrating upon ad-hoc networking and sensing applications. Attention then is given to areas of service management – specifically, monitoring and control for QoS and ***Information Assurance (IA)*** are addressed. The concept of integrated IA stands beyond the existing security scope, presenting a rule-based framework in which data security is incorporated within the enterprise-data strategy. Currently, integrated rules permit business missions to be closely interrelated with assurance requirements.

Establishing and expanding upon an integrated data and information strategy is the main thrust of this book. A knowledge-management chapter herein examines current methodologies alongside the concept of NCBO. Different advanced data fusions are profiled in the chapter as foundations for accomplishing IS. To contend with accelerating changes in technology and services, guidance per implementation and management for emergent Enterprise 2.0 technologies is given in the book's final chapter. This book concludes with a glimpse of potential NCBO applications in SOE, including: financial operations, customer-relationship management, workforce management, and telecom-business process management.

William Y. Chang
Irvine, California
July 2007
www.ncsoe.com

Foreword

Today's enterprise platforms and software businesses comprise a dauntingly complex environment that challenges nearly every aspect of corporate operations. This overall complexity is particularly apparent in the critical areas of software development, computer networking, system integration, service delivery, and quality assurance.

The core component and critical enabler of a Service Oriented Enterprise is the Service Oriented Architecture (SOA) and Common Operation Picture (COP) technologies. SOA is a style of information system architecture that enables the creation of applications built by effectively combining loosely coupled and interoperable services. An effective implementation of SOA and COP lies upon a network-centric business operation while information is collected and organized into sensible intelligence and knowledge.

The Network-Centric Service Oriented Enterprise (NCSOE) presents a system-of-systems framework that can assist the system integrators and solution vendors in establishing a feasible path for achieving operational openness and efficiency. For instance, applications of Platform as a Service (PaaS) adopts the concept that platforms are costly, therefore the ability to create a platform through a subscription service can avoid associating applications on one physical platform. As the result, the corporate applications, data, and users can be moved around more effectively and economically. While the virtualization paradigm may introduce overhead and impact the computing performance, NCSOE offers a new breed of solution that improves the speed of communication by breaking through the barriers of business domains and application segments.

Being a seasoned system integrator, the author offers a staging guidance with practical samples and methodologies for the development and fielding of network-centric, service-based solutions for different business sectors. The content of the book provides a useful background for readers who are interested in practicing service-based business, operations, engineering, networking, knowledge-management, and cross-value-chain integration. It is a reference book that architects, developers, and technical managers may well want to keep handy when designing network-centric solutions for the enterprise.

William J. Wanke
President
Service Delivery Solutions
Telcordia

Acknowledgments

Many people have played a part in the development of this book. I would like to thank Mark Jongh de at Springer for agreeing to publish this book as well as providing guidance for the manuscript development. I would also like to thank Cindy Zitter and Werner Hermens (Springer) for doing a great job of coordinating the review and correction of the manuscript into final product.

My gratitude is extended to Kenneth Evensen (PM Networking Waveforms, JTRS, USA Army), Rick Gallher, Wayne Howe (Integrated Defense System, Boeing), Richard Lau (Applied Research, Telcordia), Jim McDevitt (OSS Development, Telcordia), Benjamin Gallher, and Dave Barnes (Operations, AcuMaestro) who helped me formulate the book proposal and provide invaluable comments toward the structure and main values of the book.

I am particularly grateful to the inputs from Ram Khare (FCS Network Performance and Architecture, SAIC), Ning H. Lu (ITT Aerospace/ Communications), and Oliver Wang (FCS Network Management, Northrop Grumman Corporation) for providing their research works for my reference and verifying the technical accuracy of this book. A special thanks and recognition to Ram Khare, Harry McCabe (FCS SoS Common Operational Environment, SAIC), and Sean Harnedy (TSAT, Booz Allen Hamilton) for smoothing the rough edges of my technical prose and making many excellent suggestions that led to a lot of improvements in the book.

This book could not have been completed without referring to many TeleManagement Forum (TMF) documents. Thanks go to Ian Best and April Davis for their prompt approval of using the TMF's TOM, e-TOM, and NGOSS publications.

My sincerely thanks go to my management across several companies. I thank Eric Bick, Pete Campanella, and Curt Williams at SAIC for assisting me to obtain the publication approval from the FCS program. I also thank Don Silberg at Boeing and Mike Davenport at Booz Allen Hamilton for supporting my goal to pursue the interest in network-centric business operations. These gentlemen exemplify the highest standard of intelligence, dedication, and commitment to quality that make working with these companies a rewarding experience.

Chapter 1

INFORMATION SUPERIORITY

Information technology (IT) oriented enterprises have entered into a new era where information sharing within the company is no longer just application-to-application or machine-to-machine. Traditionally, these platform-centric computing applications offer vertical benefits that fulfill the functional requirements of a particular company within an enterprise. One of the most vibrant and revolutionary subjects in the area of business performance management today is the new network-centric view of business practice that provides bottom-line benefits. A networked business environment that can provide reliability, performance, and access to core business information and processes is an ideal environment for the next generation enterprise.

Network-Centric Business Operation (NCBO; section 1.4*)* is the integration of all stakeholders within the enterprise, and can extend to include (in a secure and controlled manner) other business partners.

NCBO is different from the telecommunication industry's "network-centric" systems that focus on the performance of physical connectivity as driver of business operations; NCBO is part of the next generation Information Management, comprising the enterprise's core technology and operational platform. NCBO thereby possesses a collection of combined business policies, techniques, and procedures to ensure that networked information is seamlessly employed to create decisive *information superiority*.

Thus information superiority and the operational spirit of NCBO go beyond telecommunications networks or computer networking; it becomes a concept of business and organizational behavior. With this new understanding, the potential applications of NCBO can contribute to the coalescence of the tactical, operational, and strategic levels of service-oriented business management.

One of the key features provided by NCBO is its capability to support speed of execution – the conversion of superior information into action that compensates for the weakness of the existing *Service-Oriented Architecture (SOA*; section 1.3*)*. The focus of this chapter is to provide insights into why marrying NCBO and SOA is critical for an enterprise's success. This chapter provides the necessary descriptions of the new concept, major functional components, and methodology that will be used throughout the entire book [1].

1.1 Information Management

Information Management (IM) is the foundation for achieving information superiority. Operational advantages of information superiority are obtained through the systematic provision of clear, accurate, and useable information. This section portrays the history, scope, and business drivers of Information Management.

1.1.1 What Is Information Management?

Information Management achieved a high visibility in the mid-1970s as the *National Commission on Federal Paperwork* was seeking cost reduction in satisfying the demands for paperwork by the Federal bureaucracies. In its early days, Information Management had limited definition. It only included data resources such as production data, market research data, and personnel records. In this limited scope, Information Management largely dealt with files, file maintenance, and life-cycle management of paper and a small number of other media. At that point in time, Information Management only encompassed the knowledge of what documents existed regarding a particular subject, where they were located, what media they were stored on, who owned them, and when they should be destroyed [2].

By the late 1990s when information was regularly disseminated across computers and other electronic devices, Information Management had evolved into a powerful resource for organizations. The information operations shifted from passive document management to a progressive business knowledge acquisition capable of collecting one or many disparate knowledge sources.

Under the new role, Information Management deals with the value, quality, ownership, use, and security of information in the context of organizational performance. The current service-oriented computing environment has given enterprises open access to common processes, application services, and information. Through a browser, business organizations can eliminate the need to support multiple interfaces, multiple versions, duplicate functionality, and fractured operational data versions.

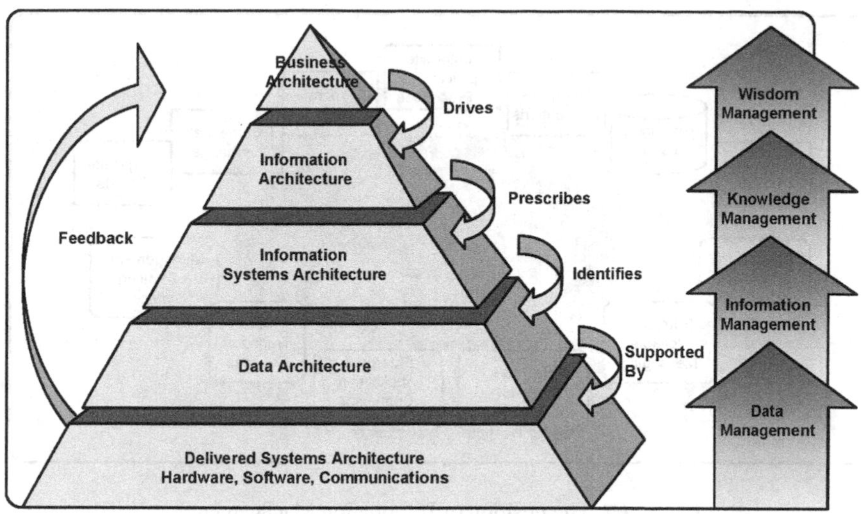

Figure 1.1. The requirements of Information Management.

Figure 1.1 uses a stacked arrow and a pyramid figure to illustrate this trend. In the arrow chart, enterprise data can be processed from the "raw" data to sensible business information, to knowledge for improving tactical business tasks, and ultimately to business wisdom upon which executives can make strategic decisions. The pyramid figure depicts a process life cycle of end-to-end Information Management. In this bidirectional flows, the business architecture [3] delineates the means by which an organization efficiently plans, collects, organizes, uses, controls, disseminates, and disposes of its business missions. Through information architecture, the enterprise ensures that the contents and values of that information are identified and exploited to the fullest extent down to the system level. Data architecture and the bottom layer deliverables, in turn, address the implementation and operational aspects of repository, translation, monitoring, reliability, performance, and accessibility of the deployed services. At every layer of the pyramid, feedbacks are essential for the adjacent higher layer to be aware of any potential gaps or areas of improvement.

1.1.2 Drivers of New Information Management Paradigm

The new Information Management can be envisioned as organizing and utilizing data, adapting to the knowledge [4] world by incorporating new responsibilities for strategic thinking that cut across organizational boundaries and business partners, and to inform executives and service managers about business conditions that demand immediate action. Figure 1.2 depicts the position of Information Management with other enterprise functionalities:

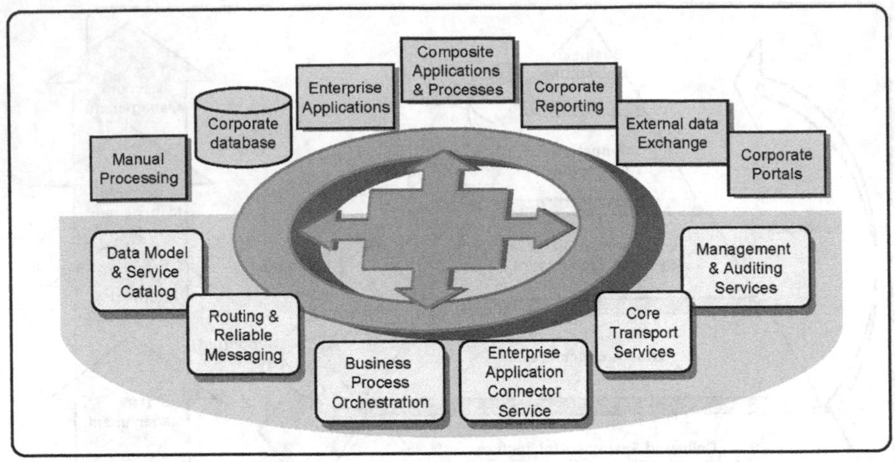

Figure 1.2. The position of Information Management.

Today, information silos are the bane of most organizations as they try to integrate and share data to get a clearer understanding of customers, products, and other objects of interest. In addition, regulatory compliance, performance management, and collaborative business relationships demand a single view of relevant information [2,5]. Expectations of the new Information Management include full capabilities of an enterprise to provide a successful balance of technologies, processes, competencies, and skills in order to ensure the managed information is focused, coordinated, measured, supported, and controlled across the business. A common goal of achieving corporate transformation to the new method can be facilitated by high-level business processes and the proper adjustment of personnel roles and responsibilities. A successful transformation can increase the enterprise's competitive positioning. Today's drivers for the improved Information Management can be summarized as Business, Technology, and Operations [6,7].

1.1.2.1 Business Drivers

The requirement of information-intensive interactions has moved underlying economics significantly. Businesses require increasing competitive advantage, and the aiding of strategies through both IT and the commercial and corporate usage of information networks. Corporations establish symbiotic relationships with their value-chain partners and belong to a part of a continuously adapting ecosystem to increase the speed and profitability in both sales and services. Integration needs to be accomplished in both the vertical as well as horizontal directions. Horizontally, timelines can be compressed by linking suppliers and customers. Vertically, demanded product and productivity can be achieved by the integration consisting of a high-powered information grid [3,8,9] a sensor grid, and a transaction grid.

Emerging industries and business collaboration requires in-depth Information Management to improve their strategic decision-making. To ensure successful execution of a tactical mission in the corporation, the enterprise needs to address the business, organization, people, processes, and culture that are suitable for cross-enterprise operations. The resources identified in the new business model may dictate the socialization of the service-system approach. To achieve this new business goal, corporate employees need a richer understanding of the data and its context above their existing practices. An example of this is that integrated information silos that realize horizontal data fusion (chapter 8).

Enterprise-level collaborated templates implement the strategy for common shared services and provide guidelines for cross-channel and cross-enterprise services. Using these can significantly reduce the turnaround time for publishing information across the organization. Furthermore, improving the organization's and the individual's visibility to accurate information can influence the quality of the products and services.

1.1.2.2 Technology Drivers

For enterprises that provide information products to their customers, the exploded and growing demands of information sharing and interactions among applications have impacted individual user's behavior as well as the service provider's strategy to macroeconomic issues. Web-based technologies, combined with high-volume, high-speed data access, and technologies for high-speed data networking are leading to the emergence of network-centric computing. For example, the emergence of the Google network publishing model allows any information to be created, distributed, and easily exploited across the extremely heterogeneous global computing environment. This so-called "Google Grid" married with on-demand service can seamlessly support in-band data delivery, broadcast, and pay-per-view services for highly profitable customer-centric businesses.

Converged network technologies allow very high-speed networks employing coaxial cable, optical, and wireless techniques to simultaneously deliver all types of content such as traditional computer data, downloaded or streaming music and radio, Internet-based telephone (e.g., VoIP), and *Video-On-Demand* (streaming video). The trend of wireless technology has gone beyond the *third generation (3G)* networks (chapter 3). Service providers aim to provide a high degree of mobility enabling users to access ubiquitous services "anywhere, any time" by a rapidly proliferating choice of high-speed wireless connectivity options. Examples of wireless mobile networks include the Institute of Electrical and Electronics Engineers (IEEE) 802.11 series for hot-spot application, the 802.16 WiMAX for longer range communications, and Bluetooth for shorter distances.

Mobile networks are spontaneous in nature and highly self-organized. This means the network can be rapidly formed or dissolved by the participating devices (chapter 3). One of the most noticeable mobile network applications is autonomic data sources, or intelligent sensors (chapter 4). The sensing applications are traditionally used for environmental monitoring (e.g., humidity for agriculture- and weather-forecast, and vibration for volcano- and earthquake-monitoring) or military applications; European and Japanese car manufacturers are beginning to incorporate ad-hoc networks with sensors in automobiles for collision protection.

Emergent networks involving on-demand alternatives such as mobile networks introduce a new level of economic benefits and tie contents and *Quality of Service (QoS*; chapter 7*)* into the service feature. The network management policies and tools which empower effective information exchange across their service sectors become essential to the enterprise's service management (chapter 5). Managing highly flexible and dynamic networked applications presents very difficult technical and operational problems to solve. Although the traditional management for a land-line network is mature in every aspect, there is still no integrated network management available that is capable of managing these new types of heterogeneous networks (infrastructure and infrastructure-less).

1.1.2.3 Operational Drivers

Information Management is shifting from being a business enabler to being a business contributor, and is playing a central role in the future of business strategy. To a certain extent, effective business management does not solve business problems unless it is tied directly to business and governance objectives. Figure 1.3 illustrates this cross-relationship where business assurance and corporate-rule compliance form a centerpiece situated between the corporation's values and operational efficiency. As shown, enterprise risk management is driven by compliance and business assurance capability. By aligning Information Management with business objectives, information becomes a business contributor and can assure the business meets its vision and goals.

At the strategic level, such assurance is applicable to legislation such as *Sarbanes-Oxley (SOX)* and *Health Insurance Portability and Accountability Act (HIPAA)* (i.e., rules and practices that corporations must follow to keep financial reports correct and reliable and securely accessible), International Financial Reporting Standards such as *Code of Federal Regulations (CFR) Part 11*, risk management, compliance management, and operational compliance.

At the tactical level, data analytics for service or production monitoring, quality, performance, satisfaction, risk, and auditability can be improved.

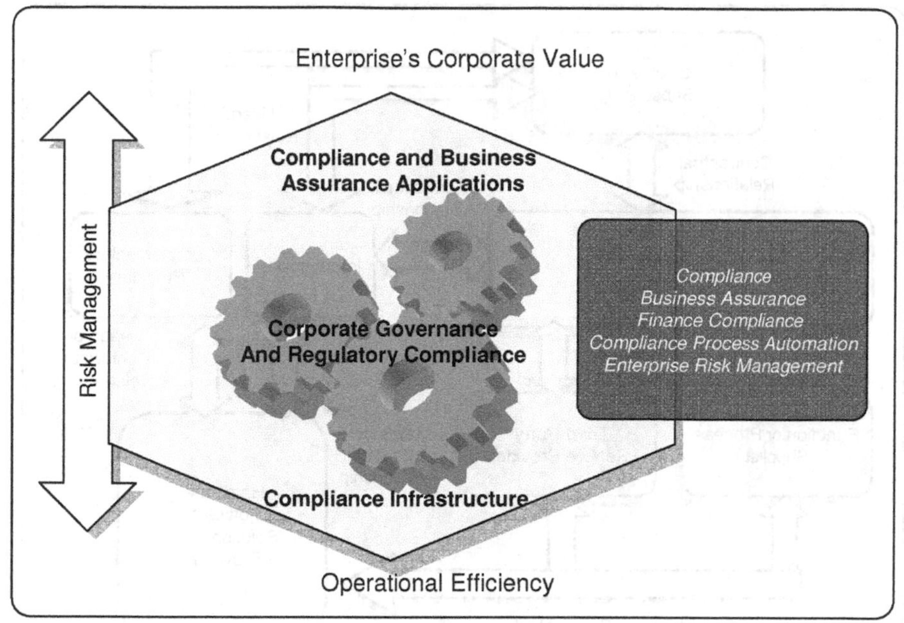

Figure 1.3. Business assurance relationship chart.

Appropriate control and feedback mechanisms can provide enterprises continuous enhancement of both new and existing processes.

A *Service Level Agreement (SLA)* [10] is a contractual agreement between a service provider and a customer, between cooperating service providers, or interorganizational; it mandates specific service objectives. The applications of SLAs in interorganizational agreements are seen in help-desk services, network performance monitoring, and other internal processes. Quality measures and penalties/costs for a specific SLA agreement are defined within and tracked by the system called *Service Level Management (SLM*; section 9.7*)*. It is important that SLM have a real-time capability to track the governance specifications including service levels, problems, improvements, and costs to enforce the compliance rules for managing business services. An effective SLM should possess a governance model mapping corporate, business, and technological policies, and ensuring appropriate resource allocation, services utilization, technology compliance, and security. Networked with *customer relationship management* (CRM), SLM can assist marketing and customer service employees to obtain a clearer understanding of customers. Figure 1.4 portrays a typical flow of a wireless carrier where a home/primary service provider has multi-ladder SLAs with different service providers in the value chain, including function and process

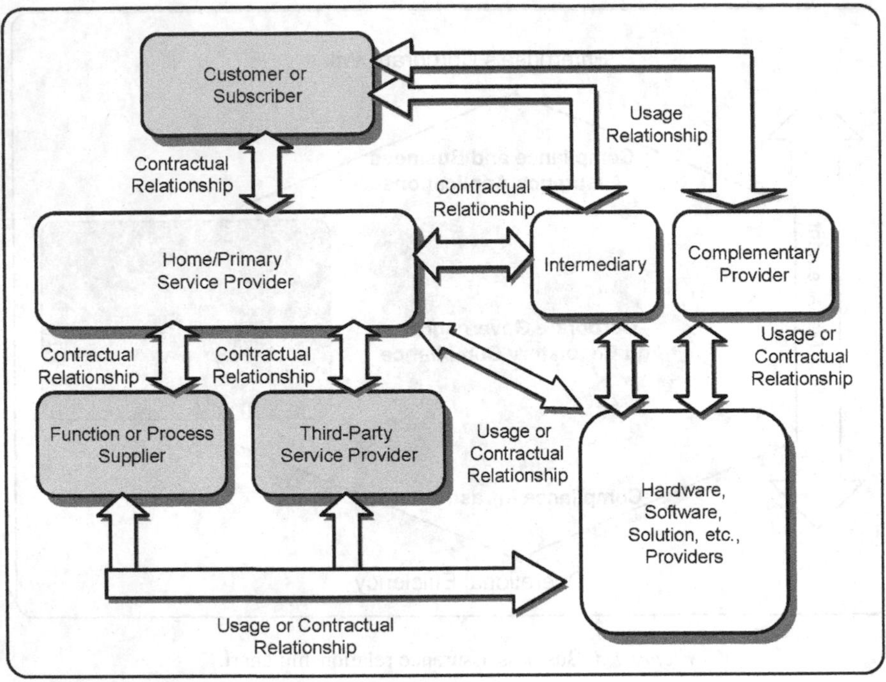

Figure 1.4. Service providers' relationship chart.

service providers, third-party service providers, hardware/software service providers, and so forth [10,11].

Service discovery occurs when a service consumer accesses information or resources during use. Discovery promotes reusability, minimizes redundant efforts, enables loose coupling through service virtualization, and facilitates the implementation of applications through service composition and orchestration. Through a standards-based registry mechanism, service users can always "plug-and-play" with the latest and greatest services offered by the providers and do not have to keep track of the location of the service provider. From the service provider's perspective, service discovery provides the registry platform for publishing and organizing networked services for discovery without having to change the configuration and architecture of the existing services. In summary, run-time discovery facilitates information exchange in a fast moving (e.g., disaster recovery mission) environment where resource discovery and traffic management can be commanded in an ad-hoc nature.

Services and capabilities can be leveraged to share work across providers for both pre-planned and ad-hoc tasks, such as *automatic farming* for on-demand computing. In mission critical applications, business transactions in an open network demand a robust security framework, including encryption and authentication. *Role management* concerns the services that are executed on behalf of some user or user role. It also manages whether a service can act as an autonomous agent acting on behalf of the enterprise or some *Community of Interest (CoI*; section 8.1.1*)*. To satisfy the new business requirements, installation of transport and message level security at multi-hop scenarios to manage across boundary conditions is important. Some intermediary examples include routers, policy enforcers, and business process coordinators.

Equally important are disaster recovery, business continuance, and disaster management. They define functions and architecture features that are critical components of the new Information Management infrastructure.

1.1.3 Achieving Information Superiority

Knowledge is power. The generation and exploitation of competitive awareness has emerged as a key enabler of effective decision-making and a principle component of competitive advantage in many sectors of the economy. Dominant competitors, as shown in many applications, can generate a high degree of awareness in their respective business domains and in extended business ecosystems. The benefits of utilizing the new Information Management are as follows [6,12]:

- With the extended information from corporate contacts, connections, and channels of communication, the enterprise users are able to expand their reach into mission terrains, service fields, markets, or suppliers that are not available in their private domains.
- By providing access to a wealth of relevant information and knowledge, including the latest analytical reports, action plans, operational picture, and the insights of *subject matter experts* (SMEs), the information users and enterprise executives can reduce information uncertainties and risks to promote a higher level of business and situation awareness.
- When available knowledge and wisdom are beyond the original scope, it can sometimes provide the enterprise executives a different perspective toward a business case. The new vision can give them the power to eliminate or reduce obstacles, or even convert potential competitors into operational partners.
- Based on the additional knowledge, the enterprise can align with larger value-chain partners to pursue broader common interests. As a result, anything that benefits one of the value-chain partners also benefits the enterprise.

- The enterprise executives can use the superior information in the partnership negotiation to produce a positive spiraling effect or downward spiral in an enterprise's favorable direction, depending upon different situations.
- The new insight of business operations or intelligence that have direct or indirect influences to one business case can reduce the amount of time, energy, systems, and services that must be devoted to conflict resolution and stress management. This result allows the enterprise users or executives to free up resources for more profitable pursuits.
- The availability of information with respect to resources, talents, and strengths that are controlled by other business identities can empower the executives by multiplying their enterprise's capabilities and compensating for their limitations.
- With continued success in the industry, the frame of positive business practices can make the enterprise a more positive, ethical, and friendly place to work. This in turn attracts better employees.

To achieve Information Superiority, this book aims to provide an enterprise level solution using the service-oriented paradigm. In section 1.2, the *Service-Oriented Enterprise (SOE)* will be articulated at the blueprint level, describing the "what" of the solution. In section 1.3, the Service-Oriented Architecture addresses how the solution will be constructed. These following two sections cover Service-Oriented Computing starting with the concept of Network-Centric Business Operations; additionally, the enabling Information Management functionalities to support the enterprise services are highlighted.

1.2 Service-Oriented Enterprises

Enterprise in the context of this book is defined as an organization or cross-organizational entity performing with a specific business scope and mission. Decision-making in an enterprise environment is heavily influenced by dynamic patterns of collaboration and associated with different levels of accountability. This requires information integration across the management processes, operational processes, and supporting processes scattering across many functional areas as different services.

1.2.1 Service and Service Types

A service is a reusable logical object that exists as an independent functionality or mixed with other services. It is offered by a service provider to a consumer or a user through a contractually defined "interface". A service can be implemented by a set of software, process, procedure, or the combination of the three. Each service can offer one or more operations or functions. In this sense, a service becomes a commodity. Thus, the consumer of a service is not concerned with implementation details [13,14].

A service interface contains some combination of syntactic, semantic, and behavioral information which specifies the provider's obliged action on behalf of the consumer and the consumer's responsibilities in using the interface. The syntactic information delineates operations that provide the functionality of the service. A separation between semantic and syntactical descriptions allows the customer to discover whether two services perform the same or similar tasks. A complete service interface should include two specifications to address the consumer and the supplier aspects. The service customer specification addresses the consumer-oriented aspect of a service including a separate specification for each interface and their associated operations, such as functionality, cost, and expected service quality. The service provider specification addresses the supplier-oriented aspect of a service describing the implementation constraints that govern a solution or solutions which realize the service.

Conceptually, the implementation of service can be an independent effort where the service customers can start utilizing portions of the offering while the providers are still delivering the same service through the same interface. It is also important to note that not all functionality needs to be offered as services although most enterprise processes or sub-processes will eventually evolve into them. The enterprise services can be classified as the following three types:

- Commodity Services are the functionally generic and stable service group for an enterprise. Examples of these services are employee salary and benefit managements. Because this type of service can be rather generic and ubiquitous for use at low risk of failure or poor performance, it is often a candidate for outsourcing.
- Core Business Services are the service group that represents the essential characteristics of the enterprise and supports their core business attributes. These services are likely to be volatile and require a certain degree of change due to the nature of business competition. Examples of this service type are pricing management and customer relationship management. These services can be self-contained but often reusable during different offering life cycles.
- Value-added Services are a set of functionalities which can reflect the special value an enterprise can offer to a target market. As a market differentiator against its rivals, the enterprise's offerings are often highly innovative and require constant changes to maintain its competitive advantage. Examples of this service type are new technology and new value-chain flows. To exploit value-added features to the market quickly,

these services should be designed with more dynamic paradigms to reduce the risk of time-to-market.

As seen in the above discussion, enterprise services involve major strategic business decisions on the sourcing and usage of services. Sourcing concerns how services should be classified and provided, for example, whether a service should be classified as core-business or value-added, or whether they should be outsourced or performed internally. Usage concerns the target customers and how the services should be offered, for example, whether an external value chain can be included as part of the offering or a scale-down market is preferable. The consideration and decision-making processes of these subjects should be part of the core operations of the enterprise.

1.2.2 What Is Service-Oriented Enterprises?

An enterprise includes interdependent resources such as people, organization, process, and technology. The category of people is represented as an abstract collection of knowledge and expertise. They are further classified and allocated into different organizations depending upon business missions. The enterprise processes are business processes and products, applications, and data. The technology category includes software and hardware infrastructure which coordinate business functions and share information in support of a common mission or set of related missions.

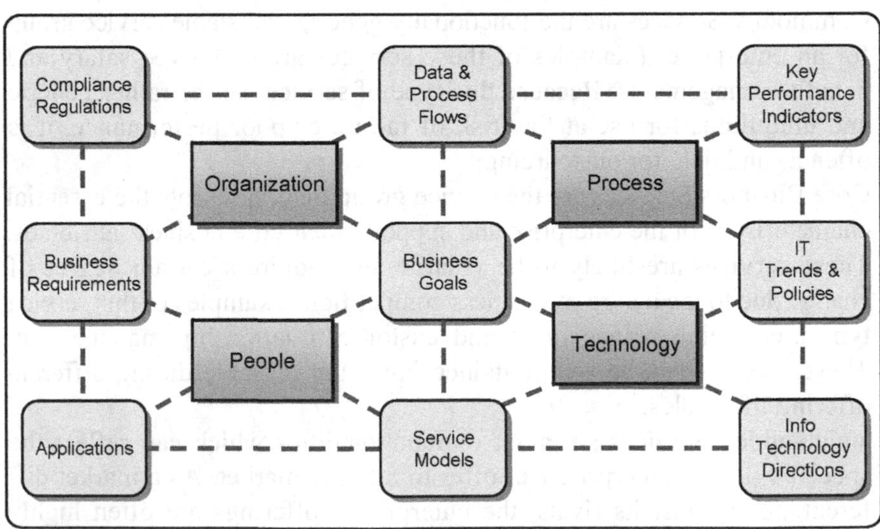

Figure 1.5. Enterprise resource relationships.

Although often associated strictly with information technology, these four interdependent resources relate more broadly to the practice of business operations. For instance, the people and organization define the mission, the information necessary to perform the mission, and the technologies necessary to carry out the mission. With the same or different sets of people, the processes for implementing new technologies then are executed in order to align with the organization's core goals and strategic direction.

As shown in Figure 1.5, business goals of a *Service-Oriented Enterprise (SOE)* are supported by the four resources in a protective environment for effective and efficient data and technologies management to conduct business. The supporting characteristics are listed as below:

1. The protection comes from the governance functions for setting priorities for investment, efforts and usage of the information, and data in accordance with the regulation and guidance.
2. The technology resource covers the enterprise-wide technical infrastructure that supports access, use, management, and delivery of data, applications, and key performance indicators for seamless business operations.
3. Decision-making can be improved by incorporating location-based approaches, data, tools, and knowledge into the business.
4. The data provides the enterprise partners, value-chain stakeholders, and corporate users the information they need to carry out the shared business processes needed for making decisions.
5. The applications provide enterprise partners, value-chain stakeholders, and corporate users with the applications (via service interfaces) to access, manage, use, analyze, present, and interpret the enterprise data to conduct business.
6. The service models situated between technology, people, and applications to establish an abstract and unified service view for the management communities inside or outside (for service providers or value-chain partners) the enterprise to effectively manage the data and technologies.

To satisfy the enterprise customers and users, the technology resource should provide appropriate services to support business operations. A *service* is typically defined as a collection of interface contracts and contractually defined behaviors that can be provided by an enterprise resource for use by any of the enterprise resources. In the telecommunications and information services industries, enterprise services can be classified as a set of capabilities provided by set of systems or utilities to their service consumers. Such service offerings may include telecommunications or network transport services, services that handle information resources including the storage, retrieval, manipulation and visualization specific to the resource, and management services including fault, configuration, accounting, performance and security functionalities, as well as service life-cycle management, service instance management, and user life-cycle management.

1.2.3 SOE Objectives

Service orientation focuses on how services support the dynamic discovery of appropriate services at run time. From a service customer's perspective, service providers are substitutable as long as the functionalities comply with the contract imposed by the service description. With this principle, a successful Service Oriented Enterprise can connect business processes both horizontally and vertically. The infrastructure supported by SOE provides an enterprise architecture and security foundation to execute any services consistently across the enterprise. The objectives of SOE can be defined as following:

- The new technology should be capable of quickly responding to a user's request or creating an environment that facilitates business-to-business commerce in a way that large volume messaging, orchestrated processes, long-running transactions, registering electronic business services, and secured messaging can be managed effectively.
- The new technology is expected to possess the capability of scalability to reasonably grow the capacity of the computing resource and the capability of predictability to add functions in increments.
- The target solution should have a certain level of insured uptime for the measure of reliability.
- In addition to scalability, the solution should be easily and cost effectively deployable and redeployable for any new or updated application.
- Any changes to the deployed solution should have the ability to be quickly changed in terms of system functionality as of the consideration of business agility.
- Any new functionality developed can potentially be reusable in other applications without major design and development efforts.
- At the system level, new services or applications can be easily integrated with other systems or solutions.

1.2.4 SOE Architecture

From the perspective of service implementation, the SOE defines "*what*" and "*with who*" of the enterprise service solution. The SOA defines the "*how*" of the service solution and the *Service-Oriented Computing (SOC)* defines "*where*" a service paradigm should be applied to software and business functions. Contrasted against traditional SOA platform architectures which have placed more emphasis on integration within the platform rather than across platforms, SOE architectures focus more on cross-platform coordination and information collaboration. The SOC assembles the realizations of the technologies such as Web services and workflow languages in accordance with the specified architecture [15].

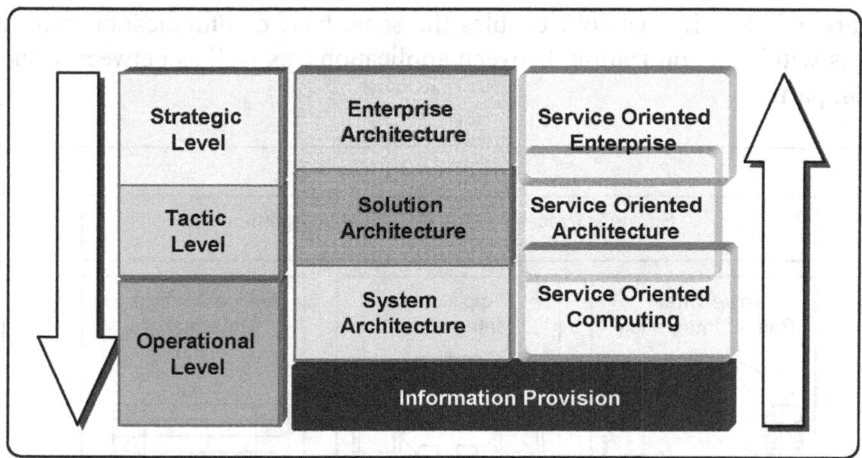

Figure 1.6. Service-oriented business framework.

In the ideal situation, services are designed top–down at the SOE level; business functionalities are defined at the Enterprise Architecture or strategic level, including the corporate level business planning and policies. These functionalities are further decomposed in lower level services at the Solution Architecture or Tactic level. The overlap between SOE and SOA at the right column of Figure 1.6 shows a seamless transition between tactical and strategic layers. From this point on, collected services are assigned to different systems where each service may interact with various other services to accomplish a certain task.

Depending upon the defined functionality, operations of one service might be a reuse and/or combination of several low-level functions. In that case, these low-level functions are not considered services. The operational level dictates the system and task-level activities as well as Information Management as depicted in Figure 1.6. The applications of the top–down approach include process modeling, functional decomposition, policy and business rules analysis, and domain specific behavior modeling of new systems enabling integration across business functions. As shown, the top–down approach can be conducted in parallel with a bottom–up analysis such as modularizing existing legacy assets for service exposure, integrating services across multiple applications for a business objective, or implementing individual Web services.

SOE brings interoperability and agility to the forefront of the enterprise solution design. A major theme for the SOE is to assume System of Systems *(SoS*; section 1.5*)* integration and can include *Business Process and Applications Management*, *Value-Chain Partner Integration*, *Application Integration*, *Service Application Development*, and *Service Network*. As shown in Figure 1.7, Service network enables the same base communication mechanisms within an application, between applications, as well as between value-chain partners.

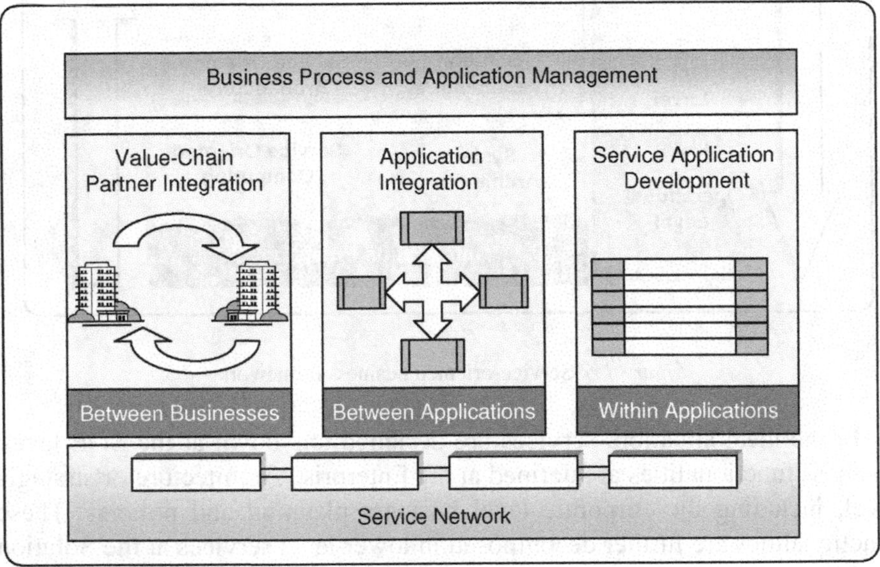

Figure 1.7. Enterprise resource relationships.

1.2.4.1 Business Process and Applications Management

The SOE is also a driver of the next generation process-driven architectures where process-driven architectures decouple the process-logic from the business logic. In a process-driven architecture, a process is broken down into activities and each activity is further broken down into tasks. Information in a process can be executed inside of a "process engine". The process-driven architecture leverages the SOE to provide a consistent means of accessing the variety of systems that are utilized across a process, and normally exists in the form of *Business Process Management (BPM)*. *Business Applications* Management *(BAM)* provides a generic means to visualize the health of SOA-based business services (chapter 10). It assists the enterprise to plan, manage, configure, and optimize service applications based on the service level contracts and ensure compliance of the business objectives. It is also responsible for tracking availability and performance of the offering services and helps the service provider to isolate, diagnose, and fix the highest-priority problems.

1.2.4.2 Value-Chain Partner Integration

Value-chain partner integration is sometimes called partner integration or trading partner integration; it exists in the form of *Business to Business Integration (B2Bi)* and encompasses the automated exchange of information between different organizations such as partners, customers, suppliers, distributors, and others. Comprehensive partner integration can:

- Automate the flow of transactions between suppliers, customers, and trading partners and represent one of largest areas of opportunities for using technology to streamline business processes.
- Enable collaborative business relationships that facilitate real-time decision-making, accelerated cycle times, and better monitoring of partner performance.
- Deal with the complexity and expense needed to integrate a wide variety of heterogeneous IT systems and business processes across existing and future business partners.

1.2.4.3 Application Integration

The function of Application Integration is to integrate information between "application silos". This is also known as "*Enterprise Application Integration (EAI)*". EAI intends to transcend the simple goal of linking applications, and attempts to enable new and innovative ways of leveraging organizational knowledge to create further competitive advantages for the enterprise.

The applications that are discussed within the scope of EAI include *supply chain management*, customer *relationship management*, and *business intelligence and integrated collaboration environments*. EAI is the process of linking these applications and others in order to realize financial and operational competitive advantages. The advantages of EAI are its capability to provide information access among systems in real time, streamline business processes, and maintain information integrity across multiple systems. Traditionally, its challenges are high-development costs, time and resource consuming, up front design requirement, and increased management as the number of applications increases. The usual set of tools for supporting EAI includes message queuing and gateways, distributed transaction monitors, communication brokers, events and states monitoring, and business process management tools. The standards related to these technologies include message-flow languages such as *Business Process Execution Language for*

Web Services (BPEL4WS), data transformation vehicles such as *Extensible Style-sheet Language Transformations (XSLT)*, and adaptors such as Web services.

1.2.4.4 Service Application Development

The paradigms of software development have moved from structured programming, to object-oriented programming, to component-based, and now to a service-oriented programming style. The new paradigm embraces the advantages from the previous generations and more emphasis is placed on asynchronous messaging, XML for identifying data types, and an increased use of protocols over *application program interfaces (API)*. Service-oriented applications are composed of the run-time loose bundling of services and apply the concepts of a SOA to the design of a single application. To create a sensible application for a SOE environment, the loose bundling is counter to the tighter compiling technique used to bind many object-oriented systems. Each individual service is compiled, but the orchestration between the services is usually hosted in an orchestration engine where run-time binding takes place.

1.2.4.5 Service Network

A Service Network is an application level network that leverages a SOA and is composed of a number of Service Network Participants and many Services. It extends beyond the firewall and may integrate with Service Networks of other companies by the standardization of the protocols used to communicate. Unlike traditional applications which were built discretely, applications and the network now become one entity in a Service Network. It is often difficult to identify where one application begins and ends.

1.3 Service-Oriented Architecture

As delineated in the previous section, the *Service-Oriented Architecture (SOA)* defines the "*how*" of an enterprise service solution will be implemented. It is an enterprise-scale IT architecture for linking resources on demand. The first SOA method was announced in 2004 *Service-oriented Modeling and Architecture (SOMA)*. The SOA consists of a set of business-aligned IT services that collectively fulfill an organization's business processes and goals. A service, in this context, is a discoverable software resource with an externalized service description. This service description is available for searching, binding, and invocation by a service consumer. In a SOA, resources are made available to participants in a value network, enter prise, or *line of business* (or LOB, typically spanning multiple applications within an enterprise or across multiple enterprises). Business process flows can be supported by choreography of these exposed services into composite applications. An integrated architecture supports the routing, mediation, and translation of these services, components, and flows by an *Enterprise Service Bus (ESB)*. The deployed services must be monitored and managed for quality of service and adherence to non-functional [16,17].

1.3.1 What Is Service-Oriented Architecture?

The concept of a SOA is based on an architectural style that defines an interaction model between three primary parties as shown in Figure 1.8. These three parties are:

- The service provider who publishes a service description and provides the implementation for the service. It is responsible for supplying service objects that implement service functionalities.
- The service consumer who can either use the *uniform resource identifier (URI)* for the service description directly, or can find the service description in a service registry and then bind and invoke the service.
- The service broker who provides and maintains the service registry. The registry contains a set of service descriptions along with references to service providers; it provides mechanisms for service publication, removal, and discovery.

The basic interaction pattern that characterizes service orientation shows in the figure where the service provider publishes a service description in a service registry. A service consumer later queries the service registry to discover services in accordance with the criteria relative to a service description. If a service provider meets the published criteria, the service registry returns the provider's references to the service consumer. If multiple responses are returned to the service consumer, it is the service consumer's responsibility to select a target service provider to which it will bind. Upon a successful bind action to the provider, a service object is returned by the service provider. After completing the service interaction, the service object can be implicitly or explicitly released.

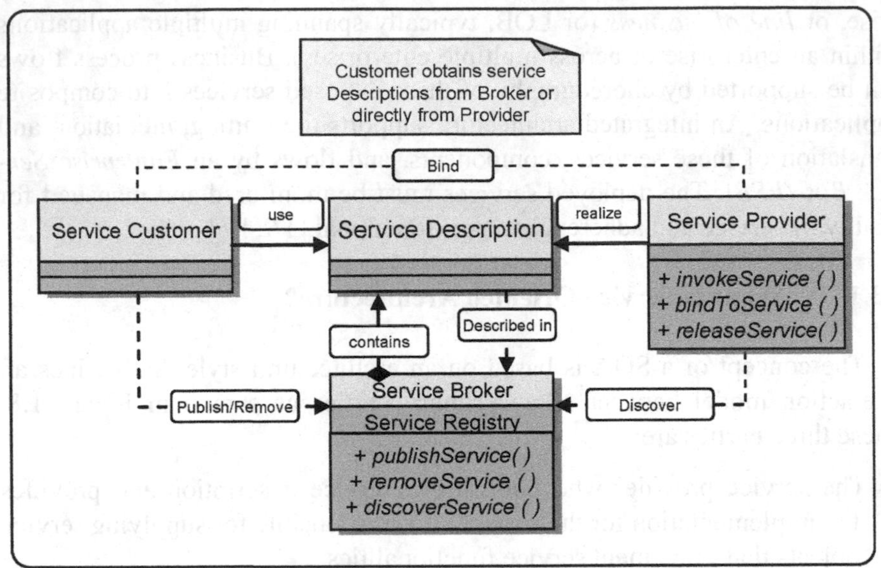

Figure 1.8. SOA interaction model.

With this flexible architecture – primarily by the separation of interfaces, implementations, and binding protocols – the choice of a service provider can be deferred until run time so that greater business agility can be achieved. This feature helps businesses respond more quickly and cost-effectively to the changing market conditions they may face by promoting reuse and interconnection of existing IT assets rather than more time consuming and costly reinvention. However, to enforce the QoS requirements to their service consumer with or without this flexibility, the service provider should ideally implement a governing framework with declarative policies to support their service commitments [17]. Chapter 7 will provide more in-depth discussion about service quality and its management.

SOA is an evolution in architecture as it captures many of the best practices or actual use of the architectures that came before it. It can be used as a business mapping tool allowing business developers to define business services and operating models, and thus provides a structure for IT departments

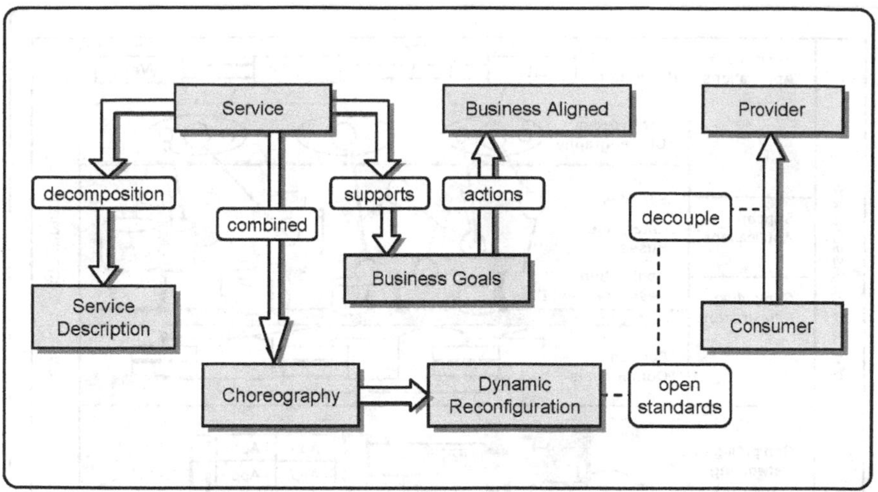

Figure 1.9. Attributes of a SOA management.

to deliver the actual business requirements. This changes the relationship between service developers and IT system developers such that services can be properly represented in the business view, not just in the way that technologists think the business services should be.

Figure 1.9 depicts sample attributes of a SOA where service is decomposed into functions and descriptions to support a decoupled relationship between providers and consumers. The detachment of a provider to their customer removes the dependency to the physical service objects, thus increasing the offering's flexibility.

1.3.2 The Layers of a SOA

The implementation of a SOA can be seen in a layered architecture. Figure 1.10 [16] depicts the vertical and horizontal layers that fit into the enterprise service architecture framework and will be used throughout the book. The naming conventions and containing components adopted in this section are purposely altered to accommodate future discussion of network-centric operations, therefore they may not be fully identical to the standard terms used in the traditional SOA.

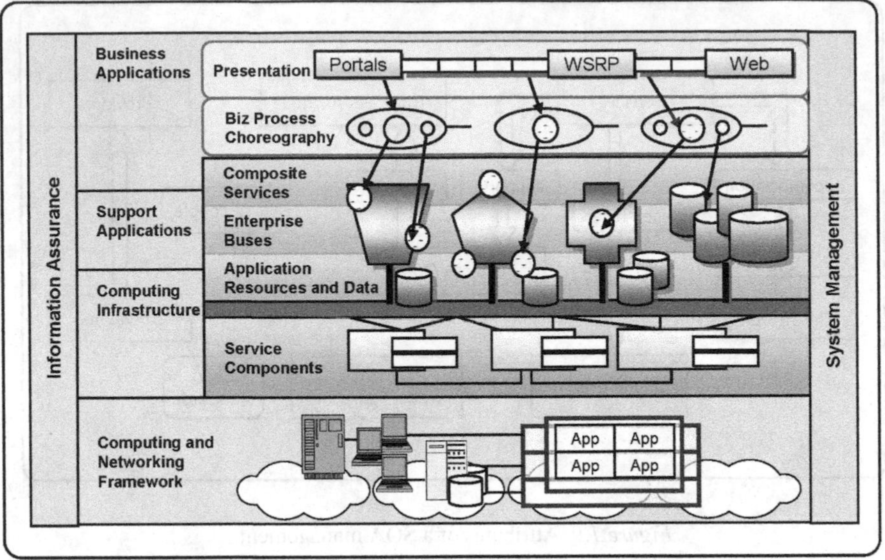

Figure 1.10. SOA layers in enterprise services.

The major SOA functionalities in the enterprise service architecture are as follows:

- *Business Application Layer*: This layer contains two major areas, namely service choreography and business presentations. Services are bundled into a flow through orchestration or choreography, and thus act together as a single application. Each application group supports specific use cases and business processes. The business presentations area bridges the user interface to the grouped application in order to establish an end-to-end solution. This can be constructed in the form of a user graphical presentation or an access channel to a service or composition of services. An increasing convergence of standards such as Web Services for *Remote Portlets* Version 2.0 and other technologies have started to leverage Web services at the application interface or presentation level.
- *Support Application Layer*: Composite service contains control and data flow that coordinates service invocation and data transfer among the different services to accomplish a particular task. A service composition is considered abstract until service providers are discovered and bound. Service compositions must handle issues relating to service discovery and service dynamics (e.g., self-adaptation). The application resources and data can be dynamically discovered or be statically bound and then invoked, or possibly, choreographed into a composite service. Service resources are exchanged through Enterprise Buses.

- *Computing Infrastructure Layer*: Service components are responsible for realizing functionality and maintaining the QoS of the exposed services. These special components are a managed, governed set of enterprise assets that are funded at the enterprise or the business unit level. As enterprise-scale assets, they are responsible for ensuring conformance to SLAs through the application of architectural best practices. This layer typically uses container-based technologies such as application servers to implement the components, workload management, high-availability, and load balancing.
- *Computing and Networking Framework Layer*: This framework layer consists of package applications (e.g., CRM and ERP) as well as the computing hardware and communication facilities. The composite layered architecture of an SOA can leverage existing systems and integrate them using service-oriented integration techniques.
- *Information Assurance Layer*: This cross-layer function provides the capabilities required to monitor, manage, and maintain the integrity and security of the offered services. Through sense-and-respond mechanisms, this background process and tools ensure end-to-end protection at the transaction and session levels.
- *System Management Layer*: This cross-layer function enables the integration of services through a set of capabilities which cover service planning, instantiation, configuration, monitoring, testing, and reconfiguration. It covers Web Services Management and other relevant communication and application managements sufficient to support any functionalities specified in the SOA.

The concept of the SOA architectural hierarchy depicted above is widely accepted as a computing paradigm and standardization of parts to realize actual business functions. To illustrate the relationship between standard SOA and the network-centric enterprise services, this model will be adopted through out the book in order to maintain a consistent theme in different subject discussions thus it should not be constrained by any SOA specific descriptions. Additionally, part of the architecture systems can be substituted or changed in specific implementations while still meeting the requirements of a SOA.

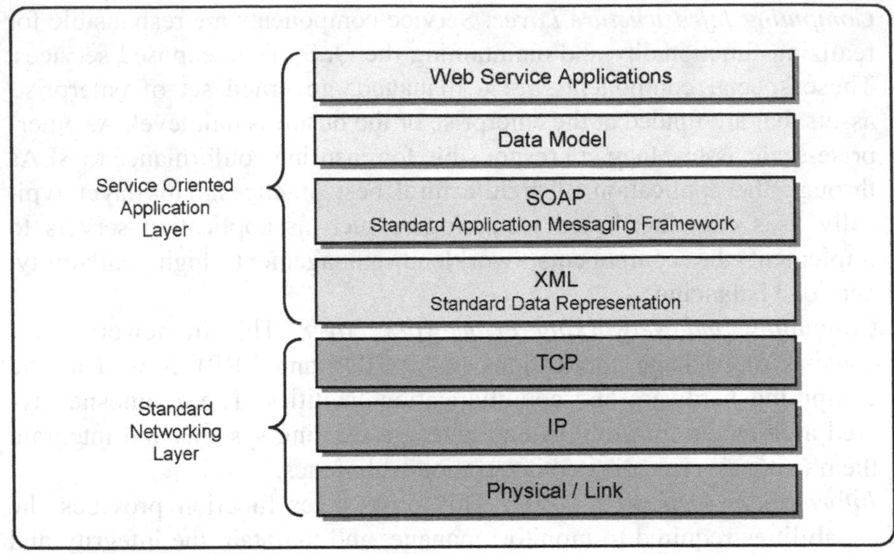

Figure 1.11. Layers of standards for service-oriented applications.

From the standards and protocol perspective, Figure 1.11 portrays the stacked relationship between SOA layers and standard networking layers. The technologies covered by the standard networking layers will be addressed in chapters 2–4. In the SOA layer, four sub-layers are shown. The *Extensible Markup Language* (XML) is a general-purpose markup language that provides a text-based means to delineate and apply a tree-based structure to information. The *Simple Object Access Protocol (SOAP)* is a protocol for exchanging XML-based messages over computer networks with HTTP. SOAP forms the foundation layer of the Web services stack, providing a basic messaging framework allowing more abstract layers to build upon it. The Data Model is an XML data model that is best delineated in XML Schema. For example, some enterprises capture everything in *Unified Modeling Language (UML)*, a general-purpose modeling language that includes a standardized graphical notation for an abstract model of a system that can be exported as XML Schemas [18,19].

1.3.3 Characteristics of SOA

SOA is a paradigm for organizing and utilizing distributed capabilities that may be under the control of different ownership domains. It provides a uniform means to offer, discover, interact with, and use capabilities to produce desired effects consistent with measurable preconditions and expectations. Its characteristics can be categorized as follows [17]:

- *Loosely Coupled*: Unlike traditional point-to-point architectures, SOAs comprise loosely-coupled, highly interoperable services. These services interoperate based on a formal definition (or contract) which is independent of the underlying platform and programming languages. Services can change and be versioned while eliminating or at least managing the ripple effect on applications consuming these services.
- *Standards based Interfaces*: Open standards are essential, as are the advertisement of the service interfaces in well known and widely accessible "service registries" or discovery services. This enforces the platform-neutral and allows services to be executed independent of their computing environment. SOA relies on the ability to identify services and their capabilities through a directory service that delineates the services available in its domain.
- *Distributed Process*: Choreography defines how a party interacts with other external parties. The relationship between a service provider and consumer is dynamic; the party may either be the client or the deployed service itself, in which multiple clients may be involved and the relationships are established at run time by a binding mechanism.
- *Services-centric*: Service-centric includes services performed in response to a specific request from a group of consumers as well as functions that consume the result of services supplied by a provider. A service represents a discrete unit of business, application, or system functionality. The intent should be to transform basic services into more complex system capabilities to deliver more valuable functionality.
- *Stateless*: Stateless means not depending on any preexisting condition. In a SOA, services should not depend on the condition of any other service. They receive all information needed to provide a response from the request. Given the statelessness of services, service consumers can sequence their business objects into numerous flows to perform application logic.
- *Coarse Grained*: Services focus on high-level business processes using standard interfaces. The coarseness of the grain appropriate to a given service depends on some degree on how that service will be most often used and the likely "network distance" between the service provider and the service consumer. Lower bandwidth and higher latency connections suggest coarser granularity while a high frequency of "single item" requests from diverse sources suggests a need for finer-grained service interfaces.

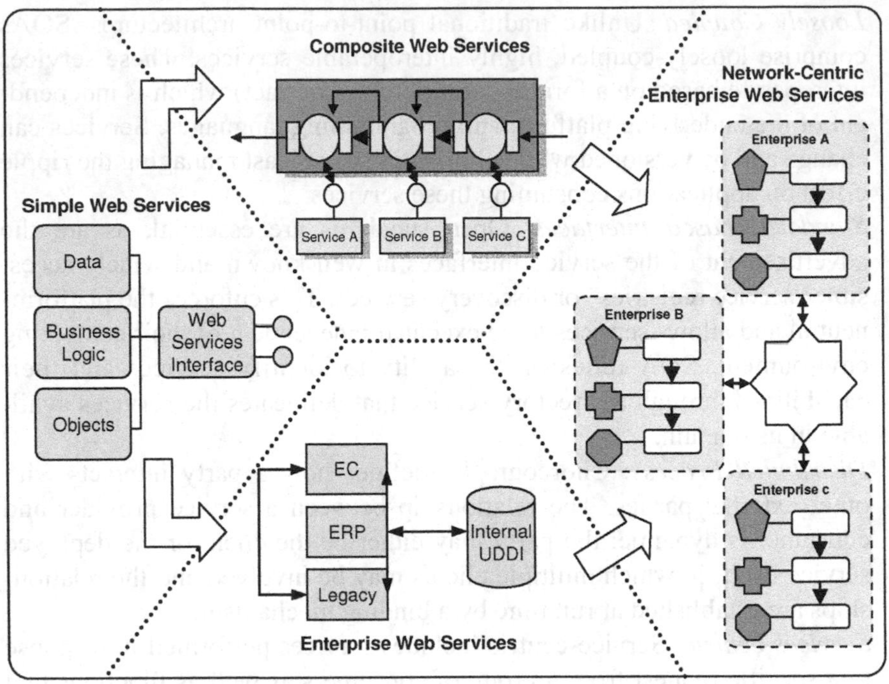

Figure 1.12. Trend of SOA development.

SOA does not require Web services, and Web services can be deployed without a consistent or universal SOA. Services that are too fine-grained or incomplete add configuration management and administrative burdens to the service user and to run-time overhead. Services that are too coarse-grained create difficulty in using only the functionality and business rules one needs. Coarse-grained services also create the potential for unintentional coupling and unnecessary run-time overhead. Figure 1.12 depicts the trend of SOAs developed from simple Web services to the network-centric enterprise Web services along with the complexity of business requirements.

1.3.4 Benefits of SOA

There are many benefits of using the SOA technology. Firstly, SOA simplifies the complexity of IT management by allowing smooth internal integration processes and facilitating information sharing across organizational boundaries. This is accomplished by detaching the dependency of an integration backbone across heterogeneous application platforms and allowing the enterprises to start small and grow as needed. With the scalable infrastructure, enterprises can more easily leverage existing IT assets and expose them as reusable services. The life-cycle of legacy investments can then be extended and the enterprise can maximize value of its IT investments while minimizing risks.

Secondly, the benefit of SOA comes from its open architecture nature which forces the IT department to implement the solution in a dynamic instead of static mindset. By exposing and sharing information across single "silo applications", the enterprise can adopt new technology innovation in real time. Adoption of emerging standards and technologies through open interfaces translates directly into benefits for improving business intelligence, increasing responsiveness, and reducing risk through freedom of choice. Internally, the enterprise can leverage existing developer skill-sets by eliminating the need to learn proprietary technologies.

Thirdly, SOA facilitates easier integration and increased agility that can lead to a better *return on investment (ROI)*. This can come from three areas: 1) Focusing on the interfaces of the overall service and service components instead of internal implementation allows the service and system designers to allocate their resource and energy on the core values and composite functionalities; 2) Limiting the involvement of component level implementation can reduce project risk and delays; and 3) Reducing the dependency of individual service component development can accelerate the service deployment and leverage best practices and methodology of the enterprise's value framework.

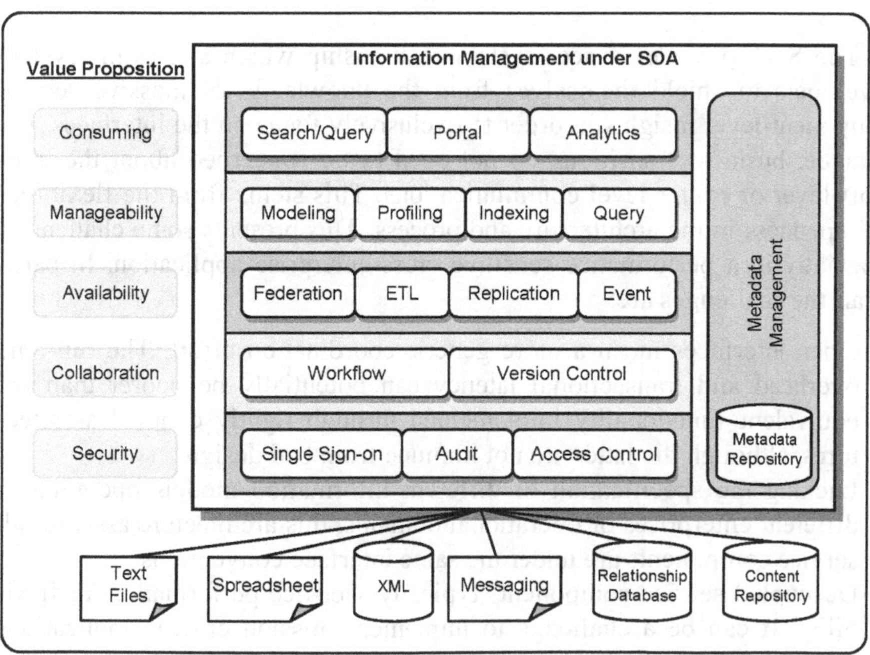

Figure 1.13. Information management stack under SOA.

Fourthly, with this robust content management feature, SOA presents opportunities for end-to-end business integration and transformation. In enterprise data management, structured information deals primarily with the data that is ordered and set to specific allowed types. Because unstructured information does not easily conform to an ordered set with strict types, the management of such information is categorized as content management. As the enterprise information converges from pure structured toward mix of structured and unstructured, SOA can help to transform existing Information Management functions into reusable services, integrate large numbers of heterogeneous information sources, reduce development costs, and expand capabilities quickly. Figure 1.13 shows the Information Management stack, a logical view or framework for categorizing Information Management services based on their value propositions: security, collaboration, availability, management, and information consumption.

In summary, SOA dramatically eases integration in heterogeneous environments and provides a transformational enhancement in agility, visibility, consistency, and interoperability that turn into better ROI. Figure 1.13 depicts the Information Management stack under SOA. On the left side of the figure, the value propositions for each application layers are shown.

1.3.5 Challenges of SOA

The SOA provides a peer system relationship which allows the system developers to shield themselves from the knowledge of massive service component-level insights in order to exclusively focus on the interfaces. For instance, business transitions do not need to be concerned about the transport layer or router level communications. This stems from the flexibility and openness in the architecture and process. This presents some challenges, especially in a performance sensitive cross-enterprise application. In particular, the challenges are:

1. Open interfaces mean a more generic coordination effort. The run-time overhead and transactional latency can potentially be poorer than the equivalent functionality implemented through tightly coupled architectures, although the latter are not immune from bad design.
2. Lacking the specification of different information models operating in different enterprises or operational domains, this architecture assumes all service components are under the same interface conventions.
3. Decoupled service components typically sacrifice performance for flexibility. It can be a challenge to implement mission critical applications with the traditional SOA technologies when the business requirements demanding real-time responses.

4. In an overly normalized interface design, all services are defined in a flat relationship. Such system design breaks the hierarchy of application components that can potentially cause inefficiency in control flow rules and slowness in troubleshooting.
5. Issues may arise relating to different identity or naming standards and regulations such as web services, security services, e-business information exchange standards, and federal identity management services and standards. This may introduce a path forward issue when standards bodies have different agendas and schedules in mind.
6. Managing and providing information on how services interact is a complicated task, especially when services metadata is designed across enterprises. SMEs for new and legacy services require new levels of skill sets to understand and utilize the constantly expanded, updated, and refined architecture.
7. Appropriate levels of security may not be addressed for on-demand mission critical applications (e.g., running over ad-hoc networks) when consumer services are external to company firewalls and become more visible to external parties than traditional monolithic proprietary applications.

From the operational perspective, services that are too fine-grained or incomplete can add configuration management and administrative burdens to the service user and to run-time overhead. Services that are too coarse-grained create difficulty in using only the functionality and business rules one needs. Coarse-grained services also create potential for unintentional coupling and unnecessary run-time overhead. The key to resolution lies in good subject matter synergy and object-oriented management.

1.4 Network-Centric Business Operations

Enterprise services may be delivered directly to the customer or to general user communities on behalf of the customer. User experience in terms of response time, completeness of the given information, and associated value-added features are keys to enterprise success in the business. In the previous section, the service architecture level discussion was given, including the pros and cons of the existing practices. As shown, the key weakness of today's SOA practice is its responsiveness to large or complex networked services, particularly to mission critical or real-time applications. This is due to its original intention of solving the interoperability of new and legacy systems. With more emphasis upon system openness to a standard framework and less focus on solution level performance and collaboration considerations.

As service-oriented solutions become more accepted by enterprises in many different business sectors, the surfaced performance limitation becomes

IT business's new challenge. With respect to the Service-Oriented Computing and Information Provision depicted in Figure 1.6, this section proposes a new paradigm called *Network-Centric Business Operations (NCBO)* to accommodate the identified problem discussed in "Challenges of SOA", section 1.3.5.

NCBO takes as a given the existing infrastructure and benefits of SOA, and applies the additional requirements and benefits of real-time processing, collaboration, interoperability, and assurance.

NCBO is a concept of human and organizational behavior based upon adopting network-centric principles and applying it to enterprise operations. NCBO focuses on business intelligence sharing that can be generated from the effective linking and networking of the intelligent enterprise [20]. The greatest value of NCBO is its support of *speed of execution* – the conversion of a superior information position to immediate action. For example, anything dealing with real-time market conditions will benefit. With NCBO, the SOA weaknesses discussed in the previous section can be well compensated. The end result will be a solution with more effective communication and better performance.

1.4.1 The Principle of Network-Centricity

While SOA focuses on the service "interface" and "interaction", network-centricity emphasizes collaboration of information sharing and information awareness that can be exploited via self-synchronization and other network-centric operations. This achieves effective and timely business executions. From a computing architecture perspective, NCBO deals with centrality of information that allows business entities to work in concert to achieve synergistic effects without requiring them to always operate in a linked fashion. Additionally, NCBO also focuses attention on the importance of the interactions among coordination entities that are necessary to generate synergistic action.

To illustrate the concept of NCBO in a service-based environment, a sensing and controlling application is used as an example for discussion. This type of application can be found in transportation, manufacturing, military, emergency rescue, aviation, and any other sector where detection, analysis, and action are basic functionalities of the application. First, this sample model is presented in stand-alone configuration. In the subsequent scenario when multiple instances are networked, the operation can be classified as either platform-centric (section 1.4.1.1) or network-centric (section 1.4.1.2).

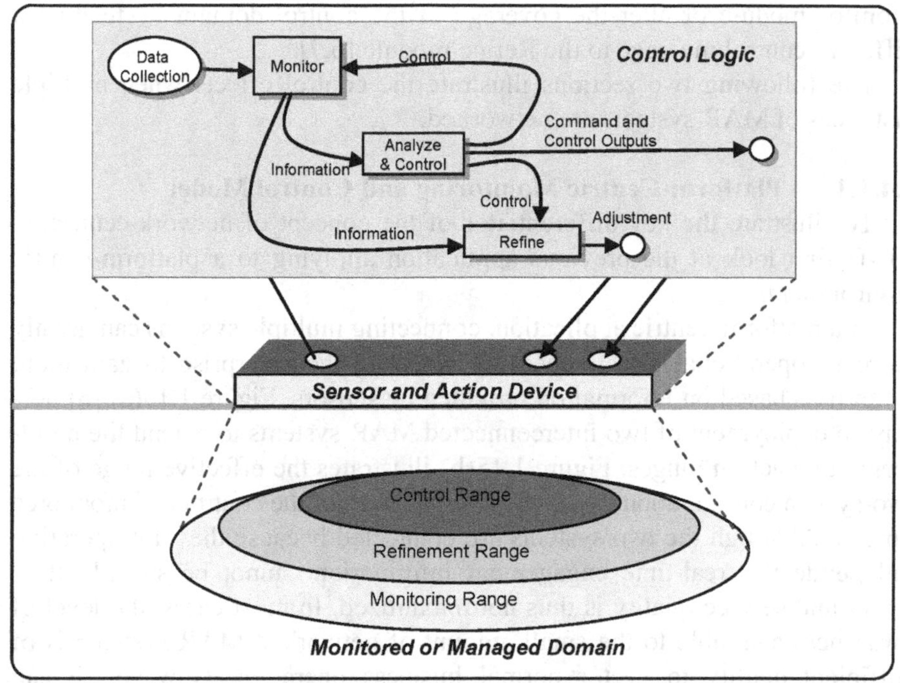

Figure 1.14. The Monitor-Analysis-Refine service model and engagement envelope.

Figure 1.14 shows a stand-alone "sensor and action device" which contains or is controlled by a control logic *Monitor-Analyze-Refine (MAR)* system. The MAR system monitors and manages an application environment marked with three gray-level radiuses. The outer radius is the complete monitoring range where the system is aware of the environmental situation. The control range in the inner radius represents the "effective" domain where the system can take action upon the event. The refinement range represented in the middle radius is the area where the system has the ability to dynamically adjust the control range making the system influential to the situation. In the MAR system, Data collection collects sensing data from the monitor range and sends it to the Monitor module. The Monitor module preprocesses the raw data into information and forwards the data to the Analyze & Control module as well as the Refine module. The Analyze & Control module conducts information analysis against the received information; if an action to the control range is needed, a command and control message will be generated and sent to the device. This command or control message will apply to both control and refinement ranges; or to change the coverage area of the refinement range. Alternatively, the analysis can conclude a decision to change the data collection period by feeding a control message back to the

Monitor module or alter the coverage of the control domain by feeding a different control message to the Refine module [6,7].

The following two sections illustrate the control effects when multiple instances of MAR systems are networked.

1.4.1.1 Platform-Centric Monitoring and Control Model

To illustrate the key differentiator of the concept of network-centricity, let us first look at the previous application applying to a platform-centric environment.

In a platform-centric application, connecting multiple systems can greatly increase operational effectiveness by allowing the enterprise to gain more awareness based on information provided by sensors. Figure 1.15(a) [6] portrays a deployment of two interconnected MAR systems to extend the monitoring and action ranges. Figure 1.15(b) illustrates the effective range of the two-system configuration. Note, the overlap areas of the control and monitored ranges. Although the two systems are connected because they are operating independently, real-time engagement information cannot be shared effectively and service quality is thus not maximized. In most cases, the level of awareness available to the small amount of networked MAR systems is of sufficient quality to vector normal business operation. However, it can potentially be extremely difficult to develop and maintain situational awareness when there are large numbers of systems operating in close proximity. In particular when the number of overlap areas increases, or number of systems that control the same area increase, the coordination of data collection as well as control and commands collaboration can become a rather complex management task.

1.4.1.2 Network-Centric Monitoring and Control Model

In contrast, network-centric operations in the same application are illustrated in Figure 1.16(a). In a network-centric environment, capabilities for sensing, monitoring, event-assessing, and action are robustly networked. The source of the increased power in a network-centric operation is derived in part from the increased content, quality, and timeliness of information flowing between the systems in the network. This collaborated information flow is a key to enabling shared service quality awareness, and increasing the accuracy of the information. This is shown in data and control flows associated with the shaded oval.

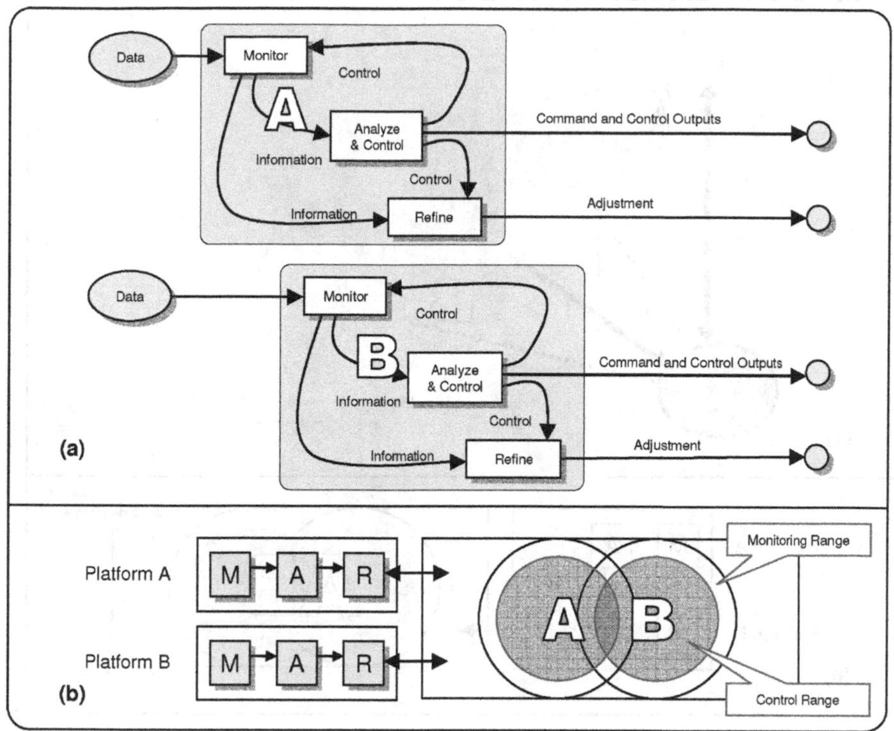

Figure 1.15. Platform-centric networked systems.

In terms of affects of the new paradigm, the improved situational awareness increases overall service capability for observing, orienting, deciding, and acting. This can be illustrated with Figure 1.16(b) [6] where near real-time information sharing among systems enables potential service quality to be increased. The robustness of the networked (A and B) systems comes from its capability to enhanced shared awareness with increased quality. Such design effectively increases the monitoring as well as the action ranges and in turn enables cooperative execution and self-synchronization of service effectiveness.

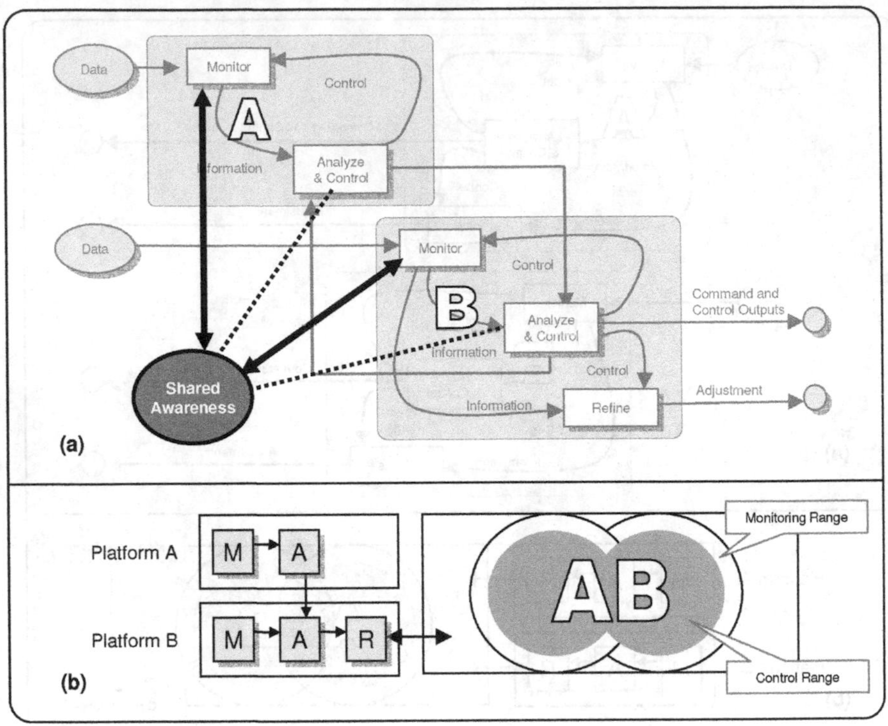

Figure 1.16. Network-centric networked systems.

NCBO possesses collaboration and decentralization in the form of self-synchronizing forces which can increase and improve awareness of the deployed applications. With this new capability, the service providers will have a better understanding of both the big picture and the local situation that the providers currently do not have. In resource-intensive applications, applying NCBO concepts to resource management can exhibit the potential for moving information instead of moving material or people. These substitutions generate considerable savings in time and resources and result in increased value in the form of informational power for a given level of investment.

1.4.2 The Merits of NCBO

In the MAR application, the network-centric model reveals the execution power of information collaboration by the creation of shared events awareness and knowledge. This awareness and knowledge is leveraged by *execution*, *monitoring*, and *enhancement* approaches and by self-synchronizing operations. There are several key features that merit attention in enterprise service development, they are [21]:

1. *The Increased Tempo of Execution*: NCBO is about information interoperability and flexibility. Through service interfaces, enterprise users and applications can access relevant information more easily. It focuses on how to derive business intelligent power from distributed interacting entities and how to improve the access to this information. The actual computing and communications are less significant to this result-oriented approach. Iterative development and implementation make it possible to change prioritization during system development and implantation.
2. *Increased Responsiveness*: The following Figure 1.17 shows the user footprint decreases and user capability increases as the enterprise services move from platform-centric to network-centric. On the left, the figure portrays the heavy capital dependency required by the users to access and exchange data that are crucial to the business operations. Moving to the right, NCBO that reveals superior business intelligence and execution co-exist to improve the user capability. The key differentiator is the focus on application execution and operations instead of communication networks or hardware enhancements.

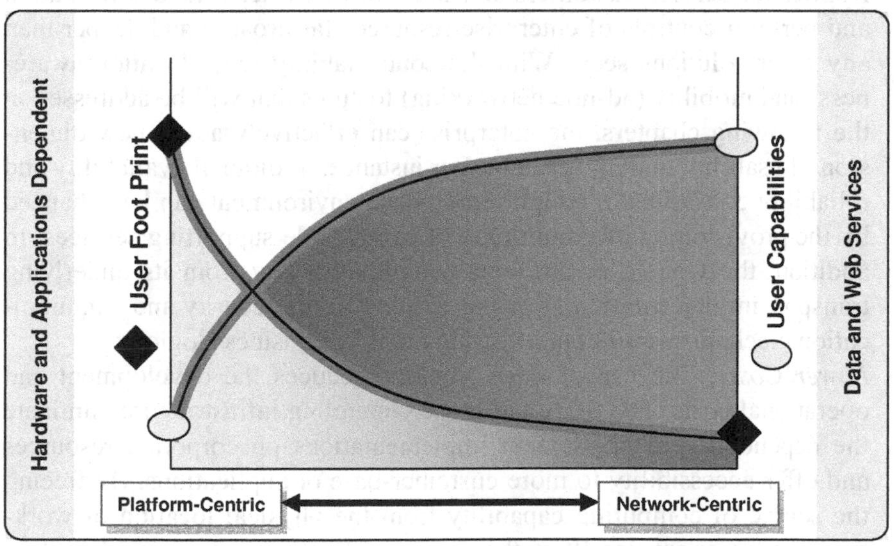

Figure 1.17. Moving from platform-centric to network-centric.

3. *Increased Operational Effectiveness*: The new method makes the information transformation and process transformation easier through a standardized interface. The capability of information fusion provides collaborated business intelligence and intelligent views for enterprise

service providers and their customers. Operational effectiveness can be improved by an effective linkage among entities with access to high-quality information services. Such linkage can bridge the dispersed and distributed entities to generate strategic and tactical synergy. Policy-based security allow flexible security level changes dependent on the situation.

4. *Lower Risks*: Empowered by the knowledge derived from a shared awareness of the business data as well as a shared understanding of business goals, the enterprise can achieve self-synchronization and be able to operate with a smaller footprint. A smaller footprint means less complexity and faster actions; in an operational term, this means less risk for failure and simpler management efforts. As a result, the business forces can perform more effectively and autonomously and lead to greater probability of success with less dependable resources. In mission critical applications such as trading systems, such an advantage can directly result in higher profit.
5. *Improved Customer Experience and Satisfaction*: NCBO opens a new frontier for service customers and users to reach networked information and perform controls of enterprise resources far broader and deeper than any other solutions seen. With the controllability (e.g., location awareness) and mobility (ad-hoc networking) features that will be addressed in the following chapters, the enterprise can effectively add a new dimension of usability to their services. For instance, traditional availability and reliability constrains in a highly mobilized environment can be enhanced by the provisioning of a multitude of comparable supporting services. In addition, the QoS layer abstracts complexity away from its underlying transport implementation allowing changes to the security and communication mechanisms without affecting the upper business logics.
6. *Lower Costs*: The use of open standard reduces the development and operational costs. The SOA and loosely-coupling infrastructure eliminate the dependency of application implementations on corporate resources and offer accessibility to more customer-base or applications. By freeing the source of computing capability from the physical location of workspace assets or entities allow the enterprise to effectively streamline their business processes and moves toward to the synergy of intelligent effects. As the enterprise can avoid presenting multiple objects for different applications, the service users can also benefit from the small resource requirement to utilize the service.

1.4.3 Major Elements of NCBO

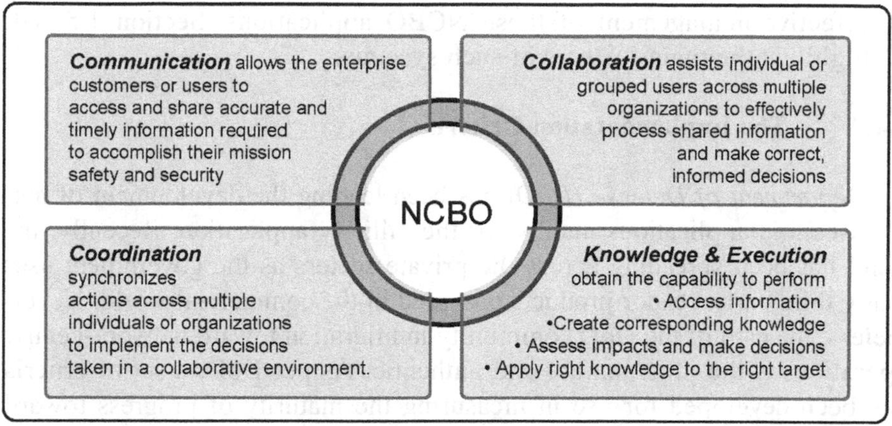

Figure 1.18. Major process components of network-centric operations.

As discussed previously, NCBO moves a step beyond traditional situational awareness to network-based decisions. It is transparent to business mission, size of operations, and geographical distribution. Furthermore, NCBO is not narrowly about technology but broadly about an emerging enterprise that is capable of responding in the Information Age. Thus NCBO has to be oriented from the standpoint of the coalescence of the tactical, operational, and strategic levels of business practices. Because a network-centric enterprise operates under a different, more modern, rule set than a platform-centric enterprise, it is essential to incorporate these new elements into the Information Management framework. The following three areas are the identified elements for the new generation solution [7]:

- Intellectual capital reveals itself in the form of enterprise information, service knowledge, and the associated processes. As will be seen in chapters 8 and 9, this revolutionary concept merges with the existing enterprise's IT skills and operational experience and presents a rather different and protracted cultural challenge to enterprises.
- Transformation process has to co-evolve with the Intellectual Capital. Figure 1.18 identifies a collected process for the transformation, including communication (technology), coordination and collaboration (organization), and Knowledge & Execution (doctrine). These essential processes are referred to throughout the entire book as applicable to the subject matter discussions.
- Dedicated or specialized systems need to be developed in order to accommodate the enterprise information, service knowledge, and new processes for the new NCBO-based services. Enterprises also need to

develop associated supporting systems and methodologies capable of accomplishing specific business and service missions, or facilitating effective management of these NCBO applications. Section 1.5 will highlight the main features of such systems.

1.4.4 The Implementation Criteria

Department of Defense (DoD) has been leading the development of network-centric applications mainly for the military application. Recently, the trend has been spreading across the private sectors as the government uses many third party vendor products provided in the commercial world. Nevertheless, the path of the DoD community in migration toward network-centric operations is the most mature and authentic. As per DoD, a set of criteria has been developed for use in measuring the maturity of progress toward achieving enterprise-level capabilities. This set of four levels is:

1. The first level pertains to systems adapting to the network-centric environment in a very basic fashion. This level focuses on user experience and can include basic network access such as HTTP, IPv4 mixed with IPv6 and data sharing.
2. The second level pertains to collaborative information sharing across systems in the enterprise. This level addresses the information process within and across systems; its scope includes systems networked as well as web and information services.
3. The third level pertains to intelligent information exchange across systems using semantically enriched publish, subscribe, query and brokering capabilities. At the solution level, or SoS level, the emphasis includes self-configuring networks, multiple security levels and combined coalition networks, data translation and mediation, service level agreements, and so forth.
4. The fourth level pertains to seamless operational awareness across systems in an on-demand distributed computing environment. The top-level implementation is a balance of technology, process, people, and organization. It includes dynamic bandwidth optimization, transparent cross-domain access, seamless data interoperability, and so forth.

Figure 1.19 depicts a transformation of an existing service-based enterprise to the fourth level NCBO practice. As shown, island business functions are grouped into three cross-related modules, namely knowledge sharing, information assurance, and network management. These modules are networked by the enterprise infrastructure to eliminate duplicate data and process and improve efficiency of sharing and communication capabilities [22].

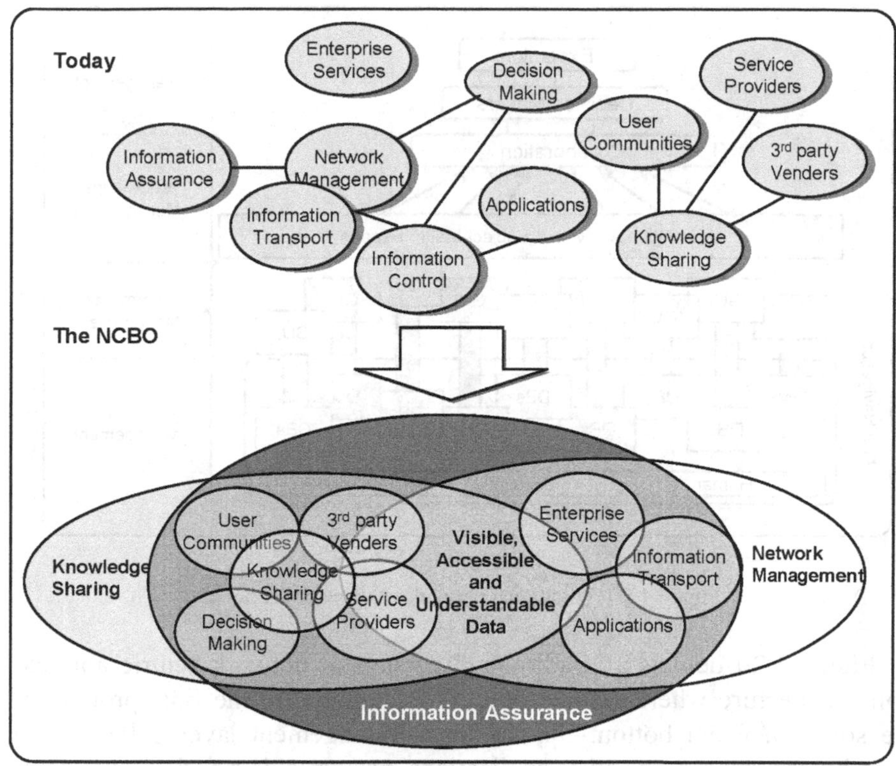

Figure 1.19. Transformation to NCBO model.

1.4.5 NCBO and Service-Oriented Computing

Service-Oriented Computing (SOC) expands the enterprise architecture specifications into a solution implementation. The goal of successful implementation of a NCBO solution is to ensure that the productivity, service quality, and efficiency of networked enterprise services can exceed the sum of individual services. This goal is applicable to both the services offered to the enterprise customers as well the services used to manage service operations. They can be seen as customer-view and provider-view SOC, respectively. Examples of customer-view network-centric SOC are an Internet Web-surfing agent which organizes Web contents into consolidated reports, military battlefield situation awareness, and emergency rescue operations. Examples of provider-view network-centric SOC are SLM, *Service Quality Management (SQM)*, and CRM.

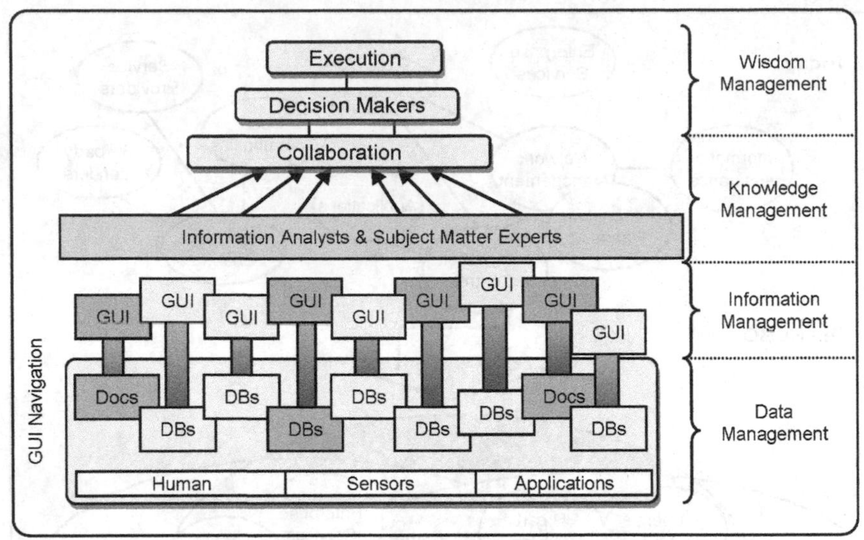

Figure 1.20. Traditional network-centric applications.

Figure 1.20 depicts a "traditional" version of network-centric application architecture where manual process is essential to the final product of the solution. From bottom–up, the Data Management layer collects data from human, sensors, or other applications, performs data fusion, and stores them in various data repositories. The Information Management layer consequently organizes these data into meaningful business information and makes them accessible to the application users via *graphical user interfaces (GUIs)*. Following the business and operational quittances, the application users form groups of information analyst or SME teams to manually analyze the information provided by the applications.

The Knowledge Management layer collaborates and consolidates information into *knowledge*. Depending upon the complexity level of the managed information, cross-references and information coordination tasks can be labor intensive and time consuming. The executives at the Wisdom Management layer perform the final analysis against the reports from the Knowledge Management teams. The final product of this layered process is a set of attributes or characteristics that can potentially impact the existing business practice or contribute to the strategic directions of the enterprise.

Evolving into the SOC implementation, application, and process silos are consolidated by the new methodology. As the result, the overall coordination efforts are significantly improved as shown in Figure 1.21 where *Web Services (WS)* are attached to the front-end of each application and open a new-paradigm of information sharing. It is important to mention that a pure SOA

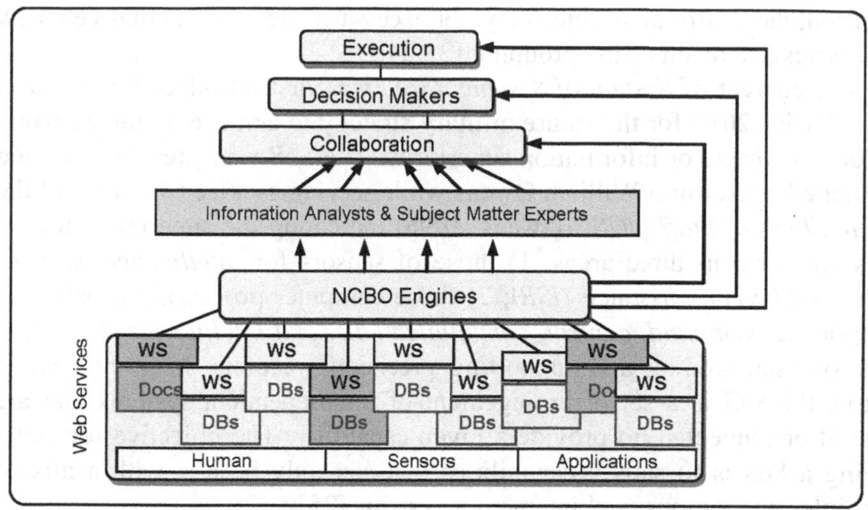

Figure 1.21. Network-centric applications with web services and an NCBO engine.

technology heavily leans upon Web services' open nature to deal with inter- and intra-entity communications. Many implementations have shown the trend of the transition by beginning with Web services and then arriving at more effective and manageable "business services" with the application of policy articulation, business rules, and process control. In this book, a more broad definition is used to address the open interface without having to depend upon specific technology.

There are many attributes and functionalities working behind the application information flows to support a seamless business practice. In the figure, an abstract box named NCBO engines is situated between the applications WS and portal WS to illustrate its relationship with other components. The deployment of a network-centric service-oriented solution takes the advantage of the "conclusive intelligent" from the NCBO concept enabling reliable, consistent, and collaborated information flows between networked services. To effectively support these goals, many of the tasks exist in the form of operational support functions or internal services performed by the service providers. Normally these tasks are invisible to the service users but occasionally offered as value-added services for external advanced functions. They will be delineated in the following section.

1.5 System-Level Integration

A traditional IT view of a family of systems is basically a grouping of systems having some common characteristic(s), but lacking the synergy of common missions. While putting together a group of systems into a suite or solution, the family of systems may not necessarily acquire qualitatively new properties as a result of the grouping [23,24].

The concept of *System of Systems (SoS)* was first introduced by DoD in Joint Vision 2010 for the future military strategy to achieve dominant battle space knowledge or information superiority. The SoS was later renewed and expanded by Admiral William Owens while serving as Vice Chairman of the *Joint Chiefs of Staff (JCS)* (Owens, 1996) indicating the superior technologies emerging in three areas: 1) those of sensors for *intelligence, surveillance, and reconnaissance (ISR)*; 2) those computer processing capabilities supporting *command, control, communications, and intelligence (C4I)*; and 3) those surrounding and supporting precision weapons. In more generic terms, the SoS is a set or arrangement of interdependent systems that are related or connected, to provide a given capability. The objective for developing a SoS is to satisfy capabilities that can only be met with a mix of multiple, autonomous, and interacting systems [25].

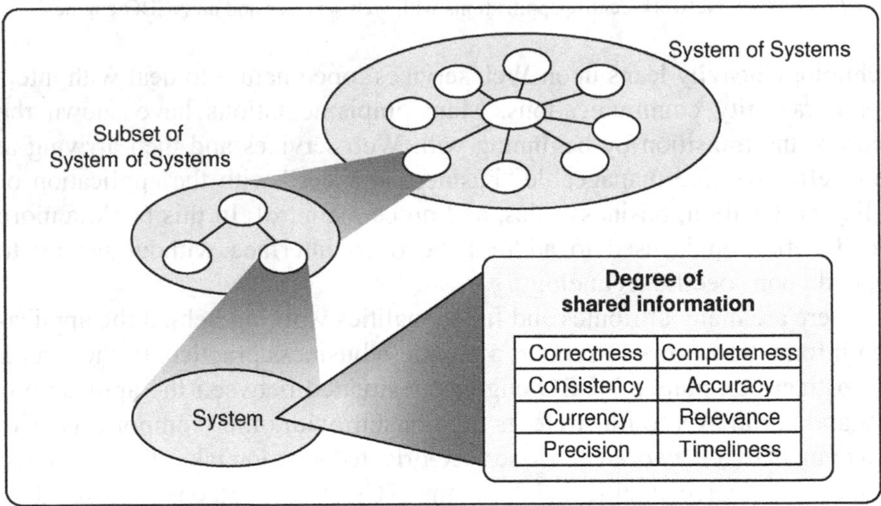

Figure 1.22. A hierarchy of a System of Systems.

The SoS is characterized by relatively more centralized management and control over development and operations, and therefore less autonomy. Under this definition, systems within a SoS, even though they are managed independently, can be subject to some uniform direction in the areas of architectural framework, guidelines, standards, development principles, and operational view. With the concept of NCBO the final effect of networked families of systems is expected to go beyond the additive sum of the individual capabilities of its member systems.

Figure 1.22 depicts a hierarchy of a SoS where the component parts can be a system or subordinate system, called subsystems. Through the relationships among its constituent systems, the SoS can achieve information and operational synergy, thus interoperability is an essential attribute of SoS [26].

1.5.1 System of Systems and Federation of Systems

A *federation of systems (FoS)* is a variation of SoS but managed without central authority and direction. The constituent systems of a FOS are independently managed, thus its authority are decentralized in management, development, and operations. Because there is no central authority for direction, the participation of the constituents occurs through collaboration and cooperation to meet the objectives of the federation [27].

- In these systems, there is little central power and authority for "command and control".
- The participation of the coalition of partners is based upon collaboration and coordination to meet the needs of the federation.
- A Federation of Systems is characterized by autonomy and heterogeneity and, often by geographic distribution.
- Consideration of success characteristics for a Federation of Systems is very desirable as well.

The technical architecture of a FOS could comprise widely varying standards and guidelines – the equivalent of multiple technical architectures used by its constituents. Accordingly, the individual systems as implemented would be more heterogeneous than a SoS in hardware components, platforms, operating systems, programming languages, software applications, and data structures. There would be more issues of interoperability.

Consequently, a FOS is generally characterized by a greater degree of autonomy, heterogeneity, and distribution.

Generally, a FOS is more heterogeneous than a SoS. Any SoS will exhibit some diversity, even one adapted to a single architectural framework. The individual systems are managed and operated independently by various organizations (e.g., services and defense agencies). When multiple communities of humans manage, engineer, and operate, there will be different interpretations of requirements, standards, and priorities.

However, a higher viewpoint needs to be taken in most planning and design situations because an enterprise-wide service-oriented solution might lead to a large, unmanageable service model. This is owing to the nature of SOE where SOA does not dictate a particular decomposition style. As stated in the discussion of the network-centric concept, the NCBO paradigm can accommodate the weakness of a pure SOA based SoS design and tighten the loosing ends in the areas of information, process, and control management.

Furthermore, by decomposing existing systems into a NCBO paradigm, it becomes possible to synthesize a set of candidate services from the components identified and synthesize others by adapting the business process flows that have been discovered at the higher layer of abstraction. As the result, the final service hierarchy can be established at mesh relationship rather than a simple tree structure, where the process flows can be realized as services and the services can be realized as process flows. This will increase the flexibility and efficiency of the enterprise information and process management.

1.5.2 SoS Features NCBO

To create an effective SOE which can justify action to gain business value, plan for adoption, and develop good strategies for implementation, a discussion on the nature of business and technical services within an enterprise is beneficial. This can help avoiding misperceptions and misunderstandings of the concept of NCBO, especially when extended to include a wider audience such as business partners.

The relationship of NCBO Engine and the affiliated services is depicted in Figure 1.23. The adoption of service-oriented SoS design provides essential values in the following areas: 1) an explicit frame of reference or data elements describing business or operational entities and concepts; 2) clear guidance and protocols for invoking a service; and 3) the data objects in and out of the service. The applications interacting with the NCBO Engine can include the following:

- *Sensor Management Services*: Sensor management deals with setting modes, etc. in the individual sensors. This is covered in chapter 4.
- *Service and Operation Management*: This feature contains services to support executives and service managers. The features include services necessary to plan and manage enterprise operations in all its phases. The services cover areas such as planning, tasking, combating, and follow up. These are illustrated in chapter 5, "Building a wireless network service".
- *Information Service*: This feature contains services that handle information about the current situation, like surveillance and reconnaissance information, weather information, and geographical information provided by sensors and other sources. The services are further divided into "Dynamic" and "Static" information. This is covered in chapter 6 Network Services Monitoring.
- *Collaborative Services*: This feature contains services allowing the user to collaborate and communicate with other users. This feature includes means for Voice, videoconferencing, messaging, chat, and white boarding. The key contributors are data communication and QoS features are discussed in chapter 7.

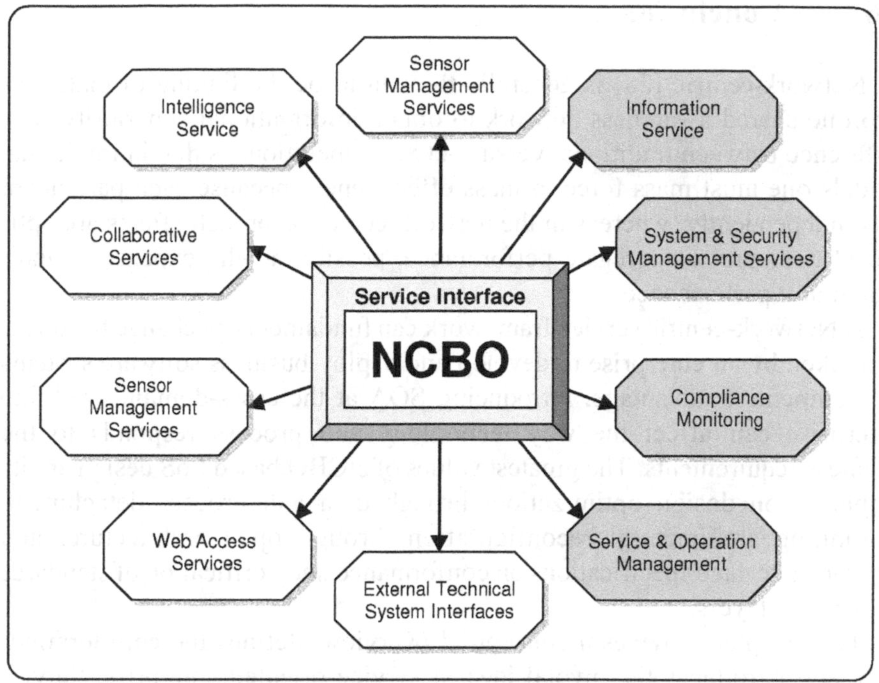

Figure 1.23. NCBO engine and affiliated services.

- *External System Interface and Web Access Service*: This feature offers services to external users or applications to access and browse the Internet or Intranet. The NCBO system offer interoperability with external systems through different bridges. This is covered in chapters 8 and 10.
- *Message System and Security Service*: This feature allows the user of the enterprise to configure and manage system, security, authorization, key, communication, and network management. This is covered in chapter 8.
- *Intelligence Services*: This feature provides all services to support intelligence gathering, processing, and presentation. This includes strategic intelligence service where information that cannot be attributed to a source must be provided and used within the system. This is covered in chapter 9.
- *Personalization and Situation Adaptation Services*: This feature contains services that provide means to choreograph services in order to tailor the system capabilities to meet different situation. The services included are choreography services and access services for the service catalogue. Other examples are Logistics Services, Training, and Simulation Services. These applications are addressed in chapter 10.

1.6 Conclusion

Network-centric [28] is generally thought to be the linking of platforms into one shared awareness network to obtain informational superiority. The difference between traditional versus network operations is that in traditional models one must mass force to mass effectiveness because each participant acts independently, whereas in the network-centric approach effects are optimized to improve aggregate performance, possibly at the expense of individual unit performance.

A Network-centric service framework can fundamentally change the direction taken by an enterprise to develop and deploy business software systems for competitive advantage. Introducing SOA at the cross-domain level, the enterprise can affect the way technology and process responds to the business requirements. The greatest values of NCBO based SoS design are its emphasis on design optimization through data and process detachment, continuing architectural reconfiguration through open architecture, and rigorous interface specifications on conformance and verification of standards at different layers.

This chapter provides a conceptual overview, defines the core terminology and introduces the pivotal idea of service oriented enterprise. Service orientation presents some massive cultural and technical challenges that cross-three areas that have traditionally worked largely in isolation from one another: business process improvement, application development, and software operations. A tangible example of how the idea of a service can provide an unifying thread for drawing together these areas is addressed along with some guidance for applying this approach to business management.

Chapter 2

ENABLER OF INFORMATION SUPERIORITY

The emergence of Web service technologies has shifted from *distributed object architecture (DOA)* to SOA. In the government and private sectors there has been a growing need for increased integration and collaboration among CoIs (section 8.1.1), often across organizational and corporate boundaries. To enable information superiority, such new service deployments have triggered the need to effectively manage these services in order to ensure a successful SOA [1].

U.S. DoD has been historically at the forefront of new technology to assure U.S. military superiority. The diversification and complexity of the government environment requires rather comprehensive and successful Information Management models to support their objectives. It is to be believed that the success story from DoD can provide good methodology and process samples to any enterprise. Designed by DoD, the *Global Information Grid (GIG*; section 2.2*)* is directed towards providing critical networking infrastructure, and is essential for achieving network-centric operations. The role of the GIG is to create an environment which is global, robust, survivable, maintainable, interoperable, secure, reliable, and user-driven. It provides significant elements in bridging business needs and traditional Information Management.

This chapter profiles architecture hierarchy and major elements of the GIG and provides history and background to demonstrate the evolutionary path of Information Management in execution, monitoring, and control. It aims at enterprises' *information technology (IT)* operations so the values provided by the GIG can leverage their current best practices in business operations and integrate the new network-centric approach to assist them remaining competitive in their information practices. *Enhanced Telecommunication Operational Maps (eTOM*; section 2.3*)* from *Telecommunication Management Forum (TMF)* are reviewed and associated with GIG functions thus the management infrastructure can be exchangeable allowing for smooth transition if desired.

2.1 Information and Computing Grid

Enterprise IT exposes the computing grill in the adoption and incorporation of *service objects (SO)* for clients, third-parties, and business partners with the SOA technology. The transformation of SOC demands the process to better assure corporate information based on business policies and rules. As a key computing element in the enterprise computing infrastructure, SOA allows enterprise processes to closely interact with the other three functions, namely collaborative computing, autonomous computing, grid computing.

Another level of SO adoption is its ability to successfully overcome interoperability issues and to integrate systems and applications using open transport infrastructure. As proprietary protocols, glue code, and point-to-point connections give way to open and standards-based protocols, SOC can now interact with other applications based on service descriptions that each system externalizes. As the result, the information modeling and data strategy which support the transport services are cross-enterprise. Expanded from Figure 1.10, the relationship of the enterprise computing infrastructure and Information Management is shown in Figure 2.1 [2].

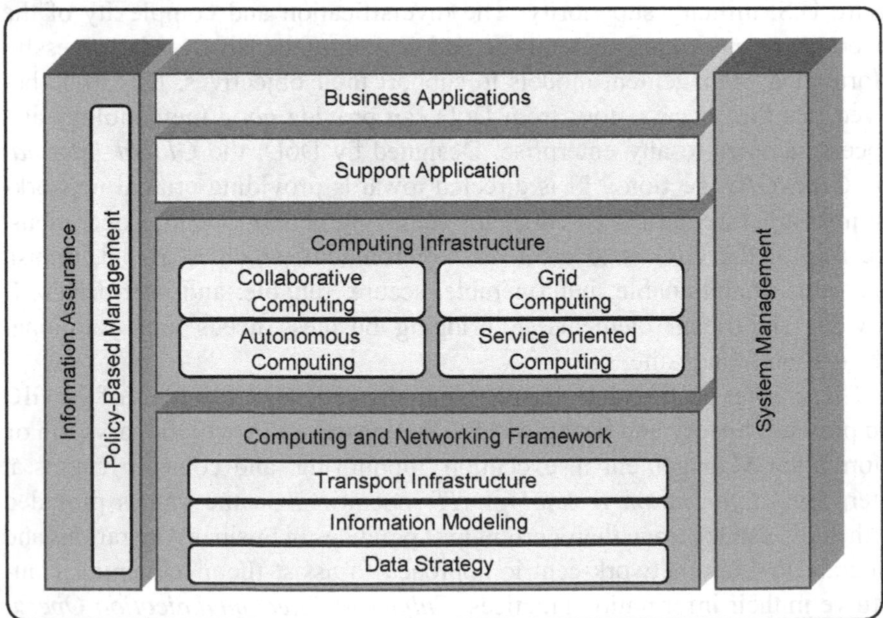

Figure 2.1. System architecture of enterprise services.

2.1.1 Service-Oriented Maturity Model

This Service-Oriented Maturity Model provides a framework to discuss the applicability and benefits of SO in an organization across five maturity levels of adoption.

From the customer-experience perspective, the task of the IT infrastructure is to ensure the specified quality of *end-to-end services* throughout the *service life cycle*. This is accomplished by managing the quality of the supporting sub-services from a service or third-party providers. Enterprise networks and the management systems that control them have become much more sophisticated and mature in recent years. The IT resources have become "smarter" through the use of embedded software controls. This has given rise to a new view of the use of management systems. The robustness of such IT management systems makes it a competitive tool that can be leveraged by operators as well as customers. This trend is emerging as a new vehicle for customer retention, adding new value to existing customer care for customer-satisfaction improvement, thereby increasing revenue per customer [3].

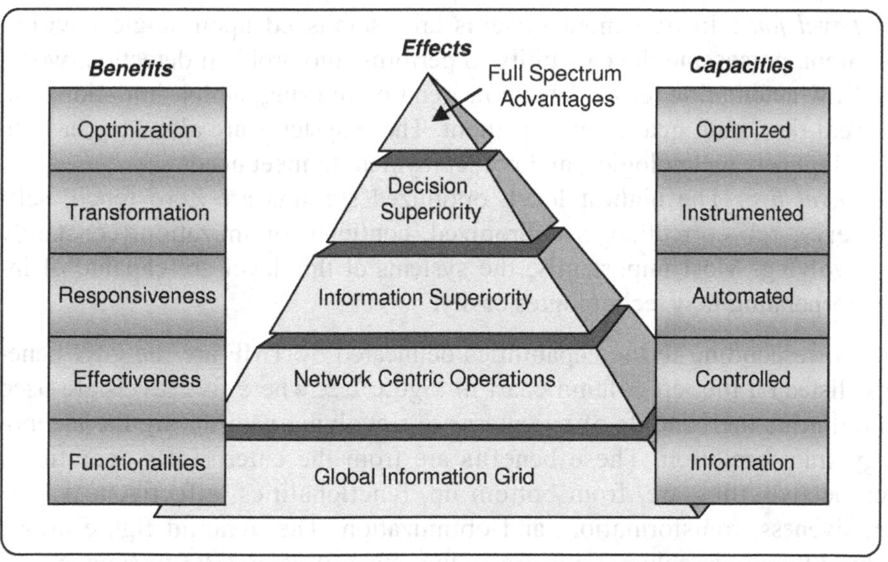

Figure 2.2. GIG as an enabling foundation and operational maturity.

Improving from today's management systems, service problems in an enterprise IT environment are identified after the fact, either after users have experienced or complained about troubles or the service providers receive abnormal service alerts. An effective service management allows IT managers to monitor and manage every detail of network usage, including user, application, and resource usage details, all in real time. It unobtrusively gathers and analyzes service data and provides real-time reporting of information pertaining to the health and security of business applications running on the network. All events in the enterprise resource are interpreted and reported intelligently; giving service operators the reports needed to improve their services.

The TMF (section 2.3) has created a road map of enterprise management systems development in five levels, depicted in the right column chart of Figure 2.2. It is a recommended direction for service providers to develop their capabilities with regard to configuration, performance, problem resolution, and billing management [4].

- *Level one*: Informal systems are highly manual, point solutions, multiple databases, difficult to change.
- *Level two*: Controlled systems are on the basis where access integrated inventory and common configuration data are available but difficult to scale.
- *Level three*: Automated systems advance towards a scaleable, cohesive data-model, and bottom–up and top–down analysis.
- *Level four*: Instrumented systems are established upon single environment, possessing the capability to perform auto problem detection, workflow automation, error detection, trend monitoring, action initiation, and real-time state quality management. These systems are also very easy to adopt new technologies, and predeployment to meet needs.
- *Level five*: The highest level, optimized systems are Zero touch, self-serve, self-correction, synchronized, continual optimization, constantly evolving. Most importantly, the systems at this level are capable of incorporating new technologies easily.

Corresponding to the capabilities delineated by TMF are the GIG benefits, listed on the left column chart in Figure 2.2, where five levels are used to delineate the benefits of an enterprise's evolving path during the technology transformation. These benefits are from the enterprise's operational perspective; they are, from bottom up, functionalities, effectiveness, responsiveness, transformation, and optimization. The pyramid figure drawn behind these two columns illustrates the effect of using GIG to support network-centric operations and obtain information superiority. The transformation can assist the enterprise to achieve decision superiority, and ultimately reach full-spectrum advantages because of highly automated knowledge and information awareness.

2.1.2 Concept of Information Sharing on Need-to-Know

In addition to the effects of the service maturity model, it is equally important that the enterprise focus on their data strategy. From a technology perspective, protecting network boundaries using firewall and certification levels for communicating classified and sensitive data over the network is a mature industry; chapter 8 will provide more in-depth discussions. However, isolating information of one community from the information of other communities sharing the same network is a challenge for information management. The larger the shared network, the greater the difficulty in providing multiple secure activities within it.

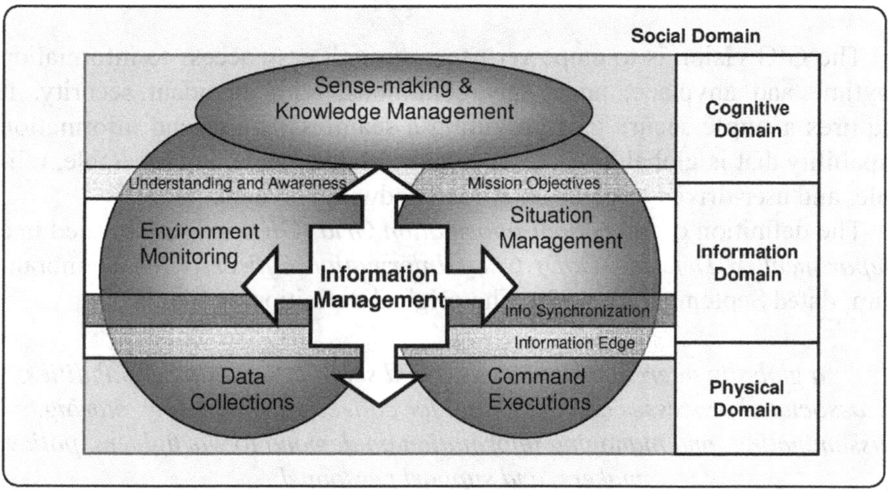

Figure 2.3. Domain relationships.

Figure 2.3 portrays a sample of layered domains and its relationship with information management. As shown in the figure, data is collected and synchronized through the information edge into an *Information Domain*. Information is further fused into knowledge via the understanding and awareness processes. At the *Cognitive Domain*, knowledge turns into an actionable plan as per the mission objectives. The action plan is consequently executed as part of the situation management and applied to the *Physical Domain* (more in chapter 9). All the flows belong to the *Social Domain* which contains all philosophical, strategic, tactical objectives and identities in the circle of data, information, and cognitive transformation [5].

Information Management is situated in the center of the circle and interacts with these three domains as a key enabler of network-centric business operations. As this circle continues to interpret data from the Physical Domain, translate the data into sensible knowledge, and apply commands to the Physical Domain, it essentially demonstrates an intelligent system with the capability to automatically adjust actions in accordance with the surrounding environment. This is the fundamental nature of information and decision superiority. In a military application, such ability enables *Command, Control, Communications, Computers, and Intelligence (C4I)* integration of joint forces, improves interoperability of systems, and increases optimization of bandwidth capacity. In a commercial application, such an ability can translate into lean-and-mean business practices in enterprise information exchanges across value-chain participants [6].

2.2 Global Information Grid

The GIG vision is to empower users through easy access to information anytime and anyplace, under any conditions, with attendant security. It requires a single secure grid providing a seamless end-to-end information capability that is global, robust, survivable, maintainable, interoperable, reliable, and user-driven (e.g., information/bandwidth on demand) [7].

The definition of the *Global Information Grid (GIG)* was established in a *Department of Defense (DoD) Chief Information Officer (CIO)* memorandum, dated September 22, 1999. The original definition of GIG is

a globally interconnected, end-to-end set of information capabilities, associated processes and personnel for collecting, processing, storing, disseminating, and managing information on demand to warfighters, policy makers, and support personnel

On May 2 2001, the extended definition of GIG reached agreement among the DoD CIO, the *Under Secretary of Defense (USD)* for *Acquisition, Technology and Logistics (AT&L)*, and the *Joint Staff.* In accordance with the updated definition, GIG components include all owned and leased communications and computing systems and services, software (including applications), equipment, data, security services, and other associated services that meet one or more of the following criteria:

- Transmits information to, receives information from, routes information among, or interchanges information among other equipment, software, and services.
- Provides retention, organization, visualization, information assurance, or disposition of data, information, and/or knowledge received from or transmitted to other equipment, software, and services.

- Processes data or information for use by other equipment, software, and services.

The GIG works at the infrastructure level providing seamless end-to-end capabilities from all operating locations (bases, posts, camps, stations, facilities, mobile platforms, and deployed sites). And therefore should include non-GIG IT, such as stand-alone, self-contained, or embedded IT that is not or will not be connected to the enterprise network. The GIG can support *plug and play* interoperability to joint, high capacity, netted operations. It makes tactical and functional fusion a reality, defenses in depth against all threats, and is fused with weapons systems necessary to achieve information superiority. It can interface to coalition, allied, and non-DoD users and systems [8].

2.2.1 Global Information Grid and Enterprise Environment

GIG was born out of concerns regarding interoperability and end-to-end integration of automated information systems. The effort is to manage issues such as streamlined management and the improvement of information infrastructure investment. GIG also includes *National Security Systems (NSS)* to support National Security, and related *Intelligence Community (IC)* missions and functions (strategic, operational, tactical, and business) in war and in peace. It is DoD's goal for its Information Management to be fully integral to the military command and control, intelligence, and mission support functions to improve interoperability of systems in order to increase optimization of bandwidth capacity as well as to improve information sharing through the robust networking.

The GIG's role is to create an environment in which users can access data through various services without having to rely on (and wait for) organizations in charge of data collection to process and disseminate the information. Figure 2.4 illustrates different GIG layers in supporting an enterprise environment. It depicts the service layer as detached from the applications and systems; the communications and infrastructure layers are supporting the transport functionality and ensure cross-system interoperability. This figure also denotes the preferred focus of enterprise operations, which is a top–down view of services.

In addition to all the operational advantages, the GIG could also reduce the substantial resources and logistics needed to bring command, control, and communications systems to a military operational environment [9].

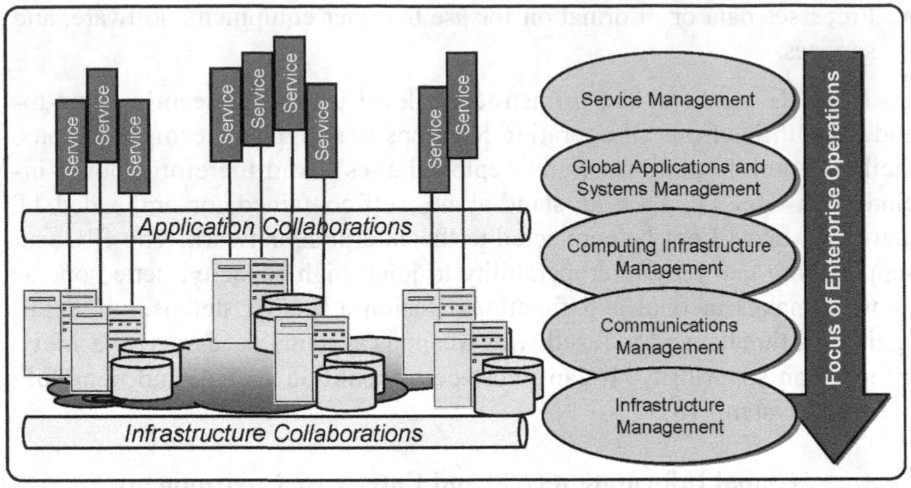

Figure 2.4. GIG enterprise environment.

2.2.2 The Goal of GIG

The goal is to increase the network-centricity of cross-silo business planning, operational intelligence, information technology, customer, and marketing management operations and can be concluded as following [10]:

- increasing reach among the users and customers,
- increasing richness in the information and expertise that can be applied to supporting operational decisions,
- increasing agility in rapidly adapting information and information technology, and
- increasing assurance that the right information and resources to do the task will be there when and where they are required.

Table 2.1 illustrates how DoD envisions the GIG will help transform current mission critical mission into technology-oriented Information Management operations [11].

The GIG can enhance operational capabilities while providing a common operational environment for conventional and the next generation command and control, enterprise mission support, service support, intelligence, and business functions. Additionally, the values which GIG can potentially benefit normal business operations include the following [12]:

- Moving information in real time before or with logical and/or physical resources, during the planning and deployment phases to ensure the levels of supplies and disposition of assets can align with the associated missions and commands.

Table 2.1. How DoD Envisions GIG Will Help Transform Military Operations.

Current	Future
Customized, platform-centric information technology	Network-centric, commercial off-the-shelf software, Web-based
Circuit-based transmission of data	Internet protocol-based transmission of data
Bandwidth limitations	Bandwidth on demand
Limited operational picture	Situational awareness
Fixed and remote command and control	Mobile, deployable, in-transit command and control
Broadcast (push) information to users	Post information on network and facilitate "smart" pull by users
Collect, process, exploit, disseminate	Collect, post, process, use
Individual	Collaborative
Stovepipe decision-making	Communities of interest
Multiple data calls, data duplication	Handle information only once
Private data	Shared data
Perimeter, one-time security	Persistent, continuous information assurance
Single points of failure	Diverse routing
Separate infrastructures	Enterprise services
Interoperability by standard applications	Interoperability designed from start ("born joint")

Sources: DoD (data); GAO (presentation).

- Establishing a rapid and seamless flow and exchange of information to enable collaborative mission planning and execution from widely dispersed locations and at different levels.
- Reduced redundant service involvements at high operational tempos where dynamic planning and redirection of assets is required.
- Performing collection, processing, storage, distribution, and display of information horizontally and vertically across organizational structures and community domains.
- Ensuring individual service user possesses the ability to obtain and use mission and administrative support information from the enterprise, internal and external organizations, value-chain partners, and other widely dispersed assets.
- Timely, assured connectivity and information availability for decision makers and their advisors to support effective decision-making.
- Integrated, survivable, and enduring communications.

Figure 2.5 depicts a logic-to-physical horizontal view where control information can travel from a conceptual space into a physical action space as well as monitoring information traveling from the physical action space back to the conceptual space. From the command and control perspective, essentially all the network-centric operational values are transforming from left-to-right in the order of information, perception, cyber or network operations, information protection, electrical action control, to the physical action. Conversely, the situation awareness intelligence travels from right-to-left [13].

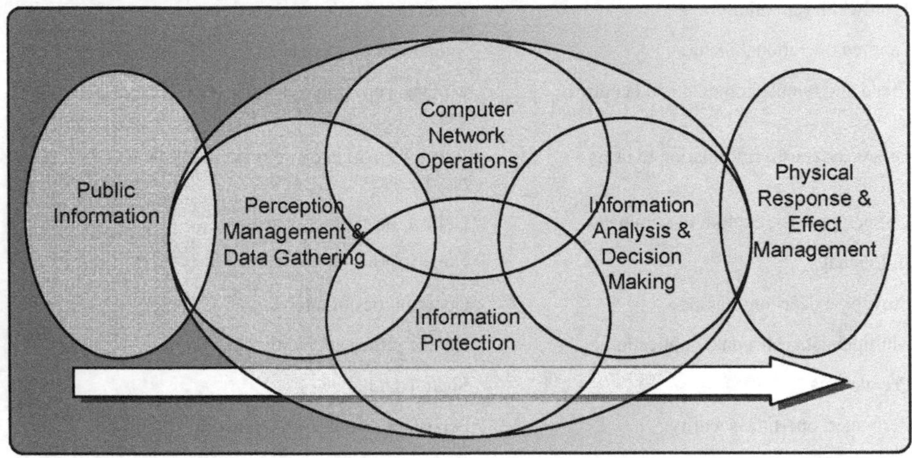

Figure 2.5. Logic-to-physical horizontal view in network-centric information flow.

2.2.3 Original GIG Operations Space

The original operational space of GIG defined by DoD was established upon the network framework much like the Internet, but with more dependence on space-based and mobile, ad-hoc systems to carry out communications functions. Figure 2.6 shows the various layers of the GIG's overall concept. At the core are communications satellites, next generation radios, and an installations-based network with significantly expanded bandwidth. These will provide the basic infrastructure through which data will be routed and shared. In addition, the GIG would employ a variety of information technology services and applications to manage the flow of information and ensure the network is reliable and secure. Various information technology tools would be available to help users determine what information is available, where to find it, and how best to use it. DoD envisions that communities of interest would be developed, linking users with common interests who would collaborate on analyzing and sharing information. Ultimately, most of DoD's sensors, weapon systems, business systems, and systems belonging to decision makers, military units, and allies would be tied into the GIG network – serving as both users and providers of data [11].

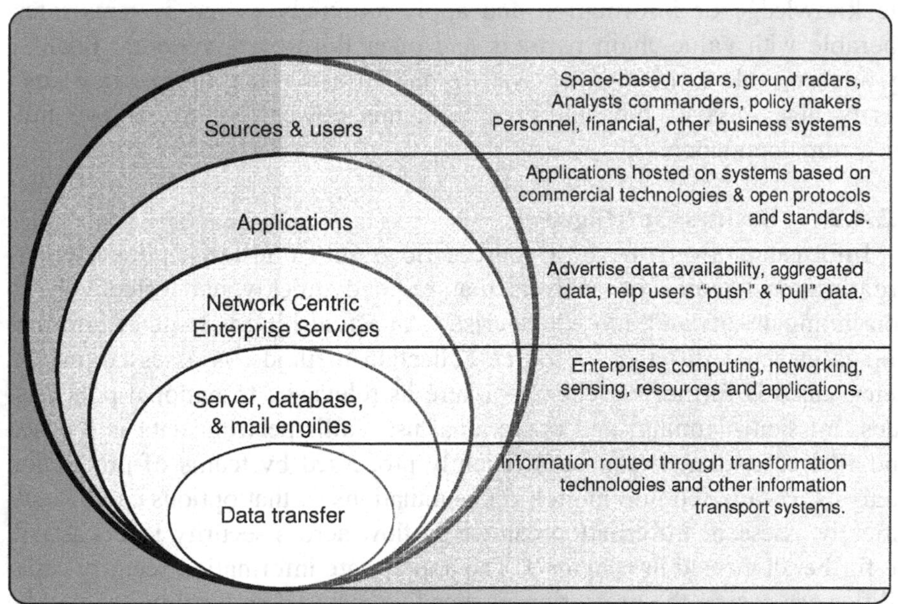

Figure 2.6. A general depiction of DoD's characterization of the GIG.

2.2.4 GIG Applications in Commercial Arena

Even thought the GIG was designed for the military applications, as the goals of better information for decision-making are common between the government and private sectors. The following scenarios and functionalities are actually applicable to applications that require rapid and seamless flow and exchange of information around the globe to enable collaborative mission planning and execution from widely dispersed locations and at different levels (to include strategic, operational, tactical, and business).

2.2.4.1 Execution, Monitoring, and Control

A fully integrated dashboard or common operating picture that provides appropriate level of broadness and depth of the mission status, operational health, and potential threats to the business operation can assist the executives and service managers to obtain a three-dimensional operation space view in near real time. This can help the decision makers to ensure vertical and horizontal integration of mission control or executions.

In an enterprise application where reaction times must be in seconds, data collectors (can be in a form of sensor) acquire target objects and pass that information directly to the actor process (computer, equipment, or human) over high bandwidth communications pipes. Through an enterprise-wide common interface or information presentation means, the enterprise users can apply the knowledge or information and apply rationally to the systems interoperable with value-chain partners and other third-party vendors. Enabled by interoperable and integrated systems and infrastructure, information superiority hence assists the enterprise with this power tool to achieve full-spectrum dominance.

2.2.4.2 Business Intelligence

Information from the best sources flows into multi-disciplined, cross-organizational teams of analysts that respond quickly and effectively to continuing threats and immediate crises. An astonishing volume of information is gathered through all source collection methods, is assessed, and in many cases is further enriched to assure its relevance to national policy issues, mission planning, and operational use. Full-spectrum data is focused and filtered so that it can be efficiently processed by teams of production analysts. Data is fed into models and simulations so that options can be realistically assessed. Information can easily flow across security levels as will be further discussed in chapter 9. The appropriate information security capabilities can ensure the protection of sensitive material and sources as will be seen in chapter 8.

2.2.4.3 Business Operation Support

Business functions, such as logistics, finance, health, and personnel, are as effective and efficient as similar functions performed in the private sector. Advanced information technology allows the users to exploit the *Reliability, Maintainability, Availability (RMA)* of enterprise services. Scarce resources are no longer wasted on unnecessary infrastructure and unique applications, and support functions multiply the effects of the RMA. Smart cards speed purchases and help streamline procurements. Logistic supply systems fill requests for supplies in hours. Asset visibility is maintained at every point of the supply chain (using advanced technologies such as bar coding and scanners). Standard interfaces, shared data, and the use of commercial standards facilitate outsourcing of activities where appropriate. People routinely telecommute, saving office space and reducing impacts on the environment. Enabling technologies are used to facilitate the most efficient exchange of the full range of business information resulting in streamlined and rapid response to supporting missions [14].

To support its customers as they improve mission performance, the enterprise community reengineers its internal processes to be more effective and efficient, and changes its culture:

- The enterprise has a customer focus and measures customer satisfaction.
- Systems and technical architectures are applied to ensure interoperability and integration.

- The enterprise acquisition process uses prototypes, demonstrations, and exercises to evolve IT capabilities in full collaboration with end users.
- IT services and products are benchmarked to achieve "world-class" performance at the lowest possible cost.
- The enterprise's organizations continually improve their internal processes, such as software design and technology insertion.
- The enterprise empowers its people and embodies the principles of a "learning organization".

A value-chain environment, working in partnership between client and provider, has redesigned how it does its business. Culture, organization, training, and processes have been reinvented. Organizations are streamlined to eliminate unnecessary headquarters staff. Individuals are empowered and accountable. Vertical stovepipes and hierarchical thinking has given way to horizontal teaming and cross-functional integration.

2.2.4.4 Networked Sensor Applications

As will be seen in chapter 4, sensor networks provide significant performance advantages over stand-alone sensors in key mission spaces by overcoming the fundamental performance limitations (e.g., coverage, accuracy, and target identification properties) of individual stand-alone sensors. The operational performance of a sensor network (a collection of networked sensor entities) in generating business awareness depends upon a number of factors including the performance of component sensors, sensor geometry (the locations of the sensors with respect to each other and the objects of interest, the velocity of information, fusion capabilities), and tasking capabilities.

The performance advantage that emerges from the enabling of sensor networks is a function of the type of sensors being employed (e.g., active, passive) and the class of objects of interest (e.g., missiles, aircraft, tanks, submarines, and so forth). Sensor networks can generate significantly increased business awareness of objects in the business operations.

The value-adding processes of data fusion and sensor tasking can partially overcome these limitations. Information technologies enable firms to create a high level of competitive awareness within their organizations and extended enterprises. Integrating across the experiences of the firms that have emerged dominant in their competitive domains, the following core themes are revealed.

1. Networking is enabling the creation of new types of information-based relationships with and among organizations that are able to leverage increased competitive awareness.
2. Time is being compressed and, as a result, the tempo of operations is being increased.

3. The cumulative impact of better information, better distribution, and new organizational behavior provides firms with the capability to create superior value propositions for their customers and dominate their competitive space.

2.2.5 GIG Functions

The GIG process is required to accommodate all Information Management tasks related to creation, acquisition, transmission, organization, storage, dissemination, presentation, protection, and disposition of information. The functions that support and characterize the information flow and exchange throughout the GIG are organized and defined as follows:

1. *Computing* has process and store functions. The process function is a set of operations to manipulate data, information, or knowledge into the desired form to support decision-making and other GIG functions. The store function retains, organizes, and disposes of data, information, or knowledge for information sharing.
2. *Communications* supports the transport function to facilitate end-to-end movement of data, information, or knowledge between operational communities.
3. *Presentation* or the *human-GIG interaction (HGI)* function supporting information interactions between human-in-control and GIG service access point.
4. *Network Operations (NETOPS)* has three main management functions. It is an organizational and procedural framework for integrating network, information dissemination, and information assurance managements. The *network management (NM)* function monitors, controls, and ensures the visibility of the various networking and internetworking components. The *information dissemination management (IDM)* function manages the dissemination and storage of information across the GIG for awareness, interoperable access, and delivery of information. The *information assurance (IA)* function protects and defends (detection, reaction, and restores) information and information systems to ensuring their availability, integrity, authentication, confidentiality, and non-repudiation.

The GIG works an infrastructure in itself with a number of added services, as illustrated in Figure 2.7 [15].

The following sections lay out the blueprint for areas that are needed to be factored into solution implementation not all systems may require all features listed.

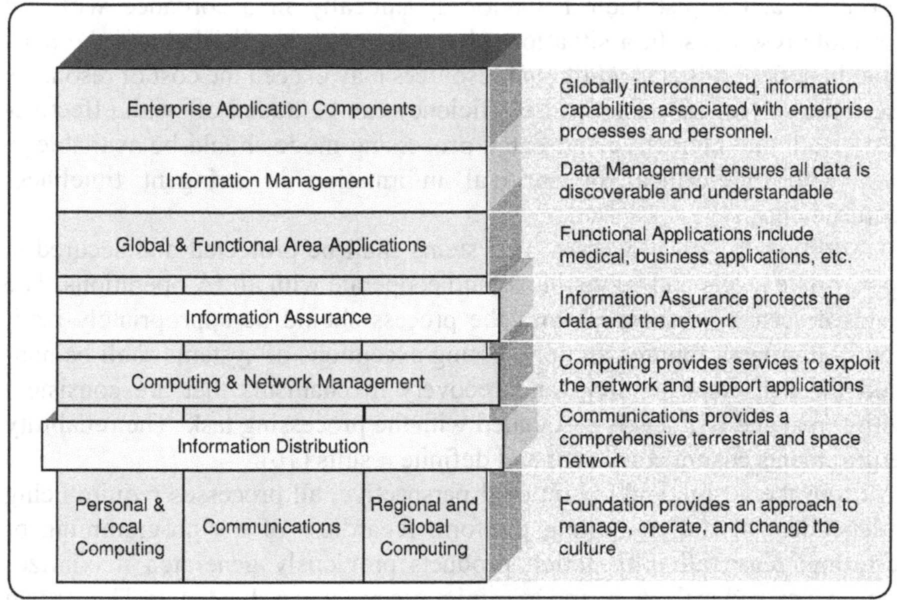

Figure 2.7. GIG reference model and GIG enterprise services.

2.2.5.1 GIG Computing

GIG computing consists of two areas, namely process and store. The specific requirements of GIG process are to support decision-making and other GIG-supported activities. The store requirements enable and support the indexing, cataloging, and storage of information and the rapid search and retrieval from repositories, all for decision superiority.

The GIG Process

The objectives of the GIG process requirements aim to alleviate IT challenges from the areas of interoperability, collaborative process, and security in a distributed computing environment.

To achieve interoperability among systems' processes, GIG requires all processes to use standardized *interprocess communications (IPC)* to communicate with local or remote processes, regardless of whether the processes resides on GIG or non-GIG systems. The functional specifications are also extended to retain GIG security and integrity while being responsive to task prioritization dynamically.

The GIG process functions support analytical and collaboration capabilities through services that support collaborative planning, decision-making aids, modeling and simulation, data mining, intelligent agents, and virtual workspaces. All critical processes shall be able to monitor the available resources and adjust their behavior dynamically in accordance with the available resources. In a situation where resources are limited and the marginal benefit of utilizing additional resources may exceed the cost of resources used, the system function ensure efficiency can be traded off with effectiveness. Both the interactive and batch processing mode should be available to deal with time-critical or survival information in stringent timeliness requirements.

Additionally, all processes of systems shall be protected and secured at appropriate levels and be visible to and cooperate with all IA operations. The level of security associated with the process should be appropriately justified. All process failures and processing exceptions of systems shall be handled through error-handling and recovery mechanisms that are consistent with threat and risk levels associated with the processing task. The reliability requirements ensure consistent and definite results [16].

From the design and operational perspective, all processes require being independent of the computing platform regardless of the programming or scripting; reuse all information products previously generated maximizes consistency and efficiency and to minimizes process redundancy. The system should adopt a modular design for a high degree of cohesion to enhance process reusability and system maintainability. Such design implies low coupling and leads to relatively independent processes to achieve the plug and play "commodities" goal. The validation requirement demands the accuracy of outputs from systems to ensure that the right system was built. The verifiability requirement focuses on a traceable path from the designed and implemented system to check for building the system the right way.

The GIG Store

The store function is responsible for the organization, retention, and disposition of information to facilitate information sharing across the GIG.

The GIG store functions include Infrastructure Management providing visibility of storage infrastructure to efficiently manage the available storage capacity and provide the capability to remove/discard/update stored data. Systems' data shall facilitate its distribution in accordance with processing and transport needs and supports the rapid retrieval of the information by the user.

The GIG store function dictates the specifications in identifying and using common standards for data and metadata representation to ensure data interoperability, e.g., XML. Using a single, discrete source of reference, future updates of that data will be able to refer back to the designated single reference source. Data and information integrity should be maintained whether they are compressed for storage or not. One of the key features in

GIG storage is its high standard of data survivability; the system function prevents the loss of stored data from physical threats such as fire, water damage, information operation threats, power outage, natural events, and *Electromagnetic Pulse (EMP)*.

The data security function includes classification and releasability criteria within the semantic tag or associated schema, including the authorization requirements of data retrieval. The short-term data retention function considers mission operational needs, while the long-term retention function includes legal or other regulatory requirements. All the data should be transparent to the user. The data disposal function allows reuse of the storage space occupied by the disposed data; the storage space is hence released for the storage of new data.

2.2.5.2 Communications

GIG Communications provide transport functions to allow the enterprise to move information or knowledge within the enterprise environment, including users, producers, and intermediate entities. As the networking technology evolves, a standards-based framework can enable the seamless and efficient insertion and incorporation of emerging technologies for fully cross-domain information exchange.

The scope of the transport framework is to conduct information sharing over the existing data links networks. In wireless applications, the utilization of the GIG communication resource in the area of electromagnetic spectrum can be optimized through efficient frequency reuse and advanced modulation, compression, and filtering techniques. In a large scale operating environment where interoperability is critical, the spectrum management will include compliance with collaborated policies to achieve the most effective result.

The framework also includes the control of information switching, routing, and transmission functions. QoS in transport services deals with priority information delivery in an overarching operating environment. Quality factors can include: response time in unicasting, multicasting, or broadcasting applications, prioritization and precedence for expedited handling, availability and reliability for service level objectives, real or near real-time latency, as well as the call throughput success rate. In a more dynamic operating environment where mobility (e.g., communications on-the-move) is demanded, the transport framework is responsible for providing an uninterrupted service both laterally and vertically. For voice applications, the framework needs to provide secure voice interoperability and high call throughput success rate also known as call completion rate. Measurable goal-achievement depends on near real-time data collection from transport elements such as switches or routers to the network management devices.

From an operational perspective, GIG can improve the service availability and reliability by possessing the capability for multiple connectivity paths (not susceptible to the same threats) and media to increase the robustness of the services to avoid any single point of failure. The service systems and their supporting systems should be designed to feature maximum mobility and ease of deployment, especially in the areas of scalability and adaptability to satisfy different deployment scenarios. In mission critical applications, survivability of information and systems against all potential threats commensurate with the operating environment is essential. To enable user confidence, all information elements exchanged should maintain a high degree of information integrity. Depending on the security requirement, sufficient secure voice cryptography is essential for enabling interoperability with other operational organizations.

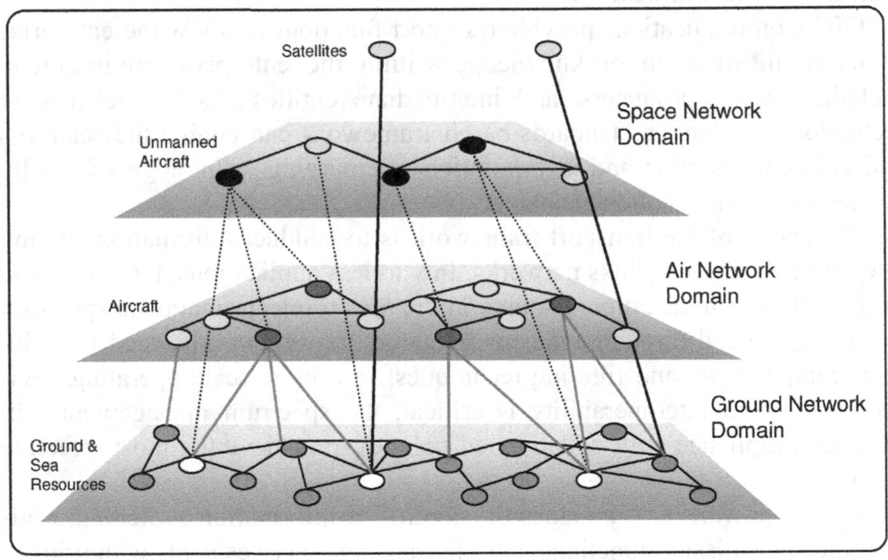

Figure 2.8. Three-Tier ground, air-space network.

Figure 2.8 depicts a three-tier ground, air, and space network The commerical applications of space communication are expanding to include global long-distance telephone service; wireless communications and wireless data links; private, wireless networks for voice, data, and multimedia; *point-of-sale* data gathering; news gathering; information distribution, videoconferencing, and employee training; entertainment services (high-quality television transmission); digital audio broadcasting; Internet services; tele-education; telemarketing; crime-prevention networks; intelligent highway services; and high-performance, special-purpose radio-frequency components, antennas, digital electronics, and digital signal processing.

2.2.5.3 GIG Network Operations

Network Operations (NETOPS) is the organizational and procedural structure used to monitor, manage, and control the GIG by means of NM, IDM, and IA. To effectively support network-centric operations, the enterprise must be able to obtain cross-organizational situational awareness of their IT assets and the information flow [17].

Network Management (NM) Function

As depicted in Figure 2.9, *network management (NM)* hierarchy, the stove-piped and multiple-domain application systems shown in level three are normally not designed to support global, end-to-end network management. In layer two, the mission specific scope offers network or sub-network based information and operational management. It is not until layer three functions are in place that network management can provide a fully integrated and distributed network management capability, offer an end-to-end view of mobile wireless computing and networking, and allow the management of common user networks from multiple locations with NCBO available enterprise wide [18].

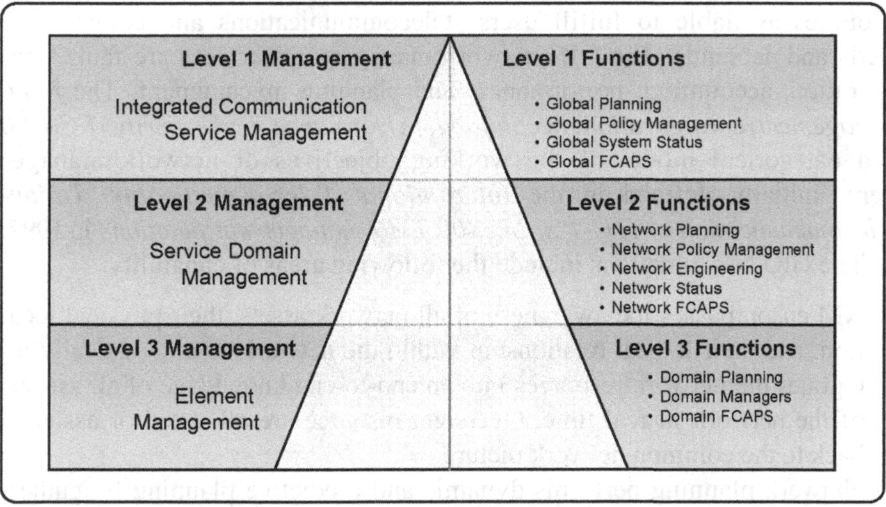

Figure 2.9. Network management hierarchy.

The goal of the GIG network management function is to enable and support distributed and partitioned network control, implement management standards, and enhance asset visibility to support integrated enterprise operations.

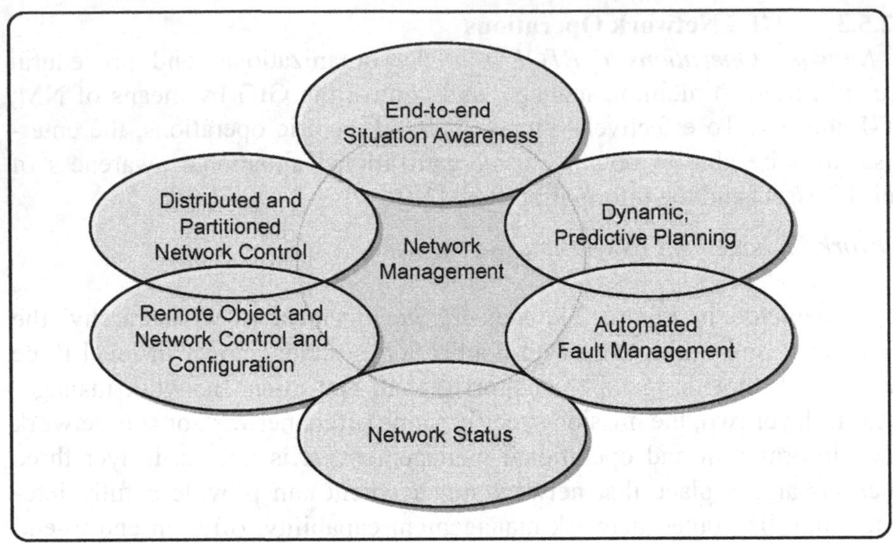

Figure 2.10. Network management functions.

NM (Figure 2.10) is the set of activities that establishes and maintains the GIG network switching, transmission, information services, and computing resources available to fulfill users' telecommunications and connectivity needs and demands. The GIG network management services are fault, configuration, accounting, performance, and planning management. The *fault-management, configuration, accounting, performance, and security (FCAPS)* is a categorical model of the working objectives of network management, initially defined in the *International Telecommunication Union-Telecommunication's (ITU-T's) M.3400 TMN management functions* in 1997.

The GIG NM functions include the following areas of capability:

- NM encompasses the awareness of all network assets, their physical location, and their logical relationship within the network. It automatically integrates the network resources into an end-to-end knowledge of all aspects of the network in real time. Oversight resource are allocated or assigned back to the common network picture.
- Network planning performs dynamic and predictive planning by gathering and processing knowledge from the GIG assets to optimize their utilization. Figure 2.11 depicts sample features in the planning function.
- NM can rapidly transfer control of one or a group of objects within and across the distributed and partitioned network. The transition of control will maintain continuous control without hindering any end-to-end visibility.

- All GIG components provide network status and metrics to the management system to assist decision-making. The NM functions monitor, configure, reconfigure, and control all aspects of the managed objects or network devices.
- The fault and performance management (as assurance) functions perform automated performance evaluation and fault analysis. These functions include problem detection, fault isolation and diagnosis, problem tracking, historical archiving, trending, and alerting. The network assurance related alerts or alarms will be correlated to eliminate duplicated or false reports. These functions also include the tasks to initiate test as well as perform diagnostics to isolate service defects.

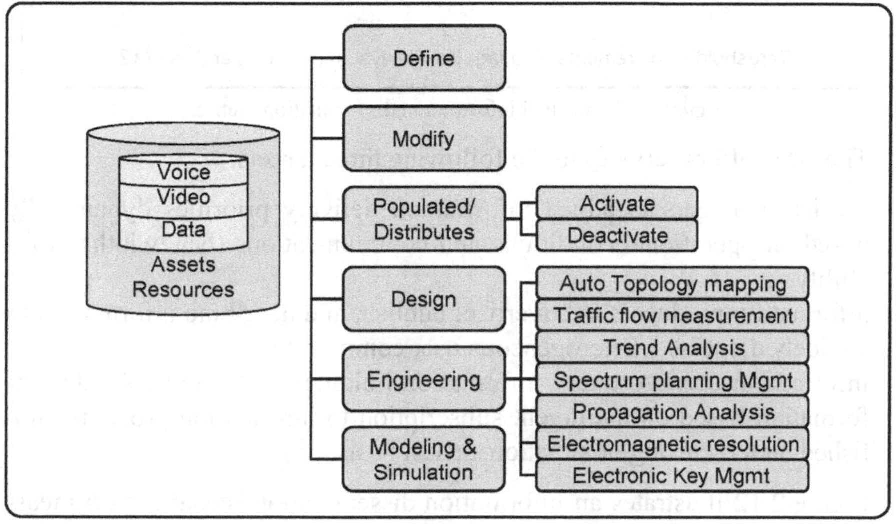

Figure 2.11. Network planning and its associated functions.

Information Dissemination Management (IDM) Function

Information dissemination management (IDM) can maximize the flow of relevant information to the user, consistent with the user's information requirements, the operational policy (to include statutory requirements), and available resources.

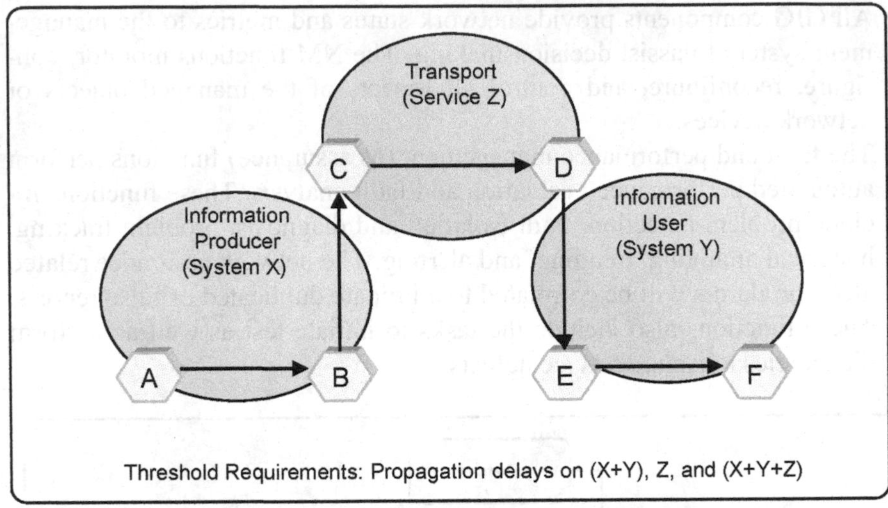

Figure 2.12. Survival information dissemination metric.

The IDM offers services to the following three targets:

- service managers to adjust information delivery priorities dynamically based on operational conditions and communications (bandwidth) availability.
- information producers to advertise, publish, and distribute information to a widely dispersed, heterogeneous user community.
- information users to query information holdings and acquire needed information based on intelligent subscription to information products published on a recurring or situation-driven basis.

Figure 2.12 illustrates an information dissemination scenario with measurement metrics. Here an Information Producer A at System X disseminates survival information, through Service Z, to an information user F at system Y. Nodes B, C, D, and E represent service access points managed by service managers [4].

The major IDM functions can be grouped into five categories and listed in the Figure 2.13. They are:

- Operational characteristics category addresses the robustness of the networks/communications transmission pathways, including the flexibility to adopt tactical and strategic operations without major software modifications, scalability for small or large deployment, and directory services for minimal personal intervention.
- Awareness category recommends desired formats on the priority of information flows in accordance with dissemination policy, infrastructure availability, and security policies. This function also assists the users to expedite the discovery of information. These functions include:

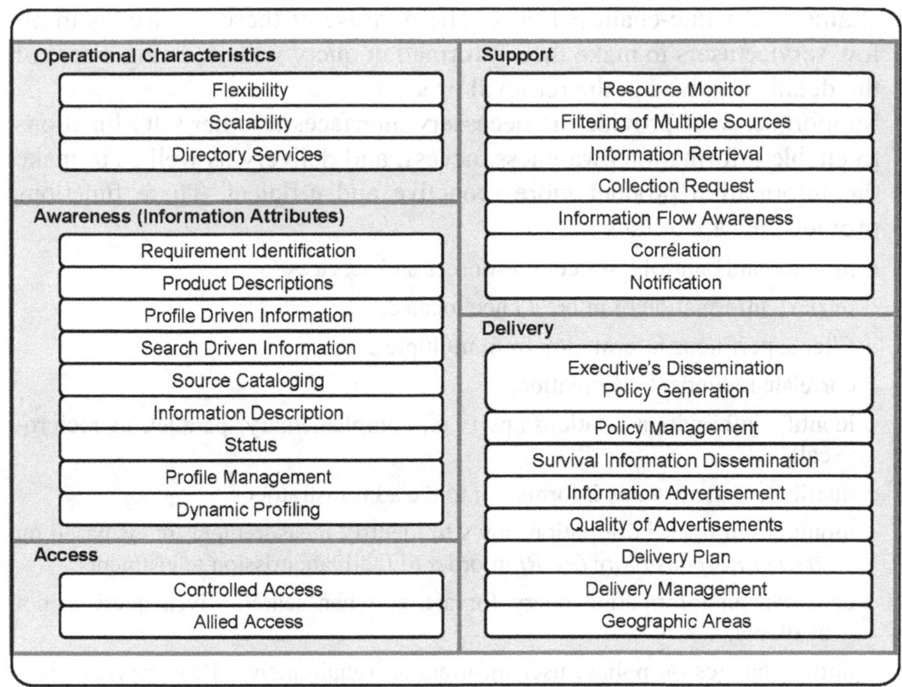

Figure 2.13. IDM functions.

- o assist the user to develop identification mechanisms for facilitating rapid awareness of existing information or for triggering new information collection,
- o use standardized metadata (including classification) to label information product,
- o use profile-driven service for speedy dissemination once a profile is posted,
- o search-driven service equipped with well-defined user queries available to search queries,
- o build and update catalogs of information products automatically based upon information products and users' profile requests,
- o allow users to access information description via standard metadata,
- o track and report the satisfaction level of the information delivery,
- o allow the users to manage profiles based on collaboration of information (e.g., mission, role, time, location, situation, and environment), dissemination policies, and other rule sets such as security, and
- o allow the users to dynamically activate/deactivate information requirements based on profiles.

- Information access services regulate access to information according to information assurance (e.g., security rules) and dissemination policies in the domains of internal organization, external organizations, supply chains, and value-chain partners. The purpose of these services is to allow service users to make their information query without being aware of the details involved in the retrieval process.

- Support services provide the necessary interfaces to other GIG functions to enable information awareness, access, and delivery as well as to make the information product more proactive and efficient. These functions provide the capabilities to
  - o monitor and control IDM core resources and services,
  - o retrieve information of interest once located,
  - o filter superfluous information from multiple sources,
  - o correlate redundant information,
  - o identify information relationships (e.g., complementary, parallel, or reciprocal),
  - o distribute system status information to the administrators,
  - o monitor and track information flows to identify measurement trends based on *Area of Responsibility (AOR)* in order to facilitate mission adjustments,
  - o construct an information query for a user when search-driven query is not available,
  - o notify changes on policy, user information requirements, IDM services, network status, provider and user system status, and
  - o notify availability of information or the delivery/receipt of information.
- Delivery category capitalizes the capability to produce and disseminate time-critical (e.g., survival) information to specific receivers. These functions provide the capabilities to 1) feature effective and intuitive functions for the users to define dissemination policy, changes to the subordinate policies should raise alerts; 2) provide a means in the policy management to quickly and dynamically modify a policy; 3) deliver (survival) information with appropriate prioritization in accordance with standard schema, dissemination policies and user profiles; 4) inform the users for information producer's new or updated products; 5) delineate information products with established search words and level of description (by information producers) for quality advertisements; 6) establish and dynamically adjust the end-to-end delivery plan based upon user information requirements, mission priorities, dissemination policy, and available transport resources; 7) use the delivery attributes (e.g., priority, QoS, Precedence) to govern dissemination treatment in the transport system throughout the GIG; and 8) disseminate information to a specific geographic area where the users are situated.

Information Assurance (IA) Functions

Information assurance (IA) protects and defends information and information systems by ensuring their availability, integrity, authentication, confidentiality, and non-repudiation. This includes the restoration of information systems by incorporating protection, detection, and response capabilities.

The following three figures illustrate the evolution of network and information assurance from the perspective of networking architecture:

Figure 2.14 portrays a security network based on *physical separation*. A separated network for each CoI in a cross companies or cross organizations situation provides absolute isolation of unwanted intends of information sharing. The cost overhead for this configuration, however, is expensive and not practical. Furthermore, the relationship with coalition partners or suppliers will not be functioning at the isolated silos. The following figure illustrates two functional communities in which users share the same work area, the system functions offered by separate networks [19].

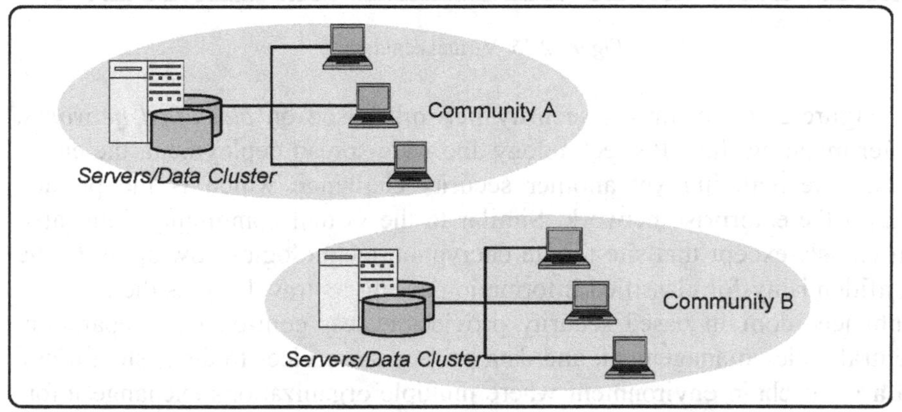

Figure 2.14. Separate networks.

Figure 2.15 portrays a security network based on the concept of *virtual community*. The virtual community uses firewalls to establish a *virtual private network (VPN)* allowing the communities to share a common network infrastructure. The firewall offers user authentication and access control to enforce secure accessibility. Role based access control restricts access of community resources only to designated users to prevent leakage of information. To improve the level of protection, encryption technologies can be deployed to prevent the data from being readable from the network. The figure below depicts two user groups that are networked into two server/data clusters. A security manager situated between the two sub-networks features access control to these two communities. Central policy based management provides control of security at low support cost.

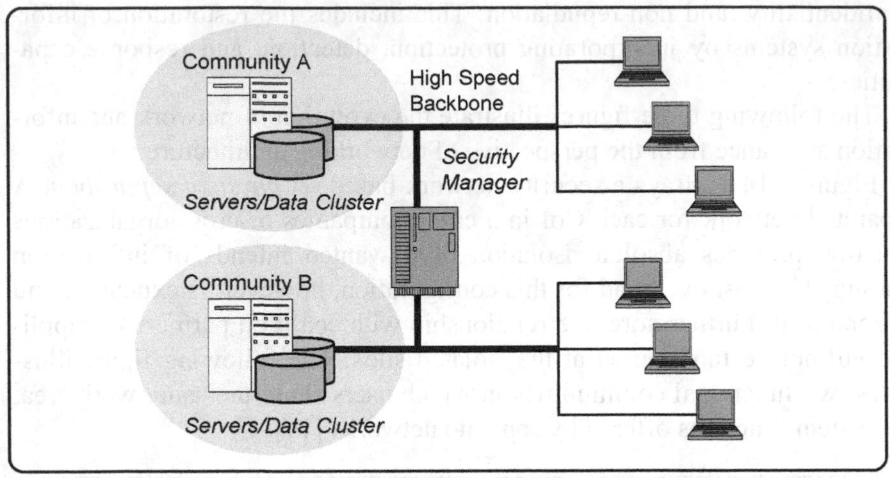

Figure 2.15. Virtual community.

Figure 2.16 portrays a security network based on *classified networks*. After maturing the VPN technology and wide-spread deployment, the enterprises are realizing yet another security challenge which is the privacy within the enterprise network. Similar to the virtual community delineated previously except that site-to-site encryption technologies now apply to the confidentiality for classified information during its travel across the Internet. Enhanced domain based security provides access control, data separation, central policy management, and data privacy as services to the system users. In a value-chain environment where multiple organizations exchange information closely, sets of collaborated rules and policies are critical to a successful information sharing architecture. The following figure depicts a coalition environment in which multiple classified user groups and server groups are connected over the Internet.

Extending from Figure 2.16, it is a general requirement for the IA functions to provide mechanisms for controlling access to specific information such as intelligence, personal, and proprietary information based on the policies and rules aforementioned [20].

In the scope of GIG information protection, IA protects the information from any unauthorized or unintended access or modification during the information life cycle including storage, processing, transmission, and presentation. It is essentially to maintain the integrity, reliability (even in the event of a denial of service attack), robustness, survivability, and rapid restoration of information and process.

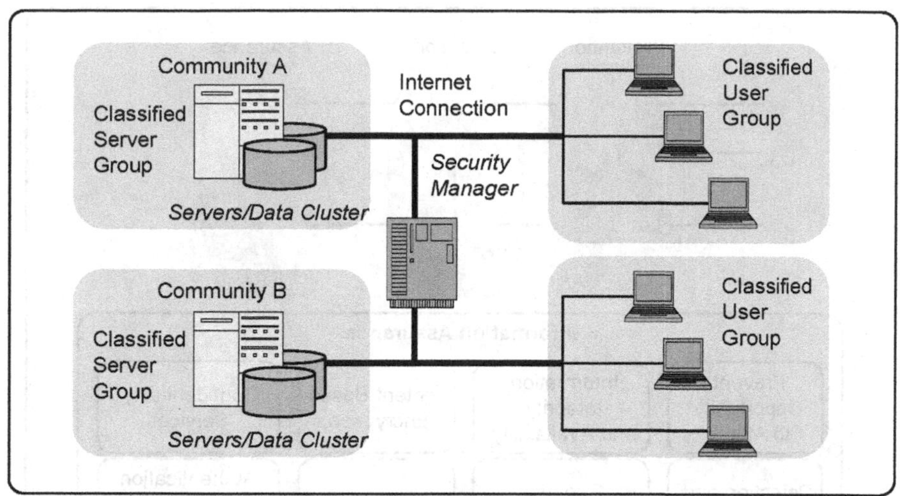

Figure 2.16. Classified networks.

There are two main subjects in these functional groups. Firstly, The GIG systems shall have the IA capability to define, control, and defend enclave boundaries. The systems should be able to operate within each security enclave and across any security enclaves in a controlled fashion using adequate assurance means. Confidentiality services should operate across security enclaves allowing users to share data at different and/or multiple security levels as appropriate. Content-based encryption of information objects should be supported at the host and the public key infrastructure should be developed for authentication, confidentiality, and non-repudiation.

Secondly, the systems should provide adequate protection to prevent or at least minimize the opportunity of anomalies, attacks, or disruptions from external threats, internal threats, and natural causes. These threats can include passive intercept attacks such as unauthorized disclosure of information or a user attempts to circumvent system access for performing unauthorized operations. In any event, the system should incorporate an infrastructure which can rapidly detect, report, and respond to all sources of such events to enable operational situation awareness and responses.

Figure 2.17 shows a *dynamic and active defense system* through layers protection where gray colored lines represent attacks and the black lines represent authorized access [13].

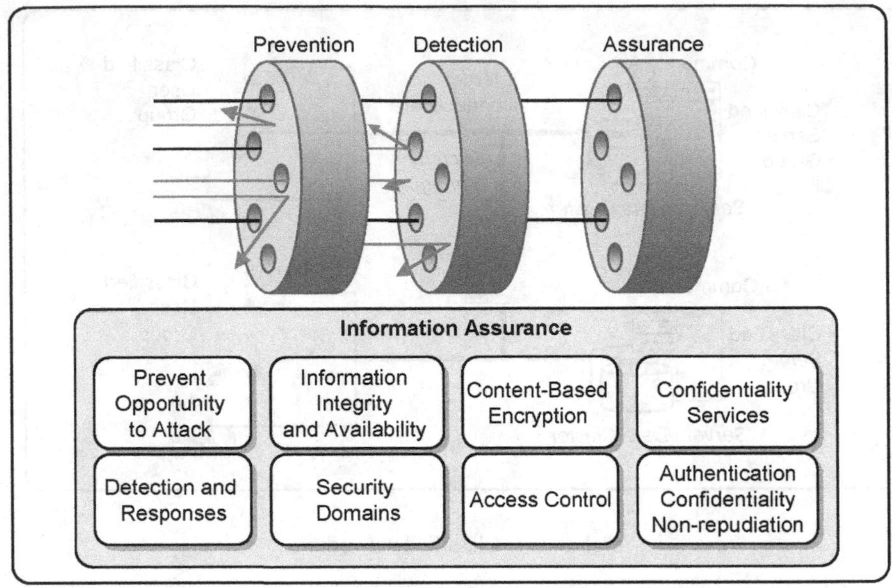

Figure 2.17. Information assurance functions.

2.2.5.4 Human-GIG Interaction

Human-GIG Interaction (HGI) is the input and output of information representations between human-in-control and GIG entry points. The system design should minimize human performance errors, interface problems, and workload (physical, cognitive, attention) requirements. All of these improvements will greatly enhance the operators' and executives' decision-making ability.

HGI specifies the requirements which present information to and accept information from humans using a combination of visual presentation (blinking lights and plain text through full-motion, stereoscopic, color imagery, and human visual inputs), aural presentation (e.g., single constant tone through multi-language, stereophonic, synthesized speech), tactile presentation (e.g., pressure, temperature, and vibration), or other unique sensory methods. The use of multimedia presentations can avoid reading voluminous textual material and expedite the decision-making process. Interface characteristics should be designed to maximize human productivity and performance, for instance, users can prioritize information inputs for review/alert or the system interface is compliant with the enterprise or mission standards to minimize user input, mechanical, and perception errors and support recovery from errors.

HGI requires unobtrusive confirmations of user input and actions, to include implicit visual, aural, and/or tactile feedback in response to user actions (e.g., push-button highlighting, mouse button or keyboard key clicks, or audible tone) as well as explicit notifications for the system response of the entered data.

All end-user skill levels should be supported in the aspects of learnability which is to minimize the time and effort invested in reaching a specified level of user performance, flexibility which provides multiple methods to accommodate changes to tasks or preferences, and tailorability which is to accommodate mission changes or skill differences. HGI also includes a user-centered design to ensure that the requirements of the end-user are satisfied and results in increased user satisfaction. A context-sensitive on-line help tools are included to eliminate or reduce the need for off-line support or documentation. Software download capabilities that provide basic user-assisted functionality such as metadata encoding, converters, fonts, rendering, and input method editors should be available as needed.

HGI shall functionally accommodate use in a specialized operating environment (e.g., cockpits, mobile environments, hand-held radios, ships, low light), for instance, for the safety of users in tactical situations. Decision aids and tools should be available to maximize user efficiency of their task and determine what interfaces will be supported in certain operating environments. HGI hardware and software elements shall be ergonomically designed to maximize productivity by reducing user fatigue and discomfort.

2.2.5.5 Mobility Common Operational Picture

With the features discussed in the previous sections, the GIG is emerging as the next generation service architecture for military command, control, communications, intelligence, surveillance, and reconnaissance information to the spectrum of users, software agents, and software systems.

To meet information needs of operational commanders, data and services available in the GIG are composed to create a *Common Operational Picture (COP*; section 9.6*)* to facilitate collaborative planning and situational awareness. The COP presents a mix of information provided by decision aids, environmental databases, platform performance data, doctrinal behaviors, and simulation processing. This data is reconciled through metadata and data mediation and merged to create the GIG COP, as will be discussed in chapter 8 [21,22].

As depicted in Figure 2.18, the GIG provides the enabling foundation for network-centric business operations, the realization of improved information positions is established upon COP that provide the basis for shared situational awareness and knowledge to help achieve fully interoperable response capability. The figure shows a high-level operational view of an organization of the logical GIG functions and their interrelationships within the GIG. Also included are the entities that the GIG is required to interface with when engaging in the exchange and dissemination of information with them [4].

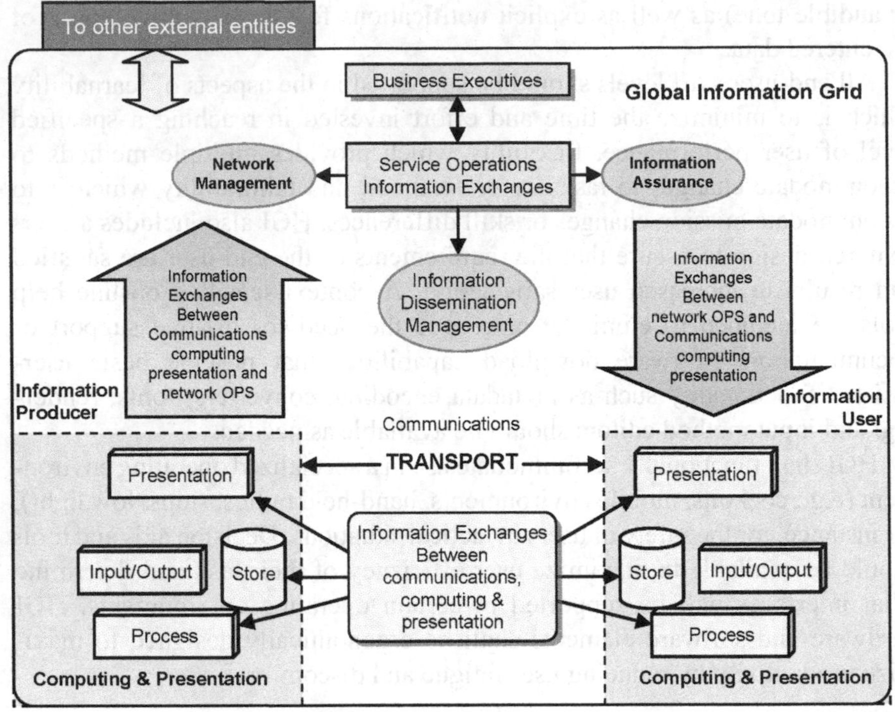

Figure 2.18. High-level operational view (OV-1).

2.3 Telecommunications Management Network Models

The service environment of a telecommunication service provider includes multi-vendor networks and a rather complex new-economy world of providers and clients in an ever-expanding value chain. As shown in Figure 2.19, the network architecture is typically designed with a number of horizontal network layers, each with a distinctly unique purpose and the connectivity service are separated from the end-user services. In addition, vertical division sets apart the network and the related service control and media gateways with diversified and vast area of communication products and technologies. All these resources aim to provide a solution capable of delivering a unified set of end-user services [23].

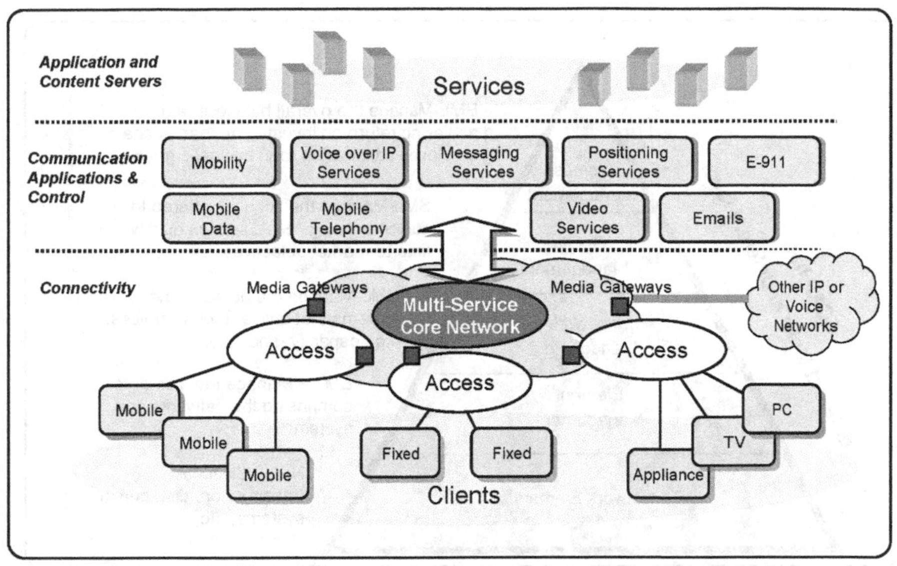

Figure 2.19. The architecture for next generation networks.

The challenge to the service provider is how to manage and operate a set of services and the infrastructure effectively. This task involves people, processes, and systems. Such systems are referred to as Operations Support Systems *(OSS)* in the telecommunication industry. The OSS provides methods and procedures to access managed service objects across the entire network infrastructure and manage the business itself. Figure 2.20 depicts the ITU-T's *Telecommunications Management Network (TMN)* model. The pyramid figure demonstrates how an OSS solution is integrated, in building-block fashion from the network element to the business management layers. This figure illustrates how each layer is dependent on the services provided by the adjacent layer below; all contribute to the overall success of the business.

From bottom up, the network elements layer contains networking equipment such as switches and transmission that constitute a single resource. The element management layer is the management functionality that is required to operate a single piece of equipment. The network management layer addresses the functionality required to control a network that is formed by multiple network elements; the management scope is typically covering an end-to-end connection. The service management layer concerns the management

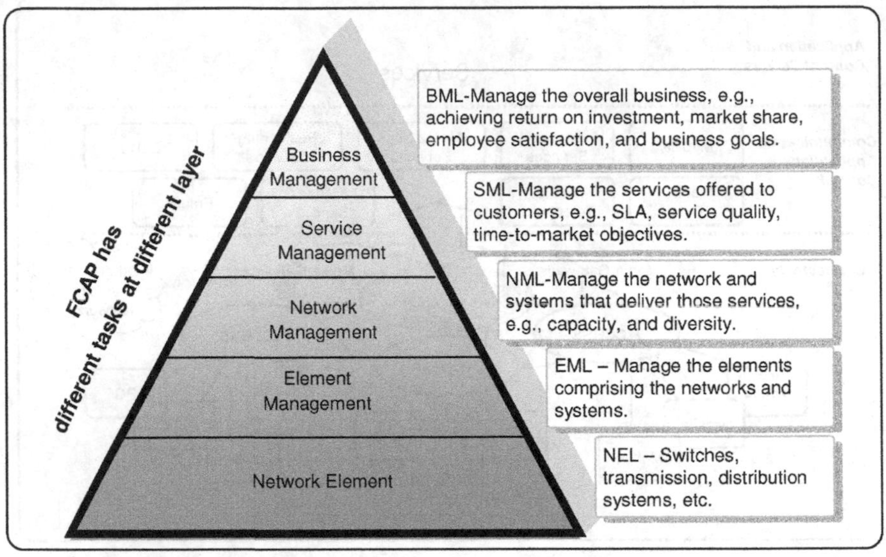

Figure 2.20. ITU-T, Telecommunications Management Network model.

capability of services that are supported by the lower-layer networks. A service can be a hotspot access, an e-mail account, or *Short Message Service (SMS)* messaging. The business management layer has two parts: the management functions that are customer-facing can include the customer management, billing, and customer center; the service provider management functions can include market research, market share, and governmental goals achievement.

Critical to the success of any integrated OSS is its capability to provide visibility of the entire managed service, and to draw the appropriate business flow that is affecting the customer experience. From that standpoint, TMF has defined TOM and eTOM to develop sets of recommendations for service providers. These will be further delved into the following sections.

2.3.1 Telecommunication Operational Maps

The TMF's *Telecommunication Operational Maps (TOM)* uses customer interface management at the top layer to drill down to the lower-layer processes. It is a framework that provides a definition of common processes, a common language, end-to-end process flow examples, and individual process inputs and outputs. It is relevant to all service types and should be technology independent. The strength of the TMN model is that it provides the capability to reach a level of abstraction that is increased through the layers. Ideally there is no need for interaction between layers that are not adjacent [24].

The TOM focuses on the direct customer processes represented by *fulfillment, assurance, and billing (FAB)*. However, FAB processes were not on the TOM framework map, they were rather an overlay. As shown in Figure 2.21, the TOM regroups the TMN model into three basic, end-to-end processes common to any service-oriented business. These three categories are referred to as FAB, as illustrated below:

- Fulfillment process grouping provides customers with their requested products in a timely and correct manner. This process translates the customer's requests into a solution, informs the customers of the status of their purchase order, and ensures completion on time. Fulfillment process also covers the overall process of implementing and activating services for a customer.
- Assurance process grouping maintains the service to ensure that services provided to customers are continuously available and compliant to SLA or QoS objectives. The assurance process also manages the service through timely responses and resolution of customer- or network-triggered problems through effective trouble ticket management and dispatching jobs for restoration and repair.
- Billing process grouping conducts timely and accurate bill preparation, knowledgeable and responsive billing inquiry support, and timely adjustment-handling and payment operations. This process grouping also supports prepayment for services.

All three end-to-end processes have interfaces among many processes across the framework. The customer predominantly initiates the fulfillment process. The assurance process can be triggered by the customer or resource elements, and the billing flow is predominantly from data collection in the resource elements to bills presented to the customer. There can be additional interfaces required with other providers and operators. All these flow elements have a certain level of integration and automation.

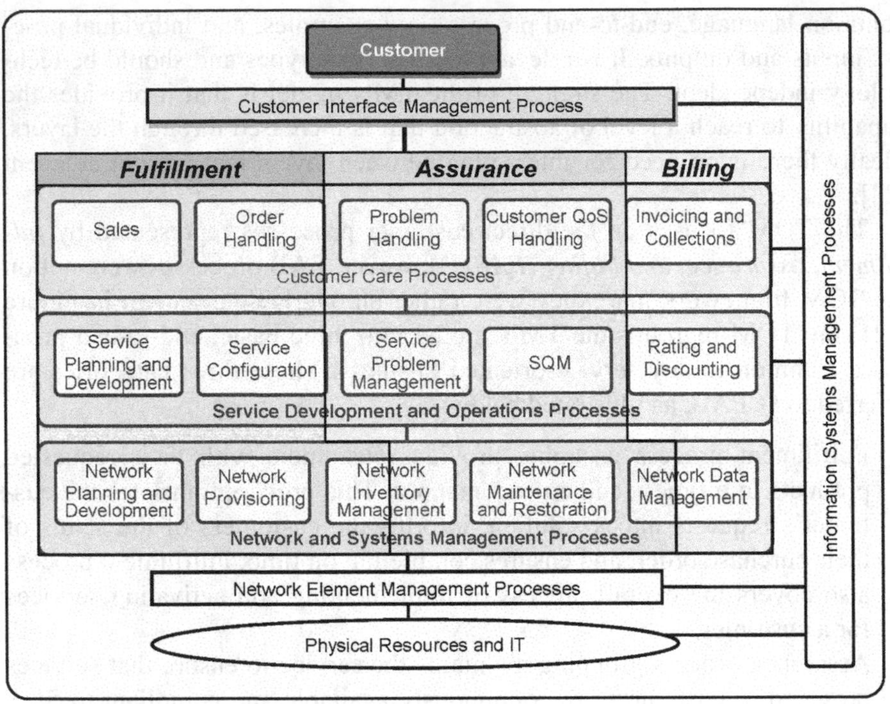

Figure 2.21. TMF Telecommunication Operational Maps.

2.3.2 Enhanced Telecommunications Operations Map

From the original TOM, TMF carries forward into the *enhanced Telecommunications Operations Map (eTOM)* and broadens to a total enterprise framework, through several generations of detail and refinement, to the current Release. The eTOM is intended to address increased complexity in a service provider's business relationships and processes. It specifically adds processes to address the needs of supply chain life-cycle management, supplier/partner relationship management, product life-cycle management, and infrastructure life-cycle management. The eTOM structure establishes as a "business process framework", rather than a "business process model" serving as the blueprint for process direction. This is because the enhanced map aims to categorize the process elements business activities so that these can then be combined in many different ways, to implement end-to-end business processes (e.g., fulfillment, assurance, and billing) which deliver value for the customer and the service provider. Because its nature of technology independence, the eTOM does not intend to address the strategic issues such as vision, mission, target customers, or market segments, and so forth.

Although the eTOM is more complex than the TOM, in some ways it is more intuitive than the TOM in that it closes gaps in enterprise management (i.e., corporate-type) processes, marketing processes, customer retention processes, supplier and partner management processes, and so forth. Currently, eTOM is being developed by TMF in areas such as further lower-level process decompositions and flows, and ongoing feedback together with its linkage with the *Next Generation Operations Support Systems (NGOSS*; section 2.5.3) program. The eTOM processes can be further divided into the following three-tier hierarchy.

2.3.2.1 Level Zero Processes

The eTOM Business Process Element Enterprise Framework represents the highest conceptual view of the eTOM Business Process Framework as well the whole of a service provider's enterprise environment. At the overall conceptual level, eTOM can be viewed as having three major areas of process, as shown in Figure 2.22 [25].

- Strategy, Infrastructure and Product which covers planning and life-cycle management.
- Operations which cover the core of operational management.
- Enterprise management which covers corporate or business support management.

The conceptual view of the eTOM Business Process Framework provides an overall context that differentiates strategy and life-cycle processes from the operations processes in two large groupings. It also differentiates the key functional areas in four horizontal layers, shown in Figure 2.22. In addition, enterprise management shows the internal and external entities that interact with the enterprise. The functional groupings reflect the major expertise and focus required to pursue the business. The four functional groupings are delineated below:

- The *Market, Product and Customer Processes* are constituted by sales and channel management, marketing management, and product and offer management, as well as customer relationship management and ordering, problem handling, SLA management, and billing.
- The *Service Processes* include service development and configuration, service problem management, quality analysis, and rating.
- The *Resource Processes* support the development and management of the enterprise's infrastructure, whether related to products and services, or to supporting the enterprise itself.
- The *Supplier/Partner Processes* support the enterprise's interaction with its suppliers and partners. This involves both processes that manage the

Supply Chain that underpins product and infrastructure, as well as those that support the Operations interface with its suppliers and partners.

- The *Enterprise Management Process* Area includes basic business processes that are required to run any large business. These generic processes focus on the setting and achieving of strategic corporate goals and objectives, as well as providing those support services that are required throughout an enterprise. These processes are sometimes considered to be the corporate functions and/or processes, e.g., financial management, human resources, management processes, etc. Since enterprise management processes are aimed at general support within the enterprise, they may interface as needed with almost every other process in the enterprise, be they operational, strategy, infrastructure, or product processes.

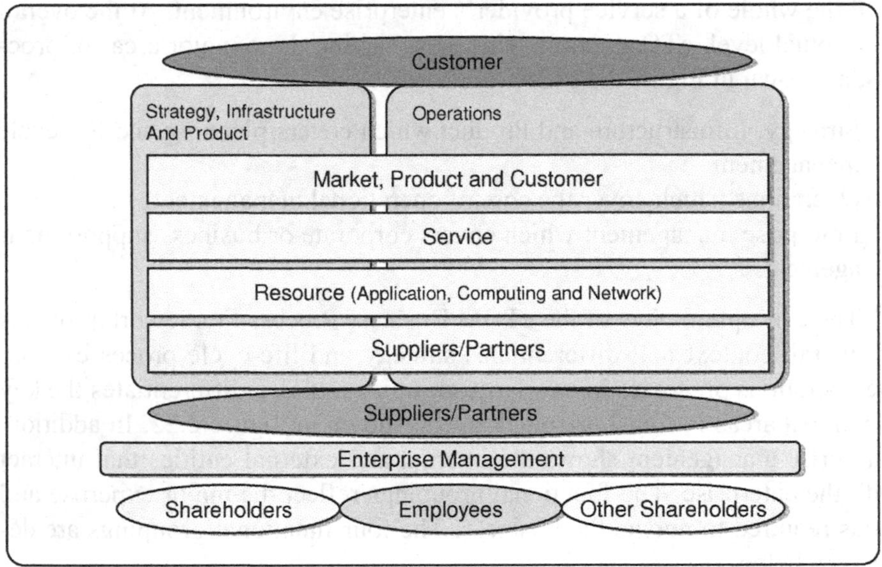

Figure 2.22. eTOM Business Process Framework – Level Zero Processes (High-level Structure).

Additionally, Figure 2.22 [25] also depicts the major entities with which the enterprise interacts. These are:

- Customers, to whom service is provided by means of the products sold by the enterprise: the focus of the business!
- Suppliers, who provide products or resources, bought and used by the enterprise directly or indirectly to support its business
- Partners, with whom the enterprise co-operates in a shared area of business
- Employees, who work for the enterprise to pursue its business goals
- Shareholders, who have invested in the enterprise and thus own stock

- Stakeholders, who have a commitment to the enterprise other than through stock ownership.

2.3.2.2 Level One Processes

Figure 2.23 shows the Level One processes in the eTOM Framework with seven vertical process groupings conducting the end-to-end processes required to support customers and to manage the business.

Starting from the right upper box, marked as Operations, Operations Support & Readiness is now distinguished from the TOM's core "customer operations processes" of FAB (section 2.3.1) to emphasize the focus on enabling support and automation in FAB, an example is customer self management. In general, The Operations Support & Readiness processes are concerned with activities that are less "real time" or customer-facing than those in FAB, thus are typically concerned less with individual customers and services and more with groups of these. As the result, not all enterprises will choose to employ this split. In addition to the FAB roles delineated in TOM, the four Operations functional process groupings also support the management of customer, service, resource, and supplier/partner interactions.

In the left upper box, the Strategy & Commit Process Grouping, Infrastructure Life-cycle Management, and Product Life-cycle Management Process Groupings are shown as three vertical end-to-end process groups that work on different business time cycles from the Operations:

- *Strategy & Commit Process* group is responsible for generating specific business strategy in support of the Infrastructure and Product Life-cycle processes as well as gaining buy-in within the business to implement this strategy. This strategy development process is heavily focused on analysis and commitment management of any market, customer, products, and services related subjects. It also tracks and adjusts the results of the strategies.
- *Infrastructure Life-cycle Management Process* group is responsible for responding to needs of the Product Life-cycle Management processes and identification, definition, planning, and implementation of all necessary infrastructures (e.g., application, computing, and network), other supporting infrastructures, or business capabilities (operations centers, architectures, and so forth) to support the provision of products to customers.
- *Product Life-cycle Management Process* group is responsible for the definition, planning, design, and implementation of all products in the enterprise's portfolio. The life-cycle processes survey the market across key functional areas, the business environment, customer requirements, and competitive offerings to create products accordingly. Product Management and Development processes develop and deliver new features or products to customers.

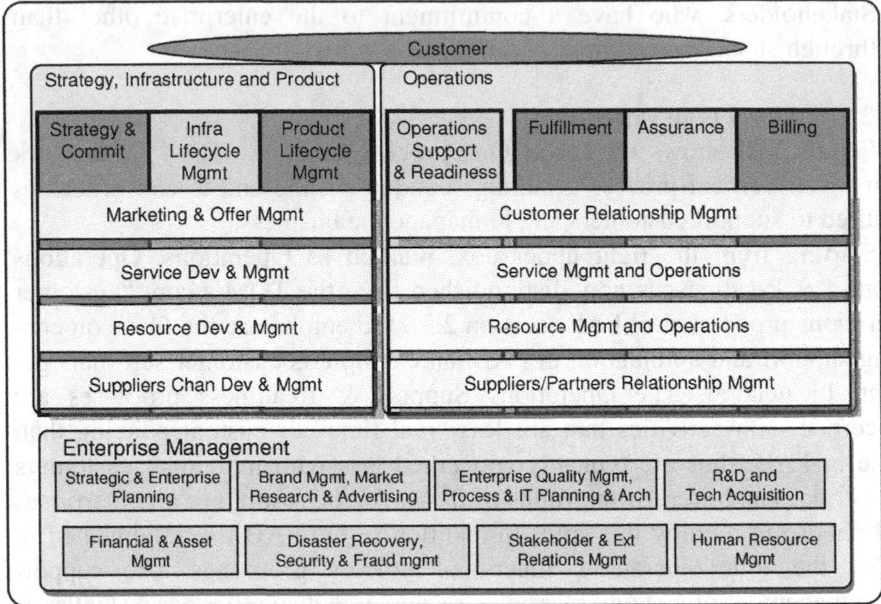

Figure 2.23. eTOM Business Process Framework – Level One Processes.

The horizontal process groupings in Figure 2.23 [25] distinguish functional operations processes and other types of business functional processes, e.g., marketing versus selling, service development versus service configuration, and so forth. The functional processes on the left enable, support, and direct the work in the Operations verticals. Details are delineated in level two processes as following.

2.3.2.3 Level Two and Three Processes

Level two processes drill down from level one and decompose the processes into function components. The purpose is to show in more detail the predominant processes that need to be involved – integrated and automated – to support the vertical end-to-end processes. This section divides the business process framework into three portions.

Some level three processes are provided as samples during the discussion of level two processes. As for comparison purposes, the level two discussion can satisfy the corresponding details to the GIG requirements thus further decomposition will not be necessary [26].

Operations

Figure 2.24 shows the Operations portion of the eTOM Business Process Framework decomposed into four functional process groups.

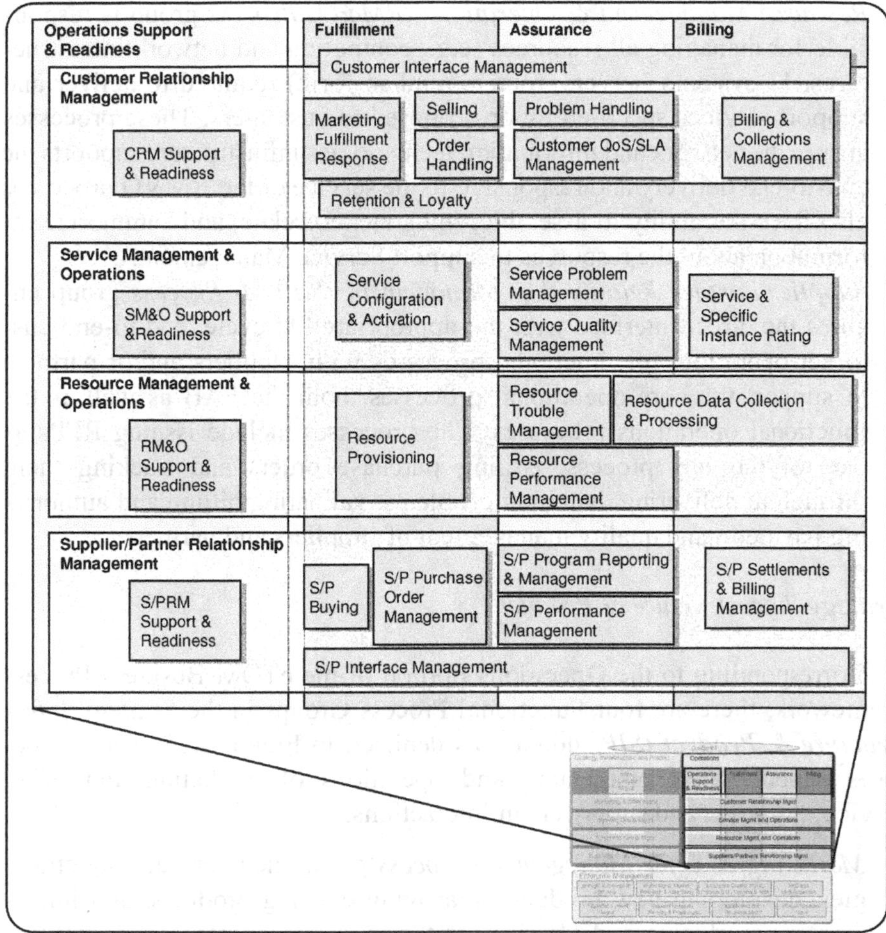

Figure 2.24. eTOM Business Process Framework – Level Two Processes.

- *Customer Relationship Management (CRM) Process* group includes the functionalities necessary for a service provider to collect customer information as well as to acquire, enhance, and retain a relationship with a customer. In a more advance feature, CRM can help the provider to identify opportunities for increasing the value of the customer to the enterprise.
- *Service Management & Operations (SM&O) Process* group includes all functionalities necessary for the delivery, management, and operations of services required by or proposed to customers. Based on customer's interest, the functions may involve some on-demand service (capacity) planning and reconfiguration.

- *Resource Management & Operations (RM&O) Process* group is responsible for managing all resources (e.g., computing and network infrastructures, IT systems, servers, routers, and so forth) required to deliver and support services specified by or proposed to customers. These processes ansure the network and information technologies infrastructure supports the end-to-end delivery and responsive to the service order. RM&O processes also have the ability to assemble, integrate, correlate, and summarize information about the resources to support Service Management.
- *Supplier/Partner Relationship Management (S/PRM) Process* group enables the direct interface with the appropriate life cycle, end-to-end customer operations, or functional processes with suppliers and/or partners to support the core operational processes, both the FAB as well as the functional operations processes. The processes include issuing RFPs as part of the buy process, issuing purchase orders and tracking them through to delivering, handling problems, validating billing and authorizing payment, and quality management of suppliers and partners.

Strategy, Infrastructure & Product

Corresponding to the Operations portion of the eTOM Business Process Framework, there are four Functional Process Groups in the *Strategy Infrastructure & Product (SIP)* domain as depicted in Figure 2.25. These processes support the management and operations of marketing and offer, service, resource, and supply chain interactions.

- *Marketing & Offer Management Process* group includes defining strategies, developing new products, managing existing products, and implementing marketing and offering strategies. These processes are enabling processes, but also the key processes that are accountable for pricing, sales, channels, marketing communications, and promotion.
- *Service Development & Management Process* group is responsible for planning, developing, and delivering services to the Operations domain. It defines the strategies for service creation and design, manages and assesses the performance of the services to meet the existing and future goals.
- *Resource Development & Management Process* group is responsible for planning, developing, and delivering the resources needed to support services and products to the operations domain. It defines the strategies for development of the network and other physical and non-physical resources, introduces new technologies and internetworks with existing ones, and manages and assesses the performance of the resources to meet the existing and future goals.

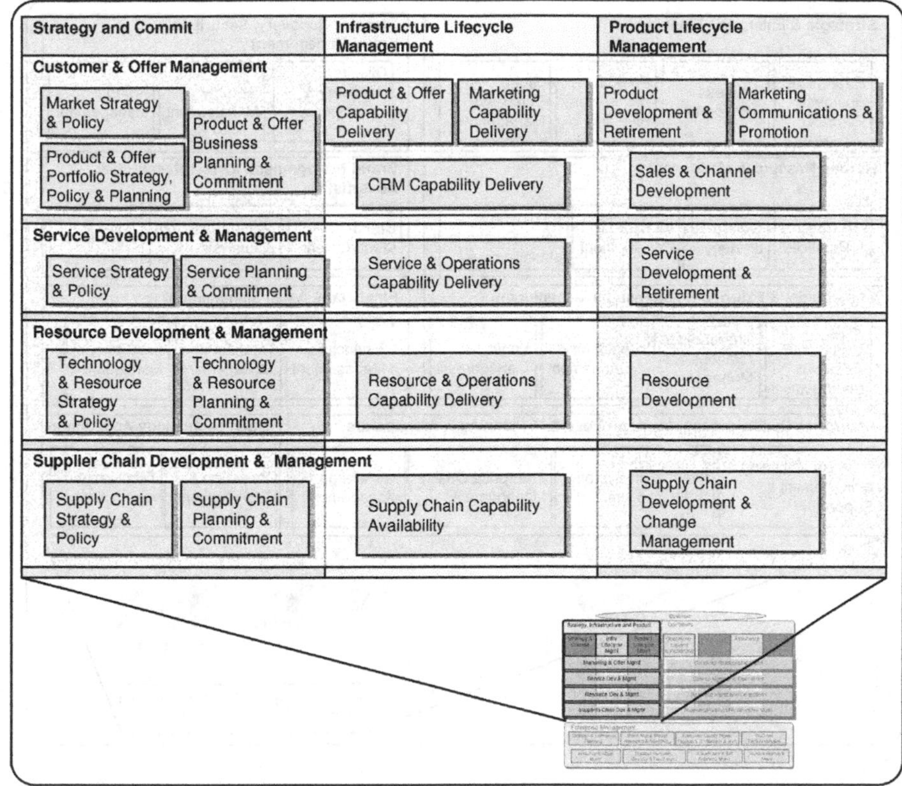

Figure 2.25. eTOM Business Process Framework – Level Two Processes.

- *Supply Chain Development & Management Process* group is responsible for the interactions required by the enterprise with the supply chain suppliers and partners. Companies are increasingly working together with suppliers and partners either to broaden their offerings or to improve their productivity. These processes assist the enterprise to have the information flows and financial flows in place and suppliers/partners available to deliver the required support in a timely manner.

Enterprise Management

Shown in Figure 2.26, *enterprise management process* group centralizes services and manages the enterprise-level actions and needs to provide a clearer focus for the relevant process responsibilities. It provides support services required throughout the rest of the enterprise. This grouping encompasses all business management processes necessary to support the rest

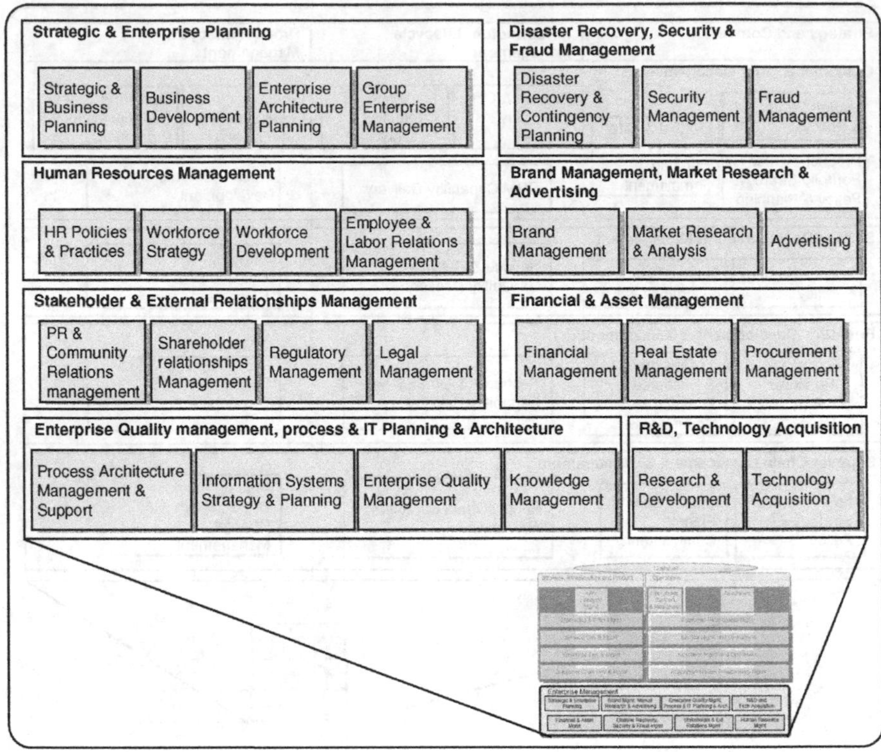

Figure 2.26. eTOM Business Process Framework – Level Two Processes.

of the enterprise, including processes for financial management, legal management, regulatory management, process cost and quality management, and so forth. Enterprise management processes are, in part, responsible for setting corporate strategies and directions and providing guidelines and targets for the rest of the business. TMF does not develop process models for these processes, since they are not processes that require significant specialization for the service providers. The eight process groups are illustrated below:

- *Strategic & Enterprise Planning Process* group drives the mission and vision of the enterprise by developing the strategies and plans for the service provider enterprise. The business and focus of the enterprise such as market direction, financial requirements, and acquisition plan are determined in accordance with the discipline of strategic planning. The process also develops and coordinates the overall plan for the business working with all key units of the enterprise.
- *Disaster Recovery Process* group focuses on assuring that the enterprise can support its mission critical operations, processes, applications, communications in the face of a disaster, from security threats and fraud attempts. These processes include priority assessment, disaster recovery

planning, and testing. Security processes have many facets and levels from entry to a building to password management and encryption. Fraud processes are closely aligned with security processes involving threshold alarms, credit verification.

- *Human Resources Management Process* group manages the people resources that the enterprise uses to fulfill its objectives. These processes includes salary structures, performance appraisal, compensation, employee benefit, labor (Union contract) relations and negotiations, safety, training, employee acquisition and release, retirement, and workplace operating policies.
- *Brand Management, Market Research & Advertising Process* group direct and support the Marketing processes in the Strategy, Infrastructure & Product and the Operations processes of the enterprise. This process group is also called knowledge management. Brand management defines the policies and strategies for the enterprise's brands. The market research processes assess product impact, determine action, and assess customer satisfaction. Advertising processes support ongoing and specific advertising campaigns which are to define overall advertising strategies and policies, work with advertising agencies, and measure effectiveness.
- *Stakeholder & External Relations Management Process* group manages the enterprise's relationship with stakeholders (e.g., shareholders and employee organizations) and outside entities (e.g., regulators, local community, and unions).
- *Financial & Asset Management Process* group is accountable for overall management of the enterprise income statement and overall corporate balance sheet. Financial management processes include Accounts Payable, Accounts Receivable, Expense Reporting, Revenue Assurance, Payroll, Book Closings, Tax Planning and Payment, and so forth. Asset Management processes set asset policies, track assets, and manage the balance sheet.
- *Enterprise Quality Management Process and IT Planning and Architecture Process* group is in charge of developing and improving the key architectures of the enterprise. It defines the enterprise's quality management processes and policies as well as providing IT guidelines and policies, funding approval.
- *R&D/Technology Acquisition Management Processes* perform research and development of technology within the enterprise and evaluation of potential technology acquisitions.

SM&O Support & Process Management processes monitor and control the SM&O processes, from a general, a cost, a Quality Performance, and an Assurance point of view. These processes are also responsible for supporting new product and feature introductions and enhancements, in development and/ or review of processes, methods and procedures in support of new products deployment, as well as conducting *Operations Readiness Testing (ORT)* and acceptance. Readiness processes develop the methods and procedures for the specific process and functions and keep them up-to-date, including making improvements. All these procedures occur before Operations accepts a new product, feature or enhancement, operations.

For service providers, it provides a neutral reference point as they consider internal process reengineering needs, partnerships, alliances, and general working agreements with other providers. For suppliers, the eTOM framework outlines potential boundaries of software components and the required functions, inputs, and outputs that must be supported by products.

Neither BSS nor service providers' enterprise management are in the focus of this book, hence, the TOM architecture is used to illustrate the operational aspect of service assurance.

2.4 Emerging eTOM and GIG

Emerging eTOM and GIG is a challenge to many enterprises, which are looking for a unified operational environment to collaborate the government and private IT industries. This section analyzes the commonalities and differences between eTOM and GIG in the application of Information Management.

2.4.1 GIG Is a guideline for DoD Network-Centric Service Management

GIG is a prescriptive specification for US DoD to specify the guidance on the implementation and continues delivery of service systems. The GIG works at the infrastructure level providing seamless end-to-end capabilities from all operating locations at a highly diversified operating environment. It can interface to coalition, allied, and non-DoD users and systems.

GIG is developed as guidance for service developers and integrators to serve a complex networked environment with many existing legacy systems, procedures, organizations. To introduce new emerging technologies and methodologies the GIG systems should accommodate many different requirements that make the detail service models rather complicated. At large, the service model is based on user hierarchy in accordance with the military commanding echelons. Even though the systems are technologies neutral, the GIG requirements have tendency of addressing wireless and mobile networks because of the nature of its applications in the military arenas. Unlike the commercial model where customers are associated with the service provider's service level objectives or agreements, the QoS in a GIG transport service focuses more on the end-to-end security, availability, and performance. The concept of high-level services has been recently integrated into the GIG architecture however it is not yet as comprehensive as in the commercial solutions.

Philosophically speaking, the service concept of GIG is based on network-centric operations where access points are less significant in comparison with the networked resources which will make the service available to the users. This is because in a mission critical environment, a user may choose to operate the same mission via different media due to mobility requirement, for instance. Measures of the success are based on the availability of the information in the network, instead of the availability of certain service access points.

GIG contains extensive requirements covering the principle, design, development, and testing criteria for the systematic implementation of DoD network-centric service management. It provides guidance for the DoD system developers and integrators to overcome potential objections raised during implementation and resolve foreseeable barriers likely to be encountered during the integration with non-GIG systems.

2.4.2 eTOM Is a Catalogue of Process Element Categories

Extending from the scope of providing standards for telecommunication service providers, the eTOM focuses on the information and communications service providers' development and integration of BSS and OSS. The eTOM analyzes all of the business activities of a service provider and categorizes them into different levels of detail, according to their significance for the business. The ratification of eTOM as an official ITU standard in 2004 has moved the eTOM into formal ITU recommendation, which is more widely accepted in private sectors.

The eTOM provides guidance for the development and management of key processes within a service provider by offering a catalogue of industry-standard names, descriptions and scopes, at multiple hierarchical levels as discussed earlier. The eTOM positions itself at commercial application and is designed as customer-centric, viewing business process from the customer services. At that level, it is difficult to differentiate some internal processes which deal with the infrastructure or business supporting tasks. By moving up from the original telecommunication operational management into business process framework, the level of detail used to satisfy the telecommunications service provider has to scarify for broader or generic standard audiences. As the result, the current eTOM model is more valuable for system architecture design than system development. Future iterations of eTOM are expected to elaborate lower-level processes as well as the linkages between them.

To accelerate enhancements to eTOM for the purpose of information superiority, reference to specialized infrastructure recommendations such as GIG can bridge these gaps with proven models. On the other hand, adding the application concepts of eTOM to the development of GIG systems can improve bottom-line sensitivity and customer-centric services. With the availability of many eTOM compliant off-the-shelf products, the government or large scale enterprise IT operations can benefit from the marriage of these two models.

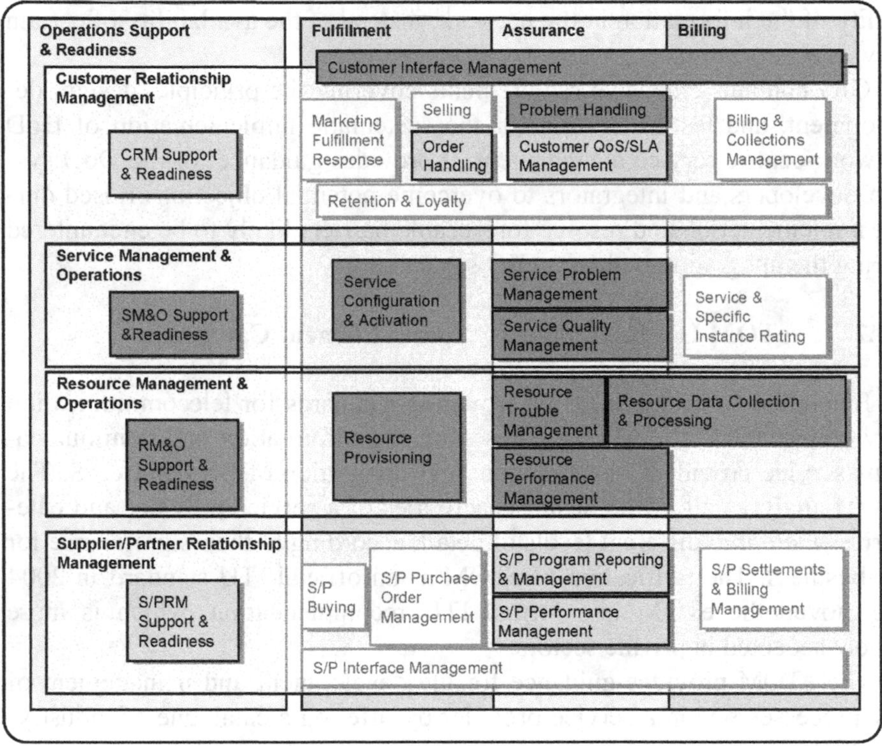

Figure 2.27. How GIG processes overlay eTOM Operations Process Elements.

2.4.3 Overlay of GIG to the Level 2 eTOM Framework

The GIG's NETOPS and Communications can be partially overlaid onto the eTOM. The following figures (Figures 2.27 to 2.29) show the eTOM level two Operations, SIP and enterprise in building GIG processes from the NETOPS and Communications specifications. The GIG processes and functions delineated earlier are of an equivalent process level to the eTOM level two decompositions [27].

It is worthwhile to point out that GIG documents provide lower-level process details for very specific applications, such as ones with high mobility and stringent security. Because GIG processes aim to guide such detailed system implementation, their overlay to the eTOM's level three process elements is the most appropriate. However, due to the incompleteness of the level three specifications in the current version, using eTOM to map GIG processes is limited. For the interest of comparison, the following figures use the shading to indicate whether GIG supports the management of internal IT services or customer services in the correlated eTOM processes.

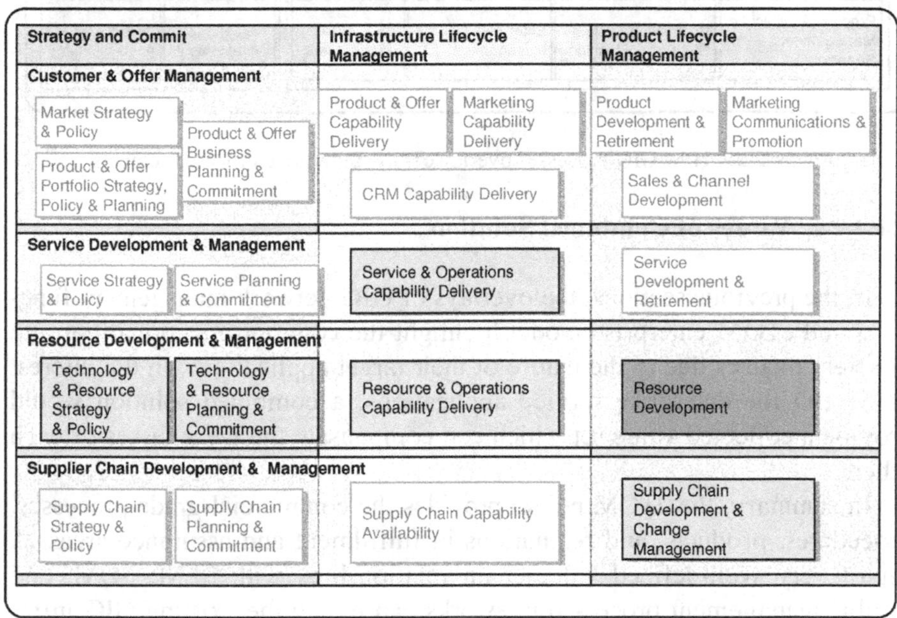

Figure 2.28. How GIG processes overlay eTOM SIP Process Elements.

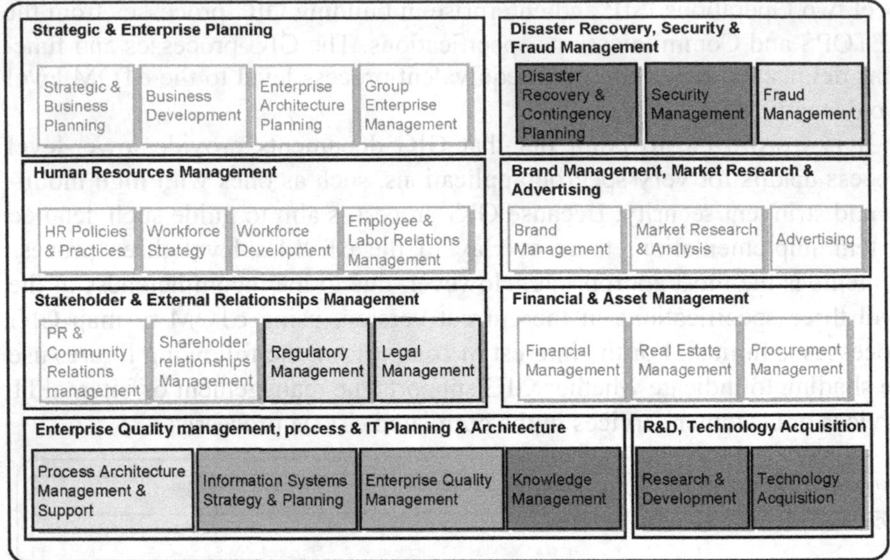

Figure 2.29. How GIG processes overlay eTOM Enterprise Process Elements.

2.4.4 Values of Combined Solution

In the previous sections, the overlays of GIG network management functions and eTOM enterprise model highlight the common functionalities and different focuses due to the nature of their target applications. In the interest of NCBO for enterprise service applications, a combined solution would provide a collected value set which can compensate the weaknesses of each other.

In summary, the eTOM model provides the commercial-grade processes, procedures, products, and regulations in fulfillment and assurance areas. A set of very well-defined value-chain relationships with SLM, SQM, and trouble management process frameworks can enrich the existing GIG infrastructure. For instance, service roaming agreement for wireless networks have been used by many operators in different countries. Additionally, vendors have created enormous amount of tools and solutions for almost every aspect of service operators' operational needs, thus the cost of available tools are relatively more affordable and reachable.

In contrast, because the planning process of eTOM based operators is typically conducted "in-house" to protect their competitiveness, the operators tend to have less interest to establish a hierarchical relationship with other service providers. Furthermore, since most commercial service providers have not yet identified a profitable business model for ad-hoc based services, such as Hot Spot or Wi-Fi, there has been few fully intergraded business-to-operation process mentioned. On the other hand, the ad-hoc network technology paired with sophisticated information assurance capability in GIG have been existing in the battlefield for many years, additionally, commanding echelons have been providing organized community-based planning to grant appropriate information and access privileges to different service users. Such valuable experiences and procedures can enrich the TMF model not only in the flexibility to adopt future technology challenges but also in a better service model for community sensitive service offerings. The service differentiators can be categorized by security level, locations, class of information, and so forth.

2.5 Current Implementation Frameworks

"Better, faster, cheaper" are three magic words that easily sum up the goals of most service business. Service providers are trimming down and rounding up their resources to get fit for the competition. Many solution ideas have been covered in this chapter so far thus there is a need to provide a glimpse of how these ideas are implemented in the IT industry. The *DoD Architecture Framework (DoDAF)* and *Federal Enterprise Architecture (FEA)* are two government-based solutions using GIG as the enabler. The NGOSS is created by TMF based on eTOM. A quick SoS view is provided as follow:

2.5.1 DoD Architecture Framework

Department of Defense Architecture Framework (DoDAF) is a framework for development of a systems architecture or *enterprise architecture (EA)*. All major U.S. Government DoD weapons and IT system procurements are required to develop an EA and architecture following DoDAF. It has broad applicability across the private, public, and voluntary sectors around the world [28].

The DoDAF provides the guiding principles for modeling and designing architectures in the DoD environment as delineated by three views, shown in Figure 2.30. There three views are:

- The operational view (OV) to delineate the tasks, activities, operational elements, and information exchanges required to accomplish missions.
- The system view (SV) to delineate system and interconnection supporting operational functions.
- The technical view (TV) includes technical standards, implementation conventions, rules, and criteria that guide system implementation.

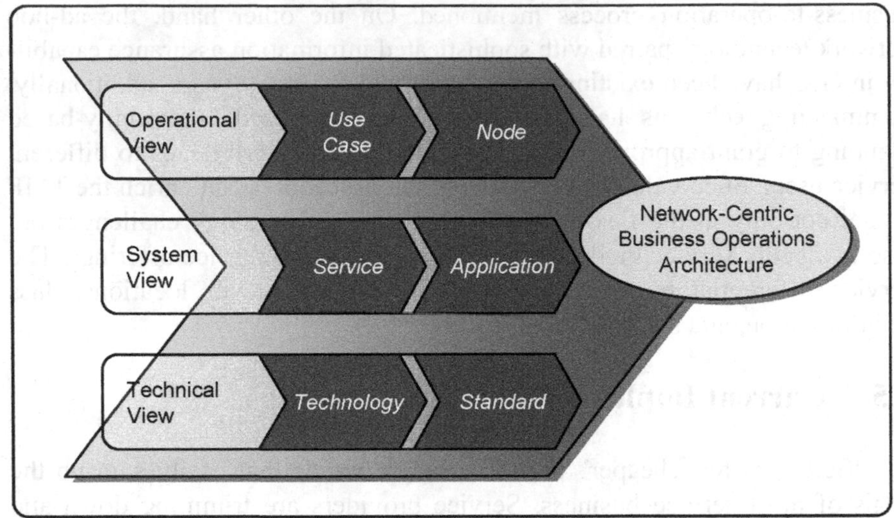

Figure 2.30. Primary objects in formulating a NCBO architecture.

Each view has a set of products. There may be multiple instances of use case, node, and so forth in service instance. These objects are linked with other architecture objects to form a comprehensive picture of a solution. The details for each of these three views will be discussed in the later chapters.

2.5.2 Federal Enterprise Architecture

Federal Enterprise Architecture (FEA) is an architectural framework recommended by the *Federal CIO Council* [Federal Enterprise Architecture Framework, Version v1.1, Federal CIO Council, 1999 www.feapmo.gov.]. It is designed to ease sharing of information and resources across federal agencies, reduce costs, and improve citizen services [29–31].

The FEA is currently a collection of reference models that develop a common taxonomy and ontology for describing IT resources. These include:

- The *Performance Reference Model (PRM)* to measure the performance of major IT investments and their contribution to program performance.
- The *Business Reference Model (BRM)* to delineate the business operations of the Federal Government.
- The *Service Component Reference Model (SCRM)* to classify service components for how they support business and performance objectives.
- The *Data Reference Model (DRM)* to delineate the data and information that support government program and business line operations.

- The *Technical Reference Model (TRM)* to categorize the standards, specifications, and technologies that support and enable the delivery of service components and capabilities.

The framework comprises the five architectural layers which follows the DoDAF specification and is depicted in Figure 2.31. In the top business architecture layer, the high-level operational concept graphics and use cases with associated activities characterize the business operation. Also, state transition and event trace delineate the dynamic aspect of the operation. Next, the information layer consists of operational node connectivity and information exchange. The data layer contains data exchange information, service contracts, and data schemas. Logical architecture or service stack diagrams, system relationship, functional decomposition, state transition, and event trace, and so forth characterize the application layer. Finally, system communications description and standard and technology profile and forecast support the infrastructure layer.

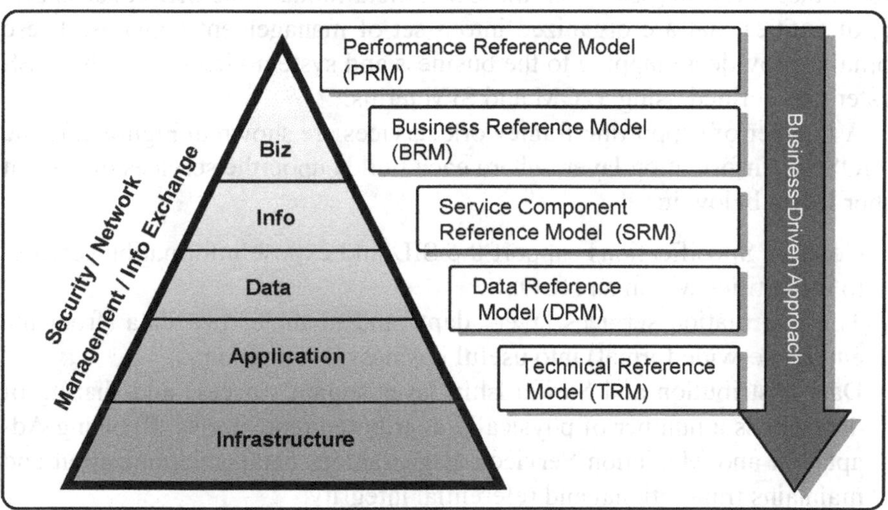

Figure 2.31. FEA architecture layers and component.

2.5.3 Next Generation Operations Support Systems

Next Generation Operations Support Systems (NGOSS) is TMF's initiative to develop a flexible plug-and-play OSS architecture, covering the integration process, information, and platform architectures that enables and facilitates the rapid deployment of new service products. An important characteristic of NGOSS is the decoupling of the services offered from the underlying telecommunications network. Through the identification of well-defined, contract-specified interfaces, NGOSS can be built by commercial off-the-shelf components and supported by a distributed processing framework [32–34].

The basic architecture underlying NGOSS is that of a *distributed, interface-oriented architecture (DIOA)*. Similar to the concept of SOA, a DIOA-based system consists of a number of run-time entities that together offer the functionality represented by a set of interfaces. Clients wishing to exploit this functionality bind to the interfaces and invoke operations over those bindings.

The NGOSS architecture is model-based. That is, information in the NGOSS is represented via well-defined models that can interact and be shared with each other. NGOSS *Shared Information and Data (SID)* model is the means by which useful information, relevant to a given set of business processes, may be factored out, shared, and operated on by multiple business processes on a system-wide basis. The NGOSS SID is a shared information model that is refining based on the UML meta-model. The SID consists of a set of entities that are organized into a set of management domains. These domains provide a mapping to the business and system views of the NGOSS system, as defined using eTOM and SIM terms.

A number of supporting framework services are shown in Figure 2.32 the NGOSS as information layer, where each builds upon the services offered at other layers below it:

- Contract Specifications support the SID and expose information services to the entities within an NGOSS.
- The information services layer adapts and mediates raw data (from the enterprise-wide format) into useful business information.
- Data Distribution and Stewardship layer supports access and sharing of data across a number of physically distributed repositories. By using Adaptation and Mediation Services, it guarantees data synchronization and maintains transactional and referential integrity.
- The separate raw repositories hold and maintain the data or act as a data proxy.

The NGOSS architecture services have two fundamental classes:

1. The *Business Services* provide elements of business functionality, which are presented through Contract Specifications. Examples: Provisioning, Billing.
2. The *Framework Services* includes services which provide standard OSS capabilities that can be orchestrated by Business Services (e.g., logging) or the capabilities needed to support the patterns of interaction between Components implementing Business Services (e.g., Naming, Registration, and Service Location).

Shared Information and Data Management Services and *Process Management Services* are basic framework services and they can be used by other services. *Process Management Service* provides the externalized process control acting as a conductor or coordinator of activities spanning across the NGOSS Components. *Policy Management Service* is an OSS framework Service containing policies to represent business rules and resulting configuration commands for configuring various feature of a device. NGOSS *Distribution Transparency* is loosely coupled distributed Components which assist NGOSS *clients* and *components* to locate other NGOSS *contracts* and the associated *components* without knowledge of their physical location.

Figure 2.32 shows the structure of the NGOSS architecture and the layering of services.

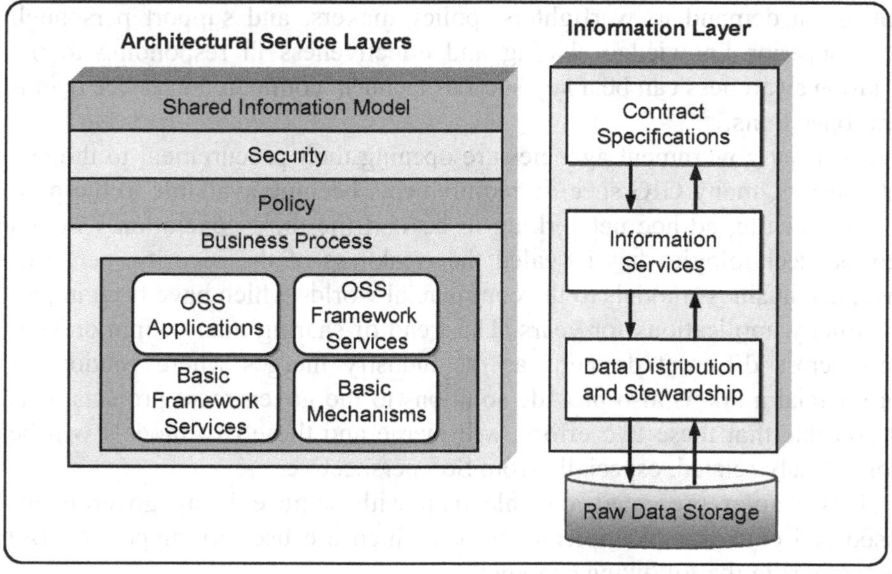

Figure 2.32. NGOSS architectural layering of services.

2.6 Conclusion

Nowadays, most enterprises place their focus upon the convergence of multiple functionalities into one seamless capability in order to respond to the increased pace of technological change as well as evolving operational demands. The GIG is defined by DoD as one of the key enablers that form the foundation of the government-based network-centric transformation. The GIG represents a globally interconnected, end-to-end set of information capabilities and processes for collecting, processing, and managing information on demand to warfighters, policymakers, and support personnel. The

GIG fulfills a fundamental principle of Network-Centric Operations by securely connecting people and systems regardless of time or place, providing vastly superior situational awareness and better access to information for accelerated decision-making. On the other hand, TMF eTOM is modeled for the telecommunication service providers to develop their OSS. eTOM brings more financial and billing processes focus for a commercial solution while the GIG being more security sensitivity for military actions, both are based on the same operational principles and are commonly exchangeable for their functional building blocks. The most noticeable differences are the focus of their customer's interest.

In critical military missions, globally interconnected end-to-end set of information capabilities allowing the associated processes and personnel to perform collecting, processing, storing, disseminating, and managing information on demand to warfighters, policy makers, and support personnel. Such superior knowledge sharing and effectiveness in responding to the situation awareness can be a key success factor in commercial service operators' operations.

As many government agencies are opening their procurement to the private sectors, many GIG specific requirements become available to the public. Meanwhile, ad-hoc networking in beyond the third generation wireless network technologies has revealed the weakness of the security, performance, and business models to the commercial worlds which have been in part of military applications for years. The trend of sharing many common subjects across different domains as the industry merges where vendors of commercial markets also provide solutions to the government projects. It is foreseeable that these two efforts will merge and these two models will be more closely related, especially from SoS perspective.

This chapter presented a viable path with some existing government-based and commercial implementations which are used to support NCBO discussions in the following chapters.

Chapter 3

WIRELESS NETWORK TECHNOLOGIES

NCBO is not limited to telecommunications networks and computer networking; however, network technologies play an essential role in supporting an enterprise's IT business operations. The GIG and eTOM models discussed in the previous chapters demonstrated how technology infrastructure can support the enterprise vision of network-centric operations in a service-oriented environment allowing the enterprises to share capability with a minimum requirement for local functionality that a single host needs to possess.

A mobile wireless network is a dynamic environment exhibiting decoupled computing, on-demand services, and physical mobility for the freedom of sharing information with many others. Incorporating mobile wireless technologies in the enterprise information management can improve the service quality and effectiveness of SOE services. As new information objects introduced by the next generation wireless technology offers auto-configuration and flexibility, enterprises can hence leverage such dynamic features arising beyond the 3G mobile systems to align with their existing business and technology frameworks to create new market opportunities never seen before.

The sections on wireless transport services represent the main thrust of this chapter; the motivation of this subject is to understand the imperatives for a viable network-centric service framework upon wireless transport services. A brief history of wireless networks, their architectures, and the current development of wireless networking standards and various implementations are discussed. The following sections delve into the ad-hoc network technology presenting the technical challenges of this technology, the hierarchy of different protocol layers, and potential interrelationships between such transport services and the achievable SOE integration. A glimpse of the wireless networks paves the technological foundation for sensor applications discussed in the next chapter.

3.1 Overview

A network-centric enterprise service framework is comprised of elements each of which fulfills a specific role in the framework. As depicted in Figure 3.1, the roles of these networking elements can directly or indirectly support the service description, advertisement, discovery, invocation, composition, and other application specific roles that will be addressed in the following chapters.

Traditional wire-line services are considered mature technologies. However, enterprise services in wireless network applications such as response coordination by firefighters and police at disaster sites or *command and control (C2)* by the military in a battlefield require a systematic rethinking of their core concepts. This is because these wireless scenarios demand reliability despite the dynamic nature of the underlying network. For instance, a key issue with the NCBO in wireless services is to mitigate the frequent disconnection and to maintain a sufficient duration of communications in order to support automatic and transparent discovery of services and the maintenance of channels across different service coverage domains, e.g., PAN, LAN, MAN, and WAN (see section 3.1.2).

A more complicated solution with the concept of "context sensitive binding" even requires the service provision channel between two entities to be maintained as they move through changing physical and logical contexts.

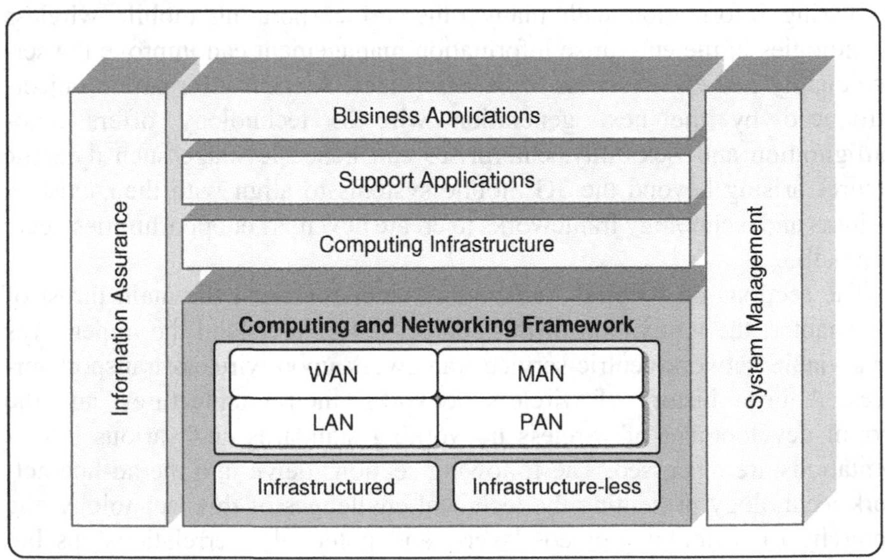

Figure 3.1. System architecture of enterprise services.

This chapter profiles different service elements that can potentially fulfill the need described. This overview section covers wireless networking categories, networking technologies, the architecture of wireless networks, and four different network coverage domains and associated applications. These are essential building blocks for an enterprise service framework. The integration aspect will be addressed in the later chapters to complete an end-to-end view of different enterprise solutions.

3.1.1 Infrastructured and Infrastructure-Less Networks

Infrastructure-less networks are also called *ad-hoc networks*, where an individual node is allowed to move freely and remain connected with others in dynamic manner. Since there is no fixed router, every node could act as a router. In Latin "*ad-hoc*" literally means "*for this purpose only*", thus an ad-hoc network can be regarded as a spontaneous network.

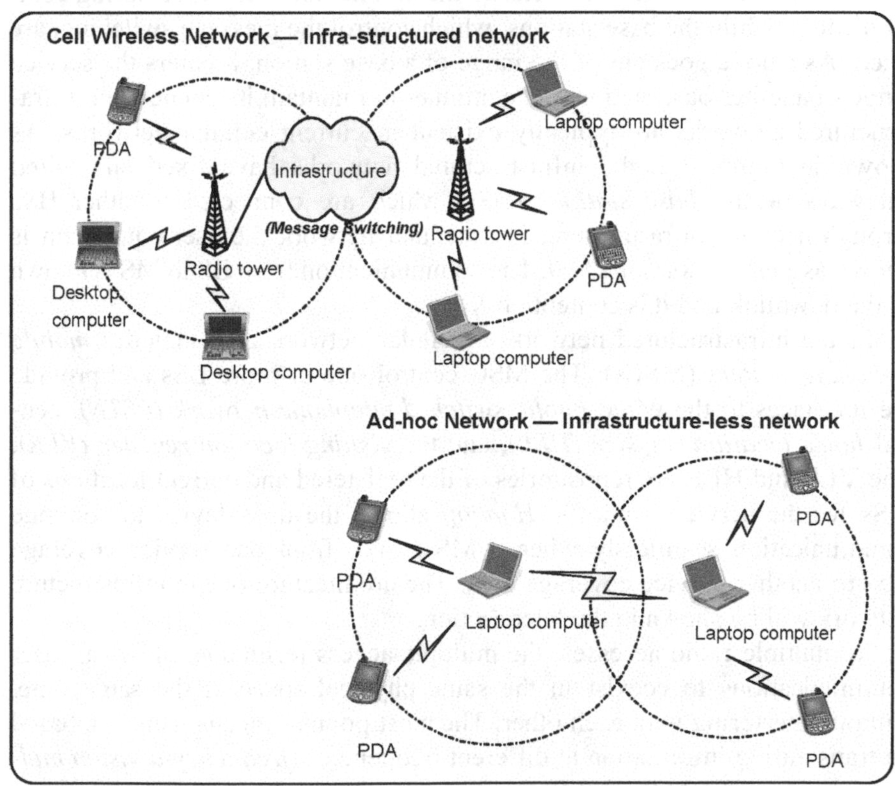

Figure 3.2. Comparison of cellular and ad-hoc wireless networks.

An ad-hoc network can be formed without predetermined organization; nodes are responsible for discovering their most appropriate neighboring nodes with which to communicate. As shown in Figure 3.2, a mobile node cannot communicate directly with the destination node, a *multi-hop* or *store-and-forward* scheme can relay the messages through other nodes. All intermediate nodes function as routers to discover and maintain the path to the destination nodes. At the network level, all nodes potentially possess identical capabilities and responsibilities in a fully symmetric environment. Each node, however, can have asymmetric capabilities such as different transmission ranges, battery life, processing capacity, and speed of movement, or application roles such as routers or root node (e.g., gateway to the backbone network). Traffic characteristics of an infrastructure-less network can be managed by different service designs such as broadcast methods (e.g., unicast, multicast, and geocast; chapters 4 and 5) and addressing schemes (e.g., host-based, content-based, and capability-based; section 4.3.5).

An infrastructured network allows the mobile nodes to move during communication while the base stations, which control the message switching, are fixed. As a node goes out of the range of a base station, it enters the service range of another base station and continues to maintain its connection. Infrastructured networks are typically existent in current cellular networks. As shown in Figure 3.2, the infrastructured networks have fixed and wired gateways or the *base stations* (BSs) which are connected to other BSs through network infrastructure. In a cellular network the user equipment is known as a *mobile station (MS)*. The communication from BS to MS is known as the downlink and it is contention-less.

In the infrastructured network, a cellular network also includes *mobile switching centers* (MSCs). The MSC control one or more BSs and provide the interfaces to the wired *public switched telephone network (PSTN)*, central *home location register (HLR)*, and the *visiting location register (VLR)*. The VLR and HLR are repositories of the registered and current locations of MSs for the service handoffs. *Handoff* allows the user device to continue communication seamlessly when a MS moves from one service coverage area to another service coverage area. The architecture of the infrastructure network will be shown in the later section.

In multiple radio accesses, the multiple-access technique allows all user communications to coexist in the same physical space at the same time, without interfering with each other. The most popular mechanisms are based on transmitting information at different frequencies (*frequency-division multiple access or FDMA*), in different time slots (*time-division multiple access or TDMA*), or using specific codes for each message (*code-division multiple access or CDMA*). These three multiple-access techniques are depicted in Figure 3.3.

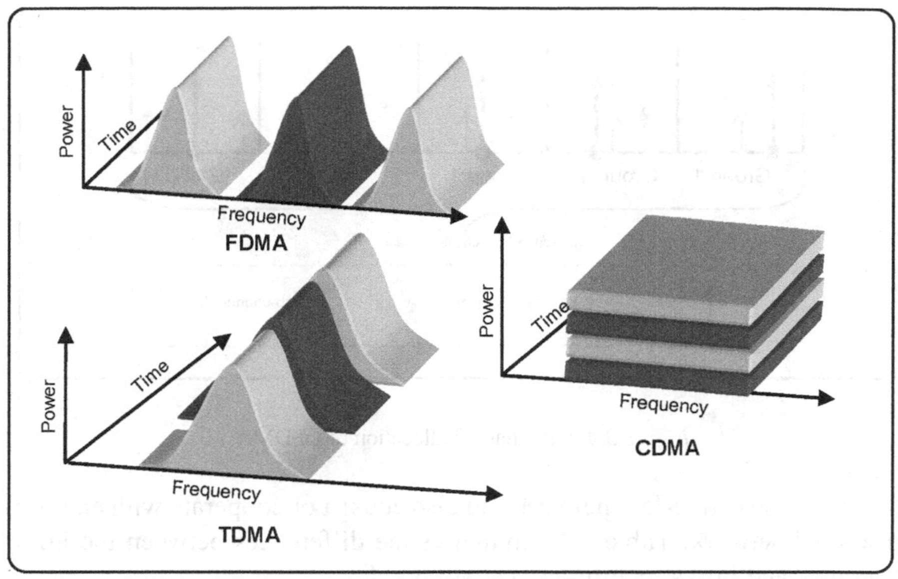

Figure 3.3. Physical-layer multiple-access techniques.

A more modern technique is called *orthogonal frequency-division multiplexing (OFDM)*, also known as *discrete multi-tone modulation (DMT)*. It uses the digital modulation scheme over the principle of *frequency-division multiplexing (FDM)*. In essence, frequency spectrum is divided into several sub-channels and each low-rate bit stream is transmitted over one sub-channel. The sub-carrier using a standard modulation scheme, for example PSK or QAM, and their frequencies are allocated so that the modulated data streams are orthogonal to each other. OFDM can eliminate cross-talk between the sub-channels thus intercarrier guard bands is not required. This feature greatly simplifies the design of the radio transmitter and the receiver.

Orthogonal frequency-division multiple access (OFDMA) is a combination of frequency domain and time domain multiple access. In OFDMA, the resources are partitioned in the time-frequency space, and slots are assigned along the OFDM symbol index and OFDM sub-carrier index. It is a multi-user version of the OFDM digital modulation scheme where a multiple number of sub-carriers (as sub-channels) can be assigned to different users. The users can achieve different data rate by assigning different code spreading factor or different number of spreading codes to each user. An example of sub-channel allocation, and an example of allocation scheduling of sub-channels are illustrated in Figure 3.4.

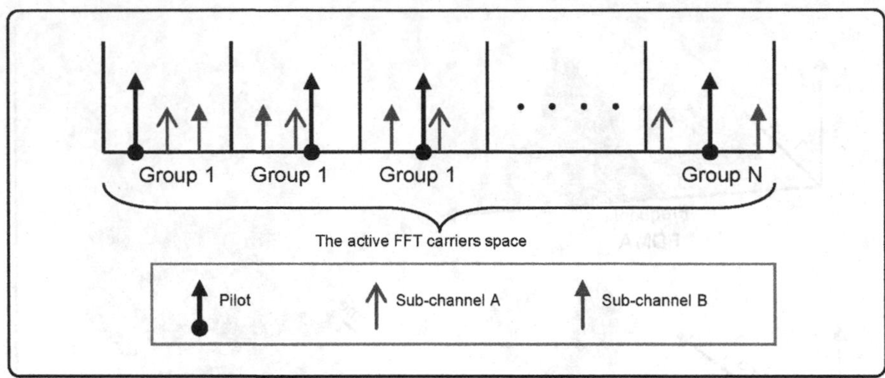

Figure 3.4. Sub-channel allocation of OFDMA.

An infrastructure-less network can also coexist or cooperate with an infrastructured network. Table 3.1 summaries the differences between the infrastructured and infrastructure-less networks [1].

Table 3.1. Differences between Infrastructured and Infrastructure-Less Networks.

Infrastructured Network	Infrastructure-Less Network
Fixed infrastructure	No infrastructure
Single-hop wireless links	Multiple-hop wireless links
Initially, circuit-switched	Initially, packet-switched
Low call drops due to handover	Frequent call drops
High cost and time of deployment	Very quick and cost-effective
Reuse of frequency via channel reuse	Dynamic frequency sharing
Bandwidth reservation is achieved easily	Complex MAC layer
Cost of network maintenance is high	Maintenance operations are built-in
Low complexity of mobile devices	Intelligent mobile devices are required
Widely deployed, evolves	Under development in commercial sector
Fixed, prelocated cell sites and base stations	No fixed base stations, very rapid deployment
Static backbone network topology	Highly dynamic network topologies with multi-hop
Relatively benign environment and stable connectivity	Hostile environment (losses, noise) and sporadic connectivity
Detailed planning before base stations can be installed	Ad-hoc network automatically forms and adapts to changes
Main application areas: civilian, commercial	Main application areas: military, rescue

3.1.2 Long-Range and Short-Range Networks

Wireless networks can be divided by the range of coverage. Figure 3.5 depicts four levels of network, where *wireless wide area network (WWAN)* and *wireless metropolitan area network (WMAN)* are long-range networks, and *wireless local area network (WLAN)* and *wireless personal area network (WPAN)* are short-range networks.

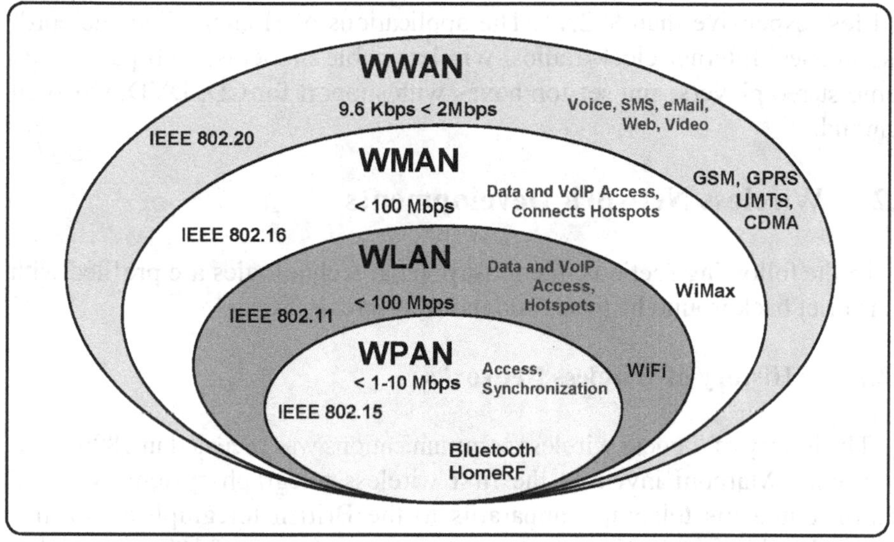

Figure 3.5. Four levels of network.

Long-range wireless networks usually require subscription to service providers who offer connectivity over geographically large areas. The broadcasting equipment is owned by the provider and the user-facing equipment is owned by the subscriber. Applications such as cell phones, pagers, wireless-enabled laptops, and handheld devices are in this category. The applications of WAN include GSM, GPRS, UMTS, and CDMA 2000. The most popular commercial MAN in the wireless arena is WiMax, defined in IEEE 802.16.

The main purpose of WLANs is used to extend a service provided by a wired network, one popular example is IEEE 802.11, *Wi-Fi* ("*wireless fidelity*" a trademark of Wi-Fi Alliance) or hotspot. IEEE 802.11 is now used as a general term for WLANs. Also, initially it was referred to as 802.11b networks, but now it refers to any 802.11 family networks including 802.11a, 802.11b, 802.11g, or dual-band. Applications of WLAN can include enabling printers, servers, and routers to be shareable with a wireless-equipped computer.

WPANs are differentiated from the WLANs by their smaller area of coverage, and their ad-hoc-only topology. In WPAN, Bluetooth is intended for point-to-point communications. A Bluetooth-enabled laptop or handheld device can access peripherals such as printers and remote security system through single access point. Another new popular application of Bluetooth is hand-free phone service in automobiles.

HomeRF is also a WPAN to support data, voice, and streaming media for home wireless networking. It is more versatile and resistant to interference, and less expensive than 802.11. The applications of HomeRF include cordless phones, Internet clock radios, wireless cable modems, web pads, MP3 home stereo players, and set-top boxes with support for CD, DVD, video on demand.

3.2 Wireless Network Developments

In the following sections, the most popular technologies are profiled with their brief background histories and main features.

3.2.1 History of Wireless Networks

The history of modem wireless communications was revealed in 1896 when Guglielmo Marconi invented the first wireless telegraph system. Marconi demonstrated his telegraph apparatus to the British telegraph authorities and applied his first British patent application on June 2 of 1896. The radiation signals were sent in July 1896 over a distance of one-and-three-fourths miles on Salisbury Plain based on long-wave (>1 km wavelength). On May 13 1897, communication was established between Lavernock Point and Brean Down England at distance of 8 miles. In 1907, the first commercial trans-Atlantic wireless service was initiated. In 1915, wireless voice transmission between New York and San Francisco was achieved [2,3].

In 1920, the first commercial radio broadcast took place in Pittsburgh, Pennsylvania. In 1927, first commercial radiotelephone service operated between Britain and the US. In 1935, the first telephone call around the world was made.

In 1946, the first public telephone service started in 25 major US cities, in the same year, first car-based mobile telephone set up in St. Louis, using "push-to-talk" technology.

In 1960, the concept of "trunking" was introduced; it allowed telephone companies to offer full-duplex, auto-dial systems. In 1962, the first communication satellite, Telstar, launched into orbit. In 1968, *Defense Advanced Research Projects Agency – US (DARPA)* selected BBN to develop the *Advanced Research Projects Agency Network (ARPANET)*. The packet-data technology used in ARPANET was the father of the modern Internet. In the same year, AT&T proposed the cellular concept to the FCC.

The history of wireless ad-hoc networks began in 1973 when the DARPA initiated a research program for interlinking mobile battlefield elements in a packet-based infrastructure-less and hostile environment called *packet radio networks (PRNet)*. In the same period, the ALOHANET, based at the University of Hawaii, was the first large-scale packet radio project. Late in that decade, the X.25 standard was defined for the packet switching technology to establish an efficient means for commercial data communications. In 1977, the *Advanced Mobile Phone System (AMPS)*, invented by Bell Labs, was first installed in the US with geographic regions divided into 'cells' (i.e., cellular telephone). Since the emergence of infrastructured and infrastructure-less mobile wireless networks in 1970's, wireless networks have become increasingly popular in the communication industry.

In 1982, the European *Global System for Mobile Communications (GSM)* was founded. In the January of 1983, TCP/IP was selected as the official protocol for the ARPANET. In 1984, the AMPS cellular system began its deploying. In 1990, Motorola files FCC application for permission to launch 77 low earth orbit communication satellites, known as the Iridium System. In 1991, *US digital cellular (USDC)*, or IS-54, released a service to support three users in each 30 kHz channel. It was later improved to accommodate six users per channel. In 1993, *Internet Protocol version 4 (IPv4)* was defined to support *Transport Control Protocol (TCP)* for reliable transmission over the Internet. IS-95 *code-division multiple access (CDMA)* was introduced in the next year. In the 1990s, the GSM and IS-95 standards evolved to include wireless data transmission as an integral part of their service.

3.2.2 IEEE 802 Series Standards

In 1985, the *Federal Communications Commission (FCC)* released the unlicensed *international, scientific, and medical (ISM)* bands, which were to become important in the development of WLANs. These so-called "garbage bands" were existing in equipment such as microwave ovens for heating food. Devices operating in these bands require using "spread spectrum" technology. This technology spreads a radio signal out over a wide range of frequencies, making the signal less susceptible to interference and difficult to intercept. In 1990s, a new IEEE committee called 802.11 (see section 3.6.4) was founded to investigate a standard. Two variants, 802.11a and 802.11b, were ratified over the next two years. Table 3.2 provides a summary of IEEE 802.11 series standards and task groups.

Table 3.2. Summary of IEEE 802.11 Series Group.

Group	Task
IEEE 802.11	The original WLAN standard supporting 1 Mbps and 2 Mbps, 2.4 GHz RF and IR standard (1999)
IEEE 802.11a	High-speed WLAN standard for 5 GHz band. Supports 54 Mbps (1999, shipping products in 2001). It operates in the Unlicensed National Information Infrastructure bands of 5.3 and 5.8 GHz
IEEE 802.11b	Enhancements to 802.11 to support 5.5 and 11 Mbps (1999). WLAN standard in the ISM band of 2.4 GHz. Supports 11 Mbps.
IEEE 802.11c	Bridge operation procedures; included in the IEEE 802.1D standard (2001)
IEEE 802.11d	International roaming (country to country) automatically configures devices to meet local RF regulations (2001).
IEEE 802.11e	Enhancements: QoS, including packet bursting (2005)
	Addresses QoS requirements for all IEEE WLAN radio interfaces.
IEEE 802.11f	Inter-access point protocol (2003)
	Defines interaccess point communications to facilitate multiple vendor-distributed WLAN networks
IEEE 802.11g	54 Mbps, 2.4 GHz standard (backwards compatible with b) (2003)
	Establishes an additional modulation technique for 2.4 GHz band. Supports speeds up to 54 Mbps.
IEEE 802.11h	Spectrum management of 802.11a for European compatibility (2004)
IEEE 802.11i	Enhanced security (2004) on both authentication and encryption protocols. It encompasses 802.1X, TKIP, and AES protocols.
IEEE 802.11j	Extensions for Japan (2004)
IEEE 802.11k	Radio resource measurement enhancements
IEEE 802.11l	Reserved but unsound
IEEE 802.11m	Maintenance of the standard; odds and ends.
IEEE 802.11n	Higher throughput improvements. Provides higher throughput improvements. Intended to provide speeds up to 500 Mbps.
IEEE 802.11o	Reserved but unsound
IEEE 802.11p	WAVE – wireless access for the vehicular environment (such as ambulances and passenger cars)
IEEE 802.11q	(reserved, typologically unsound, can be confused with 802.1q VLAN trunking)
IEEE 802.11r	Fast roaming
IEEE 802.11s	ESS Mesh networking
IEEE 802.11t	Wireless Performance Prediction (WPP) test methods and metrics
IEEE 802.11u	Interworking with non-802 networks (e.g., cellular)
IEEE 802.11v	Wireless network management
IEEE 802.11w	Protected management frames

In 1994, the Swedish communication equipment maker Ericsson proposed Bluetooth. Later *Bluetooth* (section 3.6.5) was taken over by *Special Interest Group (SIG)*. In 1998, the WPAN group published the original functionality requirement and included Bluetooth and HomeRF. Bluetooth has since been selected as the base specification for IEEE 802.15. In March of 1999, IEEE 802.15 was approved as a separate group to handle WPAN standardization. *WiMAX* (section 3.6.6) was formed in 2001 in defining the original 802.16 specification. A summary of IEEE 802 series standards and task groups is listed in Table 3.3.

Table 3.3. Summary of IEEE 802 Series Group.

Group	Task
802.1	High Level Interface (HILI) Working Group
802.2	Logical Link Control (LLC) Working Group
802.3	CSMA/CD Working Group
802.4	Token Bus Working Group
802.5	Token Ring Working Group
802.6	Metropolitan Area Network (MAN) Working Group
802.7	BroadBand Technical Adv. Group (BBTAG)
802.8	Fiber Optics Technical Adv. Group (FOTAG)
802.9	Integrated Services LAN (ISLAN) Working Group
802.10	Standard for Interoperable LAN Security (SILS) Working Group
802.11	Wireless LAN (WLAN) Working Group
802.12	Demand Priority Working Group
802.14	Cable-TV Based Broadband Communication Network Working Group
802.15	WPAN Working Group, focusing on developing standards for short-distance wireless networks. The result standard is intended to coexist with other wireless and wired networks within the ISM band.
802.16	Broadband Wireless Access (BBWA) Working Group
802.17	Resilient Packet Ring (RPR) Working Group
802.18	Radio Regulatory Technical Advisory Group
802.19	Coexistence Technical Advisory Group
802.20	Mobile Wireless Access Working Group
802.21	Media Independent Handover Working Group

3.2.3 MANET and Emerging Defense Communications Technologies

In the early 1990s, the DoD funded the *Near-term Digital Radio (NTDR)* project. The NTDR used clustering and link-state routing, and self-organized into a two-tier ad-hoc network. Now used by the US Army, NTDR is the one of the non-prototypical military ad-hoc networks in use at large deployment today.

In the mid to late 1990s, the *Mobile Ad-hoc Networking (MANET)* working group was created in the IETF to standardize routing protocols for ad-hoc networks. The development of routing within the MANET working group and the larger community forked into reactive (routes on-demand) and proactive (routes ready-to-use) routing protocols. HIPERLAN was the other standard that addressed and benefited ad-hoc networking. *Multi-hop cellular network (MCN)* and *self-organizing packet radio ad-hoc network with overlay (SOPRANO)* are based on hybrid architecture, combing the benefits of both cellular and ad-hoc network to improve the capacity of the service.

Two key programs from DoD that support next generation wireless warfighting communications for network-centric operations are the *Transformational Satellite Communications System (TSAT)* and the *Joint Tactical Radio System (JTRS)* [4–6].

Approved by a Joint Requirements *Oversight Council Memorandum (JROCM)* on October 23, 2003. TSAT is the next generation *satellite communications (SATCOM)* system. It is based on the *Transformational Communications Architecture (TCA)* and represents advancement from the current circuit based systems to support airborne and space-borne Intelligence, Surveillance, and Recon-naissance communications with high speed, secure, protected, dynamically allocated, and efficiently utilized bandwidth.

The JTRS program was initiated in early 1997 to improve interoperability between radios acquired from different vendors or operated by different military services. The JTRS radios are scalable by virtue of form, fit, and cost and are expandable using the *open software communications architecture (SCA*; section 3.5.1.2*)* standard. These radios can be used in handheld, man-pack, small form factor (embedded), vehicular, *Airborne*, *Maritime*, *Fixed or station (AMF)* settings. Waveform software runs on *software defined radio (SDR*; section 3.5.1*)* and implements the signal processing functions and protocols. If necessary, JTRS users can connect to other users via SATCOM gateway or even access the GIG information.

3.2.4 3G Networks

The *Third Generation Partnership Program (3GPP)* based network architecture grew from the 2G GSM–based architecture. The 3GPP specifications are approved as the *European Telecommunications Standards Institute (ETSI)* standards. GSM was intended for *public land mobile network (PLMN)* to provide *circuit-switched (CS)* voice services. To add data services, 3GPP developed the *2.5G General Packet Radio Services (GPRS)* network as an overlay *packet-switch (PS)* domain. The 3GPP specifications maintain GSM, GPRS (section 3.6.1), and various releases of UMTS (section 3.6.2) wideband code-division multiple access *(WCDMA)* standards.

Table 3.4. Summary of Key Features in 3GPP Releases.

3GPP Releases	Key Features
Release '99 March 2000	A major *Radio Access Network (RAN)* release. Introduced basic capabilities of UTRAN, WCDMA, and new Core Network-Access Network interface (lu-CS), *open service architecture (OSA)*, and extended *Serving GPRS Support Node (SGSN)* functions to *Radio Network Controller (RNC)*.
Release 4 March 2001	Features in Release '99 plus a minor release. Added UTRAN access with some QoS enhancements, evolved CS domain from *Mobile Switching Center (MSC)* to softswitch-based MSC servers and Media Gateways based on IP, and also added location service enhancements and *multimedia messaging (MMS)*, W*ireless application protocol (WAP)*, *Mobile Execution Environment (MExE)*.
Release 5 June 2002	Features in Release 4 plus a major core-network upgrades release. Specified IMS, made IPv6 mandatory for IMS, defined IP UTRAN but did not eliminate ATM, and included several enhancements to WCDMA, MMS, and *location services (LCS)*. The IMS phase I includes the *SIP (Session Initiation Protocol)* Session Control for IMS Signaling, Security & IMS Authentication, IMS QoS, Charging and OAM&P, OSA support, multimedia codecs, CAMEL (Phase 4) for IM-SSF, and IPv6 use for SIP signaling and IMS user traffic.
Release 6 March 2005	Features in Release 5 plus further enhancements to IMS, IMS and Internet SIP interworking, 3GPP and 3GPP2 IMS harmonization, WLAN-UMTS integration with UMTS and IMS, further enhancement to LCS and *instant messaging (IM)* services. Introduced *multimedia broadcast and multicast service (MBMS)* and *digital rights management (DRM)*, enhanced MExE, *virtual home environment (VHE)*, and OSA. The IMS phase II includes interworking with non-IMS IP networks, interworking with CS networks, UTRAN QoS optimization, dynamic QoS policy, SIP forking, WLAN/3GPP interworking, immediate and session based messaging, IMS Services combining CS and PS, Presence/Instant Messaging (SIMPLE), and full charging framework.
Release 7 and beyond	Further enhancements to IMS, and WLAN-UMTS integration for handover support and integration with legacy voice, and for MIMO antennas. The main IMS phase III enhancements contain. Emergency services, IMS local services, QoS Enhancement for IP Inter-working, *Media Resource Function (MRF)* and gateway interface enhancements, GERAN optimization for PS, IMS enhancements for Fixed Broadband access, Interim Security, and merging of TPF/FBC interfaces.

After the 3GPP was established in Europe, the 3GPP2 was created as counterpart of the WDCMA. WDCMA supports the *American National Standards Institute/Telecommunications/Industry Association/Electronic Industry Alliance (ANSI/TIA/EIA) Interim Standard (IS)*–41 and IS-95–based CDMA2000 (section 3.6.3) specifications. Mobile networks based on both 3GPP or 3GPP2 technologies are now widely deployed, and their user base is still growing. The GPRS was later enhanced in several UMTS releases, starting with Release 99, Releases 4, 5, 6, 7, and beyond, which include 3G all-IP networks, which supports VoIP and other multimedia services. Table 3.4 summarizes the main features of various 3GPP specification sets, issued as different releases. 3GPP continues to evolve including the introduction of universal terrestrial radio access network *(UTRAN)* and new capabilities of *IP multimedia subsystem (IMS*; section 3.6.7*)*. Table 3.4 summarizes the key features of 3GPP releases [7].

3.2.5 Beyond 3G and 4G Networks

Owing to the trend of global mobility and needed service portability across different standards, an integrated solution is critical for the future success of technology-based enterprises. Founded in 2001, the *Wireless World Research Forum (WWRF)* intends to integrate the existing technologies and protocols to achieve the highest throughput and lowest cost wireless network possible for the *fourth generation (4G)* wireless network. The official designation from the IEEE for 4G is *Beyond 3G (B3G)*; it incorporates other applications and technologies such as Wi-Fi and WiMAX. The B3G standard is designed to support service speeds ranging from 100 Mbps (in cellphone networks) to 1 GBps (in local Wi-Fi networks) and with mobility condition to reach 20 Mbps at top speed of 100 miles per hour. These specifications aim to provide all digital networks which can fully utilize IP and converged video and data. Table 3.5 summarizes the main differences between 3G and 4G technologies [8].

The goals for 4G networks to offer seamless connectivity and global roaming across multiple networks are achievable by the specifications that support smooth handoff across heterogeneous networks. The high data rates and highly personalized capability from the 4G network technology realize

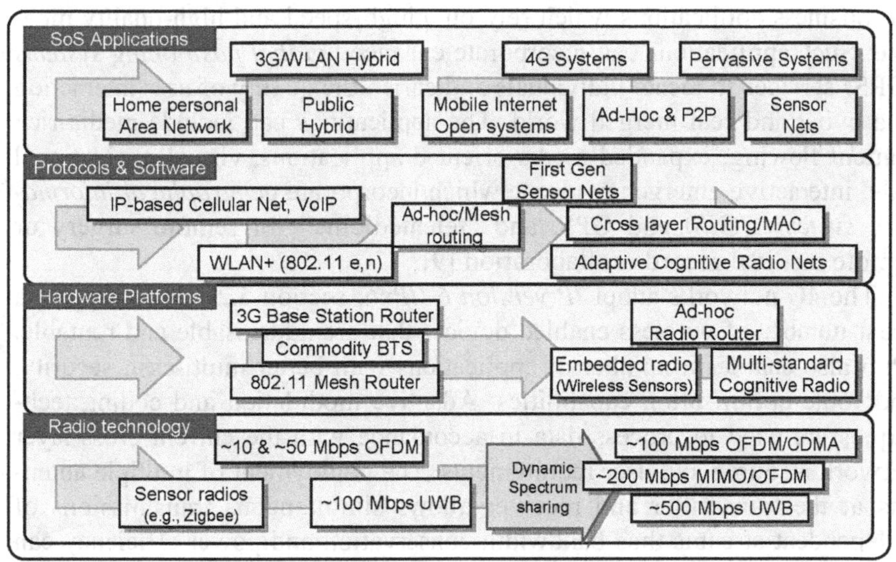

Figure 3.6. Convergence to 4G wireless technology.

Table 3.5. Key 3G and 4G Parameters.

Generation	2.5G	3G	4G
Design begin	1990	1990	2000
Operational	1999	2003	~2010
Network architecture	Wide area cell based	Wide area cell based	Hybrid – integrated WLAN, Blue Tooth, WAN
Standards	GPRS, EDGE, 1xRTT, IS-95B	WCDMA, UWC, CDMA 2000	One standard
Services	High capacity packet data	High capacity broadband	Complete IP multimedia
Access	TDMA, CDMA	WCDMA, CDMA 2000	MC-CDMA or OFDM
Switching	PSTN/Packet	Circuit/packet	Packet
Data rate	>384 Kbps	>2 Mbps	>200 Mbps
IP	Multiple versions	Multiple versions	All IP (IPv6.0)
Component design		Optimized antenna, multi-band adapters	Smart antenna, SW multi-band, wideband radios

the business applications which rely on a high-speed and high-quality pipeline. Such applications can incorporate enhanced *global positioning systems (*GPS*)* services to locate individuals and enrich the quality of user interaction at a cyber and real merged world. The applications can include media-rich content flowing, expanded media-oriented applications, virtual navigational aids, interactive emergency rescue which incorporate *geographical information systems (GIS)* and GPS, and "telemedicine" for remote surgery or remote medical records collaboration [9].

The 4G networks adopt *IP version 6 (IPv6*; section 5.2.1.3*)* to support a great number of wireless enabled devices that are addressable and routable. IPv6 also enables a number of applications with better multi-cast, security, and route optimization capabilities. Adaptive modulation and coding techniques are used to process data in accordance with the current cross-layer network resource and user requirements. The deployment of multiple antennas at the transmitter and receiver allows simultaneous transmissions of independent streams thus bandwidth conservation and power efficiency can be improved. The radio technologies for B3G systems include *multiple input multiple output (MIMO)* technology, link adaptation techniques, multi-carrier based modulation and access (OFDM/OFDMA), iterative (multi-user) processing, "cross-layer" optimization and design principles, and *ultra-wideband (UWB)*. The technology trends are illustrated in Figure 3.6.

From a security perspective, the security infrastructure of the 4G networks comprising components such as firewalls, *VPNs*, *Internet key exchange (IKE*; section 5.2.3.2*)* tunneling, and *intrusion prevention systems (IPS)* are resident at the application layer. Virtualization of security can eliminate technology dependency thus protocol changes across network domains will not impact the end-to-end services. This is especially important for IPv4 to IPv6 domain routing, VoIP secure access management, and adoption to new *physical (PHY)* level technologies such as OFCDMA, MC-CDMA, and other evolving 4G techniques.

The 4G allows a user to be simultaneously connected to several wireless access technologies and can seamlessly move between them requires a smart-radio (also known as *cognitive radio* technology; section 5.4.1) to efficiently manage spectrum use and transmission power. One application of *open wireless architecture (*OWA*)* is *software defined radio (SDR*; section 3.5*)*. SDR is a hardware independent solution constituting different standards for better utilization of available bandwidth as well as making use of multiple channels simultaneously. In summary, the 4G system will dynamically share and utilize the network resources to meet the next generation users and business needs [10].

3.3 Characteristics and Fundamental Challenges of Ad-Hoc Networks

Compared with infrastructured networks, the advantages of infrastructure-less technology include ease and speed of deployment, and less dependence on infrastructure. Additionally, the ad-hoc networking technology offers enterprise global roaming to perform fast and seamless handover across multiple networks. In the stand of NCBO, the following sections will cover the fundamental characteristics and architectures of the ad-hoc network technology to support future SoS discussions [1].

As delineated in section 3.1.1, an ad-hoc network is a collection of wireless mobile nodes that dynamically form a temporary network on user demand regardless of whether these nodes are stationary, moving slowly or at high speed. The size of an ad-hoc network can be from few nodes to thousands of nodes depending upon the configuration. Despite the long history of ad-hoc networking, its applications still have many outstanding issues because the network can merge and split dynamically, the link condition can cause error or failure, the node can enter a resource contention situation when the topology changes, and other QoS and routing challenges. Some problems can be isolated into nodal level and some belong to network level problems [11].

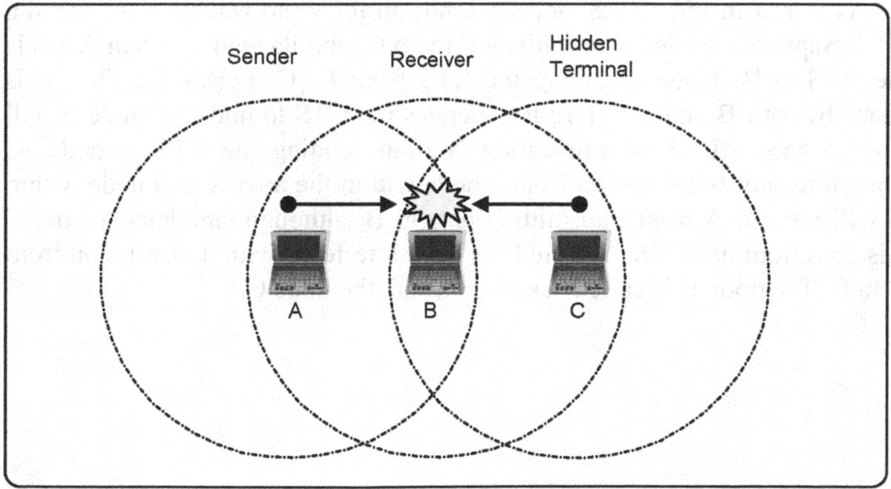

Figure 3.7. Hidden terminal problem.

3.3.1 Hidden Terminal Problem

Carrier sense medium access (CSMA) is one of the earliest mechanisms adopted for ad-hoc networks. In CSMA, a transmitter will first sense the wireless channel in the vicinity and refrain itself from transmission if the channel is already in use. When a node wants to transmit a data packet, it first transmits a *request to send (RTS)* frame. If a node is ready for receiving the data packet, it can transmit a *clear to send (CTS)* packet. Once the sender receives the CTS packet without error, it starts transmitting the data packet.

Figure 3.7 illustrates the hidden terminal problem, node B can communicate with A and C both, but node A and C cannot hear each other. When node A senses a "free" medium and is transmitting data to node B, meanwhile node C unaware of the ongoing transmission also attempts to transmit data to B. This causes collision at node B, in this case, the hidden nodes are identified as node C. It is a common practice to use a predata control information exchange (virtual medium sensing) to avoid the hidden terminal problem. One such virtual sensing mechanism is the 802.11 RTS/CTS exchange resulting in nodes getting exclusive access to the channel for a well-defined time period.

3.3.2 Exposed Terminal Problem

As shown in Figure 3.8, node A sends an RTS and waits for B to send a CTS. Suppose a node D transmits a RTS to C simultaneously when A sends the RTS to B. Upon receiving the RTS from D, C transmits CTS and is heard by both B and D before B generates the CTS to node A. Node B will enter a back-off period preventing B from sending the CTS to node A. Therefore, any transmission from a node within the area X to a node within Y will prevent A from transmitting data to B, although simultaneous transmissions from area X to Y would not have interfered with transmission from A to B. The node B is called "exposed from" the node C.

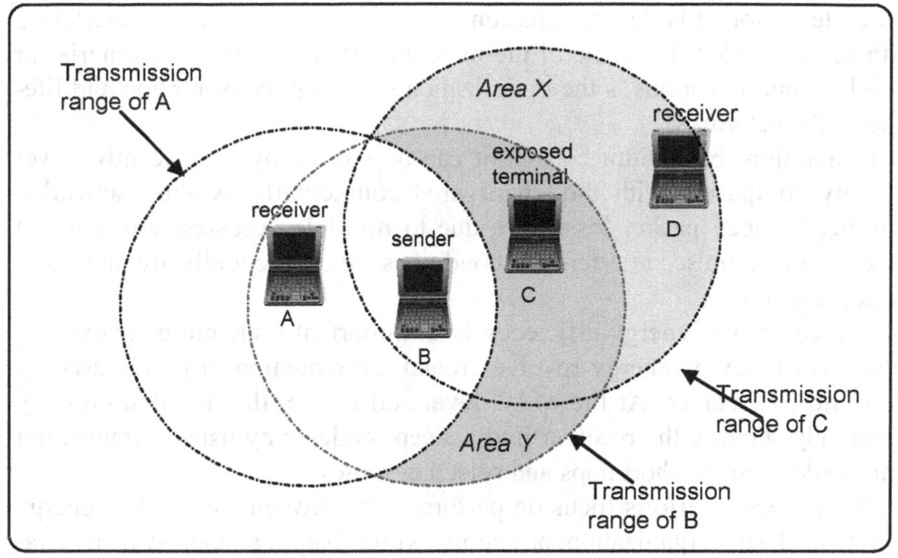

Figure 3.8. Exposed terminal problem.

3.3.3 Self-Organization

In a wireless ad-hoc network, all nodes are free to move arbitrarily at any time. As the result, the networks topology may change randomly and rapidly at unpredictable times. Mobility induced route changes make routing difficult because the topology is constantly changing and nodes cannot be assumed to have persistent data storage. Updated information through self-organization can be managed in one of the following approaches:

- Neighbor discovery – All nodes periodically transmit short packets ("*beacons*" or promiscuous snooping) to gather neighbors information.
- Topology organization – All nodes periodically gather information about the entire network or a part of the network.
- Topology reorganization – Topology update is triggered by one of the following scenarios: network partitioning, network merging, mobility of nodes, failure of nodes, or complete depletion of power sources of the nodes.

3.3.4 Resources Constrained

Resource constraints of a wireless node can include low-power, small-memory, and limited-bandwidth. Because of the nature of a mobile communication, mobile node can experience frequent topology changes. Power control of a mobile node must be well managed to ensure not only the right power level for reliable transmission but also the avoidance of interfering with nearby nodes. Thus one of the most important performance criteria for mobile communications is the optimization of energy consumption and lifetime of the networks.

In addition, bandwidth constraint can be caused by significantly lower capacity comparing with their hardwired counterparts. Ad-hoc networks' mobility induced packet losses are due to multiple accesses, transmission errors, fading, noise, interference conditions, and potentially frequent network partitions.

The concept of energy-efficiency is an important issue but most existing solutions for saving energy revolve around the reduction of power used by the radio transceiver. At the MAC level and above, this is often done by selectively sending the receiver into a sleep mode or by using a transmitter with predetermined short hops and selecting routes.

Most research efforts focus on performance between various low energy routing and self-organization protocols, while keeping other system parameters fixed. The relationship between aggregate energy consumption and non-protocol parameters such as node density, network coverage area, and transceiver power characteristics are less addressed. A better approach is to look from the SoS standpoint with the overall QoS strategy that is sensitive to the energy consumption.

3.3.5 Limited Physical Security

Mobile networks are generally more prone to physical security threats than are fixed cable networks. There are several factors of security: 1) *Availability* ensures the survivability of network services despite denial of service attacks; 2) *Confidentiality* ensures that certain information is never disclosed to unauthorized entities; 3) *Integrity* guarantees that a message being transferred is never corrupted; and 4) *Authentication* enables a node to ensure the identity of the peer node it is communicating with.

Active attacks might allow the adversary to delete massages, to modify messages, and to impersonate a node, thus violating availability, integrity, authentication, and non-repudiation. A fault diagnoses algorithm can be used to pick out the faulty nodes and at the same time remove the node from the whole network. However, this process must take place in real time to guarantee the needed performance. However such algorithms may not correctly diagnose faulty node in the presence of changing network topology during the diagnosis. More transport security attacks and resolutions can be found at section 8.5.4.

In any event, entity that has a wireless LAN should consider using security safeguards such as the *Wired Equivalent Privacy (WEP)* encryption standard, the more recent *Wi-Fi Protected Access (WPA)*, *Internet Protocol Security (IPsec)*, or a *virtual private network (VPN)*.

3.3.6 Routing

The contributing factors such as multi-hop, mobility, large network size combined with device heterogeneity, bandwidth, and battery power limitations make the design of routing protocols a major challenge.

Two main kinds of routing protocols exist today: one is called table-driven protocols (including distance vector and link state), another is on-demand protocols. In table-driven routing protocols, the protocols are consistent and up-to-date routing information to all nodes is maintained at each node, whereas in on-demand routing the routes are created only when desired by the source host.

Consider a service pattern when one node passing through the whole network very quickly, as depicted as device A in Figure 3.9. This affects to the whole network by triggering topology update on every node's routing table, and leads to the loss of packets, bandwidth consumption, and tremendous delay. Many routing protocols may create redundant routes, which will greatly increase the routing updates as well as increase the whole networks overhead. Secondly, in responding to the topology changes, periodically sending routing tables will add additional burdens to the limited bandwidth and waste battery power. Thirdly, transmission between two hosts does not necessarily work equally well in both directions therefore some routes determined by some routing protocols may not work in some environments [12].

For instance, scalability for supporting satisfactory QoS level in a large node number configuration is closely related as to how quickly network protocol can manage overhead increases as the number of nodes and links change. Scalability can be proactively accomplished by using routing or location hierarchy or perhaps limiting the control updates that are close to the changes. Dynamic route requests limitation and local broken routes repairs are norm for reactive resolution.

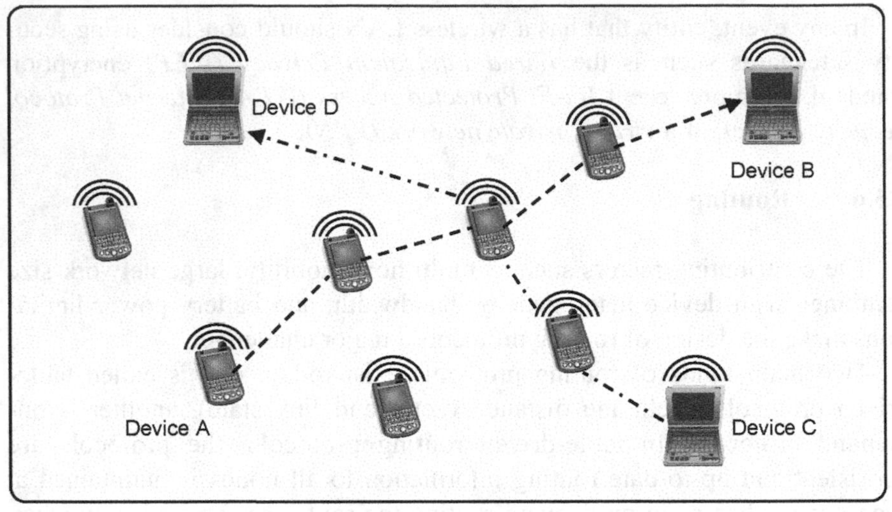

Figure 3.9. Ad-hoc routing for mobile wireless devices.

3.3.7 Multicasting

The *multicast* feature in ad-hoc networks can minimize link bandwidth consumption by transmitting data from multiple senders to multiple receivers without knowing their address. Figure 3.10 demonstrates node **A** broadcasting messages to all nodes that are connected to the network. This feature reduces bandwidth, delay, and processing in delivering traffic to a group. Regardless of the network environment, multicast communication is a very useful and efficient means of supporting group-oriented applications. Example applications include audio- and video-conferencing as well as one-to-many data dissemination in critical situations such as disaster recovery or battlefield scenarios [13].

The challenges of wireless multicast are their limited channel bandwidth, changing topology, and diverse wireless channel. In ad-hoc networks, multicasting must be able to adapt rapidly to infrastructure changes, an active networking approach can be employed: hosts can adapt in real time by downloading appropriate multicast mechanisms. Using low-power and low storage capacity hosts, the multicast can hence manage the balance between robustness versus efficiency.

- Host behavior completely independent of other hosts
- No limit on host speed
- No constraints on direction of movement
- High probability of frequent, temporary network partitions

Multicast routing protocols use two types of trees for sensing messages, namely source tree and shared tree. A source tree is directed from a single source to many receivers. In the shared tree, any node is both sender and receiver. The challenge of multicast routing protocols is to establish and maintain a tree effectively. The protocol MOSPF is a multicast extensions of OSPF, routers advertise multicast groups they service directly via IGMP, and routers maintain groups per source tree. The *Negative acknowledgement (NACK) Oriented reliable Multicast (NORM)* protocol is defined (IETF RFC 3940 and RFC 3941) to provide reliable transport of data from one or more sender(s) to a group of receivers over an IP multicast network by using NACK operations with optional *Forward Error Correction (FEC)*.

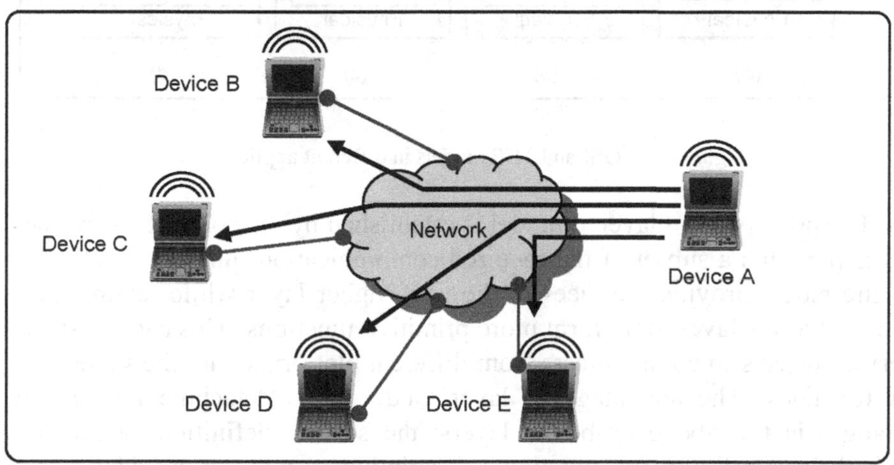

Figure 3.10. Multicasting.

3.4 Communication Protocol Layers

Managing a wireless transport services can include aspects of standards, processes, technologies (including hardware and software), and systems. In network-centric enterprises, one of the most significant service objectives has been to achieve service inter-dependency especially in information gathering and information processing. A hybrid computing environment may contain legacy and modern services that are linked but not fully integrated. The efficiency of an interdependency feature in such an environment relies upon a modularized and abstracted service relationship. One of the most commonly referred methods is the layer model.

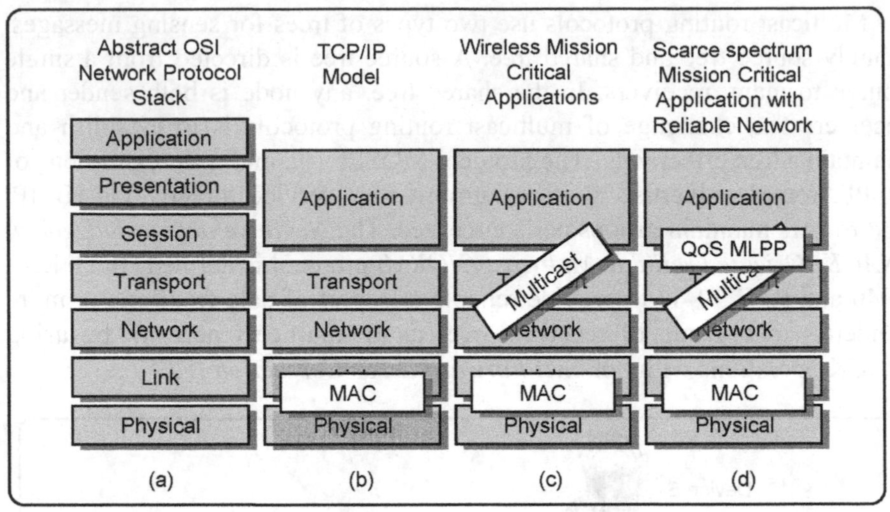

Figure 3.11. OSI and TCP models in different applications.

The principle of a layered model is established by the concept where each layer performs a subset of the required communication function. Each layer in the model provides services to the next higher layer while relying upon the next lower layer to perform more primitive functions. This can assist two service objects to communicate from different platforms with the same layer of functions. The advantage of layer model is its detachment from any changes in the above or below layers; the service definitions within the model focus only on the functional description of what is provided to the next upper layer.

In Figure 3.11(a) *Open Systems Interconnection (OSI)* Reference Model shows the abstract model with seven protocol stacks. These seven layers were presented as the optimal number of layer for telecommunication industry in 1984. During the same period, TCP/IP model has become the de facto standard in common IT industry. The TCP/IP model addresses only the bottom four layers with an abstract application layer as shown in Figure 3.11(b). Although no OSI-based protocol survived as a commercial product, the model is generally accepted as design guidance from theoretical perspective.

Because the TCP/IP model is commonly identified as the standard communication protocol in the community of NCBO, this model will be primarily referred as the "transport service". Furthermore, although TCP/IP applications are widely spread among wireless and wire-line service segments, the emphasis will be placed more upon the wireless side. This is shown in Figure 3.11(c) and (d) as mission critical application stacks where additional functions are required, e.g., multicasting and QoS, and MLPP (section 7.4.3). Details of QoS are explained in chapter 7.

3.4.1 Physical Layer

The physical layer is the most basic network layer, providing only the means of transmitting raw bits. General physical layer functions include connection establishment/termination, resources management, error control, coding schemes, data conversion/filtering/compression, diversity techniques, TRANSEC, timing and synchronization, and broadcast frequencies. The physical signaling sub-layer is the portion of the physical layer that interfaces with the MAC, performs character encoding (e.g., Unicode), and optional performs isolation functions.

A wireless network includes radio, position information (GPS receiver) and antennas applications in either directional antennas (One-to-all communications) and smart antennas (One-to-one/many communication) that are essential to a service deployment. The capabilities include sectored antennas (fixed beam positions), beam steering, and tracking a transmitter; this may require MAC and routing protocols support in a heterogeneous network. Frequency allocation, whether it is identical, different but fixed, or hopping (Bluetooth, Ultra-Wide Band) also impacts the actual utilization of radio resources.

The RF and baseband layers of Bluetooth are located in this layer. If the modulation scheme is transparent to MAC layer, MAC's awareness of time duration required for data transfer can result in better service efficiency. The IEEE 802.11 standard provides data rates of 1 Mbps with *binary phase-shift keying (BPSK)* modulation, or 2 Mbps with *quadrature phase-shift keying (QPSK)* modulation, for direct-sequence spread spectrum. The IEEE 802.11a and HiperLAN2 physical layer will feature essentially the same physical layer and uses the same modulation schemes. Frequency-hopping spread spectrum uses 2–4 level *Gaussian frequency-shift keying (FSK)* as the modulation signaling method. The choice between frequency-hopping spread spectrum and direct-sequence spread spectrum will depend on a number of factors related to the user's application and the environment in which the system will be operating.

An effective energy management scheme can reduce interference caused at other nodes, preserve energy at battery-powered hosts, and most importantly, allow greater spatial reuse. Figure 3.12 depicts the power control introduces asymmetry. In the figure, D transmits to C at low power, but B uses high transmit power to transmit to A. However, B may not know about D-to-C transmission, but can interfere with it. An ideal solution will reduce energy consumption, and maximize spatial reuse.

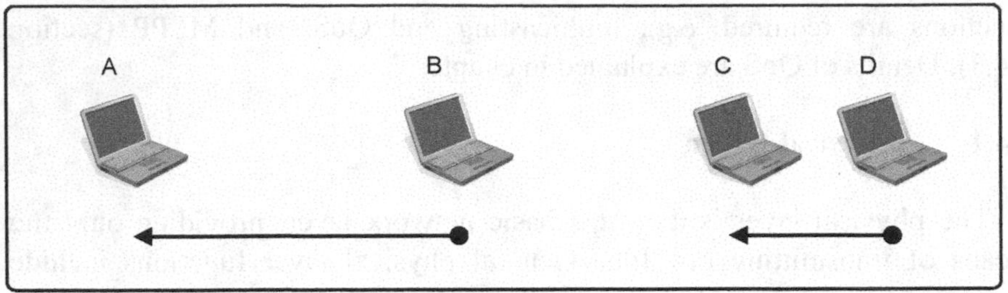

Figure 3.12. Power control introduces asymmetry.

3.4.2 Data Link Layer

The link layer transfers data between adjacent network nodes and provides the means to detect and possibly correct errors that may occur in the physical layer. This layer provides logical link management, network formation, scheduling, segmentation, adaptation, neighbor discovery, synchronization among nodes for bandwidth reservation, adaptive data rate control that is sensitive to neighbor nodes, QoS support for real-time traffic, power management, efficient allocation and utilization of the available bandwidth, capability to support distributed environment, contention window for congestion control, scalability to large networks, support directional antennas for higher spectrum reused lower power consumption, fare bandwidth allocation or weighted allocation to nodes, and low control overhead.

In this layer, the data transfer might or might not be reliable. Many implementations rely on the network or transport layers to support flow control, error checking, acknowledgments, and retransmission.

IEEE 802 splits the OSI data link layer into the upper sub-layers called *logical link control (LLC)* and the lower sub-layers called *media access control (MAC)*. The LLC provides multiplexing, flow control, acknowledgment, and error recovery. The MAC manages the access to the media. The media access control can be either distributed or centralized.

The MAC protocols can be roughly categorized into three broad classes: 1) the fixed assignment class will have schemes like TDMA, CDMA, and FDMA. Lacking the flexibility in allocating resources and thus these protocols are unsuitable for dynamic and bursty wireless packet-data networks; 2) the random assignment class consisting of ALOHA and CSMA are very flexible thus is predominantly used in wireless LAN protocols. For instance cellular networks use ALOHA to get the code when entering a cell and CDMA for subsequent communication; and 3) the demand assignment class with schemes like *Token Ring*, *group allocation multiple access (GAMA)*, and *packet reservation multiple access (PRMA)* attempt to combine the features from the above. These protocols are typically based on CSMA/CA and multi-hop TDMA for broadcast.

It is the data link layer's common goal to strike the balance between maximizing the channel capacity utilization and minimizing of latency on the same broadcast media. The issues with MAC for multiple channels include how to split bandwidth into channels and how to use the multiple channels. For instance, the MAC in Bluetooth is a fast frequency-hopping spread spectrum/CDMA/time-division-duplexing system that employs system polling to establish a link. Frequency-hopping CDMA allows tens of piconets to overlap in the same area providing an effective throughput that is greater than 1 Mbps. The access method in each piconet is TDMA.

QoS at this layer concerns the achievement of fairness by providing equitable sharing of a channel. Typically a probabilistic framework with centralized protocol (such as 802.11 point coordination function) is more effective than a distributed protocol even though distributed MAC appears to be more suitable for ad-hoc networks. Additionally, it should minimize the effects of hidden and exposed terminal problems.

3.4.3 Network Layer

In the TCP/IP reference model the network layer is called *Internet Protocol (IP)* layer, it responds to service requests from the transport layer and issues service requests to the link layer. The network layer deals with end-to-end (source to destination) packet delivery whereas the data link layer is responsible for node-to-node (hop-to-hop) packet delivery. The key feature in this layer centers about topology control, QoS, and routing.

Topology control includes neighbor discovery, network organization and formation (neighbor and link), geometric structures, network partitioning, data/service replication, scheduling node activity, *sub-network dependent convergence function (SNDCF)*, backbone formation (clustering and dominating sets), IP addressing for mobile merge/split networks, and application specific approach such as Bluetooth scatternet formation (e.g., sparse, dense, and planar). Topology management also supports service monitoring and troubleshooting.

The quality of connectivity is extracted from the pair of the best nodes. The network layer QoS handles time-sensitive traffic and supports data distribution to avoid single point of failure. This includes managing the adaptivity to frequent topology changes, quick access to routes for minimum connection setup time, reliable broadcasting to avoid packet collision, and power management. Dynamic and fair channel access can maximize simultaneous transmission to improve latency, nodal availability, and stability can benefit the preferred neighbor election and further optimize network and routing performances.

Routing is about finding a path from a source to destination, transmission options can be broadcasting (send packets to all nodes), multicasting (send packets to several nodes), or geocasting (send packets to all nodes inside a region). Functionally routing capabilities include routing computation and maintenance, localized status maintenance to avoid state propagation control overhead, loop-free and free-from-stale routes, and converging optimal routes from the topology information. The routing management must be able to dynamically accommodate the topology changes, antenna shadowing, terrain masking, interference, battery-power metrics, or individual nodes processing loads.

Routing information can be managed either reactively or proactively. The reactive mechanisms maintain routes between nodes that need to communicate while the proactive approaches maintain routes between all node-pairs. The reactive routing approaches depend on the source to initiate route discovery on demand thus the overhead is lower but route determination may generate flooding or bursts at times for global search that cause delay. On the other hand, the proactive routing requires periodic updates to eliminate delay for route determination. The overhead for continuous updates for all routes whether needed or not can consume unnecessary bandwidth consumption. A hybrid approach based on mobility patterns of the nodes and traffic characteristics is preferable.

Address assignment in this layer for wireless communications is also a challenge. Static assignment makes it easier to guarantee unique addresses, but dynamic assignment is more flexible. Time synchronization is another challenge in ad-hoc network when GPS timing is absence. These subjects will be addressed in chapter 4 (section 4.5).

3.4.4 Transport Layer

The transport layer responds to service requests from the application layer and issues service requests to the network layer. This layer provides transparent transfer of data between service nodes. To turn the unreliable and basic services from the network layer into more effective and useful services, the transport layer is responsible for end-to-end connection, error recovery, flow control, and ensuring complete data transfer. In the case where a large data transmission is required, this layer can fragment user data into smaller packets; each fragment is assigned a transport header to ensure delivery. As per the definition of the Internet protocol suite, *Transmission Control Protocol (TCP)* is specified for connection-oriented communication while *User Datagram Protocol (UDP)* is specified for connectionless service.

The TCP protocol is sender-centric, providing a reliable point-to-point connection coupling with efficient load balancing and congestion control. It guarantees ordering of delivery, detects and recovers from errors, and adapts to the network traffic well with flow control thus can help end users to accomplish reliable and cost-effective data transfer. On the other hand, UDP provides the datagram-type transport, offering neither error recovery nor flow control and leaving these to the application. Thus, UDP's delivery is not guaranteed.

The concept of ports introduced in TCP/IP model is identical to the ports in the session layer of OSI model. Computer applications can each listen for information on their own ports directly from the transport services. In the flow control, congestion avoidance such as slow-start is used to keep the bandwidth consumption at a low level to avoid potential packet drops. Existing transport protocols support only point-to-point and point-to-multipoint (multicast broadcast) connections.

Due to the increasing number of Internet-based applications over both wired and wireless networks, the media transmissions have been gradually unified into the TCP network protocol, and TCP has become a mainstream media for transport layer communications. The services involving voice, data, multimedia, and related to the associated QoS criteria are keys to a successful transport layer implementation. The main features at this layer are flow control and congestion control.

In wired networks, errors are mainly due to congestion. In wireless networks, the error rate is increased because of frequent disconnection due to mobility or power failure. In wireless applications, TCP may misinterpret packet losses and retransmission timeout caused by location-dependent contention, hidden terminal problem, packet collision, route change/failure and due to congestion, therefore improved feedback schemes such as reducing the congestion window in response and unnecessary degradation (timeout) in throughput are used to help identify the problem. But because a new route may differ significantly from old route, how to choose the appropriate timeout and congestion window after detecting a route change would have to come with more careful design considerations. TCP has several variations over ad-hoc applications, these enhanced protocols will be addressed in chapter 5 (section 5.2.1).

3.4.5 Application and Cross-Layering Layer

The behaviors of RF channel characteristics including unpredictable changes, the difficulty of sharing the channel medium with many neighbors, and potentially nodal level QoS requirement changes all impact end-to-end QoS requirements. A promising method for satisfying QoS requirements is a more unified approach of cross-layer or vertical-layer integration. The idea is to violate many of the traditional layering styles to allow different parts of the stack to adapt to the environment in a way that takes into account the adaptation and available information at other layers. For instance, the overhead introduced at the transport layer when congestion control, reliability, and flow control are active is handled separately (e.g., to release one intermediate link under congestion), thus higher-level coordination will be preferable to improve end-to-end performance.

The application layer functions include information fusion and coordination of the lower-layer management supports. These can include:

- security and cooperation in ad-hoc networks,
- energy management,
- end-to-end QoS,
- context awareness and layer triggers with signals to notify other layer,
- network status at all layers,
- application level service discovery, and
- spontaneous networking.

Unlike the wired network transport's decoupled approach, the cross-layer interaction in an ad-hoc network between the transport layer and lower layers such as the network and the MAC layers are important to adapt to the changing network environment. For instance, throughput unfairness at the transport layer due to the throughput or delay unfairness existing at the lower layer can be more effectively managed at the transport layer.

For instance, *Ad-hoc Transport Protocol (ATP)* is specifically designed for ad-hoc wireless networks and is not a variant of TCP. The major aspects by which ATP defers from TCP are 1) coordination among multiple layers; 2) rate based transmissions; 3) decoupling congestion control and reliability; and 4) assisted congestion control. Similar to other TCP variants proposed for ad-hoc wireless networks, ATP uses services from network and MAC layers for improving its performance. ATP uses information from lower layers for: 1) estimation of the initial transmission rate; 2) detection, avoidance, and control of congestion; and 3) detection of path breaks. Unlike TCP, ATP utilizes a timer-based transmission, where the transmission rate is decided by the granularity of the timer which is dependent on the congestion in the network. The congestion control mechanism is decoupled from the reliability and flow control mechanisms. The network congestion information is obtained from the intermediate nodes, whereas the flow control and reliability information are obtained from the ATP receiver. The intermediate nodes attach the congestion information to every ATP packet and the ATP receiver collates it before including it in the next ACK packet.

3.5 Radio Development

A radio performs a variety of functions in the process of converting voice or data information to and from an RF signal. These functions include processing the analog RF signal, waveform modulation/demodulation, and processing of the baseband signal.

The processing of the analog RF signal consists of amplification/deamplification, converting to/from intermediate frequencies, RF up-conversion/down-conversion, and noise cancelling. Waveform modulation/demodulation depends on the waveforms used in that radio. The waveform generally includes error correction and interleaving of the signal. The baseband signal processing part adds the networking protocols and routes the signal to the output devices.

Analog radios perform these functions on analog signals. Using analog signal processors and heterodyne filters, the analog signal can be processed at different frequencies by a chain of analog functional blocks. Digital radios transform the analog radio signal to a digital signal at some point in the chain with an *analog-to-digital converter (ADC)* using *digital signal processors (DSP)*. The digitally processed signal is converted back to analog by a *digital-to-analog converter (DAC)* and transmitted through the antenna.

The process of impressing the information for transmission is known as modulation. *Amplitude modulation (AM)* means changing the amplitude of a wave in a way corresponding to the sending information. Instead of modulating the amplitude, if we change the frequency of the signal, the resulting modulation is called *frequency modulation*, FM. There are other types of modulation techniques that are variations of AM and FM. These include *Single Sideband (SSB)*, *Double Sideband (DSB)*, *Vestigial Sideband (VSB)*, *Frequency Shift Keying (FSK)*, *Gaussian Minimum Shift Keying (GMSK)*, and others.

As will be seen in the following section, the *Software Defined Radio (SDR)* is a reconfigurable radio; the same hardware can be used to perform different functions at different times by the definition of its running software. It provides a flexible radio architecture allowing the radio functionalities to be highly personalized in real time.

3.5.1 Software Defined Radio Technologies

Software defined radio (SDR) is a new technology that allows a single terminal to support various kinds of wireless systems. A separation of hardware and software allows the various control applications to run largely independent on the actual physical *electronic control unit (ECU)*. This kind of "virtual machine" can be internally organized as a fairly complex and highly dedicated sensor/actor network. To accomplish this goal, the existing node-centric solutions need to be replaced by a network-centric operating system extended by dedicated automotive middleware. This radio software is based on the *Software Communications Architecture (SCA)*, an open architecture defined by the *Joint Tactical Radio System (JTRS) Joint Program Office (JPO)* [14,15]. SDR is the underlying technology behind the JTRS initiative to develop software programmable radios that can enable seamless, real-time communication across the U.S. military services, and with coalition forces and allies.

SDR refers to wireless communication in which the transmitter modulation is generated or defined by a computer, and the receiver uses a computer to recover the signal intelligence. To select the desired modulation type, the proper programs are required by microcomputers that control the transmitter and receiver. This action will also request an over-the-air service reconfiguration update to the network to request that the required information is re-purposed to suit the new display and then a reconfiguration command is delivered to divert the content.

Typically, the antennas for transmitting and receiving, the series of signal and RF amplifiers, and human interface devices are not part of SDR. In voice application, for instance, ADC and modulator in the transmitter as well as DAC and demodulator in the receiver are four computer-controlled circuits thus their parameters can be controllable by software. Functionally, ADC converts the voice audio to ASCII data, the modulator impresses the ASCII intelligence onto a RF carrier, the demodulator separates the ASCII intelligence from the RF carrier, and the DAC generates a voice waveform from the ASCII data.

3.5.1.1 Benefits and Opportunities

A wireless terminal (phone, PDA, and so forth) that is reconfigurable via software. It enables wireless devices to be easily updated to new or later versions of the air interface and allows multiple interfaces to be supported. For example, a software defined cell phone could be used across in any country in the world (see also soft phone).

In the technology beyond 3G wireless network, future wireless devices will need to support multiple air interfaces and modulation formats. SDR enables such functionality in wireless devices by using a reconfigurable hardware platform across multiple standards. The most significant asset of SDR is versatility. Changing the service type, the mode, and/or the modulation protocol involves simply selecting and launching the requisite computer program.

- Radio (terminal and base station) manufacturers and operators can increase profit margins to use one design for the radio part for global markets.
- Ease of upgrades and fault correction has direct costs and logistics benefit on a mass-market.
- Dynamic network reconfiguration depending upon the nature of the traffic or customer demand.
- Seamless spectrum management in different technology domains for roaming subscribers.
- Offer content provision opportunities for third-party service providers to form a commercial relationship with other parties in the value chain.
- Common look and feel of services for service providers to maximize the brand projection.
- Enabled over-the-air reconfiguration offers opportunities to service personalization.
- Customization on-demand for special needs or operating in special environment.

3.5.1.2 Software Communications Architecture

The *Software Communications Architecture (SCA)* provides a common open architecture used to build a family of radios across multiple domains that are interoperable and reusable. The radios built upon SCA can use a wide range of frequencies and enable technology insertion. As the result, JTRS radios can improve interoperability by providing the ability to share waveform software between radios and reduce development and deployment costs. The special attributes of SCA can be concluded as following:

- *Common Open Architecture* holds the advantages of promoting competition, interoperability, technology insertion, quick upgrades, software reuse, and scalability.
- *Multiple Domains* supports operations in a wide variety of domains, including airborne, fixed, maritime, vehicular, dismounted and handheld.
- *Multiple Bands* allows a JTRS radio to replace and interoperate with a number of existing radios that use a wide range of frequencies.
- *Compatibility* guarantees the new radios to communicate with legacy systems in order to minimize the impact of platform integration.
- *Upgrades* enable technology insertion. New technologies can be incorporated to improve performance.
- *Security* such as programmable cryptographic capability, certificate management, user identification and authentication, key management, and multiple independent levels of classification are part of the new architecture.

- *Networking* with legacy network protocols for the purpose of seamless integration as well as with new wideband networking capabilities, e.g., voice, data, and video.
- *Software Reusability* allows the maximum possible reuse of software components by supporting plug and play behavior with waveforms being portable from one implementation to the next.

The SCA is designed to be an open, standardized architecture providing interoperability, technology insertion, quick upgrade capability, software reuse, and scalability.

The SCA specifications define the *Operating Environment (OE)*, the services, and interfaces that the applications use from the OE. The interfaces are defined by using the CORBA IDL, and graphical representations are made by using UML.

The OE consists of a *Core Framework (CF)*, a CORBA middleware, and a POSIX-based *Operating System (OS)*. The OS running the SCA provides services and interfaces that are defined as mandatory in the *Application Environment Profile (AEP)* of the SCA. The CF delineates the interfaces, their purposes, and their operations. It provides an abstraction of the underlying software and hardware layers for software application developers. An SCA compatible system following these interfaces to interact with JTRS radios.

The interfaces are grouped as Base Application Interfaces, Framework Control Interfaces, and Framework Services Interfaces.

- The Base Application Interfaces are used by the application layer. They provide the basic building blocks of an application. The interfaces in this group are: Port, Life Cycle, TestableObject, PropertySet, PortSupplier, ResourceFactory, and Resource.
- The Framework Control Interfaces provide the control of the system. The application layer can reach the OS through these control interfaces. The interfaces in this group are: Application, ApplicationFactory, DomainManager, Device, LoadableDevice, ExecutableDevice, AggragateDevice, and DeviceManager.
- The Framework Services Interfaces provide the system services. These interfaces support both core and non-core applications. They include: File, FileSystem, FileManager, and Timer.

The CF uses a Domain Profile to delineate the components in the system. The Domain Profile is a set of XML files that define the identity, capabilities, properties, interdependencies, and location of the hardware devices and software components that make up the system. The software component characteristics are contained in the *Software Package Descriptor (SPD)*, *Software Component Descriptor (SCD)*, and *Software Assembly Descriptor (SAD)*. The hardware device characteristics are stored in the *Device Package*

Descriptor (DPD) and *Device Configuration Descriptor (DCD)*. The Properties Descriptor contains information about the properties of a hardware device or software component. The Profile Descriptor contains an absolute file name for a Device Configuration Descriptor, a Software Package Descriptor, or a Software Assembly Descriptor. Finally, the *DomainManager Configuration Descriptor (DMD)* contains the configuration information for the DomainManager.

Although the SCA uses the CORBA middleware for its software bus, the application layer can reach the OS by other means. CORBA adapters can be used to wrap the legacy software components. Figure 3.13 shows the relationship between the AEP, the application, and the OE.

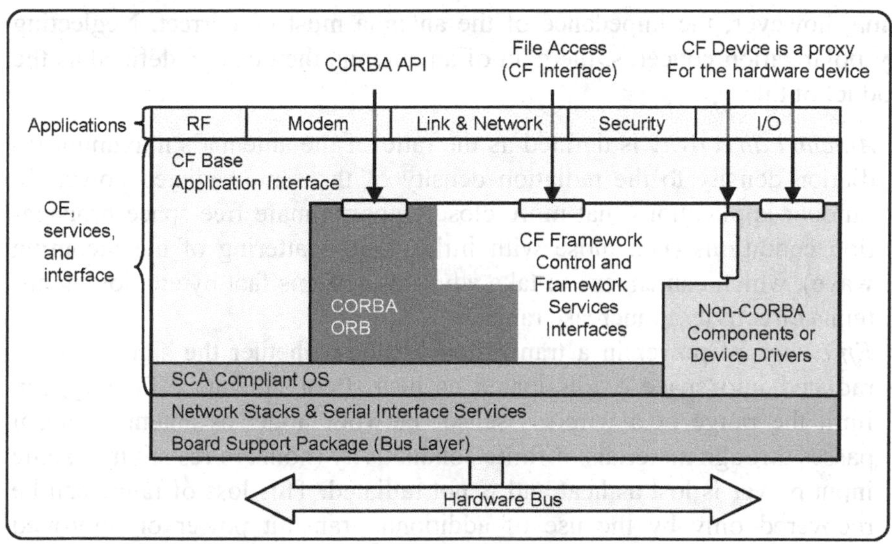

Figure 3.13. Relationship between SCA components.

CORBA is the interoperability backbone of the SCA. Efficient use of CORBA, such as avoiding ORB-dependent features can increase compatibility with other CORBA compliant ORBs. New radio software (known as a *waveform*) on the radio system is deployed as a new application and uses the CF services like the *FileSystem* to increase reusability. The waveform specific behavior can be implemented by function overloading. Scalability is provided by software component assemblies. A waveform application creates a CF Resource for each functional unit, connects these resources to each other using CF Ports, and deploys these resources on CF devices. When a new hardware device is installed on a system, a new logical CF Device is created as a software proxy for this hardware device, and the Device is registered to a CF *DeviceManager*.

3.5.2 Antennas Characteristics

The most underappreciated component of a wireless sensor network node is often its antenna. Most wireless sensor network nodes are designed to be physically small, with low-power consumption and low product cost as the primary design metrics. These requirements make the design of the node's antenna system both important and difficult. This situation is often exacerbated by the need to adjust the antenna design to fit aesthetics of the network node's physical design, which often forces the antenna to be the last electrical component designed in the system.

The efficiency of an antenna considers only power accepted by the antenna from the source. For maximum power transfer from transmitter to antenna, however, the impedance of the antenna must be correct. Neglecting any polarization concerns, the gain of an antenna then can be defined as the product of the:

1. *Antenna directivity* is defined as the ratio of the antenna's maximum radiation density to the radiation density of the same radiated power. In outdoor applications that more closely approximate free-space propagation conditions (i.e., those with little or no scattering of the incoming wave), which can choose to take advantage of this fact by employing antenna directivity to increase range.
2. *Efficiency* of power in a transmitter dictates whether the signal can be radiated into space or dissipated as heat. Poor antenna efficiency can limit the range of a wireless sensor network node; as antenna current passes through materials of finite conductivity (nonzero resistivity), some input power is lost as heat and is not radiated. This loss of range can be recovered only by the use of additional transmit power or improved receiver sensitivity, both alternatives that can increase power consumption significantly. Batteries, displays, sensors, circuit boards, and other materials having significant loss at RF must be kept out of this near-field region. The preceding range discussion omitted any discussion of efficiency. Real antennas, of course, are not perfectly efficient; in fact, when a fixed limit is placed on physical size, a lower-frequency antenna is less efficient than a higher-frequency antenna, due to the higher circulating currents in the lower-frequency antenna.
3. *Mismatch effects* implies that the input impedance of an electrically small antenna of fixed physical length has a reactive component that increases as the frequency of operation is lowered. The reactance may produce large mismatch losses if some type of impedance matching network is not used. The increasing reactance makes the design of a low-loss impedance matching network increasingly difficult as the frequency of operation is lowered.

3.6 SoS Views of Network Architectures

The following sections profile the systems view and architectures of the most popular infrastructured wireless network technologies, namely GSM, GPRS, UMTS, CDMA 2000, Wi-Fi, WiMax, Bluetooth, and IMS applications. The discussion in the following sections provides a most likely available communication backbone to support enterprise infrastructure-less services.

3.6.1 GSM and GPRS

Global System for Mobile communication (GSM) is a digital mobile telephone system that is the most popular standard for mobile phones in the world. GSM open standard is developed by the 3GPP allowing network operators to offer roaming services which means subscribers can use their phone all over the world. GSM is a cellular network that uses a variation of TDMA to allow eight speech channels per Radio frequency channel. There are eight burst periods grouped into what is called a TDMA frame. It operates at either the 900 or 1800 MHz frequency band. The exception to the rule is networks in parts of the Americas (including the USA and Canada) that operate at 850 or 1900 MHz.

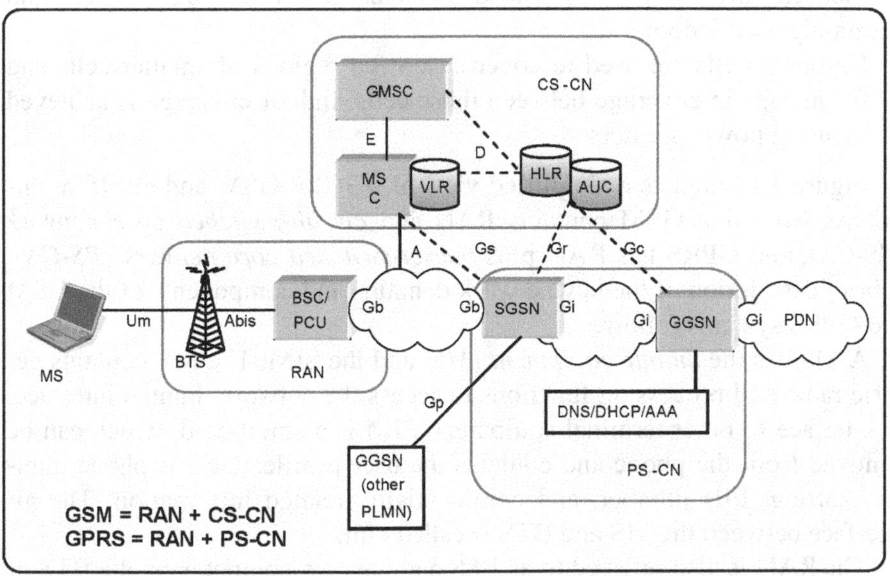

Figure 3.14. GSM and GPRS network architecture.

Based on GSM, *General Packet Radio Services (GPRS)* is a packet-based wireless communication service that promises data rates from 56 up to 114 Kbps and continuous connection for video conferences and multimedia when use with mobile handheld devices or notebook computers. GPRS will complement existing GSM services such as circuit-switched cellular phone connections and the *Short Message Service (SMS)*. As GPRS becomes available, mobile users of a *virtual private network (VPN)* will be able to access the private network continuously rather than through a dial-up connection. GPRS will also complement Bluetooth, a standard for replacing wired connections between devices with wireless radio connections. In addition to the IP, GPRS supports X.25, a packet-based protocol that is used mainly in Europe. GPRS is an evolutionary step towards *Enhanced Data GSM Environment (EDGE)* and *Universal Mobile Telephone Service (UMTS)*.

Cell radius varies depending on antenna height, antenna gain, and propagation conditions from a couple of hundred meters to several tens of kilometers. There are four different cell sizes for different coverage area in a GSM or GPRS network:

- Macro cell is regarded as "cell" where the base station antenna is installed in a mast or a building above average roof top level.
- Micro cells are cells whose antenna height is under average roof top level and typically used in urban areas.
- Picocells are small cells whose diameter is a few dozen meters and mainly used indoors.
- Umbrella cells are used to cover shadowed regions of smaller cells and fill in gaps in coverage between those cells. Indoor coverage is achieved by using power splitters.

Figure 3.14 depicts a simplified view of a 3GPP GSM and GPRS architecture. Note that GSM contains RAN and *circuit-switched core network (CS-CN)*, and GPRS has RAN plus *packet-switched core network (PS-CN)*. A brief description of the key network domains and components of the GSM and GPRS systems follow.

A MS has the *mobile equipment (ME)* and the SIM. The ME contains generic radio and processing functions to access the network, human interface, or interface to other terminal equipment. SIM is a smart card, which can be removed from the phone and contains the user profile, such as phone number, barring, PIN number, and confidentiality-related information. The air interface between the MS and BTS is called Um.

The RAN is also referred to as BSS and has two components: the BTS or simply BS, and the BSC. The BTS is responsible for the radio transmission and reception from antennas to the radio-interface-specific signal processing, and it can handle several radio carriers at a time. The purpose is to modulate, amplify, filter, and transmit the downlink signals (and perform the reverse on the uplink). The BSC is responsible for the radio interface management, allocation and release of radio channels, and handover management of several BTSs. The BSC handles handoffs, cell rankings, locating MSs, power control, channel allocation, frequency/code allocations, coding, and limited switching. The links that connect the BTS and BSC are T1/E1 circuits (*Abis* in Figure 3.14); the connections of RAN to PS-CN are *frame relay (FR)* links (*A link* in the same figure).

The CS-CN also called the mobile switching subsystem (MSS) or the network switching subsystem (NSS) consists of a mobile services switching center (MSC) and a gateway MSC (GMSC). MSC also called mobile switch (MS), or mobile telecommunications switching office (MTSO), performs the basic switching function, coordinates the setup of calls to and from GSM users, manages communications between GSM and other telecommunications networks, and collects billing information. A GMSC passes CS-traffic between fixed and mobile networks. The GMSC is an MSC that is able to find the corresponding HLR based on the called number. The GMSC and MSC/HLR may physically be one unit. It interfaces with the HLR, public switched transport network (PSTN), other public land mobile networks (PLMNs), and other networks such as packet-data networks. The MSC and GMSC support both transport and control plane functions. The HLR is a central, permanent location and maintains a management database that holds subscriber information relevant to the provision of telecommunications services, some information related to the location information of the subscriber, such as MS roaming number, VLR address, MSC address, and the local MS identity for routing and charging of calls towards MSC. The VLR is a temporary location and the management database of MSC and is utilized to handle mobility and roaming. It interacts with the HLR in obtaining the subscriber data when needed. The VLR includes all users currently located in the system, including roamers and non-roamers. The HLR and VLR work together to allow both local operation and roaming outside the local service area. The authentication center (AuC) is a database that maintains and manages security, authentication and encryption, and related information for each subscriber. The equipment identity register (EIR) is a database that keeps track of all mobile stations (often implemented with AuC) and their identities in order to prevent the use of stolen or faulty equipments.

The underlying network that connects MSC and GMSC comprises TDM links, and the network that connects MSC/GMSC and HLR/VLR comprises *signaling system number 7 (SS7)* links. In 3GPP Release 98, HLR, AuC, and EIR databases are also considered part of CS-CN.

An overlay PS-CN was added to GSM by modifying BSC to include the *packet control function (PCF)* to support packet-switched data for the GPRS architecture. PS-CN has *serving GPRS support nodes (SGSN)* and the *gate-*

way GSN (GGSN). The SGSN performs mobility management, encryption, and charging functions, and also supports SMS over GPRS. GGSN is the gateway that connects to a *packet-data network (PDN)* such as the Internet or corporate intranet. Also, for roaming support, border routers, in private IP networks connecting SGSN and GGSN, are used to connect with other PLMNs or a *GPRS roaming exchange (GRX)*. The underlying networks that connect PS-CN elements, as well as inter-PLMN links, are part of private *managed IP (M-IP)* networks. The links between PS-CN elements and the HLR are SS7 links. The PS-CN also includes IP utility servers, such as DNS, DHCP, and AAA, to support data services.

3.6.2 UMTS

Universal Mobile Telecommunications Service (UMTS) is a 3G broadband, packet-based transmission of text, digitized voice, video, and multimedia at data rates up to 2 Mbps. Based on the GSM communication standard, UMTS is the planned standard for the future; meanwhile, users can have multi-mode devices that switch to the currently available technology. The electromagnetic radiation spectrum for UMTS has been identified as frequency bands 1885–2025 MHz for future IMT-2000 systems, and 1980–2010 MHz and 2170–2200 MHz for the satellite portion of UMTS systems. The IP running on UMTS means it has the capability of providing new services, such as alternative billing methods (pay-per-bit, pay-per-session, flat rate, asymmetric bandwidth, and others). The higher bandwidth of UMTS promises other new services, such as videoconferencing. UMTS promises to realize the *Virtual Home Environment (VHE)* in which a roaming user can have the same services to which the user is accustomed when at home or in the office, through a combination of transparent terrestrial and satellite connections. Figure 3.15 depicts a simplified view of such 3GPP UMTS systems architecture. A brief description of the key network domains and components of the UMTS system follows.

The *User Equipment (UE)* is the UMTS term for MS. It contains generic radio and processing functions to access the network, human interface, or interface to other terminal equipment. UE supports two *UMTS terrestrial radio access (UTRA)* air interfaces called WCDMA and *time-division synchronous CDMA (TD-SCDMA)* and contains a *removable user identity module (R-UIM)* called the *user identity module (UIM)*.

The RAN has two components: *NodeB* (new name for BTS), and *radio node controller (RNC)* (new name for BSC). At times the combination of NodeB and RNC together are called the *radio network system (RNS)*. Underlying network links that connect NodeB and RNC are ATM *private virtual circuits (PVCs)*; these links in an all-IP network will be IP over ATM.

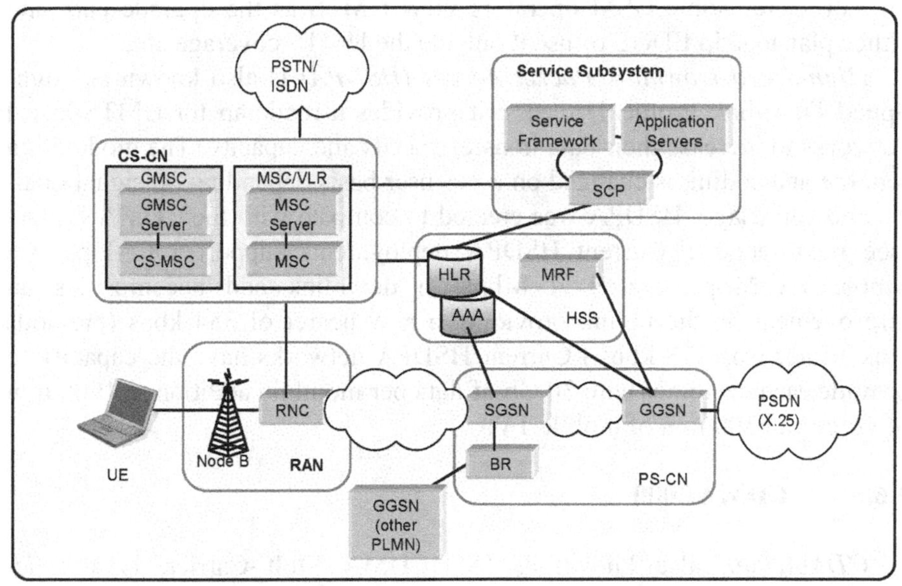

Figure 3.15. UMTS network architecture.

CS-CN components are enhanced in UMTS to support new interfaces to RAN; otherwise, the components remain the same as in GPRS CS-CN. In 3GPP UMTS Release 5, the transport and control functions of the MSC have been logically split into two components, MSC server and *circuit-switched media gateway (CS-MGW)*.

The HLR is enhanced and now called *home subscriber system (HSS)*; it consists of HLR, VLR, AuC, and EIR databases, and *Authentication, Authorization, and Accounting (AAA)* functions. The underlying support network for HLR, VLR, AuC, and EIR is SS7 with GSM *mobile application part (MAP)* protocol; however IP networks support the newer HSS elements such as AAA and *home agent (HA)*.

The components of PS-CN are essentially the same as in GPRS. However, the SGSN is upgraded to support new ATM interfaces.

Enhanced Data rates for GSM Evolution (EDGE) or *Enhanced GPRS (EGPRS)* included in Release 7 of the 3GPP standard is a digital mobile phone technology that allows to increase data transmission rate and to improve data transmission reliability. It was introduced into GSM networks around the world since 2003 and can be used for any packet-switched applications such as an Internet connection and high-speed data applications such as video services and multimedia. On March 14, 2007, Ericsson announced plans for EDGE Evolution, an upgrade to EDGE that permits 1 Mbps peak speeds and latencies down to 100 ms with the existing network infrastructure. Some GSM operators view UMTS as the upgrade path and either plan to skip EDGE or use it outside the UMTS coverage area.

High-Speed Downlink Packet Access (HSDPA) is also known as High-Speed Downlink Protocol Access; it provides a roadmap for UMTS-based networks to increase their data transfer speeds and capacity. The modulation scheme and coding is changed on a per-user basis depending on signal quality and cell usage. HSDPA was created to compete with the CDMA EVDO (see next section). Current HSDPA deployments support 1.8 Mbps, 3.6 Mbps, 7.2 Mbps, and 14.4 Mbps in downlink and accompanies an improvement on the uplink providing a new bearer of 384 kbps (previous max bearer was 128 kbps.) Current HSDPA networks have the capacity to provide each customer with 30 Gb of data per month in addition to 1000 min of voice and 300 min of mobile TV.

3.6.3 CDMA 2000

CDMA2000, also known as IMT-CDMA Multi-Carrier, is a *code-division multiple access (CDMA)* version of the IMT-2000 standard developed by the *International Telecommunication Union (ITU)*. As depicted in Figure 3.16, the CDMA2000 standard is 3G mobile wireless technology evolving from the existing cdmaOne services, including speech coders, packet-data services, circuit- data services, fax services, SMS, and *Over the Air Activation and Service Provisioning (OTASP)*. CDMA2000 can support mobile data communications at speeds ranging from 144 Kbps to 2 Mbps and have the following three phases: 144-Kbps packet data and voice (1XRTT), 384-Kbps packet data, voice, and video (3XRTT), and fixed wireless access at 2 Mbps. The 1X-RTT is based on IS95A/B technology and has two different implementations, 1X-EVDV and 1X-EVDO.

Although the specifications of 3GPP WCDMA are identical to 3GPP2 CDMA2000 3X, these systems are not compatible. The difference is the chip rate, the frequency at which the transceiver resonates. CDMA2000's chip rate needs to be a multiple of cdmaOne's chip rate, while WCDMA's chip rate has to fit the GSM framing structure. Unlike UMTS's/WCDMA's wide bandwidth of 5 MHz, CDMA2000 is based around a single-frequency 1.25-MHz channel (for reuse of existing spectrum used by IS-95A/B system) band (1X-RTT), or three consolidated 1.25-MHz bands (3X-RTT). Both cdmaOne and CDMA2000 use global positioning system (GPS) signals for network timing.

Table 3.6 summarizes a comparison of mobile network terminology used by GSM/GPRS, UMTS, and CDMA2000.

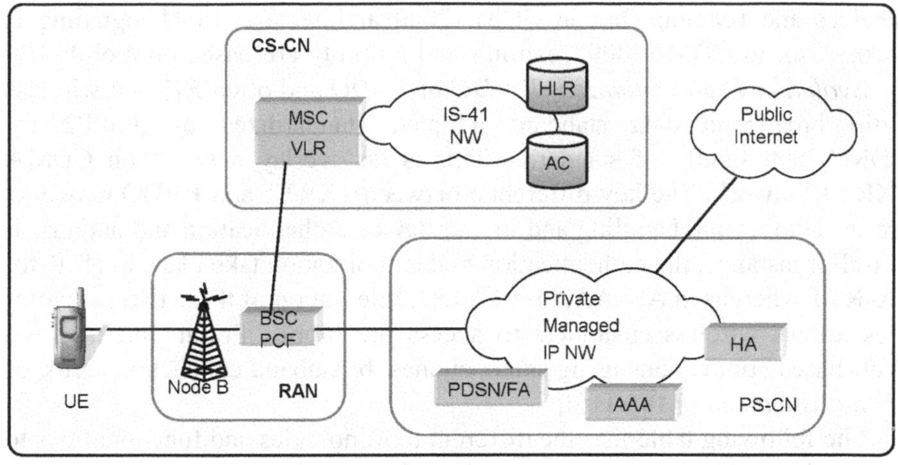

Figure 3.16. 3GPP2 CDMA2000 systems architecture.

The primary function of the PCF in the RAN is to establish, maintain, and terminate layer 2 connections to the PDSN.

The PDSN is equivalent to both the SGSN and GGSN in UMTS and incorporates several functions in one node. The major function of the PDSN is to route packets to IP networks or directly to HA. The PDSN also assigns IP addresses and maintains *point-to-point protocol (PPP)* sessions to the MS. It also initiates AAA for the MS packet session. Usually, the PDSN incorporates the *foreign agent (FA)* functions. The FA functions support mobile IP roaming and mobility and include functions such as reverse tunneling, registration, and dynamic HA and home address assignments. The HA is an important component of mobile IP, it redirects packets to the FA and receives and routes reverse-tunneled packet from the FA. The HA also provides security by authentication of the MS through *mobile-IP (MIP)* registration and maintains connection with the AAA server to receive subscriber profile data.

The AAA server performs at least three types of functions depending on the type of network: In the *home network*, the AAA server authenticates and authorizes the MS based on requests from the local AAA server. In the *visited network*, the AAA server's function is to pass authentication requests from the PDSN to the home network, and authorize responses from the home network to the PDSN. The AAA server also stores accounting information for the MS and provides user profiles and QoS information to the PDSN. In the *intermediary* or *broker network*, the AAA server forwards requests and responses between visited networks and the home network that do not have bilateral agreements and AAA associations.

There are two other differences between UMTS and CDMA2000 architectures. In UMTS, GSM *mobile application part (MAP)* supports CS-voice services and roaming, but in CDMA2000 architecture, IS-41 signaling is used. Also, in CDMA2000, roaming and mobility are based on mobile IP.

Evolution-Data Optimized (EV-DO or *EVDO* and often *EV)* is a wireless radio broadband data standard adopted standardized by 3GPP2 for CDMA2000 family of standards. This is an overlay network on CDMA 1XRTT network. The key difference between 1XRTT and EVDO networks are in radio airlink handling and in end device authentication and authorization. For instance, the authentication and authorization take place in HLR for 1X-RTT whereas in AN-AAA for EVDO. Integration of these two technologies allows wireless customers to access the Mobile Portal, Internet, and Web-based applications using smart phones, broadband connection cards, or *phone-as-modem (PAM)* [16].

The following table lists the different terminologies and functionalities to summarize the discussion of the previous three sections.

Table 3.6. Mobile Network Terminology.

Network Component	GSM/GPRS	UMTS	CDMA2000
Base station	BTS	NodeB	BS
Base station controller	BSC	RNC	RNC or BSC/PCF
Circuit switch	MSC	MSC	MSC
Tunnel switch	SGSN	SGSN	—
Network access gateway	GGSN	GGSN	PDSN/FA
User profile and authentication	HLR/AC	HSS/HLR/AC	AAA/HA
Visitor profile and authentication	VLR	VLR	FA
Multimedia support	—	IMS	MMD
Roaming and mobility	SS7/GSM MAP	SS7/GSM MAP/SIP	IS-41 Mobile IP
Back-haul network	FR/managed IP	ATM/managed IP	Managed IP
Signaling network	SS7/GSM MAP	SS7/GSM MAP → IP	ANSI-41 → IP

3.6.4 WLAN and Wi-Fi

As depicted in Figure 3.17, WLAN use high-frequency electromagnetic waves that are either *infrared (IR)* or *radio frequency (RF)* to transmit information from one point to another. RF is more practical than IR as it can propagate through solid obstacles useful for indoor applications. Traffic from multiple users is modulated onto the radio waves at the transmitter, and extracted at the receiver. Multiple radio carriers can coexist in the same physical space, and at the same time, without interfering with each other by using FDMA, TDMA, or CDMA. Wireless LANs have been standardized by the IEEE 802.11 standards subgroup. With the OFDM defined in IEEE 802.11a and 802.11g, the real-world wireless LAN speed limit is moving to 50 Mbps and beyond.

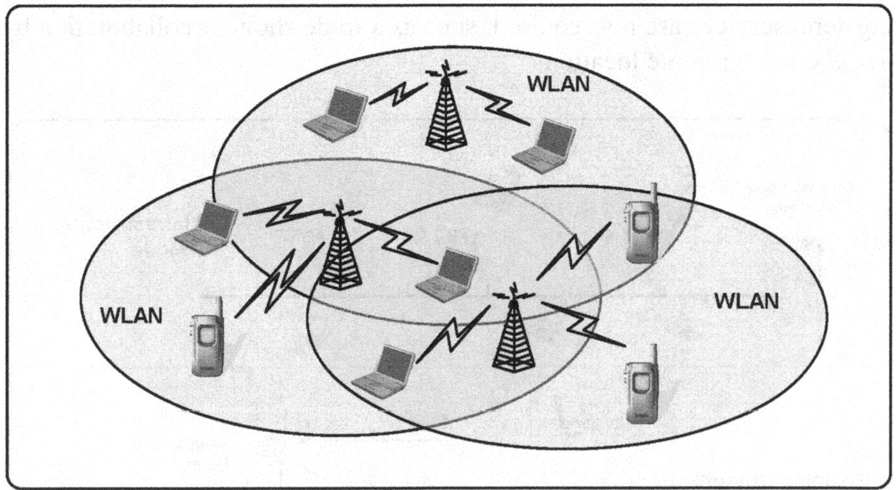

Figure 3.17. Multiple wireless local area networks.

Wireless fidelity (Wi-Fi) is a type of WLAN that uses specifications in the 802.11 family, designed to seamlessly integrate with Ethernet (IEEE 802.3) networks. The term Wi-Fi was created by an organization called the Wi-Fi Alliance, which oversees tests that certify product interoperability. Originally, Wi-Fi certification was applicable only to products using the 802.11b standard. Today, Wi-Fi can apply to products that use any 802.11 standard. An interconnected area of hot spots and network access points is known as a hot zone. IEEE 802.11 specifies two, incompatible, techniques for radio wave transmission: *frequency-hopping spread spectrum (FHSS)* and *direct-sequence spread spectrum (DSSS)*; the latter offers higher raw transfer speeds, up to 11 Mbps (comparable to 10Base-T Ethernet). Major challenges 802.11 faces include limited service range (about 300 ft without physical obstructions), performance degradation when the unit is far from the network, data throughput speeds, security, and QoS.

Figure 3.18 depicts the Wi-Fi networking modes in common use and supported by 802.11 MAC layer implementations. Figure 3.18(a) shows the ad-hoc mode, also referred to as *independent basic service set (IBSS)* topology;

it is a *peer-to-peer network* in which no dedicated system is required to assume the role of a gateway router. Several wireless nodes will communicate directly with one another in a mesh or partial-mesh topology. Typical instances of such an ad-hoc implementation do not connect to a larger network and cover only a limited area. If a client in an ad-hoc network wishes to communicate outside the peer-to-peer cell, a member must operate as a gateway and perform routing. Configuring a Wi-Fi network in *ad-hoc mode* establishes a network where wireless infrastructure does not exist or where long-term services are not required, such as a trade show or collaboration by coworkers at a remote location.

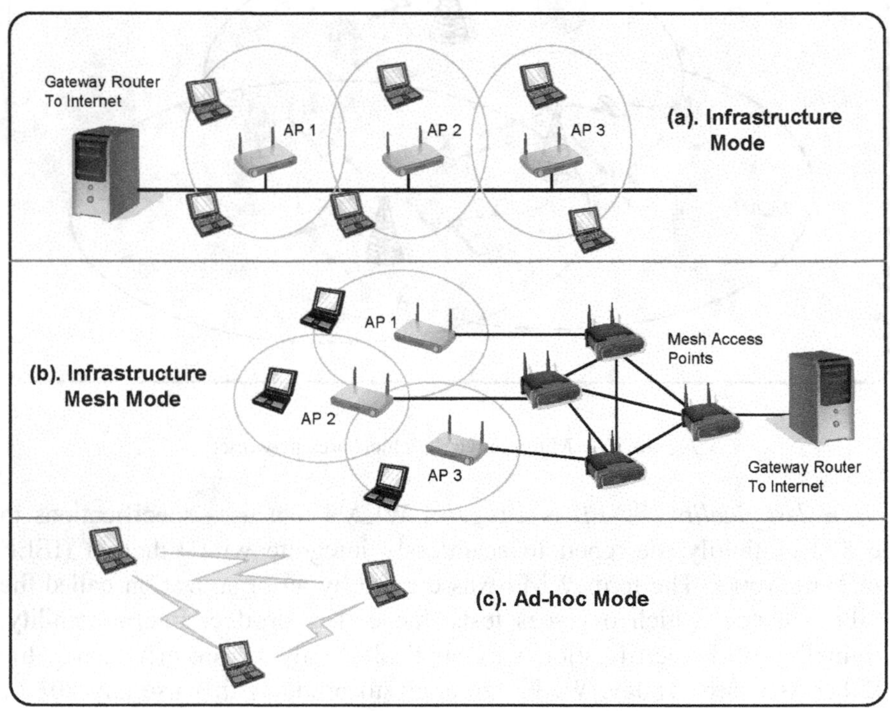

Figure 3.18. Three Wi-Fi networking configurations.

Figure 3.18(b) is the *infrastructure mode*. This most basic configuration is referred to as a BSS topology and requires at least one wireless AP (also referred to as a base station) to the wired network infrastructure, called the *distribution system (DS)*, and a set of wireless nodes or computers. The access point then bridges the traffic between the computers on the wireless network it controls, assuming the role played by an Ethernet hub in a basic star-shaped wired network. Other general access point parameters include range, access controls, maximum number of simultaneous wireless connections, and if the access point supports multi-access point roaming – the ability to create a single network from multiple-access points, enabling wireless clients to seamlessly hop from coverage cell to coverage cell.

APs act as a bridge between the wired and wireless networks aggregating access for multiple wireless stations onto the wired network and are under the control of the same MAC function. Communication between wireless nodes, wireless computers, and the wired network is by the AP. All APs transmit a beacon management frame at fixed intervals. To associate with an AP and join a BSS, a client listens for beacon messages to identify the APs within range. The client selection of which BSS to join is carried out in a vendor-independent manner. A client may also send a probe request management frame to find an AP associated with the desired *service set identifier (SSID)*. Multiple BSS (or APs) that share the same ESS ID and DS form an ESS. Cells in an ESS may overlap, or there may be gaps. The Wi-Fi networks with multiple APs can use the same channel or different channels to boost aggregate throughput. Full overlap provides for both an increase in aggregate bandwidth and redundancy. Each AP and *mobile unit (MU)* has a unique MAC and IP address. The MU, also called *mobile node (MN)*, *mobile station (MS)*, or *mobile client (MC)*, can roam from AP to AP. In 3G terminology, an MU is called *user equipment (UE)* or handset. Although the Wi-Fi standard defines how a wireless computer communicates with an AP, it does not define how roaming should be conducted and supported within an ESS topology network, in particular when a roaming user crosses a router boundary between subnets. In theory, it is possible to implement *dynamic host configuration protocol (DHCP)* across the network and force users to release and renew their IP address as they migrate from one subnet to another, but this is not a desirable solution. Roaming between APs is largely reliant on vendor-specific implementations and management. Most corporate WLANs operate in infrastructure mode and access the wired network for connections to printers and file servers. The public hotspots provide Wi-Fi service, free or for a fee, from a wide variety of public meeting areas, including coffee shops and airport lounges, and also operate in infrastructure mode.

Figure 3.18(c) shows the *infrastructure mesh mode* combining features of ad-hoc mode with infrastructure mode. It is a router network without the cabling between nodes and supports the inherent rerouting for fault tolerance that such networks deliver. The infrastructure mesh is built of peer nodes that are not required to be cabled to a wired port like traditional Wi-Fi APs. Rather, each simply plugs into a power supply. It automatically self-configures and communicates with other nodes over the air to determine the most efficient multi-hop transmission path. Today, most mesh implantations are vendor specific, until the 802.11s standard specifications for mesh networking are completed.

The infrastructure mesh uses dual-radio mesh APs, which have two radios operating on different frequencies in two different mesh topologies. One radio supports user access, while the other provides back-haul. A typical configuration uses 2.4-GHz Wi-Fi for local access and 5-GHz band wireless for back-haul. The access capacity is not impacted by the forwarding traffic since it is done with a separate radio on a separate RF channel.

In an enterprise environment, infrastructure wireless meshes are important since these cut out the need for costly, wired back-haul to be provisioned to every node.

3.6.5 WPAN and Bluetooth

WPANs use RF technologies similar to those of WLANs, but short-distance (10s of meters versus 100s) and low-power radio. WPAN can be deployed in full mesh topology where nodes are connected directly with each others or partial mesh topology where some nodes are only connected to certain nodes. Mesh networks have the capability to provide extension to network coverage without increasing transmit power or receive sensitivity, with enhanced reliability via route redundancy, easier network configuration, and better device battery life due to fewer retransmissions.

WPAN is beacon-enabled mesh; multiple coordinators send beacons periodically to coordinate communications. Self-organized or predetermined beacon arrangement should be deployed to avoid direct and indirect collisions. A time synchronization mechanism is needed for beacon alignment. Signaling and management in mesh WPAN is more complicated than in a star-topology, energy consumption is a big concern in WPAN.

IEEE 802.15.5 task group defines the necessary mechanisms presenting in the PHY and MAC layers of WPANs to enable mesh networking. Bluetooth radio operates in the unlicensed ISM spectrum in the frequency range of 2.402 to 2.480 GHz. A Bluetooth network can exist in three ways: Point-to-point (e.g., Bluetooth mobile phone with Bluetooth headset) as shown in Figure 3.19(a), Point-to-multipoint, this is called a piconet as shown in Figure 3.19(b), and Linked point-to-multipoint, this is called a scatternet as shown in Figure 3.19(c). In a scatternet, the master computer is also connected to another master computer. The other master computer is slave to the 'central' master computer. But, this slave computer is master to its Bluetooth networking slave computers. An example PC configuration of scatternet is portrayed at the bottom figure of Figure 3.19.

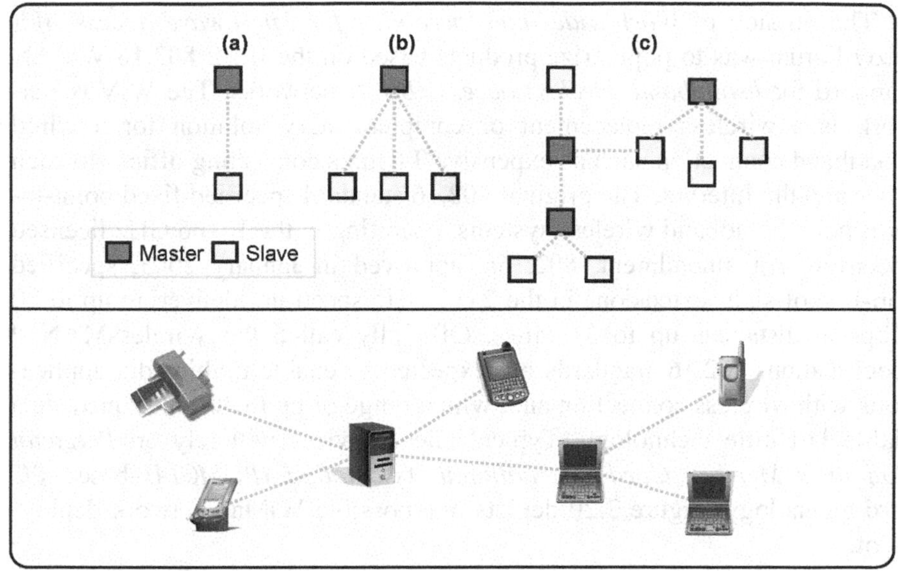

Figure 3.19. Bluetooth configurations.

Bluetooth uses 79-hop frequencies, spaced 1 MHz apart. If the transmission encounters interference, it waits for the next frequency hop, and retransmits on a new frequency. Two or more units sharing the same channel form a piconet. One Bluetooth unit acts as the master of the piconet, whereas the other units act as slaves. Up to seven slaves can be active in the piconet. Each piconet is assigned a specific frequency-hopping pattern. The pattern is determined by the piconet identity and the master clock of the master station. The overall hopping pattern is divided into two 32-hop segments, odd and even. Each 32-hop pattern starts at a point in the spectrum, and hops over a pattern that covers 64 MHz. The 32-hop segments are concatenated, and the random selection of the index is change, for each new segment. After completion of each segment, the sequence is altered, and the pattern is shifted 16 frequencies in the forward direction.

3.6.6 WMAN and WiMax

A WMAN covers a geographic area such as a city or suburb; it is targeted for use in metropolitan and regional networks. WMANs have much longer range than WLANs, as much as several kilometers and more, as opposed to the nominal 100 m of WLANs. These networks offer support for roaming and support applications requiring both low-latency data and real-time voice services.

The mission of *Worldwide Interoperability for Microwave Access (WiMax)* Forum was to popularize products based on the IEEE 802.16 WMAN standard for *broadband wireless access (BWA)* networks. The WiMax network is a wireless replacement or complementary solution for a wired broadband connection such as expensive T1 links connecting offices to each other and the Internet. The original 802.16 standard specified fixed point-to-multipoint broadband wireless systems, operating in the 10–66 GHz licensed spectrum. An amendment, 802.16a, approved in January 2003, specified non-line-of-sight extensions in the 2–11 GHz spectrum, delivering up to 70 Mbps at distances up to 31 miles. Officially called the WirelessMAN™ specification, 802.16 standards are expected to enable multimedia applications with wireless connection and, with a range of up to 30 miles, provide a viable last mile technology. Typical client devices will rely on *Personal Computer Memory Card International Association (PCMCIA)*–based PC card technology. Figure 3.20 depicts one possible WiMax network deployment.

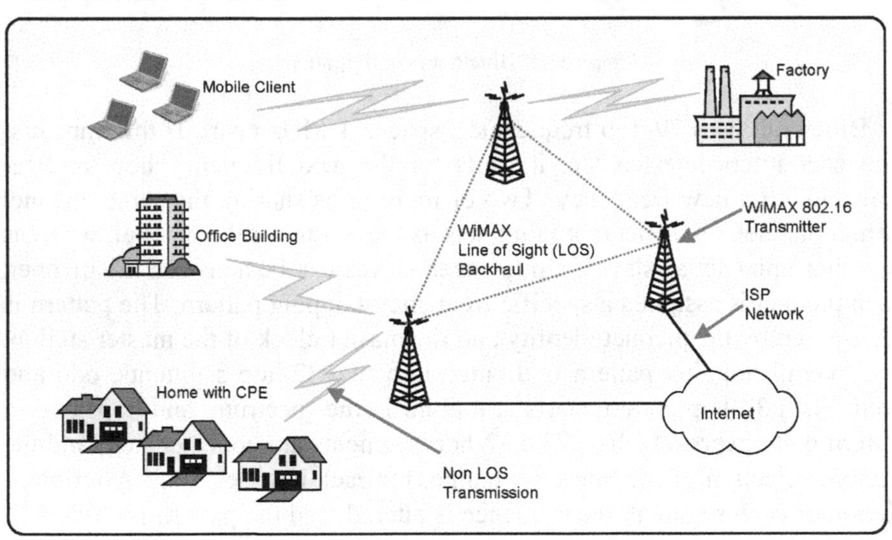

Figure 3.20. WiMax.

WiMax uses highly directional antennas, whereas Wi-Fi uses omni-directional antennas. These two standards also use different approaches for QoS and security. WiMax 802.16d is suitable for fixed point-to-multipoint networks, and WiMax 802.16e is suitable for mobile both peer-to-peer and ad-hoc networks.

Another competing standard in the works is the IEEE 802.20 mobile broadband wireless access standard. It is expected to support data rates of greater than 100 Mbps at ranges of 15 km or more. 802.20 will operate in licensed bands below 3.5 GHz (500 MHz to 3.5 GHz). It will incorporate global mobility and roaming support between base stations. The standard will support real-time traffic with the low latency of about 20 ms or less required for VoIP. Typical channel bandwidth will be less than 5 MHz.

One deployed commercial example of WiMax is the *Wireless Broadband (WiBro)*, provided by two Korean Telco (KT, SKT) in June 2006. The target digital *consumer electronics (CE)* includes MP3P, PMP, game player, digital camera, and telematics. The converged terminals have various form factors such as PDA, Mobile Phone, PCMCIA card, and PC.

Based on the wireless broadband Internet technology, WiBro adapts TDD for duplexing, OFDMA for multiple access with 8.75 MHz channel bandwidth. Operating in 2.3–2.4 GHz band, WiBro provides portable high speed Internet connection, both in stationary and mobile mode.

WiBro base stations offer an aggregate data throughput of 30 to 50 Mbps and cover a radius of 1–5 km allowing for the use of portable Internet usage. In late 2005 ITU reflected WiBro as IEEE 802.16e. However, the inclusion of QoS in WiBro for stream video content and other loss-sensitive data appear to be and may be the stronger advantages over the WiMAX standard. The WiBro network architecture is illustrated in Figure 3.21.

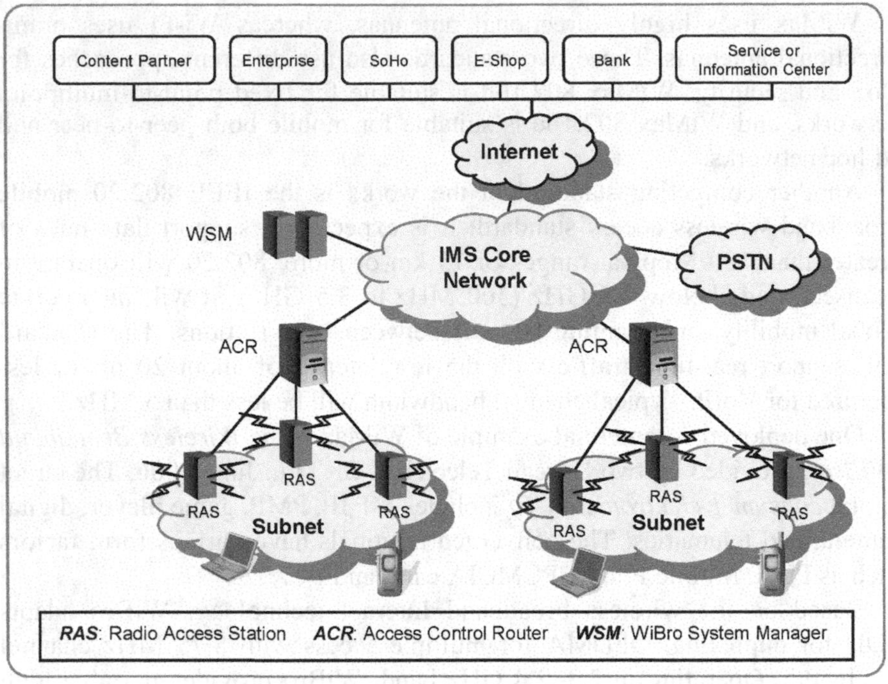

Figure 3.21. WiBro network architecture.

High performance radio metropolitan area network (HIPERMAN) is a European alternative to WiMAX. Created by the *European Telecommunications Standards Institute (ETSI) Broadband Radio Access Networks (BRAN)* group, HIPERMAN provide a wireless network communication in the 2–11 GHz bands across Europe and other countries. It enables both *point-to-multipoint (PMP)* and mesh network configurations for ATM and IP networking.

HIPERMAN is optimized for supporting packet-switched networks such as broadband Wireless DSL in frequency bands below 11 GHz (mainly in the 3.5 GHz band) primarily for residential and small business environments. It offers various service categories, full QoS, fast connection control management, strong security, fast adaptation of coding, modulation, and transmit power to propagation conditions and is capable of non-line-of-sight operation. The technology supports both FDD and TDD frequency allocations and H-FDD terminals.

3.6.7 IP Multimedia Subsystem

The *IP Multimedia Subsystem (IMS)* is a standardized open systems architecture in the network domain that supports a wide range of IP-based services over the existing phone systems (both packet-switched and circuit-switched). It uses *Voice-over-IP (VoIP)* based on SIP protocol defined in 3GPP and employs both mobile and fixed multimedia services [17].

IMS is at the heart of Next Generation Convergent Networks, it intends to merges the Internet with the cellular world. Service users can use all their services whether they are mobile or not. Because of the open-nature of IMS, multimedia sessions among IMS community or non-IMS users can be established end-to-end with the same protocol. Applications and services can be supported seamlessly across all networks. This feature gives network operators and service providers the ability to control and charge for individual services.

As mentioned earlier, the primarily designed (3GPP R5) of IMS is to provide services upon GPRS using SIP signaling. 3GPP R6 was extended to incorporate non-GPRS based access and SIP TEs, especially to harmonize with the 3GPP2 (CDMA 2000) IP *Multimedia Domain (MMD)*. The later releases emphasize on the integration of more services and adaptation of fixed networks. Figure 3.22 depicts a high level systems view of an IMS network. At the transport layer, three 3GPP releases are addressed.

In the access network, the user can connect to an IMS network using various methods via standard IPv6. A direct IMS terminal (e.g., mobile phone, PDA, and computer) with a SIP user agent can directly register into an IMS network. Fixed access (e.g., DSL and cable modems), mobile access (e.g., W-CDMA, CDMA2000, GSM, and GPRS), and wireless access (e.g., WLAN and WiMAX) are all supported. Non IMS-compatible VoIP phone systems like the POTS (the old analogue telephones) and H.323 can be supported through gateways.

Call Session Control Function (CSCF) is a collected function to process SIP signaling packets in the IMS.

A *Proxy-CSCF (P-CSCF)* is a SIP proxy that is the first point of contact for the IMS terminal. It authenticates and generates charging records of the user and establishes an IPsec security association with the IMS terminal. It can be located either in the visited network (in full IMS networks) or in the home network (when the visited network is not IMS compliant yet). Some networks might use a *Session Border Controller (SBC)* for this function. The terminal will discover its P-CSCF with either DHCP, or it is assigned in the PDP Context (in GPRS). It may include a *Policy Decision Function (PDF)* to authorize media plane resources such as QoS.

An *Interrogating-CSCF (I-CSCF)* is a SIP proxy located at the edge of an administrative domain. Its IP address is published in the DNS of the domain, so that remote servers can find it, and use it as an entry point for all SIP packets to this domain. I-CSCF queries the *home subscriber server (HSS)* to retrieve the user location; it's the HSS that assigns an S-CSCF to

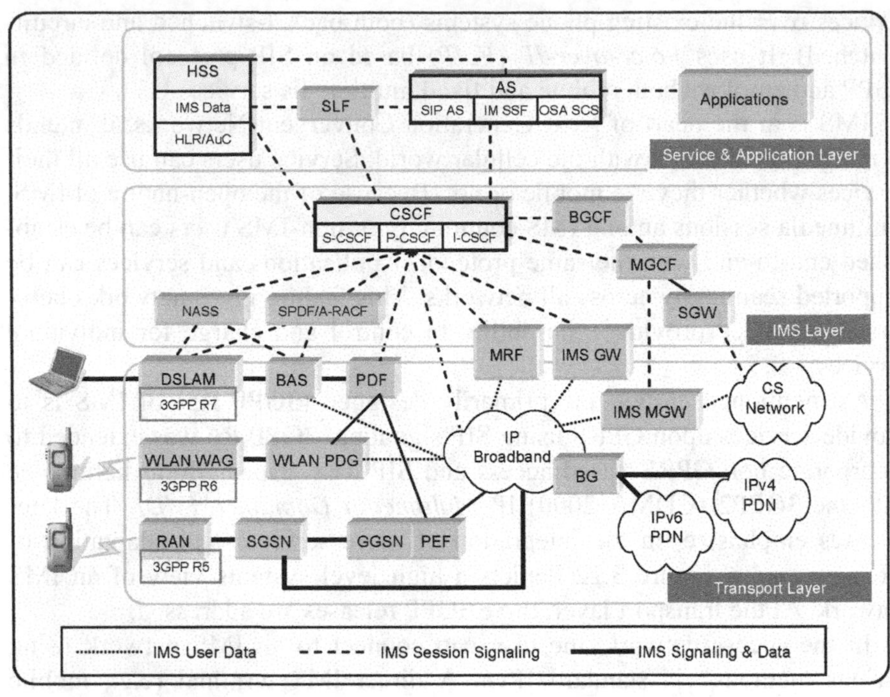

Figure 3.22. IMS architecture.

the user. A *Serving-CSCF (S-CSCF)* is the SIP server for signaling and session control as well. It's always located in the home network. The S-CSCF interfaces to the HSS to download and upload user profiles. It handles SIP registrations and provides routing services. Multiple S-CSCF can be deployed in the network for load distribution and high availability consideration.

The core network contains the HSS and *subscriber location function (SLF)*. HSS is the master user database containing the subscription-related information (user profiles) and performs authentication and authorization of the user. It is similar to the GSM HLR and AUC. In case when multiple HSSs are used, the SLF is required.

The *application-server (AS)* interfaces with the S-CSCF using SIP. It hosts and executes IMS services allowing third party providers an easy integration and deployment of their value added services to the IMS infrastructure. Three components are shown in Figure 3.22. The SIP AS is a native IMS application server. The *open service access-service capability server (OSA-SCS)* is an interface with OSA application servers using Parlay. The *IP multimedia service switching function (IM-SSF)* interfaces with CAMEL application servers using CAP.

The media servers located at the IMS layer is called *media resource function (MRF)*. It provides a source of media in the home network. It can be used for playing of announcements (audio/video), Multimedia conferencing (e.g., mixing of audio streams), *text-to-speech conversion (TTS)* and speech recognition, and real-time transcoding of multimedia data (i.e., conversion between different codecs).

A *breakout gateway control function (BGCF)* is a SIP server that includes routing functionality based on telephone numbers. It's only used when calling from the IMS to a phone in a circuit switched network, such as the PSTN or the PLMN.

PSTN gateways interface with PSTN *circuit switched (CS)* networks. For signaling, CS networks use ISUP (or BICC) over MTP, while IMS uses SIP over IP. For media, CS networks use PCM, while IMS uses RTP. A *signaling gateway (SGW)* transforms lower layer protocols as SCTP (which is an IP) into MTP (which is a SS7 protocol), to pass ISUP from the MGCF to the CS network. A *media gateway controller function (MGCF)* does call control protocol conversion between SIP and ISUP, and interfaces with the SGW over SCTP. A *media gateway (MGW)* converts between RTP and PCM.

Veizon's *Advances to IMS (A-IMS)* architecture aims to fill gaps that standard IMS leaves open. This will ease the transition from legacy networks to the all-IP networks in the future. The key principles include uniform treatment of SIP and non-SIP applications, comprehensive security, and three-layer peering, dual anchoring, and multi-tiered service interaction management. The concept of dual anchoring is to support two IP address to a mobile terminal where the service provider can assign latency sensitive applications to the visit anchor (in the form of IP) and applications which require greater levels of service controls to the home anchor. The disadvantages of A-IMS are its dependency upon the CDMA technology than the GSM technology, as well as the acceptance from other operators [18].

The *Next Generation Mobile Network (NGMN)* [19] was established in 2006 by leading mobile operators to complement and support the technological roadmap for the next generation of mobile networks beyond HSPA and EVDO. This effort is to assist operators conducting transitions of the existing wireless broadband services and systems, including planned enhancements, to the next generation technologies with minimum impacts to their competitive edges.

3.7 Conclusion

While service-oriented operations reach a certain level of maturity in wired networks, it remains nascent in wireless networks. In this chapter, the history of wireless networks, technical challenges, and path-forward developments are presented.

Mobility protocols are used to support routing to and from mobile nodes. When mobility becomes the norm rather than exception, it is imperative for interoperability between implementations, i.e., dealing with large-scale mobile delivery, discovery management, and security. Examples are authentication and access control schemes for mobile users. Current access control schemes allow the specification of who can do what (e.g., send and receive.) With mobility, the scopes are extended to address the issue of who can do what, where, and when.

This chapter starts by introducing the notion of network-centric services and their applicability in wireless networks. Mobile ad-hoc networks are an ideal technology to establish in an instant communication infrastructure-less service base for mission-critical applications or overcome a flawed architecture. The existing wireless technologies were highlighted with the ad-hoc feature as a communication foundation of service-oriented enterprise. The discussions were then moved to the practical aspects of the ad-hoc wireless technologies, as they potentially pertain to each of the salient elements of an enterprise service offering. For each of these elements, the challenges and characteristics of ad-hoc wireless network was distilled.

Finally, the highlights and trends of the most popular radio and service architectures in the recent research and development were revealed. This chapter is intended to give a perspective on the issues, challenges, and imperatives of designing and implementing a wireless communication framework for enterprises services, one that will serve as a building block of infrastructured and infrastructure-less technologies for the next subject.

Chapter 4

WIRELESS SENSOR NETWORKS AND APPLICATIONS

A sensor network is a computer network of many spatially distributed devices using sensors to monitor conditions, such as sound, temperature, pressure, vibration, motion, or life-threatening pollutions (e.g., radiation and biochemical). A complete sensor device is normally equipped with sensing, computation, and communication capabilities. This configuration allows sensor devices to communicate with each other, and also relies upon the peer sensors to transport data to a monitoring computer. Usually sensor devices are small so that they can be produced and deployed in large numbers. However this attribute also severely constrains the availability of their resources in terms of energy, memory, computational speed, and bandwidth.

In the foreseeable future, everyday objects such as automobiles and home appliances will connect the living environment to information networks. Pervasive computing devices will allow applications to gather and share a large amount of information. Sensor networks will soon be able to track everything from industrial control and monitoring, home automation and consumer electronics, security and military sensing, asset tracking and supply chain management, intelligent agriculture, and health monitoring. Such information that was not available before will open up new markets for a large range of new services and applications. The viability of the new information-driven business lies in the enterprise's capability to unify wireless network technology with tangible knowledge service applications.

This chapter is situated as a key building-block of an enterprise service to support customer-facing or environment-facing applications as part of a situation awareness system. The first part of this chapter provides a general look at the sensor applications, sensor network architecture, data dissemination methods, antennas, and waveform management. The second part introduces the existing standards most popular in the sensor industry and several associated applications. Lastly, the SoS view of a wireless sensor network provides technical foundation sufficient to establish a sensor-integrated enterprise information management solution.

4.1 Overview

Sensor technologies play an essential role in supporting information collection and object management as part of the integrated enterprise services architecture. Traditional sensor applications rely on a "data-centric" networking paradigm for data sharing. For instance, wireless database technology allows sensors to query data from other sensors with multi-hop routing protocols.

Owning to the technology maturity and pervasive market growth, massive production and deployment of sensors have reduced the operational cost dramatically. The increasing number of sensors per managed site, with far more complex and rich information, has introduced new challenges such as heterogeneity, privacy, scalability, and security which are unseen in a "data-centric" environment.

Nowadays, an enterprise system is expected to collect data from a very large number of sensors attached to vehicles, traffic lights, road surface, buildings, and so forth. Such complex and large sensor networks need to be managed by a network-centric operating system as a "melting pot" of various solutions. The ability to federate different products and sub-systems can significantly increase environmental awareness and knowledge which corresponds to a new core competency, a competency that is fundamental to achieving information superiority.

Defining this mentioned core competency calls for new generation operational capabilities in design, deployment, and operation of the sensor networks. Figure 4.1 depicts the functional building blocks of a wireless sensor application within the enterprise services. As shown, establishing upon the active and passive sensors is the sensor network where sensor nodes are managed network-centricly. This network-centric operations and managements of wireless sensor network need to incorporate power management, mobility, discovery, configuration, security, and data fusion. The collaborated capabilities form essential service elements which impact the enterprise operations in technology, organization, and doctrine. The technology aspect of these subjects will be portrayed throughout this chapter. Broader influences to the rest of the enterprise services will be delved in detail in the following chapters.

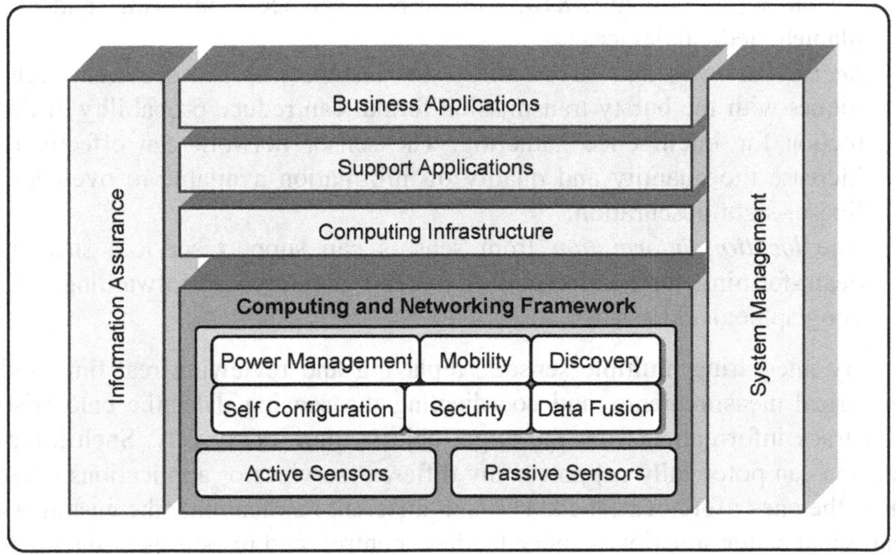

Figure 4.1. System architecture of enterprise services.

4.1.1 Networked Sensor Applications

To achieve higher efficiency of data management, sensor networks may employ distributed capability with multiple routing paths. In mission critical scenarios, the connectivity may require the attributes of self-healing and self-maintaining to support resiliency from any threats to the managing environments. From a data traffic perspective, the sensor applications typically have relaxed throughput requirements and are often measured infrequently. This section profiles some sensor applications [1]:

- *Environment monitoring and control* of industrial safety, soil condition, farm or barn temperature, *heating, ventilating, and air conditioning (HVAC)* of a building, security in disaster relief, and building structure analysis.
- *Tracking and responding* to the target environment for disaster relief, to the location of animals in the ranch, to the shipping containers in transport business, to the packages in shipping industry, to the maintenance schedule of machinery, and to the enemy's attempt to avoid attack.
- *Life quality improvement* such as intelligent *personal computer (PC)* peripherals or appliances, PC-enhanced toys, "*universal*" remote control of home electronic equipment, networked biological (e.g., weight or blood sugar) sensors for health monitoring, location-aware tourism and shoping,

remote keyless entry (RKE), athletic performance monitoring, and implanted medical devices.

- *Secured sensing and accessibility*, for instance, spread spectrum techniques with the bursty transmission format can reduce probability of detection for intelligence gathering. The sensor network can effectively increase the quantity and quality of information available to overcome line-of-sight obscuration.
- The *location information* from sensors can support services such as beam-forming for localization of targets, geographical forwarding, and geographical addressing.

By integrating multiple sensors, replaying and reviewing real time and historical measurements, and coordinating the sensing data, the enterprise can track information from the target objects more effectively. Such information can potentially support many different services or applications other than the ones aforementioned. Through different applications, the customers can yield better situational understanding, control, and responses of the managed environments.

4.1.2 Category of Sensor Nodes

As discussed in the previous section, the effectiveness of stand-alone sensors can be improved through employment of multiple sensor units against the managed objects. The combination of sensor fusion and dynamic sensor tasking can lead to more accurate measurements. Because multiple sensor deployment does not require all sensors to possess identical operational roles, for efficiency sake, sensors are thus grouped and act in complementary functionalities to constitute a sensor network. These different functions can be roughly divided into the following categories:

- *Generic and special sensors* support the heterogeneity of information gathering in enterprise services. There are two basic types of sensors, passive and active sensors:
  - An active sensor is a measuring instrument that generates a signal, transmits it to a target, and detects the returned signal reflecting off the target objects. Against objects moving in air and space, active sensors are an effective means of providing very accurate ranging measurements. The most common active sensors used in remote sensing are radar and sonar. A sample application of active sensor is depicted in Figure 4.2.
  - A passive sensor provides detection without emitting any energy signal that can themselves be detected. Most passive electromagnetic spectrum sensor systems operate in the visible (image recognition), infrared (detecting emitting infrared radiation even in the dark), thermal infrared (temperature change), seismic (earthquakes), acoustic (sound), strain (applied forces), salinity (concentration of chlorides in the water), neutrino (emissions of un

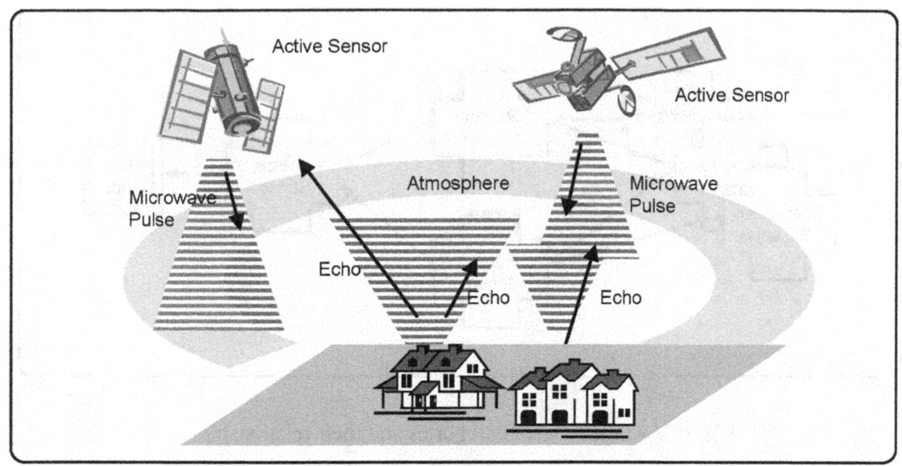

Figure 4.2. Active sensor.

shielded reactors), humidity, temperature, and microwave portions of the electromagnetic spectrum to provide sufficient information for pattern recognition applications to profile the presence, characteristic, or shape of a target.

- *Router sensors* are used as routers or can be used as data dissemination nodes in the sensor network in addition to its sensor role. These nodes self-organize themselves to form the backbone of the sensor network and hold the following advantages:
    - Certain specialized sensors may be expensive to build; detaching the routing capability from those specialized sensors allows the designer to emphasize on the sensor function then the networking function. This can potentially reduce the density of the specialized sensors in the network to achieve cost-effectiveness.
    - As performance of specialized sensors is separated from the router sensors, the router sensors can be specialized on networking specific features such as best paths selection. Additionally, the number of routers can be increased to improve the service durability and the fault-tolerance of the network.
- *Aggregator nodes* perform self-configurable aggregating functions within a sensor environment. This functionality can be deployed in a router sensor or a special sensor node.
- *Sink nodes* normally have relatively high processing power, and high storage capacity, and can connect to the enterprise inter- or intra-networks for transmission of collected data. The sink nodes are sometimes called gateway nodes. Depending upon the applications, they may hold the responsibility of sending specific control messages to certain nodes, broadcasting messages within the managed sensor group, or relaying data among sensors.

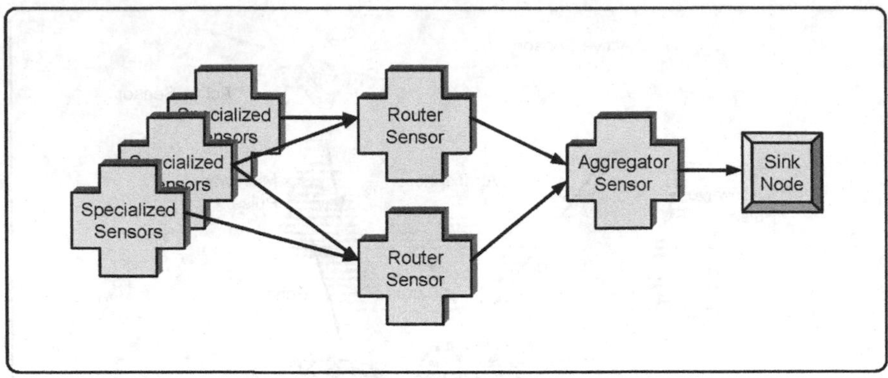

Figure 4.3. Four sensor categories and their relationships.

Figure 4.3 depicts the relationships of these four sensor categories. Because *generic* and *special sensor* nodes generate data thus they are called *sources*; the information to be reported is called an *event*. Through router sensors, the events are transmitted to an *aggregator*. The sink node collects the events and forwards them to the back-end enterprise services or applications. In a less complex configuration, a sink node can be a *sensor base station (SBS)* hosting an application system or systems.

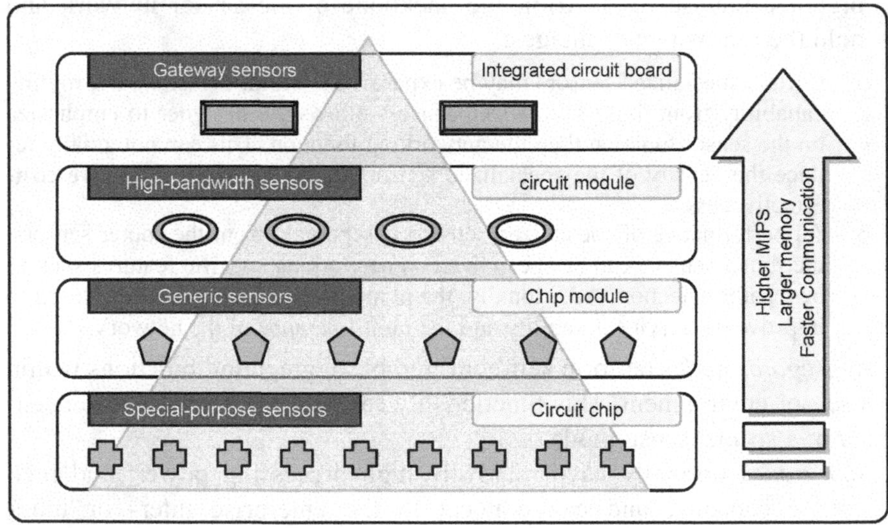

Figure 4.4. Hierarchical deployment of wireless sensor networks.

A network-centric wireless sensor network offers a decentralized data fusion and control paradigm to establish a unified yet flexible architecture suitable for a wide range of services. The trend of this new sensing functions lies at the *integrated circuit (IC)* technology for increased robustness, lower cost, and smaller size. From the design perspective, a sensor is a self-contained modular electronic system that is equipped with a radio transceiver, a small microcontroller, and an energy source, usually a battery. The microcontroller can perform data analysis such as beam forming or aggregation of related data. It can also include routing computation overhead. The radio transceiver involves transmission and reception between multiple nodes. Figure 4.4 shows a sample hierarchical deployment of a sensor network. Dependent upon the computing complexity and resource levels, sensors can be situated inside a circuit chip, chip module, circuit module, or even as an independent component in a gateway sensor. The sensors at the higher layers of the pyramid tend to hold higher computing speeds (millions of instructions per second or MIPS), larger memories, and faster communication speeds [2].

4.1.3 Sensor Networks

A large number of networked sensors can provide better spatial coverage, higher responsiveness, survivability, and robustness. Sensor fusion enables measurements from multiple sensors to develop a composite picture of the situation. The composite picture decreases the time required to generate situation and service awareness. In addition to the sensor fusion, dynamic sensor tasking is a proven method for improving accuracy of the measurement by reducing error or unwanted data. A complex sensor network may feature multi-hop and a self-configured wireless network consisting of many sensor nodes. Fine-grained localization (section 4.5.2) and time synchronization (section 4.5.3) can be added to enhance detections across nodes.

Table 4.1 lists the basic attributes of the Internet and sensor network. In particular, sensor networks primarily focus on dissemination, collection, aggregation, and gradient-directed services, whereas the Internet principally focuses on end-to-end communication. By comparing these two networks, the enterprise can rationally allocate resources between sensor and backbone networks separated by the gateway nodes.

In a sensor network, data traffic can be categorized into data collection and data dissemination (diffusion). These two types of traffic are depicted in Figure 4.5.

Data collection can be either periodic or on-demand. The sensed data is transmitted from sensor nodes to the data sink or the base application. In the context of data collection, a "*round*" is defined as the base application collecting data from all the predetermined sensor nodes once. Generally, the routing protocol must be energy-efficient in order to maximize the system

Table 4.1. Internet and Sensor Networks.

The Internet	Sensor Networks
Independent hosts and applications	Collaborative nodes, gateways, and specific applications
End-to-end flows (static)	Collect, disseminate, routing, synchronization (dynamic)
Infrastructured	Infrastructure-less (ad-hoc networking)
Human-interaction, throughput can be high	Even driven, low utilization with occasional spike
Power supply by AC/DC	Often battery-powered
Latency depends on the QoS of session, normally is small and expectable	Delays caused by wake time (power management), broken path (interference or mobility), and routings (traffic patterns) thus not expectable
Bandwidth is relatively cheap	Bandwidth is expensive
In-network state is less significant, service behavior is rather stable and predicable	Service behaviors are influenced by the limitation of physical computing resources (e.g., memory, antenna, and battery)

lifetime. Energy efficiency is primarily accomplished by using the best routing path and by turning off unneeded components of the node. Such design and operational objectives are to maximize the *number of rounds* of communication with minimum resource consumption.

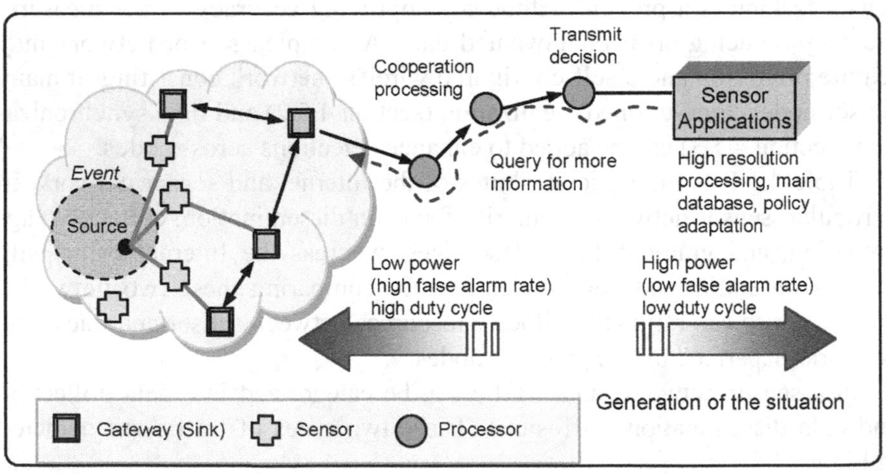

Figure 4.5. Data collection, processing, and queuing reflect dynamic policy.

Data dissemination (or *data diffusion*) includes any queries from the data sink to the sensor nodes as well as the replies from the sensor nodes back to the data sink. Intelligent data diffusion may consist of a multiple-step process including *interest propagation* and *data propagation* to filter and consolidate traffic. The process starts from a sink broadcasting the events of interest to its neighbor nodes. This interest is further propagated across the entire network. All receiving nodes maintain an interest cache for the needed events. The sink node can periodically refresh its interests. When an event is detected and fits the profile of interest, this event is prorogated back to the interested node. Depending upon the design, all intermediate nodes can either maintain a data cache or further fuse the reporting data.

4.1.4 Service Requirements in NCBO

In an NCBO environment, it is a general practice that wireless sensor networks are formed and managed in an infrastructure-less design in order to reduce dependency on the potentially high cost of network infrastructure. The sensor tasking enables sensor resources to be dynamically focused on high priority sectors of the managed space; it helps the enterprise ensure the right mix of sensors is available at the right time. The following are some design and operational considerations for sensors and sensor networks in an NCBO environment:

- The capabilities of node can be homogenous, heterogeneous, or a mixed of nodes dedicated to a special function such as sensing, routing, and aggregation. Divided functionalities for specific sensor nodes can save on energy consumption. Message traffic from different sensors may be at different rates, however, unbalanced traffic makes data routing more challenging.
- Deployment of sensors relates to the topology and scalability of the sensor network. The deployment can be either *deterministic*, where the sensors are *manually* placed, or self-organizing, where the sensor nodes are scattered randomly in an ad-hoc manner. The performance of sensor network coverage is contributed to by the range and sensitivity of each node, as well as the location and density of the collected nodes in the given region. The redundancy strategy can be used to enhance overall system lifetime. Support detectability can assist the enterprise to determine where to add or move nodes for maximized coverage.
- Because sensors and gateways can be mobile or stationary, *network dynamics* dictate the stability of the routing path, which eventually influences QoS (such as energy and bandwidth). Sensed events can be either proactive or reactive, and either static or dynamic depending upon the application. Without depending upon central control, *self-organized* operation can yield better situational awareness by adapting to changes in the network topology, and even avoid failed nodes in the communication paths.
- Networking can be either peer-to-peer or overlay; data delivery from sensors to the sink node can be continuous, event-driven, query-driven, or

hybrid. In an infrastructure-less network, preserving energy and maintaining route stability are highly influenced by the data delivery methods. The data transmission should meet the performance criteria in delay, bandwidth, queuing, and accuracy for optimal QoS.

- *Data fusion* aggregates the raw data from sensors and helps the sensor network to reduce data redundancy for traffic optimization. Data aggregation techniques can include suppression, basic mathematical calculations, noise reduction, or data combination. Data fusion improves context awareness which in turn improves the adaptation and management in network-centric operations. When a global identifier is not available, attribute based naming is normally used for nodal coordination. Sensors should reduce the amount of state maintained in the nodes and increase localized operations to improve network-centricity.
- Also in the aggregation process, the *location information* of sensors (from *Global Positioning System* or GPS, for instance) typically provides key data to the report. In the situation when GPS is not feasible due to environmental or configuration constrains, alternate position synchronization such as *collaborative detection* should be included.
- *Service exposure* is a measure of expected ability to monitor a target in the sensor field. It is the integral of the sensing function on a path from source node to the sink node. This requires complete synchronization across different layers to impose multiple-access schedules; thus detected events can be performed without ambiguity. *Broadcasting* capability in the network should be considered in a transparent manner thus important data can be broadcasted to all the sensor nodes.
- Because networked sensors can be operating remotely, sensor nodes are failure prone due to malfunction, destruction, depleted battery stores, and human damage. Security and trust management in ubiquitous networks, systems, and applications are essential for service assurance.
- Energy management in network-centric applications is essential to the durability of the services. As the transmission power of a wireless radio is proportional to distance squared or even higher order in the presence of obstacles, direct connection is preferable in sensors close to sink. In randomly scattered networks, multi-hop routing is unavoidable with the added price of overhead from topology management and medium access control. With discrete power levels in sensors, a communication paradigm sensitive to energy consumption and QoS is an essential requirement for an infrastructure-less service network.

4.2 Wireless Sensor Network Architecture

In a sensing field where sensors are deployed in a functional group or domain group, introducing hierarchical architectures can provide common abstraction for sensor applications. While the control node, or gateway, can act as a relay or entry point to a larger network and complicate the final network plan, sensor deployment actually differs by grouping consideration.

The very nature of a wireless ad-hoc network is that its routers are free to move randomly and organize themselves to form an arbitrary topology. One of the connection options is called mesh network. The concept of a wireless mesh network relies upon its capability to cooperatively communicate between massive amounts of individual wireless nodes. In a mesh network, all nodes are connected to each other and form a fully connected network. It can be decentralized with no central server for less scalable applications or centralized and controlled by a server for highly scalable applications. Both of these two configurations are relatively inexpensive and very reliable. The mesh networking technology can support either a part or the entire service coverage of a sensor network deployment, regardless of the network architectures.

This section profiles three network architecture options: layered, clustered, and tiered, and addresses their design considerations from functional and operational perspectives [3].

4.2.1 Layered Architecture

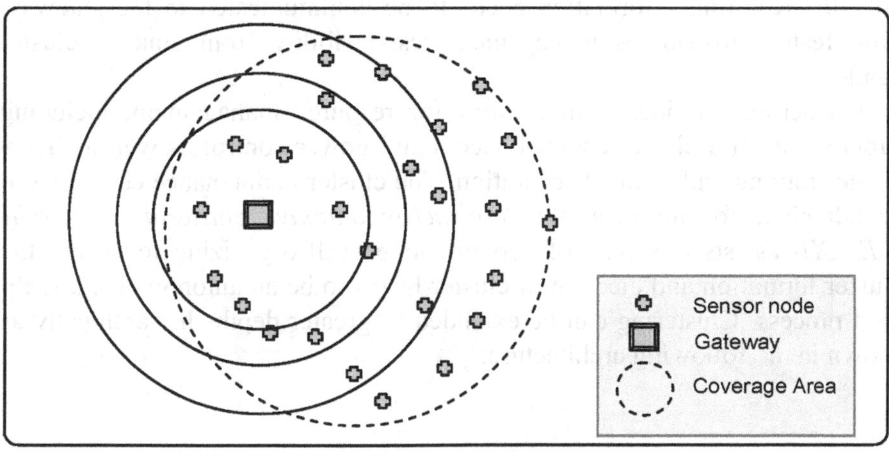

Figure 4.6. Layered architecture.

Figure 4.6 portrays a layered architecture containing a single powerful gateway and the layers of sensor nodes around it. The definition of a layer is a group of nodes that has the same hop-count to the gateway. The gateway acts as an access point to a larger network and can also be a data-gathering and processing entity. The advantage of a layered architecture is that each node is involved only in short-distance, low-power transmissions to nodes of the neighboring layers.

This architecture has been used with in building wireless backbones and in military sensor-based infrastructures.

4.2.2 Clustered Architecture

A clustered architecture organizes the sensors nodes into groups, each governed by a cluster-head. The nodes in each cluster are involved in message exchanges with their respective cluster-heads, and these heads send messages to a sink node, which can be a gateway node or an application station. Figure 4.7 depicts a clustered architecture where any message can reach the sink node in at least two hops.

Clustered architecture is especially useful for sensor networks because it provides a framework for data fusion, local decision-making, local control, and energy savings. Location awareness using GPS and a longer-range radio are two useful additions. During the process of distributed detection/ estimation and data fusion, the radio transmissions are among nodes within a cluster, under the control of their affiliated cluster head. The data gathered by all members of the cluster can be fused at the cluster-head, and only the resulting information needs to be communicated to the gateway. This feature distributes management responsibility from sink to cluster heads.

Clustering provides a framework for resource management, including support for intra-cluster channel access and power control as well as inter-cluster routing and channel separation. The cluster maintenance can be fixed or adaptive; for instance, the *low-energy adaptive clustering hierarchy (LEACH)* assists this type of network to be self-organizing to ensure the cluster formation and election of cluster-heads to be an autonomous, distributed process. Clustering can be extended to greater depths hierarchically as shown in the following architecture.

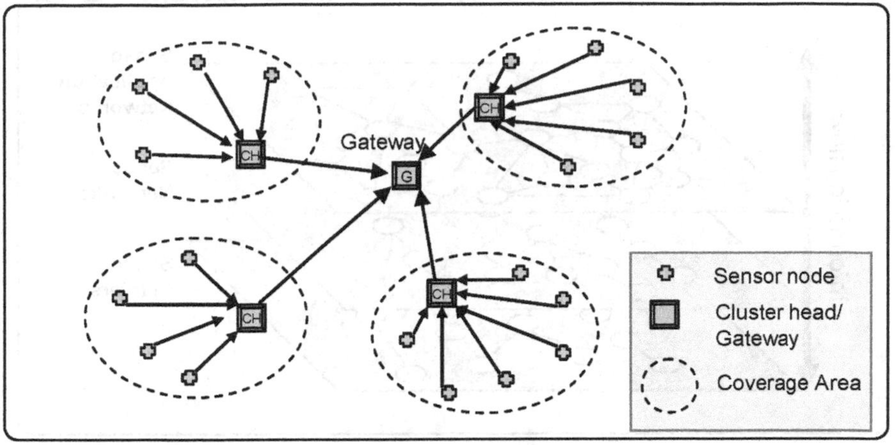

Figure 4.7. Cluster architecture.

4.2.3 Tired Architecture

Figure 4.8 shows a conceptual diagram of a three-tier sensor network. The sensor clusters are responsible for the collaborative signal processing of the observation and perform data reduction if appropriate. This processing can include beam-forming, distributed detection/estimation, and data fusion. One tier above the sensor clusters, the sensor networks are responsible for relaying data and performing domain level control messages. The top level sensor application networks are responsible for routing and disseminating the information to other enterprise entities for information sharing.

Conceptually the sensor application networks are larger than the sensor networks, because they include additional nodes such as data receiving users and other data processing nodes. From an architecture perspective, a successful integrated sensor cluster design should consider collaborative signal processing at each sensor node, management of multiple hop networking, synergy between the sensor requirements and communications performance requirements, security to support resistance to jamming and reliability of data, and balanced power distribution.

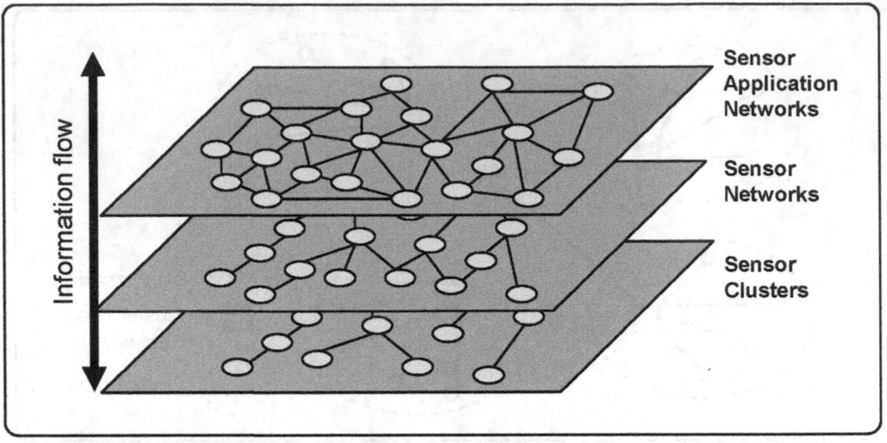

Figure 4.8. Three conceptual tiers in a wireless sensor network.

4.3 Sensor Data and Communication Protocols

Mobile nodes in an ad-hoc network communicate with each other in a peer-to-peer fashion that poses a challenge in data dissemination among the mobile peers, each having limited transmission range and unpredictable mobility. A network-centric operation requires the data dissemination to be non-uniform and can be integrated into a new information management middleware for large scale sensor networks.

The routing architecture connects all the sensors as an interconnection network between the router nodes. Sensor nodes transmit the messages to their adjacent router nodes, and the message specifies whether it is to be delivered to a specific node or a node group. A node along a path can manipulate received data locally in accordance with the data contents. This in-network processing can reduce communication while keeping higher level semantic requirements. As the result, the data can be transformed or suppressed before forwarding to the next hop. In the cases when a group of nodes are addressed, multicasting data between specialized nodes of a certain type can be supported over the broadcast infrastructure. Once the message reaches a router node reachable to the target destination, it is sent to the destination node. Key architectural issues that support the enterprise services include route discovery and maintenance, naming, and the packet forwarding rules [4].

The spirit of network-centric services is its capability to collaborate information from many different sources and forms. In the following sections, numerous sensor data and communication protocols will be discussed. It includes traditional data-centric, event-triggered, location-based, QoS-sensitive, and power-sensitive approaches. These approaches are not limited to MAC or network layers, with some of them designed for the application layer. For the enterprise to establish a service-oriented framework, all these implementations can serve as building-blocks offering data to support the information management functions, which will be illustrated in the following chapters.

4.3.1 Data Dissemination

A sink node sends queries to the managed regions and waits for replies from sensors. In many configurations, the number of nodes deployed makes the sensor network infeasible to assign global identifiers on the nodal basis. Lack of global identification plus random deployment of sensor nodes often prevent the nodes from making specific identification of their targets. As the result, the network routing exploits the queries posed for specific data rather than a particular sensor. This reveals the significance of aggregate data over individual sensor nodes. Thereby, data is usually transmitted from all sensor nodes within the deployment region with significant redundancy. The following subsections profile some popular routing designs based on data-centric and address-centric schemes.

4.3.1.1 Flooding

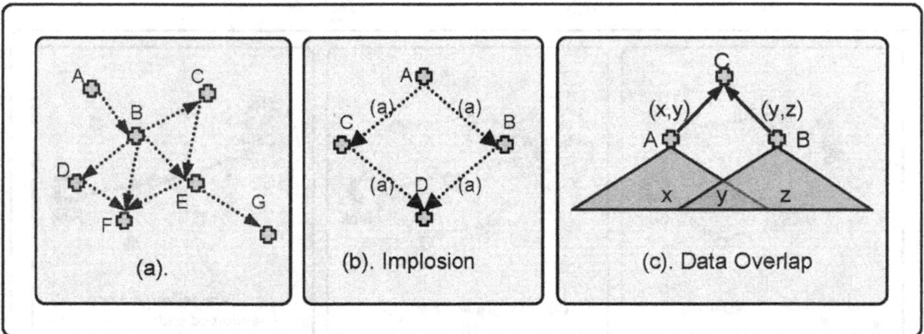

Figure 4.9. Flooding and its problems.

As shown in Figure 4.9(a), a sensor broadcasts messages to all of its neighboring nodes in the flooding method. The neighbors in turn broadcast to their neighbors and so on until the message is propagated to the destination or reaches the maximum number of hop limit. Because messages are blindly broadcasted to the neighboring nodes, the knowledge of topology or routing at each node is not necessary. Although flooding is very easy to implement, it introduces two problems. Figure 4.9(b) depicts the first problem called *implosion*. Sensor node A starts by flooding its message to its neighbors B and C. The sink node D eventually receives the same message twice. Duplicated messages arriving at the same node will result in a bottleneck at the sender. Figure 4.9(c) illustrates the *data overlap* problem where two nodes sensing the same region send similar packets to the same neighbor. These two cases demonstrate resource blindness by consuming a large amount of energy without consideration for the energy constraints.

4.3.1.2 Gossiping

Gossiping is an enhanced version of flooding. It avoids the problem of implosion by just sending messages to a randomly selected neighbors rather than broadcasting. Each node forwards messages with some probability, therefore it does not maintain routing or state info and the overhead is reduced. The fraction of executions in which most nodes get the message depends on the gossiping probability and the topology of the network. However, this cause delays in propagation of data through the nodes relating to flooding.

4.3.1.3 Directed Diffusion

Directed Diffusion queries the sensors in an on-demand basis by using a naming scheme such as name, data type, time interval, duration, geographical area, and so forth to eliminate unnecessary operations of network layer routing. As shown in Figure 4.10(a), the interest is disseminated by a sink to correct area through its neighbors.

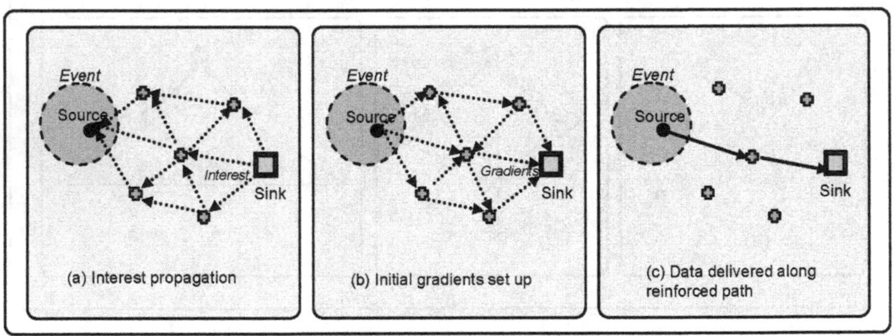

Figure 4.10. Directed diffusion.

A *gradient* in directed diffusion is a reply link to a neighbor from which the interest is received. A gradient is considered an established path where events of interest will be delivered back to originating node. Interests and data are propagated along routes with strong gradients. Gradient strength depends on the quality of the routing path. The indicator is initially small from source to sink and increased during reinforcement; good routes are inherently reinforced so the best path can be picked. The initial gradient establishment is depicted in Figure 4.10(b).

Each node has the ability to do in-network data aggregation and combination based on the interest previously cached, shown in Figure 4.10(c). Even though this method may require caching data on each node, it provides good energy efficiency and low delay. Additionally, this neighbor-to-neighbor mechanism can eliminate complicated global addressing. However, this query-driven method is not idea for applications requiring continuous data delivery or event-driven data because of the overhead from data matching and queries.

4.3.1.4 Rumor Routing

When geographic routing criteria are not applicable to diffuse tasks, Directed Diffusion floods the query to the entire network while *Rumor Routing* provides a trade-off between query and event flooding. The Rumor Routing algorithm employs long-lived packets, called agents. It is the agent which propagates or floods the events to distant nodes. When a node detects an event, it adds such an event to its local event table and generates an agent. This idea is when a node receives a query it checks the local event table, and replies with the source-to-destination path to the query originator.

Figure 4.11(a) shows a scenario when a query is originated from the query source and searches for a path to the event. The nodes that know the route can respond to the query by referring their local event tables. Because Rumor Routing maintains only one path between source and destination, the need for flooding the whole network can be avoided. Figure 4.11(b) illustrates when an agent prorogating the path to event 2 comes across a path to event 1, the agent begins to propagate the aggregate path to both.

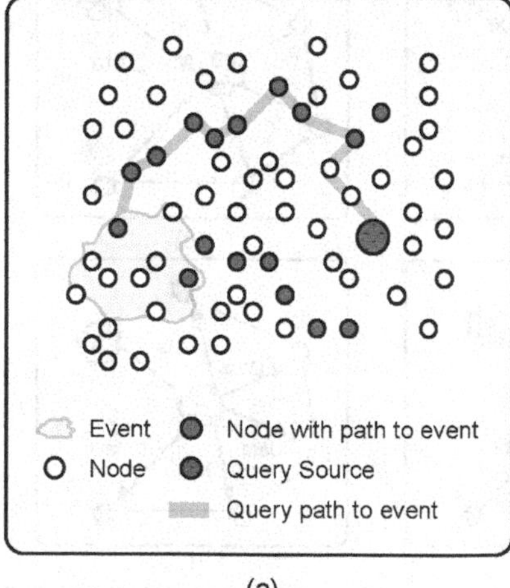

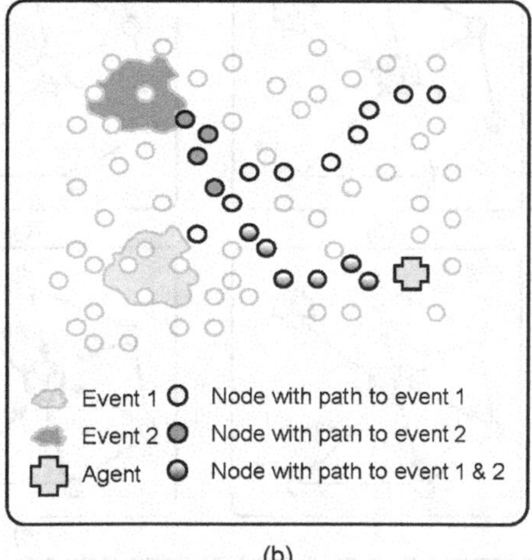

Figure 4.11. Rumor routing.

The advantages of Rumor Routing are its efficiency in handling a small number of event failures, and energy savings by limiting event flooding. For a large number of events, its drawback comes from the overhead to maintain agents and the event table, in particular when there is not enough interest on those events from the sink. The overhead can be managed by using tunable parameters such as time-to-live for queries and agents. Poor configuration may cause the nodes to make wrong observations and potentially worsen the efficiency.

4.3.1.5 Sensor Protocols for Information via Negotiation

As the first data-centric protocol, *Sensor Protocols for Information via Negotiation (SPIN)* utilizes data negotiation between nodes to eliminate redundant data and save energy. To solve the classic problems of flooding such as redundant information passing, overlapping of sensing areas, and resource blindness, SPIN adopts high level descriptors or meta-data for negotiation.

Before transmission, meta-data is exchanged among sensors via a data advertisement mechanism. As seen in Figure 4.12(a) through (c), upon receiving new events, node A advertises (with Advertise or Adv meta-data) it to its neighbor B, node B issues a *Request (Req)* message to request specific event, and node A replies with a Data message carrying the actual requested data. Figure 4.12(d) through (f) illustrates the request is extended to interested neighbors with the same sequence of handshaking.

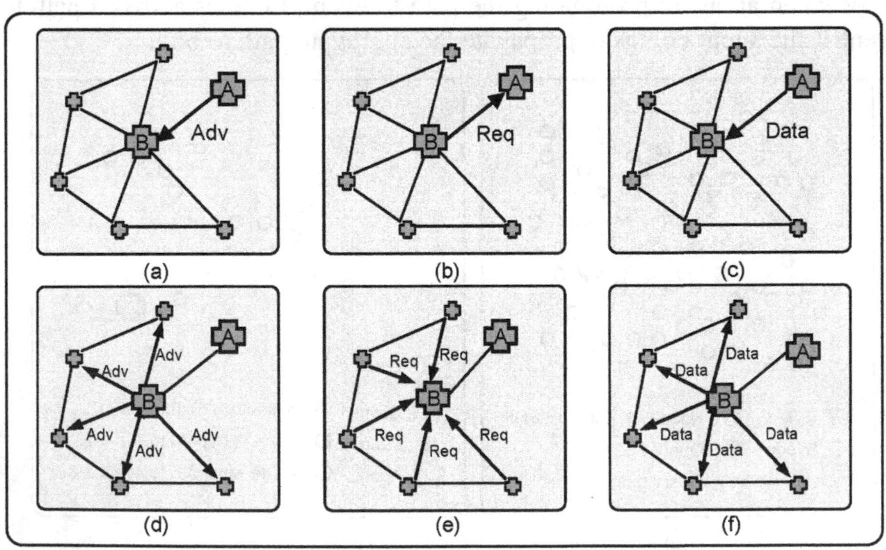

Figure 4.12. SPIN.

Because each node needs to know only the single-hop neighbors, topological changes can be localized. In comparison to flooding, SPIN halves the redundant data thus makes the energy efficiency achievable. However, if the source and destination nodes happen to be separated by the nodes that are not interested in that data or not within the reachable distance, SPIN's data advertisement will not provide guaranteed delivery.

4.3.1.6 Energy-Aware Routing

Energy-aware routing conditionally uses a set of sub-optimal paths to increase the lifetime of the network. Similar to the discovery process of Directed Diffusion where data is sent through multiple paths, Energy-aware routing selects a single path randomly from the multiple alternatives with energy as the primary consideration. These paths are chosen by means of a probability function reflecting energy consumption. The approach intends to unload traffic from the constantly used or preferred paths even these paths consume minimum energy. The philosophy is to balance the overall energy sensibility so that the whole network lifetime increases.

This sub-optimal path approach may require complicated setup calculations involving the location and types of the nodes for address identification. During the route maintenance, localized flooding is performed infrequently to keep all the paths alive; this may hinder the ability of recovering from a node or path failure as opposed to Directed Diffusion.

4.3.1.7 Gradient-Based Routing

Gradient-based routing (GBR) is a slightly changed version of Directed Diffusion, it keeps the number of hops to the sink (called height of the node) when an interest is diffused through the network. The difference between a node's height and its neighbor's height is the gradient on that link. A packet is forwarded on a link with the largest gradient; hence each node can communicate with the sink with the minimum number of hops. The application of GBR with some auxiliary techniques such as data aggregation and traffic spreading can balance the traffic uniformly over the network and eventually increases the network lifetime. Three different data spreading techniques have been proposed:

- Stochastic scheme chooses a node randomly when there are two or more next hops with the same gradient.
- Energy-based scheme increases a node's height when its energy level is below a certain threshold in order to discourage data traffic to that node.
- Stream-based scheme increases a node's height that is currently part of other existing streams in order to divert new streams away.

4.3.1.8 Constrained Anisotropic Diffusion Routing

Constrained anisotropic diffusion routing (CADR) is a general form of Directed Diffusion. CADR activates only the sensors that are close to the event of interest and dynamically adjusts data routes to maximize the information gain and minimize the latency and bandwidth. Different from Directed Diffusion, CADR measures information gain with standard estimation theory in addition to the communication cost. Every node evaluates its information-and-cost objective and routes data in accordance with its local information-and-cost gradient and application requirements. Thus it is more energy efficient than Directed Diffusion.

4.3.1.9 COUGAR

COUGAR introduces a new query layer between the applications and the sensor network. This layer uses declarative queries to abstract query processing from the network functions and treats the network as a distributed database system. In the gateway, a query plan specifies the data flow and in-network computation for the incoming query, the relevant sensor nodes, and a leader node. The leader node is selected to aggregate and transmit the data to the sink node.

This data-centric approach provides in-network computation ability for all the sensor nodes thus the energy efficiency can be ensured, especially in large sensor deployments and complex data traffic flows.

The disadvantages of COUGAR are the overhead of the additional query layer for energy consumption and storage, complexity of the synchronization in network data computation, and dynamic maintenance of leader nodes to prevent failure [5].

4.3.1.10 Active Query Forwarding in Sensor Networks

ACtive Query forwarding In sensoR nEtworks (ACQUIRE) also treats the sensor network as a distributed database but with a more complex hierarchical query process. In this method, a sensor node receiving a query from the sink tries to respond partially with its precached information and then forwards the information to a neighbor. If the precached information is neither up-to-date nor satisfactory, this sensor node will try to update the information from its neighbors. A tunable parameter representing look-ahead-hop number is introduced. This parameter dictates how many hopes the sensor can reach-out to refresh its information. Once the query is resolved, it is sent back through either the reverse or shortest-path to the sink.

This data-centric approach is ideal for one-shot and complex queries for response which may be provided by many nodes. ACQUIRE provides efficient querying by adjusting the value of the look-ahead-hop parameter. However, if the parameter is equal to the network size, the traffic behaves similar to flooding. On the other hand, the query has to travel more hops if the setting is too small.

4.3.2 Hierarchical Protocols

Scalability is one of the important deployment considerations when mobility or mission dynamic is a requirement in the sensor network. A single-tier hierarchy is easy to manage but can introduce traffic and accessibility problems with increasing sensor numbers. Overload from high-density nodes within the same managed domain can cause major latency in message delivery. The single-gateway may not be economic to install with over-size computing power to satisfy long-haul sensing coverage. For the sensor network to cope with unpredicted load and without degrading the service, hierarchical routings aim to arrange multiple clusters with domain-based data aggregation and fusion. As seen in the following subsections, multi-hop communication within a cluster is used to efficiently maintain overall energy reserves as well as decrease the number of the total messages to the sink.

4.3.2.1 Low-Energy Adaptive Clustering Hierarchy

Low-energy adaptive clustering hierarchy (LEACH) is the first and one of the most popular hierarchical routing approaches for sensor networks. A sensor network can have multiple clusters, each has a cluster head. A LEACH network is illustrated in Figure 4.13. The selection criteria of a cluster head is determined by the strongest received signal strength. Each cluster head maintains its transmission schedule and routers events to the sink. Application-specific data processing such as data fusion and aggregation are performed locally at the cluster head.

A LEACH network is capable of adaptive and self-configuring cluster formation; cluster heads rotate randomly over time to balance the energy dissipation of nodes. Because the network is completely distributed, there is no need of global knowledge of the network. Additionally, the computing process of each sensor node is relatively simple because of its local focus, thus the lifetime of the network can be increased. The disadvantages of LEACH are its overhead for dynamic clustering such as advertisements, and single-hop routing within the cluster may not be applicable for networks in large regions.

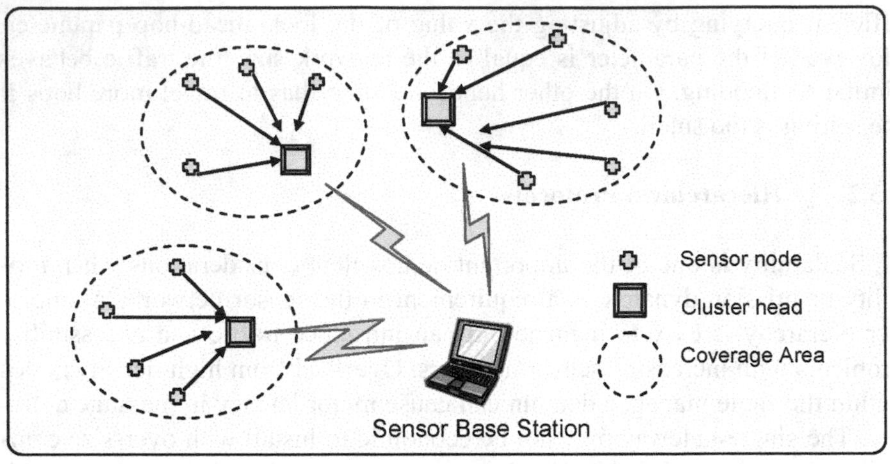

Figure 4.13. LEACH.

4.3.2.2 Power-Efficient Gathering in Sensor Information Systems

Power-Efficient GAthering in Sensor Information Systems (PEGASIS) improves the LEACH approach by forming chains from sensor nodes rather than clusters. Each node transmits and receives from a neighbor and only one node is selected from that chain to transmit to the sink. As depicted in Figure 4.14, node n3 is the leader and it passes the token along the chain to node n0. Node n0 passes the event to node n1; n1 and n2 aggregate the event and transmit it to node n3. After receiving the information, node n3 passes the token to node n6, node n6 transmits its event to node n5, and n4 for further aggregation. Node n3 waits to receive data from both neighbors and then conducts final aggregation. Eventually, the data is aggregated in the chain and sent to the sink node.

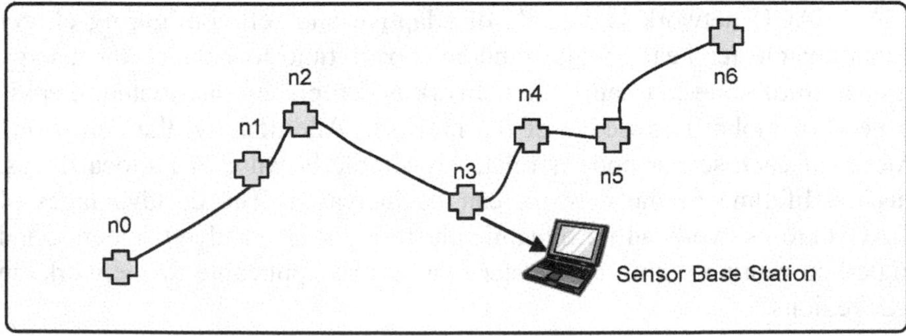

Figure 4.14. PEGASIS.

A PEGASIS network can outperform a LEACH network. Although overhead from LEACH clustering can be reduced, PEGASIS still requires dynamic topology adjustment and it can introduce significant overhead, especially for highly utilized networks. It can also introduce excessive delay for distant nodes in the chain. In addition, the single leader can become a bottleneck.

4.3.2.3 Threshold Sensitive Energy Efficient Protocols

Threshold sensitive Energy Efficient sensor Network protocol (TEEN) is a hierarchical and data-centric approach designed for time-critical applications. The rule to form clusters is based on close nodes, and the hierarchical grouping repeats on the next level until the sink node is reached. A sample hierarchy is depicted in Figure 4.15, where five clusters form two-tier network and connect to a sensor base station.

Upon the completion of network formation, the cluster head (or gateway node) broadcasts two thresholds to the nodes. The "hard threshold" specifies the minimum sensed attribute value that a sensor will trigger an event to the cluster head. The "soft threshold" further qualifies the event based on the attribute's change amount; this can reduce the number of transmissions in case changes in the sensed attribute are little or no change. This method is not applicable for applications which need periodic reports.

The Adaptive Threshold sensitive Energy Efficient sensor Network protocol (APTEEN) is an extension to TEEN. APTEEN extends the event trigger criteria to cover both capturing periodic data and reacting to time-critical events. This is accomplished by broadcasting more information from the *cluster heads* (gateways) to all nodes; the message includes the attributes, the threshold values, and the transmission schedule. Cluster heads perform data aggregation to save energy and support three different query types: the historical type query is to analyze past data values, the one-time query is to take a snapshot of the network measurement, and persistent query is to monitor an event for a period of time.

Figure 4.15 depicts the architecture of TEEN and APTEEN.

The main drawbacks of the two approaches are the overhead and complexity of forming clusters in multiple levels, implementing threshold-based functions and dealing with attribute-based naming of queries.

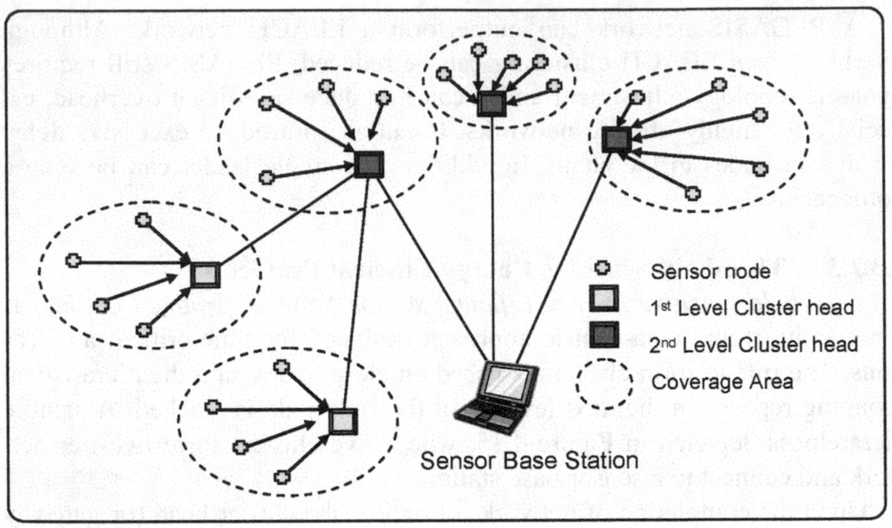

Figure 4.15. TEEN and APTEEN.

4.3.2.4 Energy-Aware Routing for Cluster-Based Sensor Networks

The energy-aware routing for cluster-based sensor networks is based on a three-tier architecture. This approach assumes that sensors are grouped into clusters prior to network operation, and the cluster heads (gateways) are less energy constrained and know the location of the sensors. Gateways maintain the states of the sensors and set up multi-hop routes for collecting sensing data. A TDMA based MAC is used for nodes to send data to the gateway and controlled by the gateway. The sink node communicates only with the gateways. The sensing and processing circuits are assumed to be capable of operating in an active mode or a low-power stand-by mode. Both the radio transmitter and receiver can be independently turned on and off. This approach can achieve higher scores in energy consumption, delay optimization, and throughput than the non-energy sensitive protocols.

4.3.3 Location-Based Protocols

Because sensors are spatially deployed in a region, location information can assist sensor nodes in determining the distance to their neighbors. Location of a node can be determined by using GPS, *trilateration* via *ultrasonic*, or *beacons*. Such information allows a sensor node to estimate energy consumption of communication paths and potentially assist the node to calculate the most energy-effective route to its target nodes. For the coverage areas that are not in immediate need, certain sensor nodes can be temporarily inactive to save energy in accordance with their location information. Furthermore, the location of sensors can help the sensor application to determine where and when to diffuse data. The appropriate level of data fusion in a well-designed coverage domain not only improves the performance of traffic but also streamlines the data query process.

4.3.3.1 Minimum Energy Communication Network

Minimum energy communication network (MECN) uses low power GPS to establish and maintain a minimum energy network. This approach self-configures a minimum power topology which will have less numbers of nodes and require less power for transmission between any two nodes. MECN assumes a master-site as the information-sink and identifies a relay region for every node. The relay region consists of nodes in a surrounding area where transmitting through those nodes is more energy efficient than direct transmission. The network is dynamically adaptive for minimum power paths globally without considering all the nodes. This is performed using a localized search for each node considering its relay region. This method performs well in stationary nodes.

4.3.3.2 Small Minimum Energy Communication Network

Small minimum energy communication network (SMECN) is an energy efficient enhancement of MECN. In MECN, it is assumed that broadcasting is allowed, which is not possible every time. In SMECN possible obstacles between any pair of nodes are considered.

However, the network is still assumed to be fully connected as in the case of MECN. The sub-network constructed by SMECN for minimum energy relaying is provably smaller (in terms of number of edges) than the one constructed in MECN if broadcasts are able to reach to all nodes in a circular region around the broadcaster. As a result, there are fewer hops per transmission and fewer maintenance costs of links. However, finding a sub-network with a smaller number of edges introduces more overhead in the algorithm.

4.3.3.3 Geographic Adaptive Fidelity

Geographic adaptive fidelity (GAF) is an energy-aware location-based routing algorithm. It conserves energy by turning off unnecessary nodes in the network without affecting the level of routing fidelity. It forms a virtual grid for the covered area. Each node uses its GPS-indicated location to associate itself with a point in the virtual grid. Nodes associated with the same point on the grid are considered equivalent in terms of the cost of packet routing. Such equivalence is exploited in keeping some nodes located in a particular grid area in sleeping state in order to save energy. Nodes change state from sleeping to active in turn so that the load is balanced. There are three states defined in GAF. These states are discovery, for determining the neighbors in the grid, active reflecting participation in routing, and sleep when the radio is turned off. The state transitions in GAF are depicted in Figure 4.16.

GAF can substantially increase the network lifetime as the number of nodes increases. This approach performs well in handling mobility, latency, and packet loss.

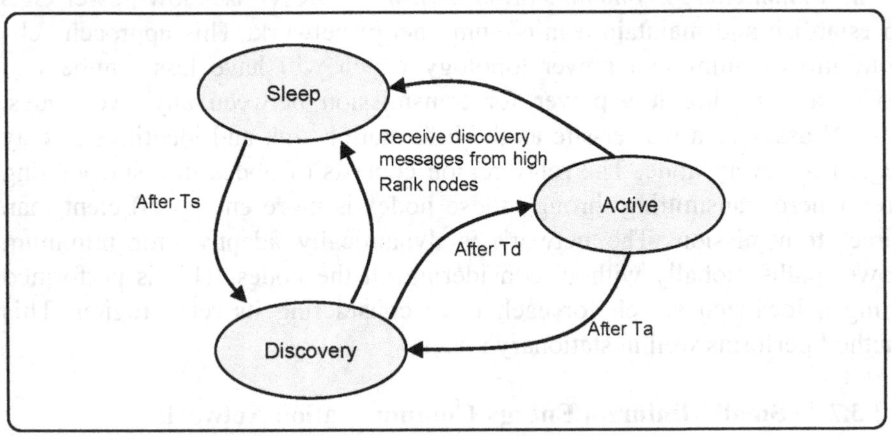

Figure 4.16. GAF.

4.3.3.4 Geographic and Energy Aware Routing

Geographic and energy aware routing (GEAR) uses energy aware and geographically informed neighbor selection heuristics to route a packet towards the target region. This method is the same as Directed Diffusion but restricts the number of interested nodes by region, rather than sending the interests to the whole network. GEAR compliments Directed Diffusion in this way and thus conserves more energy.

In GEAR, each node keeps an estimated cost and a learning cost of reaching the destination through its neighbors. The estimated cost is a combination of residual energy and distance to destination. The learned cost is a refinement of the estimated cost that accounts for routing around holes in the network. If all nodes have at least one closer neighbor to the target region, the estimated cost is equal to the learned cost. The learned cost is propagated one hop back every time a packet reaches the destination so that route setup for next packet will be adjusted.

4.3.4 QoS-Based Protocols

QoS-aware methods consider end-to-end delay requirements while setting up the paths in the sensor network. The considerations of a link performance include the energy level, traffic patterns, connectivity, and so forth. The end-to-end awareness may require more nodal level knowledge about its neighbor nodes and their relationships with the sink.

4.3.4.1 Maximum Lifetime Energy Routing

Maximum lifetime energy routing (MLER) intends to maximize the feasible time the network lasts. It measures link cost based on the network flow as a function of node remaining energy and the required transmission energy. The traffic distribution information assists the node to identify the least cost path whose residual energy is largest among all the paths. The absolute residual energy is calculated with *minimum transmitted energy (MTE)* algorithm. The Bellman-Ford shortest path algorithm is used to calculate the least link (path) cost to the sink. This approach can optimize the traffic distribution based on the existing network flow plus the relative residual energy that reflect the forecasted energy consumption rate.

4.3.4.2 Maximum Lifetime Data Gathering

Maximum lifetime data aggregation (MLDA) and *maximum lifetime data routing (MLDR)* intend to maximize data aggregation and lifetime data routing based on a polynomial time algorithm. The MLDR is used whenever the data aggregation is not possible and the network flow is a concern, e.g., steams from video sensors.

The data-gathering schedule specifies how to collect and route data to the sink. A schedule is represented as one tree for each round where the sink is the root and spans all the nodes. The number of rounds or periodic data readings from sensors without exhausting any single node is called the *lifetime* of the system. The ability to maximize the lifetime of the system depends upon the duration for which the schedule remains valid. The result of this method is a schedule plan called *optimal admissible flow network*. Both MLDA and MLDR are computationally expensive for very large sensor networks, thus a cluster-based enhancement can assist their scalability.

4.3.4.3 Minimum Cost Forwarding

Minimum cost forwarding (MCF) uses a back-off based algorithm to identify the minimum cost path in a large sensor network. This method is simple and scalable as it limits the number of messages exchanged. There are two phases in the protocol.

In the setup phase, the sink diffuses through the network for setting the cost value in all nodes. In the predetermined period, the nodes wait for the message with minimum cost to arrive. The cost function in the algorithm captures the effect of delay, throughput and energy consumption and identifies optimal cost of any node to the sink with only one message at each node.

As the result, this method does not require addressing or forwarding paths; next-hop states for the nodes can be eliminated.

In the data collection phase, the source broadcasts the event to its direct neighbors. The receiving nodes determine whether to forward or drop the event based on the transmission cost calculation. Data flows over the minimum cost path and the resources on the nodes are updated after each flow. Optimal forwarding can be achieved with a minimum number of advertisement messages.

4.3.4.4 Sequential Assignment Routing

Sequential assignment routing (SAR) is the first protocol in the sensor application with the notion of QoS in its routing decisions to achieve energy efficiency and fault tolerance. SAR uses trees to manage the paths from sink to sensors. Multiple table-driven trees are created where the root of each tree is a one-hop neighbor of the sink. Thus, SAR maintains multiple paths from nodes to sink. The information with respect to QoS, energy resource, and packet priority level are incorporated within the management trees in order to assist path selection. Path or node failure is recovered locally by enforcing routing table consistency between upstream and downstream nodes on each path automatically. SAR offers more effective power consumption than the typical minimum-energy metric algorithm because of the additional consideration of packet priority.

The advantages of fault-tolerance and easy recovery offset the overhead of maintaining the tables and states at each sensor node, especially when the number of nodes is huge.

4.3.4.5 Energy-Aware QoS Routing Protocol

Energy-Aware QoS Routing Protocol identifies a least cost and energy efficient path that meets certain end-to-end delay requirements. The link cost measurement is a function of nodal energy reserve, transmission energy, error rate and other communication parameters. Figure 4.17 depicts the class-based queuing model; it resides in all the router nodes to support both best effort and real-time traffic simultaneously.

A bandwidth ratio parameter with an initial value is used by the gateway to manage traffic flow. This parameter dictates the amount of bandwidth dedicated to the real-time and non-real-time traffic on an outbound link in case of congestion. Consequentially, the throughput for normal data cannot be influenced by this parameter. This protocol uses an extended version of *Dijkstra* algorithm to select a path from the candidate list which meets the end-to-end delay requirement.

The problem of the basic EAQR is lack of flexibility to adjust the ratio parameters for different links. An enhancement was made later to provide configurable parameter for each node in order to achieve a better utilization of the links.

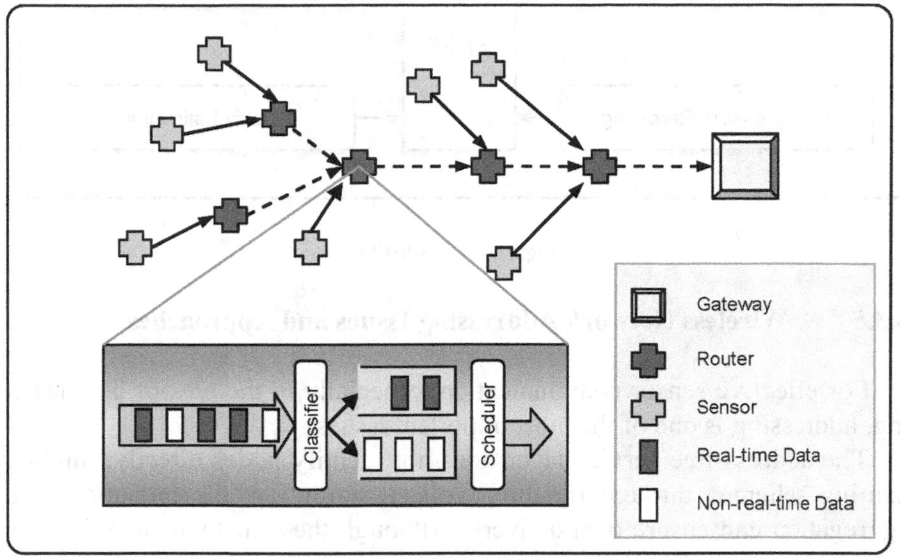

Figure 4.17. Queuing model in Energy-Aware QoS Routing Protocol.

4.3.4.6 SPEED

SPEED is a QoS routing protocol that provides soft real-time end-to-end guarantees. It intends to assure predicable end-to-end delay for the packets. The admission decision for routing is made with the consideration of the distance to the sink and the speed of the packet, called *stateless non-deterministic geographic forwarding (SNGF)*. This protocol requires each node to maintain information about its neighbors and uses geographic forwarding to find the paths. SNGF works with four other modules at the network layer, as shown in Figure 4.18. From the left upper corner, the Beacon Exchange module collects information about the nodes and their location. The backpressure-rerouting module is used to prevent the cases such as when a node fails to find a next hop node, or the congestion caused by the source node to receive back its messages. In either case the module will pursue new routes. The Neighborhood Feedback Loop module gathers the miss ratios from its neighbors to evaluate if the neighbors can in fact meet the desired speed. This measurement is provided to SNGF for the decision of whether the relay ratio is acceptable or the packet should be dropped. Delay estimation calculates the elapsed time based on the reception of an ACK from a neighbor. The delay values can assist the SNGF to select the node which meets the speed requirement. With such complexity, SPEED can provide congestion avoidance.

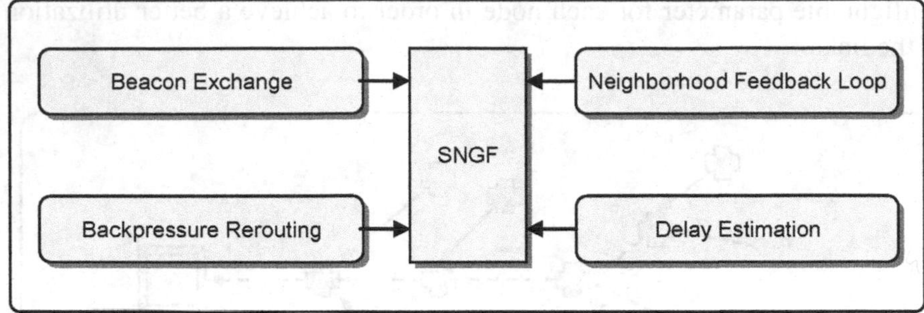

Figure 4.18. SPEED.

4.3.5 Wireless Network Addressing Issues and Approaches

For effective sensor communication, especially in the area of broadcasting, addressing is one of the most important issues.

The address-free service layer does not identify nodes directly; implicit naming schemes through flooding, collection routing, dissemination, and aggregation can ensure data delivery. Although these methods may include names to refer to data items, such as sequence numbers or dispatch identifiers, the actual routing occurs at the underlying protocols where basic topology (e.g., tree or direct neighboring) encapsulates this naming and hides it from applications [4].

The name-based service layer encompasses multi-hop communication based on destination identifiers. Both of the broadcast and dissemination protocols in this category rely on implicit naming provided by local connectivity. This includes approaches such as geographic routing, logical coordinate routing, as well as more abstract and flexible naming schemes such as directed diffusion, which use data identifiers. In most cases such functions rely on the underlying (e.g., MAC layers) support to provide an efficient local broadcast primitive [6].

Regardless of whether it is an address-free or name-based service, network addressing is a critical issue for effective network communication. In a cluster hierarchy, for instance, all member nodes plus the non-member one-hop neighbors of all member nodes in a cluster are deemed necessary to have distinct addresses. The scheme of dynamic addresses assignment requires the same addresses to be reused. Since the network has to remain operational, address assignment must acquire a valid address and tracks the topology changes in a near real time.

The transport layer identifications such as IP addressing utilize global unique addresses. However, the limited IP4 addresses and frequent disconnections and reconnections in an ad-hoc network presents a change of physical address identification. Allocating and keeping track of IP addresses can be a cumbersome task; furthermore, many addresses may be wasted as a result of network planning for mid- to large size sensor networks. When abstraction is needed for ease of application management, an external directory to map logical identity to physical address may be needed to manage the global addresses. Such an external directory will introduce dependence and centralization challenges in the areas of scalability and robustness [7,8].

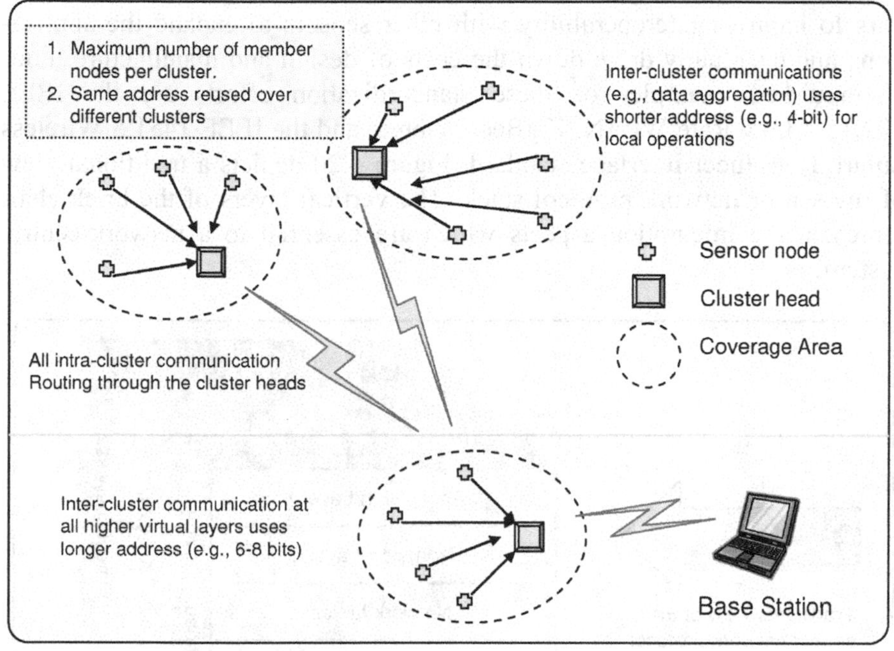

Figure 4.19. Sensor addressing in a cluster network.

The MAC layer may be a more effective alternate solution because a sensor network in essence requires only local unique addresses. It can be more feasible to achieve a self-contained directory in a self-organizing fashion with self-healing properties at the link layer. However, MAC addresses identify the target node at the hop level; its functionality is restricted to the node's direct neighbors. Random identifiers cannot serve the purpose of MAC addresses, as they do not guarantee the absence of collisions.

Alternatively, application attributes such as location can be used directly by the routing protocol instead of a network address. The reason is that common attributes can be encoded in only a few bits. This will be a great advantage to compact the packet payload.

Careful spatial reuse greatly reduces the number of distinct addresses, which can therefore represented by a smaller number of bits. As shown in

Figure 4.19, the payload for a message should have a network address for intra-cluster, inter-cluster, and next-hop communications.

4.4 Wireless Sensor Network Standards

The special features of wireless sensor networks rest on their low cost and distribution in large numbers. Standardization can assist different vendors to improve interoperability with other sensors to expand the applications and eventually drive down the costs of design and manufacture. Four distinguished examples of these standardization efforts are the IEEE 802.15.4 Low Rate WPAN, ZigBee, Wibree, and the IEEE 1451.5 Wireless Smart Transducer Interface standard. Figure 4.20 depicts a traditional view of the sensor network protocol stack. The vertical layers of the brick chart represent the integration aspects which are essential to a network-centric system.

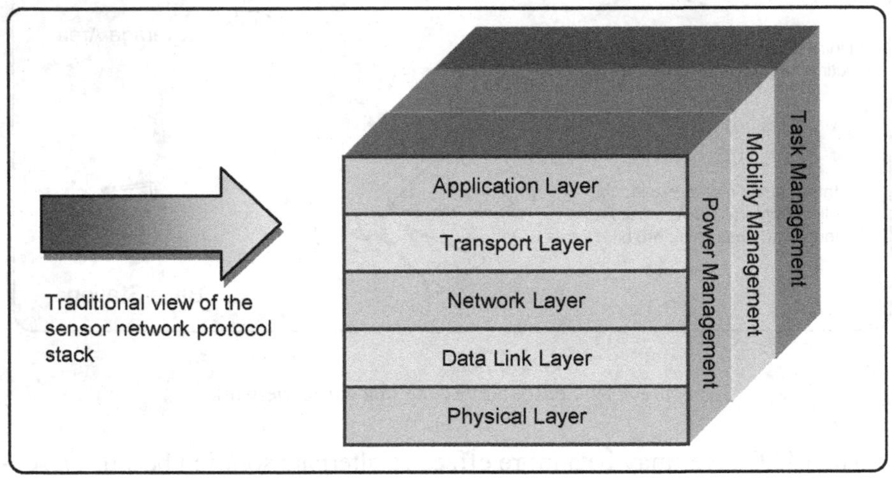

Figure 4.20. Sensor network and service layers.

4.4.1 The IEEE 802.15.4 Low-Rate WPAN

The IEEE 802.15.4 standard specifies the *physical (PHY)* and MAC layers at the *industrial, scientific and medical (ISM)* bands for low power, low data, high density, and with fixed or moving devices in the *personal operating space (POS)* of 10 m. The purpose of the specification is to provide ultra low complexity, ultra low cost, ultra low power consumption and low data rate wireless connectivity among inexpensive devices. The raw data rate will be high enough to satisfy a set of simple needs such as interactive toys, but scaleable down to the needs of sensor and automation needs for wireless communications. The protocol hierarchy of the standard is portrayed in Figure 4.21 [9].

The IEEE 802.15.4 standard supports both star and peer-to-peer connections, and is therefore able to support a wide variety of network topologies and routing algorithms. These applications vary from those requiring high data throughput and relatively low message latency, such as wireless keyboards, mice, and joysticks, to those requiring very low throughput and able to tolerate significant message latency, such as intelligent agriculture and environmental sensing applications. When security is used, the AES-128 security suite is required.

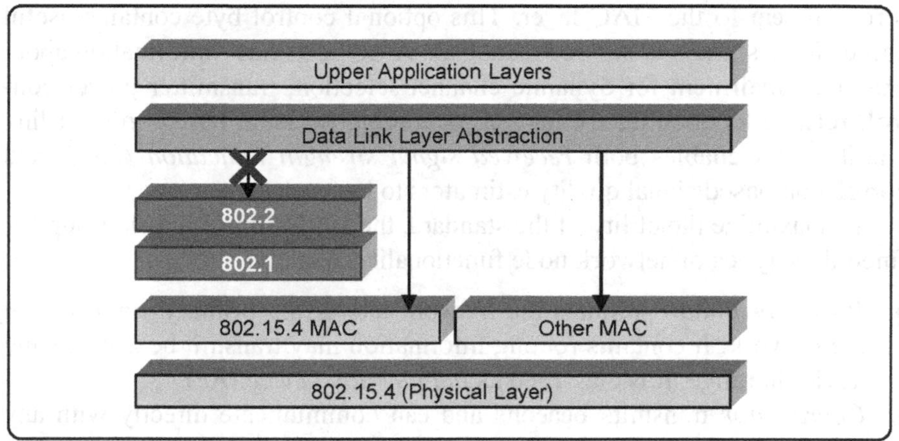

Figure 4.21. IEEE 802.15.4.

The air interface is *Direct Sequence Spread Spectrum (DSSS)* using *binary phase shift keying (BPSK)* for 868.0–868.6 MHz (for Europe) and 902–928MHz (for much of the Americas and the Pacific Rim), and *offset quadrature phase shift keying (O-QPSK)* with half-sine pulse shaping for 2.400–2.485 GHz (substantially worldwide).

At the MAC layer, *CSMA mechanism with Collision Avoidance (CSMA-CA)* provides reliable communications between a node and its immediate neighbors. It also supports beacons and synchronization to improve communications efficiency. The beacon is followed by a *contention access period (CAP)* and thus allows optimum trade-off between message latency and network node power consumption for each application. A "battery life extension" mode is also available that limits the CAP to a fixed time of approximately 2 ms. The IEEE 802.15.4 MAC handles network association and disassociation, has an optional super-frame structure with beacons for time synchronization, and a *guaranteed time slot (GTS)* mechanism for high priority communications. The IEEE 802.15.4 standard uses long beacon periods and the battery life extension mode for power management, additionally the active period of a beaconing node can be reduced (by powers of two), allowing the node to sleep between beacons. The MAC layer also manages packing data into frames prior to transmission, and then unpacking received packets and checking them for errors.

The PHY includes receiver *energy detection (ED)*, *link quality indication (LQI)* and *clear channel assessment (CCA)*. Both contention-based and contention-free channel access methods are supported. The standard has a both 16-bit address field as well as with 64-bit extended addresses. Message transmission can be optionally acknowledged for reliable communication.

A LQI byte is attached to each received frame by the physical layer before it is sent to the MAC layer. This optional control byte contains useful values for designers or service managers. A LQI can carry information about channel impairment for dynamic channel selection, transmitter power control, relative location determination, or routing decision based only on link quality. This enables both *received signal strength indication (RSSI)* and correlation-based signal quality estimators to be used.

To maximize the utility of the standard, the IEEE 802.15.4 task group defined three types of network node functionality, namely:

- *PAN coordinator* initiates the network and is the primary controller of the network. It contains routing information may transmit beacons to any device in range. It is classified as *full function device (FFD)*.
- *Coordinator* transmits beacons and can communicate directly with any device in range. It may become a PAN coordinator if it should start a new network. It is also classified as a FFD.
- *Device* does not transmit beacon and can directly communicate only with a coordinator or PAN coordinator. It is classified as *reduced function device (RFD)*. It must be as inexpensive to produce as possible, is likely to be battery-powered, and has very limited functional requirements, needing to communicate only with a FFD.

In the star network, the master device is the PAN coordinator (an FFD), and the other network nodes may either FFDs or RFDs. In the peer-to-peer network, FFDs are used, one of which is the PAN coordinator. RFDs may be used in a peer-to-peer network, but they can only communicate with a single FFD belonging to the network, and so do not have true "peer-to-peer" communication.

4.4.2 ZigBee

Because the IEEE 802.15.4 does not standardize the network, transport, and application layers, ZigBee Alliance was formed to assure interoperability between devices operating the IEEE 802.15.4 standard. In addition to the creation of higher layer specifications, the ZigBee Alliance is also the marketing and compliance arm of IEEE 802.15.4 – similar to the relationship between the Wi-Fi Alliance and the IEEE 802.11 WLAN standard [10].

ZigBee defines the network (NWK), security, and application layers upon the IEEE 802.15.4 PHY and MAC layers, and also provides interoperability and conformance testing specifications. Table 4.2 compares Zigbee wireless technologies with Wi-Fi and Bluetooth technologies. ZigBee standard provides the following features:

- Providing low power consumption thus can be last for month or years. Unlike Bluetooth, ZigBee has only active or sleep states for transmission and reception, this simplify the implementation of power management.
- Allowing for inherent configuration and redundancy, thus offers low device cost, low installation cost, and low maintenance.
- Allowing high density of nodes per network, a critical benefit for massive sensor arrays and control networks.
- Offering simple protocol, about 1/4th of Bluetooth's or 802.11's, advantages on cost, interoperability, and maintenance.

Table 4.2. Comparison of Wireless Technologies.

	Wi-Fi	Bluetooth	ZigBee
Frequency bands	2.4 GHz	2.4 GHz	2.4 GHz 868/915 MHz
Stack size	~1 Mb	~1 Mb	~20 kb
Raw data rate	11 Mbps	1 Mbps	250 kbps (2.4 GHz), 40 kbps (915 MHz), 20 kbps (868 MHz)
Number of channels	11–14	79	16(2.4 GHz),10(915 MHz), 1(868 MHz)
Data types	Digital	Digital, audio	Digital, key-value pairs
Inter-node range	100 m	10—100 m	10—100 m
Number of devices	32	8	255/65535
Power requirement	Medium-hours on one battery	Medium-days on one battery	Very low-years on one battery
Current market penetration	High	Medium	None
Architecture	Star	Star	Star, tree, cluster
Best applications	Internet inside building	Computer and phone peripherals	Low-cost control and monitoring

Table 4.2 compares ZigBee protocol with Wi-Fi and Bluetooth. Note that these three protocols are very similar in architecture but target different implementation and application considerations.

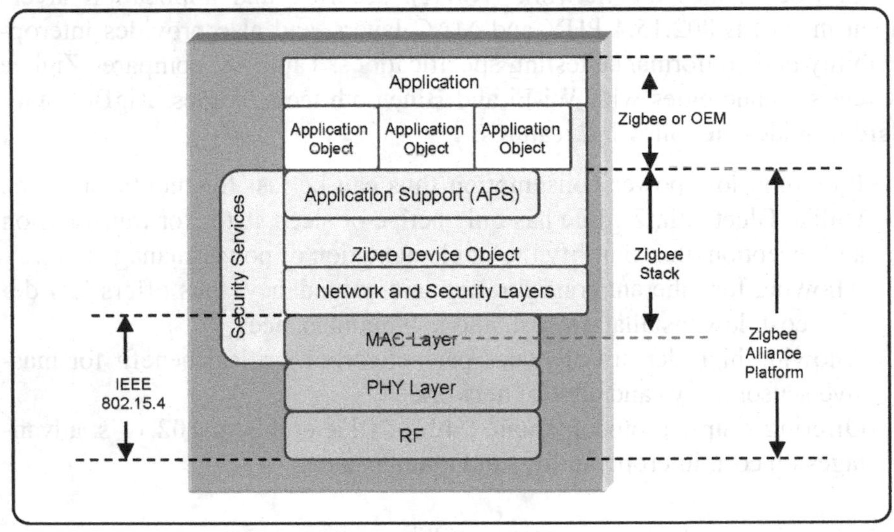

Figure 4.22. Zigbee layers.

Figure 4.22 illustrates four Zigbee related layers upon the IEEE 802.15.4.

The Zigbee network layer handles network configuration, neighboring device discovery, routing map building, routing and multi-hop capability, and supports three networking topologies: Star, mesh (peer-to-peer) and cluster-tree (hybrid star/mesh), as showed in Figure 4.23. Zigbee-enabled products will be based on physical (full function device and reduced function device), logical (coordinator, router and end device) and application (application profile) device types. PAN coordinator uses the NWK layer to start a new network and assign network addresses to new devices when they join the network for the first time. Perhaps the most straightforward way to think of the ZigBee routing algorithm is as a hierarchical routing strategy with table-driven optimizations applied where possible.

ZigBee Device Object (ZDO) is responsible for overall device management as well as security keys and policies. The ZDO is like a special application object and resides on all ZigBee nodes. ZDO has its own profile called *ZigBee Device Profile (ZDP)*; it contains the services for device discovery, etc. and serves as an access points to the upper applications. As shown in the figure, ZigBee application may add an application object to a ZigBee stack by direct call to the ZDO or through the *application support layer (APS)* in order to access other ZigBee devices on the network or services such as binding, security, or network settings. The ZDO dictates the security policies and configurations implemented by the security services. Applications should negotiate with the ZDO to specify the security settings required for the ZigBee stack.

The APS routes messages on the network to the different application end points running on the node. This includes maintaining the binding tables and forwarding messages between bound devices. Another responsibility of the APS is discovery, which is to identify the role of the device within the network (e.g., ZigBee coordinator or end device). APS initiates and/or responds to binding requests and establishing a secure relationship between network devices.

The Security Services are about providing security services for establishing and exchanging security keys, and using these keys to secure the communications. At the MAC layer, ZigBee uses the *Advanced Encryption Standard (AES)* as its core cryptographic algorithm for single-hop security processing. For multi-hop message transmission, ZigBee relies upon upper layers (as shown in Figure 4.22, NWK, ZDO, or APS layers) to set up the keys, determine the security levels to use, and control the security processing.

The Applications Object is a software component or an application building block at an end point, which achieves what the device is designed to do.

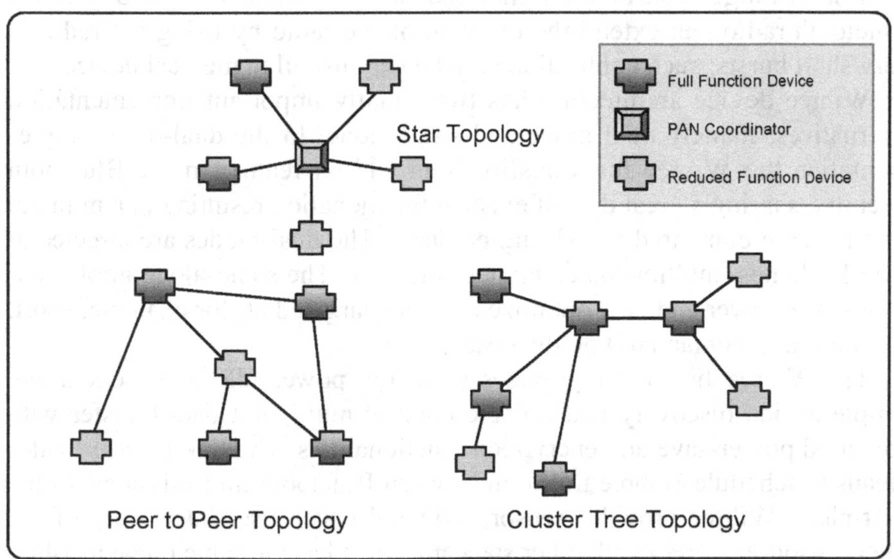

Figure 4.23. Possible Zigbee network topology configurations.

4.4.3 Nokia Wibree

Wibree is the first open technology offering connectivity between mobile devices or Personal Computers, and small, button cell battery power devices such as watches, wireless keyboards, toys and sports sensors. Its radio technology enables smaller and less costly implementations and being easy to integrate with Bluetooth solutions. It can be used in conventional mobile phones as well as emerging wireless markets, such as watches. It is perceived as a complement to Bluetooth [11–13].

CSR, Broadcom, Epson, Nokia, and Nordic Semiconductor jointly announced the specification will be used to transmit data at 1-megabit rates across short distances of up to 10 m, and that it will use about a tenth the power of Bluetooth. Wibree operates in 2.4 GHz ISM band with physical layer bit rate of 1 Mbps and provides link distance of 5–10 m. It is the first wireless technology to solve the following needs in a single solution:

- Ultra low peak, average, and idle mode power consumption
- Ultra low cost and small size for accessories and *human interface devices (HID)*
- Minimal cost and size addition to mobile phones and PCs
- Global, intuitive and secure multi-vendor interoperability

When smart-home-applications were factored in – using a mobile phone as a short-range control for lights and other devices. A hybrid Wibree/ Bluetooth radio can extend the duration of the radio by using the radio in very short bursts; such applications can be very useful in medical devices.

Wibree device architecture has two equally important implementation alternatives, namely dual mode and stand-alone. In the dual-mode implementation the Wibree functionality is an add-on feature inside Bluetooth circuitry, sharing a great deal of existing functionality, resulting in a minimal cost increase compared to existing products. The dual modes are targeted at mobile phones, multimedia computers and PCs. The stand-alone implementations are power and cost optimized designs targeted at, for example, sport, wellness, and human HID product categories.

The Wibree link layer provides ultra low power idle mode operation, simple device discovery and reliable point-to-multipoint data transfer with advanced power-save and encryption functionalities. The link layer provides means to schedule Wibree traffic in between Bluetooth transmissions. In the first phase Wibree provides sensor, HID and watch user interface profiles. There is some overlap with other standards, as it has the same range as Bluetooth, and is ultra-low power like ZigBee in devices powered by small batteries that have to last a long time, such as wireless mice and keyboards. Wibree is for more sporadic transmission of small amounts of data.

4.4.4 THE IEEE 1451.5 Wireless Transducer Interface Standard

The development of IEEE 1451 "*smart sensors*" is developed by the IEEE and the *National Institute of Standards and Technology*, a division of the U.S. Department of Commerce, to address the issue of transducer compatibility. This suite of interface defines a smart transducer interface which provides a unified communication protocol for a smart transducer interface [14,15].

IEEE 1451.2 defines a standard *transducer electronic data sheet (TEDS)* to facilitate the use of smart sensors by standardizing the interface between the sensors and the *network capable application processor (NCAP)*. Figure 4.24 depicts the relationships of NCAP, TEDS, and the *smart transducer interface module (STIM)*. NCAP is the protocol-handling processor between the sensor and the network. TEDS provides the transducers a means to delineate themselves (e.g., parameters associated with the transducer) to measurement systems, control systems, and any device on the network. IEEE 1451.3 specifies the protocols and architectures associated with a distributed multi-drop transducer bus via a single NCAP. IEEE 1451.4 adds analog transducers to the existing digital signaling interface.

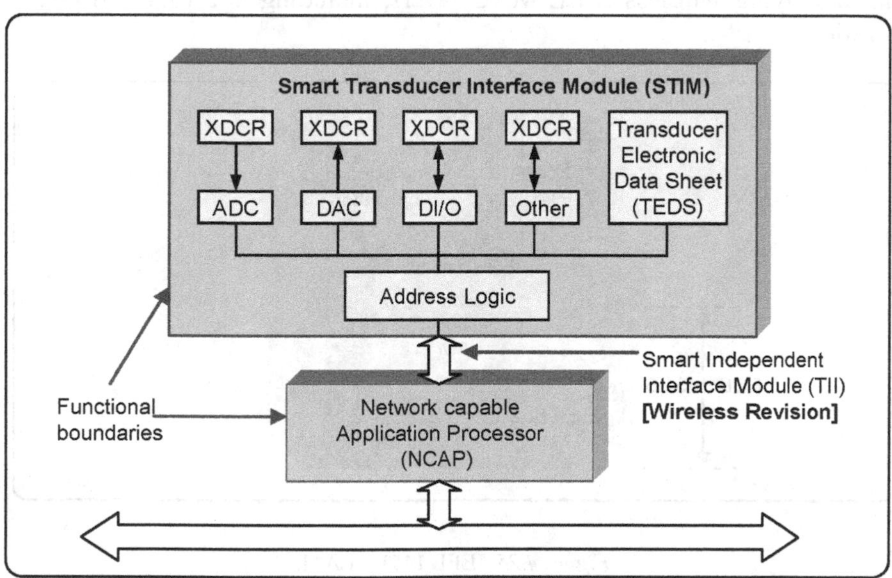

Figure 4.24. IEEE 1451 specifications.

The goal of IEEE 1451.5 is to provide reliable wireless communications between STIMs and NCAP to replace the existing *transducer independent interface (TII)* for wireless networks. The specification includes auto-configuration, session management, data transfer, and reliable multicasting and/or broadcasting. The following table (Table 4.3) summarizes the difference between TII and IEEE 1451.5.

Table 4.3. Difference between TII and P1451.5.

	Transducer Indep. Interface	Wireless Interface (P1451.5)
Association (NCAP-to-STIM)	One-to-one (physical)	One-to-many (logical)
Addressing (in module level)	No	Yes
Channel reliability	High	Low
Power supply	Mains powered	Battery powered
Transmission mechanism	Bit level	Packet level
Sleeping mode	No	Yes
Bandwidth	No constrain	Limited

As shown in Figure 4.25, the scope of IEEE 1451.5 is to define the *link adaptation and management (LAM)* Layer between the application layer and the underlying wireless IEEE MAC layers, including 802.15.4 and 802.11 families.

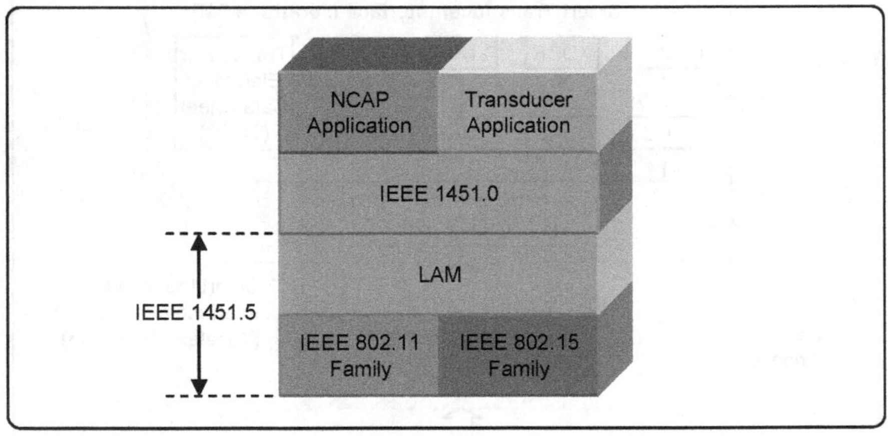

Figure 4.25. IEEE 1451.5 LAM.

Supporting “plug and play” configuration of the network the LAM management services include NCAP Startup, STIM Startup and Addressing, Service Discovery, STIM Disassociation/Detach, STIM Orphan, Unexpected STIM Detach, and Dynamic Channel Adaptation.

The LAM data service has four major areas, they are:

- *Data Transmission Mechanism*: Star topology network with centralized control at the coordinator. The *superframe* structure supports both contention-based and contention-free medium access, with Beacon based channel synchronization mechanism.
- *Application Functions Supported*: From P1451.2 standard, it covers functional Addressing and channel Addressing, data Transport to the STIM, global or channel triggering, Interrupts (masks, status registers), STIM or channel control, and optional functionality such as self-calibration. From P1451.3, standard, it supports multiple STIMs.
- *Data Scheduling*: *packet pending queue (PPQ)* for NCAP to send data to more than seven STIMs. Differentiated Services to three priority level (high, medium, and low). Data Aggregation to consolidate packets from NCAP to the same STIM.
- *Reliable Broadcasting/Multicasting*: NCAP sending global triggers, controls and commands to all/multiple STIMs. NCAP sending reprogramming files to all/multiple STIMs.

In comparison of LAM and ZigBee, IEEE 1451.5 supports multiple MAC (e.g., IEEE 802.11 and 802.15.4), reliable end-to-end transmission, reliable broadcast/multicast support, data aggregation, differentiated service, and sleeping mode that are lacking in ZigBee.

4.5 SoS Views of Wireless Sensor Networks

One novel aspect of the network-centric sensor network solution is the concept of cross-layer services. The services cut across layers or arise within multiple layers providing different "service elements" to support on-demand queries from different enterprise applications. Instead of being fully encapsulated at one layer, only visible to the layers above and below, this cross-layer operational environment is accessible to all the layers in the solution. To accomplish this business goal, many technologies and methods are required in order to formulate a seamless computing and management framework. Figure 4.26 demonstrates a high level functionalities and hierarchy of an enterprise-grade sensor application.

In this section, the SoS functionalities required for supporting sophisticated sensor networking are addressed. Bear in mind, not all the subjects covered in the section are necessary. The enterprise should carefully exam in the pros and cons of the delineated methodologies and chose the most appropriate ones sufficient for their implementations.

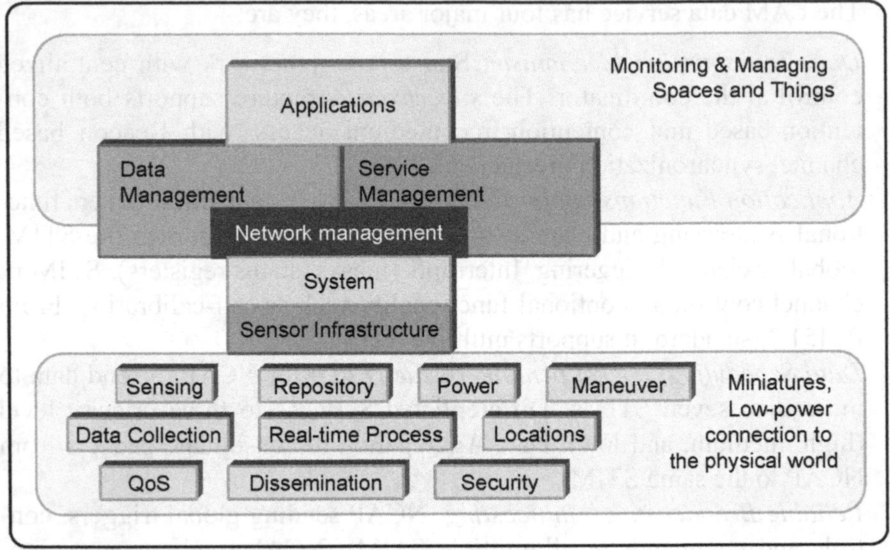

Figure 4.26. High level functionalities and hierarchy of sensor application.

4.5.1 Power Management

As stated in the earlier section, radio hardware in sensor nodes usually have limited bandwidth, memory, and processing capabilities; the placement of sensor nodes into a monitored area so that the full coverage is achieved with minimal energy consumption is critical to success of the enterprise's business operations. System designer should consider energy consumption from other sources such as computation or mobility requirements in addition to the known source from a wireless interface communication [16]. Energy efficiency can also be improved in the software or protocols such as MAC, routing, topology management protocols, and in-network processing. It is where network-centric concepts can assist the collaboration between sensor service attributes such as higher tolerance to latency, low sampling rates, and shorter the transmit distance to recognize the power efficiency. Figure 4.27 depicts the operational concept of sensor energy management, where the sensor node switches between wake and dormant states depending upon the application needs [17].

4.5.1.1 Node Level Power Management

Power conservation can be managed at local level. The power consumption level can be affected by operational configurations such as transmission frequency, node activation cycle, data polling, data sampling frequency, transmission range, and node mobility [18]. The energy efficiencies in hardware can be determined at microcontroller, radio, signal processing, sensors, and power supply [19].

At the communication protocol level, the power management is possible by adjusting the duty cycles of nodes in accordance with the changing workload. The duty-cycling between active and low power modes for the purpose of performance/power scaling as the power consumption of low power mode is negligible. For instance, the contention based MAC protocols require the neighboring nodes periodically exchange their listen schedules through a signaling channel to coordinate listen/sleep cycles. The TDMA based MAC protocols posses natural idle times built into their schedules thus they do not have to keep the radio on to detect contention and avoid collisions.

A more sophisticated method such as dynamic voltage scaling, the radio can learn the energy profile at run time, adapt the power consumption level, and fine-tune the power scaling behavior for better battery efficiency., Prediction filters (e.g., *Exponentially Weighted Moving Average* or *EWMA*) can be added in a stable monitoring environment to predict the energy availability in the near future.

4.5.1.2 Network Level Power Management

The network level power management concerns how the network as a whole can be power managed to address the spatial variations.

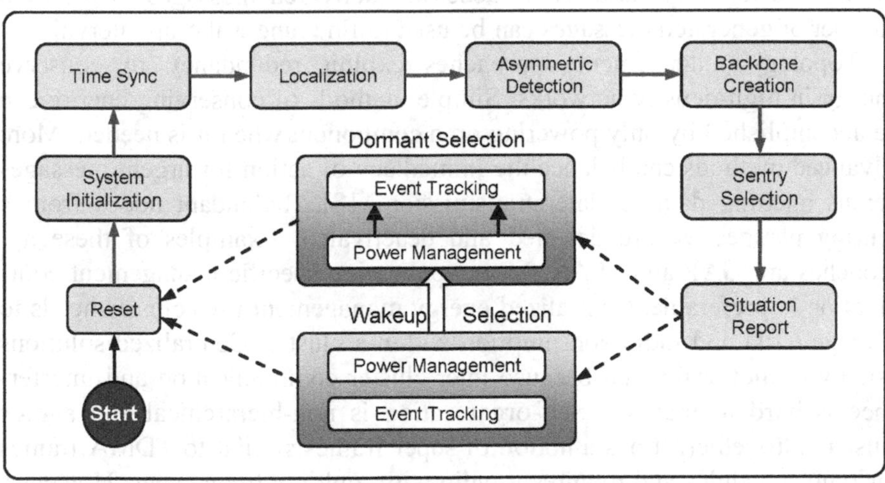

Figure 4.27. Sensor application concept of operations.

Because the energy cost of the radio's idle mode differs little from the receive mode the radio must actually be turned off. The sensor network must coordinate the sleep schedules of different nodes and maintain sufficient QoS such as end-to-end communication delays. To save energy while discovering contacts, a radio has three power management modes: *search*, *contact*, and *dormant* modes. In the search mode, the radio wakes up periodically to discover a contact. This period is called a *wake-up interval*. In the contact mode, the radio stays awake to exchange messages with other nodes that it previously discovered in the search mode. In the dormant mode, the radio is not used and remains asleep, as shown in Figure 4.27.

It is assumed that contacts must be discovered by one or both radios of the nodes. To discover contacts, a radio broadcasts messages called beacons periodically. To conserve power, a node can opt to use only one long-range radio with periodical sleeps and wakes while discovering contacts. A more complex and effective option is to use multiple radios or radio channels for power management, where low-power radios with more frequent wake-up interval are for discovering contacts, and high-power radios are for data exchanges. If a low-power radio detects a contact, it wakes up the high-power radio, which then enters the contact mode. Meanwhile the low-power radio continues to search for other contacts. The high-power radio can also be awaked by the application messages from other high-power radio directly; it stays awake until the beacons indicate that the contact is ended. The indication can be derived by not receiving a certain number of beacons consecutively from the source node. In this case, the high-power radio returns to the dormant mode. Metrics such as normalized energy consumption across a subnet and delivery ratio from successful delivered messages to the total number of generated messages can be used to fine tune wake-up interval.

Topology management approaches exploit redundancy to conserve energy in high-density networks. Simple methods of conserving energy can be accomplished by only powering on a component when it is needed. More advanced methods can balance the immediacy of action for urgent messages versus queuing data for later transmission [18]. Redundant nodes from a routing perspective are detected and deactivated. Examples of these approaches are GAF and SPAN. More application specific management coordination is preferable. Centralized energy management uses cluster-heads to manage CPU and radio consumption within a cluster. Centralized solutions usually do not scale well because inter-cluster communication and interference is hard to manage. Self-organization is non-hierarchical and avoids clusters altogether. It has a notion of super frames similar to TDMA frames for time schedules and requires a radio with multiple frequencies. However, it assumes a stationary network and generates static schedules [19]. Energy aware routing protocols typically use battery energy based routing cost metrics. The objective is to choose data routes appropriately such that the routing load is distributed uniformly across the network to leverage the total battery resource for maximizing lifetime. The routing cost metrics must not be limited to solely residual battery level to select the best routes; potential battery level prediction is also an important factor to the decision.

All of the power management approaches need some form of time synchronization to schedule communication. Nodes have synchronized clocks from a source such as GPS to synchronize the beacon windows for common and discrete intervals. In the case where fine resolutions or the global clock federation is not necessary, a simpler local synchronization protocol can also be satisfactory.

4.5.2 Auto- and Self-Configuration

For efficiency consideration at large deployment sites, most of the wireless ad-hoc networks are expected to be self-configurating. Self-configuration refers to two aspects, one is during the first construction of the network, the self-configuration network is supposed to be forming the network itself. The other aspect is when one host moves in or moves out the wireless ad-hoc networks, the network should have the ability to reconfigure the topology of the whole network. Although many works have been done on this topic, a satisfied answer is still lacking because the question is never tackled in systematic way.

A wireless sensor network deployment can be large, complex, heterogeneous, and dynamic. The sensor application globally aggregates large numbers of independent computing and communication resources and this may require the capability to let the sensor nodes to manage themselves with minimum human intervention. This makes a need to create self-configuring network protocols to form network topologies, routing, media access, and beacon systems. In sensor networks, nodes may be participating in many self-configuring tasks at different network layers. Self-configuration is enabled through dynamic discovery and composition of new components and component reconfiguration at run time.

Achieving autonomic self-managing behaviors requires programming and middleware support for context and self-awareness, knowledge and context based analysis and planning, and plan selection and execution [20,21]. NCBO supports wireless sensor networks with a generic framework with self-configurable applications where a large number of sensors coordinate among themselves to achieve a large sensing task. Auto- and self-configuration can occur in two phases of the sensor application life cycles, one is at the deployment phase and the other is at the reorganization phase.

- *Deployment phase*: At the ad-hoc type wireless network, sensors can be deployed incrementally. The sensor node with radio would normally go through four states. They are: 1) Initialization state to deploy some starting points or anchors of the network for other following nodes; 2) Selection state to form a common map of the environment according to data from the deployed sensors; 3) Assignment state to identify the follow-up and available nodes; and 4) Execution state to activate the follow-up deployment of nodes to their target locations [22].

- *Reorganization phase*: After node deployment, the sensor network may require reorganization in cases when a node/link fails, a network partition occurs, or a node rediscovery occurs. In a node/link failure, the routing table in the affected node needs to be updated, and broadcast of a tree/graph may be required. Group partition is caused by failure or disconnection of some crucial nodes, which forces the network to reorganize itself into new groups. Node rediscovery typically happens when nodes are coming back from sleep mode (see power management) and find new topology relationships with their neighboring nodes. Any of the above events can be managed by the following sequential sub-phases: 1) each node independently discovers its set of neighbors; 2) nodes aggregate themselves into groups, self-assign location-based address, compute routing tables, and construct broadcast tables/graphs; 3) handshaking messages are exchanged among nodes to ensure routing and broadcast information is up-to-dated; and 4) a node or nodes detect group partitions or node failures and update their routing table based on the new topology. This may include reorganize subgroups or join with new groups. In either case, group reorganization is required to balance the network hierarchy [21].

At the application level, the design of a localization system is largely influenced by application requirements. Node localization can leverage having a few nodes at known *positions* (also known as *beacons*) and compute the relative positions with other nodes or form a completely independent coordinate system. The beacon periodically transmits a packet containing its unique ID and position. These beacons constitute the underlying infrastructure of the localization system. The system can be either "tightly coupled" where beacons that are wired to a centralized controller and placed at fixed positions or "loosely coupled" where beacons that are wireless and coordinate in a scalable, decentralized manner. Such a localization system must autonomously measure and adapt its properties to environmental conditions in order to achieve ad-hoc deployment and robust, unattended operation in any environment.

Auto- and self-configuration is an essential feature to reduce human engagement in sensor deployment and maintenance. In addition to the configuration feature, the enterprise can also consider additional features such as Self-optimization, Self-healing, and Self-protection to add values to the exiting resources. Self-optimization is based on dynamic switching of workflows and components using composition rules, balancing of workload and resource utilization, and definition of component interaction patterns. Self-healing is about restarting or replacing failed components. Self-protection can preventing the loss of data or tasks or services by reactions defined to defend the system integrity from undesired operations of malicious agents.

4.5.3 Time Synchronization

A strong link now may become weakening later because of changes on environmental condition, e.g., new obstacles, unanticipated interferers, and other factors. Such impact causes the network to react to the external factors that impact the time synchronization can be concluded into the following major reasons: RF interference, changes in the physical environment that block communication links, loss of individual nodes, and prescheduled sleep/wake cycle for power management. From the functional perspective, interferences can come from the changes of temperature, phase noise such as access fluctuations, frequency noise due to the unstable clock crystal, asymmetric delays between the outgoing and the return paths, and clock glitches caused by hardware or software anomalies. All of the above reasons can cause major time synchronization challenges [23–25].

A general time synchronization scheme requires synchronization messages to be exchanged to obtain multiple pairs of corresponding time instants. Either a receiver-receiver approach or a sender-receiver approach can be used in the synchronization protocol. In intra-cluster communication, the members only need to synchronize with the root node.

- *Reference-broadcast synchronization (RBS)* is a receiver–receiver synchronization scheme to provide instantaneous synchronization among a set of receivers that are within the reference broadcast of the transmitter. A node sends beacons to its neighbors using physical-layer broadcast. The recipients use the arrival time of the broadcast as a reference point to compare their times. Least square linear regression is used to estimate the clock skew and phase offset. RBS achieves significantly better precision than traditional synchronization protocol because the nondeterministic roundtrip delay is removed from the critical path. However, this protocol may suffer from the uncertainties of the overlapping transmission and reception times and the accuracy in multi-broadcast domains or large scale ad-hoc network deployment [26].
- Network time protocol *(NTP)* is used to provide network-wide synchronization among networked nodes in the Internet. However, the sensor nodes may loss the accuracy when power management and topology maintenance protocols (e.g., SPAN and LEACH) are employed. Temporary disjunction of node due to mobility or other environmental reasons can also cause undisciplined clocks. Additionally, the accuracy of NTP

for round-trip communications is designed in the order of milliseconds time while the MAC layer of the radio stack can introduce several hundreds of milliseconds delay at each hop. Thus NTP is suitable only for low precision demands.

- *Timing-sync protocol for sensor networks (TPSN)* performs sender-receiver time-stamps synchronization at the MAC layer. It eliminates errors caused by access time and propagation delay via two way message exchange. However, it does not estimate the clock skew of the nodes. A revised TPSN is based on similar methodology as the NTP, where the sensor nodes are organized into multiple levels and synchronized to the root node of the hierarchy. Similar to the problem in NTP, nodes at different levels responsible for synchronization may fail or disrupt. Similar to RBS, this protocol can also suffer from the uncertainties of the overlapping transmission and reception times.
- Time-diffusion synchronization protocol *(TDP)* provides network-wide time synchronization within a certain tolerance. The tolerance levels can be adjustable in accordance with time differences among the sensor nodes before protocols requiring time-stamps. This protocol enables applications to coordinate sensor nodes, for instance, the sink to detect the time difference between multiple sources so the temporal differences can be adjusted. In addition, it allows the sink to issue a start time to the sensor nodes allowing interactive sensing and monitoring for better target tracking, data fusion, and decision fusion. This is especially beneficial for better performance when multiple sources are sending data back to the sink through flooding or directed diffusion [17].
- *Flooding time synchronization protocol (FTSP)* is designed to improve the time accuracy in MAC layer at the network level. FTSP provides multi-hop synchronization by synchronizing the time of a sender to multiple receivers with a single radio message time-stamped at both the sender and the receiver sides. Linear regression is used in FTSP to compensate for clock drift. FTSP maintains the global time in a single, dynamically elected root node; all other nodes synchronize their clocks to that of the root. This ad-hoc tree is robust against node and link failures and dynamic topology changes. A problem of this centralized synchronization method is its single point of failure and the complexity of root node reelection.
- Unlike TDMA's time synchronization where all nodes must share a common sense of time so that they know precisely when to talk, listen, or sleep. *Time synchronized mesh protocol (TSMP)* nodes maintain a sense of time and exchange offset information with neighbors to ensure alignment. These offset values ride along in standard ACK messages and cost no extra power or overhead. TSMP slice the wireless media across time

or frequency. This provides robust fault tolerance in the face of common RF interferers as well as providing a tremendous increase in effective bandwidth.

4.5.4 Data Fusion

Elementary information or measurements reside in different collection nodes and need to be collected and collaborated in sensible and understandable forms. Data fusion combines information from different sources into a single data set for further data mining. The applications of data fusion can include autopilot of aircrafts, self-steering gear for ships, dynamic positioning for ship sailing, inertial guidance for missiles and aircraft, radar tracking (track is determined by comparing the new measurements with history), navigation system, *simultaneous localization and mapping (SLAM)* for robots to build a map within an unknown environment, econometrics applications, and so forth. The following subsections profile some popular data fusion mechanisms.

This section focuses on the level zero fusion which is the initial process at or near the sensor that organizes the collected data into usable information.

4.5.4.1 Data Association

The data association method is used at level one fusion. Its main application is to produce an estimate of a target's kinematics for localizing a target. Some example factors are position, velocity, and rate of acceleration for a target object. A fundamental challenge of data association is to decide which data should be selected. Two common techniques used to eliminate outliers are establishing a *figure of merit (FOM)* and gating. The distance between an established track for a target and a single data can be represented by the Mahalanobis distance, offering a normalized index by measurement and track error variances.

4.5.4.2 Kalman Filter

Kalman Filters is a sequential approach used for positional estimation at the level one fusion. It is an efficient recursive filter which predicts and matches the state of a dynamic system from a series of incomplete and noisy measurements in order to provide accurate continuously-updated information. Kalman filters are based on linear dynamical systems discretised in the time domain. They are modeled on a Markov chain built on linear operators perturbed by Gaussian noise. As discrete time increment, a linear operator mixes some noise and known control factors to the current state in order to generate the new state. Consequently, another linear operator mixed with more noise generates the visible outputs from the hidden state. This algorithm can remove noise from sensor signals to better estimate the smoothed values of position, velocity, and acceleration of an object given only a sequence of observations about its position. A wide range of engineering applications supported by Kalman Filter covers from radar, computer vision, and three-dimensional-map-making, to robot location.

4.5.4.3 Bayesian Decision Theory

Without a probabilistic means of fusing data, sensors are typically limited to a definitive answer such as yes and no. Revised probabilities called "posterior probabilities" can consolidate and interpret overlapping data to provide a greater measure of confidence by quantifying the uncertainty behind sensor decisions. *Bayesian decision* models theory [27] is a common technique at level two data fusion for guiding human decision-making. With this method, sensor data is weighted according to their known accuracy level, often inversely proportional to the variance of each sensor's response.

A Bayesian network is a form of probabilistic graphical model representing a set of variables with a joint probability distribution and explicit independence assumptions. Optimization based search method can be used to understand the structure of the network. This requires the techniques of a scoring function and a search strategy. A common scoring function is the posterior probability. A local search strategy makes incremental changes aimed at improving the score of the structure. A global search algorithm like Monte Carlo methods, delved into the next subsection, can avoid getting trapped in local minima.

4.5.4.4 Monte Carlo Methods

Monte Carlo samples (ensemble) estimates an approximate of the forecast means and variance/covariance of sensor data. It assesses the stability of computations due to the expected noise mechanisms present in the data. These are then used in the linear Kalman filter update formulas to obtain the analysis distribution.

A computer simulation generates data within the expected measurement distribution, passes through the algorithmic computation, and distributes of resulting values around their true values accumulated. The results can then be used to quantify the expected error distributions on the data. The advantage of such approaches is that examples of realistic images can be used as a starting point to define which features are likely to be present. An example of this technique would be in the assessment of feature detection.

One of the Monte Carlo methods is called Bootstrapping, a *sequential importance resampler (SIR)*. Bootstrapping is a statistical method for estimating the sampling distribution of an estimator by sampling with replacement from the original sample. It is used often in the purpose of deriving robust estimates of standard errors and confidence intervals of a population parameter like a mean, median, proportion, odds ratio, correlation coefficient or regression coefficient. It is a rather popular alternative to provide complicated formulas for the calculation of standard errors.

4.5.4.5 Dempster–Shafer Evidential Reasoning

Dempster–Shafer evidential reasoning (DSER) is a generalization of the Bayesian theory of subjective probability which produces superior results in working with data uncertainty. The Dempster–Shafer theory is a mathematical theory of evidence based on belief functions and plausible reasoning to calculate the probability of an event. Dempster–Shafer theory obtains degrees of belief for one question from subjective probabilities for a related question, and Dempster's rule for combining such degrees of belief when they are based on independent items of evidence. The degree of belief in a proposition depends primarily upon the number of answers (to the related questions) containing the proposition, and the subjective probability of each answer. Also contributing are the rules of combination that reflect general assumptions about the data. In this formalism a degree of belief (also referred to as a mass) is represented as a belief function rather than a Bayesian probability distribution. Probability values are assigned to sets of possibilities rather than single events: their appeal rests on the fact they naturally encode evidence in favor of propositions.

4.5.5 Sensor Database

Uncertain data and streams of data are two main data characteristics of a sensor network. This is because a sensor network can have a large number of nodes, no global knowledge about the network, node failure and interference is common, and the data can be transmitted across multiple hops before arriving at the destination node. To accommodate the nature of such data, the existing database techniques may not be fully applicable. The design consideration of a sensor database starts from the appropriate representation of sensor data and sensor queries. The trade-off of executing the query fragments locally on sensor nodes or distributing the query fragments over a changing network needs to be carefully measured. The database management system should also consider the deployment and management of a sensor database system where the sensors may not be available all the time due to link failures and other environmental conditions. Two popular sensor database architectures are illustrated below.

4.5.5.1 Warehousing Data Repository

The warehouse approach is the traditional method of collecting all events into a central repository, as shown in Figure 4.28. Applications can invoke database queries against the central data location for all the information. The query processing takes place on the server side.

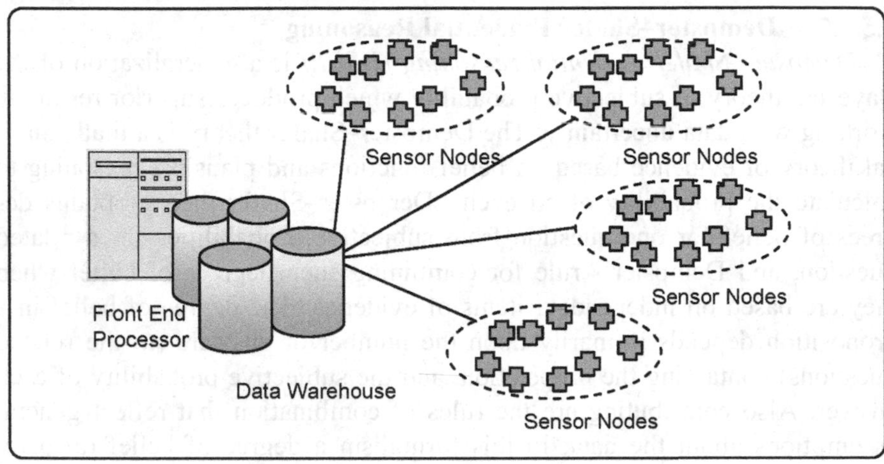

Figure 4.28. Data warehousing.

4.5.5.2 Sensor Database System

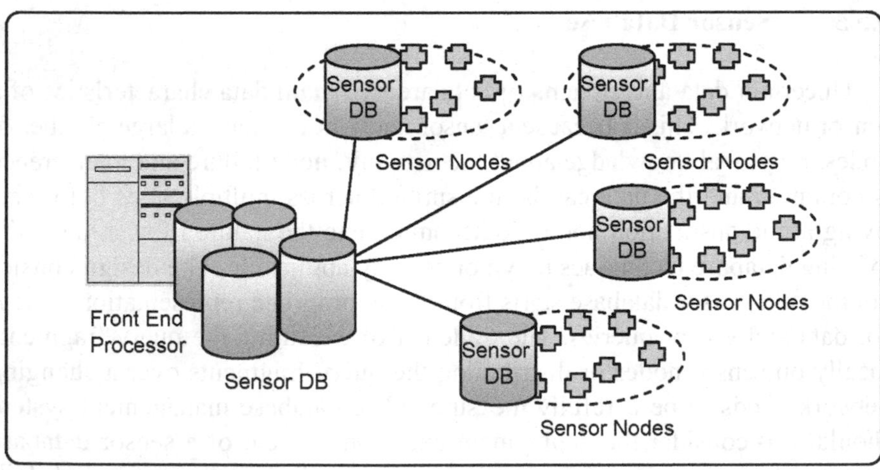

Figure 4.29. Sensor data source, event, and sink.

Figure 4.29 depicts the sensor database system that supports distributed query processing over sensor network. Every node has its own set of data and can be shared among the networked nodes. The Front End node coordinates queries specified by the application missions and exercises individual queries against a node, group of nodes, or the entire network of nodes.

4.6 Conclusion

NCBO enables the use of sensors to generate and leverage information supplied in many family, commercial, or military environments. In this context, sensors are growing in significance as they provide sensed inputs to assemble a better understanding of managed fields or even to support a *common operating picture (COP)* in critical business or military missions. The increasing incidence of asymmetric situations in modern operations is leading to the growing importance of ground- and air-based surveillance. The development of sensor systems that provide network-friendly solutions is expected to fuel the growth of the *intelligence, surveillance, target acquisition, and reconnaissance (ISTAR)* markets whether in commercial or defense segments.

A fundamental challenge with data collection, processing, and dissemination is the task of deciding which technologies should be combined into the SoS solution. Several data communication protocols have been devised by the researchers to assure the transport networking with the balance of energy and QoS considerations. To facilitate better integration, four industry standards are discussed including IEEE and vender-driven specifications.

Even though the sensor applications are situated at the bottom level of the NCBO system architecture as depicted in Figure 4.1, it does not prevent the sensor applications from being deployed at the Business Application layer and directly interacting with the end-users or customers. In fact, the need for such systems exists in many applications involving tasks in which timely fusion and delivery of heterogeneous information streams is of critical importance, e.g., remote Web-based building monitoring. It is for the sake of the service hierarchy that the additional layers are needed to emphasize the value of the service-oriented enterprise. Section 4.5 addresses many functional subjects which are generic for an integrated sensor network.

Chapter 5

BUILDING A WIRELESS TRANSPORT SERVICE

The key features of the next generation wireless transport services that distinguish them from the traditional distributed environment are mobility, network awareness, situation reactivity, community autonomy, self-learning, service intelligence, temporal continuity, and management flexibility. An effective transport fulfillment must be able to support both strategic and tactical requirements in a dynamic environment and cover both the access domain as well as the core network whether these networks are infrastructure or infrastructure-less. Successful fulfillment can only be achieved through careful planning which lays down in an organized and structured approach to ensure the deployed services are in functional consistency.

From an operational perspective, instantiation of a service plan is also part of the fulfillment process, which includes initializing service parameters and service models, as well as establishing a service inventory database for operational management. Once the service parameters and models are created, configured, and initiated, an instance of the planned service is created. The network service instance will then be functioning according to the activation schedule.

This chapter outlines the service requirements, transport service functionality, and deployment considerations sufficient to support a general understanding of design criteria and implementation guidelines for IP based wireless network services. The QoS and the IA subsections provide basic pictures of the key enterprise service functions and will be expanded fully in the later chapters.

In the telecommunication industry, the fulfillment process requires close integration of many peer level *Operation Support Systems (OSS)*. On the other hand, military applications typically separate network planning into high-level planning and detailed planning according to the echelon hierarchy and mission organization. In the interest of supporting NCBO, both scenarios will be briefly discussed in the SoS approach section.

5.1 Overview

Transport service management is to execute a set of functions required for controlling, planning, allocating, deploying, coordinating, and monitoring network resources. Building a wireless transport service requires the service providers to investigate options based on the business drivers, budget allocations, available technologies, and time tables for the services.

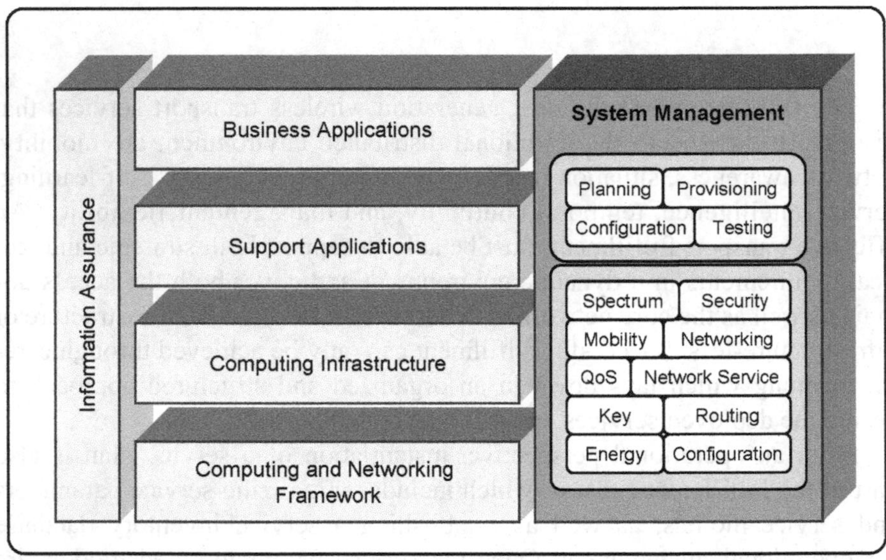

Figure 5.1. System architecture of enterprise services.

A transport service can be categorized based on attributes such as ownership, usage, and technology. Ownership may be private or public. Usage based is influenced by a combination of physical transmission characteristics and enterprise usage such as fixed wireless, movable wireless, or wire-line communication. When deploying in geographically separated areas, it is further broken down into WAN, MAN, LAN, and PAM (see section 3.1.2).

As shown in Figure 5.1, the network management function of a wireless transport service is situated at the System Management layer of the enterprise service system architecture which contains two functional groups. The upper functional group contains planning, provisioning, configuration, and testing. The bottom group categorizes the service requirements into frequency spectrum management, security, mobility, networking, quality of service, network service, key management, routing management, energy (or power) management, and service and network configuration.

As will be illustrated in the SoS Views section, there are other functional areas that are part of the enterprise's service management interacting with these shown functions to support seamless solution integration (e.g., sales). In a distributed computing environment, many of these systems, functions, or technologies are spread across different domains owned by various value-chain participants.

The main scope of this chapter is to lay down a preliminary set of technologies, processes, and systems by which the service providers can establish a network-centric and service-oriented management framework. Applications for wireless transport services vary depending upon the business segments, purposes of the deployment, and type of business the network will be serving, therefore they are not in the scope of this book.

5.1.1 Wireless Transport Services

Ad-hoc networks (see section 3.3) have gained popularity in the fourth generation networks because of their independence of any existing infrastructure. However, lacking the standards to specify complete operational functions, methods, and protocols (e.g., auto-configuration of IP address and other network parameters) in a multi-hop packet forwarding environment has prevented this technology from accelerating into the commercial world with the similar wide installation base as the infrastructure-based networks. Nevertheless, the emerging technology has shown many successful footprints in different deployment scenarios; the following three configurations are generally seen in an enterprise environment.

1. Stand-alone ad-hoc network which is not connected to any external network.
2. Ad-hoc network at the edge of infrastructured network through gateways. The gateways may be either fixed or mobile, single or multiple.
3. Ad-hoc network occasionally connects to an infrastructured network.

In cases two and three, at any moment of time the ad-hoc network may merge with other into a single ad-hoc network or be partitioned into several sub-networks.

Within an ad-hoc network, connectivity can use mesh or non-mesh architecture. In earlier mesh networks, one dedicated node was providing both backhaul and client services. An enhancement to this architecture allowed this node to relay messages over multiple hops while another provided client access; this significantly improved backhaul bandwidth and latency. A more effective architecture uses multiple nodes for the backhaul to achieve higher bandwidth and low latency; hence, it is more satisfactory for demanding applications such as voice and video where messages have to be over many hops.

The general rules for networking requirements include the consideration of supporting *connectivity*, *services*, and *applications*. In a hybrid networking environment, the wireless network connectivity and gateway operations have to incorporate all environment resources, whether it is intra-domain or inter-domain, to support the seamless flow of information.

Figure 5.2 portrays a sample multi-layer hybrid network service. The physical and data link layers considerations include different connectivity technologies covering waveform software, link, and inter- or intra-network protocols. The link and network layers include the adaptive routing and delivery of message traffic within a single domain or across multiple domain scenarios. The session manager focuses on the QoS and interaction of customer communication sessions. The applications support services layer provides some basic service primitives allowing the service operators to construct sophisticated composite services. Such flexibility can realize dynamic data

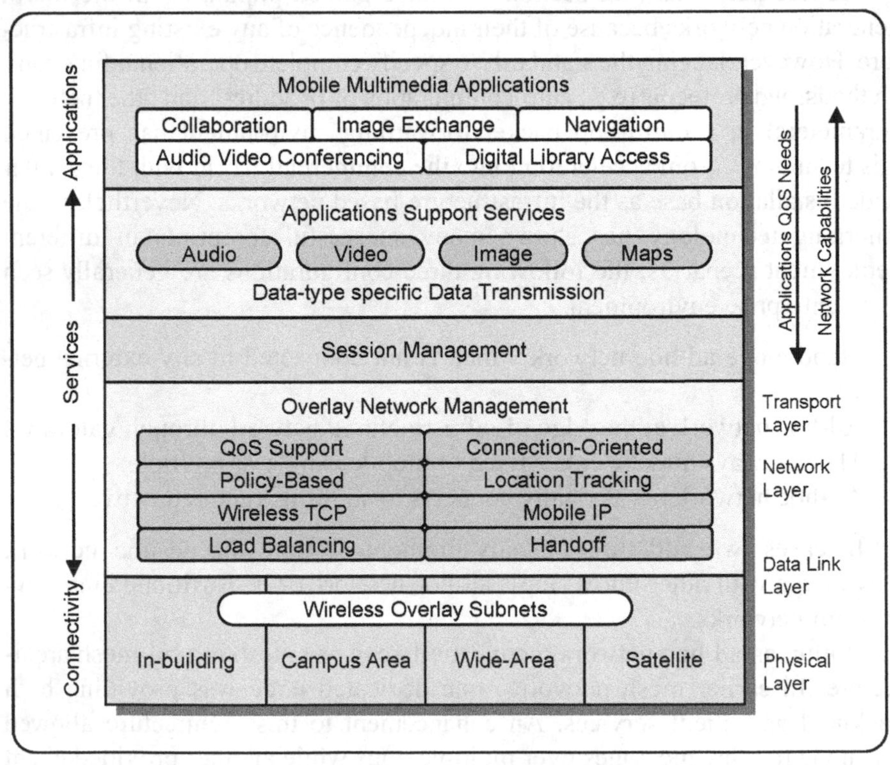

Figure 5.2. Multi-layer hybrid services.

federation and distributed queries in a virtual compartment. The top level applications can include collaboration, image exchange, navigation, audio video conferencing, and digital library access [1].

From the business perspective, service requirements are to construct an efficient transport framework for open access and control. In a service-oriented framework, the providers should provide a service infrastructure so that their customers can configure and reconfigure the service usage in real time or near real time. To accomplish this feature, the infrastructure has to build upon an open architecture with high degree of data transparency (more discussions in chapter 8) where the service related data sources are available for the controlling customers through open control interfaces.

5.2 Network Service Functionalities

In the following sections, the TCP/IP protocols and their associated standards are addressed to support the transport services as well the higher layers applications.

5.2.1 Common Functions

Technology evolutions has introduced new elements and features to the enterprise and impacted the transport management. However, with the layer model it is expected that the impacts can be minimized. The following subsections profile some core functions for the enterprise transport services, its consequent sections will address the management aspect of these functions.

5.2.1.1 TCP Protocols

TCP is the most predominant transport layer protocol in the data communication industry. Its reliability, end-to-end congestion control mechanism, byte-stream transport mechanism, and simple design have made TCP an influencing protocol in the design of many protocols and applications. Section 3.4 has highlighted main features of TCP protocol. This section is extended to address the functionalities of some variations specific for ad-hoc networks.

- *TCP Feedback (TCP-F)* uses a feedback-based approach thus requires the support from reliable link layer and a routing protocol to provide feedback to the TCP sender about path breaks. *Route failure nodes (RFN)* and *route reestablished notification (RRN)* are used in the intermediate nodes to provide feedback. TCP-F was designed to minimize frequent path breaks and does not need to invoke congestion control when links fail. Its disadvantages include potential synchronization problem of the congestion window during path state changes and the mistreatment of BER with congestion [2].

- *TCP Explicit Link Failure Notification (TCP-ELFN)* is similar to TCP-F and can manage path break with link failure notification without using congestion control, however, is less dependent on the routing protocol. Except when a sender receives an *explicit link failure notification (ELFN)*, it periodically sends probe packets to detect the route reestablishment. Its disadvantages include the congestion window may not catch up with the link state changes, mistreatment of BER, and path failure can last longer when the network is temporarily partitioned [3].
- *TCP with buffering and sequence information (TCP-BuS)* is similar to the TCP-F and TCP-ELFN in using feedback information from an intermediate node on detection of a path break. TCP-BuS takes advantage of the underlying routing protocols, especially the on-demand routing protocols such as *associativity based routing (ABR)* to identify partial paths and localize query for queuing. It extends *retransmission timeout (RTO)* time to allow path reestablishment and avoid fast retransmission. *Explicit route disconnection notification (ERDN)* and *explicit route successful notification (ERSN)* are used to manage path breaks. Its disadvantages include the increased dependency on the routing protocol (compared to TCP-F and TCP-ELFN) and the buffering at the intermediate nodes, thus it may be more vulnerable on the end-to-end performance. Using ERDN and ERSN also introduces overheads to this protocol [4].
- *Ad-hoc Transport Control Protocol (ATCP)* acts as a transport layer between TCP and IP, and maintains the end-to-end semantics of TCP. It uses a network layer feedback mechanism from the intermediate nodes to make the sender aware of the status of the network path. ATCP uses *explicit congestion notification (ECN)* and *Internet control message protocol (ICMP)* to monitor the state of the network. By invoking congestion control only when needed, ATCP provides a feasible and efficient solution to improve throughput in ad-hoc wireless networks. Its disadvantages include the requirement of an implementation-dependent network layer protocol for detecting the route changes and partitions, additional ATCP layer on the TCP/IP protocol stack, and the modification in the standard interface [5].
- *Split-TCP* splits a long TCP connection into a set of short concatenated TCP segments to enhance the throughput and throughput fairness, thus provides better resilience to impact of mobility. *Proxy* nodes are introduced as terminating points at these segments. *Local acknowledgment (LACK)* is used to confirm receiving. The buffering function in each segment enables dropped packets to be recovered from the most recent proxy. The rate control helps the congestion management on inter-proxy

segments. Combining the buffering and rate control enhances reliable packet delivery from end-to-end and thereby achieves better parallelism. Its disadvantages include the requirement to modify the TCP protocol (violating compatibility with the standard), the failure on a proxy node may lead to throughput degradation, and the overhead from the LACK between proxy nodes [6].

- *TCP-RENO* uses a closed-loop, end-to-end, and window-based congestion control. By doubling congestion window size on every RTT, TCP-RENO implements slow-start scheme to achieve equilibrium gradually but quickly; both sender and receiver maintain sliding windows for flow control. To avoid congestion, TCP-RENO uses *additive-increase-multiplicative-decrease (AIMD)* to adjust window size based on the receiving duplicate ACKs, time-out, or round-trip time to ensure fast recovery of the lost packet. Its advantage includes the independence of lower layers to generate messages. The disadvantage is its inefficiency to solve non-congestion-caused losses, thus can be counter-productive if not used correctly [7].
- *Ad-hoc Transport Protocol (ATP)* does not maintain any per-flow state at the intermediate nodes, instead, it collects congestion information directly from the nodes in a congestion situation. ATP's rate based transmission solves burstiness issues inherent in the traditional window-based transmission. The improvements to the standard protocol include better performance, decoupling of the congestion control and reliability mechanisms, and avoidance of congestion window fluctuations. The disadvantages of ATP are the lack of interoperability with standard TCP, thus the fine-grained per-flow timer may become a scalability bottleneck and the dependency on the notification and feedback from lower layers.

5.2.1.2 The Internet Protocol v4

Published in 1981, the *Internet protocol (IP)* version 4 [8] was defined for transmitting blocks of data called *datagrams*. The source and destination nodes of the IP communication are hosts identified by fixed length addresses. This protocol also specified the fragmentation and reassembly of long datagrams, if necessary, for transmission through packet networks.

IPv4 uses 32-bit addresses, many of which are reserved for special purposes such as local networks or multicast addresses, thus reducing the number of available (4.2 billion addressable) addresses for public Internet addresses. The IPv4 header is depicted in Figure 5.3.

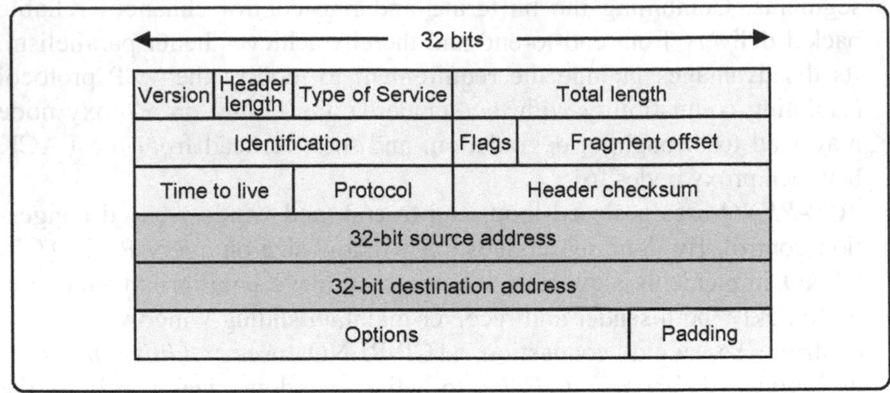

Figure 5.3. IPv4 header.

An 8 bits allocation called *type of service (ToS)* field in the IP header allows the sending host to specify preference (e.g., prefer low delay vs. high reliability) for how the datagram would be handled through an internetwork. These bits have been redefined by the DiffServ working group in the *Internet Engineering Task Force (IETF)* and the *explicit congestion notification (ECN)* codepoints (see section 7.3.3.2) [9]. New technologies such as v*oice over Internet protocol (VoIP)* requiring real-time data streaming for interactive data voice exchange; the ToS field is used to ensure the communication efficiency. The Message Prioritization is shown in Figure 5.4 where different messages sent by computers in the *service cluster* are prioritized by the *advanced scheduling* node and forward to the appropriate destinations with predefined orders.

Time to live (TTL) field is an 8-bit control byte. It helps prevent datagrams from persisting (e.g., going in circles) on an internetwork by putting an upper limit on the time (in seconds) or "hop count" that the datagrams can exist in an Internet system. The TTL field is set by the sender and reduced by every host on the route to its destination. If the TTL field reaches zero before arriving its destination, the datagram will be discarded, and an ICMP (section 5.2.1.5) error datagram will be sent back to the sender.

The *Protocol* field defines the protocol used in the data portion of the IP datagram which includes ICMP, TCP, and UDP.

IPv4 supports router nodes to determine if a packet is too long for the next link and to break the data into fragments if necessary. A standardized procedure at the destination host will reassemble the fragmented packets that arrive separately. This standard procedure includes recovery from loss and further fragmentation during the transmission.

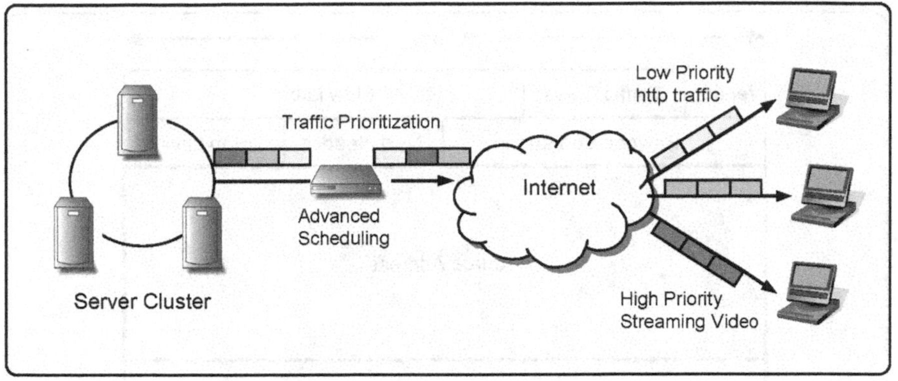

Figure 5.4. Message prioritization in IP protocol.

5.2.1.3 The Internet Protocol v6

The *Internet protocol (IP)* version 6 [10] is the second version of the IPv4. It was invented by Xerox PARC and adopted by the IETF in 1994. It was called "*IP next generation*" *(IPng)* during the period of standardization process. Incidentally, IPv5 was not a successor to IPv4, but an experimental flow-oriented streaming protocol intended to support video and audio. The new features in addition to IPv4 can be summarized as following [11]:

- Addresses in IPv6 are 128 bits long to avoid potential exhaustion of the IPv4 address space. IPv6 addresses this problem by supporting 340 undecillion addresses. The drawback of the large address size is its inefficiency in bandwidth usage. The header structure is illustrated in Figure 5.5.
- Supporting stateless auto-configuration of hosts; a host sends a link-local multicast (broadcast) request for its configuration parameters when it first connects to a network; the routers respond back with a router advertisement packet containing network layer configuration parameters. If IPv6 auto-configuration is not suitable, the host can either use stateful auto-configuration [12] or manual configuration.
- Multicast on the local link and across routers is part of the base protocol suite in IPv6. This is an optional feature in IPv4.
- Supporting payload packet size over the 64Kb limitation posted by IPv4. The "jumbo-grams" can improve communication performance over high-throughput networks.
- Using a simpler and more systematic header structure to improve the performance of routing.
- IPsec (section 5.2.3.1) is an integral part of the base protocol suite in IPv6.

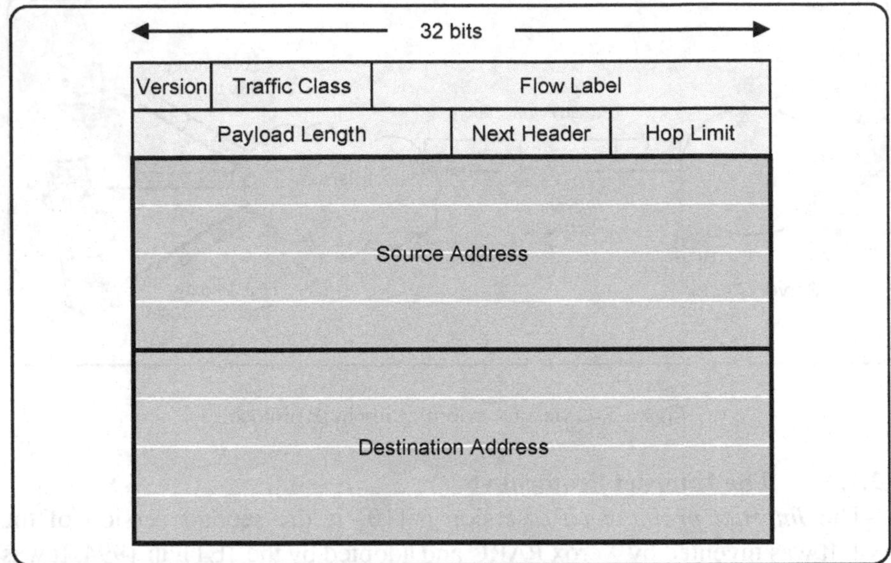

Figure 5.5. IPc6 header.

To reach an IPv6 Internet, the existing IPv4 infrastructure must be able to carry IPv6 packets. A technique known as *tunneling* encapsulates IPv6 packets and transmits them over the IPv4's link layer. *Automatic tunneling* refers to a technique where the tunnel endpoints are automatically determined by the routing infrastructure. *Configured tunneling* is a technique where the tunnel endpoints are configured explicitly. Figure 5.6 portrays the internetworking between IPv4 and IPv6 networks.

To integrate IPv6 and IPv4 nodes smoothly and seamlessly, the transition mechanisms can be categorized into the following four groups:

- *Dual-stack* or "*dual-stack IP layer solution* [13]" implements both the IPv4 and IPv6 protocol stacks in every node of the network.
- *6to4* is an IPv4 tunnel-based transition mechanism [14] which allows different IPv6 domains to communicate with other IPv6 domains through IPv4 clouds without explicit IPv4 tunnels. The only configuration is done on the host side. The server side can accept 6to4-encapsultated packets coming from any host.
- *4to6* allows different IPv4 domains to communicate with other IPv4 domains through IPv6 clouds [15].
- *6in4* encapsulates IPv6 packets into IPv4; it requires an explicit tunnel on both ends of the tunnel, at the host and at the server (6in4 router) sides [16].

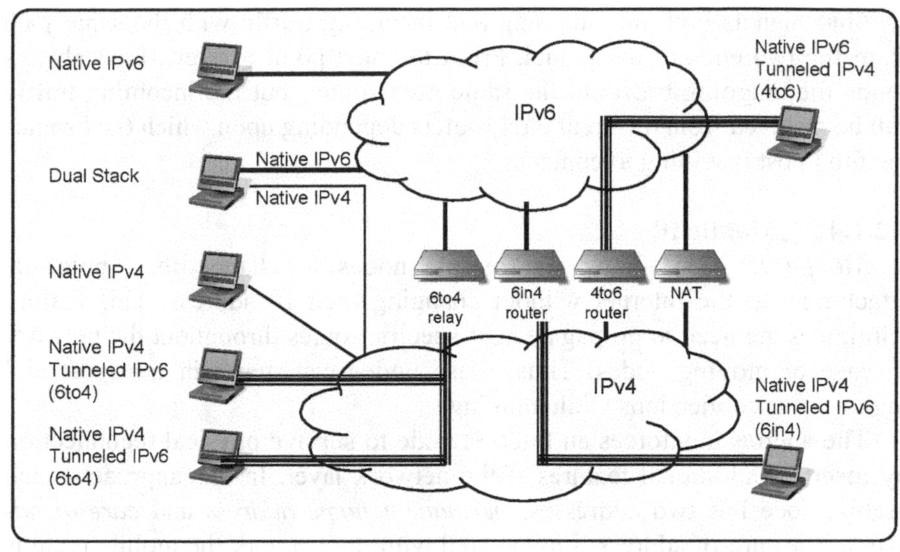

Figure 5.6. IPv4 and IPv6 integration.

IPv6 is most useful for mobility, QoS, privacy extension, and so forth. IPv6 is intended to address the concern of IPv4 address exhaustion. The introduction of *network address translation (NAT)* was intended to support direction translation between IPv4 nodes and IPv6 nodes. The translation can be stateful or stateless depending upon whether state information is kept or not. However, NAT makes it difficult or impossible to use some peer-to-peer applications, such as VoIP and online games.

Table 5.1 lists the core specifications of IPv6.

Table 5.1. IPv6 Core Specifications.

Standard Number	Description
RFC 2460	Internet Protocol, version 6 (IPv6) specification (obsoletes RFC 1883) [17]
RFC 2461/RFC 4311	Neighbor discovery for IP version 6 (IPv6) (4311 updates) [18,19]
RFC 2462	IPv6 stateless address auto configuration [20]
RFC 4443	Internet Control Message Protocol (ICMPv6) for the IPv6 Specification (obsoletes RFC 2463) [21]
RFC 2464	Transmission of IPv6 packets over Ethernet networks
RFC 4291	Internet Protocol version 6 (IPv6) addressing architecture (obsoletes RFC 3513) [22]
RFC 3041	MAC address use replacement option [23]
RFC 3587	An IPv6 Aggregatable Global Unicast Address Format [24]

6in4 tunnels both the outgoing and incoming traffic with the same path from the two ends of the tunnel. From the host point of view, 6to4 always sends the outgoing traffic to the same 6to4 router, but the incoming traffic can be received from different 6to4 routers depending upon which 6to4 router the 6to4 host is willing to contact.

5.2.1.4 Mobile IP

Mobile IP [25] allows the mobile nodes to change their point-of-attachment to the Internet without changing their IP address. This feature eliminates the need to propagate host-specific routes throughout the network in case of moving nodes. Thus, these nodes can maintain transport and higher-layer connections while moving.

The approach enforces an Internet node to survive physical reconnection by inserting additional features at the network layer. In this approach, each mobile node has two addresses: *permanent home address* and *care-of address*. The care-of address is associated with the network the mobile node is visiting. The mobile node is always addressable at its home address. A *home agent (HA)* stores information about the mobile nodes whose permanent home address is in the home agent's network. A *foreign agent (FA)* stores information about mobile nodes visiting its network and advertises care-of addresses [26].

When a node is ready to communicate with the mobile node, it uses the home address of the mobile node to send packets. These packets are intercepted by the home agent, which tunnels the packets to the mobile node's care-of address with a new IP header while the original IP header is preserved. The packets are de-capsulated at the end of the tunnel in order to remove the added IP header and delivered to the mobile node.

When acting as sender, the mobile node simply sends packets directly to the other communicating node through the foreign agent. The foreign agent could employ reverse tunneling by tunneling mobile node's packets to the home agent if needed. The home agent in turn forwards them to the communicating node.

The additional features to the standard IP protocol include the following:

- An authenticated registration procedure by which a mobile node informs its home agent of its care-of address.
- An extension to ICMP router discovery allowing mobile nodes to discover prospective home agents and foreign agents.
- The rules for routing packets to and from mobile nodes. This includes the specification of one mandatory and several optional tunneling mechanisms.

Enhancements to the mobile IP technique, such as Mobile IPv6 [27] and *hierarchical mobile IPv6 (HMIPv6)*, are to improve the security and efficiency of this approach in IPv4. In mobile IPv6, three operational entities are defined: *mobile node (MN)*, *correspondent node (CN)*, *home agent (HA)*. New destination options for IPv6 include: *binding update option*, *binding acknowledgement*, *binding request*, and *home address option*. The additions to the ICMP message for the *dynamic home agent address discovery* include a set of request and response messages. The advertisement interval option and home agent information option are added for the *neighbor discovery* [28].

5.2.1.5 Internet Control Message Protocol

Internet control message protocol (ICMP) [29] is an integrated part of the IP suite. It is used by the IP gateways or destination hosts in response to errors in IP datagrams processing [30]. This protocol is also capable of supporting connectivity diagnosis or assisting routing decision. ICMP messages are usually processed as a special case of IP instead of a normal sub-protocol of IP.

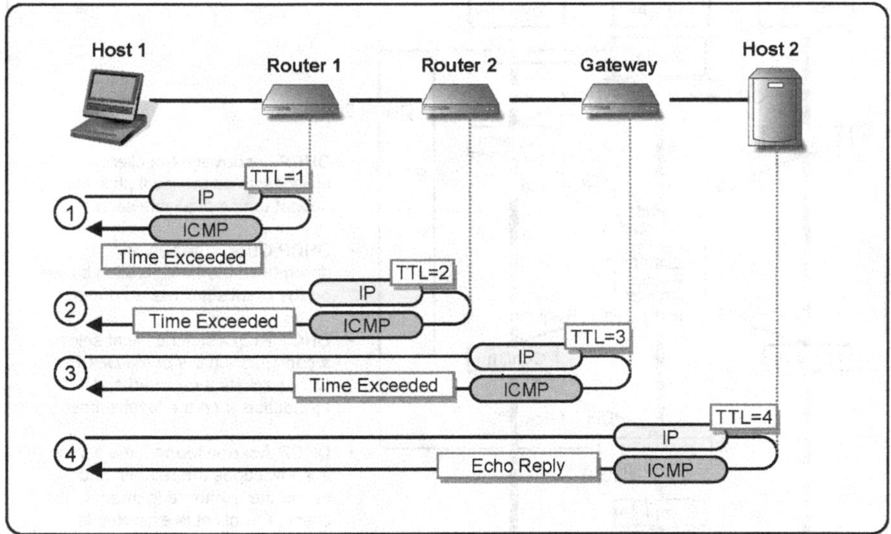

Figure 5.7. Traceroute command.

Commonly used network utilities such as *traceroute* (Figure 5.7) and *ping* are based on this protocol. The *traceroute* command transmits UDP datagrams with specially set IP TTL header fields; it looks for ICMP *Time to live* exceeded in transit or *destination unreachable* messages in response. The *ping* command sends ICMP Echo Request messages (and receives Echo Response messages) to determine if a host is reachable, and how long the packet takes to make a round-trip with that host [21].

5.2.2 Mobility

The mobility section addresses the standard protocol to support IP level configuration parameters that can satisfy mobility requirement.

5.2.2.1 The Dynamic Host Configuration Protocol

Dynamic host configuration protocol (DHCP) [12,31] is a client and server structure to provide configuration parameters to the Internet hosts. DHCP consists of a protocol set providing host-specific configuration parameters from a DHCP server to a host as well as the associated mechanism that allocates network addresses to a host. Figure 5.8 depicts the DHCP commands and the communication flow between two servers and a client. The DHCP protocol provides three methods of IP-address allocation:

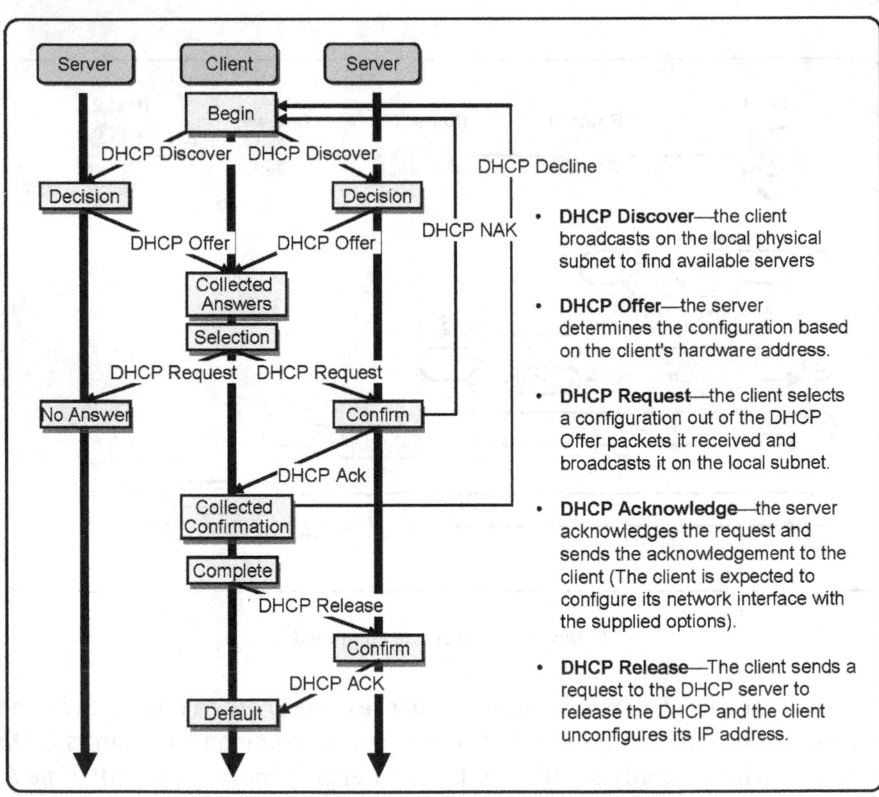

Figure 5.8. DHCP commands and flows.

- *Manual allocation*: The MAC and IP address pairs are manually entered into the DHCP server by the server administrator. Clients query the IP addresses by providing the requesting MAC addresses.
- *Automatic allocation*: The DHCP server permanently assigns the requesting client an IP-address from a range given by the administrator.
- *Dynamic allocation*: The network administrator assigns a range of IP addresses to the DHCP. The clients are configured to request IP addresses from the DHCP server when they start up. The request-and-grant process uses a lease concept within a controllable time period.

The Dynamic allocation approach eases network installation procedure on the client side considerably. By making use of the DNS update protocol [32], DHCP server can automatically update the DNS names associated with the client hosts to reflect new IP address.

5.2.3 Networking Functions

The networking functions include Internet Protocol Security, Internet Key Exchange, and Encapsulating Security Payload.

5.2.3.1 Internet Protocol Security

Internet protocol security (IPsec) [33] specifies the base security architecture for IPsec. IPsec is usually implemented in the kernel of the operating system and is accessible by both Web and non-Web applications (e.g., file sharing and backup).

IPsec is a set of network layer cryptographic protocols to ensure that computing nodes are communicating with a trusted entity and the protected traffic (e.g., password) will not be monitored or modified. It contains two portions:

- Securing packet flows: The *Encapsulating security payload (ESP*; section 5.3.3.3*)* provides authentication, confidentiality, and message integrity. The *authentication header (AH)* provides authentication and message integrity.
- Key exchange: The *Internet key exchange (IKE*; section 5.2.3.2*)* protocol.

IPsec support two security modes: the tunnel mode provides portal-to-portal security from a node to several machines, and the transport mode allows end-to-end security. Either mode can be used to construct a VPN, shown in Figure 5.9, where two security gateways connect two private networks in the tunnel mode, or the other two hosts are connected in the transport mode.

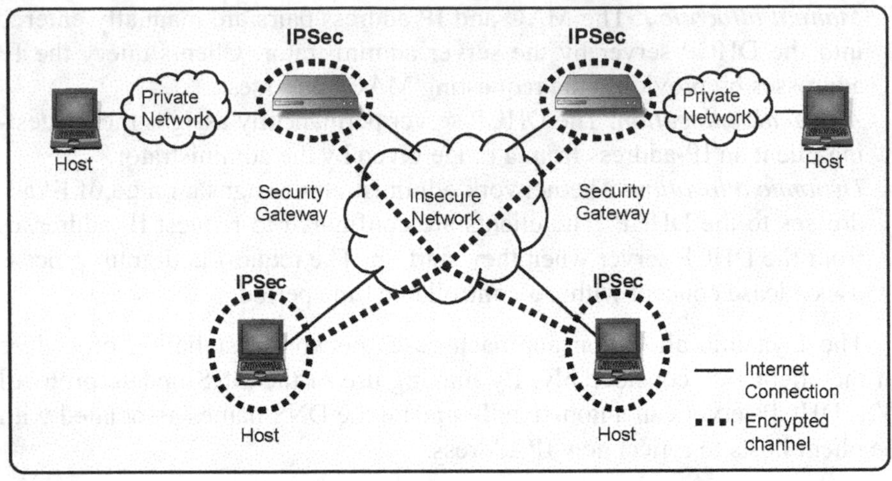

Figure 5.9. A virtual private network via tunnel mode.

5.2.3.2 Internet Key Exchange

Internet key exchange (IKE) [34] is defined for two communicating nodes to establish a *security association (SA)* that enables the applications to authenticate users, negotiate the encryption method, and exchange the secret key. IKE is derived from the ISAKMP framework for key exchange and uses the *Oakley* and *SKEME* key exchange techniques.

IKE uses public key cryptography to provide secure transmission of secret keys to the recipient so the encrypted data can be decrypted at the other end. The purpose of this feature is to mutually authenticate the communicating parties.

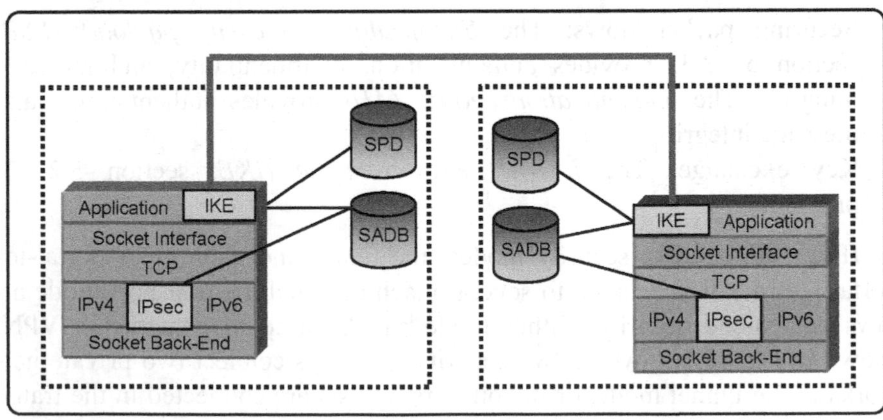

Figure 5.10. IKE in IPSec applications.

Figure 5.10 depicts the relationship of two communicating nodes using IKE. As shown, the embedded IKE generates keys and distributes them securely. IKE stores the keys in a *security association database (SADB)*. IPSec fetches the necessary keys from the SADB in the form of a *security association (SA)* when it needs to apply security to an IP packet. An SA contains the encryption keys, a specification of the IPSec protocols, and the lifetime of this SA.

The IKE daemons negotiate and setup SAs. The *security policy database (SPD)* is consulted on the initiating side to determine what SAs to establish. On the receiving side the SPD is consulted before accepting a proposed SA. The accepted SAs are then inserted into the SADB on each side respectively. Thereafter, the applications can communicate with the target systems using IPsec security.

5.2.3.3 Encapsulating Security Payload

Encapsulating security payload (ESP) [35] *extension header* provides origin authenticity, integrity, and confidentiality of an IP packet. The *authentication header (AH)* protects only intermediate devices changing the datagram. ESP encrypts the contents of a datagram to ensure only the intended recipient can see the data. It contains three components: *ESP header* in front of a protected datagram, *ESP trailer* follows the protected data, and *optional ESP authentication data field* provides authentication services similar to those provided by the AH. ESP may be applied alone, in combination with the IP AH, or in a nested fashion, for instance, through the use of tunnel

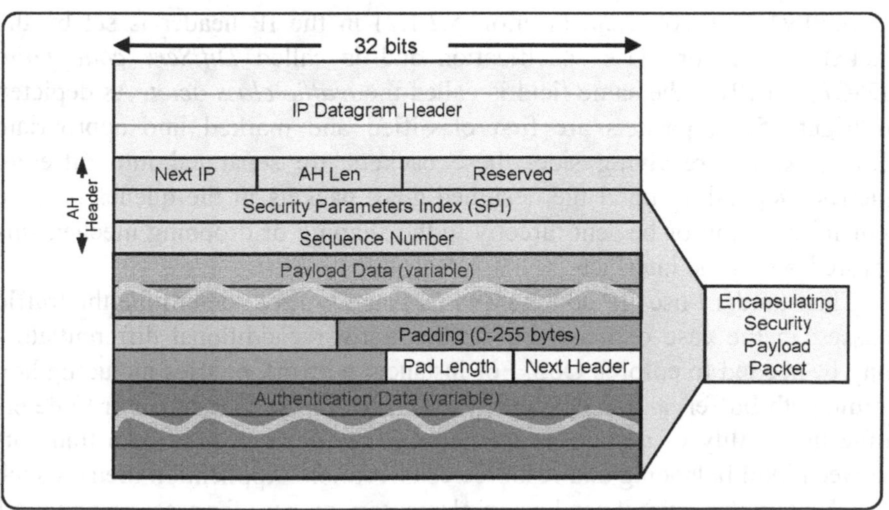

Figure 5.11. Encapsulating security payload.

mode. Unlike the AH header, the IP packet header in the ESP application is not accounted for. Figure 5.11 shows the ESP in an IP header.

5.2.4 Quality of Service

Differentiated services enhancements to the IP are intended to enable scalable service discrimination without the need for per-flow state and signaling at every hop. The purposes of QoS are to provide the managed network with predictable response times (e.g., quantitative performance requirements), setting of traffic priorities (e.g., "class" differentiation), dedication of bandwidth on a per application basis, avoidance and congestion management, management of loss during traffic burst, and management of delay and jitter [36].

QoS can be thought of as operating on one or more of three levels: 1) best effort; 2) differentiated service to deal with differing levels of QoS on a packet by packet basis; and 3) integrated quality service for applications.

5.2.4.1 Differentiated Services

Differentiated services (DiffServ) [37] defines the IP traffic management by classifying packets at the sender and policing (see section 7.3.3.4) at the receiver. The contractual agreements between the sender and the receiver are called SLAs; they specify what classes of traffic will be provided, what guarantees are needed for each class, and how much data will be sent for each class. Multiple flows can hence be managed in a multitude of ways depending upon the requirements of each flow.

In IPv4, the ToS field (section 5.2.1.2) in the IP header is set by the packet sender for class specification and is called *DiffServ code point (DSCP)*. In IPv6, the same field is called the *traffic class octet*. As depicted in Figure 5.12, packets are first classified and marked into appropriate DSCP. At the receiving side, these packets are separated into different queues. Depending upon the designed goal, packets in the queues may be sent for marking or be sent directly to the shaping or dropping mechanisms before leaving the interface.

This standard uses IP address and message types to determine the traffic classes; in the case of managing ad-hoc network additional differentiators may be needed to enforce QoS. For instance, network metrics including hop count, path buffer, and path stability can assist the service operator to determine the quality of a path. These network metrics can provide a trade-off between load balancing and resource conservation. Application metrics such as delay and throughput can be complementary metrics for assessing network quality.

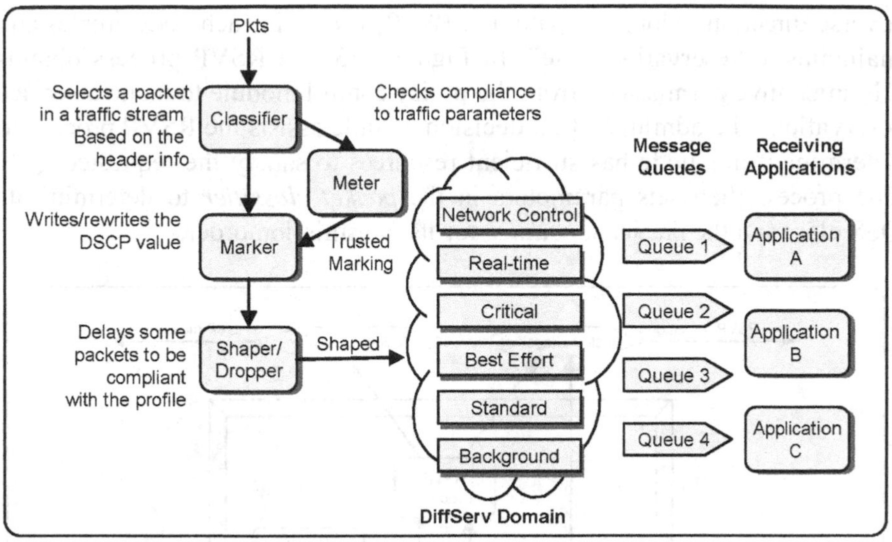

Figure 5.12. DiffServ process and sample message levels.

5.2.4.2 IP Precedence

Data precedence [38] is considered the *best effort* QoS at the network layer. It specifies a three-bit field in the ToS byte of the IP header to provide shaping, policing, drop priorities, and admission control of user traffic based on the *precedence levels*. The classification range is 0–7, where 0 is the lowest and 7 is the highest priority. With IP precedence configured, the network packets traverse through IP precedence devices and receive appropriate priority treatment according to the specified priority. Priority traffic is always serviced before traditional traffic.

This function allows the network operator to assign values to classify and prioritize types of traffic. IP precedence is being phased out in favor of DSCP, but is supported by many applications and routers.

5.2.4.3 Resource-Reservation Protocol

Resource-reservation protocol (RSVP) [39] signals the router to clear a path for application traffic in order to eliminate annoying skips and hesitations. RSVP carries the request through the network, visits each node the network uses to carry the stream, and attempts to make a resource reservation for the stream at each node.

The receiver host of a data flow is responsible for sending RSVP *reservation request (Resv)* upstream towards the senders. The reservations request is composed of a *flowspec* for specifying the requested quality of service and describing the data flow, and a *filter spec* for the packets to be filtered. The path of this request flow will later be used for the actual data flow in the reverse direction. Along the path, the *RSVP process* in each node creates and maintains a "reservation state". In Figure 5.13, the RSVP process obtains administrative permissions from the policy control module to make a service reservation. The administration decision module assists the RSVP process to determine if this node has sufficient resources to satisfy the requested QoS. The process then sets parameters in the *packet classifier* to determine its QoS class and the *packet scheduler* for its transmission order.

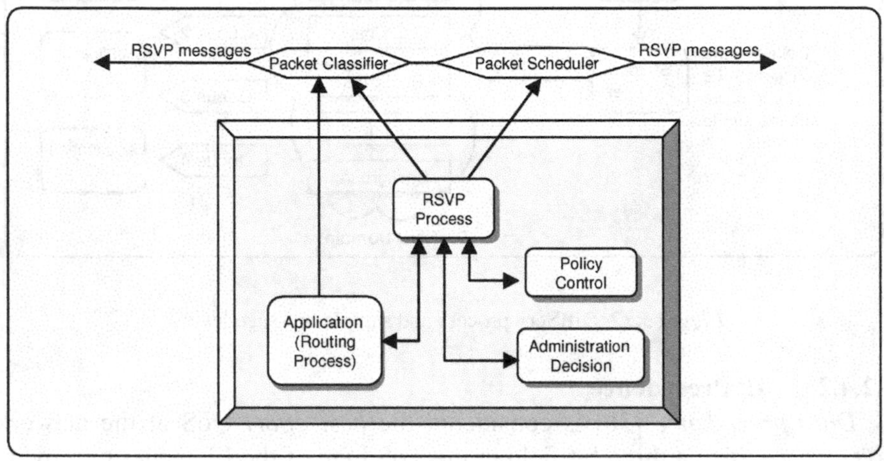

Figure 5.13. RSVP process and two local decision modules.

At the other end, each sender host transmits RSVP *path* messages downstream along the unicast or multicast routes provided by the routing protocol following the paths of the data. These Path messages store "path state" in each node along the way. A path state includes at least the unicast IP address of the previous hop node to ensure hop-by-hop connection in the reverse direction.

As routing paths can change to adapt to topology changes in a wireless network, RSVP is also capable of adopting reservation to the new paths automatically.

5.2.5 Network Services

The network service functions includes the support of unicast, multicast and broadcast traffic types of any multimedia and control messages for the enterprise intra-domain and inter-domain network services and gateway operations.

5.2.5.1 Internet Group Management Protocol

Internet group management protocol (IGMP) [40] manages multicast traffic. It generates *IP multicast group memberships* to neighboring nodes searching for the routers which have interest in receiving the multicast packets. IGMP includes the function called "source filtering" to receive inclusive or exclusive packets from specific source addresses.

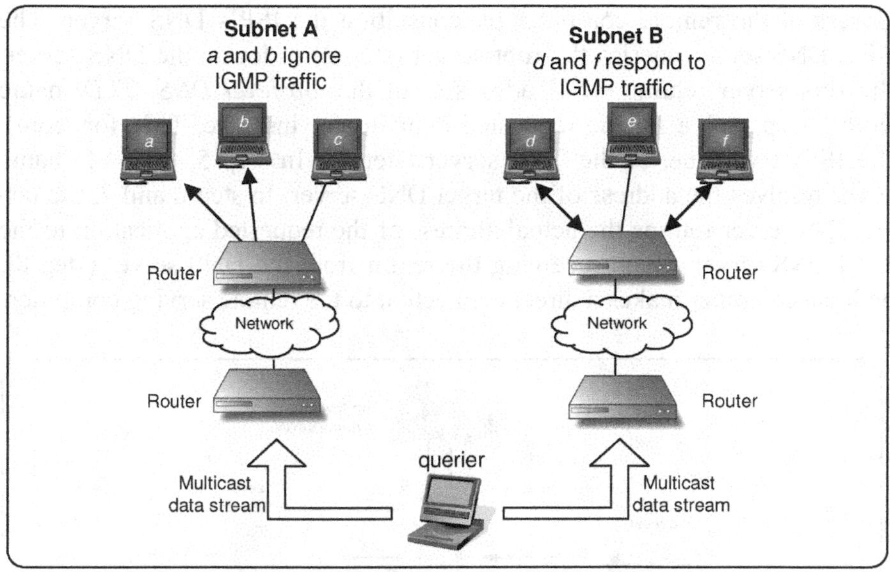

Figure 5.14. Three IGMP messages and a host management flow.

IGMP identifies members of the multicast group per "subnet". A "querier" is a network node which periodically broadcasts *IGMP query* messages onto the link. The network nodes respond to the query messages with *IGMP report* to inform their membership or to join a new multicast group. The *leave group* message is sent when a host wishes to leave the multicast group. Figure 5.14 shows the *querier* sends the IGMP queries to nodes a, b, d, and f. Only d and f determine to stay in the group and respond with IGMP reports.

5.2.5.2 Domain Naming System

Domain naming system or *domain name server (DNS)* [41,42] stores information about *domain* names in a distributed database on networks and enables service users to refer to an application by the domain names rather than the actual addresses. The most important feature of DNS is its capability to provide a worldwide keyword-based redirection service by translating the domain name to the actual addresses of the destinations.

The domain name space is constructed in a tree structure. Each node in the tree is associated with resource information and a domain name. The domain tree can be divided into zones; each zone contains a collection of nodes that are authoritatively served by a dedicated DNS name server. Figure 5.15 depicts a sample system and a query flow of a typical domain name service configuration. In step 1, an Internet application (e.g., Web browser) receives a user entered address, and attempts to resolve the network layer address of the remote computer by consulting the ISP's DNS server. The ISP's DNS server queries the root server (step 2) to locate the DNS server. The root server returns the IP addresses of the *top level DNS (TLD)* name servers responsible for the requested domain (for instance, TLD for .com). The ISP server queries the TLD server (step 4). In step 5, the TLD name server resolves the address of the target DNS server. In step 6 and 7, the target DNS server returns the actual address of the requested application to the ISP's DNS server. Upon receiving the return from the DNS server (step 8), the local computer makes a direct connection to the remote serving computer.

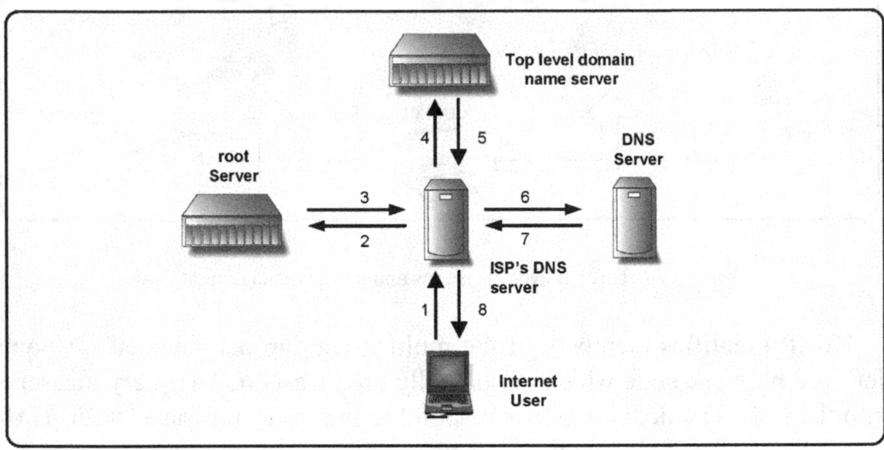

Figure 5.15. Multiple-tier domain naming system.

5.2.5.3 Network Time Protocol

Network time protocol (NTP) [43] synchronizes time and coordinates time distribution through the Internet network. Distributed time servers use *returnable-time* design to synchronize network clocks with time standards in a self-organizing and hierarchical-master-slave configuration. This method also works with local routing algorithms and time daemons to distribute reference time in case the standard time is not available. The main characteristics of NTP are the following:

- Fully automatic, continuous synchronization
- Capable of synchronizing single or networked computers
- Generally available on any computer
- Dynamically auto-configuring
- Independent of time zones and daylight saving by using the *coordinated universal time (UTC)*
- Accuracy in the range of 1 ms

An NTP primary server, also known as the first stratum, is connected to a high precision reference clock. Other computers with compatible NTP software can automatically query the primary server to synchronize their system clocks. This computer in turns can synchronize other computers until the 16th stratum. Each computer can be a server of their lower stratum computer and meanwhile a client for its upper stratum computers. Because each server can handle some hundreds of clients, the system can virtually support an unlimited number of computers. Additionally, a client can be configured to subscribe to more than one server in order to enhance reliability and accuracy. The NTP software can always switch to the server with the best accuracy automatically.

5.2.6 Routing in Wireless Network

The routing functions include routing information protocol, open shortest path first protocol, border gateway protocol, and two protocol independent multicast modes.

5.2.6.1 Routing Information Protocol

Routing information protocol (RIP) [44] is a distance-vector routing protocol running above the network layer of the IP network to exchange routing information among gateways and hosts. Using RIP within an *autonomous system (AS,* a collection of IP networks under the control of a single entity*)* is referred to as an *interior gateway protocol (IGP)*. The other protocol addressing the interface between two AS's is the *exterior gateway protocol (EGP)*.

RIP employs hop count as a routing metric, the maximum number of allowable hops is 15 thus 16-hops is the limit in a subnet. Figure 5.16 depicts a RIP deployment with hop count of four. A RIP router periodically (default at every 30 seconds) sends announcements, which contain the routing table entries to inform other local RIP routers about the networks it can reach. RIP version 1 uses IP broadcast packets for its announcements. RIP version 2 uses multicast or broadcast packets for its announcements. *RIPng (RIP next generation)* is designed for the IPv6 network.

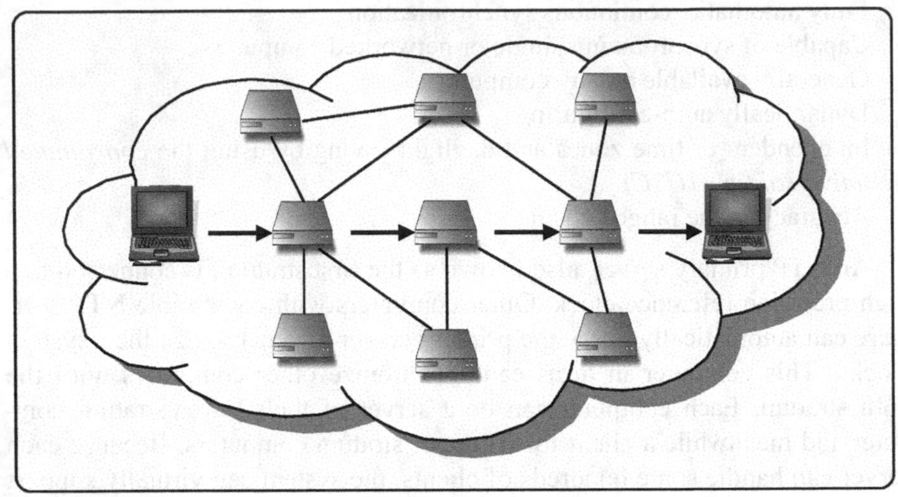

Figure 5.16. RIP with hop count of four.

Each RIP router transmits full updates thus can generate large amounts of network traffic in a bandwidth sensitive network environment. A mechanism called *split horizon* (prohibiting a router from advertising a route in the direction from which it was received/learned) with limited "poisson reverse" (advertising the route back to the router that is used to reach the destination, but marks the advertisement as unreachable) is used to avoid routing loops.

It is extremely simple to configure and deploy a RIP. The disadvantage of RIP is its inability to scale to large network due to the limited hop count, the convergence time needed for RIP routers to reconfigure to a new internetwork topology, and the excessive traffic caused by its periodic announcements.

5.2.6.2 Open Shortest Path First Protocol

Open shortest path first protocol (OSPF) is another type of IGP (see section 5.2.6.1) used for routing in a single *autonomous system (AS)*. OSPF uses *link-state technology* allowing the routers to exchange information about the direct connections and links between routers.

Unlike RIP which exchanges the entire routing table, OSPF maintains a database describing the internetwork topology and only updates the database when the topology changed. Based on this topology database and the link state database, a routing table is calculated with a *shortest path first (SPF)* algorithm to obtain loop-free routes. Neighboring OSPF routers form an adjacency to ensure the link state database on each router is synchronized

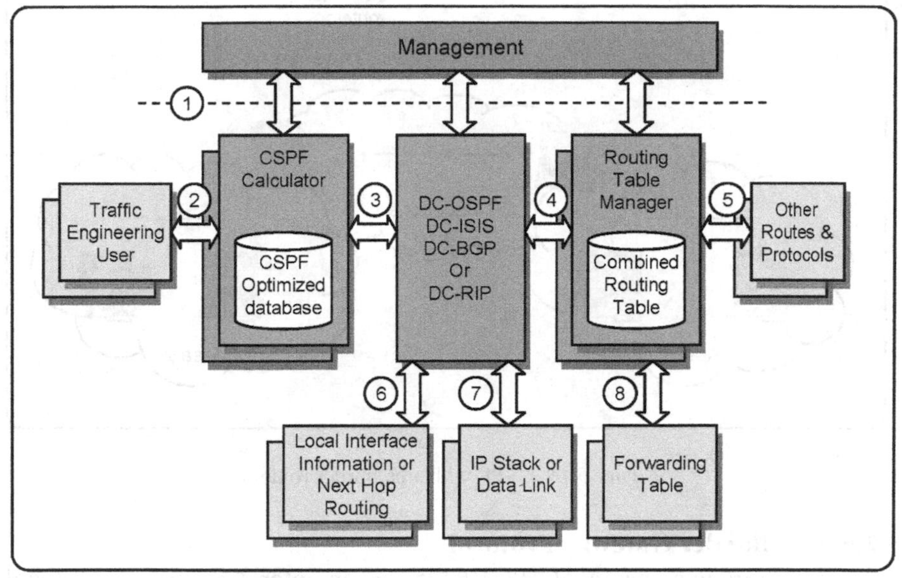

Figure 5.17. OSPF functional diagram.

in real time. OSPF also provides authentication of routing updates, and utilizes IP multicast for updates. Changes to the link state database will trigger recalculation of the routing table. The functional diagram of OSPF is depicted in Figure 5.17.

OSPF introduces the concept called *area to improve scalability*, which groups nodes into sets of networks to reduce traffic exposure to all the nodes. Each router only keeps a link state database about the local areas. *Area border routers (ABRs)* connect the backbone area to other areas, as shown in Figure 5.18. The topology of each area is hidden from others in order to reduce the amount of traffic introduced by the topology updates. Because the routing within an area is independent, it also offers protection of the local area preventing bad routing data from other areas. In addition, all OSPF routing protocol exchanges are authenticated.

With the *variable length sub-netting* technology, OSPF uses different masks (i.e., different sizes) on the same IP network number to reach different subnets; this enables OSPF the flexibility to configure IP subnets.

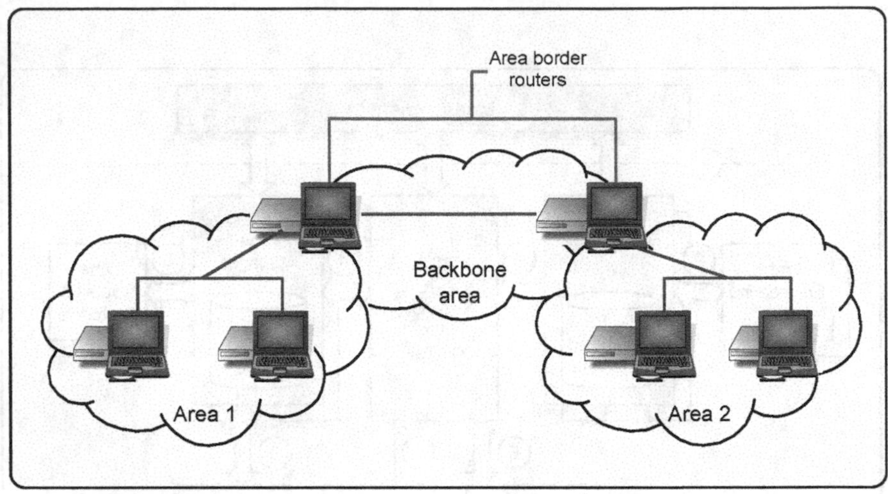

Figure 5.18. OSPF with area border routers.

5.2.6.3 Border Gateway Protocol

Border gateway protocol (BGP) [45] is an inter-AS routing protocol. BGP was created with the experience gained from EGP to exchange network reachability information with other BGP systems. BGP can help the Internet to become decentralized, the routing loops to be pruned, and the policy decisions at the AS level to be enforced. A *BGP speaker* periodically sends keepalive messages to maintain the connection.

When BGP is running inside an AS, it is referred to as *internal BGP (iBGP)*. When BGP runs between AS's, it is called *external BGP (eBGP)*. A BGP router that routes iBGP traffic is called a *transit router*. Router that sits on the boundary of an AS and uses eBGP to exchange information with the ISP is called *border* or *edge routers*. Figure 5.19 shows three interconnected AS's.

BGP supports *classless inter-domain routing (CIDR)*; it uses the route aggregation of AS paths to decrease the size of routing tables. For instance, BGP can be used to join a large OSPF network as OSPF by itself cannot scale to size.

Route reflectors [46] and *confederations* [47] are included in BGP to manage the scaling problems in a full mesh AS domain. Route reflectors reduce the number of connections required in an AS. A router can be configured as a route reflector while others in the AS can be peers to it. Confederations are used in very large networks where AS can be configured to encompass many smaller, and more manageable internal AS's.

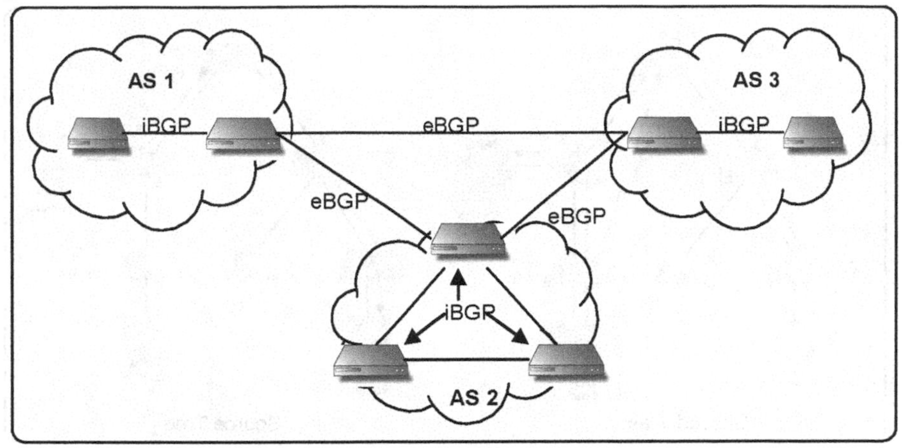

Figure 5.19. BGP over three autonomous systems.

5.2.6.4 PIM-SM: Protocol Independent Multicast-Sparse Mode

Protocol independent multicast-sparse mode (PIM-SM) is a multicast routing protocol designed with the assumption that the recipients for any particular multicast group are sparsely distributed throughout the network, and most subnets in the network do not desire to receive multicast packet.

PIM-SM is a router-to-router protocol that maintains the traditional IP multicast service model of the *receiver-initiated multicast group membership.* It supports both shared and shortest-path trees, and uses soft-state mechanisms to adapt changes on network conditions in the form of *routing information base (RIB)*. Routers use PIM's *join* and *prune* messages to join and leave multicast distribution trees.

By default, PIM-SM uses a multicast distribution tree called *shared tree*, as seen in Figure 5.20(a), with *rendezvous point (RP)* as the root of the shared tree. The source host encapsulates data into PIM control messages and sends it by unicast to the RP, which in turn forwards the packets through a common tree to all members of the group. A host can use *static configuration, bootstrap router, auto-RP, anycast RP*, and *embedded RP* methods to discover the address of a RP for a multicast group.

PIM-SM also supports the use of *source-based trees* as shown in Figure 5.20(b). In this case, a separate multicast distribution tree is built for every source. It directly connects sources to receivers. Each tree is rooted at a router adjacent to the source, and the source sends data directly to the root of the tree. *Source-specific multicast (SSM)* allows the host to specify the source

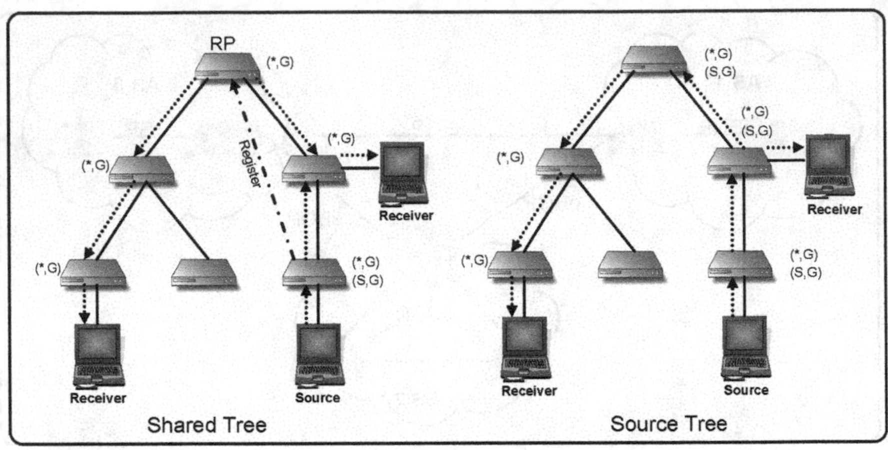

Figure 5.20. Protocol independent multicast-sparse mode.

from which they wish to receive data or the multicast group they wish to join. A host identifies a multicast data stream by a source and group address pair (S,G), rather than by group address only (*,G). The source tree is considered the shortest-path tree from the perspective of the unicast routing tables.

PIM-SM is a soft-state protocol. Unless refreshed, the router's state configuration is short-term and expires after a certain amount of time. In other words, all state will time-out at some time after receiving the control message that instantiated it. To keep the state alive, all PIM join messages are periodically retransmitted.

5.2.6.5 PIM-DM: Protocol Independent Multicast-Dense Mode

Protocol independent multicast-dense mode (PIM-DM) is mainly designed for multicast LAN applications, while the PIM-SM is for wide area and inter-domain network. Unlike PIM-SM, the receivers in multicast groups of PIM-DM are distributed densely and assume the majority of subnets desire to receive multicast packet.

Multicast data is initially sent to all hosts in the network, routers on the source's LAN forward them to their PIM neighbors. In order to prevent forwarding loops from occurring, any packets arrive other than the upstream interface of the router will be dropped. The data is thus flooded to all parts of the network. Routers that do not have any interest hosts must send PIM prune messages to the upstream router to detach themselves from future messages, as shown in Figure 5.21. After the prune state at the routers time-out, data traffic will flow back into the nodes previously pruned. This mechanism can ensure the data only sent to the parts of network that require it.

PIM-DM can use the routing table populated by any underlying unicast routing protocol, therefore the service operators does not need to introduce and manage a separate routing protocol to perform *reverse path forwarding (RPF)* checks.

PIM-DM only uses *source-based* tree. Because it does not use RPs, the implementation and deployment are generally simpler than PIM-SM. PIM-DM is an efficient protocol when most receivers are interested in the multicast data, however, it does not scale well across larger domains when most receivers are not interested in the data. As the result, it is less commonly used than PIM-SM.

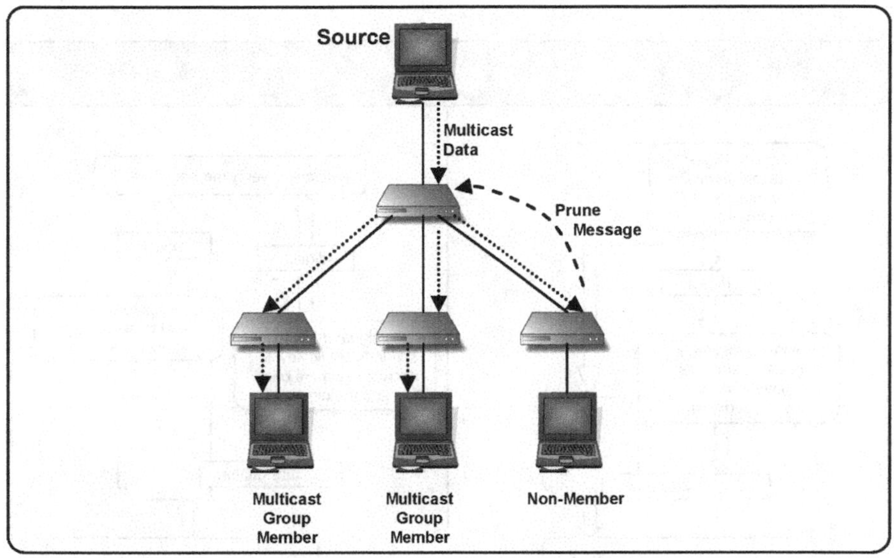

Figure 5.21. Protocol independent multicast-dense mode.

5.2.7 Transport Information Assurance

An encryption method can choose to use asymmetric-key or symmetric-key cryptography. Using the asymmetric-key approach, the sender uses a public key to encrypt the message. To decrypt the message, the recipient uses the private key or secrete key. This is in contrast with the symmetric-key cryptography where the same key is used to encrypt and decrypt the message (see section 8.5.5.2). The message flows are portrayed in Figure 5.22 [48].

To create a digital signature that ensures the integrity of a message, the keys are used in reverse. The private key is used to sign the message (encrypt the digest), and the public key is used to verify it (decrypt the digest).

5.2.7.1 Symmetric-Key Algorithm

The keys represent a shared secret between two or more parties that can be used to maintain a private information link. The symmetric cryptography requires all parties to obtain a single- and private-key.

Symmetric-key algorithms are less computationally intensive than asymmetric-key algorithms. However, the algorithms require sharing one secret key at each end. Since keys are subject to potential discovery, they need to be changed often. The symmetric-key algorithms can be divided into stream ciphers and block ciphers. Stream ciphers encrypt the bits of the message one at a time, and block ciphers take a number of bits and encrypt them as a single unit. Section 8.5.5 will delve further into this subject.

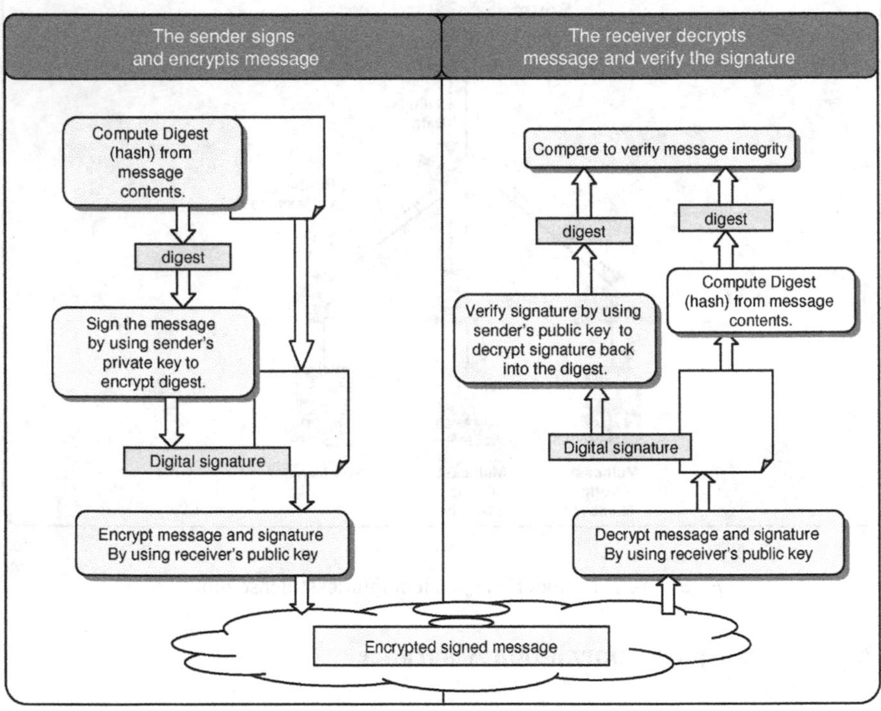

Figure 5.22. Message integrity and privacy.

5.2.7.2 Asymmetric-Key Algorithm

Asymmetric-key cryptography is a synonym for public-key cryptography. With this algorithm, all parties can communicate securely with a public key. This method requires a pair of cryptographic keys related mathematically, they are public key and private key. The public key "locks" a lock and the private key unlocks it. There are many forms of public-key cryptography. The public key encryption keeps a message secret from anyone that does not possess a specific private key. The public key digital signature allows anyone to verify the message created with a specific private key. The key agreement allows two parties that may not initially share a secret key to agree on one.

Public key techniques are typically more computationally intensive than purely symmetric algorithms. A quality asymmetric-key algorithm can be many times slower than a quality symmetric-key algorithm.

Because neither asymmetric-key algorithms nor symmetric-key algorithms are better than the other, these two algorithms are not always used alone. In modern cryptosystem designs, both algorithms are used to take advantage of the virtues of both.

5.3 Planning and Deployment Considerations

The purpose of network plans for a transport service is to create a data product which specifies the network resources, service requirements (e.g., QoS), and service policies (rules and guidance). The purpose of the service configuration and reconfiguration is to instantiate the services in accordance with the new or updated network plans. The policies defined in the network plans also specify how the services should be controlled and managed, for instance, the SLA thresholds, quality objectives, and radio frequency adoption policy. The enterprise can have option of automatically changing configurations of the managed resources with little or no operator interaction. To provide dynamic contexts to a plan, tradeoffs from different design options must be considered. Some sampled design considerations for ad-hoc wireless services can include [49]:

- The bandwidth balance between high QoS and low probability of intercept (or detection).
- Coordination of slot assignment at layer 2 with DiffServ allocations at layer 3.
- Consideration of the relay placement versus OSPF area design to minimize interarea traffic in a multi-hop connection.
- In a multi-hop connection, some nodes may be used to operate as gateways or relays on behalf of others with less battery life.
- Spectrum management and power control to prevent denial of service from "friendly interference".
- High data rate applications trade for lower frequency RF propagation.
- Appropriate resource allocation to ensure access privileges and fairness in time-critical applications.
- Awareness of the limitations with respect to allowable frequency bands due to terrain limitations, line of sight, weather, and environment.
- Flexibility of role change of a network resource.

- Automated feedback loop of communication nodes (e.g., radio) to provide input for service reconfiguration.

Furthermore, in a wireless mobile network where the operations are based on multiple administrative control authorities, the network planning and management must be responsive to topology changes, intermittent connectivity, and murky boundaries for administrative control authority, network congestion, and transition between domains.

In the following sections, some key operational considerations are highlighted.

5.3.1 Radio Resource Allocations

Radio waves are part of electromagnetic waves which have two important characteristics that can be changed. One is the *amplitude*, or *strength* of the wave, and the other is the *frequency*, or how often the wave occurs at any point. Electromagnetic waves with certain frequencies are called radio waves. The *radio frequency (RF)* spectrum [50,51] is a multi-dimensional concept involving radio frequency bandwidth, time span, geometrical volume, polarization, and in a satellite application – a segment of the satellite orbit in space applications.

The use of radio frequency spectrum is now coordinated and regulated worldwide through the *International Telecommunication Union (ITU)*, a specialized agency of the United Nations since 1947. In 1963, the first World Space Radio-communication Conference integrated the satellite orbit with the radio frequency spectrum into three geographical regions (Figure 5.23). Region 1 includes the whole Europe, Africa, Middle East and northern part of Asia. Region 2 covers the Americas, and Region 3 covers the southern part of Asia, Australia and Oceania. Each region has its individual frequency allocations but some services have worldwide frequency allocations.

The radio frequency spectrum has been divided into a number of specific frequency bands allocated to specific services in each of the three regions. Each frequency range has a band designator; each range of frequencies behaves differently and performs different functions. The frequency spectrum is shared by civil, government, and military users of all nations according to the ITU radio regulations, as shown in Table 5.2.

For a given service, the frequency allocations and restrictions may also depend upon the communication direction, e.g., uplinks and downlinks in different frequency bands. Additionally, all reserved frequency bands may remain unused for many years and for various reasons, even though other applications cannot find free frequencies.

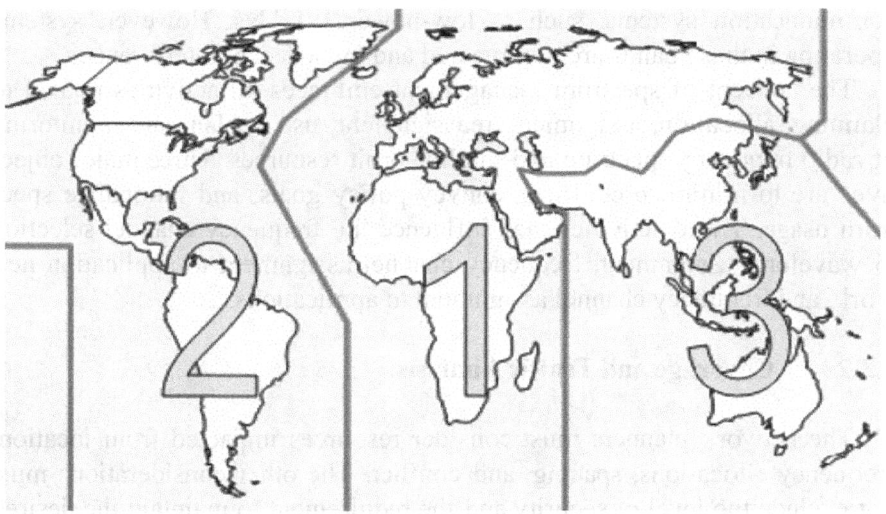

Figure 5.23. For the purpose of Radio Regulations, the world has been divided into three geographical regions numbered 1, 2, and 3.

Table 5.2. The ITU Frequency Bands.

Band No.	Symbol	Frequency	Wavelength
1	ELF	Extremely low – 3 to 30 Hz	100,000 to 10,000 km
2	SLF	Super low – 30 to 300 Hz	10,000 to 1,000 km
3	ULF	Ultra low – 300 to 3000 Hz	1,000 to 100 km
4	VLF	Very low – 3 to 30 kHz	100 to 10 km (myriametric)
5	LF	Low – 30 to 300 kHz	10 to 1 km (kilometric)
6	MF	Medium – 300 to 3000 kHz	1000 to 100 m (hectometric)
7	HF	High – 3 to 30 MHz	100 to 10 m (decametric)
8	VHF	Very high – 30 to 300 MHz	10 to 1 m (metric)
9	UHF	Ultra high – 300 to 3000 MHz	100 to 10 cm (decimetric)
10	SHF	Super high – 3 to 30 GHz	10 to 1 cm (centimetric)
11	EHF	Extremely high – 30 to 300 GHz	10 to 1 mm (millimetric)
12	THF	Tremendously high – 300 to 3000 GHz	1 to 0.1 mm (decimillimetric)

The radio regulations allocate some frequency bands for non-telecommunication purposes. These are known as *industrial, scientific and medical applications (ISM) frequencies*, *free-radiation frequencies*, or *non-licensed* bands. Some ISM bands have been used by interference-immune communication systems, such as low-power WLANs. However, systems operating in these bands are unprotected and must accept interference.

The concept of spectrum management embraces all activities related to planning, allocation, assignment, reassignment, use, replan, and monitoring of radio frequency spectrum and satellite orbit resources. Three major objectives are to minimize conflicts, convey policy goals, and rationalize spectrum usage. These activities may influence the frequency channel selection to waveform assignment, frequency channel assignment to application network, and frequency channel assignment to applications.

5.3.2 Coverage and Traffic Analysis

The network planners must consider resources impacted from location, frequency allocations, spacing, and conflict. The other considerations must not exclude the level of security and the requirement to maintain the desired performance with minimal impact to wireless channel capacity.

Introduction of wireless capabilities imposes a spectrum management function in the network management. Mobility requirements complicate spectrum management because of the spatial nature of spectrum allocations.

Network partitioning has the tendency of introducing monitoring problem; meanwhile, remerging can introduce risk in address confliction. Appropriate management mechanism should ensure integrity of the network operations when topology changes.

Coverage and capacity analysis are two keys performance considerations for wireless network planning. The coverage-oriented analysis includes propagation path loss predictions for available sites and their antenna locations. Other coverage and traffic requirements can include some or all of the following considerations:

- The locations of available sites, competitor locations, timing, logistic criteria, logistic contingencies, technical criteria, technical contingencies, and proximity to potential and current service users.
- Density of deployment. If the traffic load (average up- and down-link load) is too high in some regions, they should be localized with domain selection criteria. For instance, rescue applications require high availability of the network, making redundancy a high priority.
- Installation selection such as antenna configurations can be employed at different antenna locations.
- Mobility of nodes deployed may concern: 1) individual nodes move in and between networks, sub-networks, and network infrastructure; 2) a network detaches from one part of a stable network and reattach to another part of that network; and 3) management functions associated with mobility requirements (monitoring topology and auto-configuration).

- Power assignment includes transmission powers in uplink and downlink as well as the smart-antenna's pilot powers. Power constrains should consider various power options, for instance, replenishable power source (wearable sensors that can be replaced), non-replenishable power source (once the network is replaced, it cannot be replenished), and regenerative power source.
- Data fusion may be considered in mission areas where limited bandwidth and power constrains may require local aggregation of data at the intermediate relay nodes.
- Traffic pattern analysis can dictate the traffic distribution plans and requires layer three data and control planes; subjects of interest may include routing from IP upward, intra- and inter-domain routing, routing security, and routing performance in control and data planes (rate of topology change effects).
- Multicast requirements identify the multicast members' needs as mobile nodes or networks traverse within the network infrastructure. Service design considerations include the management function to handle branch distribution and reconstruction within mobile network infrastructure.

5.3.3 Mobility Requirements

Mobility requirements rise by the need to operate the enterprise resources in a mobile environment. Mobility is the capability to maintain system functions while there are changes in the locations and relationships between system entities. From a service design perspective, these changes are limited to the geographical or logical movement of enterprise recourses (for instance, system entities). Several major areas for requirement considerations can be summarized in the following:

- *Maintaining Functions*: The service consumers and service producers can carry on the network functionalities while the device, system, network, and other entities are moving. Examples of the service providers are enterprise applications, sensor services, Web services, and mission executives. Examples of the service (or information) consumers are applications and users. The services can be voice, data, or hybrid services.
- *Handling Autonomy*: The ability of service operators to maintain local or regional services (e.g., e-mail, voice, situation awareness) as an autonomous unit or sub-network while a portion of the services (e.g., connectivity to the corporate backbone network) is lost and the ability to synchronize and operate when the lost service is recovered.
- *Limited Resources*: To manage the limited resource from bandwidth on wireless links, *size-weight-and-power (SWaP)* on mobile platform,

physical security, processor power, and so forth. Some factors may be related, for instance, limited processor power may reflect a need to conserve battery power to meet stringent SWaP requirements for a wearable device.

- *Maintaining Connectivity and Security*: Mobility opens up new possibility for network attacks, security should not comprise due to mobility. The security of information and the ability to perform the user's tasks are two essential features of IA, thus the ability to secure information, identify entities, and perform physical security should be included.
- *Information Synchronization*: To satisfy network-centric operational needs, the enterprise has to obtain common shared data assets, however, certain information objects used for synchronized activity may be available only in mobile units. Adequate protection of sensitive information coupled with mobility requirements can drive whole new requirements for controlling and limiting specific data sets. The goal is to coordinate and keep current of information assets assuring the information and system integrity.

5.3.4 Energy Management

Mobile communication applications typically require network components to consume power substantially lower than the static wireless networks. For instance, industrial and medical sensors, smart tags, and badges are powered by small coin cell batteries, thus can last from several months to many years. Some industrial monitoring and control applications may expect longest monitoring period possible to reduce the equipment (e.g., battery) maintenance efforts.

In a wireless network node, *active power consumption* of the transceiver is much greater than its *standby power consumption*. The node must consider operating its transceiver in a low duty cycle mode possible in order to achieve low average power consumption.

In addition to the consumption consideration, *power sources* dictate the average and peak power consumption therefore it should be considered in the system design and physical deployment. The power sources can come from ambient sources of energy, such as solar, RF, and mechanical vibration. Each has its limitation, for instance, solar-powered devices need to be lit, and vibration-powered devices need to have vibration. The battery technologies include manganese–zinc, alkaline–manganese, lead–acid cells, lithium–ion cells, zinc–zinc oxide cells, lithium–aluminum, and iron sulfide.

As for the *charging schedule*, the charge recovery effect can extend the battery life of mobile devices. A battery undergoing pulsed discharge has a greater capacity than an identical battery undergoing a constant discharge.

From an operational perspective, the lower the duty cycle of the pulsed discharge, the greater the battery longevity will be. In practice, taking advantage of the charge recovery effect means that the device should activate high-power dissipation components (e.g., the transceiver) in infrequent bursts (resulting in a low duty cycle of operation). Furthermore, the bursts should be separated from each other if all possible in order to give the communication nodes the maximum possible time to recover before the next discharge pulse.

An appropriate communication protocol at the physical layer can also ease the hardware design. For instance, *channel frequencies* and *spacing* allows a high synthesizer reference frequency to be used for fast lock time, this feature can reduce or eliminate the requirement for narrow bandwidth filtering (e.g., in channel selectivity filters). This gives wide bandwidth systems, such as *direct sequence spread spectrum* systems, an advantage over *narrowband* systems for low duty cycle networks. An additional advantage of *direct sequence* systems is that their implementations have a high digital circuit content, and relatively low analog circuit content. A SoS level power management discussion can be found in section 4.5.1.

5.3.5 Planning Procedures

In the transport service planning procedure, the initial task is to gather information, resource, and signal information. Gathering interface and signaling information may include: 1) types of deployment mechanism; 2) equipment and physical interface connecting to the router; and 3) software configuration for each interface connecting to the enterprise resources. In the entire life cycle of network service planning, there are several different phases of planning to support the initial and on-going operations of the new network. These phases are:

- *Initial Planning* involves the creation of plans for new service configurations prior to the initial deployment.
- *Post Deployment Plan* is generated as an addition or changes for the new service configurations after the initial deployment, but before instantiation.
- *Dynamic Plan Change* allows modifications on business missions after instantiation. Alternating plans can affect the behaviors and performances of localized regions. This procedure also allows the service operators to reconfigure the entire service as needed.

Network system planning must be derived from the coordinated service plans in accordance with the developed scenarios. The service plans contain detailed information on aspects relevant to network planning; they can be classified as follows:

- *Radio and environment* includes radio propagation, radio bearers, information on the terrain and background noise.
- *Infrastructure* includes all aspects that are to some extent under the control of the network operator. This includes base station hardware, antennas, potential sites and antenna locations, radio resource management, DNS, billing application, and so forth.
- *User demand* relates to users, such as offered services (e.g., video telephony, media streaming), user mobility, usage specifics, and traffic data.
- Security concerns keys for encryption and identifiers for service discovery.
- *Provisioning resource* includes IP addresses, sub net masks, frequency allocations, routing algorithms, broadcasting rules, and other QoS parameters.

5.3.6 Configuration Dissemination

Network configuration is the process by which a set of service configuration files is loaded onto the device or communication node and made available to the service operations or users. The network supporting the devices is required to support appropriate interfaces and protocols that are used during provisioning. To configure network nodes, the provisioning system should perform the following series of steps, check the results, and provide feedback about the progress.

1. The network planning system converts the service configuration files from its transport format (e.g., encrypted format) before it can be used.
2. The information in the service configuration files may include the vendor name, version, size attributes, security keys, network address, frequency, application identifiers, and other task related parameters.
3. If the service configuration files were previously installed on the managed nodes, this will be treated as a potential upgrade. As part of the updating process, the persistent data preconfigured in the nodes may be preserved for use by the updating data.
4. The provisioned nodes initiate the newly download of the service configuration files by the service operators or users.
5. The managed nodes must be able to verify that the new configuration files are qualify for the action and can be instantiated. The user or operator should be alerted when exceptional condition occurs. Examples of exception are insufficient memory, mismatch the specified file sizes, in-

consistent mandatory attributes such as version number, or lost connection during provisioning.

Figure 5.24 illustrates an abstract flow of configuration. The above provisioning procedures can be deployed either manually or via an *over-the-air (OTA)* scheme. For a large customer based or complex network configuration, provisioning the network after initial configuration (preset) can be a complicated and time-consuming process. For instance, reprovisioning the existing service profile (such as changing the IP address or telephone number) is operationally difficult and impractical. Therefore, OTA management can simplify the provisioning process and made efficient to a large extent.

Whether it is manual or OTA, the provisioned nodes or devices are expected to provide mechanisms that allow the operators or users to discover the configuration files that can be loaded into the device. During the download and installation process, the engineers or users should be able to control the download, determine which versions of software are installed, updates the service instance, and obtain status about the new instance on the node. In any operation, the user should be informed of progress and be able to cancel the activity.

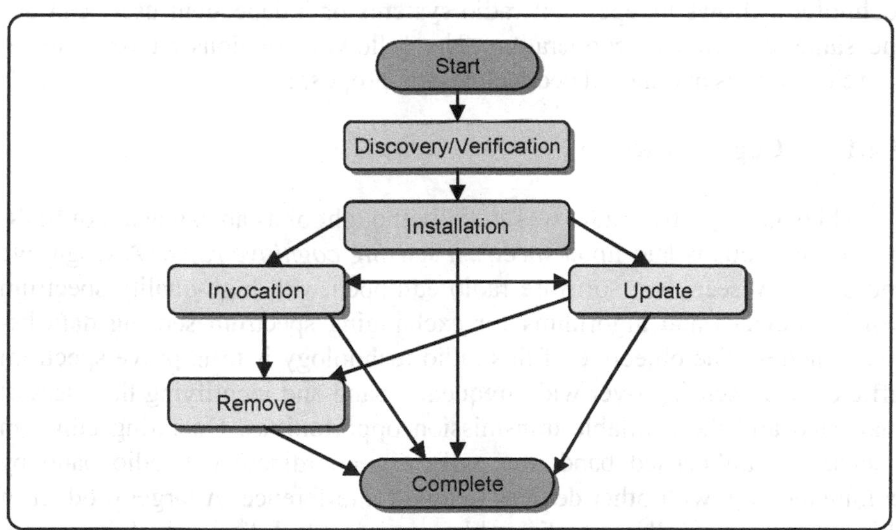

Figure 5.24. Configuration flows.

5.4 Evolving Radio Technology

There has been extensive research on channel allocation, particularly on base station frequency and channel assignment in cellular networks. These works mainly for reducing the probability of call blocking with the assumption of equal channel-weighting treatment.

In the recent development of wireless service, cellular network bands are overloaded in most parts of the world meanwhile other frequency spectrums such as amateur radio and paging are still far from saturation. Driven by the inefficiency of the frequency utilization, the recent researchers have move on to a new focus of heterogeneity with respect to the availability of spectrum and rewards (e.g., bandwidth and throughput) from occupying different ranges of spectrum.

The new spectrum management aims to achieve non-interference by using either non-collaborative or collaborative means. In either case, the solution has to provide spectrum availability for short periods of time [52].

By increasing the available spectrum and capacity, the service operators can increase link range and enable more access. The most immediate applications can take place in the areas such as emergency, sporting event, itinerate event, disaster, and even general Internet access in medium and low population density areas.

Built based on the technology aforementioned in chapter 3, the SDR (section 3.4.1) make this dynamic spectrum management possible. SDR technology allows independent radio systems or independent users can use the same spectrum in cooperation. The following sections address the research activities and the related technology proposals.

5.4.1 Cognitive Radio

Although cognitive radio was initially thought of as an extension of SDR, the recent focus is laid upon *spectrum sensing cognitive radio*. A Cognitive radio is now seen as a software radio equipped with high-quality spectrum sensing devices and algorithms for exchanging spectrum sensing data between nodes. The objective of this radio technology is to improve spectrum efficiency by sensing over wide frequency band and identifying the users of that band and the available transmission opportunities. Operating either in licensed or unlicensed band, the radio can coordinate the radio band by communicating with other devices to avoid interference. A target product of this concept is a fully reconfigurable wireless black-box, which can automatically change its communication variables in response to any network or user demands.

Depending upon the set of parameters taken into account in deciding on transmission and reception changes, the radio can be in either full cognitive or frequency spectrum sensing cognitive.

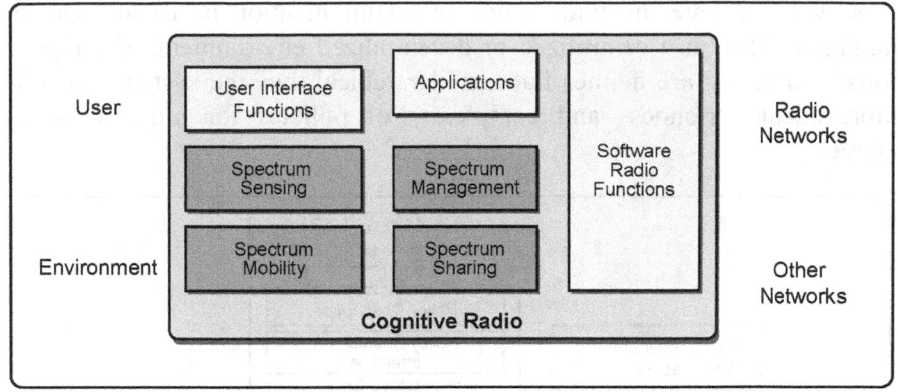

Figure 5.25. Cognitive radio.

As depicted in Figure 5.25, there are four major components in a cognitive radio. These four components interact with SDR, user interface, and applications, they are:

- *Spectrum sensing* detects the unused spectrum or spectrum holes. The detection techniques can be based on the presence of transmitter, matched filter, energy, cyclostationary feature, interference, or information from multiple radios.
- *Spectrum management* conducts spectrum analysis and makes spectrum decision to capture the best available spectrum that meets the QoS requirements.
- *Spectrum mobility* allows the radio terminals to maintain seamless transition to other spectrums.
- *Spectrum sharing* providing the fair spectrum scheduling methods.

Filling free radio frequency bands adaptively *(OFDM)* are generally used with this type of radio to increase the number of cooperating sensing nodes and decrease the probability of false detection.

5.4.2 DARPA XG Program

The *DARPA next generation (XG) communications program* was established to manage spectrum policy-making for dynamic spectrum usage. Although the life cycle of XG program was from 2002 to 2006, it provided a technical framework to improve the efficient use of spectrum over the current static allocations. The main principle of the XG program was to create an architectural implementation which can offer a flexible policy framework in order to separate policies from engineering. The separation can avoid advocacy for specific sharing policies. As the result, such policies can effectively achieve the wide range of communication needs and can be managed either in a centralized or decentralized environment. The regulations of a policy are neither flat nor hierarchical thus the system can offer unprecedented richness and complexity of policies for multiple policy sources.

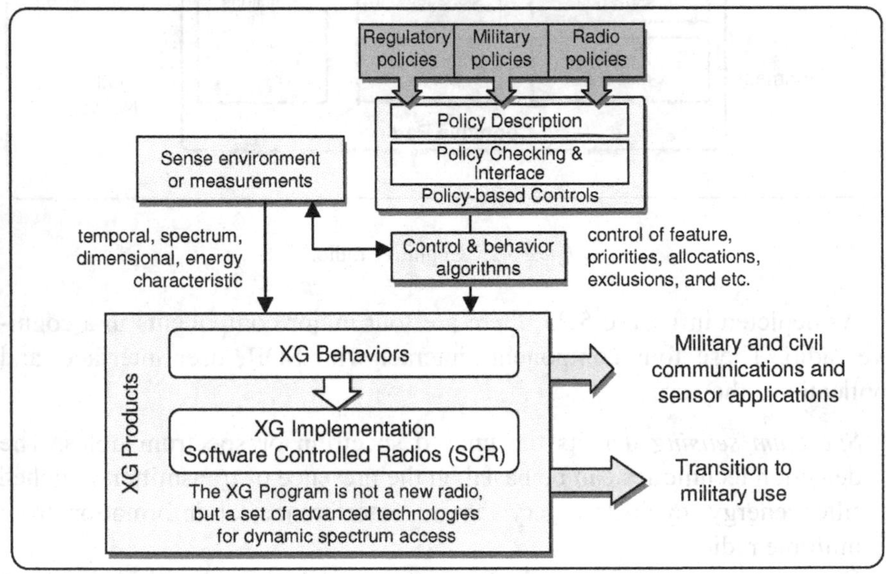

Figure 5.26. DARPA XG program.

Furthermore, the system can provide a general means that allows rapid deployment for diversity of policy sources. For instance, the peer-to-peer authorities are suitable for small- to medium-size commercial value-chain processes, while the hierarchical policy authorities are idea for the current military planning process (see section 5.5.1) or any enterprise which has to manage complex hierarchical networks.

Figure 5.26 portrays the scope of the XG program. The policy-based control module coordinates policies from three distinguished sources, namely *regulatory policies*, *military policies*, and *radio policies*. These high-level specifications are based on an expressive and extensible policy language, with executable semantics that meet the different regulation bodies. The policy language uses *multiple inheritance class structures* and *meta-policies*.

Outputs of the controlled policies are fed into a set of control and behavior algorithms for optimization. These algorithms check the compliance of the candidate transmissions using efficient, state-of-the-art rewriting technology. These algorithms interact with the sensing module and optimize the policies in both the presence of conflicts as well as the absence of complete information. This system uses fast decision procedures to yield the candidate parameter bindings for satisfactory policies. The same set of sensed data, containing the information about temporal, spectrum, dimensional, and energy characteristic, in conjunction with the outputs from the optimization algorithms, are provided to the *XG behavior module*. The SCR can therefore manage the radio behaviors in accordance with the rules and policies from the XG behaviors module.

5.4.3 NSF NeTS Programmable Wireless Networking

The Programmable Wireless Networking (ProWiN) of *NSF NeTS* program supports the creation of new wireless networking systems based on programmable radios. This type of network devices aims to route messages through the network and interoperate with the larger Internet, manage spectrum resources dynamically, self-organize with a rapid initial configuration, accommodate mobility, support a variety of network services, use adaptation to ensure QoS, and support multiple users and domains. To achieve the above goals, the new device must be wireless, multimodal (multi-interface) and frequency-agile with rich control and monitoring interfaces. The major functional blocks of the program are depicted in Figure 5.27, and include [53,54]:

- Dynamic spectrum management architectures and techniques
- Topology discovery and optimization, and network self-configuration
- Interaction between routing, topology, and administration/management
- Programmable radios for the community

This technology allows the radios to perform inter- or intra-domain operations in various topologies, where the wireless networks and protocols are programmable to adjust configuration changes dynamically. This method can manage topology changes such as convergence and division in an environment which contains dynamic spectrum access and overlapping networks. In this platform solution, topology formation, routing, interlayer interaction are incorporated with the requirements of mobility, power management, and *command and control (C2)*. With its programmable capability, the degree of management of overlapping networks can now be raised to conduct bottom-line improvements on the wireless communications to include connectivity quality and resilience when exploiting to different systems and administrative domains.

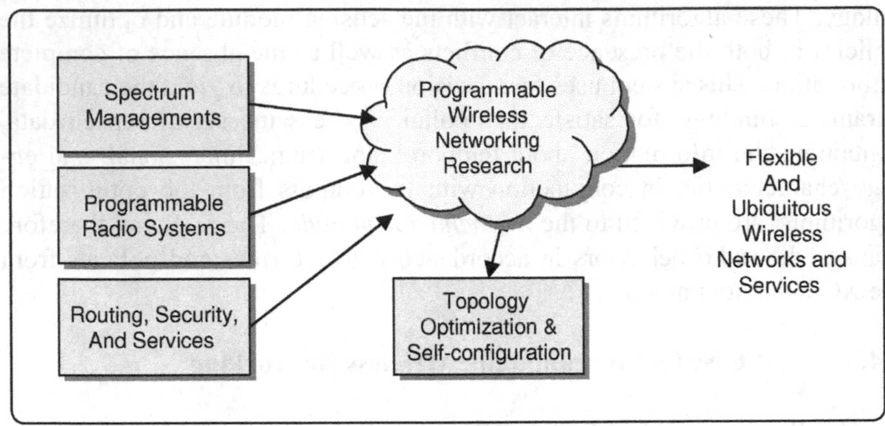

Figure 5.27. NeTS program.

5.5 SoS Views of Network Initialization

The SoS view section illustrates a typical flow of a fulfillment process from receiving a customer inquiry, to service order creation, to the configuration of the service and its installation. The service fulfillment processes starts with presale activity and ends with on-time and correct installation of a customer's requested service (Figure 5.28). Support information is required to manage any SLAs, to provide for problem or trouble management, and to produce an accurate bill. Depending upon the individual service provider's process, orders can be placed through the sales process or directly through the order management process. For bulk sales or resellers, the service provider would use a dedicated sales function to manage customers. Interfaces to the customer are shown, as well as the output interfaces required to support service assurance (e.g., trouble or problem management, SLM) and billing processes. Interfaces are required with other service providers or network operators when the service offered to a customer involves joint service arrangements.

It is not necessary to complete the entire fulfillment flow for services that have preassigned service arrangements. For instance, for configured and tested facilities that are preprovisioned, the network provisioning flow can be skipped.

In other cases, more process activities may be required for reasons such as SLA requirements or a complex bundled offering. The flows necessary are determined by the provider's operational processes and policies.

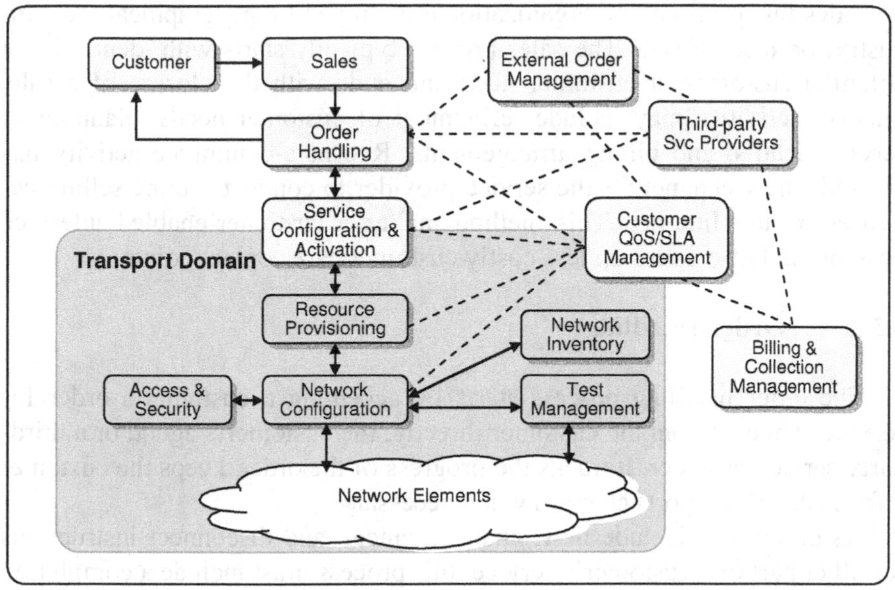

Figure 5.28. Fulfillment flows.

Additionally, security and test management are critical and can apply at every interface. Both functionalities can be applied as a sub-process across the entire OSS or can be managed as a dedicated process. In the following sections, the associated functional blocks will be delved individually.

5.5.1 Sales

The functional goals of the sales process are to respond to market needs quickly, sell the correct service to suit the customer's need, and set appropriate expectations with the customer via SLAs, if necessary. To accomplish this, the processes should be able to assess the needs of each customer and be capable of educating the customer about the service products that match those needs. A complete sales process should include the activities of selling and field support that can create a match between the customer's expectations and the service provider's ability to deliver that service. Some service providers implement the sales process as pure sales; some include various levels of technical sales or back-office support. As the sales intervals are sharply decreased, technical sales support is engaged early in the cycle (this may include preorder work and interfaces) to reduce costly order errors, especially for customized solutions.

Sales functions can be organizationally aligned by geographical area, industry, or account size. The sales process typically starts with identifying a potential customer or customer need and ends with the closure of a sale. Support activities may include refinement of customer needs, planning of service details, and billing arrangements. Recent e-commerce activity has created a new channel for the service provider to conduct routine selling activities on the Internet. This method makes a customer-enabled interface possible and also opens up less costly customer care contact points.

5.5.2 Order Handling

The order handling process starts by accepting a customer's order for service, whether from the customer directly, the customer's agent, or a third-party service provider. It tracks the progress of the order, keeps the customer informed, and supports changes when necessary.

As orders can include new, change, cancel, and disconnect instructions for all or part of a customer's service, this process must include a completion acceptance from the customer. The process should ideally include a follow-up or notification to ensure that the service is working properly. A completed order should include sufficient information to build or update a customer account record in trouble or problem handling, performance reporting, and billing processes and systems.

This process is also accountable for initiating and receiving credit information for new customers according to the service provider's business rules. When customization is available for complex bundled offerings, this process should also support preliminary feasibility inquiries and optional pricing estimates. Sometimes this requires the development of an order plan. Modern CRMs typically include the entire order handling process and tracking capabilities for preorder activities and can perform channel management and market research.

5.5.3 Network Provisioning

The network provisioning process starts with a configuration (or reconfiguration) or installation request from either the network management layer processes or the service configuration process. This process includes the configuration of the network to ensure that network capacity is available and is ready for provisioning, maintenance, and tests to ensure operational readiness. This process essentially administers the logical network and interfaces with the network inventory manager for physical installation or implementation in the network or associated services. The physical installation or implementation may include network and service additions, changes, deletions, and configuration changes. For a new service, the result of the process is the network and associated operations' being logically configured.

If a network resource has been preconfigured, the provisioning process can be managed directly through service provisioning or customer care processes, as the physical resource and should be ready for service. In order to keep the inventory identifiable throughout the OSS process, the network provisioning process is responsible for assigning and administering identifiers for provisioned resources and making them available to other processes.

The sequence of operations starts with a network provisioning request from the service configuration process within the service management layer and finishing with the configuration result. It then shows the start of monitoring with messages being sent to the service configuration and network data management processes, respectively.

5.5.4 Service Configuration System

There are three triggers for the service configuration process. The first is a service infrastructure need to maintain performance or to add service-specific capacity; thus it is not customer specific. The second trigger is customers' requests for service installations or service configurations. The third trigger is a response to a reconfiguration request due either to a customer demand or a problem resolution after the initial service installation. The service configuration process interacts with the network provisioning process and the network inventory process to perform physical implementation or installation work in the network or an associated service resource.

5.5.5 Network Configuration and Routing

The network configuration and routing process is responsible for installing the initial network configuration and subsequent network reconfigurations. Any configuration-related works can use this process to issue work orders to the workforce management process for coordinating the tasks.

When an order from network provisioning indicates that a reconfiguration (e.g., rerouting) is needed in the operational network, this process will need to coordinate with high-level processes to apply business rules for the utilization of the network in order to design the service appropriately. To ensure data integrity, the network configuration process has to maintain the configuration information stored in its routing and connectivity tables and keep it synchronized with the network configuration information stored in network management and administrative systems.

5.5.6 Network Inventory

Inventory functionality includes the ability to add, change, decommission, assess the status of, and reconcile inventory related data. The network inventory process is responsible for installation and administration (acceptance) of the equipment in accordance with the physical implementation of the network. This process also manages spare parts, software and hardware upgrades, and repair process records that may impact the network provisioning process. The trigger for this process is typically a work order request for installation often initiated by a network problem. It can also be triggered by the repair, fault, or spare part sub-processes. Some service providers outsource portions (e.g., site work, repair, software upgrades, or equipment or software inventory) of this process to suppliers.

5.5.7 Testing

The test process is responsible for verifying the operational status of a service and determining the cause of any faults. This process maintains a collection of hardware and software test suites and a database for test scenarios, which should identify the component under test and the expected test results. The test scenarios should cover the goals of the test, test criteria, test approach, testing process, test schedule, test routines, result collection, and result expectations. Depending upon path and equipment characteristics, the test results should align with the service metrics specified in any associated SLAs. It should also coordinate schedules with the trouble ticket management process to provide traceability and audit capability against all activities, such as MTTR.

5.5.8 Military Resource Planning

The service management staff in the military planning units must address spectrum supportability, operation compatibly, and *electromagnetic environmental effects (E3)* throughout the mission life cycle. The resource planning include [55,56]:

- The impact analysis of the electromagnetic environment upon the operational capability of military forces, equipment, systems, and platforms. A plan typically encompasses all *electromagnetic disciplines, electromagnetic compatibility and electromagnetic interference (EMC/EMI), electromagnetic vulnerability, electromagnetic pulse (EMP), electronic protection (EP), hazards of electromagnetic radiation to personnel (HERP), hazards of electromagnetic radiation to ordnance (HERO)*, and

hazards of electromagnetic radiation to fuel (HERF), and natural phenomena effects of lightning and *precipitation static (p-static)*.
- Planning, coordinating, and managing joint use of the electromagnetic spectrum through operational, engineering, and administrative procedures without causing or suffering unacceptable interference.

Figure 5.29 depicts a sample resources flow in a military operation. The flow starts from functional area analysis, functional needs analysis, functional solution analysis, and lastly the functional area plans [57,58].

There are four levels of plans in an adaptive planning procedure. Under adaptive planning, plan creation can be expedited by guidance that specifies the level of detail required for each plan. The amount of detail required is tied to the plan's importance, the likelihood of being executed, and the details of planning required. The guidance can be classified into the following:

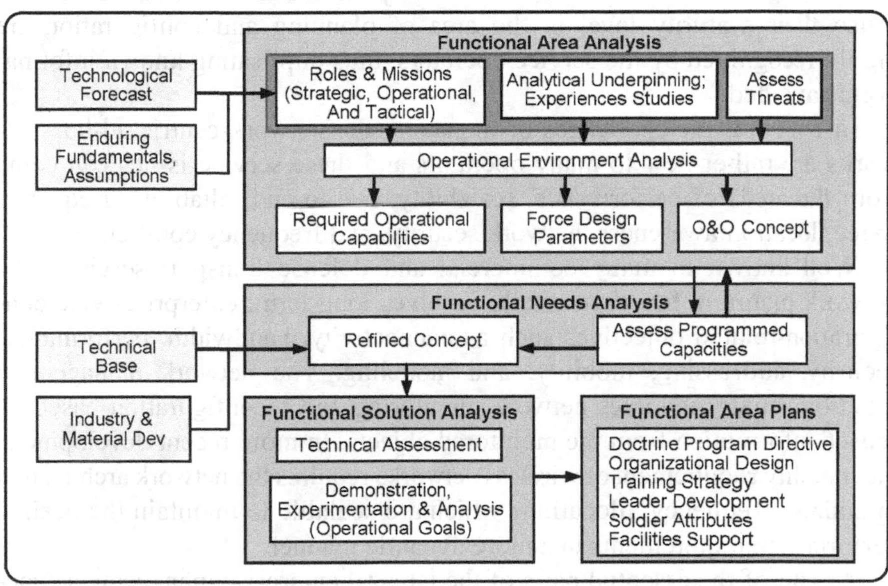

Figure 5.29. Military resource planning.

- *Level 1 plan* requires a developed course of action *(COA)*. The resultant product can be a COA briefing, a command directive, a commander's estimate or concept, or a memorandum.
- *Level 2 plan* culminates in a base plan, a briefing, and *intellectual property rights (IPR)* to the higher commanders. Level 2 plans provides sufficient detail to describe the *concept of operations*, major forces, concepts of support, and anticipated timelines for completing the mission. This is also called *base plan*.

- *Level 3 plan* includes the base plan from the level 2 plan, and a combatant commander's estimate of the plan's feasibility with respect to forces logistics, sustainment, and transportation. This is also called *concept plan (CONPLAN)*.
- *Level 4 plan* requires a base plan, a complete set of descriptions, and a detailed force flow data. This is also called *operations plan (OPLAN)*.

5.6 Conclusion

In the context of transport service management, the scope of network planning and management is always domain specific. This chapter focuses on the infrastructure-less networks and services which could be attached to or detached from traditional wireless networks. The reason why tradition methods or landline networks are less emphasized in this chapter was because their maturity level in the area of planning and configuration are highly recognized by the service operators, thus duplicating known information is avoided.

In contrast, the challenges of managing the network-centric ad-hoc networks are rather new to many operators and these service issues can come from the areas of performance, scalability, end-to-end reliability, frequency space, location awareness, network security, and frequency conflict.

Well known to many commercial and defense transport services, the network planning function usually involves long term, enterprise-wide configuration-related objectives such as connectivity, bandwidth, performance, security, addressing, mobility, and modeling. The network management function usually involves network monitoring and reconfiguration based on sensed information from the monitored objects. In more recent development, the mobility requirement of wireless networks requires the network architecture to address frequency allocations which are scalable to maintain the desired performance requirements in a more dynamic manner.

As one of the essential parts of the integral enterprise management functions in the network-centric services, the emphasis of this chapter is placed upon SoS integration of many fulfillment features in the OSS framework. The fulfillment systems that can cover the requirements of network service planning include waveform, spectrum, key, power, security, QoS target, and routing protocols. The deployment and deployment consideration section highlighted the processes and design flows about how to initiate and instantiate a workable network plan. The evolving radio technology sections provide a path-forward viewpoint for where strong technical drivers are arising to trigger changes to the processes and methods of the enterprise service management.

Chapter 6

NETWORK AND SERVICE MONITORING

Enterprises services are critically reliant on their networks to function in a distributed, diversified, and complex environment. Historically, wireless service providers place a heavy emphasis on segmented network measurements and domain specific metrics. Recent technology evolutions in network management have improved the capability in measurement coordination and data collection. This improvement significantly expands the awareness of the horizontal networking technologies, as well as the vertical service domains. As a result the growing recognition of the service behavior has enlighten the service providers to start correlating services with revenue for potential measurable customer satisfaction, employee satisfaction, and other non-traditional metrics.

Measuring performance in an over-arching environment challenges the degree of accuracy and completeness of the managed services and thereby continuously pressures system developers and standard bodies to improve new skills for better and faster awareness of end-to-end service performance. Until recent years, service monitoring had been playing a passive business role in reporting and acknowledging service troubles. As the service awareness is entering a new era when service providers not only tactically respond to problems but also strategically anticipate need, service providers are no longer competing based upon a limited set of service parameters. In the spirit of network-centric business operation, service vendors are now creating their own Blue Ocean [1] strategy as a corporate culture and differentiator.

This chapter delineates the latest and most effective means to monitor and measure all parts of a geographically dispersed enterprise network, including its equipment and associated resources. It constitutes the management of diverse functionalities including fault, performance, accounting, testing, and security management. Most popular data collection mechanisms are summarized and discussed. The SoS section portrays a workable SoS approach to implement an integrated service monitoring and enterprise network data solution.

6.1 Overview

Network and service monitoring is one of the most essential enterprise features which can assist the service providers in obtaining important intelligence about the offered services for both business and operational reasons. Although traditional IT monitoring is commonly referred to as the data collection of computing and network components (e.g., applications, operating systems, desktops, servers, routers/gateways, and switches) recent practices have revealed much other hidden information from the existing measurements.

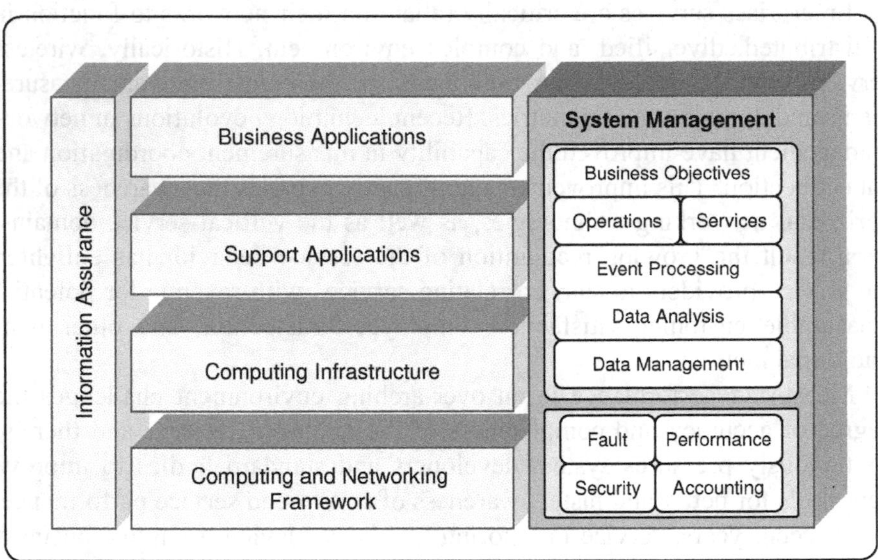

Figure 6.1. System architecture of enterprise services.

For instance, some measured parameters from the managed network resources can potentially be used to derive into meaningful knowledge such as network traffic patterns, QoS-based performance, and network behaviors. Similar techniques are widely adopted into the application and business arenas where business transactions, Web service traffic, and mission results become the center of the service monitoring function; these higher level implications and methods will be addressed in the following chapters.

As depicted in Figure 6.1, the network and service monitoring feature possesses more features and values than merely data acquisition and embellished reports. The *hard (raw) data* controllable by collection agents and distributable over local or global networks can be categorized into fault, performance, security, and accounting as shown in the bottom box in the System Management layer. This data from a group or groups of managed resources provide limited, localized, and sometimes fragmental measurements or events. It may require time-based and address-based correlations to mediate data from different sources in the Data Management functions located at the upper box in the System Management layer. If the data acquired from multiple heterogeneous sources is done with indirect or illogical relationships, the Data Analysis and Event processing can provide level one or level two fusion functions to improve the level of understanding about these measurements. In a more advanced solution, further processes can produce operational or service information that benefit service evaluation, system integration, maintenance, performance monitoring, mission monitoring, and diagnostic/prognostic performance arenas.

6.1.1 Monitoring Framework

The network and service monitoring framework captures events, measurements, and logs from the managed service resources for display and analysis. This framework should possess the capabilities to extract data from defined protocol interfaces and analyze them in operator- or user-defined methods. The operational goal is to provide accurate, detailed, and adaptive monitoring of all of distributed service components end-to-end and perform performance analysis and fault detection in a Grid computing environment.

From the data flow perspective, service data is gathered from local collection agents and these agents then route the data to a regional repository for preliminary data fusion and organization. The data including faults, errors, violations, and application triggers; they are captured and processed in real-time mode. While the performance metrics are polled from the networks periodically, this type of data is processed in a "near" real-time manner. Both acquisition methods can be configured to perform either reactive or proactive monitoring, depending upon the nature of services and the availability of the information. The monitor system then examines the captured data in real-time mode, detecting specific service conditions and generating service notifications as required.

The four functional blocks concerning the monitoring functions are managed system, management services, measurement system, and management information models, as shown in Figure 6.2. They are:

- The managed system is managed by the measurement system; it uses management services to communicate with the management system. The managed systems can optionally contain local instrumentation tools and sensor management for streamlined problem diagnosis and status reporting. Local agents in a managed system can form cluster-based functionalities such as detection, location, isolation, information routing, and data dissemination to deal with a larger domain base service for further advanced processes.
- The management services enable transport of any management data between managed systems and the management system by a common set of protocols which describe, exchange, and locate monitoring data. Depending upon the implementation requirements, such services can support repetitive and on-demand measurements with appropriate security measures. This includes archiving and access to data, evaluation, validation, analysis, and reporting of data for ease of comprehension and usage.
- The measurement system is responsible for coordinating with other management systems to manage all systems. It contains functions for monitoring, information distribution, policy management, user interface, and so forth. Through the management services, the measurement systems can obtain the configurations, relationships, and dependencies of the software and hardware resources in the information models where the events, measurements, or logs are defined. This model-driven information allows the SoS to cultivate systematic studies of problems, causes, and potential bypass in order to conduct an impact analysis of the managed services. It can provide well-understood and accepted metrics to SLM or SQM systems for tracking realistic and enforceable service objectives. Additionally, an event analysis and visualization tool can provide service operators a means of performing more effective command and control of the SoS.
- The management information models contain process reference models which explain the business context of the data. It interacts with other operation support systems such as incident management, problem management, configuration management, and change management. The models offer a common representation (e.g., naming conventions) and schemas allowing the SoS to share information among multiple measurement systems. In the SoS where multi-disciplinary functions are needed, the management information models can provide a means to enforce monitoring collaborations.

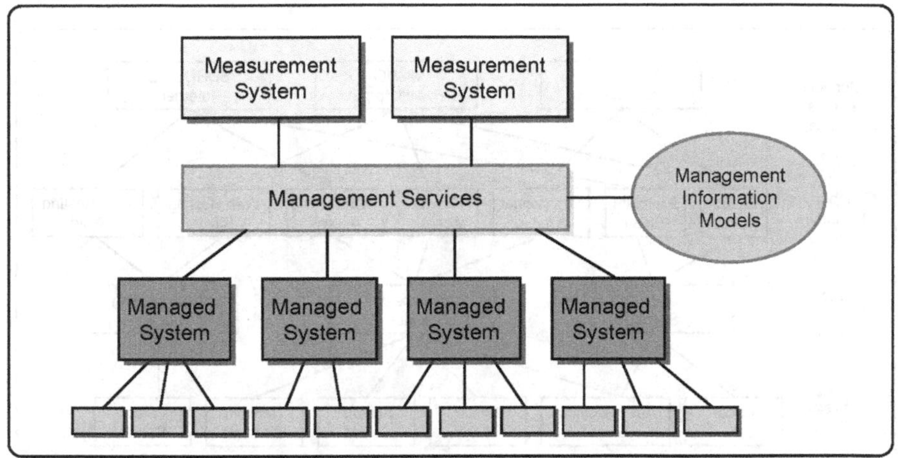

Figure 6.2. Four major functional blocks of the monitoring functions.

6.1.2 Monitor Domains

There are two dimensions concerning network and service monitoring. As depicted in Figure 6.3, a set of four-layer plane is introduced. From the top of the figure:

- *Service (Offer) plane* contains composite service (or product) components and has direct interaction with the customers or service users.
- *Collaborated functional plane* incorporates distributed service elements into business or operational groups that are most sensible to service offering.
- *Distributed functional plane* contains individual service building-blocks or elements that are logical notation of physical resources or functionalities.
- *Physical plane* can be wireless networks, wire-line networks, application servers, content servers, or management systems.

The physical plane can further divided into different domains, depicted in Figure 6.4. According to the previous discussion of network architecture and configuration, these domains may not be applicable to every implementation or deployment. For instance, a large, multiple-service, and multiple-vendors network can include the access network, core network, content network, and management network. In a simpler enterprise networking environment, the content network can be eliminated. These four domains discussed now [2].

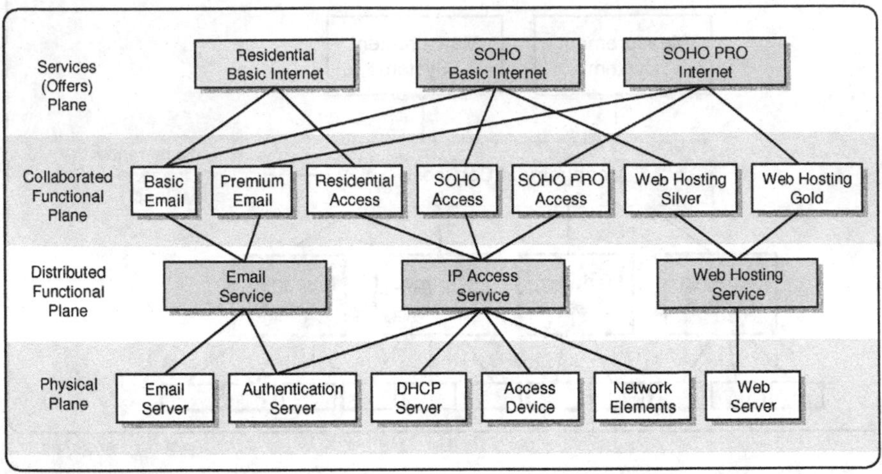

Figure 6.3. Vertical relationships of service and network resources.

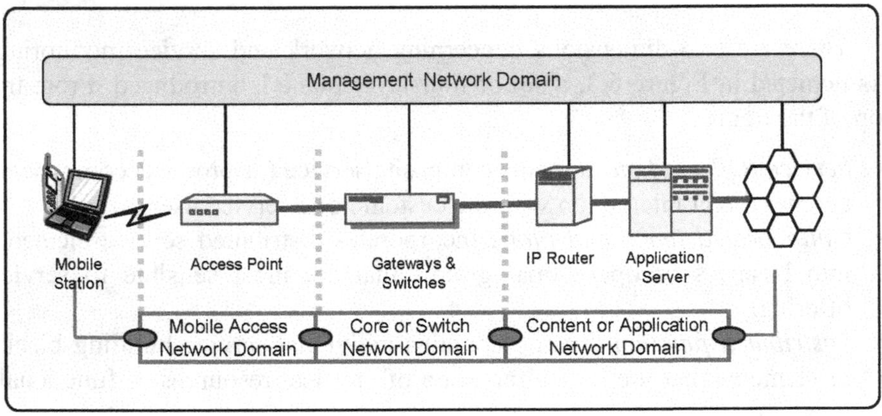

Figure 6.4. Four domains in the physical plane.

6.1.2.1 Access Network Domain

The access network domain mainly concerns the user and application facing experiences. To measure the access network metrics, the considerations are placed upon adjacencies, statistics of data and voice traffic received and transmitted counts, MAC traffic (RTS, CTS, and so forth), throughputs, packet drops/discards and reasons, TTL expired, queue limited, and so forth. For metrics with respect to applications (e.g., WWW, e-mail, a distributed RDBMS, a spreadsheet accessing a distributed file system), the measures of interest include host resource utilization, logical network topology, statistic of good packets, bandwidth (e.g., in Kbps or Mbps), packet size distribution, error rate/type, QoS (buffer/controller overflows), availability of critical networking services (e.g., mail, WWW, name, font, NFS and others) and most active resource consumers.

The RF performance between the antenna and transceiver is a measure of power (e.g., dBm). The RF performance on the other side of the antenna is measured by electric field strength (e.g., dBμV/m) or magnetic field strength (e.g., dBμA/m) at a specified distance. The antenna performance can be *in band* RF parameters like receiver sensitivity and transmitter output, as well as *out of band* parameters like spurious responses and transmitted noise.

The conventional definition of *receiver sensitivity* for wireless data networks is the minimum input power level required to achieve a given average received *bit error rate (BER)*. Two types of sensitivity are:

- The signal level necessary for symbol and frame synchronization to occur at the start of a frame.
- The signal level necessary for a certain average received BER of payload data once synchronization has been achieved.

In a sensor application, for instance, measurements data gathering can be direct transmission, gateway (relay) collection, chain-based scheme (binary scheme which classified nodes into different levels), and chain-based multi-level scheme (see chapter 4).

The other important information in this domain includes security violation, a proactive tool to identify security threats, and a response mechanism to trigger protection or prevention logics. These are a must for the enterprise.

6.1.2.2 Core or Switch Network Domain

The core or switch network delivers local traffic to the remote applications or accesses to other regional networks. Acting like the SS7 network for the traditional telephone network, the core or switch network can be very complex when end-to-end QoS is required. VPN with other special assurance functions are typically required.

From the monitoring and control perspective, statistics, alarms, and events are similar to the access network with focus more on delay, speed, and quality. The speed measures may include buffer overflow, and traffic burst. The quality can include throw away bad packets (packet loss), response time, host unreachable, hop counts, and number of simultaneous users or connections. Key information to the service operators is a consolidated service and network topology across different technologies, vendors, and protocols.

Because the number of network resources can grow rapidly, the needs for more network coverage implies that traffic flows and patterns may no longer follow the original network plans. Monitoring functions give the service providers a useful reference to align the plan with the actual deployment or utilization.

6.1.2.3 Content or Application Network Domain

The purpose of a content or application network is to form one or more service communities in order to support remote or local users. Typically, they are in part of the enterprise LAN or a special purpose content server group. The measurements of interest focus on the application layer concern security, delay, and other transport QoS measurements. For instance, Web services for business transactions may require a test driver to intrusively inject management traffic to obtain the delay measurement. At the transport level, the data collection function monitors and collects data from Server (e.g., TCP/IP, ICMP, IPX/SPX, database, event log, SQL query, HTTP URL), TCP port, routers, switches, servers, and any other IP devices. At the application level, CPU load, memory utilization, available disk space, and application processes (http, https, ping, SMTP, POP3, IMAP4, FTP, TCP), availability, and performance.

For applications, such as VoIP or videoconference, and *Internet protocol television (IPTV)*, performance monitoring against the protocols such as SIP or H.323 should be extended to the end-to-end network and host levels. Two of the most popular modes in these applications are passive call quality monitoring and active QoS management. Some monitoring units can be embedded into end-systems, management devices, or DSPs to perform non-intrusive monitoring. The results are used to improve the model of time-varying impairments and their effects on end-user-perceived quality in real time [3].

6.1.2.4 Management Network Domain

Management Network is an *out-of-band network*. This domain means not to process user application data or voice messages but to connect all the systems and server hosting operational systems (e.g., OSS) that manage the application networks. The collected information can highlight the awareness of the monitored network in the area of performance, behaviors, and troubleshooting. The network operators can look at such formation from a managing center for a particular network segment and perform needed control functions accordingly. The OSS can include but is not limited to fault management (alarm surveillance, testing), configuration management (provisioning, rating), performance management (QoS monitoring, traffic control), security management (managing access and authentication), and accounting management (rating and billing) as part of the OSI model. Depending upon the business arrangement, the management network can be connected across many companies.

In fact, network data collection is the crucial first step to establish an intelligent management system. A variety of different networked applications can run on different protocol suites (TCP/IP, DEC, AppleTalk, Netware, and so forth) over different routing protocols, bridging, and tunnels. With networked *raw* data, it is not sufficient to become "intelligent" about the managed service. To realize the awareness of service performance, the management system at the network level should integrate and correlate different information from different vendors, suppliers, and carriers. This should cover element, network, and service management applications (trouble ticket, probe management, and so forth) running on different server platforms. Once the physical resources are connected and management data is collectable, the management system can then obtain detailed knowledge about traffic patterns in the network and determine how the traffic is growing and changing. The network operator can therefore ensure that users and resources are placed in the correct locations. Additionally, the resource can be optimized and costs can be reduced regardless of their hardware or software differences.

6.1.3 Service Monitor in NCBO

A modern network typically constitutes many networks where services are chained or interacted to form a value-chain offering to target user communities (CoIs, see section 8.1.1). It is becoming the norm for many IT-based corporations to focus on their strength, and outsource other functionalities (see section 1.2.1). As a result, individual network can potentially be owned and operated by different organizations. Monitoring such network arrangements is much different than monitoring a single network because resources are now under the control of many different systems. From another perspective, network such as the Internet, even though based on the same technology, it may contain different base layer platforms and is managed by different management systems.

The ability to identify a commonality of static or dynamic characteristics of a managed network is essential for network modeling. Organizing these characteristics in a knowledge hierarchy is an important aspect of network management. These advantages are shown in Figure 6.5.

- *Corporate Customer View* provides a common understanding of the knowledge domain between network resources. This model can promote interoperability and integration of the corporation's network and results in reduced communication costs and improved competitive advantages.
- *Network Carrier View* builds upon and reuses specifications and implementations known to the network. This model can facilitate faster provisioning of advanced services and enhance the revenue stream.

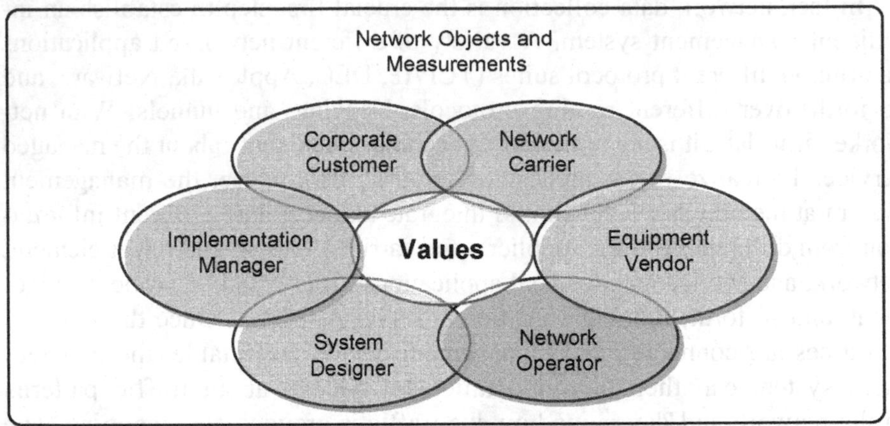

Figure 6.5. Business relationships concerning network objects and measurements.

- *Equipment Vendor View* assists in flexible and modular representations of network element architectures. The model can facilitate the engineering design process, speed up product development cycles, and result in faster time-to-market.
- *Network Operator View* facilitates similar operating and administrative functions on the network resources. The model can ease the process of integrating and managing diverse components of the networks.
- *System Designer View* imposes a clean modular decomposition on the design process of a management system, thereby reducing the development effort.
- *Implementation Manager View* provides a vehicle for reusability of the design modules, speeding up the development process and easing the evolution and maintenance of network products.

6.1.4 Monitoring Difficulties

The modern network is becoming more difficult to monitor because the rapid growth of the user base and a lack of quality measurements for the serving networks as a whole.

For instance, there are neither standardized monitoring tools nor standardized metrics for monitoring the Internet. The most common Internet monitoring tools are public domain software available for the Internet and easily customized. Several common public domain software programs used in network monitoring are *ping*, *ftp*, and *traceroute*. They are usually used to measure host response time, time delay, and loss rate. *Ping* sends a packet of user data to a specific node and the packet is echoed back. This provides metrics for response time and the percentage of packet loss. *Ftp* transfers a file from one host to another. This allows the measurement of the data transfer rate. *Traceroute* sends Internet Control Message Protocol (ICMP) messages to the host. This allows for the measurement of number of hops to another host and the performance of the route. Other public domain software products include *arpwatch*, *nslookup*, and so forth.

The challenges of these approaches are: 1) these public software are not intended for monitoring; because their usage eats up network capacity thus only limited amount of monitoring activities can be allowed to avoid impacting application traffic; and 2) monitoring the network is not straightforward; problems are not often recognizable and consequently are solved infrequently. As a result, the overall Internet performance is degrading.

Owing to the fact that most enterprise networks are beginning to rely fully or partially on the Internet to communicate with the outside information world, challenges as aforementioned can cause tremendous amount of productivity loss when performance impacts take place.

6.2 Measured Metrics

Figure 6.6 portrays a typical manager and agent relationship in a network monitoring application. The Manager can either push commands to or pull the data from the agent; it can also receive traps or events from the managed network. In a complex network deployment when scalability is a critical consideration, the agents can be configured in hierarchical architecture to improve efficiency. This figure shows two subagents associated with the agent.

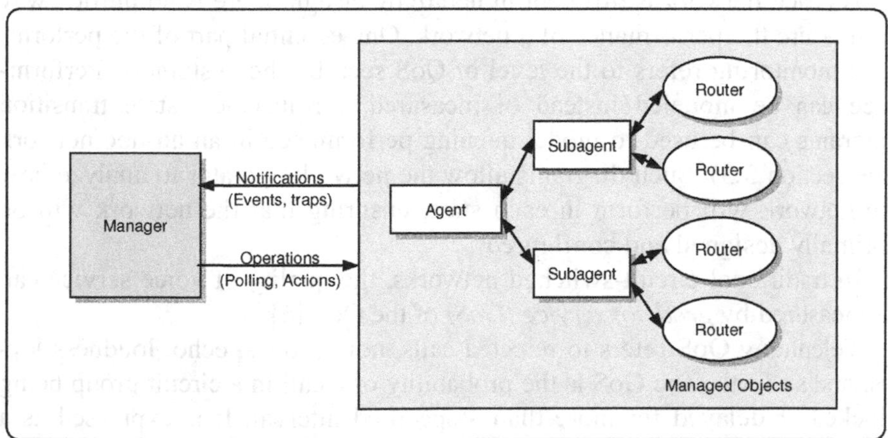

Figure 6.6. Manager–agent relationship in network management.

The following sections illustrate a generic set of metrics that are applicable to the majority of enterprise IT environments. Application variances defined in the SLA for different service customers can dictate the monitored parameters and polling cycles.

6.2.1 Faults

Faults can be a failure of an abnormal condition or a defect that causes a reproducible or catastrophic malfunction at the component, equipment, subsystem, or system level [4,5] Symmetrical faults can be an abstraction that is possible to be analyzed via a similar or even the same analytical method. Asymmetrical faults are unbalanced and difficult to analyze, thus analysis of asymmetrical faults is typically built up from a thorough understanding of symmetric faults.

Failures can also be classified as random faults or systematic faults. The occurrence of random faults cannot be determined. The rate for such faults to occur can be predicted with statistics (e.g., average) approaches. Systematic faults are often a result of errors in the equipment specifications of a system. Failures in software are always systematic; software bugs are often the result of mistakes or errors in source code or design. Bugs may have a subtle effect and lie undetected for a long time, sometimes causing the program to crash or freeze. Some bugs can lead to security problems.

6.2.2 Performance

As each network is different in nature by design, there is no unified way to measure the performance of a network. One essential part of the performance monitoring refers to the level of QoS seen by the customers. Performance can be modeled instead of measured, for instance, state transition diagrams can be used to model queuing performance in an ad-hoc network (see section 3.3). Such diagrams allow the network operator to analyze how the network will perform in each state, ensuring that the network will be optimally designed and configured.

In traditional circuit-switched networks, the quality of voice service can be measured by *grade of service (GoS)* of the QoS [6].

Telephony QoS refers to rejected calls, noise, tones, echo, loudness levels, and so forth. The GoS is the probability of a call in a circuit group being blocked or delayed for more than a specified interval. It is expressed as a vulgar fraction or decimal fraction. Additionally, GoS may be viewed independently from the perspective of incoming versus outgoing calls or between different source–destination pairs.

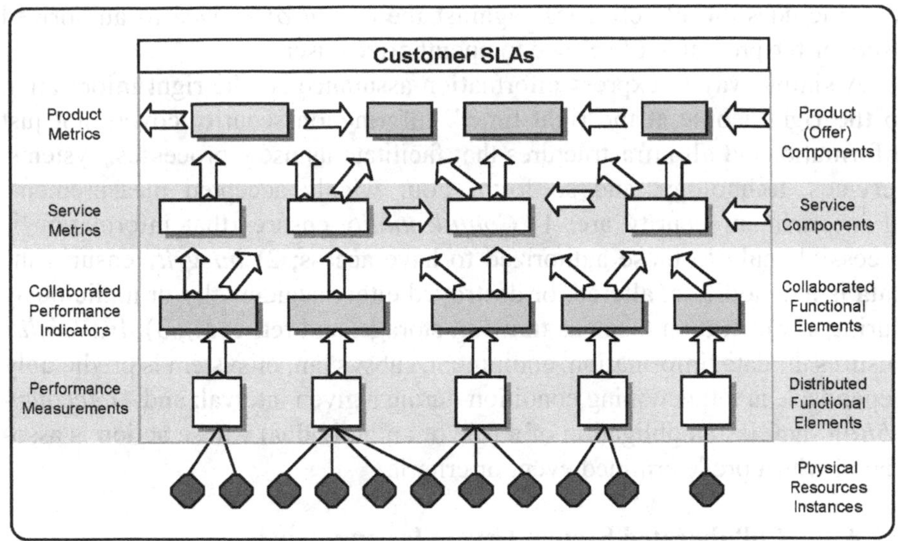

Figure 6.7. Performance measurements in different service monitoring layers.

In data packet networks, performance can be measured by bandwidth, data throughput, delays, connect time, stability, and so forth. The QoS refers to the probability of the network meeting a given SLA. Criteria for different QoS may include *bandwidth* and *latency* where the *bandwidth* is the amount of data that can be transferred through a connection in a given time period and the *latency* is the time interval for a message to travel from source to destination. Performance measurements are always with reference to the busy hour when the traffic intensity is the greatest. The complexity of data monitoring and collection can be seen in Figure 6.7 where data is aggregated and processed into different layers for service monitoring [7].

The QoS of an ad-hoc network is normally represented by network efficiency for time spending on network *formation* (collection of nodes to automatically organize itself and transmit the first message reliably), *join time* (an entering node or group of nodes to merge into an already formed network), *depart time* (reform after losing one or more nodes), *self-healing* or *recovery time* (a collapsed or fragmented network becomes functional again), and *reorganization time* (reorganization after being reconfigured).

6.2.3 Information Security Violations

Information security is referred to as an information assurance factor dealing with different "trust" aspects of information. Information security includes safeguarding or protecting the SoS against unauthorized access to or modification of information, whether in storage, processing, or transit. It also includes the effectiveness against the *denial of service* to authorized users or the provision of service to unauthorized users.

A simple way to express information assurance is "the right information to the right people at the right time". Information security covers not just information but all infrastructures that facilitate its use – processes, systems, services, technology, and so forth. Four widely accepted measurements of information security are: 1) *Confidentiality* ensures that information is accessible only to those authorized to have access; 2) *Integrity* ensures the data is not modified, altered, or destroyed either accidentally or maliciously during any operation (such as transfer, storage, and retrieval); 3) *Availability* ensures the data, information, equipment, subsystem, or system is predictably dependable in a functioning condition during a given interval; and 4) *Accountability* signifies an obligation of a role or an individual whose action is associated with a predetermined event or criteria.

6.2.4 Collaborated System Level Measurements

System level metrics are either application-specific or end-to-end experiences which support applications. The most noticeable metrics in this area are: 1) *Reliability* or *service continuation*; 2) *Scalability* is the ability to scale to support larger or smaller service environment or more or less users without impacting performance; and 3) *SoS availability* is the degree to composite service that is operable and in a committable state at a given time when the mission is called. It is the proportion of time a service is in a functioning condition.

6.2.5 Operational Measurements

Operational metrics are important indicators for any stakeholders in a value chain to gain more revenue opportunities from their valued customers. For instance, service providers' view of operational metrics are: 1) *mean time to repair (MTTR)*; 2) *mean time between failures (MTBF)*; 3) *over-provisioning bandwidth*; 4) *end-to-end view* with confidence and threshold levels of certain key statistical or performance metrics; and 5) degree of *self-configuration*. Systems operators can value operational metrics differently. For instance the measurements can include: 1) unnecessary capital expenditures from the usage patterns; 2) monitor promised versus delivered variances in SLAs; 3) maximized availability of mission-critical business applications; 4) fraud detection through real-time detection of illicit usage; 5) level of wasted bandwidth on non-business applications that is reclaimable; and 6) degree of *self-maintenance*.

6.2.6 Service Accounting

Service accounting can be described by the following attributes: 1) *Intangibility* is about the level of visualization of system behaviors that were traditionally difficult to be planned ahead, conceptualized, organized, or analyzed by typical tools. This indicator assesses if the system can provide concrete images or indicators for evaluation or comparison purposes; 2) *Perishability* measures unsold service time that is *lost* and cannot be regained; 3) *Lack of transportability* bases on feature, role, or user to assess how many offered services are not consumed at the point of "production"; 4) *Lack of homogeneity* is the ratio of sold services that required customization; 5) *Labor intensity* indicates required human involvement for sold services; 6) *Demand fluctuations* estimates demands based on the historical statistics; and 7) *Buyer involvement* measures the degree of interaction between client and service provider during service provision.

6.3 Resource Management Model

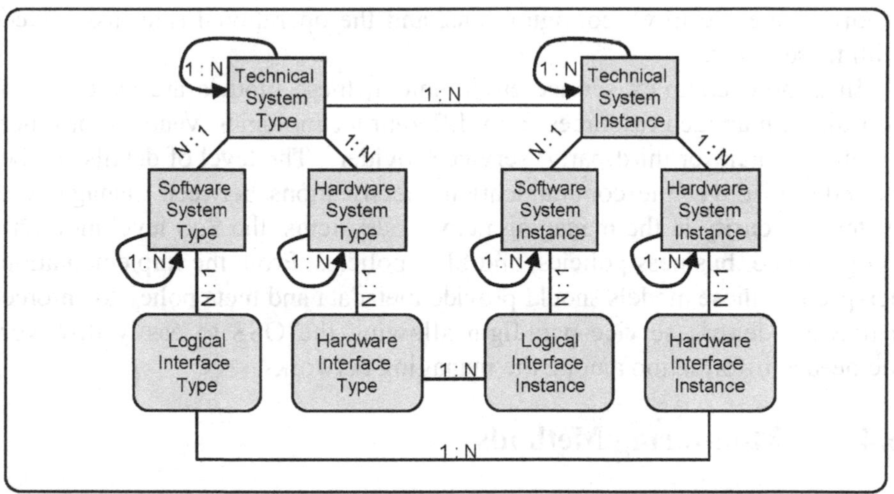

Figure 6.8. Relationships between types and instances of systems and interfaces.

A managed network or service component (see Figure 6.2) can contain one or more software or hardware system types, a system type can contain one or more system instances, and a technical system instance can contain one or more software or hardware system interfaces. The software systems can be used through different logical interfaces (information exchange models, formats, and protocols). Because a system can contain the same or different types of systems, they can be assembled into either SoS or

FoS architecture as discussed in chapter 1. These relationships are illustrated in Figure 6.8 [8].

As aforementioned in section 6.1.1, Management Information Models are used to describe the business and operational context of the management systems. By collecting the relationships and resource attributes of the managed networks or services, the service operators can establish a collaborated view of the service environment. Figure 6.8 only depicts a generic resource or asset management model. The network or service architectures and topology models briefly discussed in chapters 4 and 5 will not be repeated here. A service model which addresses more advanced information and knowledge management will be described in chapter 9.

To facilitate resource management, the service operators should ideally hold the complete information describing the managed assets. Through a comprehensive model set, the operators can increase their awareness of the resource locations, vendors, asset types, expected behaviors, how the services are configured, and the policies these assets should follow. Furthermore, these models can also provide knowledge about the dynamic aspect of the managed asset, which is also known as the *situation information*, i.e., states of operations (e.g., start, stop, connect, request, configure, available, report, create, destroy), configurations, and the operational rules associated with these states.

In a more complex service environment, these models are expected to coordinate managed resources from different technologies, vendors, or other (complementary or third-party) service providers. The level of details can be extended to cover the communication specifications between management systems, security in the managing networks/systems, the SoS level monitoring guidance, business policies, and SLA policies. From the implementation perspective, these models should provide metadata and meta policy to enforce a network-centric service paradigm allowing the OSS to easily discover the needed information among the managing networks.

6.4 Monitoring Methods

To monitor networked services, the considerations should cover from the physical layer, link layer, network layer, up to the application layer. It is important that an end-to-end service view is measured proactively and reactively. In the case when remote monitoring is applicable, an agent that interacts with the managed nodes must be able to translate that data into some predetermined protocols such as SNMP and HTTP and deliver the conditioned data to the monitoring systems. In mission critical applications where measurement data contains financial implications as part of the SLA, the

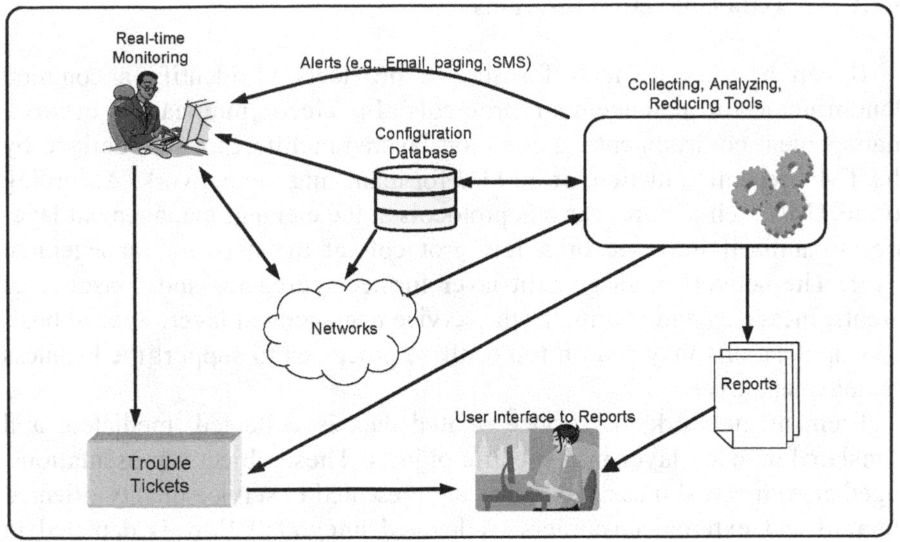

Figure 6.9. Monitoring and controls workflow.

control channels to deliver these data should be reliable, bandwidth controlled, automated, and secure.

The monitoring process provides essential service data to other OSS; therefore it is closely integrated with other functional processes such as event management for event filtering, escalation, field force automation, reporting, trouble-ticketing, and help desk support to fulfill a complete operational cycle. Integrating with inventory management system, the monitoring capability can provide up-to-date service maps to display service (network) topology and capture traffic routing status. An auto-discovery feature of the monitoring system can detect unavailable services or update communication paths as needed. Figure 6.9 illustrates a sample monitoring and control workflow.

The measurement process typically includes the capabilities for real time and historical information on faults, assets, performance and security across networks, systems, and applications. Traditionally, objective-driven monitoring is a concept of utilizing the knowledge base to control a large number of data collection agents for monitoring a distributed computing environment. These agents can be deployed to different parts of network and work together to monitor diversified classes of traffic and traffic patterns. In NCBO, this paradigm is further enhanced; the collaborated management models are now center to the operations coordinating all the managed resources. After measurements are conditioned by the preliminary data fusion functions (see section 6.5), they will be available in the managing COI ready for any OSS's access.

6.4.1 Data Collection Methods

It can be very difficult for service providers to identify a common denominator for management protocols. In telecommunication network management environments, a common layered architecture was defined by the TMN recommendations from ITU for managing the network. According to the TMN architecture, various protocols at the element management layer are streamlined into one or a few protocols at the network management layer. The network management layer further aggregates and consolidates events, messages and alarms for the service management layer. Special business applications may run on top of these processes to support the business management layer.

Element, network, or service related data is collected, mediated, and translated on each layer into specific objects. These object representations, together with actual measured values are presented to service quality-oriented internal and external customers. A layered integrated flow is depicted in Figure 6.10 [6].

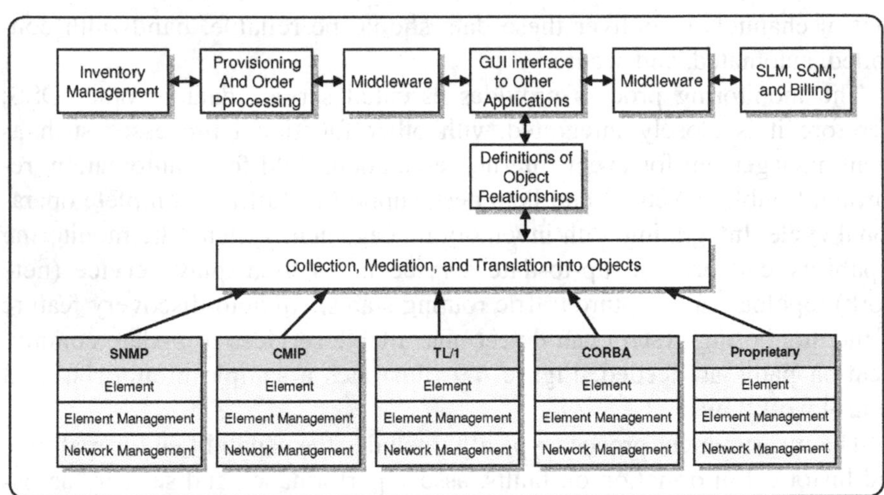

Figure 6.10. Layered integration architecture.

6.4.1.1 Packet Sniffer

The *Packet Sniffers* (also known as *network analyzers*) can be either software programs or computer hardware which captures network packets passing through physical network interfaces. The Packet Sniffer monitors Ethernet and WLAN traffic in real time and translates complex protocol negotiation into natural language according to the appropriate RFC or other specifications in order to assist in troubleshooting and debugging mixed-platform, multi-protocol networks. When operating in *promiscuous mode*, it listens to everything on the wire.

If the managed node has a so-called monitoring port, which mirrors all packets passing through all ports of the node, a single sniffer instance is sufficient. Otherwise, multiple instances will be required to capture traffic from other systems on the network.

The applications of sniffer includes analyzing network problems, isolating traffic problems and congestions, detecting network intrusion attempts, gaining information for effecting a network intrusion, monitoring network usage, filtering suspect content from network traffic, spying on other network users and collect sensitive information such as passwords, and reverse engineering protocols used over the network.

Coordinating with the *sniffers*, some organic tools such as *tcpdump* (creating TCP/UDP trace file), cyrptography-based sanitization tools, *flstats* (extracting flow statistics from trace files), *snuffle* (capturing the protocol messages, internal protocol states, and measuring implementation performance on networking nodes), and *libpcap* (tracking sessions maintaining transaction state and collecting metrics of server/network response times) can add value to the monitoring strategies.

6.4.1.2 Ping

The *Ping* facility uses ICMP Echo mechanism to send a packet of a user selected length to the remote node, and have it echoed back. The echo responder runs at a high priority hence can provide a better measure of network performance than a user application. This method has very modest network bandwidth requirements.

There are many tools available using this facility for measuring network performance. A popular one is known as *ping end-to-end reporting (PingER)* [9]. It is developed by the *end-to-end performance measurement (IEPM)* project at the *Stanford Linear Accelerator Center*. There are over 17 Monitoring Sites with more than 300 remote sites being monitored, and over 1000 monitor-site remote-site pairs included worldwide. Figure 6.11 depicts this multi-layer ping architecture to measure availability of remote hosts. The The architecture of the monitoring architecture includes three components.

- The remote monitoring sites provide passive remote-hosts with the appropriate operational requirements.
- The monitoring site contains PingER local monitoring tools (Figure 6.11) to perform short-term analysis. The ping data collected is available to the archive hosts via HTTP.
- The archive and analysis sites complement each other by HTTP and create analysis reports from the data gathered.

The performance reports from this architecture includes: 1) the Packet Loss represents quality of the link for TCP-based applications concerning congestion or imperfect packet formation; 2) the *round trip time (RTT)* is related to the distance between the sites as well as the delay at each hop, along the path between the sites. The delays at each hop are a function of three major components: the speed of the router, the interface clocking rates, and the queuing in the router; and 3) the TCP throughput can be obtained by using the Mathis formula for deriving the maximum TCP throughput from MSS/(RTT*sqrt(loss)).

Based on these reports, recommendations can be made to the service operator to make the appropriate arrangements.

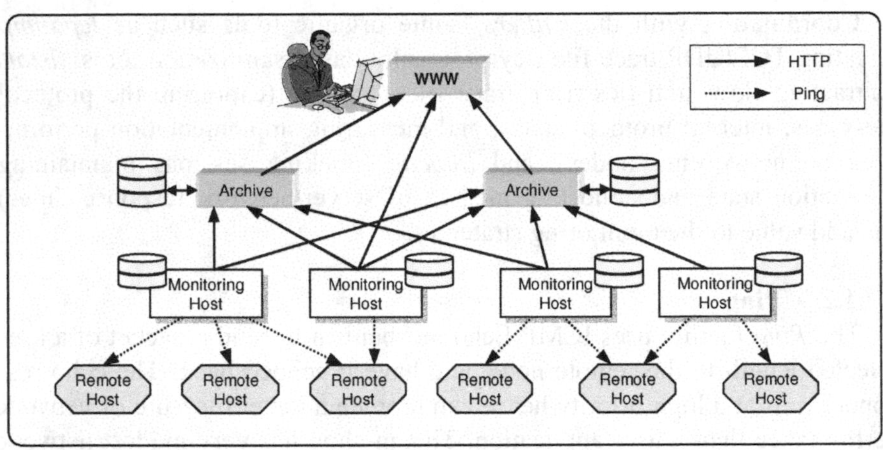

Figure 6.11. Architecture of PingER.

6.4.1.3 Transaction Language 1

Transaction Language 1 (TL1) uses a standard *man–machine language (MML)* to manage *network elements (NEs)* as defined in GR-831 by *Bellcore* (now *Telcordia*). MML is readable by machines as well as humans to replace the diverse ASCII-based protocols used by different NE vendors. It is the most widely used management protocol that manages optical (SONET) and broadband access infrastructure in North America. It has been considered one of the most popular "legacy" protocols which supports cross-vendor and cross-technology management in telecommunications.

Originally Bellcore implemented TL1 as the element management protocol in their fault management OSS called *Network Monitoring and Analysis (NMA)* for the *Regional Bell Operating Companies (RBOCs)*. As the result, TL1 support became mandatory for all NEs to be manageable by NMA. Eventually, TL1 deployments became widespread in all regional telephone companies.

The TL1 language consists of a set of messages. They are:

- *Input message* is the command sent by the user or the OSS.
- *Output/Response message* is reply sent by the NE in response to an input message.
- *Acknowledgment message* is an acknowledgment of the receipt of a TL1 input message and is sent if the response message will be delayed by more than 2 s.
- *Autonomous message* is asynchronous message (usually event or alarm) sent by the NE.

6.4.1.4 Common Object Request Broker Architecture

The *common object request broker architecture (CORBA)* is created and controlled by the *Object Management Group (OMG)* to provide platform and location transparency for sharing computing objects across a distributed computing platform. CORBA defines APIs, a communication protocol, and object/service information models to enable heterogeneous applications running on various platforms to interoperate. It uses an *interface definition language (IDL)* to "wrap" code into a bundle containing data type information and how to call it. It provides the language independent semantics in machine-readable documentation format regardless of implementation.

The architecture defined by OMG for interoperable distributed computing is called *Object Management Architecture*. According to this architecture, any relationship between distributed objects has three components: the client, the server, and a distributed object bus called *object request broker (ORB)*. The *server* provides a remote interface, the *client* calls a remote interface, and the *ORB* enables object to transparently make and receive requests and responses. Any application can be a server for some objects, and a client of others.

Figure 6.12 demonstrates how a distributed object is shared between a CORBA client and server to implement a classic query application. On the client side, the application includes a reference for the remote object. The object reference has a stub method, which is a stand-in for the method to be called remotely. Calling the stub can invoke the ORB connection capabilities to forward the invocation to the server. On the server side, the ORB uses skeleton code to translate remote invocations into method calls on the local object. The skeleton translates the call and any parameters to implementation-specific format and calls the method being invoked. When a method returns, the skeleton code will transform the results or errors, and send them back to the client via the ORBs. The *Internet inter-ORB protocol (IIOP)* is used to communicate between the ORBs based on the Internet protocol.

In addition to the described simple distributed object capabilities, ORBs also supports a number of Object services defined by the OMG. These include services for looking up objects by name, maintaining persistent objects, supporting transaction processing, and enabling messaging. ORBs also include common facilities (i.e., system management), domain interfaces (market vertical specific services), and application objects (vendor provided or custom object implementation).

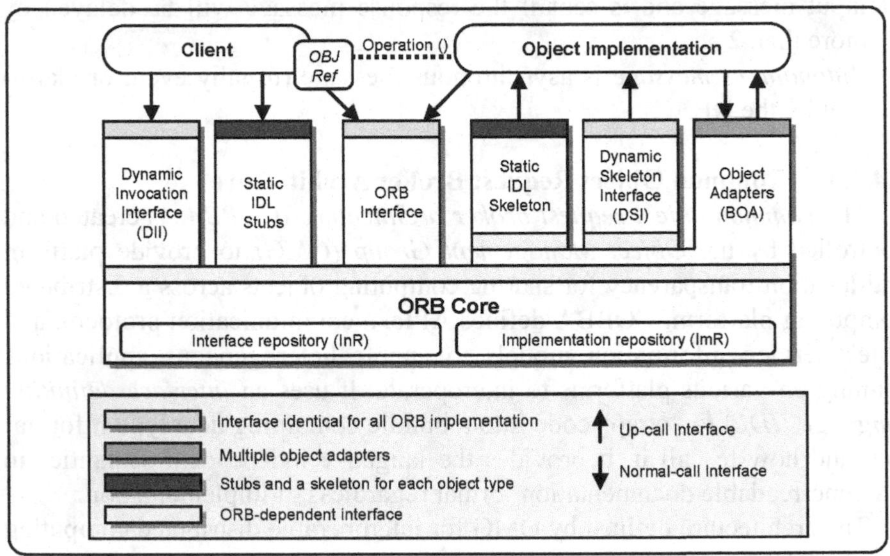

Figure 6.12. CORBA architecture.

6.4.1.5 Common Management Information Services

The common management information services (CMIS) is part of the *Open Systems Interconnection (OSI)* body of telecommunication standards. The CMIS message set is known as the *common management interface protocol (CMIP)*, a protocol (ITU-T X.700) for the communication between network management applications and management agents [10].

CMIS defines the structure and the content of a message set such that they can be used by compatible open systems. It defines management information for the managed objects to facilitate modification and actions on managed objects. Managed objects are described using *guidelines for the definition of managed objects (GDMO)* and are identified by a *distinguished name (DN)*. Information services are used by peer processes to exchange information and commands for network management. CMIP provides good security (supports authorization, access control, and security logs) and flexible reporting of unusual network conditions.

As shown in Figure 6.13, CMIS environment (CMISE) was designed as an enabler for the *Telecommunications Management Network (TMN)* featuring cross-organizational and cross-vendor network management. Using CMIS, a management system can perform the following operations [11]:

- *CREATE* an instance of a managed object.
- *DELETE* an instance of a managed object.
- *GET* the value of a managed object instance.
- *CANCEL_GET* to cancel an outstanding GET request.
- *SET* the value of a managed object instance.
- *ACTION* to request an action to occur as defined by the managed object.

The management agent can perform this operation:

- *EVENT_REPORT* to send notifications or alarms to the NMS.

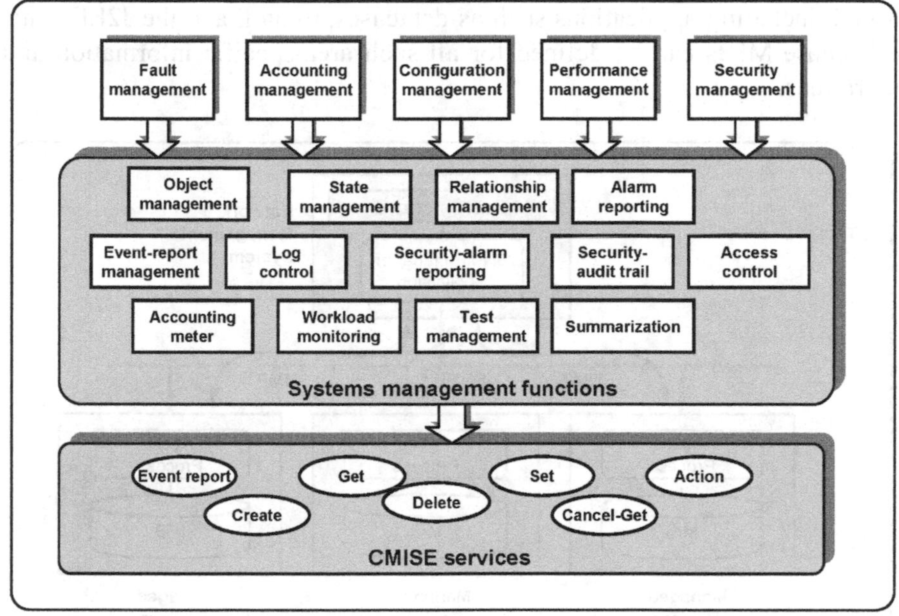

Figure 6.13. CMIS Environment.

CMIP was designed in competition with SNMP. It has far more features and complexity than SNMP. For example, SNMP defines only *SET* actions to alter the state of the managed device while CMIP allows the definition of any type of action. However, because of the complexity and resource requirements of CMIP agents and management systems, most TCP/IP devices support SNMP instead of CMIP. CMIP is only seen on telecommunication devices.

6.4.1.6 Simple Network Management Protocol

The Internet Engineering Task Force (IETF) simple network management protocol (SNMP) protocol operates at the application layer (layer 7) of the OSI model. It forms part of the Internet protocol suite as defined by the IETF. The protocol is used by network management systems for monitoring networked devices for conditions that warrant administrative attention.

The SNMP protocol is extensible by design, achieved through the notion of a *management information base (MIB)*. An MIB specifies the management data of a specific subsystem of an SNMP-enabled device. It uses a hierarchical namespace containing object-identifiers, defined by Abstract Syntax Notation Number One (ASN.1). The MIB hierarchy can be depicted as a tree with a nameless root; each level is assigned by different organizations. This model permits management across all layers of the OSI reference model, including applications such as databases, e-mail, and the J2EE. This is because MIBs can be defined for all such area-specific information and operations.

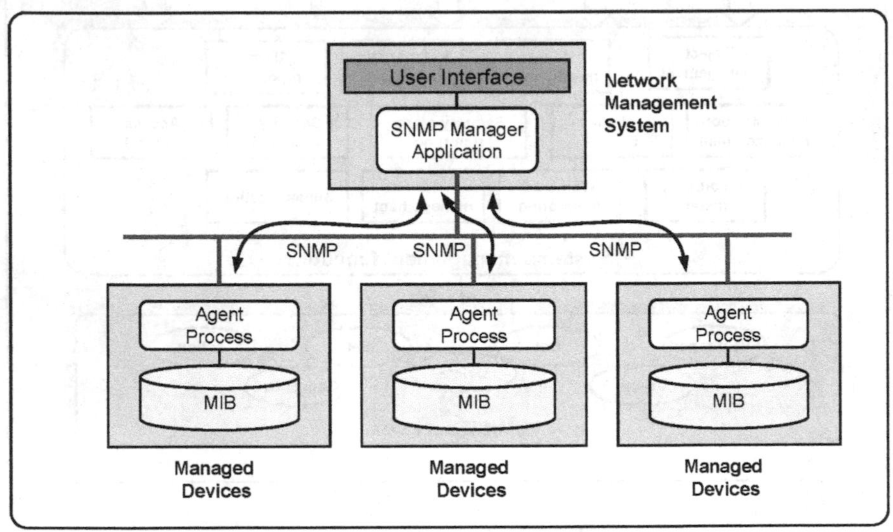

Figure 6.14. SNMP Framework.

As shown in Figure 6.14, the SNMP framework has three fundamental software components architecturally; they are: master agents, subagents, and management stations.

- *Master agent*, also referred to as *managed objects*, acts as a server and responds to SNMP requests made by a management station. A master agent relies upon subagents to provide information about the management of specific functionality.

- *Subagent* implements the information and management functionality defined by a specific MIB of a subsystem (i.e., the Ethernet link layer). Some subagents gather information from managed objects, configure parameters of the managed objects, respond to managers' requests, and generate alarms or traps.
- *Manager* or *management station* functions as a client. It issues requests for management operations on behalf of an administrator or application, and receives traps from agents as well.

SNMP version 1 was created to solve the problems from OSI CMIS effort (see section 6.5.5) which was perceived to be neither implementable nor workable due to the complexity and over emphasis upon theoretical operations. SNMP was designed as an interim protocol towards large scale deployment of the Internet. As the result, SNMPv1 was criticized for its poor security. Authentication of clients is performed only by a "community string" (a type of password), which is transmitted in clear-text. SNMPv1 specifies five core *protocol data units (PDUs)*. They are [12–14]:

1. *GET REQUEST* to retrieve management information.
2. *GETNEXT REQUEST* to retrieve sequences of management information.
3. *GET RESPONSE* to retrieve an action result.
4. *SET* to make a change to a managed subsystem.
5. *TRAP* to report an alert or other asynchronous event about a managed subsystem.

SNMP version 2 known as SNMPv2, includes improvements to performance, security, confidentiality, and manager-to-manager communications over its predecessor. However, it was not widely adopted due to disagreements over the overly complex security framework. SNMPv2 renames asynchronous event reports from traps to notifications with improved message format. It also added GETBULK and INFORM to the supporting PDUs. GETBULK is an improvement to GETNEXT for retrieving large amounts of management data with multiple rows in a table by a single request. INFORM allows one managing system to send trap information to another managing system [15–26].

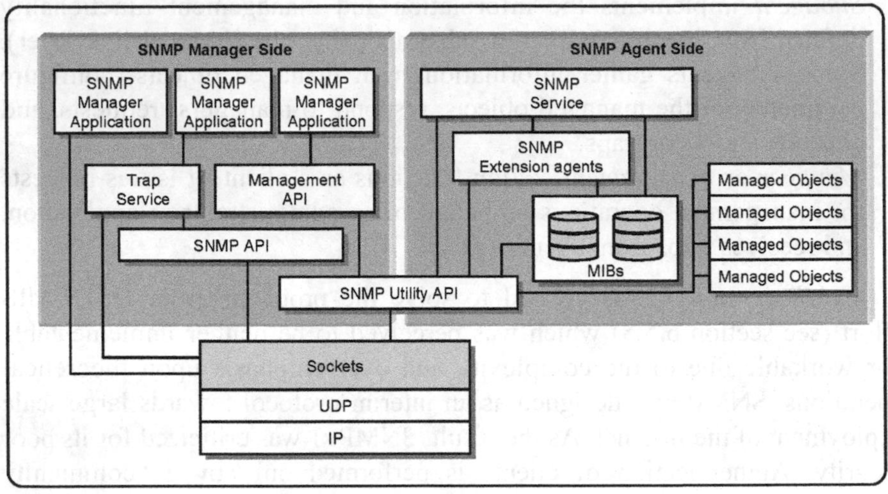

Figure 6.15. SNMP information overview.

Table 6.1. MIB Standards.

RFC Numbers	Descriptions
RFC 1155	Defines the Structure of Management Information (SMI) [27]
RFC 1157	SNMPv1
RFC 1212	TCP SMIv2 MIB
RFC 1213	UDP SMIv2 MIB
RFC 1227	SNMP Multiplexing (SMUX) protocol
RFC 2011	SNMPv2 MIB for IP
RFC 2012	TCP SMIv2 MIB
RFC 2013	UDP SMIv2 MIB
RFC 2096	IP Forwarding Table MIB
RFC 2741	Agent Extensibility (AgentX) protocol
RFC 1850	OSPFv2 MIB
RFC 1657	BGPv4 MIB
RFC 2246	The Transport Layer Security (TLS) protocol, version 1.0
RFC 2274(Obsolete)/3414	User-based Security Model (USM) for SNMPv3
RFC 2932	IPv4 Multicast Routing MIB
RFC 3289	DiffServ MIB
RFC 3410-3418	SNMPv3
RFC 3584	Coexistence between SNMPv1, SNMPv2, and SNMPv3
RFC 2274/2574/3414	SNMPv3 User-based Security Model

Community-Based SNMP version 2, or SNMPv2c [28–35], comprises SNMPv2 but replaces the controversial SNMPv2 security model with community-based security scheme of SNMPv1. The User-Based SNMPv2, or SNMPv2u [36,37], offers better security than SNMP v1 without incurring the complexity of SNMPv2. The mechanism was eventually adopted as one of the two security frameworks in SNMPv3.

SNMP version 3 [38–46] contains the specification of the *user-based security model (USM)* describing the elements of procedure for providing message level security. This document also includes a MIB allowing remote monitoring and management of the configuration parameters for the security model. Sample SNMP information architecture is depicted in Figure 6.15. It portrays a relative location of MIB and necessary interactions with other management processes.

A MIB is a collection of information that is organized hierarchically and accessible by SNMP. It is comprised of managed objects and is identified by object identifiers. There are two types of managed objects in the MIB: scalar and tabular. The *scalar* object defines a single object instance and the *tabular* object defines multiple related object instances that are grouped in MIB table. Each MIB can contain more than one object instance. The SNMP MIB standards are listed in Table 6.1.

6.4.1.7 Remote Network Monitoring

The *remote network MONitoring (RMON)* was developed by the IETF to support monitoring and protocol analysis of Ethernet and Token Ring LANs. It includes open and comprehensive network analyzers, and possesses protocol analyzer capabilities for network fault diagnosis, planning, and performance tuning features.

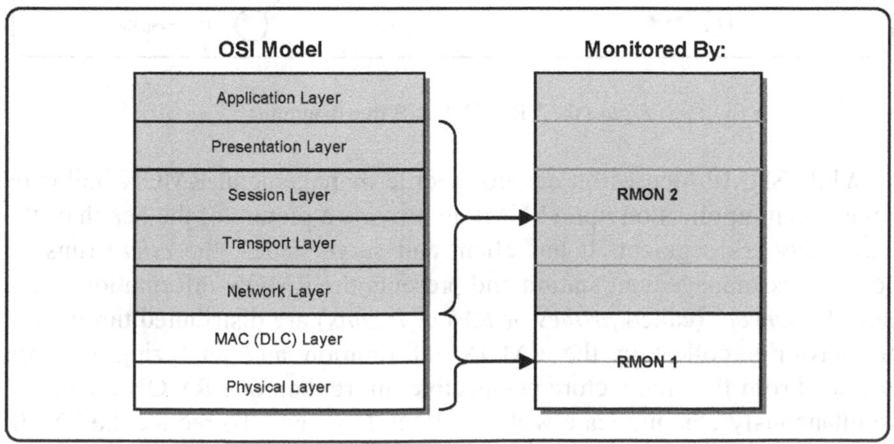

Figure 6.16. RMON Model.

RMON has two versions to monitor the full seven layers of OSI model, namely RMON1 and RMON2. RMON1 provides the data for segment monitoring and protocol analysis against layers one and two of the OSI model. RMON2 monitors above the MAC layer, supporting protocol distribution and providing a view of the whole network rather than a single network segment. As shown in Figure 6.16, RMON2 is not a superset of or replacement for RMON1.

The first RMON1 focused specifically on Ethernet. The updated release was extended to support the *Token Ring*. The RMON1 MIB supports current and historical traffic statistics of a network segment and a specific host domain, a threshold-driven versatile alarm and event mechanism, and flexible filters to capture focused measurements. Figure 6.17 shows a listing of the RMON1 groups and where RMON fits within the *International Standards Organization (ISO)* and IETF standards organization.

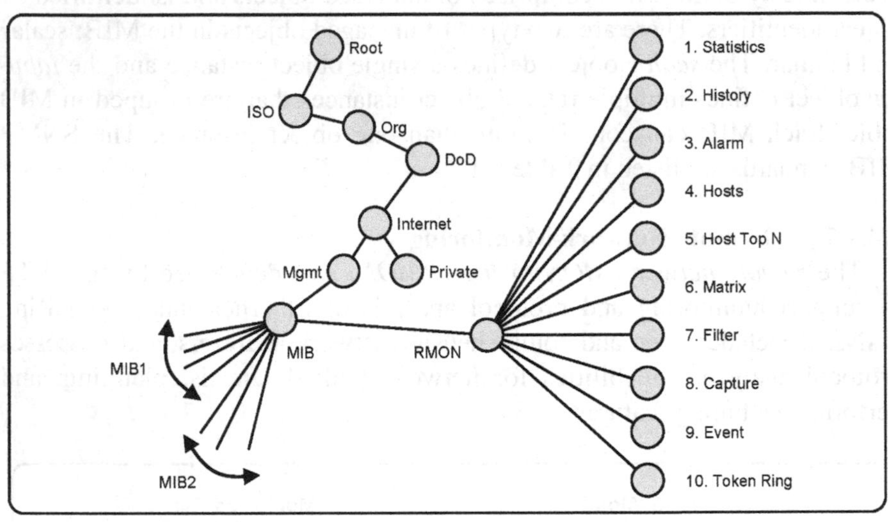

Figure 6.17. RMON1 MIB tree diagram.

While SNMP focuses on device-specific management, RMON builds its management application upon SNMP to provide a picture of the health of the whole network segment. It has client and server sides: the *client* runs on the network management station and presents the RMON information to the user; the *servers* (called *probes* or *RMON agents*) are distributed throughout the networks collecting the RMON information and analyzing network packets. From the architecture perspective, more than one RMON *client* can simultaneously communicate with one RMON *server*. To reduce the SNMP traffic on the network and ease the processing load on the management station, RMON agents only transmit collected and processed data to the management station as necessary. RMON1 includes a protocol analyzer to allow for distributed troubleshooting tools.

The RMON2 brings benefits to the interoperability between independently developed solutions by moving up the protocol stack to analyze the network- and application-layer traffic. By monitoring the higher protocols, RMON2 can provide the information beyond segmented connectivity and present an internetwork or enterprise view of network traffic. RMON2's capabilities include higher layer statistics, address translation (binding between MAC-layer addresses and network-layer addresses), configurable historical data studies, improved filtering, and remote probe configuration.

The *protocol directory* of RMON2 supports a simple and interoperable scheme to establish associations with other RMON2 agent implementations. This is especially important when the application and the agent are from different vendors. This protocol directory feature allows RMON applications to:

- Define an open, extensible structure for collecting the traffic, host, and matrix data for each protocol and application.
- Map the data collected by a probe to the correct protocol name that can then be displayed at the network manager.

6.4.1.8 Flat Files and File Transfer Protocol

Data stored in a flat file has no structural relationships in contrast to more complex models such as a relational database. The data is generally stored one record per line. Individual fields of a data may simply have a fixed width with padding or a delimiter such as whitespace, tab, comma, or other characters.

As per this definition, a flat file database should consist of only data and delimiters. However in broader application cases, flat file refers to any database in the form of rows and columns, with no relationships or links between records and fields. Nowadays, XML is a popular format for storing data in plain text files. As XML allows very complex nested data structures, it requires special software tools to decode the content. Therefore XML based data files are not usually classified as standard flat files.

Flat files are used internally by many computer applications to store configuration and monitored data. Many applications allow users to store and retrieve their information by flat files using a predefined set of fields. The advantage of flat file is its simplicity. However, when the file size grows over a certain limit or the relationship among data item reaches a certain level of complexity, the data management can immediately become a challenge. Furthermore, the data management of files is structural- and data-dependent. *Structural dependence* implies that any file structure change will force all the programs that use the data structure to be modified. *Data dependence* implies that any changes in the characteristics of the data (such as from integer to decimal) also require all the programs that use the data definition to be modified. As the result, turn-around time for any update can be unpredictable.

File transfer protocol (FTP) is the file transfer protocol in the TCP/IP protocol suite to move or copy a file from one location to another. FTP was originally designed for peer-to-peer file transfer. The user utilizes ftp to copy a file from one computer to another computer with the same account or known user account and password.

The FTP demon allows machines to transfer files without the user's interaction. However, this approach has a major security disadvantage on intrusive file transfer because anonymous FTP does not require having an account on the remote machine for exchanging files with.

6.4.1.9 Database

A database is a collection of related pieces of data. The structural description of managed objects and the relationships among them in the database is known as a *schema*. Database models (or data models) are the ways to organize a schema to model the database structure. There are three common models: relational, hierarchical, and network. The relational model represents data in the tabular format consisting of rows and columns. The hierarchical data model organizes data into a tree-like structure limiting the number of relationships. The network model allows each record to have multiple parent and child records, forming a lattice structure. For service assurance and monitoring purpose, only the relational model is considered due to its commonality.

A relational database is structured in accordance with the relational model containing predicate logic and set theory. A complete database system requires managing software called the *relational database management system (RDBMS)*. Figure 6.18 demonstrates the database layers and RDMS.

The *structured query language (SQL)* is the most popular computer language used to create, modify, retrieve, and manipulate data from relational database management systems. It is a set-based and declarative computer language. *Procedural language/SQL (PL/SQL)* is Oracle Corporation's proprietary server-based procedural extension to the SQL database language. It grows the SQL specification into a full-fledged programming language while maintaining the advantages of SQL. SQL keywords can be classified into the following groups:

- *Data retrieval* is used to retrieve zero or more rows from one or more tables in a database.
- *Data manipulation* is the subset of the language used to add, update, and delete data.
- *Data transaction* is used to wrap around the DML operations.
- *Data definition* to define new tables and associated elements.
- *Data control* handles the authorization aspects of data and permits the user to control who has access to see or manipulate data within the database.
- *ANSI-standard SQL* supports as a single line comment identifier.

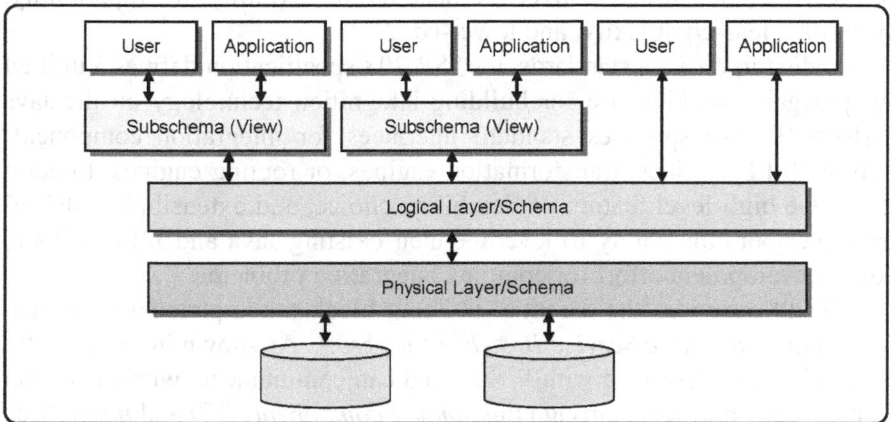

Figure 6.18. Database and RDMS.

The concept of a dimensional database is to convert the data presentation from multiple two-dimensional tables into multiple-dimensions. Such multi-dimensional database systems offer an extension to the relational system to provide a multi-dimensional view of the data. The advantages to this database model are its ability to analyze large amounts of data with very fast response times. For instance, an application can "slice and dice" through data, and "drill down or roll up" through various dimensions of the defined data structure. This capability allows the monitoring process to quickly identify trends or problem areas. From the management perspective, a multi-dimensional database offer intuitive spreadsheet-like views for clear presentation, easy navigation, and ease of maintenance because data is stored in the same way as it is viewed. Additionally, this approach can achieve better performance than the relational systems with a similar data requirement.

In summary, multi-dimensional database systems are a complementary technology to enrich relational systems. In some circumstances it makes more sense to use multi-dimensional arrays rather than relational tables.

6.4.1.10 Java Business Integration

The Java Business Integration (JBI) specification is known as *Java Specification Request (JSR)* 208 [47]. The JSR 208 Expert group, chaired by Sun Microsystems, was organized through the *Java Community Process (JCP)* program and *Java 2 Enterprise Edition (J2EE)* developers. The business mission of JBI is to serve the integration space like J2EE does for Java applications. The goals are to deliver the benefits of flexibility, interoperability, reusability, less-complexity, and lower-cost.

Building upon Java standards, the JSR 208 specification defines a unified and pluggable architecture for building integration technology on the Java platform. It also specifies standard interfaces for integration components such as BPEL engines, transformation engines, or routing engines. In addition to the high level feature of flexibility, choice, and extensibility, JBI offers developers the ability to leverage their existing Java and J2EE skills to reduce development effort for complex integration problems.

JSR 208 provides the essential building block for implementing a standard-based *Enterprise Service Bus (ESB)* for SOA. As shown in Figure 6.19, JBI services are described with WSDL and can communicate with each other over different protocols through the *binding component (BC)* and *normalized message service* (e.g., a network management system):

- BC can bind the service to a specific protocol like JMS, SOAP, IIOP, and so forth. For instance a SOAP BC transforms normalized messages received from the application into a SOAP envelope and pushes the envelope on the connections. Similarly, when it receives a SOAP envelope, it transforms the envelope into a normalized message and hands off the normalized message to the applications.
- JBI also provides a *service programming interface (SPI)* allowing the service to push and pull normalized messages. Normalized messages contain XML data (message payload) and contextual information (e.g., transactional context and security context). The application offloads the service from having to deal directly with the contextual information.

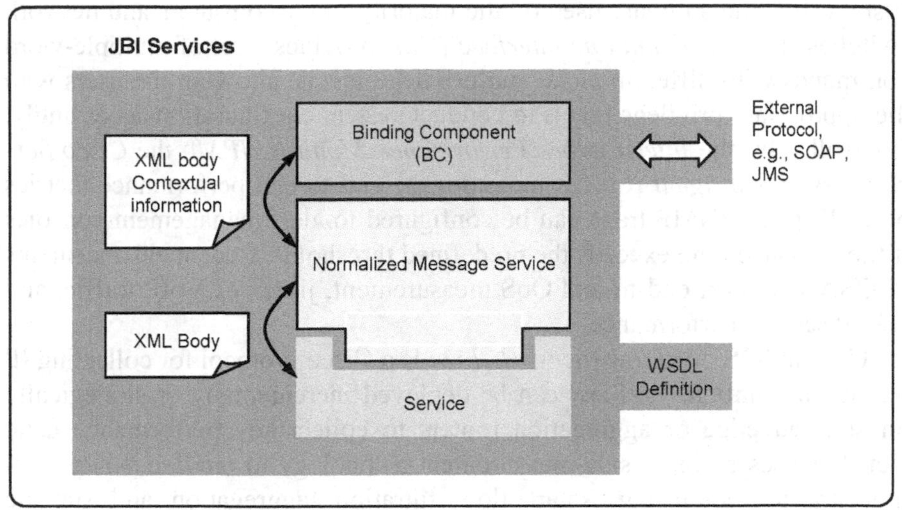

Figure 6.19. Java business integration.

6.4.2 Other Private Implementations

This section profiles two commercial monitoring tools which are frequently seen in IT department of many enterprises. They are *BMC Patrol* and *Cisco Internetwork Operating System (IOS)*. Both of these two products aim to support servers, routers, and corporate applications, as well as desktop services.

BMC Patrol is a popular tool which provides performance management of many generic and private IT solutions. It consists of Patrol Console, Patrol Agents, Patrol Knowledge Modules and Patrol View. The Patrol Con*sole* is the central management tool for monitoring and managing the application, workstations, routers, and servers. It provides a graphical user interface to display all monitored resources in the distributed systems. The console interacts with *Patrol Agents* on remote machines through event-driven dialogs. The agents collect management data from the managed resources and only send event messages to the console on a state change. Pa*trol Knowledge Modules* gather health metrics on the managed resources and provides service relationship and availability information to both the console and agents. The advantage of the Patrol approach is its relative autonomy of the agent operations. When loaded with instructions from the Knowledge Modules, the agents can start, monitor, alert, record, and manage the IT resources without a connection to the console.

Cisco IOS is a package of routing, switching, internetworking and telecommunications functions tightly integrated with a multi-tasking operating system. It is the software used on the majority of Cisco routers and network switches. The *command line interface (CLI)* provides a set of multiple-word commands with different *mode* and privilege levels, allowing the users with the appropriate privilege levels to conduct system configuration accordingly. Controlled by the *Internetwork Performance Monitor (IPM)*, the *Cisco Service Assurance Agent (CSAA)* measures the end-to-end performance metrics of an IP path. SNMP traps can be configured to alert management consoles if the response time exceeds the predefined thresholds. Recent enhancements of CSAA support end-to-end QoS measurement, jitters of VoIP traffic, and HTTP service performance.

Used in IOS, *NetFlow (network flow)* is a Cisco protocol for collecting IP traffic information. NetFlow can be deployed incrementally or strategically on selected edge or aggregation routers to collect key performance data. NetFlow uses an input side-measurement technology to provide nearly real-time traffic monitoring, smart flow filtration, aggregation and statistic evaluation, and multi-criterion data flow selection for network planning, monitoring, and accounting applications. The *NetFlow Monitor (NF)* and NetFlow Analyzer process and evaluate abnormal network activities (such as security attacks, routing troubles, and so forth).

6.5 Data Analysis

Historically, fault management provides basic event (e.g., trap) management often with some alarm de-duplication. Performance management provides statistical process of service measurements from the managed objects (e.g., network elements and application processes).

Data fusion in enterprise services play a critical role in creating service knowledge for better situation understanding and decision-making. The data can be gathered at the sensor level (as described in chapter 4), the transport networks (as described in chapter 5), or at the application level (further discussed in chapter 9). In essence, data fusion is an abstract processing function which holds different incarnations. According to the categories defined by the defense industry, level one fusion takes new inputs, normalizes the data, identifies or correlates the data to reduce redundancy, provides the last known disposition or status of the managed service resource, and makes them available in a data repository. The level two fusion aggregates the individual entities, analyzes these aggregations, and resolves conflicts at the group level. Upon aggregating the data with others references, the service providers can identify or derive events or actions from the collaborated management environment. These schemes make advanced processes for service management possible.

This section profiles some advanced analytical methods and portrays the path forward of converging methods for performance and fault management.

6.5.1 Advanced Analytic Methods

The "event" data from monitored objects require additional process to be turned into more meaningful information. The following functions can be added to the service assurance functions as extensions of data collection and additional preliminary analytical functions.

6.5.1.1 Event Process

Event process can be as simple as "pinging" an IP node for its availability. In a more sophisticated system, event process can also include polling managed events to discover a variety of conditions based on policies. This may sometimes require complex behavioral aberrations, including those sensitive to performance, and user experience and service impact. For instance, policy-based suppression can eliminate duplicate alarms (also known as *alarm de-duplication*). It sometimes requires complicate event correlation and event automation. Another example is the *downstream alarm suppression*. It is essentially to capture the hierarchic idea that devices downstream from a failed router or failed server can potentially appear to fail.

In the *event correlation* process, root cause analysis can isolate a single point of failure, by a laborious rules development cycle to define unique conditions. The rule set enables correlation across multiple event conditions to isolate problems.

Alerts can be created to reflect insights into nodal behavior where threshold conditions are bound to time-sensitive events and performance-related conditions. Sometimes the rules are based on specific service behaviors focusing upon customer experiences or reflecting unique operational situations. Because the rule development is labor intensive and not quite adaptive to changing conditions, the price to maintain the needed skill set and to manage the content updates is high.

After an event or alert is identified, *event automation* provides consoles for integrating and managing events from a range of sources. It displays the level of alarm reduction and alarm de-duplication along with insight into business or service impact, such as SLA penalty analysis. Comprehensive topology depends upon *event automation* to integrate networking information sensitive to physical layer connections. This technique can help the service operator to identify failure location in a node, a component of a node, an application, or a line.

6.5.1.2 Artificial Intelligence in Process

Artificial intelligence (AI) describes problems solving methods that traditionally are only processed by humans. It is a branch of machine theory that has spawned such ideas as fuzzy logic, rules-based systems, case-based reasoning, and neural networks.

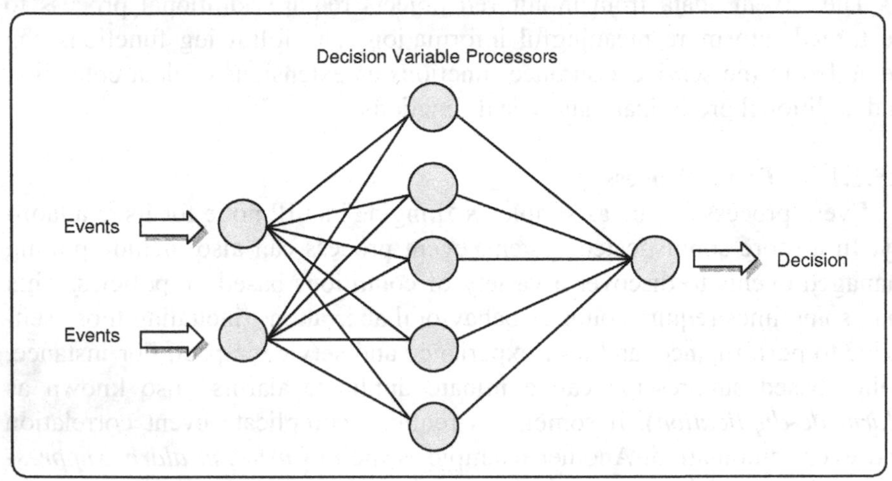

Figure 6.20. Fuzzy logic.

Unlike a binary approach to truth and falsehood, the *fuzzy logic* (Figure 6.20) is a form of logic where decision variables have degrees of truth and falsehood. It allows the system to grapple with possible conditions of failure that need the ambivalence of "maybe" versus "yes" or "no". Fuzzy logic is derived from fuzzy set theory dealing with reasoning that is approximate rather than precision. Fuzzy sets are based on vague definitions of sets instead of randomness, thus fuzzy truth represents membership in vaguely defined sets and in unlikelihood of some event or condition. Degrees of truth are often confused with probabilities. However, they are conceptually distinct.

Case-based reasoning is a form of AI. It is the process of solving new problems based on the solutions of similar past problems. The case-based reasoning system looks for keyword matches and adapts the most successful solutions to the current situation. Once the current problem is resolved, it contributes to the history of best cases and stores them in the database. This allows the system to learn and adapt to unique conditions over time. Case-based reasoning is a prominent kind of analogy making. It has been popular among help desk solutions. For instance, service centers keep the task resolutions and treat them as a database of solutions to problems.

Case-based reasoning has been formalized for purposes of computer reasoning as a four-step process:

1. *Retrieve*: Given a target problem, retrieve cases from memory those are relevant to solving it.
2. *Reuse*: Map the solution from the previous case to the target problem.
3. *Revise*: Having mapped the previous solution to the target situation, if necessary, revise.
4. *Retain*: Store the resulting experience as a new case in memory.

6.5.2 The Convergence Trends in Performance and Fault

Traditional network monitoring solutions include two separated rudimentary performance and fault management systems. An enterprise purchases a reporting solution for performance and a trap management system for availability. These two systems do not have much in common. To improve the service quality awareness or service behavior under certain circumstances, service operators need to obtain the ability to navigate quickly and easily between fault and performance management. A collaborated management solution has shown strong operational and business values. This is driven mainly by the need to police service levels for business contract compliances, operational efficiency, and customer behavior analysis. As the result, fault management becomes a part of a broader performance and service management solution.

From an integration perspective, fault management needs inputs from performance related data to be able to proactively prevent faults from happening. Fault management can leverage time-specific data with thresholded measurements or trend and analyze time-stamping faults much like performance data. In another event, jitter triggers an alarm after it has been above a certain threshold for a certain time.

The other important aspect for speedy troubleshooting lies upon the capability to automate the connection between isolating a point of failure to view relevant historical performance data in time and with relevant device context. This has two advantages. Firstly it can improve the root-cause analysis from identifying “where occurred” to determine “what caused”. Secondly, the interdependencies and relationships between the events, behaviors statistics, topological and configuration awareness, and network references can add much insight into accuracy of trouble analysis and error eliminations. Finally, for competitiveness and service level management such features can offer real-time values to the service providers. The combined tool immediately consolidates performance and fault management investments with less equipments and monitoring agents which directly imply fewer loads to the service environment thereby operational efficiency is improved. In chapter 9, more service knowledge will be further illustrated.

6.6 SoS Views of Service Monitoring

From an SoS perspective, different levels of data aggregation, high availability and high scalability of the managing architecture are required to support flexible service monitoring in a complex enterprise networking solution. In addition to the data collection function, advanced analytical tools which can translate the measurements to service related indicators are part of the management architecture. It allows the operators to perform end-to-end evaluation on a pre-scheduled processing cycle, predict (with trending techniques) and optimize the performance, and report service status in accordance with different types of SLA arrangements. Figure 6.21 portrays an integrated monitored data flow in a normal service assurance application where SLAs are the driver of the process. Detail SLA management functionalities will be covered in chapter 9 (section 9.7) [2].

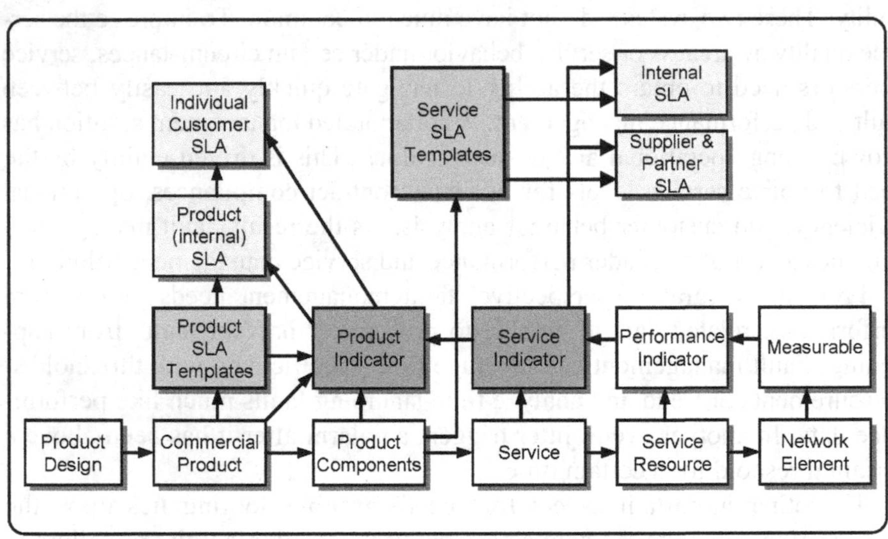

Figure 6.21. Integrated monitored data flow.

6.6.1 Event Management

Events identify problems at a low abstraction level and thus must be managed across the many possible types of enterprise resources. Typically the event console serves as the hub for availability and performance solutions. The event console consolidates and processes thousands of events that occur in the environment. This includes events from network devices, hardware systems, middleware, and applications. The event console uses the mechanisms discussed in section 6.5 to provide intelligent, multi-level analysis and correlation to filter out misleading or redundant events, highlight the essential information, and provide indications of the root cause of each problem quickly and accurately. It can respond automatically based on the indication of the root cause, allowing automated correction of problems without the need for involvement by an individual. This helps preliminary data fusion to offer the benefit of cost reduction by reducing the staff required to maintain the systems and by reducing the time to resolve issues.

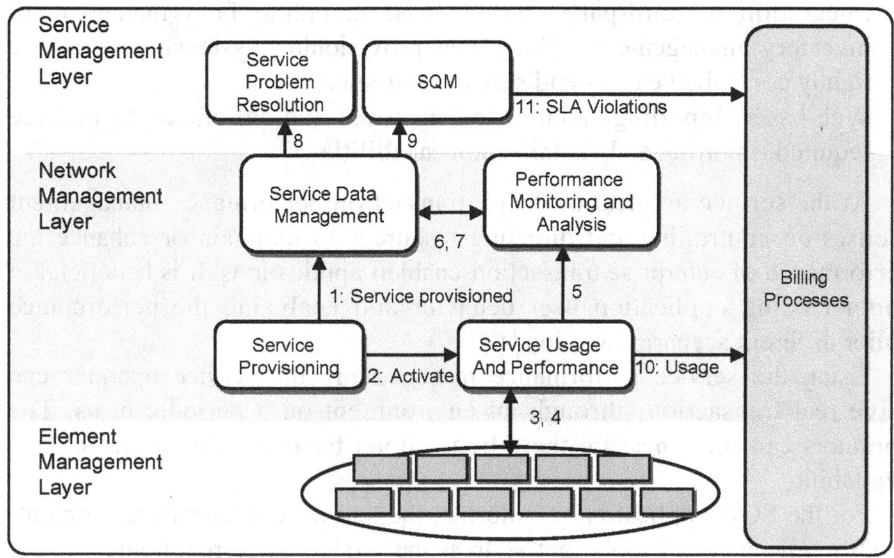

Figure 6.22. Detailed flow of network data management.

As part of the enterprise COP, the event console can include the network management solution, which helps operators track and resolve problems down to the network layers. It provides those events that the operators need to react to in the order of severity. Thus can be tightly integrated with help desk systems to automatically create trouble tickets based on events it receives.

6.6.2 Performance Management

Organizing information from networks in silos by vendor, hardware type, region, or application may not satisfy the need for a typical central control. As consolidation has brought together many types of heterogeneous networks, the need to centrally manage performance data and gain a single, integrated view of network operations has become important to deliverer consistent, quality service. Only by having the ability to view consolidated data as well as the capability to dynamically manipulate and compare more discrete data sets, can the service operators understand key performance indicators that link to the business bottom-line values. Key features of performance management include:

- To support multi-vendor and multi-technology integration into an enterprise-wide view of a network.
- A single network view, featuring enterprise-wide reporting that can deliver key performance indicators and key quality indicators.
- Integration to third-party applications, including fault management, inventory management, billing and provisioning systems, to create a tightly controlled end-to-end service assurance.
- Web-based reporting, administration tools and interfaces to provide required reporting and visualization capabilities.

At the service application level, transaction performance management focuses on controlling and directing resources to maintain or enhance the performance of enterprise transaction-enabled applications. It is beneficial in understanding application user behavior and analyzing the performance under different scenarios and loads.

Using the service performance management, the service operator can drive real transactions through an environment on a periodic basis. The operators can then measure these transactions for overall performance and availability.

For the SOA application monitoring, the service operator needs content-specific management tools that address the performance requirements. The performance management should provide understanding of the relationships between services instrumented in the environment and to: 1) discover and provides topology visualization of Web services and service relationships; 2) extract service patterns; 3) provide the understanding of Web services relationships, flows, and message content; and 4) aggregate Web services log files.

6.6.3 Service Data Management

Service data management [4] is responsible for the collection of usage data and events primarily for the networked resource maintenance and restoration process, billing process, and other service management level applications. Figure 6.22 shows the service data management flow after a service is provisioned and the trigger to service data management is activated.

There are two main uses for the performance and service behavior information in the service maintenance and restoration process. The first is to conduct service performance and traffic analysis and optimization. Changes in traffic conditions or equipment failures may trigger changes to the service via service provisioning for the purpose of traffic control. Reduced levels of service capacity or performance can result in multiple requests, such as service planning for more resources, service provisioning for a reconfiguration, or nodal management systems for specific actions in the elements themselves. Second, the collected data with appropriate analysis will be useful to support proactive customer care such as supporting proactive trouble ticket management via the service maintenance and restoration process.

The service data management also provides usage information to billing processes for rating and discounting.

Other than the above two paths, this process also provides service intelligence to verify compliance with SLAs and QoS levels. Because SLAs are not known at this management level, QoS specifications must be translated into indicators and corresponding thresholds. After translation, this process must ensure that the service performance goals are tracked and that notification is provided when they are not met (e.g., a threshold is exceeded or performance degrades).

6.6.4 Service Problem Management

The service problem management process is triggered by a service problem identified by: 1) the service infrastructure; 2) a customer-specific problem or service issue from the problem handling process; or 3) the analysis of service and service trouble data. If the identified problem affects multiple customers, resolution may include immediate reconfiguration and corrective action or longer-term service design changes.

If the problem is referred by the problem handling process, this process is then accountable for providing expertise and support to the problem handling process to resolve a customer-specific problem. If the problem is from the service infrastructure or the analysis of service and network trouble data, it may need alarm correlation to detect symptoms, isolate the problem, and repair malfunctions in the service. The problem handling process is responsible for receiving service complaints, resolving them to the originator's satisfaction, and providing meaningful status on repair or restoration.

Problem reports can be originated from the service or customers. Several reported problems may be related to a single fault, or a service resource failure may be caused by a failure from elsewhere. Proactive problem handling begins with a service-resource-generated problem and the creation of a trouble ticket.

The service problem correlation function identifies faults and traffic problems in the service. It can use problem reports from the service maintenance and restoration and service data management processes. Based on this information, this function can then request actions in accordance with predetermined service policies.

The ticket can optionally be used to notify the service users in the event of a pending service-affecting disruption. Proactive management also includes working with customers on planned maintenance outages.

The problem handling process uses the trouble ticket to trigger the root-cause location process to localize the fault, work with the service problem resolution process to resolve the problem, and provide status on repair or restoration activity. A complete trouble ticket, at this stage, should delineate activities, dependencies between activities, plans, and time frames for repair tasks. Correlation functions can apply to the repair records to inhibit duplicate activities from subsequent related complaints. This process should be concluded with a completion acceptance by the customer and an internal record to support both SLA reporting and outage credits, if applicable. A follow-up contact to the customer to ensure repair quality should also be part of the process.

The service root-cause location function identifies the location of the fault and determines whether it is service affecting. It must implement immediate fixes if required, or identify quality improvement efforts. A trouble report will then be created containing all relevant details of the fault for the problem handling process. These reports will be sent to the task owners in the form of pager, SMS, or E-mail, as shown in Figure 6.23.

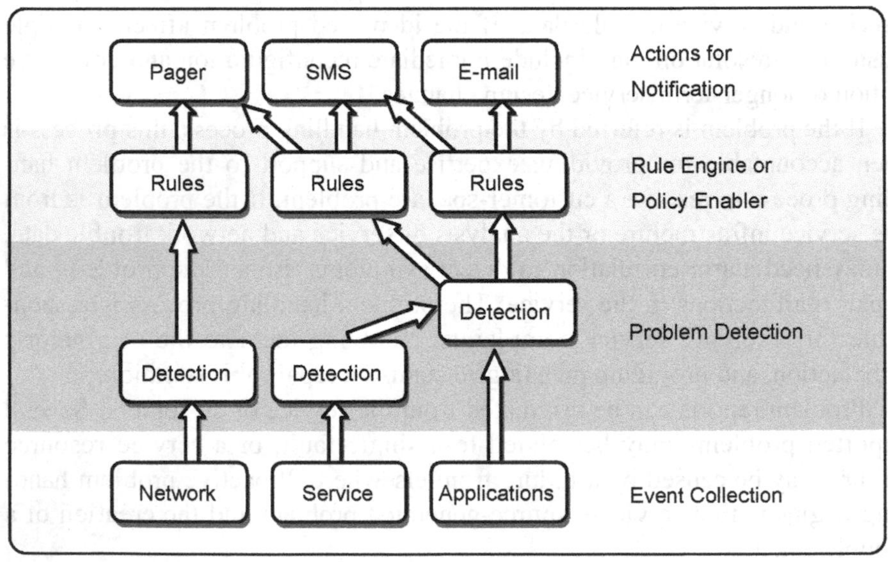

Figure 6.23. Detailed flow of problem management.

6.7 Conclusion

The technology of data acquisition by itself cannot satisfy the basic requirement of network and service monitoring in the context of NCBO. In a hybrid and wireless network, the sources of the management data, types, of collected data, architectures of management network, and availability of information may potentially present inconsistent, fragmented, and unrelated information from the collected data. This prevents the service operators from drawing a rational picture about the managed services.

For instance, managing a SoS involves activities for keeping each system updated with the correct configuration and ensures the service availability. In a mobile network where SDR radio configurations are altered automatically to reflect the environment condition changes, the synchronization between the local network topology and the central management system can present different levels of challenges. The measurement systems are in favor of supporting the change, configuration, incident, and problem management processes in a more dynamic manner. In other words, the management systems should be capable of maintaining the topology in real time while an intrusion detection system monitors a service for threats from the outside, and a network monitoring system monitors the network for problems due to performance or failures.

At the SoS level, the performance, fault, and security information should be collaboratively rationalized into events that are applicable to the service level objectives or operational objectives. Such processes are categorized as level one and level two data fusions of the system. The output products from the data fusion functions can be further extended into the knowledge management discussed chapter 9, or fed into the monitoring console for better situation awareness and service assurance. The systems that can potentially be interacting with the network and service monitoring function are illustrated in the SoS view section.

Chapter 7

SERVICE QUALITY MANAGEMENT

Quality of service (QoS) is an essential element in the enterprise transport infrastructure. The concept of QoS is loosely defined across different enterprise service management layers such that it can be used to evaluate and control the performance of a link, a domain sub-network, or the entire network. There are three aspects of QoS management: control, monitoring, and adjustment. QoS control includes planning and configuring performance attributes such as bandwidth, delay, loss, and traffic priority. An effective QoS planning and configuration function should include a policy registry and enforcement engine leveraging on open interfaces for policy descriptions. The QoS policies dictate the behaviors of the adjustment function. QoS monitoring works hand-in-hand with service monitoring functions depicted in chapter 6 to provide quality indicators of the managed services. The collected and organized indicators permit the adjustment function to arrange different amount of traffic being injected into the network in accordance with the QoS classes. The adjustment function drives vendor specific access facilities for access control in responding to the policy rules.

Appropriate planning and execution of QoS management at the transport layer allows an enterprise to achieve a truly dependable network, gain service intelligence, and identify and provide new, profitable value-added services. This chapter portrays the QoS functions, services, and QoS management framework in an IP-based network environment. From the viewpoint of end-users, QoS should be provided on an end-to-end basis with the capability for interactive service negotiation in the form of SLA. Any updates on an SLA should reflect the changed QoS policies and parameters in or close to real time during a communication session. The SoS approach section illustrates the QoS management flows and system-level interactions among SQM, and the customer QoS manager.

7.1 Overview

Quality of Service (QoS) concept originated from ATM technology and was designed to manage the provisioning of defined predictable data transfer characteristics. QoS is about data traffic on a network that is subject to scrutiny and control. The idea of distinguishing service quality is comparable among different service domains and technologies that center on classifying the processes and information in an enterprise. This section expands the definition and scope of a service first introduced in chapter 1 into service classification management.

The benefit of service quality management is attractive in essence because it offers the service customers a "window" on how their applications are performing in accordance with the agreed service level objectives. In a more advanced implementation, such function even allows the customers to manipulate or reconfigure the service for their application needs.

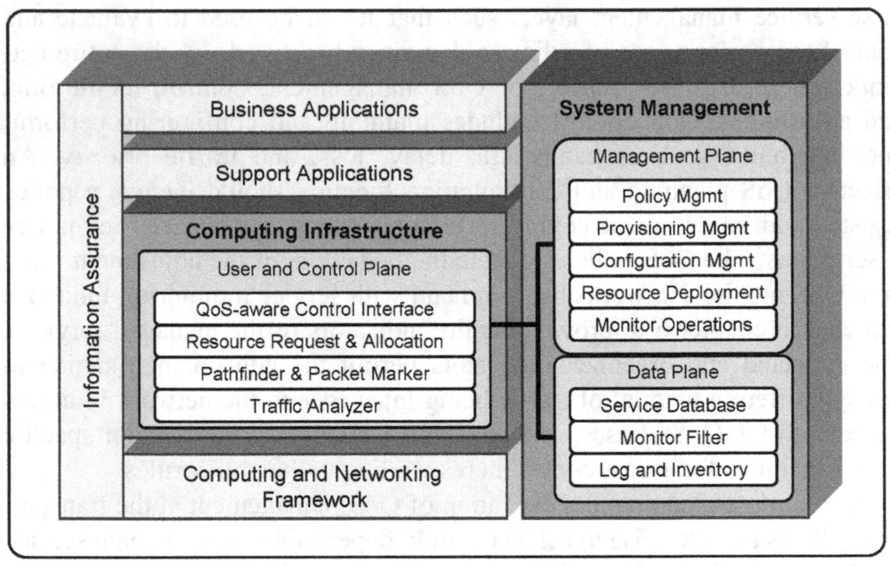

Figure 7.1. System architecture of enterprise services.

In Figure 7.1, three major functional blocks that translate key features into the system architecture are portrayed: User and Control Plane, Management Plane, and Data Plane. As part of the Computing and Infrastructure layer, the User and Control Plane offers a QoS-aware control interface, resource request and allocation, pathfinder and packet marker, and traffic analyzer. In the Service Management layer, the Management Plane contains policy management, provisioning management, configuration management, resource deployment, and monitor operations. The Data Plane interacts with the data acquisition functions discussed in the previous chapter and the enterprise resource management for service configuration and contains the following three sub-functions: service database, monitor filter, and log and inventory. These will be addressed in the following sections.

7.1.1 Service and Service Level Agreement

To support a manageable and profitable QoS to their service users, the enterprise service provider's supporting infrastructure is perceived by their operators to be much more complicated. As discussed in chapter 1, services can be classified into three types: commodity, core business, and value-added services. These three services are depicted in the left block of Figure 7.2 as offer contents and supports part of an offering. Value-add and core business services are often self-evident from the strategy perspective. They leverage the enterprise's core competency and maintain the organization's specialized knowledge and capability to innovate. In contrast, a commodity service with some part of core business services represents only the cost of market participation and might be outsourced. Commodity services are usually common to several processes and highly reusable. Examples of the commodity services include third parties contents service or human resources management.

Value-added services are critical to business success, often highly reusable and yet at the same time volatile as they are most subject to change. It is critical that these services are agile to support ongoing changes without disruption. For example, prices can frequently and quickly change according to market conditions. Because prices are reused in many different business contexts, the volatility of a change in price can pose a key business risk.

The right block demarked as offer agreement is about SLA. An SLA (or traffic contract) specifies guarantees for the ability of a network or protocol to give guaranteed performance bounds based on mutually agreed measures, this is usually done by prioritizing traffic. Often times, different types of network traffic requirements are defined in QoS and specified in an SLA. For instance, inelastic applications require a certain level of bandwidth to function, typically much more than actual utilization. By contrast, elastic applications can adapt to however much or little bandwidth is available. From a service operator perspective, the concept of composing multiple instances of a service for parallel processing for performance gains is useful in ad-hoc networks. This is because the connections may exist for short periods of time only.

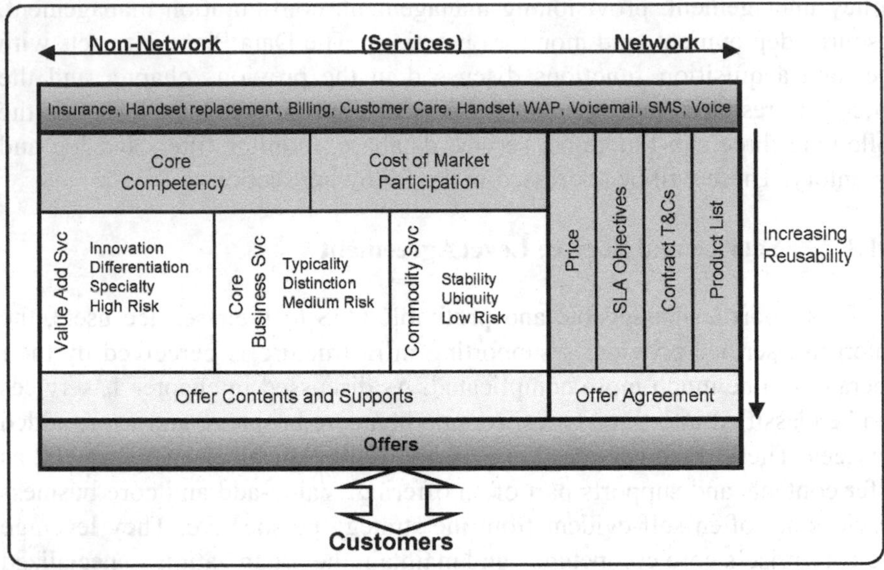

Figure 7.2. The relationship between service agreement and service management.

7.1.2 Business Drivers of Service Quality

The business drivers of QoS have many different aspects. This is mainly due because the values are across different layers of technology, processes, and procedures which impact the enterprise's marketing, operations, even business mission and objective [1, 2]. The business drivers of service quality can be concluded as:

1. Customers' expectations can be quantified in SLA. The SLA is closely integrated with corresponding service models, which suitably map various types of services onto different technologies, classes of service, and business operation policies.
2. More advanced models can associate with provider's inventory with the capability to assess service impact proactively. This feature assists the provider to quickly determine what services are related to the problems and what the SLA cost impact will be for affected customers.
3. Proactive end-to-end management is a key to ensure high quality of services and achieve quality without over-provisioning the bandwidth. Role-based management allows the enterprise customers to customize their ordered services based on the definition and assignment of roles.
4. From a user perspective, satisfaction is measured by how effective a trouble is managed. The service monitoring function can assist the provider in understanding performance trends to improve current or future

planning. The measured data can be directly applied to performance tuning for service improvement.

5. Fast turn around allows the provider to demonstrate a commitment to product quality and customer value. Demonstration of the provider's accountability and continuous process improvement can develop a stronger customer-to-supplier relationship.
6. When a service product is composed of many service objects from different providers, such a relationship is called value chain. Accurate management of the value chain can guarantee the best utilization of service resources hence the provider can enhance its competitive position while increasing its ROI.

Figure 7.3 depicts a sample value chain which is constituted by content providers, portal providers, network providers, and the primary service provider. The QoS offered to a customer can be presented in the form of *customer level agreement (CLA)*, *service level agreement (SLA)*, or *business level agreement (BLA)*. All providers have obligations to satisfy the service criteria committed in the QoS offered. The performance measurements collected by the providers are consolidated into QoS achievement reports and presented to the customers. Based on the level of perceived service, the customers will be charged accordingly.

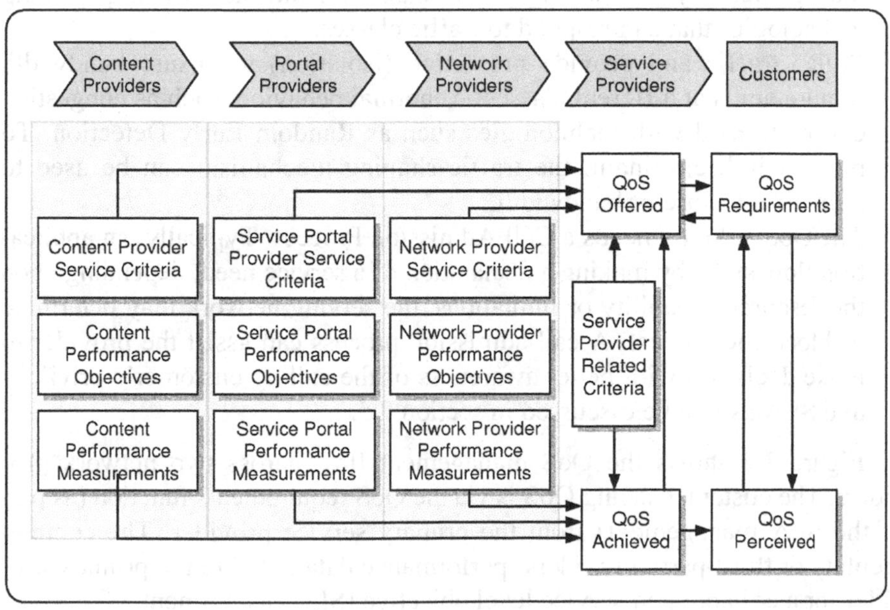

Figure 7.3. A sample service provider QoS relationship.

7.1.3 Principles of QoS

The main principle of quality service is that the network can support traffic streams with different levels of "quality of service", allowing service applications to support predictive or differentiated services, strong guarantees on the level of service in real time, as well as best-effort messaging services.

From the management perspective, the set of services that is supported on a specific network can be viewed as a service model. Models interpret interactions between services map to selective services and can reflect cost versus performance trade-offs. Service models are dictated by traffic characteristics, bandwidth specifications, and service requirements. Guaranteed service enforcement may sometimes require admission control at service resources. The principles of QoS can be concluded as:

- The QoS treatment can force the allocation of a set portion of bandwidth to each application flow. While providing isolation, fragmentation, and compression, packets can be used to maximize the use of resources as efficiently as possible.
- Mark and Classify for router to distinguish between different classes according to policies and the behaviors of the traffic. Perform congestion management by prioritizing traffic based on the marks using queuing technologies that can respond to traffic classes.
- Police traffic and provide protection (isolation) to ensure bandwidth requirements at different classes. Abnormal behaviors such as congestion can be treated with technologies such as Random Early Detection. To prevent indiscriminant, the traffic shaping mechanism can be used to maximize the use of bandwidth.
- The QoS solution needs a Call Admission Process. Typically, an application flow starts by making a declaration of a service need; depending upon the resource capability or limitations, the serving network may determine to block the request. A call admission process can assist the provider to make decisions with better awareness of the calling customer's privilege and SLA as will be discussed in section 7.5.

Figure 7.4 shows the QoS management flow across two network providers. The customer-facing QoS is via the QoS requirements function (as part of the SLA management) from the primary service provider. The complementary or third-party providers' performance data is fed to the primary provider for a collaborated service level objective (SLO) assessment.

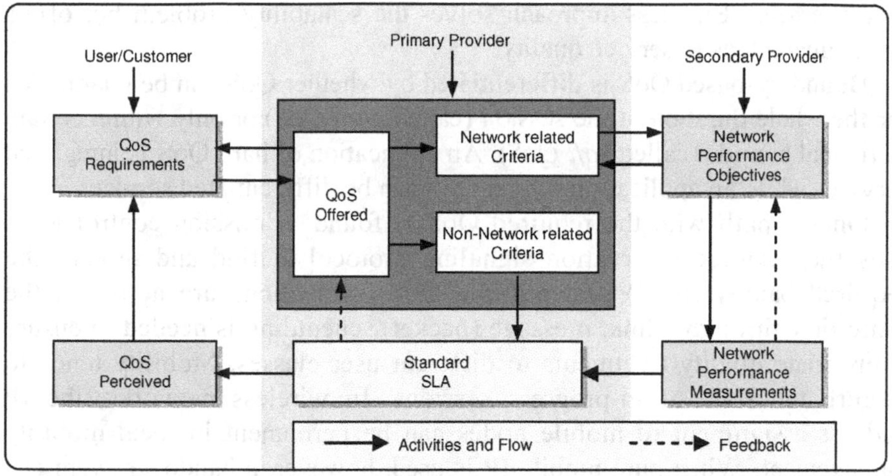

Figure 7.4. QoS management flow.

At the SoS level, the QoS management depends upon the ability to integrate multiple data sources to support a collaborated picture of service quality. An end-to-end view of service based upon customer performance criteria sometimes involves multiple user groups with different levels of SLA. This maintains up-to-date of the related service models with affiliated business rules. This management function should also be equiped with a reportig system to provide customers timely service information in their preferred format. For the service operator, this management system should manage the service components and sub-services based upon internal performance criteria, providing the capability for root cause analysis of potential service degradation, or changes of the service configuration if necessary.

7.2 QoS Management

State information includes topology and flow-specific information. In a *hard state QoS*, resources are reserved at all intermediate nodes along the path from the source to the destination throughout the duration of the QoS session. Call blocking ratio will be high at high network load. In a *soft state QoS*, resources reservations for small time intervals are used; the resources are managed in a decentralized manner without incurring any control overhead. Call acceptance rate is higher at a gracefully degraded fashion. A *stateful approach* means each node maintains either global state information or only local state information. Global state helps the source node to use centralized routing algorithm to route packets to the destination. However, control overhead can be significant. Local state uses distributed routing algorithms with less overhead. Stateless approach solves the scalability problem but offers fewer guarantees to service quality.

Boundary-based QoS is differentiated by whether QoS can be guaranteed for the whole duration of the session (called *hard QoS*) or only within certain statistical bounds (called *soft QoS*). An application of hard QoS is integrated services while an application of soft QoS can be differentiated services.

Once a path with the required QoS is found, admission control logic uses the resource reservation signaling protocol to find and reserve the required bandwidth. When multiple QoS connections are active at the same time through a link, message (packet) scheduling is needed to ensure appropriate quality treatments to different user classes. Mobility tends to perturb the state of in-progress sessions. In wireless networks, the IP address assignment to mobile nodes can be permanent in local mobility management. When pure mobile IP is used, however, a handover event can trigger the IP address to be changed based on the routing tables in the access network. As the result, each handover forces the path to remove all old reservations and initiate new reservations for the mobile node. Furthermore, local mobility management protocols may use anchor points and tunneling to forward downstream flows to mobile nodes and may lead to congestion. As the result, the setup of the access nodes influences the end-to-end performance. The strategy for buffering and queuing becomes a tremendous effect: buffers provide reliability but suffer the transmission delay. As will be seen in the following sections, when traffic is shaped at the edge of the network and no cross-over traffic exists, the rest of the network remains reliable and fast.

There are three planes in QoS management: control, data, and management.

7.2.1 Data Plane

In the data plane, user-specific flow is identified and the relative information is available to the underlying QoS process. The main objective of the data plane is to ensure flow information management. Users can register their application to the *QoS database* to obtain QoS treatment. The QoS data can include queuing and schedule specifications, as well as packet marking and traffic policing. Thereafter, the application can establish communication sessions with destination applications by referring to the predefined flow management specifications defined in the QoS database. The *application monitor filter* collects the traffic information for policing, buffer management, congestion avoidance, and further adjustment. This information is available to the control plane for QoS session establishment. The *log and inventory* is the repository for the service resource, performance measurements, and service logs available for system-level flow management.

7.2.2 Management Plane

The management plane is responsible for policy establishment and service monitoring. *QoS policy planner* lays out service specific resource arrangement based on specific policies or policy groups. *Policy configuration* allows the service operator to define and maintain QoS policies. It can include queuing and scheduling policies, flow classifiers, resource monitoring, and reports to detail QoS statistics. The policy configurations are saved in the *QoS management database* for the traffic analyzer to compare and analyze the system records with the measurement from *application monitor filter*. *QoS resource management* includes a global resource inventory for all the resources on which QoS configurations are demanded. This inventory can be a mirror of the entire managed network or a dedicated database for QoS management.

7.2.3 Control Plane

The control plane is able to setup QoS sessions on behalf of applications. Three components are presented in control plane to transparently specify and control desired QoS parameters. In IntServ with RSVP, *Resource Allocator* reserves network resources by signaling RSVP messages. In DiffServ, Packet Marker redirects IP packets for differential marking. These two logical modules are not functionally exclusive. They are interchangeable depending upon the service policy and specification. Traffic Analyzer collects traffic characteristic reference from the network and supports the other two models for better service decision-making in real time. QoS-aware Pathfinder assists the communication nodes to determine the best-fit QoS routes. The control plane constitutes the following five key modules:

- *Service Resource Allocator* is responsible for establishing RSVP sessions. By interacting with the QoS flow database, it can allocate resources based upon the flow parameters for flow identification and QoS parameters to delineate desired resource for QoS guarantee. For more intelligent allocation decision, Allocator will need information of traffic characteristic from the Data Plane to predict desired resource for the requesting applications.
- *Packet Marker* marks packets in DiffServ according to marking algorithms, which mark packets with different QoS requirements to different service classes. For multiple flows with the same QoS level, Packet Marker simply marks packets at each individual flow to facilitate the QoS definition. For single flow with multiple QoS levels, Packet Marker

redirects IP packets of a user-specific flow, updates DSCP value, and sends them back to the network protocol stack for transmission.

- *Traffic Analyzer* analyzes the efficiency of the traffic going through the interfaces in the network after deploying QoS policies. It monitors the user-specific flow on a real time or on a periodic (historical) basis in order to provide feedback about the QoS policy configurations for Service Resource Allocator to decide whether resources are appropriately allocated.
- *QoS-aware Pathfinder* is application specific and is useful for a mobile network. In supported routine protocols, it utilizes the available QoS parameter at every link to select a path with necessary "match". This function references the performance measurements from the Traffic Analyzer and coordinates with Service Resource Allocator to reserve the required amount of bandwidth for that connection.
- *QoS Control Interface* provides a normalized control interface while supporting sufficient control that reaches the controlled service resources. It protects the controllability of the control plane against potential hardware or software changes in the mission plans.

7.3 QoS Functions

Components offer services and indicate and guarantee the quality of those services. Therefore, it is necessary to facilitate the publication, selection, measurement, and validation of component and QoS values.

7.3.1 QoS-Based Design

Enterprises operating in modern markets, such as e-commerce activities and distributed Web services interactions require appropriate classification in creation of quality products and services. This can help the enterprise to determine how the QoS will exhibit to the target applications. QoS metrics of different service policies on large networks can perform a semi-automatic or automatic management scheme to decide the best configuration. In a typical *Internet Service Provider (ISP)* scenario, service quality can be largely divided into the following three commercial levels:

1. *Enterprise level* has the best performance. It offers rigid bounded delay guaranties thus suitable for applications such as videoconferencing.
2. *Standard level* offers minimum QoS guarantees whereby the network seems lightly loaded.
3. *Basic level* is characterized by its occupation of whatever network bandwidth is left.

Mission-critical applications may demand more level of service in accordance with the customer's roles and responsibilities.

Since most user traffic in the application layer traverses multiple network domains, the end-to-end QoS becomes crucial to support various network services. DiffServ (section 7.4.2) is considered a dominant QoS protocol in the network layer that is supported across different network interfaces. In wireless and wired LAN, IEEE 802.11e, and IEEE 802.1d technologies QoS is handled in the MAC layer. To ensure end-to-end service quality, these differrent QoS techniques must be coordinated under common QoS specifications.

Mobile and wireless networks exacerbate QoS design issues because these networks tend to be resource sensitive, the availability of the bandwidth tends to be highly variable, and the network topology tends to be unstable. These factors influence the overall quality of message delivery, session state, and information assurance such as security (identification/authentication) and cryptographic associations as well as multicast delivery.

In QoS-based design, routing protocol is an important feature that locates a suitable path from the source to the destination and to forward the data packet to the next intermediate relay node that satisfies the QoS service requirements. This function should consume minimum resources and be flexible to respond to network topology and (network and flow) state changes with minimum control overhead.

Even in an overly-engineered network with well designed topologies across different domains (e.g., core and access) there could still be issues of speed mismatches between technologies, jitter, or traffic prioritization as traffic pattern (e.g., peak demand) changes. The convergence of multimedia traffic with traditional data streams can also demand different data treatments. As a rule of thumb for a QoS-based design, the following factors should be considered:

- The setting of traffic priorities including dedicated bandwidth on a per application basis. This requires buffering, and therefore leads to a requirement to queue and prioritize traffic. For instance, streaming multimedia may require guaranteed throughput.
- Predictable response times including the ability to avoid or manage congestion situation. This can be extended to the management of delay sensitive or jitter sensitive applications, for instance, IP telephony may require strict limits on jitter and delay.
- Control of packet loss when congestion occurs during a burst. For instance, voice packet loss in a conversation may be preferable to lose it or smooth it over.

7.3.2 QoS Monitoring

Services must be rigorously and constantly monitored throughout their life cycles. This function assures service compliance with the targeted QoS objectives by allowing adaptation strategies to be triggered when undesired metrics are identified or when threshold values are reached.

The need for quality factors increases complexity in emerging technologies. It is important to possess the ability to monitor and control the QoS factors in the enterprise operational environment. For instance, multimedia services are most sensitive to bandwidth, delay, and delay jitter; military applications are most interesting in security, availability, and mobility (e.g., forming network); emergency search and rescue demands high availability and less errors. As demonstrated in Figure 7.5, QoS information can be managed through three layers, from CLA, SLA, to physical resource measurements. The CLA has business and financial implication, the SLA has service and traffic management implication, and the resource measurement has load and fault implications [3].

The following sections list a majority of QoS related parameters at different service levels. It is not practical to design in all the parameters listed; instead, they should be carefully correlated across the different levels to provide the most sensible and usable information with the service operator to ensure effectiveness and accuracy that is sensible for the SLA across service chains or to the service customers.

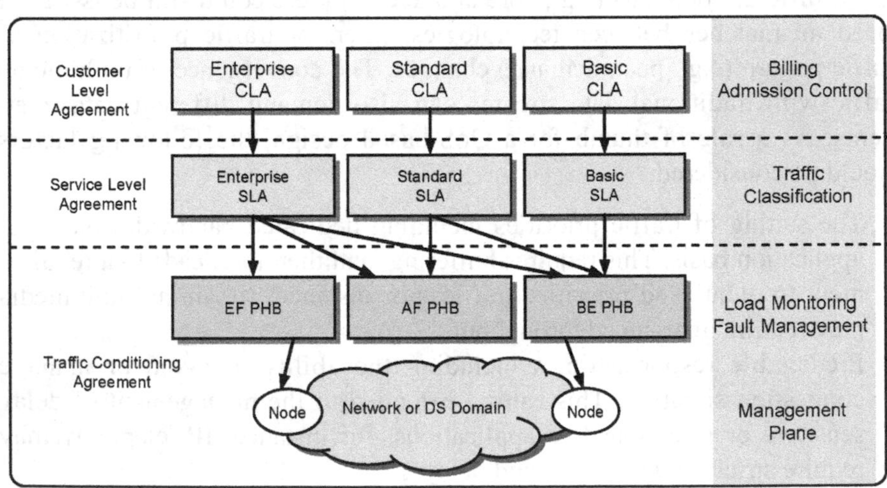

Figure 7.5. QoS monitoring at different operational levels.

7.3.2.1 Business QoS Measurements

The flexibility of SOA opens up the enterprise's applications to cope with hugely increased volumes of service requests across rapidly expanding geographical and organizational boundaries. Capacity management is a discipline that can cost-effectively align IT processing and enterprise resources in the face of changing business.

- The *business capacity* indicators are sets of trend-based metrics indicating the future business requirements for services that are considered, planned, and implemented in a timely fashion. This requires a wide knowledge that includes existing service levels and future SLAs, business and capacity plans, modeling techniques (such as simulation and trend forecasting), and application sizing methods. The knowledge management in chapter 9 will address this subject.
- The *service capacity* is aggregated service related quality indicators that are provided to customers as detailed in SLAs, including systems, networks, service throughput and performance, tuning, and demand management.
- The *resource capacity* is the measure on the utilization of service components of the service infrastructure. It goes deeply into the use of current and future technologies and their utilization.
- *Security* focuses on the confidentiality and integrity of services, ensuring that the services are available when needed and free from denial of service attacks. In addition, security must also address three underpinning principles: authenticity, authority, and non-repudiation.

7.3.2.2 Application QoS Measurements

This level of QoS metrics are the closest indicators for the service users. Three basic indicators (throughput, responsiveness, and information capacity) and three derived indicators are listed below. QoS levels apply to each operation of the Contracts Service. The basic indicators are:

- *Throughput* indicates the ability of a service to process units of an application message (e.g., business transactions or trading records) per unit time (worst, average, and best).
- *Responsiveness* indicates the operation response time (worst, average, and best) per unit time.
- *Information capacity* indicates the (worst, average, and best) size of service (message) content in units of storage.

The three derived indicators are:

- *Scalability* indicates the ease of a service to retain its intended capabilities of the three basic indicators under increasingly demanding conditions.

This can be presented as percentage increase of an indicator over specified time period.

- *Variability* indicates the degree (rate) of acceleration or deceleration of the three basic indicators over unit time.
- *Consistency* indicates the degree of stability of the three indicators over unit time. This is the opposite of the Variability indicator.

7.3.2.3 Session and Operational Measurements

The enterprise service customers may have many simultaneous sessions established for their applications, thus the total number of sessions can scale up very quickly. In an NCBO environment, the supporting technological infrastructure may evolve into complex, highly distributed, and dependent service components that requires sophisticated operational process and procedure. This group of indicators is composed of the following metrics:

- *Session availability* indicates the percentage of accumulated available serving period over the specified time period. The availability, in a broad sense, can comprise reliability, maintainability, and resilience.
- *Reliability* indicates the minimization of interrupts to the service operation. It can be presented in *mean time between failures (MTBF) measurement*.
- *Maintainability* indicates the ease that service errors can be restored back to normal condition. It can be presented in a *mean time to repair (MTTR)* measurement.
- *Resilience* indicates the ability of a service to continue to operate properly in spite of subsystem failures or triggers from resilience failover. It can be presented by the number of (additional) functional blocks needed to withstand the failures.
- *Variability* indicates the degree of acceleration or deceleration of other given measurements over a specified time period.
- *Consistency* indicates the degree of stability of other given measurements over a specified time period. This indicator is the opposite of the Variability indicator.

7.3.2.4 Transport QoS Measurements

The transport measurements concern the quality of messages as they travel from origin to destination. These metrics can be used to identify potential effects of service disruption or failure that may expand to impact greater numbers of customers, or linked with SLA to reflect the transport performance measures. The definition of quality at the transport layer can be quantified as follows:

- *Error* indicates the rate of misdirected, combined, or corrupted packets during the transmission. Retransmission of packets due to error will introduce delays.

- *Dropped-packets* indicate the rate of undeliverable packet counts owing to the buffer's limitation or loss of battery power. Retransmission of packets due to this cause will also introduce delays.
- *Out-of-order* indicates the overhead needed to rearrange out-of-order packets which are routed through a network on different paths and arrive in an incorrect order.
- *Delay* measures slowness for packets to reach their destination. Fixed delays come from switch, encoding, decoding, packetization, serialization, network propagation, processing, and de-jitter buffer. Variable delays come from message being held up in queues or routing to avoid congestion or failures.
- *Jitter* is the variation in any type of delays. Streaming audio and video are very sensitive to jitter.

7.3.2.5 Network and Routing QoS Measurements

The QoS measurements at the network layer are critical to the service operators because they directly support the transport layer QoS. An enterprise network normally comprises different technologies from many vendors. These measurements usually require some level of conditioning or data fusion process in order to mediate their differences:

- *Bandwidth constraint* indicates the reasoning of loss impact which prevents the service from reaching its achievable bandwidth requirement.
- *Error-prone and share channel* indicates the (additional) channels required to maintain certain level of error thresholds.
- *Location-dependent contention* represents the maximum density and topology arrangement that can maintain the continuation of the service within a specific location.
- *Resource constraint* represents the minimum resource dependencies to satisfy given performance requirements. The resource constraints can be influenced by battery, memory, CPU, storage, antenna, and so forth.
- *Route acquisition delay* measures how fast a path can be established and ready for communication.
- *Route reconfiguration* represents how effective a route can be changed based upon the new mission plan.
- *Loop free routing* measures if there is any existing or potential routing loop. A routing loop can prevent or delay messages to be forwarded to the right destinations thus have performance implication.
- *Minimum control overhead* indicates the additional traffic or resources allocated for network or service managements.
- *Scalability* measures how well the service can hold up the given performance criteria when sizes of the service are changed.

- *Support time-sensitive traffic* indicates the ratio of time-sensitive traffic over the total traffic. The other measure represents the ratio of time-sensitive traffic that are maintained above the performance criteria.
- *Security and privacy* will be discussed in chapter 8.

7.3.2.6 Multicasting QoS Measurements

Multicasting is a very important feature in IP-based network, especially in the area of communication coordination and control in wireless networks and data dissemination in mission-critical applications. The QoS measurements can include the following:

- *Robustness* indicates how effective the messages can be delivered to the designated receiver, receiver group, or all community members.
- *Efficiency* indicates how fast the broadcasting messages can be delivered to the designated receiver, receiver group, or all community members.
- *Control overhead* measures how much additional bandwidth is required to coordinate the multicasting feature.
- *Time-sensitive QoS* indicates the delay, error, and bandwidth of time-sensitive traffic used for multicasting.
- *Efficient group management* represents the efficiency of accepting multicast session members and maintaining the connectivity among them until the session expires with minimal exchange of control message.
- *Scalability* measures how well the multicasting can continue to function during network scale changes.
- *Security* will be discussed in detail in chapter 8. The highlights of multicasting specific measurements are *denial of service*, *resource consumption*, *energy depletion* (directing unnecessary traffic through some critical node to deplete the energy power), *buffer overflow* (filling the routing table with unwanted routing entries or by consuming the data packet buffer space with unwanted data), *host impersonation* (a compromised internal node acts as another node and responds with appropriate control packets to create wrong routing entries), *information disclosure* (a compromised internal node acts as informer by deliberate disclosure of confidential information to unauthorized nodes), and *interference* (wide-spectrum noise to attach the application, using a single wide-band jammer, sweeping across the spectrum).

7.3.2.7 Wireless Ad-hoc Network QoS Measurements

Wireless ad-hoc networks have many technology specific QoS considerations that are uncommon to other networking approaches. These measurements can include:

- *Distributed operations* measure how many communication nodes and interfaces have polling-based MAC protocols with partial coordination.

- *Synchronization* measures how well the communication nodes can manage transmission and reception slots in TDMA-based systems.
- *Hidden terminals* measure how effective the network can avoid collisions from hidden terminal situation (see section 3.3.1).
- *Exposed terminals* measure how effective the network can avoid the problem from exposed terminal situation (see section 3.3.2).
- *Throughput* measures how an ad-hoc network can minimize the occurrence of collision, maximize channel utilization, and minimize control overhead.
- *Fairness* measures how well the network can support an equal share or weighted share of the bandwidth to all competing nodes in the multi-hop relaying environment.
- *Real-time traffic support* measures if the network can be functioning with limited bandwidth and location-dependent contention while supporting time-sensitive traffic.
- *Resource reservation* measures bandwidth, buffer space, and processing power and their impacts to bandwidth, delay, and jitter.
- *Bandwidth and battery power* measures the sensitivity of increased collisions when the power level is raised.
- *Adaptive rate control* represents the variation in the data bit rate achieved over a channel.
- *Use of directional antennas* represents whether the network uses the directional antennas to increase spectrum reuse by reduction in interference and power consumption.

7.3.3 QoS-Based Selection and Execution

To better fulfill customer expectations, QoS-based selection and execution of services must be performed based on the QoS objectives defined in CLA or SLA.

As service-oriented systems carry out complex and mission-critical applications, different service classes coupled with the affiliated serves can ensure that application meets their CLA requirements. In terms of QoS Selection, they can be largely grouped into no-QoS and QoS-enabled. The non-QoS is also known as "best effort" service. The QoS-enabled group includes state-based and boundary-based QoS.

7.3.3.1 Queuing

When congestion occurs there needs to be way of sorting the traffic. Packets that have been marked can be identified and placed in queues. The queues can vary in how much and when they can load up the link with the packets contained within their queue. The shorter the queue length, the lower the latency will be. Even the fastest of links on the fastest of layer 2 switches can suffer from congestion if the data packets are large.

The following discussion profiles some of the most popular mechanisms in IP networks. The contents are meant to provide reference for enterprise service designers that have exposure to low level activities, and these mechanisms can be a source of reference when developing higher level service applications.

For instance, the simplest method of queuing is *round robin (RR)* where each queue is serviced one packet from each at a time. Another method called *weighted round robin (WRR)* allows higher priority traffic to be given a low weight thereby allowing it access to greater bandwidth.

First-in, First-out (FIFO)

First-in, first-out (FIFO) is known as *best effort (BE)* and stores packets when the network is congested and they are then forwarded in order of arrival. No queues are involved thus there is no-QoS. This is often the default mechanism of an enterprise service as it is the fastest method of queuing, and is effective for links with minimal congestion. With FIFO, ill-behaved sources can consume all the bandwidth, bursty sources can cause delay in time-sensitive traffic, and important traffic can be dropped because less important traffic fills the queues.

Weighted Round Robin (WRR)

Weighted round robin (WRR) is also a best effort connection scheduling discipline. It is the simplest emulation of *generalized processor sharing (GPS)* discipline. While GPS serves infinitesimal amount of data from each non-empty connection, WRR serves a number of packets for each nonempty connection with *number = normalized (weight/mean packet size)*. To obtain normalized set of weights, a mean packet size must be known. Only then can WRR correctly emulate GPS. To achieve an acceptable accuracy, it is best to know this parameter in advance, however, this is very uncommon in IP networks. Another problem with WRR is that it may not provide fair link sharing.

Head-of-the-Line (HOL)

Head-of-the-line (HOL) is a priority-based buffer sharing system. Newly arriving packets of priority P will join the queue behind all packets of priority P or better, and in front of all packets of priority P+1 or worse. This means that arriving packets with the highest priority have at most one packet service time of delay. HOL provides absolute preferential treatment to high-priority traffic to ensure mission-critical traffic can traverse various networks and get priority treatment. It also means that high-priority streams can starve lower priority ones of service. This approach does not attempt to give quality to any of the other streams, and thus must overprovision in order to handle the most important data.

Weighted Fair Queuing (WFQ)

Weighted fair queuing (WFQ) can allocate bandwidth according to IP Precedence using weightings. The number of WFQ queues depends upon the number of flows. WFQ flows are the traffic for a single transport layer session or network layer flow across a given device interface. IP traffic is classified based upon source IP address and port, destination IP address and port, and IP Precedence. Once the priority queues are serviced, the other IP traffic is weighted and queued accordingly. WFQ favors the shorter packets; therefore low bandwidth traffic takes priority over high bandwidth traffic. This can guarantee a certain minimum bandwidth per priority class and has the advantage of sharing unused bandwidth equally between the active flows. Because this approach does not guarantee all packets will be serviced, the potential problem with WFQ is that when the number of flows increases, a large number of dynamic queues can cause latency for high-priority traffic. WFQ across a number of interfaces is called *distributed weighted fair queuing (DWFQ)*. A graphical presentation of a WFQ process is shown in Figure 7.6.

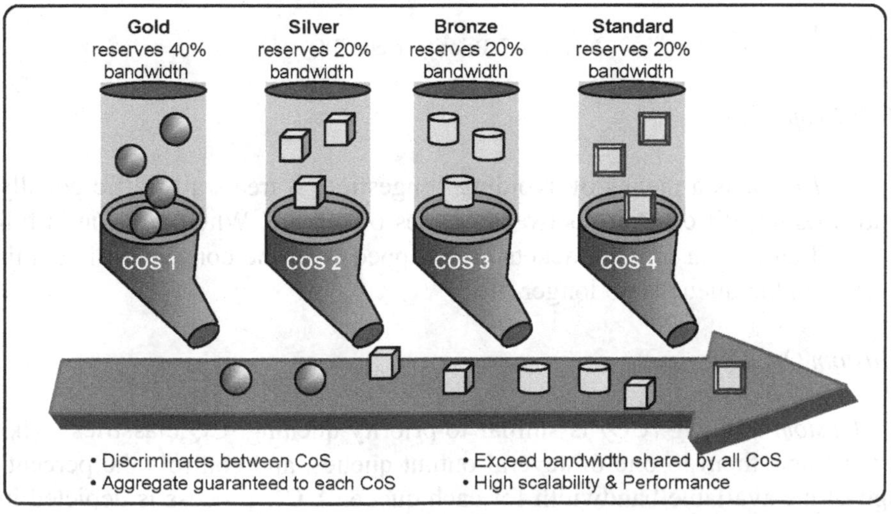

Figure 7.6. Weighted fair queuing (WFQ).

Priority Queuing (PQ)

Priority queuing (PQ) classifies packets based on certain criteria and assigns the packets to one of several output queues, serving these strictly in priority order. PQ ensures one type of traffic will be sent, possibly at the expense of others. The higher priority queues have to be emptied before the lower ones. Potentially low-priority traffic may not get forwarded at all. This is called Protocol Starvation. When a queue becomes longer than the specified limit, subsequent packets trying to enter that queue are dropped indiscriminately (tail drop). The top priority queue used for RSVP is not respected by PQ (Figure 7.7).

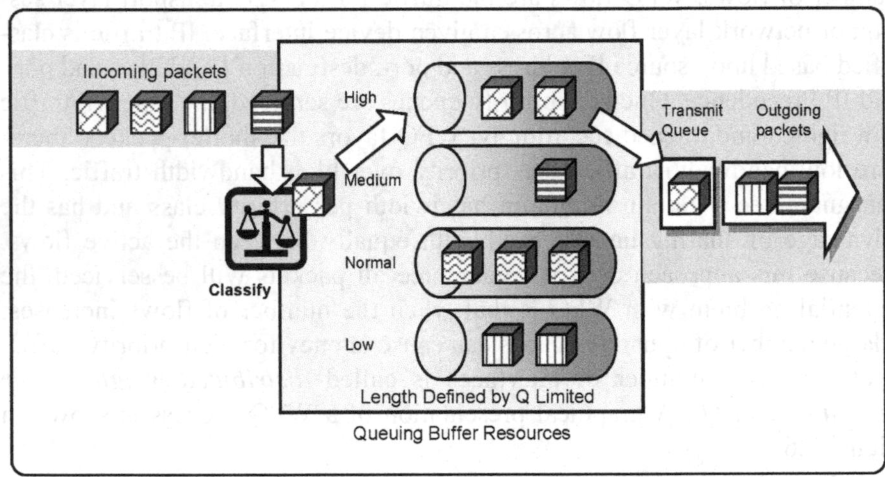

Figure 7.7. Priority queue (PQ).

Tail Drop

Tail Drop is a means of avoiding congestion. It treats all traffic equally and does not differentiate between classes of service. When a queue is full and tail drop is in effect, packets are dropped until the congestion is eliminated and the queue is no longer full.

Custom Queuing (CQ)

Custom queuing (CQ) is similar to priority queuing. CQ classifies packets, assigns them to one of several output queues, and controls the percentage of the available bandwidth for each queue. A CQ process is depicted in Figure 7.8. This method deals with queue in a *Weighted Round Robin* fashion allowing the configured amount of traffic from each, hence avoiding any queue from monopolizing the bandwidth. When a queue becomes empty, the extra space is dynamically shared out amongst the other queues. This method is used for assigning queue space based on the protocol. Sequential servicing can avoid the starvation problem of PQ and ensure that some traffic of all categories is sent. Queue 0 is reserved for control communication while queues 1 to 16 are for the applications. The top priority queue used for RSVP is not respected by CQ.

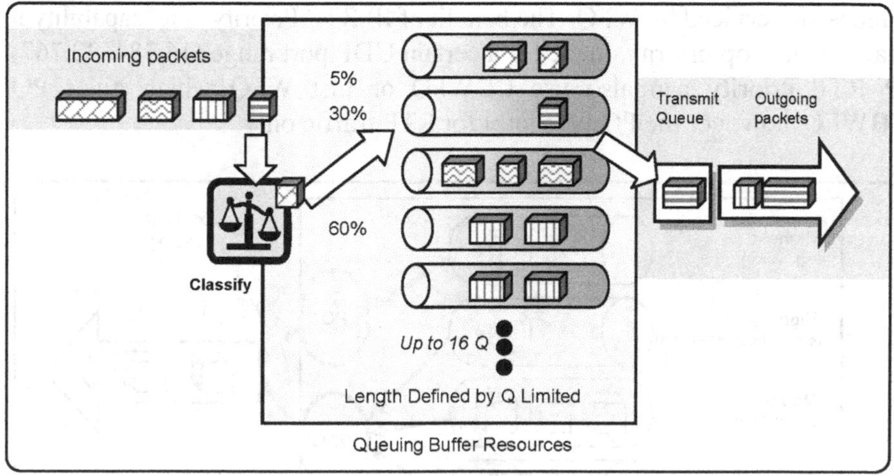

Figure 7.8. Custom queuing (CQ).

Class-Based Queuing (CBQ)

Class-based queuing (CBQ) scheduler is sensitive to the selection of parameters, possibly having a damaging effect on the results.

Class-Based Weighted Fair Queuing (CBWFQ)

Class-based weighted fair queuing (CBWFQ) extends the standard WFQ functionality to provide support for user-defined traffic classes. Traffic classes are weighted based upon match criteria including protocols, *access control lists (ACLs)*, and input interfaces. These are used by the WFQ mechanism to provide guaranteed delivery. Each class can specify the exact amount of bandwidth to be allocated for specific traffic types, and add characteristics such as the maximum number of packets (queue limit) and a drop policy. If the number of packets from a matched flow exceeds the queue limit, tail drop will take place. Unused bandwidth for one class can be shared amongst the other classes. Unclassified traffic is assumed to be in the

Default Class and is acted on by WFQ and is treated as best effort. However, this does not ensure fair treatment within a class.

IP RTP Priority

IP real-time protocol (RTP) Priority runs over UDP and gets serviced once the ports have been recognized. As depicted in Figure 7.9, IP RTP uses PQ/WFQ method therefore it is not a generic PQ as delineated. The other queues are serviced by WFQ. The benefit of IP RTP Priority is its capability to maintain the top priority queue for a certain UDP port range (16,384–32,767). IP RTP Priority can also use CBWFQ or just WFQ which gives PQ/CBWFQ, however the PQ is strictly for RTP traffic only.

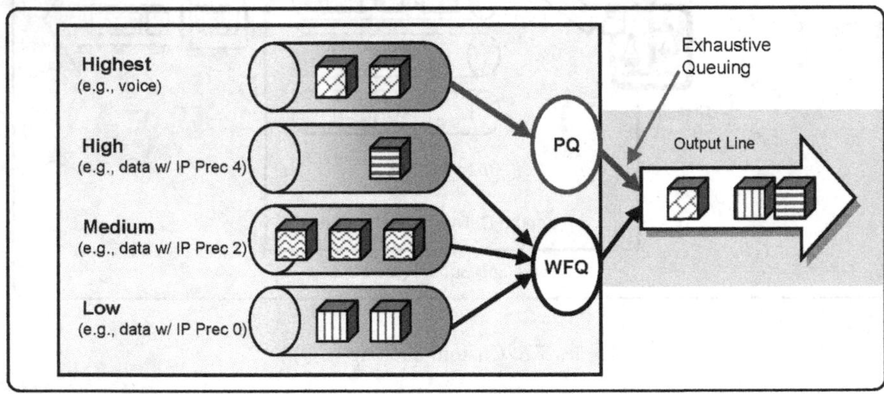

Figure 7.9. IP RTP priority.

Low Latency Queuing (LLQ)

Low latency queuing (LLQ) brings strict priority queuing to *class-based weighted fair queuing (CBWFQ)*, it is also known as PQ/CBWFQ. The strict priority queuing approach allows delay-sensitive data such as voice to be dequeued and sent first before packets in other queues are sent. Unlike IP RTP priority, the single PQ within LLQ can deal with TCP exchanges thus it is a preferred choice to use when queuing all types of traffic. When a router is configured with both IP RTP priority and LLQ, IP RTP priority takes precedence. In such case, jitter sensitive traffic should avoid this type of configuration. Figure 7.10 shows the layer two subsystem processes and the low latency queuing. The layer three subsystem processes the link fragmentation and interleaving, respectively.

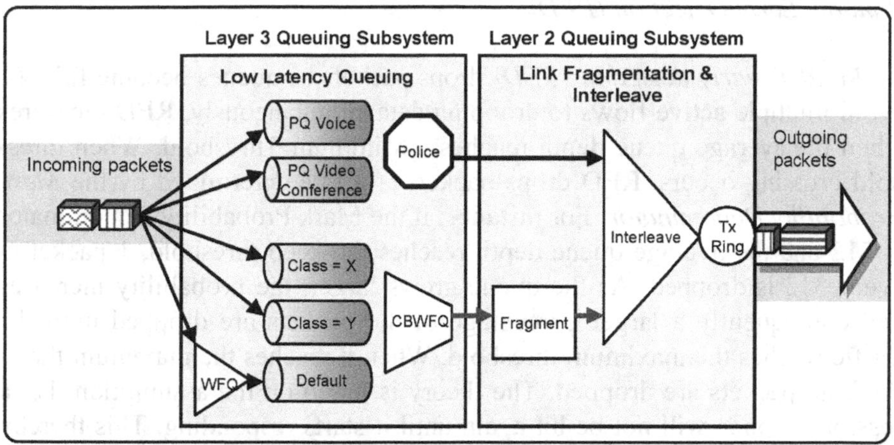

Figure 7.10. Low latency queuing (LLQ).

7.3.3.2 Congestion Avoidance

The congestion avoidance features can be profiled into the following approaches:

Global Synchronization

Global synchronization is needed when queues are constantly full and the messages are likely to be dropped indiscriminately. If there are multiple TCP flows through a congested link, chances are many flows will be dropped at the same time. The TCP slow-start mechanism for all the flows that were interrupted can lead to global synchronization. GS triggers waves of congestion followed by waves of under utilization of the link. This is not an efficient use of the link to balance the traffic pattern [4].

Partial Buffer Sharing (PBS)

Partial buffer sharing (PBS) is a mechanism for determining whether or not to admit an arriving packet to the queue. It is a popular method in an ATM network. In a priority based buffer sharing system, a number of thresholds are set corresponding to different priority levels; once the length of the queue is beyond a particular threshold, only packets with a higher priority level are admitted. This method can ensure that a high load in low-priority streams will not cause excessive loss for more important flows. However, limiting the loss with high-priority streams increases traffic pressure at this level. As a result, more high-priority packets released into the queue eventually make the average delay longer than when low-priority packets are admitted.

Random Early Detection (RED)

Random early detection (RED) drops packets as queues become full. To avoid multiple active flows to dropping data simultaneously, RED measures when the average queue depth reaches a Minimum Threshold. When threshold crossing occurs, RED drops packets at a rate determined by the *Mark Probability Denominator*. For instance, if the Mark Probability Denominator is 512 and the average queue depth reaches the keep threshold, 1 packet in every 512 is dropped. As the queue grows larger, the probability increases and consequently a larger percentage of the packets are dropped until the traffic reaches the maximum threshold. When it reaches the maximum threshold, all packets are dropped. The theory is based on the assumption that a session hit once will not be hit again until it starts responding. This thereby minimizes global synchronization and makes more efficient use of the link bandwidth during congestion.

Weighted Random Early Detection (WRED)

Weighted random early detection (WRED) drops packets selectively, generally based on DSCP/IP precedence. Packets with a higher IP precedence are less likely to be dropped than packets with a lower precedence. Figure 7.11 depicts that WRED can selectively discard lower priority traffic when the interface begins to get congested and provides differentiated performance characteristics for different classes of service. WRED uses the Drop Preference portion of the *per-hop behavior (PHB*; section 7.4.2*)* to determine the drop probability and minimize the chances of tail-dropping, high-priority packets as well as TCP global synchronization. Because WRED

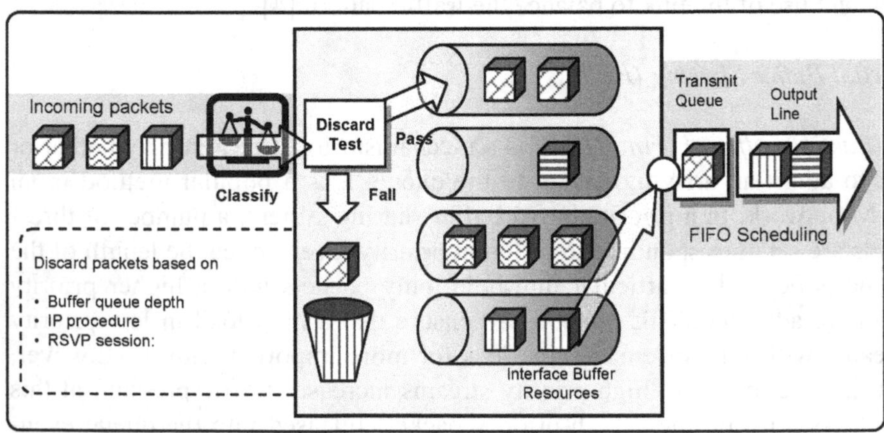

Figure 7.11. Weighted random early detection (WRED).

does not preclude the chances of dropping voice packets, therefore is not a recommended technology in a voice network [5].

WRED discards packets, and that is one way for the router to indicate congestion. *Random early detection (RED)* was designed for a router to signal that it was approaching congestion by marking packets, thus allowing early avoidance of both congestion and retransmission delays. When a router receives a packet marked as *explicit congestion notification (ECN)* capable and anticipates (using RED/WRED) congestion, it will set a flag notifying the sender to decrease its window size (sending rate). The intent is to avoid resending packets. ECN uses the 2 last bits in the ToS byte to indicate whether a device is ECN capable, and if so, whether congestion is being experienced. The position of ECN bits in an IPv4 Packet header is shown in Figure 7.12. This is a better way than the indirect packets delete congestion notification performed by the RED/WRED algorithms. However, it requires explicit support by both hosts to be effective [6,7].

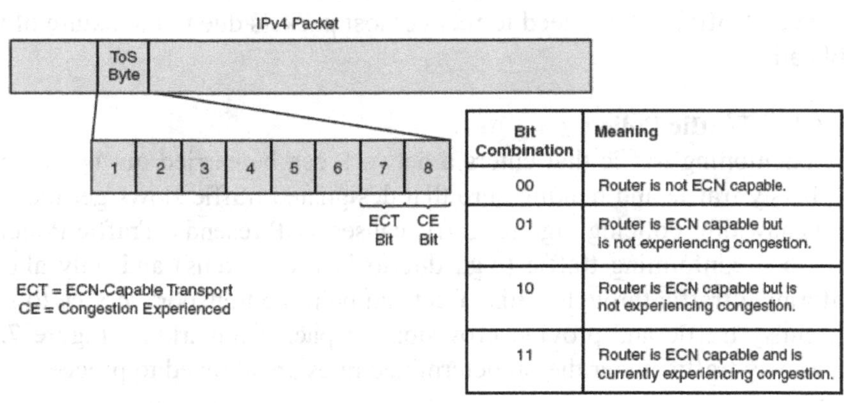

Bit Combination	Meaning
00	Router is not ECN capable.
01	Router is ECN capable but is not experiencing congestion.
10	Router is ECN capable but is not experiencing congestion.
11	Router is ECN capable and is currently experiencing congestion.

Figure 7.12. Explicit congestion notification (ECN) bits.

ECN is a far more robust way to achieve closed-loop control at the packet level than loss detection, and given designs using closed-loop control tend to be far simpler than open-loop [8].

Flow-Based Weighted Random Early Detection (FRED)

In *flow-based weighted random early detection (FRED)* a flow is made up of a 5-tuple, which are source address and port, destination address and port, and IP Precedence. FRED can track flows and penalize flows that exhaust more than their fair share of the buffer space. FRED monitors each flow in turn and observes how each flow uses the queues. FRED then increases some bursting space by scaling up the number of packets allowing for each flow in the queues. If a particular flow exceeds the allowance, FRED increases the probability of packets from that flow to be dropped.

7.3.3.3 Link Efficiency

Smaller data packets used for applications such as voice and telnet are susceptible to jitter (delay variation) when large data packets are traversing the same interfaces. *Link fragmentation and interleaving (LFI)* at layer two is a standard mechanism where large packets are fragmented and the smaller data packets interleaved with the fragments. Potential serialization delay from the data fragments must be controlled to reduce the time that delay-sensitive packets have to wait in a queue.

In a VoIP environment, Real-Time Transport Protocol (RTP) is [9] used to transport real-time data, whereas TCP is used for signaling protocols such as H.323 or SIP. RTP uses UDP for transport. The RTP header is 12 bytes in length and follows the 8-byte UDP header and the 20-byte IP header. However, VoIP does not need to recover lost packets due to the nature of the application.

7.3.3.4 Traffic Policing

Conditioning traffic that enters a network can be carried out by controlling bursty traffic and making sure that designated traffic flows get the correct bandwidth. Policing ingress traffic causes TCP resends. Traffic Policing drops non-conforming traffic (e.g., due to lack of tokens) and only allows conforming traffic through. This effect can help the transport service to sustain bursty traffic and provide provision for packet remarking. Figure 7.13 shows only traffic under the predetermined rates are allowed to proceed.

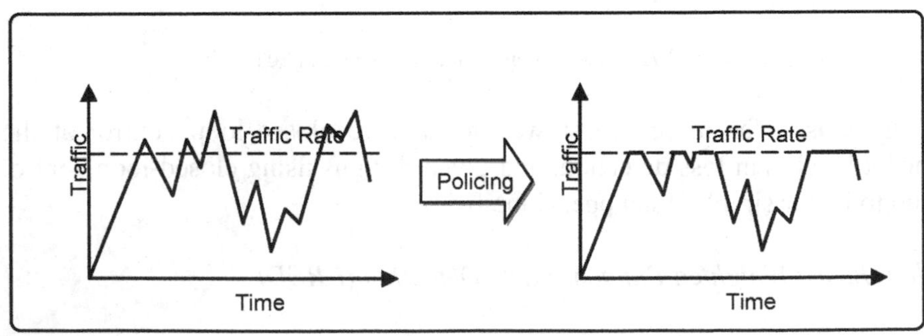

Figure 7.13. Traffic policing.

Token Bucket

Token bucket combines policing and shaping to enforce compliance with a traffic specification. It tries to solve the limit average rate and size of bursts with three components: a burst size, a mean rate, and a time interval (Tc) [10].

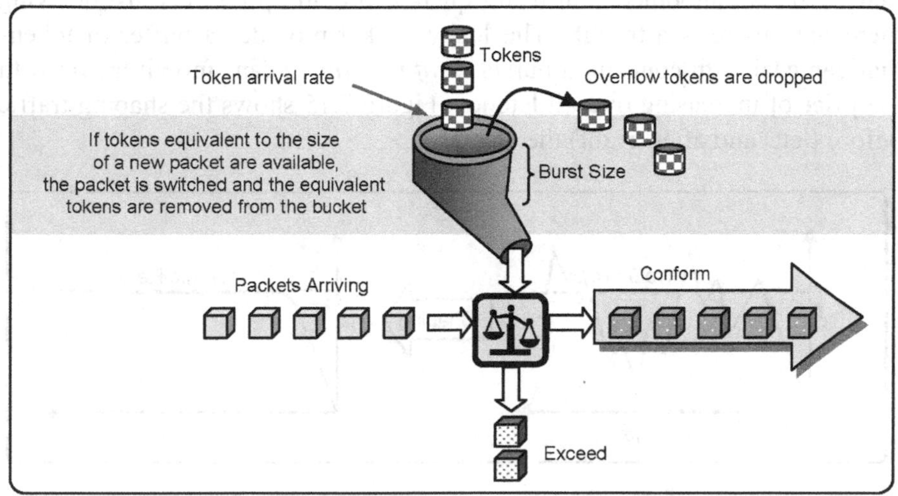

Figure 7.14. Token Bucket in Traffic Shaping (IntServ).

The token bucket approach means that any bursts are limited to the bucket capacity and the transmission rate is governed by the rate at which tokens are added to the bucket. The concept of Token Bucket or Leaky Bucket is taken from *Frame Relay Mean Rate (CIR) = Burst Size (Bc)/Time Interval (Tc)*. Imagine a bucket which is being filled with tokens at a certain rate and each token has permission to send a fixed number of bits. As shown in Figure 7.14, a packet arrives and matches the class for that bucket, and then it is added to the queue and released from the queue with the specified rate. If the bucket is full then new tokens are discarded ('leaked' out) and cannot be retrieved for use by subsequent packets. If there are not enough tokens in the bucket, the system may wait for enough tokens before sending the packet (this is traffic shaping) or the packet may be discarded (traffic policing).

Hierarchical Token Bucket (HTB)

Hierarchical token bucket (HTB) [11] is a combination of Token Bucket Filters and a Weighted Round Robin scheduler. It allows flexible allocation of bandwidth to classes with very few parameters. In HTB, each packet class has an assigned priority, and the scheduling resembles the classical Head-of-Line. If a class has no packets or is not able to send due to the assigned limit, the next class is granted the turn.

7.3.3.5 Traffic Shaping

Traffic can also be conditioned by *Shaping*. Shaping the traffic means that traffic is 'smoothed' out using queues to hold up packets just delaying them until there is a trough. The leaky bucket provides a buffer of tokens that can deal with controlled bursts. *Traffic shaping* can smooth traffic with the price of increasing overall latency. Figure 7.15 shows the shaping traffic before (left) and after (right) the effect.

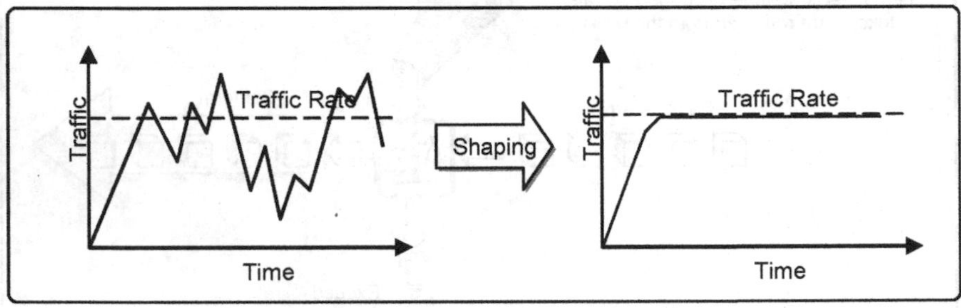

Figure 7.15. Traffic shaping.

Generic traffic shaping (GTS) applies to any outbound interface and operates with *switched multi-megabit data service (SMDS)*, ATM, Frame Relay, and Ethernet. Outbound traffic can be shaped to meet the requirements of the receiving node(s), and the DSCP values can be set accordingly. *Backward explicit congestion notification (BECN)* is used with an access list to determine the traffic to shape.

Frame relay traffic shaping (FRTS) can shape outgoing traffic on a per VC basis and set up queues such that different traffic types can be treated appropriately on the same VC. Edge nodes set the *discard eligibility (DE)* bit when there is congestion so that high precedence traffic does not get dropped, otherwise all traffic within a PVC is treated the same by the frame relay switch. FRTS even allows occasional bursting provided that the average utilization is adhered to over a specified period of time [12].

TCP Rate Control

TCP rate control modifies the window size for a TCP traffic flow. Delaying acknowledgement packets effectively slow down the traffic and avoid congestion. It is designed to ensure that all TCP flows transmit with a preconfigured rate allowing greater control over the loss and delay prioritization of packets. Most TCP rate control implementations are easy to overload simply by sending more traffic than the link can allow. For example, sending 55MB to a 50MB pipe would almost immediately cause a complete drop in all traffic.

7.3.4 QoS-Based Adaptation

It is necessary to expect to adapt, replan, and reschedule a service in response to unexpected progress, delays, or technical conditions. QoS-based adaptation allows the service providers to evaluate alternative strategies. To adjust a service from its initial QoS requirements, a set of potential alternatives is generated, with the objective of changing a service as its QoS continues to meet initial requirements. Prior to carrying out the adaptation in a running services environment, it is necessary to estimate its impact on the services QoS.

System adaptation can be modeled as a set of events. The event trace actually is a model of the system's temporal behavior. Event grammar forms the basis for system adaptation models. An event represents any detectable action found during the service life cycle. Actions (or events) evolve in time, and system behavior represents the temporal relationship among actions.

Figure 7.16 depicts a multi-layer technique for QoS enforcement in voice application. Multi-application rate shaping allows cooperating applications to adjust their behavior based on shared notions of their relative importance to the user. In an IP network, call admission control techniques such as "bandwidth brokers" are another proposed option. Finally, QoS-aware middleware can be used to leverage both application layer and network layer QoS management techniques.

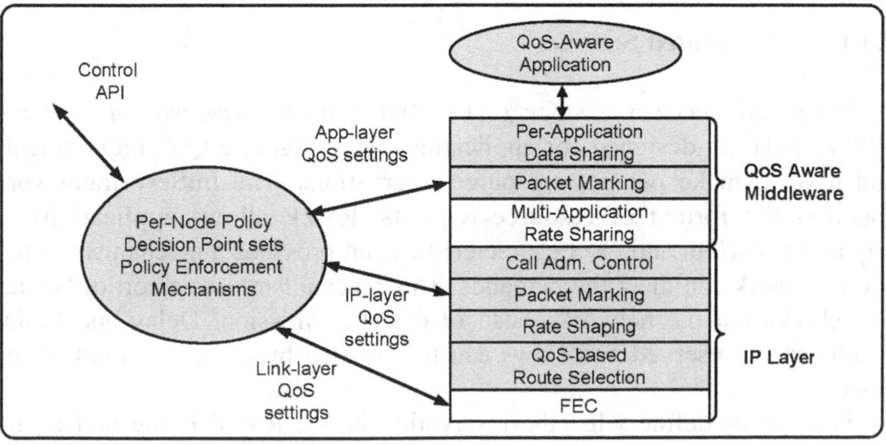

Figure 7.16. Policy decisions on a voice application.

Admission control is a major aspect of Service QoS. Admission Control may be *implicit* or *explicit*, as detailed below:

- *Explicit admission control* is based on signaled resource reservation. Applications must send a request to use the network through the resource reservation signaling mechanism. The admission control is based on the application's QoS requirements, available resources, performance criteria, and network policy. This mechanism is used in many real-time applications (such as Voice over IP) that are designed to utilize signaling such as H.323 or *session initiation protocol (SIP)* to initiate a session.
- *Implicit admission control* has no explicit resource reservation signaling. The admission control mechanism relies on a priori bandwidth provisioning and traffic conditioning mechanisms, such as traffic shaping and policing, at the network edge to control the admission of packets to the network. For instance, the connectionless and stateless architectures such as Web, HTTP, FTP, and e-mail do not employ signaling, and must rely on implicit mechanisms within the network to enforce their QoS requirements.

7.4 QoS Implementations

QoS management is about making reservations and only accepting the reservations if the network resources are able to serve them with certain performance criteria. Because service quality can be differentiated, the service providers therefore are able to charge customers for making different levels of service classes. This section will cover the three most popular QoS implementations, namely integrated services, differentiated service, and multilevel precedence and preemption.

7.4.1 Integrated Services

Integrated services (IntServ) [13] and *resource reservation protocol (RSVP)* [14] are designed for applications which require QoS requirements and have to make per-flow resource reservations. The IntServ framework specifies the format of resource requests. RSVP allows applications to request bandwidth and QoS characteristics and provides a mechanism to tell if the network can meet the demands. This mechanism uses a sort of 'scout' that checks out the network ahead of data transmission. Delay and Bandwidth can be reserved and flows can be signaled by the end station or the router.

Flow specs define what the reservation is for. RSVP is the underlying mechanism to signal it across the network. IntServ defines two parts to a flow spec:

- *Traffic specification (T-SPEC)* defines the traffic characteristic of a service. Both token rate and the bucket depth are configurable parameters that control the token bucket algorithm. The *token rate* dictates the average rate of traffic flow, and the *depth of the bucket* dictates how *bursty* the traffic is permitted. For instance, a conversation would need a lower token rate but a higher bucket depth because of frequent pauses in conversations and the required compensation for burstier traffic.
- *Request specification (R-SPEC)* specifies levels of guarantees: 1) *Best effort* is the native IP traffic, no reservation is needed. It can request retransmissions of any data lost or damaged in transit; 2) *Controlled load, guaranteed bit-rate*, or *rate-sensitive* requires a guaranteed transmission rate from its source to its destination, e.g., VoIP and videoconferencing. For instance, RSVP enables constant bit-rate service in packet-switched networks via its rate-sensitive level of service; and 3) *Guaranteed* or *delay-sensitive* service is bound in delay and dropped criteria; it requires timeliness of delivery and that varies its rate accordingly, e.g., MPEG-II video. RSVP services supporting delay-sensitive traffic are referred to as controlled-delay service (non-real-time service) and predictive service (real-time service).

7.4.1.1 Resource Reservation Protocol

RSVP supports multicast and allows reservations to be aggregated, in other words, each receiver in the group need not have to reserve. It is based on the assumption that different receivers have different capabilities and want different QoS. RSVP requests resources for simplex flows; that is, a traffic stream is always in one direction from sender to one or more receivers.

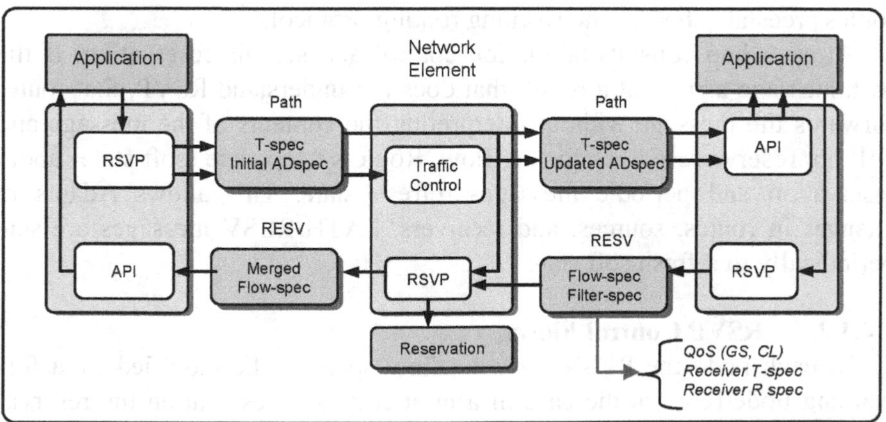

Figure 7.17. The use of RSVP objects during the resource reservation phase.

RSVP is a network-control protocol enabling Internet applications to obtain differing QoS for their data flows. As depicted in Figure 7.17, RSVP is used during the resource reservation phase. Network performance requirements can be sensitive to reliability but not time-sensitive (e.g., traditional interactive and batch applications) or timely but not necessarily reliable (e.g., videoconferencing, IP telephony, and other forms of multimedia communications). RSVP is intended to support the divergent applications.

There are five primary types of messages:

1. *Path message (PATH)* includes the IP address of the previous node, format of the sender data, *traffic specification (T-spec)*, and advertising data (ad-spec) [15].
2. *Reservation message (RESV)* carries receiver's *request specification (R-spec)*. It contains the receiver's flow-spec data object identifying the requested resources (delay and bandwidth), filter specification, and reservation style.
3. *CONFIRMATION message* is generated only upon request. Unicast to receiver when RESV reaches node with established state.
4. *TEARDOWN message* is created once the data stream has completed. PATHTEAR and RESVTEAR are triggered to terminate the call and release resources back to the mainstream traffic.
5. *ERROR message* is used in error situations. If resources are not available, for example, the sender and receiver are notified with error messages.

In RSVP, a data flow is a sequence of datagrams that have the same source, destination (regardless of whether that destination is one or more physical machines), and quality of service.

A RSVP host that needs to send a data flow with specific QoS will transmit a RSVP path message that will travel along the unicast or multicast routes preestablished by the working routing protocol.

At each hop consults admission control and sets up reservation. If the path message arrives at a router that does not understand RSVP, that router forwards the message without interpreting the contents of the message and will not reserve resources for the flow. Routers keep state (soft state) about reservation and periodic messages refresh state. This allows Adapts to changes in routes, sources, and receivers. PATH/RESV messages are sent periodically to refresh soft state.

7.4.1.2 RSVP Control Flows

At each node the RESV message flow spec can be modified by a forwarding node (e.g., in the case of a multicast flow reservation the reservations requests can be merged). When router admits a RESV message, it will install a packet filter into forwarding database, pass flow parameters to the scheduler, activate packet policing if needed, and forward the RESV message upstream. In terms of the reservation styles, three filters are available, they are:

- *Wildcard/No filter* does not specify a particular sender for group.
- *Fixed filter* allows the sender to be explicitly specified for a reservation, e.g., video conference.
- *Dynamic filter* allows valid senders to be changed over time, e.g., audio conference.

When the destination router receives the path message, it will make a reservation based on the request parameters. The admission control and policy control at this node can process the request parameters and can either instruct the packet classifier to correctly handle the selected subset of data packets or negotiate with the upper layer how the packet handling should be performed.

At each node the IP destination address of the RESV message will change to the address of the next node on the reverse path and the IP source address to the address of the previous node address on the reverse path.

Reservations from multiple receivers for a single sender are merged together at branching points. Reservations for multiple senders may be added up. Reservations for multiple senders may add up the traffic.

7.4.2 Differentiated Services

Differentiated service (DiffServ) [16] is designed to overcome the difficulty of implementing and deploying IntServ and RSVP in the Internet backbone [17]. DiffServ provides a limited number of aggregated classes in order to avoid the scalability problem of IntServ.

DiffServ defines an architecture and a set of forwarding behaviors. In DiffServ, forwarding resources are allocated to packet aggregates. In the IP protocol [18] specification, IP precedence is a mechanism to associate priorities to packets. This is considered a pre-DiffServ mechanism, because the definition of the *per-hop behavior (PHB)* code points is TOS compatible. Traditionally, IP Precedence has used the first 3 bits of the TOS field to give 8 possible precedence values. A packet is marked in the TOS field in IPv4, and Traffic Class in IPv6. A comparison comparing of IP TOS and IP DSCP is depicted in Figure 7.18 [19].

DiffServ is built on the deprecated ToS (or *traffic class*) to provide distinct services. DiffServ introduces the concept of the *DiffServ code point (DSCP)* [20] that uses the first 6 bits of the TOS field thereby giving $2^6 = 64$ different values. These map to the IP Precedence values in the TOS field of the IP datagram. DiffServ typically uses WRR, RED, WRED, and Traffic shaping for congestion management (Table 7.1).

Table 7.1. DiffServ Bit Specifications.

Per-Hop Behavior (PHB)			DiffServ Code Point (DSCP)		IP Prece-dence
Default		000000 (0)			0
Assured Forwarding		Low Drop Probability	Medium Drop Probability	High Drop Probability	
	Class 1	AF11 001010 (10)	AF12 001100 (12)	AF13 001110 (14)	1
	Class 2	AF21 010010 (18)	AF22 010100 (20)	AF23 010110 (22)	2
	Class 3	AF31 011010 (26)	AF32 011100 (28)	AF33 011110 (30)	3
	Class 4	AF41 100010 (34)	AF42 100100 (36)	AF43 100110 (38)	4
Expedited Forwarding		EF 101110 (46)			5

Packets from different sources can have the same DSCP value and so can be grouped in the same behavior aggregate (BA). The decimal IP Precedence value is derived from the first three-bit portion, or the *most significant bits (MSB)*. This is also called the *class selector (CS)* and maps directly to the IP Precedence bits. The following 3-bit 010 is the *Drop Probability* and is ignored by IP Precedence-only devices. The final section or the *least significant bits (LSB)* is always '0' and is ignored.

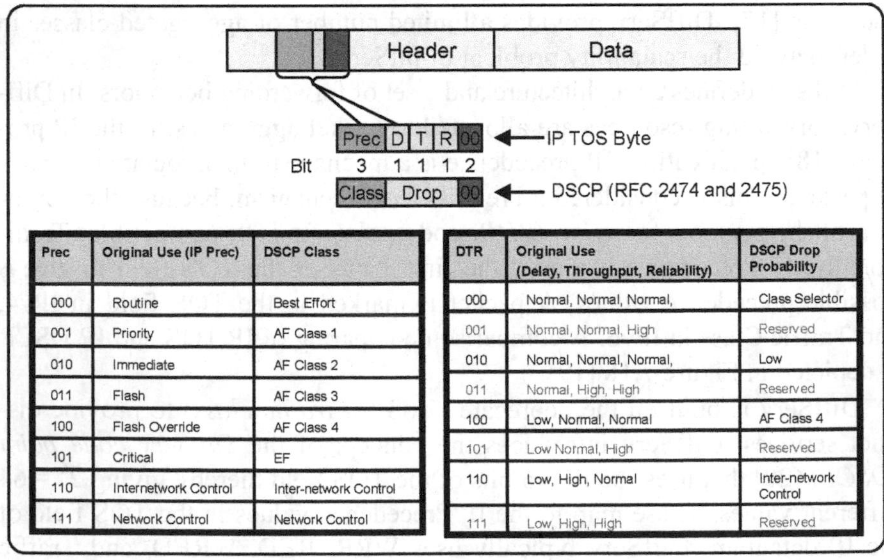

Prec	Original Use (IP Prec)	DSCP Class
000	Routine	Best Effort
001	Priority	AF Class 1
010	Immediate	AF Class 2
011	Flash	AF Class 3
100	Flash Override	AF Class 4
101	Critical	EF
110	Internetwork Control	Inter-network Control
111	Network Control	Network Control

DTR	Original Use (Delay, Throughput, Reliability)	DSCP Drop Probability
000	Normal, Normal, Normal,	Class Selector
001	Normal, Normal, High	Reserved
010	Normal, Normal, Normal,	Low
011	Normal, High, High	Reserved
100	Low, Normal, Normal	AF Class 4
101	Low Normal, High	Reserved
110	Low, High, Normal	Inter-network Control
111	Low, High, High	Reserved

Figure 7.18. IP TOS versus IP DSCP.

Any packet with a DSCP not defined in the above PHB will be given the default PHB of 000000.

Assured forwarding (AF) [21] defines four classes with some bandwidth and buffers allocated to them (e.g., Gold, Silver, and Bronze). Each class has three drop priorities in case of congestion. Non-conformant traffic is remarked.

Expedited forwarding (EF) [22] is similar to IntServ as it guarantees certain levels of loss, latency, jitter, or bandwidth. Some level of isolation is installed to avoid traffic being influenced by other traffic classes. It works It works on the basis of packets admitted at the peak rate. Non-conformant traffic is either dropped or shaped.

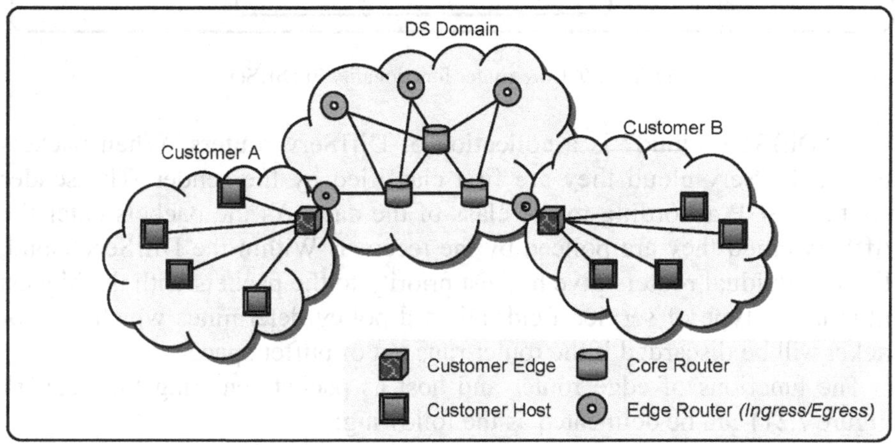

Figure 7.19. DiffServ architecture.

The main aim of the architecture of the DiffServ service is to keep the core of the network simple, focusing on supporting QoS for flow aggregates at the edges of the network, shown in Figure 7.19 [23]. The core of the network uses only the type field for QoS management; with a small number of types and well defined forwarding behavior to improve management efficiency. The forwarding treatments, formally PHB, on each network element can manage a particular flow or group of flows (behavior aggregate, or BA) of traffic for whether the routing interface should: 1) Drop the message; 2) Send the message; or 3) reclassify it [24]. As shown in Figure 7.20, BA Classifier selects packets based on the DSCP field in the IP header and determines the appropriate queues for transmission.

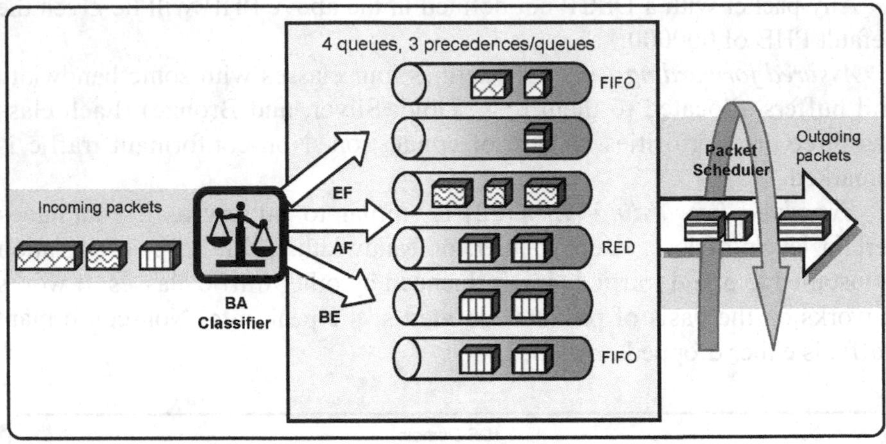

Figure 7.20. Core router functionality in DiffServ.

A "DiffServ cloud" is a collection of DiffServ routers. When packets enter a DiffServ cloud they are first classified by the sender. The sender sets the DSCP according to the class of the data. As the packets enter the DiffServ cloud they are policed by the receiver. Within the DiffServ cloud, all the individual routers give highest priority to the packets with the highest value in the type of service field. Discard policy determines which type of packet will be discarded if the router runs out of buffer space.

The functions of edge router and host as packets entering the network (Figure 7.21) can be delineated as the following:

1. *Classifier* marks packets according to classification rules and determines DSCP based on per domain flow policies defined by source and destination IP Addresses, source and destination ports, existing DSCP, and the transport protocol. The packet is marked in the first 6 bits of TOS (IPv4) or *traffic class* (IPv6). Then the packets are separated into paths where one path may be routed via a marking mechanism (3) and another path may be examined more closely (2).
2. *Policing* compares traffic rate of this class to the configured polices for this class. This is called Metering. A sub-function called conditioning then determines if the message is in or out of profile and treats the message with delays and then forwards, discards, or remarks other traffic.
3. *Marker* writes or rewrites the DSCP values on the packet to reflect drop precedence based on service policy and profile.
4. Shaper and Dropper determines the treatment of the outbound queue and perform queuing and scheduling against the queue based on configured rates, buffer, and resource allocation. Dropper discards some or all of the packets in a traffic stream to ensure compliance with the traffic profile.

5. *Media Access* includes transmitting the packet to the next node (the message may need to be transmited over multiple RF hops to get to next IP hop).

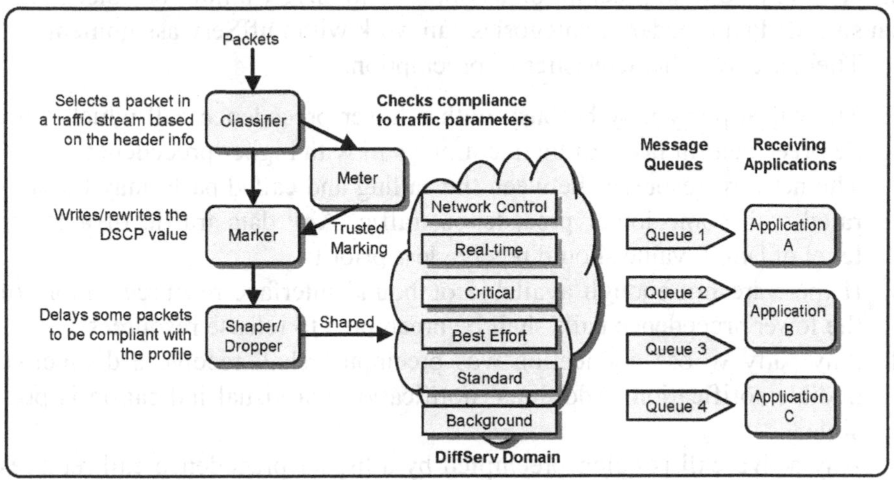

Figure 7.21. DiffServ flow control.

7.4.3 Multilevel Precedence and Preemption

Multilevel precedence and preemption (MLPP) defines a priority scheme for assigning precedence levels to specific calls or messages so that the system handles them in a predetermined order and time frame. MLPP allow the service users to gain controlled access to network resources in real time so that calls and messages can be preempted only by higher priority calls and messages. The priority defined in MLPP determines ranking order of call flows on a hop-by-hop basis through a voice and data network [25–27].

MLPP was created before electronic switching in the U.S. Government AUTOVON network. It is designed so that normal telephone traffic would not cause problems in times of emergency in the relevant NATO and DoD commands.

The scope of MLPP applications include: network or internetwork control (routing, signaling, discovery), network management, continuous interactive voice (telephony), continuous interactive video (multimedia conferencing), multimedia streaming and multicast, short block and transactional (interactive low-latency data), batch transfer (long blocks of high-throughput bulk data), and best effort. The implementation of queuing, buffering, per-hop/domain behaviors, and drop probabilities are not part of the proposal [28].

The basic function of MLPP is to cause some number of lower precedence calls to be dropped, or not started, so that higher precedence calls get placed. Remaining lower precedence calls stay at acceptable quality and parties on preempted calls receive clear feedback on why their call is being dropped (e.g., due to preemption as opposed to circuit failure or other trivial cause). MLPP precedence categories can work with DiffServ assignment.

There are five characteristics of preemption:

1. The called party may be busy with a lower precedence call which must be preempted in favor of the incoming call with higher precedence.
2. The network resources between the calling and called party may be saturated with some lower precedence traffic. Any data traffic of a lower level of DSCP value should receive less priority.
3. If there are not enough available outbound interface resources, more of the lower precedence calls shall be preempted to release resources.
4. Any party whose connection was preempted shall receive a distinctive audible notification. Additional notification via visual indication is possible.
5. Any active call is being preempted by a higher precedence call requires to acknowledge the preemption before switching to the new calling party.

If there is a user or SIP device that is configured to disable the ability to be preempted, that user or SIP phone device will not experience preemption of calls by higher precedence calls, if the cause of preemption would be due to called party busy condition (e.g., call waiting is enacted here). However, the user may still experience preemption of calls due to a lack of network resources other than the user's own access resources.

7.4.3.1 MLPP Precedence Levels

Precedence indicates the priority level that is associated with a call. Precedence assignment is ad-hoc in that the user may choose to apply or not to apply a precedence level to a call attempt. MLPP precedence does not relate to *call admission control (CAC)* or *enhanced emergency services (E911)*. In ANSI T.619-1992, five levels of precedence (or priority) for MLPP networks are defined as Table 7.2.

Table 7.2. MLPP Precedence Levels.

Precedence Level	Bits	Precedence
0 (highest)	0000	Flash override
1	0001	Flash
2	0010	Immediate
3	0011	Priority
4 (lowest)	0100	Routine
	0101 to 1111	Spare

In any case, a call session of any given precedence level or value can preempt any precedence level of a lesser level or value. If these values are equal, then other mechanisms, if any, can react according to their individual capabilities (e.g., call waiting).

- *Flash Override* is used to declare the existence of a state of war, defense Condition One, defense emergency, air defense emergency, and other national authorities in conjunction with worldwide security conferences. The President, the Joint Chiefs, and some select theater commanders would use this precedence for the most important commands. Communications within the Corps and Theater commanders would use this level of precedence as well.
- *Flash* is reserved generally for telephone calls pertaining to command and control at the field grade (e.g., brigade, battalion, and division).
- *Immediate* is reserved generally for lower level command traffic pertaining to situations that gravely affect the security of national and allied forces.
- *Priority* is reserved for calls requiring expeditious action by called parties and/or furnishing essential information. This is typically used by a Company commander to reach his or her platoon leaders.
- *Routine* is designated for normal government communications.

7.4.4 Feature Comparisons

IntServ can have parallel independent connect and disconnect actions, thus providing per-flow granularity. However, this method is commonly regarded to have performance and scalability problems due to the per-flow reservation. The amount of state information increases proportionally as the number of flows increases. This can result in a huge storage and processing overhead on routers. As discussed in the previous section, IntServ imposes high requirement on routers. All routers must have the four basic components: RSVP, admission control routine, classifier, and packet scheduler.

DiffServ operates on packet aggregates, thus does not employ any signaling protocol or maintain state info, therefore, requires less processing power. All the policing and classifying are done at the boundaries between DiffServ clouds. Because each network element can minimize its computing overhead. This makes this approach very scalable. It performs well in fixed and relatively high speed networks. However, lacking the feedback mechanism the end host is not capable of specifying the required service level dynamically thus it can only provide approximate, statistical guarantees for the service. Additionally, the detail of how individual routers deal with the type of service field is somewhat arbitrary and it is difficult to predict end-to-end behavior. The situation can become complicated if the link should cross two or more DiffServ clouds.

In MLPP, when a call is preempted, the user is informed by an audible signal and expected to try again later. The user can decide to hang up and call again in an attempt to get another circuit. This behavior will cause the network more pressure on resource competition. When a call experiencing significant loss in a measurement-based counterpart to the MLPP, the management systems will treat this phenomenon as a signal of a network problem and drop the call. If all calls at a precedence level are experiencing loss, many and perhaps all calls at that precedence level will be dropped.

7.5 Voice Service Quality Control

Admission control is one of the key QoS procedures. It determines how bandwidth and latency are allocated to data streams based on various requirements in order to prevent congestion. The procedure requires the knowledge about the characteristics of the traffic and the QoS requirements to be exchanged between network edges and core to control the traffic. The network judges whether it has enough resources available to accept the connection, and respond to the connection request.

Admission Control in ATM networks is known as *connection admission control (CAC)*; in 802.11 networks it is known as *call admission control (CAC)*. This section showcases the CAC feature in the voice and video applications.

7.5.1 Call Admission Control

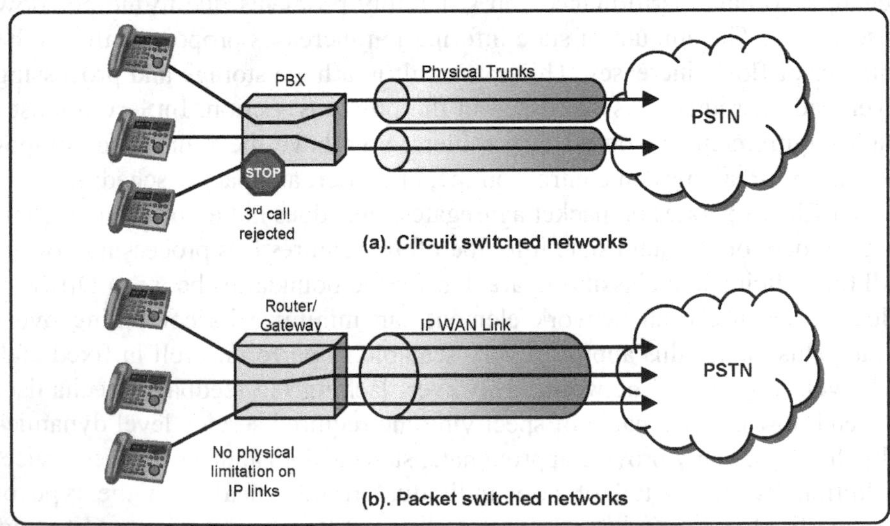

Figure 7.22. Call admission control.

Voice and video traffic, or calls, can be restricted by way of CAC tools that determine whether or not there is sufficient bandwidth. One too many calls on a link would cause the quality of the other calls to suffer so the extra call is prohibited. The use of CAC is to prevent congestion from voice and video occurring in the first place, before QoS tools are called into play.

As depicted in Figure 7.22(a), a traditional call is managed by the PBX. Any calls intended for network are limited by the preconfigured trunk limitation. In Figure 7.22(b), An IP WAN link provisioned for two VoIP calls (equivalent to two "virtual" trunks.) However, the third call can go through but the voice quality of all calls degrades. Call admission control prevents this problem by using a call manager linked to the router or gateway from the calling side. CAC can be implemented in a number of ways:

- Local CAC is not aware of the topology of the network and cannot guarantee QoS. Benefits include no messaging overhead and no delay. It offers the maximum number of connections, bandwidth on Voice over Frame Relay, and Trunk Conditioning and *Local Voice Busyout* (*LVBO* monitors LAN and WAN ports for failure and then busy out voice ports or the trunk to the PBX).
- *Measurement-Based CAC* is not topology-aware nor does it guarantee QoS.
  - Delay and Packet Loss are used to calculate the ITU G.113 *International Calculated Planning Impairment Factor (ICPIF)* for an application on a given network. This value can be used to make CAC decisions. *Advanced busy out (AVBO)* supports H.323, MGCP and SIP environments and can busy out voice ports or trunks based on ICPIF values.
  - PSTN Fallback applies to individual call setups rather than ports or the trunk. IP addresses are cached along with their ICPIF values so that SAA probes are only required on an initial call to a new IP address (therefore introducing a postdial delay just for the new entry).
- *Resource-Based CAC* such as *resource availability indicator (RAI)* and H.323 Gatekeeper Zone Bandwidth examine the resources at the time of the call request and then make a single CAC decision at that time. The resources examined will include available timeslots, Gateway CPU use, memory use, DSP use, and bandwidth availability.
  - RAI is used in H.323 networks with a Gatekeeper. The Gateway informs the Gatekeeper when it is running low on resources. The Gatekeeper then makes routing decisions based on these RAIs.
  - In an H.323 Gatekeeper environment, gatekeepers can be grouped into zones. The gatekeeper in each zone can limit bandwidth usage within its own zone and also between its own zone and other zones. Using Gatekeeper CAC is the only method available in distributed H.323 zone environments.

7.6 SoS Views of Service Quality Management

Figure 7.23 demonstrates two integrated QoS solutions. Figure 7.23(a) depicts an end-to-end operation control with Inter-domain resource negotiation.

The centralized service control solution allows the service provider to offer predictable end-to-end service quality. Figure 7.23(b), on the other hand, requires each network to support a limited range of QoS services by negotiation. The former solution provides higher controllability of service quality with the tradeoff of higher overhead and less flexibility. The latter solution has better scalability with less controllable service quality. In the following sections, an integrated QoS system in an ad-hoc network and two SQM solutions will be addressed.

7.6.1 Integrated QoS Management Architecture

QoS features provide better and more predictable network service by:

- Supporting dedicated bandwidth for critical users and applications
- Controlling jitter and latency (required by real-time traffic)
- Avoiding and managing network congestion
- Shaping network traffic to smooth the traffic flow
- Setting traffic priorities across the network

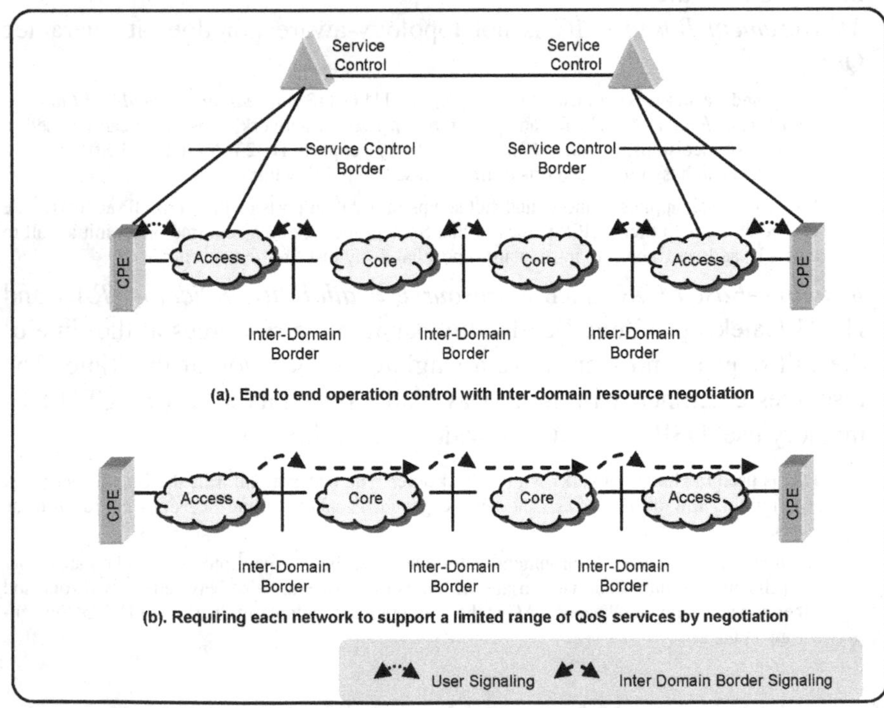

Figure 7.23. Integration of differentiated and integrated services.

This is illustrated in Figure 7.24 where the network is divided into three regions. The DiffServ is used in the core network, and IntServ is used in both ends of the access networks.

DiffServ possesses scaling advantage from the perspective of the network, but does not support an accurate service response to the application, so an application may not be aware of a particular service state. The lack of end-to-end signaling facilities makes a pure DiffServ approach very difficult to operate in isolation within any environment. Enhancements of signaling from the boundary to the client application can improve the end-to-end service; the additional signaling messages can include binding update, binding acknowledge, and binding request to build a response model [29].

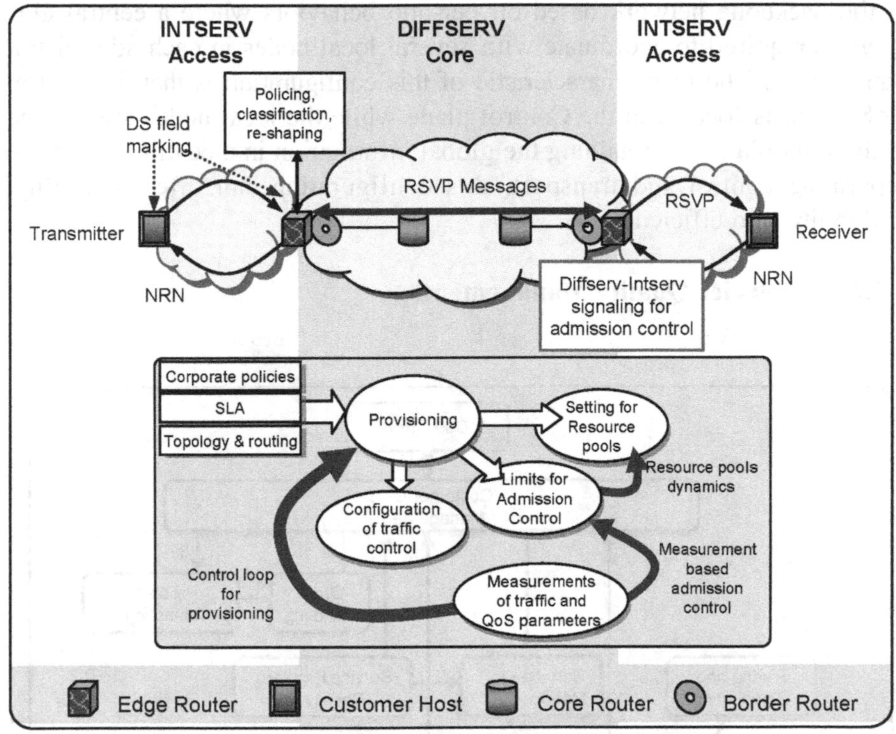

Figure 7.24. Integrate IntServ and DiffServ.

To ensure QoS in ad-hoc radio networks, *resource management (RM)* can be used for managing wireless link resources and allocating air interface resources to traffic flows. In a traditional wireless scenario, RM functions reside at the link layer performing local measurement, resource allocation and admission control decisions. This is not sufficient to meet the dynamic ad-hoc environment. Additionally, a centralized RM server coordinating resources across multiple cells is no longer applicable to meet the dynamic ad-hoc mobility requirement. In such a case, RM functionality takes place in the network layer with mechanisms to coordinate inter-RM communication. Furthermore, RM entities monitoring the load above the link layer on all air interfaces must be supported by a terminal device to determine whether a traffic flow can be supported and what QoS can be provided.

To ensure to smooth handover, QoS routing, and admission control, the resource availability of neighboring domains and potentially nodes a few hops away must be monitored. Finally, the provisioning of resources at the link layer must be coordinated across multiple hops to avoid interference between cells.

To support differentiated services, traffic are aggregated and forwarded to the backbone network based on per-hop behaviors where a central *QoS agent* is required to coordinate with several local nodes in each administration domain. The main characteristic of this configuration is that the central QoS agent is located in the Control plane while the local nodes are located in the User plane. By retaining the global information in a central server and separating control and transport, this configuration can offer flexibility, scalability, and efficiency.

7.6.2 Service Quality Management

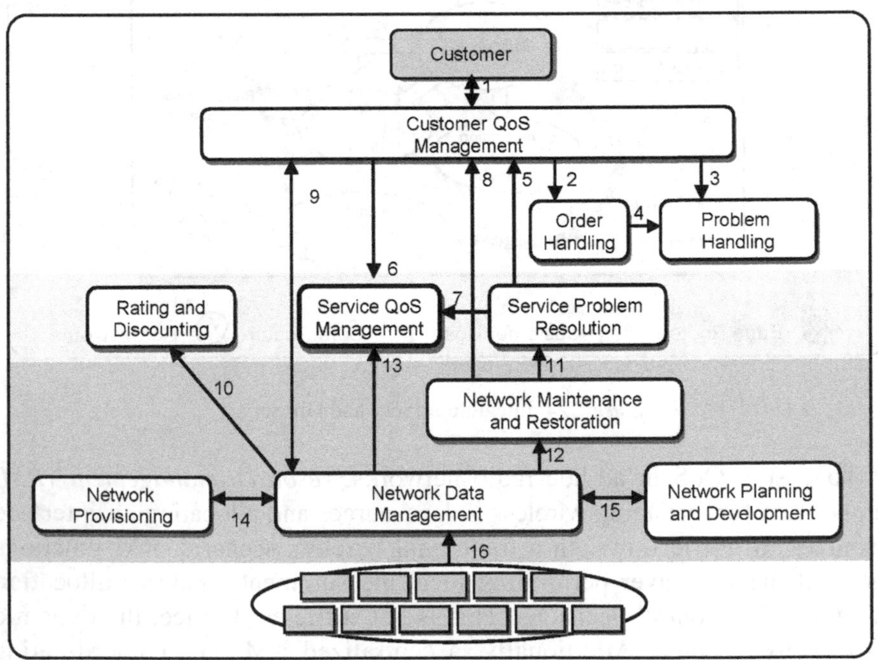

Figure 7.25. SQM flows and interfaces.

SQM manages the service life cycle from service introduction to retirement. Depending upon the service provider's OSS architecture, the SLM function may be implemented as part of an SQM subsystem. In either event, service models plays a key role here to relate the customer's view of the service to the actual service or network configurations.

Figure 7.25 depicts the data flows and interfaces of performance analysis, management, and reporting for SQM and SLM [1].

Quality measures and costs for a specific SLA agreement are defined within and tracked by the SLM. It is important that SQM have a real-time capability to track the service levels, problems, improvements, and costs for management purposes. Because of the nature of new technologies, pure connectivity service is no longer the only option for customers.

Often time, bundled services can enable the service provider to create more value-added offerings. Source quality statistics may need to be aggregated into service indicators, based on service dependencies. Therefore, SQM monitoring should incorporate quality statistics from multiple sources to infer the quality of services as delivered helping to identify or prioritize problems. This information about whether the service results meet or exceed the committed operation objectives can be referenced by internal management or ment or by customers through the customer QoS process.

In addition to the ongoing reporting capability, SQM is also responsible for managing service performance to quality and cost targets. If improvements are required for the service resource to maintain service levels per service class, SQM will provide recommendations and track the progress of the improvements or alert the sales process to slow sales.

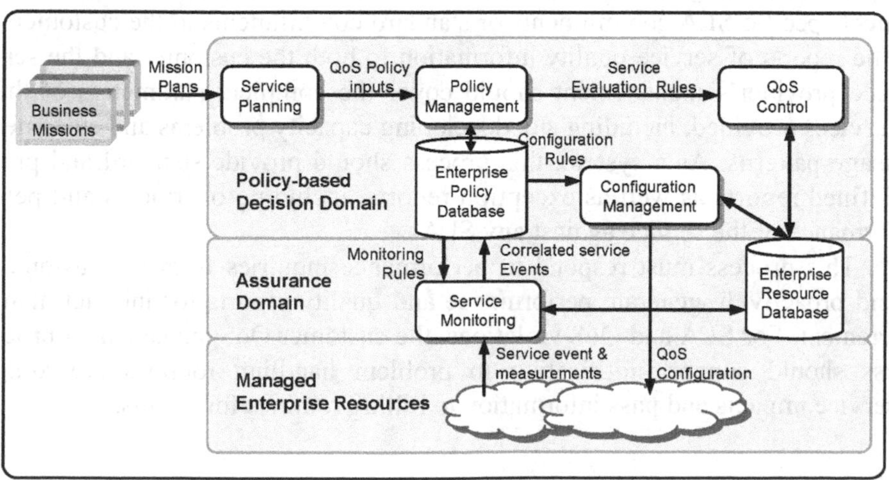

Figure 7.26. Service quality management across several domains.

Figure 7.26 depicts a SQM across three horizontal domains. The policy-based decision focuses on the business and financial aspects. The assurance domain addresses the service aspects. The managed enterprise resources focus on the physical resources. In the case where SLM is part of the SQM process, the business objective of SLM is to allow the service provider to manage its customer SLAs. Similar to SQM, the SLM system is not an independent process; it coordinates the SLA negotiation, determines appropriate QoS levels to take care of customer performance requirements, provides customizable QoS reports, and tracks the rebates and reconciliation due to service violations. Additionally, SLM provides network usage analysis by using the usage data collected by the data-collection function. It performs arithmetic and statistical calculations to evaluate traffic handling. SLM performs trend analysis on the traffic data and compares historical and predicted future levels against established threshold levels. The trend analysis enables early identification or predictions of problems before they become service affecting. This can result in a request to trouble ticket management or notifications to service managers.

7.6.3 Customer QoS Management

The customer QoS management process can be triggered by performance reports from the service problem resolution process, the SQM, or third-party service providers. QoS includes network performance as well as performance across all of a service's parameters, e.g., *orders completed on time (OCOT)* and MTTR. The goal of this process is to provide effective monitoring and reporting on action planned and taken to assure service levels that meet specific SLA commitments or standard commitments to the customers. The reports of service quality information to both the customer and the service provider's management should cover the complete parameters of the services provided, including any developing capacity problems and customer usage patterns. As a system, this process should provide standard and predefined reports as well as exception reports, including overviews and performance of the service against any SLAs.

This process must respond to performance inquiries from the customer and proactively generate performance and quality reports for internal management. For SLA and QoS violations, the customer QoS management process should support notification to problem handling routines regarding service impacts and pass information to billing routines for credits.

7.7 Conclusion

End-to-end QoS is important to enterprise users because it affects the application traffic as it attempts to optimize or provide priority to service sessions. QoS mechanisms deal with policing and shaping of network traffic with the challenge to adaptively change when congestion occurs or an instance of a SLA dictates traffic priority. This can be very challenging when the wireless service has a mobility requirement and the communication paths are changing due to the topology updates. As a result, end-to-end latency is expected in wireless services due to path adjustments or corrections caused by the roaming and hand-off features. The IP traffic schemes, thus, need the Management Plane to consider spatial resource demands and arrangement while maintaining the compliance of service objectives with any unpredictable path rearrangement.

In the context of service quality management, one of the most important differentiators that set the QoS management in network-centric enterprise service apart from the tradition schemes is the capability to handle data priorities across different vertical service layers and horizontal service domains. For instance, most mission-sensitive information needs to distinguish the priority of data as well as to mediate the conflict within and between missions, such service rules at the application layer may not have one-to-one mapping to the traffic rules at the transport layers. Meanwhile, the traffic rules may not be transparent to different transport technologies and implementations across various network domains, e.g., access, switching, and content domains. The concept of "multi-layer and multi-domain" QoS management and enforcement that spans all of these layers and domains are the fundamental stand of this chapter. This coordination requires application-independent techniques which can tailor enterprise data flows with different schemes described in section 7.3 to the current mission-state and the current network-state. A component-based implementation that provides modularity, scalability, flexibility, and compatibility is a favorite design for commmunications and data-processing systems. This is particularly important for an SOA application where the publish/subscribe architecture decouples information providers (publishers) from information consumers (subscribers) and the QoS measure will be rather unconventional.

The QoS implementation section reviews three of the most popular QoS standards, namely IntServ, DiffServ, and MLPP. The SoS View section addresses the service assurance operational support systems which either deal or interact with the service quality management function. In the next chapter, the SoS view will be raised to the next level of Information Management in dealing with integrated information assurance.

Chapter 8

INTEGRATED INFORMATION ASSURANCE

Enterprise data is the most valuable asset of a company. In a more restricted definition, data is bits of factual information and information is organized data. Thereby, enterprise information can be referred as a form of corporate data containing business sensitive relationships and processes. The essential functions of *information assurance (IA)* include the information operations that protect and defend information and information systems. The objectives of IA are to provide availability, integrity, authentication, confidentiality, and non-repudiation of corporate information. The process includes protection, detection, reaction, as well as the capability to incorporate information restoration. These objectives rely heavily upon a structured approach to sustain and improve the survivability of information, the constituent computing systems, and networking infrastructure components. From the user front, a common operation picture containing unified assurance indices to support cross-functional and aggregated effectiveness reports can be tailored to provide a higher degree of operational awareness. Its real-time business insights allow service consumers and operators to interactively acquire timely, conclusive, and secure business intelligence for enforced assurance and continuous improvement. Thus IA is one of the most critical building blocks in enterprise service architecture.

The wireless communication medium for mobile network is inherently exposed to attacks or other security related concerns. Mobility presents problems such as rights and privileges management, maintaining security associations, and perhaps adds a *location-specific* attribute to business assurance concerns. The emerging "ad-hoc" nature of mobile, wireless networks amplifies many of these problems particularly for the identification and authentication of mobile nodes, for the distribution and management of cryptographic keys, and for credentials management.

The foundation of an effective network-centric enterprise IT environment has to be built upon a unified IA capability that crosses business silos. This chapter starts with the definition and principle of enterprise data strategy, followed by the reiteration of the concept of *communities of interest (CoIs)* in the context of IA for a network-centric environment. Next, the chapter illustrates the main IA capability in the role of GIG framework, as well as the detailed security management technologies at different transport layers.

The SoS approach section offers as a practical system an example in building a networked service environment with multiple layers of assurance.

8.1 Overview

The core of the network-centric business environment is the data that enables effective decisions. This is driven by an integrated information assurance infrastructure that can be divided into two separate but interrelated areas: data and security. The data architecture helps the enterprise to handle governance of data strategy and guide cross-system integration, common reporting, and data warehousing. The security architecture provides the integrity, availability, access control, and audibility of the enterprise data assets. Today most of the "data strategies" focus on unifying data representation but lack assurance rules in the information models. In order to provide an "actionable" data model, the service management data and the information model needs to equip the knowledge base (chapter 9) in order to generate sensible business events.

Fully integrated information assurance is established upon the premise that data integrity and assurance are interrelated with planning, policy, procedures, and practices necessary to operate asset representation, asset identification, human factors, regulation compliance, personnel security, risk assessment, and computing and networking security. The system architecture that provides the framework to support the business mission of an enterprise with unified and secured information assurance is depicted in Figure 8.1.

As shown in the figure, the Information Assurance and Computing Infrastructure layer plays an essential role in the system architecture of enterprise services. These cross-layer functions closely work with the Computing and Networking Framework and System Management to ensure a collaborated view on the service contents as well as the management contents. Three functional blocks reside in the information assurance layer. They are: enterprise information for different groups of information models, Control Plane to control and protect information (based on the risk assessment and vulnerability analysis), and Management Plane to manage data, key, and security (based on incident response from the assurance policies and rules). The Computing and

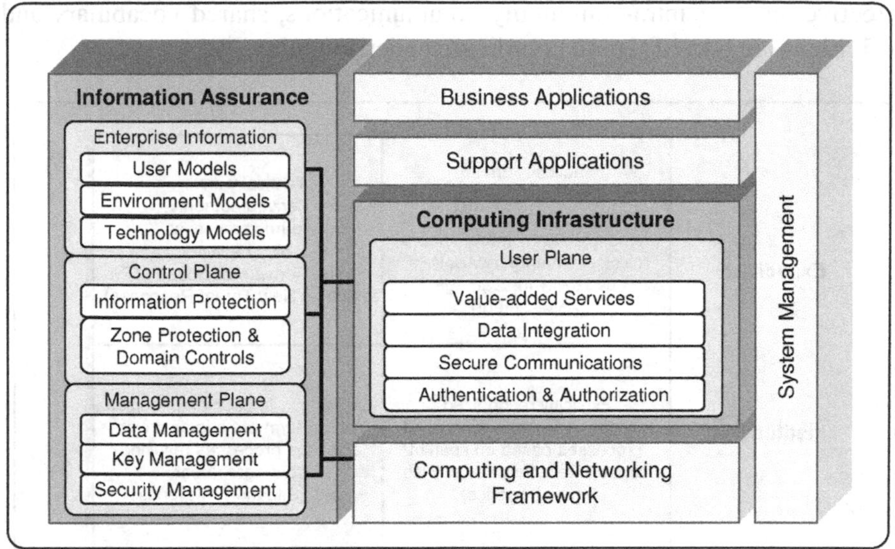

Figure 8.1. System architecture of enterprise services.

Infrastructure layer contains the User Plane functional block, responsible for the certification, accreditation, and compliance of the integrated data or with value-added services for interacting with upper layers.

The essential value of integrated information assurance is to provide the enterprise with abilities to conduct collaborative decision-making and business operations with a high degree of confidence that communication exchanges can be verified. This will serve as a sound technological and operational foundation for the knowledge management discussed in the next chapter.

8.1.1 Communities of Interest

Based on the definition from DoDı, *communities of interest (CoIs)* are collaborative groups of service users who need to exchange information in pursuit of their shared goals, interests, missions, or business processes. A CoI may have authority from explicit chartering or implied authority in accordance with their existing organization or operational hierarchy. The responsibilities of a community can be persistent or more transitory depending upon whether the business operations are ongoing or on contingency. In layman's terms, a CoI is a functional-based user group; their existence is driven by the common objectives defined in the business data and rules [2].

CoI provides an organization and maintenance construct for data, operational processes, and mission capabilities. It crosses enterprises' boundaries to access grouped information and functions relevant to the community. For effective inter- or intra-community communications, shared vocabulary and definitions are part of CoI to coordinate understandings.

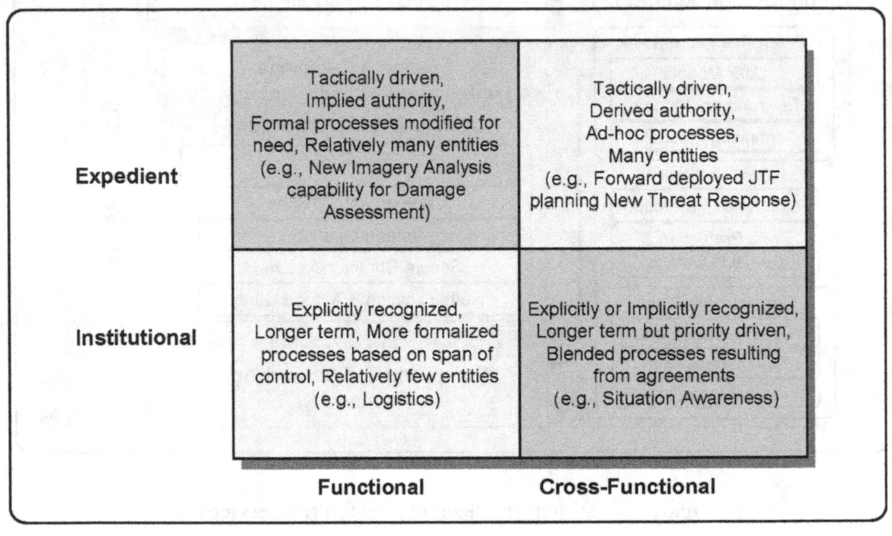

Figure 8.2. CoI characteristics.

As vertically divided in Figure 8.2, CoI can be either institutional or expedient. Shown horizontally, some CoIs may be large functional or cross-functional groups, while others may be smaller groups focusing on more localized or short-term missions [1].

- An *institutional CoI* exists to address an enduring and established organizational responsibility. Typically, an institutional CoI is established by the most important participants to execute or manage specific strategic tasks. A sample of functional institutional CoI is logistic management system and a cross-functional sample is customer relationship management.
- An *expedient CoI* has a shorter life cycle mainly for tactical tasks and missions. A sample of functional expedient CoI is a market survey for a new service introduction. A cross-functional sample is a new service deployment.

Because of the need for user participation, CoIs typically register themselves in a registry to facilitate their visibility and collaboration. The information listed in the registry can include CoIs missions or objectives, its sponsors and members, and links to CoI-related service or products. CoIs can discover individuals according to their skills and experiences, and invite particular individuals to join the CoI. Both the CoI registry and the public profiles are examples of enterprise capabilities that facilitate collaboration and provide discoverable information. CoIs consist of the following major elements:

1. Information providers and consumers who share information in pursuit of shared goals, missions, or business processes. The Information providers are responsible for registering their service descriptions in services registries to support service discovery and usage.
2. The processes and capabilities to capture, manage, and share the enterprise offerings such as enterprise (discovery, messaging, mediation, and collaboration) services, reports, data schemas, recorded collaboration and actions/decisions from the sponsors' information repository (section 8.4).
3. Service specifications containing the CoI vocabulary (data definitions, data structures, and the community ontology) and documents in the metadata format are registered in the appropriate registries allowing the listed services to be discovered for data sharing. Based upon the diversity of CoI characteristics and roles, a variety of operating processes and procedures will be used by CoIs to accomplish their data activities (section 8.3).

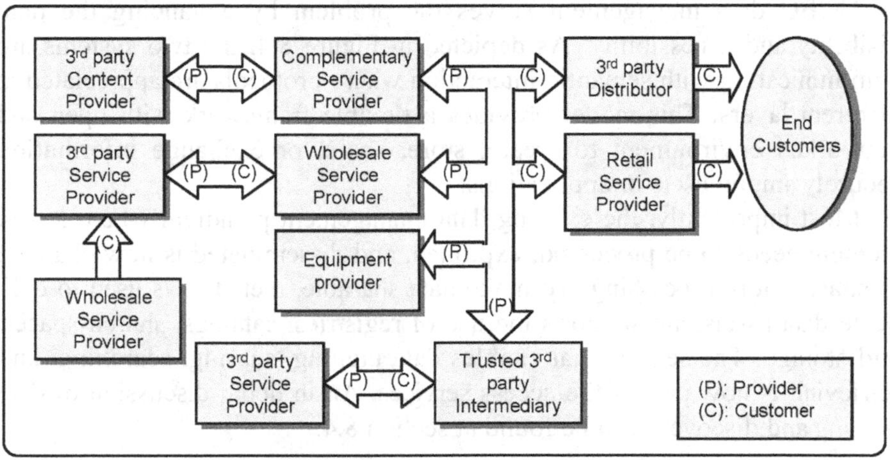

Figure 8.3. Service providers and distributors interactions.

Figure 8.3 depicts the CoI concept in the value chain of a wireless service provider in the telecommunication industry. The services are provided in layer relationships depending upon the functions of providers. The information provider and consumer relationship is marked as (P) and (C), respectively.

8.1.2 Data in the Network-Centric Environment

Enterprise data assets can exist in the forms of system files, databases, documents, official electronic records, images, audio files, web sites, text, voice, fax, e-mail, paging, notification, and alerts. In a more loose definition, the data assets include business intelligence, non-business intelligence, raw materials, and processed information. Modern enterprises rely heavily upon the ability to connect their applications and operational functionalities to the right data, and to share the data among different users, organizations, and even companies.

Additionally, the effort to accomplish the goals of eliminating data duplication and minimizing potential data translation in a hybrid environment can be very expensive and complicated. This is because traditional mechanisms require very stringent processes involving overall standardization and control of data elements, definitions, and structures across the enterprise to achieve interoperability. Furthermore, the client and server model in mobile environments may not sustain business needs as the types of network access available vary widely. Managing the enterprise-level data and reducing the dependence on a fixed infrastructure is a challenge, especially when the locations of users and data are not fixed [3].

NCBO data management solves the problem by enhancing the data visibility and accessibility. As depicted in Figure 8.4, the two systems are communicating with semantic interaction where protocols are appreciated at different layers. This model provides a flexible framework with open and networked environment to create, store, share, or exchange information securely among users or applications.

Most importantly, the existing data management paradigm where a data element needs to be processed, exploited, and disseminated is now changed to share before processing. To make data sharable, metadata is used to delineate data assets and supports the use of registries, catalogs, shared spaces, and storage. The service that enables data tagging, sharing, searching, and retrieving is now part of the access services. An in depth discussion of data posting and discovery can be found at section 8.4.

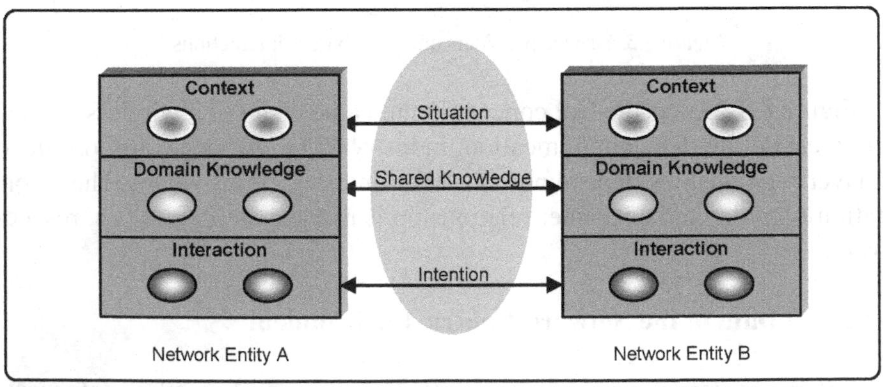

Figure 8.4. Semantic interaction elements and relationship.

8.1.3 Data Strategy

The network-centric data strategy connects disparate systems and provides the basis for coalition interoperability to achieve rapid processing or transformation. Following the paradigm described above about *share before process*, authorized users and applications have immediate access to data posted to the network without process, exploitation, or dissemination delays. Depending upon the functional requirements, the data consumers can also receive alerts when the subscribed data is updated or changed.

An enterprise's information systems architecture has many interrelated aspects, including applications, hardware, networks, business processes, technology choices, and data. As shown in Figure 8.5, the data strategy outlines the business objectives for improved collection and use of data. It dictates business process improvement and influences the decisions on the application integration, business integration, and system rationalization. The data strategy can improve the enterprise uses of communications, computation, information assurance, and Web technologies. To a certain degree, this new approach in using trust and data sharing can also introduce a cultural impact which did not exist before [4].

For instance, through discovery services, users use smart pull to retrieve data directly from the networked resources. A non-repudiation feature provides protection against false denial in a communication ensuring success rate of a mission-sensitive transaction such as security auditing. Additionally, the data management's capability for storing, sharing, exchanging, and processing information can assure that the data is correct and valid.

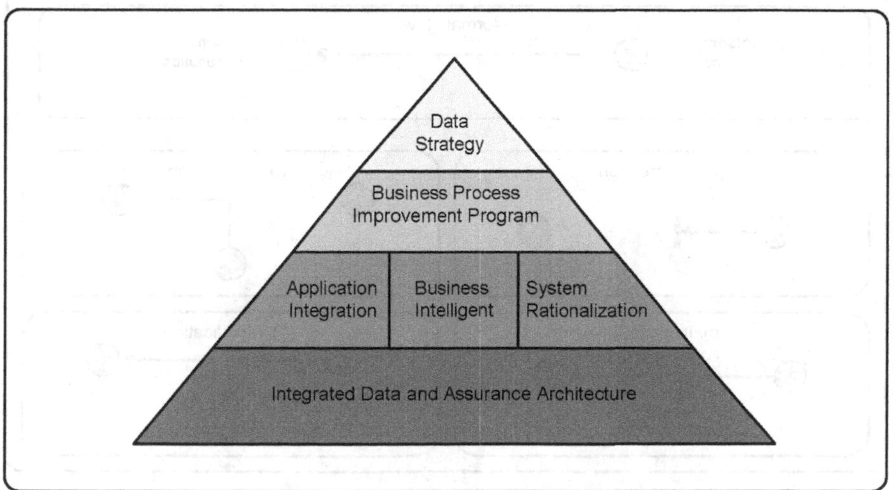

Figure 8.5. Enterprise data architecture models – support a variety of common IT and business improvement initiatives.

8.1.4 Information Assurance Strategy

In complex technology-based enterprise organizations, achieving a high level of business collaboration is fundamental to fully realizing the benefits of a service-oriented enterprise. Information sharing requires that the same producers and consumers define, manage, and register the service specifications with a secured and agreeable protocol in order to provide users with timely, reliable access to processes and data even in the event of a denial of service attack. As depicted in Figure 8.6, four examples of attacks are given to illustrate how a message can be impacted during transmission.

Defending enterprise information assets requires appropriate tools, processes, and procedures to detect unauthorized activity that may affect information sharing and collaboration. The same principle is also applicable to maintain enterprise services and access to information while under attack, or to prevent attacks. Defending systems and networks implies the protection of all enterprise management and control functions from cyber-attack, the recovery from cyber attack, and the reduction of vulnerabilities by monitoring system and data status. The goal is to achieve confidentiality by ensuring information and process integrity in accordance with mission criteria.

In a highly mobilized enterprise, the abilities to assign, prioritize, modify and revoke user- or system-roles, access rights, and resources in a timely and coordinated fashion is critical for the success of business missions. The technology evolution of computer security can be divided into the following three periods, each has its own functional and objective significances.

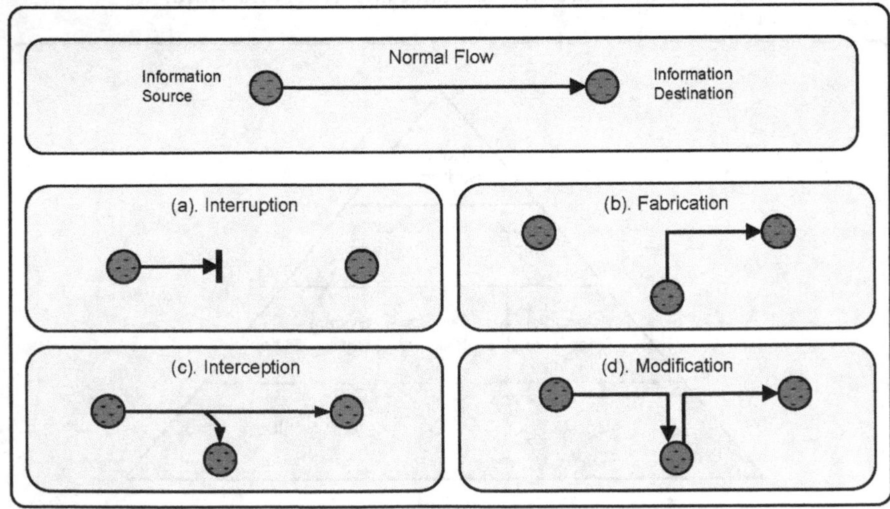

Figure 8.6. Information attacks during transmissions.

- The first generation computer security aims to prevent unauthorized release or modification of sensitive information. As depicted at the bottom box in Figure 8.7, multiple-level securities are established to prevent data from leaking or being contaminated by other sources. This generation is based on a trusted computing environment with access control and physical security to divide security levels. Cryptography is used for securing data communications.
- The second generation security focuses on detecting intrusions and limiting damages. Firewalls, *intrusion detection systems (IDSs)*, *virtual private networks (VPNs)*, and *public-key infrastructures (PKIs)* are used to establish access controls outside the managed systems or computing community. This phase uses cryptography for overall authentication, confidentiality, and integrity.
- The third generation security technology aims to achieve *tolerance of cyber attacks* as well as *continuation of critical functions*. It recognizes potential security flaws in the SoS environment and makes proactive observation against flaws at the broader view of protection. Because flaws are unlikely to be eliminated from the enterprise environment, this technology utilizes real-time situation awareness and response to prevent

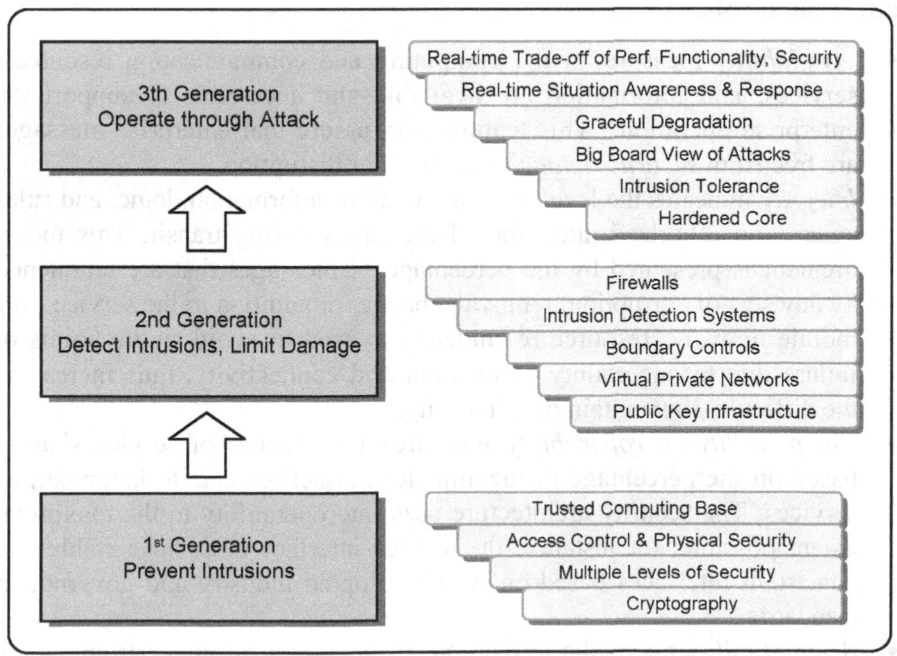

Figure 8.7. Three generations of security technologies.

attack opportunities. When service degradation avoidance becomes impossible, this technology performs trade-offs of the overall performance, functionalities, and security measures and determines the best areas to gracefully downgrade the service in real time. In a degraded mode, all the mission critical tasks can continue to function while an attack is in progress. This feature is also known as survivability.

An IA solution should be flexible enough to leverage existing IT investments in order to avoid redundant development efforts. Seamless integration with existing security tools and applications can also increase the overall stability of the enterprise.

8.1.5 Feature Objectives

Assured is defined as having grounds for confidence where an enterprise service meets its certainty or security objectives. This section illustrates the constituent feature attributes of data and service integrity and security. These attributes can provide an enforcement of enterprise-wide data and service quality. These values may be overridden or specialized at varying levels of detail. In practice, integrated information assurance is much more than data definition, availability, or security and can be extended to cover the overall information policy [5, 6].

- *Availability* measures if the computing and communication resources, services, and information are available and accessible to support the enterprise operations. This feature is to assure that enterprise messages are free from *security outage time (SOT)* or disruption.
- *Integrity* indicates the level of consistency of information, logic, and rules against unauthorized alteration of messages during transit. This measurement is presented by the percentage of messages that are untouched by any sort of corruption, removal, change, or addition to the service. In a mobile network, resource redundancy is used to avoid single points of failure due to uncertainty of location and connectivity, thus increasing the difficulty to maintain data integrity.
- *Compatibility/Interoperability* measures impedances of service sharing based on the percentage of incomplete transactions due to incompatible services. The security architecture uses interoperability to the maximum extent possible; for instance, the service interface must have stable and consistent interfaces based on widely adopted industry and government standards.
- *Accountability* traces the utilization of enterprise resources from secure logging and auditing. It is also required to support non-repudiation claims.

- *Non-repudiation* measures the percentage of messages which senders are provided with proof of delivery and the recipients are provided with proof of the sender's identity. It is to assure that transaction will not be denied on either side of the business participants.
- *Confidentiality* reflects the level of protection of the message that is carried over the underlying communication transport from unauthorized access or exchange. It is measured by the percentage of messages that are not penetrated by unauthorized consumers. The overhead associated with encryption will be an issue due to lower communications capacity in mobile wireless networks. The impact of lost header information due to data loss potentially worsens the quality of services.
- *Authority* is measured by the percentage of messages requiring authority that are successfully authorized. It is to ensure an authenticated user can have the right permission to use a message or access service elements.
- *Survivability* measures the range of conditions over which the entity will survive the minimum acceptable-level functionality and the maximum acceptable outage duration after disturbance. It represents the level of operational or functional condition of a system, subsystem, equipment, process, or procedure during and after a natural or man-made disturbance.
- *Resilience* measures how well a resource can recover from or adjust to malfunction (misfortune) or change. This indicator works closely with survivability because resilience can help the service designer to adjust resource allocation at the new service planning or replanning.
- *Authenticity* measures the validity of a message sender or recipient in compliance with business and regulatory security policies. *Single sign-on (SSO)* management is an increasingly important feature. In a mobile environment, limited network capacity and quality will make overhead of authentication costlier than for fixed wired network.

It is essential that assurance operations can be conducted across multiple CoIs and security domains. To support this requirement, systems shall have an integrated information capability that ensures information is not misrepresented or disclosed to unauthorized entities or processes in the network and infrastructure. Systems shall also have an integrated IA capability to share data among users operating at different or multiple service domains at the levels as appropriate.

8.2 Network-Centric Enterprise Data Strategy

The principle of the network-centric data strategy is to establish a logical framework enabling different systems to access the same data and providing assistance to manipulate, process, format, or translate that data if necessary.

The framework should include the basis for coalition interoperability in order to provide the best data available on the network. The goal is to allow the data sources (e.g., sensors or monitored systems) to post their data on the network at the first point when it becomes consumable and to enable the data providers and consumers to directly interact with each others through the network. Users can get the data they need for decision-making, or alternatively process the data by the knowledge management systems they choose.

8.2.1 Data Strategy for Network-Centric Data Sharing

As shown in Figure 8.8, the communication between system A and system B is based on predefined point-to-point interfaces where system B is a known user of system A data. This interface focuses on existing data administration policy, thus the data is exchanged across well-defined interfaces. Meanwhile, the system X is an anticipated user of system A and relies on an open protocol to exchange data. In the grayed area marked as Shared Space, all community users and applications across the enterprise can advertise their data assets to the network by cataloging their data with metadata in the Registry and Catalog. In this case, system A registers its metadata, and creates access services for system X's access. Any data consumers have access to the shared space can search the preregistered metadata from the CoI catalogs and pull data as needed.

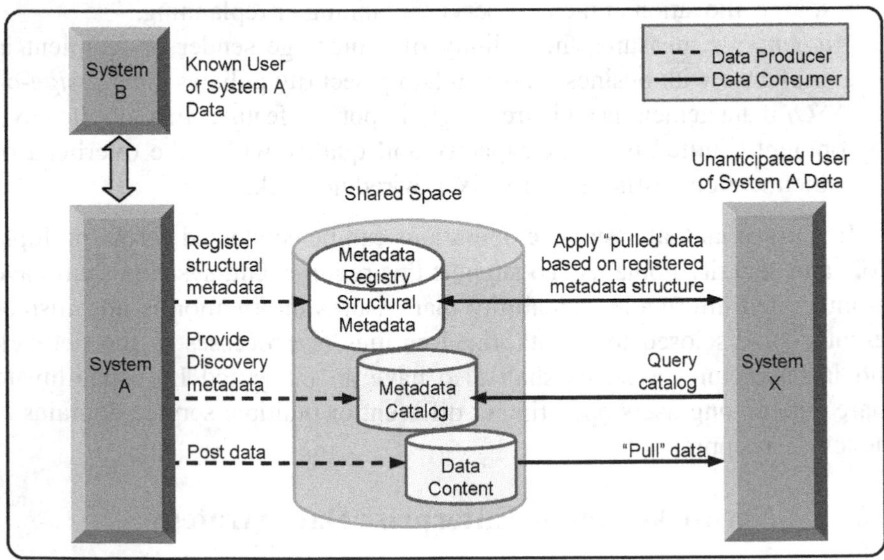

Figure 8.8. Network-centric data strategy enables unanticipated users.

Data assets in this context pertain to all legacy and new data assets which include files, databases, documents, official electronic records, images, audio files, web sites, and data access services, as well as business organizations and functions. Data strategy which can support the service scenario discussed above is crucial for service-oriented enterprise's operations. To ensure network-centricity, the strategy should possess the capability to increase the data that is available to the communities as well as to ensure that data is usable by both anticipated and unanticipated consumers. The usability of data is determined by the data quality and accuracy.

A broader definition of the enterprise data strategy concerns the plan for improving the way an enterprise leverages its data, allowing the enterprise to turn data into information and knowledge. In turn, the knowledge can be further processed into wisdom to produce both strategic and tactical improvements in business and operational performance. For instance, such transformation can assist the enterprise to achieve increased resource utilization or decreased costs. In mission critical operations, the enhanced information can improve the effectiveness of task fulfillment. The process of realizing data into "information" or "wisdom" level will be addressed in later chapters. However, once the end products (whether it is data, information, or wisdom) are produced by the systems, they will be treated as a piece of "data" for sharing and, therefore, can be folded back into the discussion here in this chapter.

8.2.2 Major Components of Data Strategy

The network-centric data strategy can enhance enterprise's existing IT paradigm in the areas of data and security management. The new strategy expands the focus to interoperability, availability, visibility, and accessibility of data rather than just standardization and cell-based data protection. To accomplish this goal, the new approach must be based upon an integrated policy-based model which can recognize the need for data to be sharable among community applications whether they are unanticipated or predefined. The flexibility in data exchange can avoid the requirement of predefined and pair-wise interfaces between or among large groups of new or legacy applications. While the new approach offers the objective of increasing the potential for many other systems to leverage the same data without anticipating development effort, this feature also maintains the service integrity and demands no exclusiveness of the legacy communication systems, depicted as system A and B communication in Figure 8.8.

There are four major components involved in a data strategy, namely information plan, data management, data model, and data control. With a data strategy in place, the information plan can drive the other three components to effectively create an integrated data and access architecture as portrayed in Figure 8.9 [7].

Data Model has conceptual, logical, and physical schemas that address the organization or structure of the data, their relationships with other data items or sub-items, rules applicable for accessibility and applications, and the actions when certain rules are satisfied. Typical strategies for structuring data include the use of data warehouses, data stores, and data marts as part of the interactive repository to support dynamic data sharing. Typical strategies for moving data across the enterprise rely on high-level service-oriented technologies (e.g., SOA) to provide real-time push-and-pull and on-demand computing schemes. In the case of interoperability between legacy and the modern systems, the SOA offers an open infrastructure to improve implementation independency.

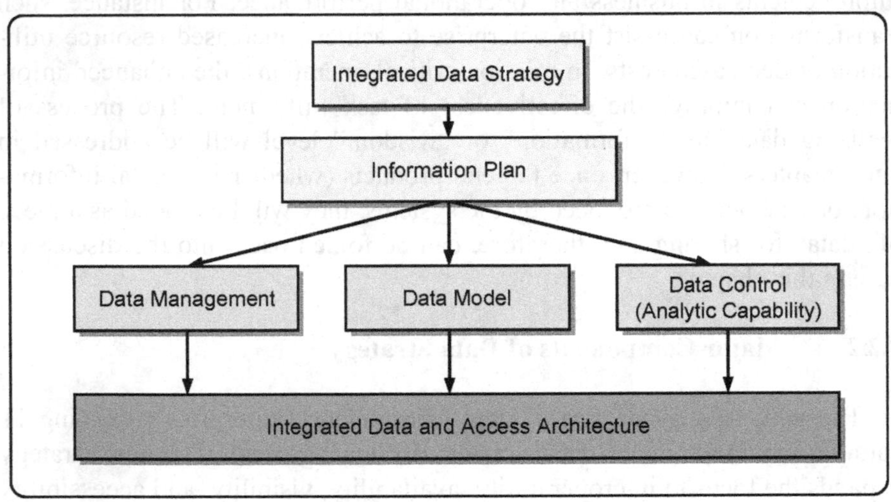

Figure 8.9. Enterprise data strategy.

Data management refers to the requirements with respect to the care, feeding, and policing of production databases. To achieve information superiority, data management plays an important role in the planning, fulfillment, operational, and assurance of enterprise service operations. It encompasses the management of data models to guide the design and building of the data architecture and to identify service boundaries across the enterprise. The service boundary can be addressed through the use of SLM technology to improve synchronization among different service providers. Additionally, the data management components can include comprehensive data quality and data guidance functions. The data quality function recognizes the values from transparency, visibility, and availability which can enforce the decision quality. The data guidance function provides understandable policing and monitoring criteria as part of the service-level objectives or operation-level objectives defined in the SLM and SQM systems (section 9.7). The guidance function supports and mentors the customers to comprehend the common goals and purpose of relevant data for better knowledge creation and decision-making.

Data control is an analytic capability to control networking architecture, service identity, customer relationship, supply chain, access policy, and business rules. The networking architecture exists in the form of a service model (section 9.3) that maintains a pair of logical and physical topology sets of information which dynamically adjust the location and connectivity according to the serving resources. This feature can assist the data transparency and availability in a highly mobilized environment. The service identity manages the attributes and policies of individual or composite services, which can ensure the integrity of the data representation in a CoI environment. The customer relationship focuses on customer behaviors and preferences to achieve better product developments and more effective marketing programs. The supply chain manages SLA to improve the efficiency and effectiveness of manufacturing and inventory management. The business rules controls can improve the allocation and accessibility of resources through appropriate role assignments and policy definitions.

It is essential that such architecture relies strongly on a well designed data strategy with the good balance of tightly-coupled and loosely-coupled distribution. A well-designed data strategy can provide obvious returns at the performance of data flow, completeness of data content, quality of data representation, and security of information protection [1].

8.3 Enterprise Data Models

An enterprise data model describes the structure and the associated underlying structure of the data within a given domain including "grammar" for a dedicated artificial language for that domain.

Inconsistency of data or information representation can delay and often prevent response to actionable business intelligence information. The integrated data models intend to solve fragmented information, reflecting the data islands of information that exist in an operational environment. Applications can now talk to each other by posting data, users can pull multiple applications to access same data or choose the same applications (e.g., for collaboration). Business process owners can make their data available on the network as soon as it is created; the system is capable of accepting post data from multiple sources in parallel.

8.3.1 Hierarchy of Modeling

Data modeling brings the data structures of interest together into a cohesive and inseparable information base by eliminating unnecessary data redundancies and by relating data structures with relationships. A data model instance may have a conceptual, logical, or physical schema. A conceptual schema describes the semantics of an organization. This consists of entity classes (representing things of significance to the organization) and relationships (assertions about associations between pairs of entity classes). A logical schema describes the semantics, as represented by a particular data manipulation technology. This consists of descriptions of tables and columns, object-oriented classes, XML tags, and other objects. A physical schema describes the physical means by which data is stored. Storage technology can change without affecting either the logical or the conceptual model. The table/column structure can change without (necessarily) affecting the conceptual model [8].

Various constraints and influences have an effect on the data architecture design. These include enterprise requirements, technology drivers, economics, business policies, and data processing needs. Enterprise requirements usually include economical and effective system expansion, acceptable performance levels, transaction reliability, and transparent management of data. In addition, conversion of raw data such as transaction records and image files into more useful information formed through such features as data warehouses is also a common organizational requirement. Data processing requirements may cover accurate and reproducible transactions performed in high volume data warehousing, repetitive periodic reporting, ad-hoc reporting, and the support of various organizational initiatives as required.

Figure 8.10 depicts a sample modeling hierarchy for a typical IT service, where Business Operations is build upon the network, system, and technology layers. Depending upon industries or applications, these layers can be expanded or merged in accordance with the specific attributes matching the business values and functionalities of the enterprise. In a network-centric environment, functions or attributes in each layer can have many-to-many relationships with other functions or attributes as the layers can reside anywhere in the CoI or event in an affiliated CoI. As mentioned in section 8.2.1, predefined interfaces between systems will continue to exist. For example, tightly engineered and real-time systems can offer "exposure" services that work "behind the scenes" collecting real-time data, storing it, and providing access and discovery through an enterprise interface. Exposure services can be designed to have little or no effect on performance critical processes or predefined interfaces and still provide access for unanticipated users.

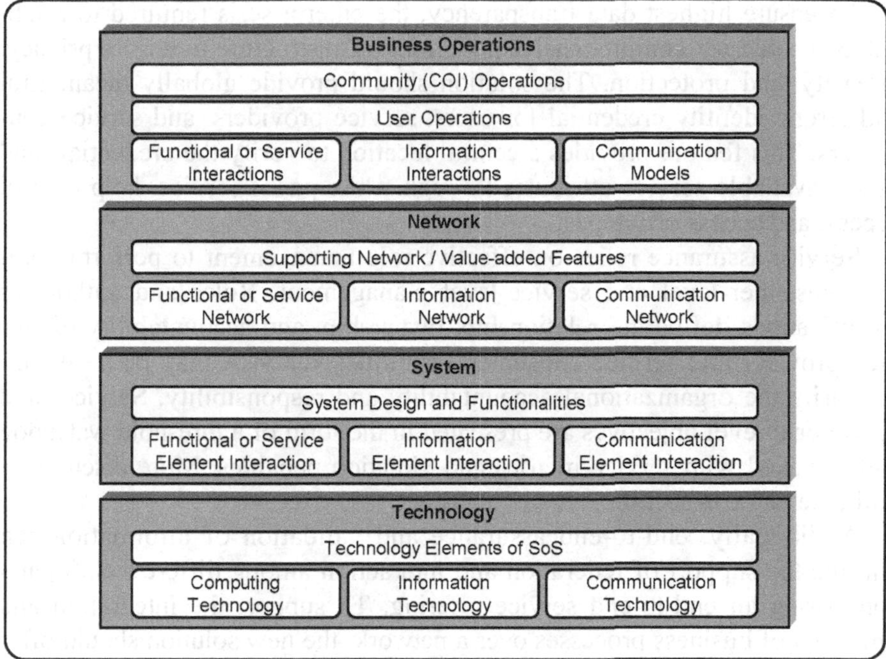

Figure 8.10. Semantic interaction layers in an enterprise service environment.

Figure 8.11 signifies the IA protection strategy evolution from current to the future. Four areas are identified by DoD and many solutions are undergoing development. The principal subjects will be covered in the following sections.

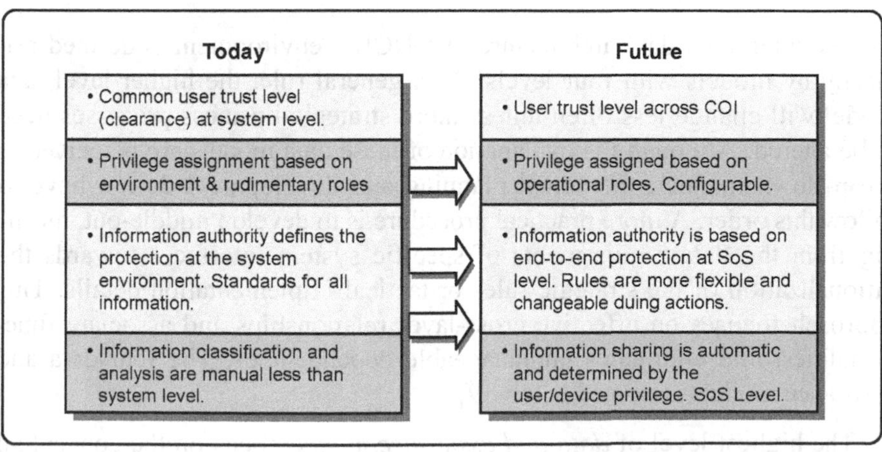

Figure 8.11. IA protection strategy evolution.

To ensure highest data transparency, the enterprise is required to establish a flexible yet comprehensive governing infrastructure to ensure privacy, integrity, and protection. The solution should provide globally meaningful and strong identity credential for users, service providers, and service consumers. This feature provides a central location to verify the credentials and locate available service attributes through white pages service, help control access, and access privileges.

Service assurance relies on effective role management to perform complex customer-level and service-level management. Roles and authorities specifications define the relationship, ownership, and accountability of service provider and service consumer. A multi-layer SLA may be necessary to clarify the organizational accountability and responsibility. Service- and operational-level objectives are presented in the form of a threshold watchdog and is linked with service metrics and violation penalties. More discussions will take place in section 9.7.

Additionally, end-to-end assurance and validation of information can enforce the support of federation and interaction among different SoS parts comprising an end-to-end service offering. To support the integration and operation of business processes over a network, the new solution should offer autonomy and decentralized management capable of abstracting the actions and concerns of different players in the service value chain to avoid any confusion or interference in individual actions. Furthermore, it should establish and maintain dependencies and trust between information providers and consumers while guaranteeing data discoverability and performance predictability.

8.3.2 Four Data and Assurance Models

The integrated data architecture in a NCBO environment is defined primarily by models with four levels. As a general rule, the higher-level data model will change less often unless more strategic business processes need to be altered. Although the explanation of these data models are perceived in a top–down manner, the actual planning and development do not have to follow this order. A more practical procedure is to develop middle-out, meaning from the data requirements of specific system interfaces towards the rationalization of the strategic rules or tactical implementation details. This approach focuses on effective cross-layer relationships and associate functionalities, and eliminates unmanageable dependencies. The four data and assurance models are listed below [9].

- The highest level of *data and assurance models* focus on the conceptual perspective, independent of any actual methods or systems. This model represents the business- or enterprise-level information strategy and consists of collected business attributes, including semantics (meaning), syntax (format), and constraints. A more modern approach typically uses a *Unified Modeling Language (UML)*-like class model to define business entities and their relationships. Although attributes and data structures are specified, class methods are not essential at this level.

- The *realization model* establishes relationships between the conceptual entities from the above model and the key data objects of the target systems. This model realizes the data items and determines how they will be propagated across the various CoI entities. The key feature of this model aims to provide visible data structures at the SoS level, including the data structure that will be exposed by the user interfaces or service interfaces. Integration with any older legacy systems can be hidden behind these interfaces.
- The *source and consumer model* details the relationships of the previous data item. The focus of this model is on identifying the role, provenance, and evolution of each data item. This model dictates how attributes are organized and managed by classes. It should also describe how the data objects will be propagated across various systems and what custodians should be applicable to these data elements when certain events occur.
- The *transportation and transformation model* specifies how the data is transformed when moved between systems. The rules for transportation and transformation are defined at the attribute level, including interface driver, constraint, and timing policies. The physical class and attribute structure of system interfaces are defined here with interaction or sequence diagrams.

These models also support validation and execution of target business processes. It includes the identification of the enterprise data with well-defined interfaces and processes that spread across several SoS entities or multiple CoIs.

8.3.3 Metadata

Metadata is "data about data". In a data strategy, metadata makes data understandable and enables interoperability. It is part of management functions rather than the architecture because the management of metadata supports the management of processes to accomplish critical data management functionalities. Additionally, metadata is more comprehensive than data architecture and data management, describing the components of applications, technology, and the information itself. Figure 8.12 shows how metadata lies across three management and architecture areas, namely data, application, and technologies. Each category has the architecture sitting on a backplane of their corresponding management. The full breadth of metadata spans these three areas.

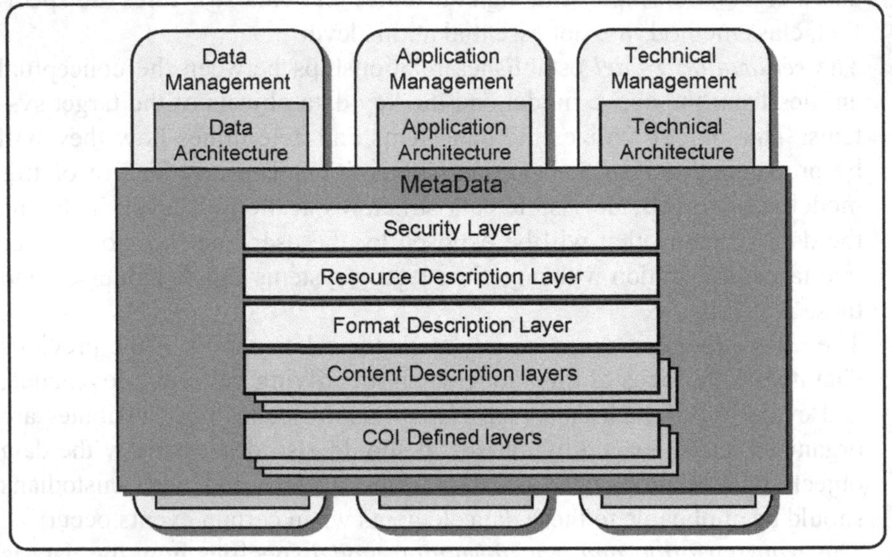

Figure 8.12. Position of metadata.

Various mechanisms are used to store and process different types of metadata and data. Metadata registries, metadata catalogs, and shared spaces are three mechanisms used to store data and information about data to enable discovery, support interoperability, and enhance data asset understanding. The metadata registry allows community applications to register their metadata agreements, thus information consumers can understand the semantics and structures of the sharable data. This framework supports interoperability and provides a richer semantic understanding of the associated data. As seen in the Figure 8.12, five layers of metadata are portrayed overlaying the data, application, and technology areas. They are security, resource, format, content, and CoI specific layers. The top layer is a security markings layer. The resource description layer is for resource maintenance and administration metadata (e.g., publisher, date for creation, and subject). The format description layer specifies format-specific metadata such as type, size, count, duration, and so forth. The content description layer defines content descriptive metadata information for discovery. Finally, the community-specific description layer defines metadata extensions which are specific to certain communities. Even though it is community-specific, the process is required to integrate the domain data with enterprise-wide capabilities.

8.4 Data Management

The need for information sharing and communication within or among enterprises is blurring the boundaries between organizations and companies. The objective in a NCBO environment is to increase the potential for many systems to leverage the same data without having to anticipate new development. The data can thus enable effective knowledge transformation and better decision-making.

8.4.1 Increase Enterprise and Community Data over Private Data

In a complex networked environment, enterprise data can potentially lose its integrity over time when data is accessed by different applications or different community users via different channels. This is because a portion of the data items held by private applications are not visible to other applications, therefore, when changes take place the key information will not be updated. To solve this problem, all data should be available in the shared spaces except when limited by security, policy, or regulations. The shared data must be visible, accessible, and understandable in order to accelerate decision-making. Additionally, the data must be organized around CoI applications and their respective domains and provides metadata to enable discovery by known and unanticipated users or applications.

8.4.1.1 Make Data Visible

The most effective way of making the data visible for community usages is through open discovery method. Users and applications can discover the existence of data assets through catalogs, registries, and other search services. The data assets must be made compliant with the enterprise data approaches to support data advertisement through metadata containing asset descriptions. The shared spaces allows the users or applications in the CoI to submit or post data, as well as provides the capabilities to ensure the data is maintained, secured, and staged as necessary. It provides virtual or physical access to any number of data assets.

Figure 8.13 is the extension of the metadata layers portrayed in the previous figure. The logical layers and elements of the *DoD Discovery Metadata Standard (DDMS)* specify structured attributes to support search tools for data discovery. The discovery metadata indicates the existence of a data object but not necessarily describes the contents of the data. As shown in the figure, the core layer of DDMS includes the attributes of data asset that can be commonly described across the community. The extensible layer provides a mechanism for supporting task specific metadata requirements. These two metadata sets are used to support search and retrieval of entities and to inform on search data. The elements in these two layers are optional; selections are subject to application requirements. Other types of metadata can include vocabularies or taxonomic structures used for organizing data assets, interface specifications, and mapping tables.

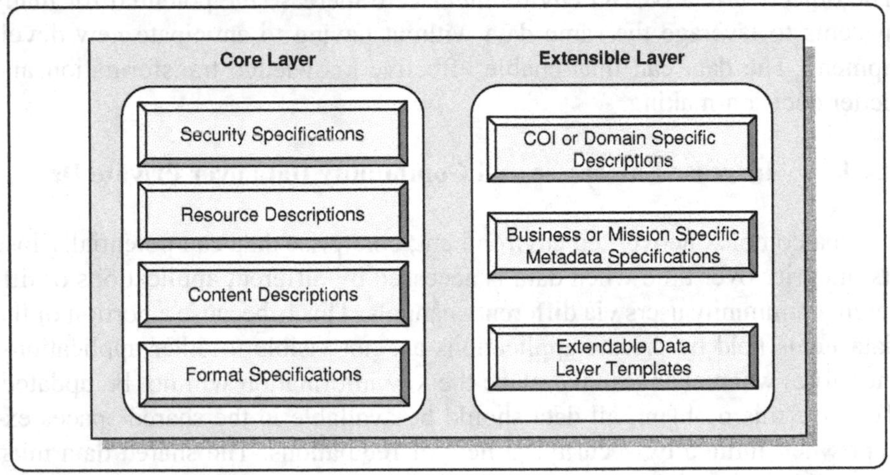

Figure 8.13. Discovery metadata standard.

Discovery metadata elements are incorporated into metadata catalogs to represent data asset in the associated shared space. Catalogs will be searchable by applications or through user-friendly, web-based interfaces. Meanwhile, register metadata contains all metadata related to data structures, models, dictionaries, and schemas. Registration of such metadata provides semantic and structural agreements to promote interoperability and understanding.

8.4.1.2 Accessible

Figure 8.14 signifies the accessibility function of NCBO in a data sharing environment where the enterprise network and global network serve as transport providing enterprise data to their information customers.

As shown in the figure, the *Developers* who understand the data formats can build the applications that post, process, exchange, and display information. The information includes the relationship between specific parts of the data asset and what elements, or fields, are used in its definition. The developer then creates shared spaces and data access services on the Network. The data access services facilitate access to database stores, business logic processes, and system data. They are a collection of software applications and data include connectivity, web sites, metadata catalogs, security services, metadata registries, and application services.

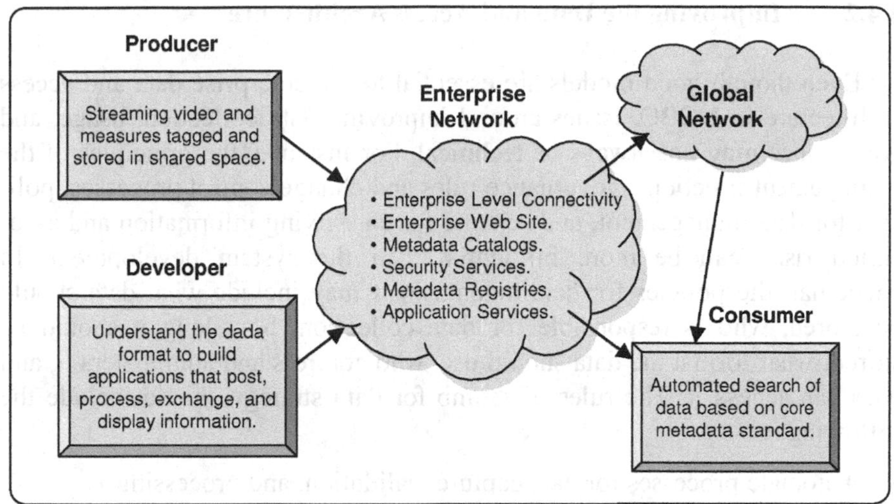

Figure 8.14. Example uses of metadata.

The data *Producer* can then post documents, images, and videos on the Network via the access services. Data assets are made available to any user or application except when limited by policy, regulation, or security. Through the metadata catalogs, search portals or applications can be used by the information *Consumer* to quickly look through a wide range of data assets to identify needed assets. Metadata also support the specification of privacy restrictions, quality property of an entity, and interoperability requirement. The services can permit access using security metadata, technologies such as *public-key infrastructure (PKI)*, and role- and permission-based access processes if adopted (section 8.5). Additionally, the associated function can add notification function to inform the service operators when encounters predetermined conditions.

8.4.1.3 Institutionalize

To incorporate the data and assurance strategy into the enterprise processes and practices, institutionalization is an effective way for the enterprise to adopt potential cultural changes. This can occur from the planning, programming, budgeting, SoS functional requirement, system policies, and implementation processes. Adoption of the network-centric data and assurance strategy can be governed by clearly defined goals and metrics. The goals are set to foster participation for the new method, and the metrics are for tracking and evaluating progress. Policy should be applicable to many areas in enterprise services implementation. Policy management and enforcement can be improved by conducting strategy awareness campaign or promoting and educating users about their responsibilities and the benefits of participation.

8.4.2 Improving the Data and Access Architecture

Even though good models are essential to the enterprise data and access architecture in NCBO, issues around improving data collection, usage, and governance may not always be technical. For instance, the principles of the management functions, governance rules and change control processes, policies for data management, and scheme for classifying information and associated risks can be more influential than the system development. In particular, the policies for data management may include what data should be stored, who is responsible for data collection, how long it should be stored, what format the data should use, who controls and administers it, and who can access it. The rules of thumb for data strategy should include the following:

- Automate processes for data capture, validation, and processing.
- Enterprise-level standard processes to update enterprise data items.
- Clear accuracy, integrity, and security responsibility assignment of each data source with corresponding custodian (a business role).
- Security of data must be protected from unauthorized access and modification.
- Data integrity should manage duplicate data if permitted. The master and copies should be treated differently, for instance, copies must not be modified.
- Changes to data structures must be coordinated at the enterprise level to avoid impacts to inter- and intra-CoI interoperability.
- Governance models and references are important to guide the data and access architecture into standards.
- Whenever possible, adopt international, national, or industry standards for common data models. For instance, ISO 11179 defines a framework for specification and standardization of data elements, the Dublin Core initiative specifies standardized metadata for resource's title, creator and date, the Universal Data Element Framework (UDEF) specifies classification for metadata based on the object class and properties concepts of ISO 11179, the World Wide Web Consortium specifies the *Web Ontology Language (WOL)* for humans understandable resource descriptions, and the European Interoperability Framework of European Commission's *Interchange of Data between Administrations (IDA)* group specifies generic standards in respect of organizational, technical and semantic interoperability.

8.4.3 Data Management Facilities

Data management is an essential function in the integrated IA environment. Figure 8.15 shows the contents of a typical data management scopes and their relationships with the enterprise data architecture. As aforementioned, the scope of data management is purposely scoped in the following areas:

Data warehousing is the main repository of the enterprise's current and historical data. A data warehouse can provide existing and history information to applications such as knowledge management to perform complex queries and analysis without degrading the operational systems. To qualify as useful data warehousing, data in the database must be organized to reflect subject matters, changes to data objects must be traceable, data must not be volatile once committed, and data must maintain consistency across the CoI.

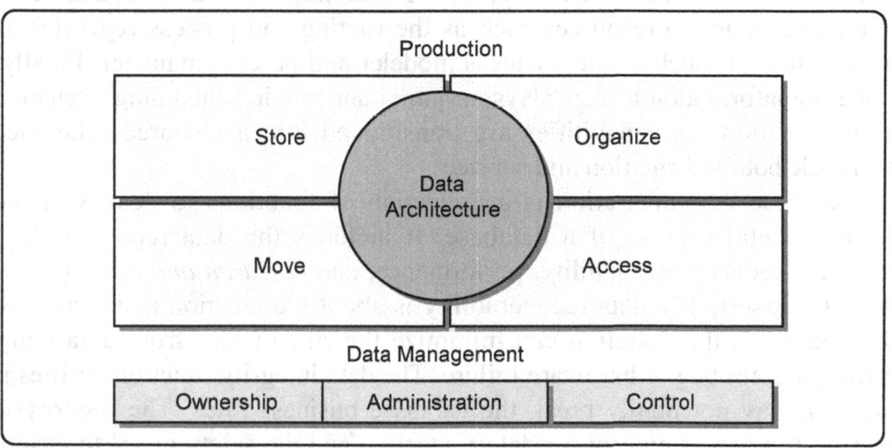

Figure 8.15. Data management framework.

The design of a data warehouse can be either dimensional or normalized. The dimensional approach partitions data into measures (or *facts*) or reference information (or *dimensions*). The advantage of this approach is its efficiency because data is prejoined into the dimensional form thus is easy for users to understand with limited technology knowledge. However, this approach is based on an optimized data representation; the flexibility for changes is its major disadvantage. On the other hand, the normalized approach uses database normalization. Tables are grouped based on general definition of the data. It provides the flexibility for modifying data relationships with the price of performance in producing information and reporting. Additionally, this method requires the database user to have precise understanding of the data structure when need to make changes to the database. This can be a challenge particularly in a large and complex database system.

Data movement consists of the *extract, transform, and load (ETL)* functions to deal with importing external data into the database. ETL can extract data from outside sources, transform it to fit business needs, and load it into the data warehouse. It is an important feature to initiate a newly created database, perform database transformation, or support bulk load to the database. For an integrated enterprise database, the ETL tool must be able to support different database systems and be able to read various file formats. Many tools also incorporate data profiling, data quality, and metadata capabilities. Data quality assurance is the process of profiling the data to discover inconsistencies and perform data cleansing activities.

To support on-demand computing with a unified resource model, data management must provide a standardized handling of both information and services, and incorporate them into a resource registry. Process creation and execution also must evolve to support the handling of resource models. This requires changes to resources such as the routing and process registries as well as to tools such as the business modeler and process manager. Finally, since the information broker plays an important role in scheduling exchange of information, its capabilities are transitioned into a resource scheduler to handle both information and services.

Database Administration is a collection of functions to deal with the environmental aspects of a database. It includes the data recoverability, integrity, security, availability, performance, and *research and development (R&D)* support. The data recoverability is about the creation and testing of data backups, this function can minimize the risk of loss from data entry error, program bug or hardware failure. The data integrity function verifies if the data may potentially break the database business rules. The security is pertinent to access control for data protection and the safety guard to ensure privacy and prevent corruption. The availability is a means to ensure maximum uptime. The performance provides effective data availability and accessibility under given resource constraints. The R&D effort is to assist the engineering team to efficiently utilize the database.

8.5 Assurance Management

The paradigm shifting towards service-oriented collaboration and composition has brought fundamental changes to the approach used to define security architectures. Under a SOE, a set of network-accessible operations and its associated resources are abstracted as a "service". To access this service, systems shall have an IA capability to operate either within each security domain or across any security domains, while ensuring the operations comply with the security requirements.

Figure 8.16 depicts potential treats of information integrity and security from different levels and areas. This figure also illustrates the vulnerability of the environment can be managed by three security plans. They are User, Control, and Management Planes.

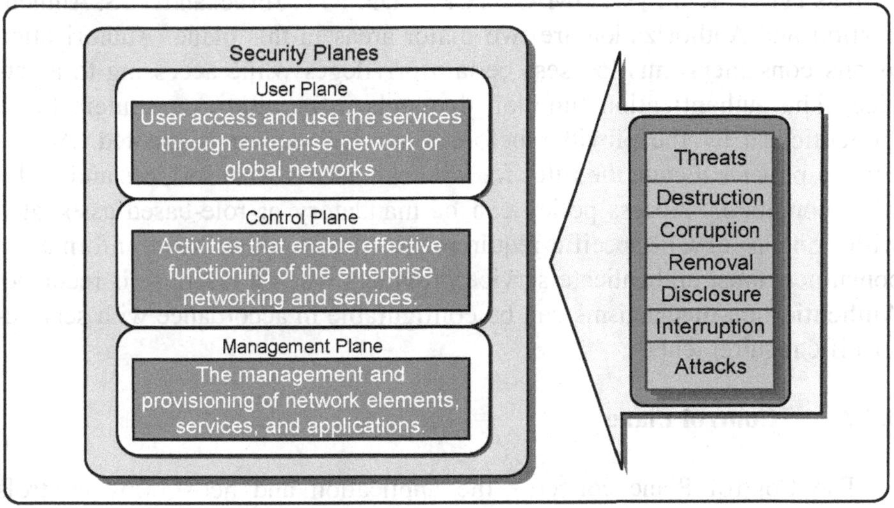

Figure 8.16. Attacks to the Security Planes.

Extended from the previous picture, Figure 8.17 portrays the three sub-plans with different emphasis and functional scopes. Each provides different protection of enterprise information. They are addressed in the following section.

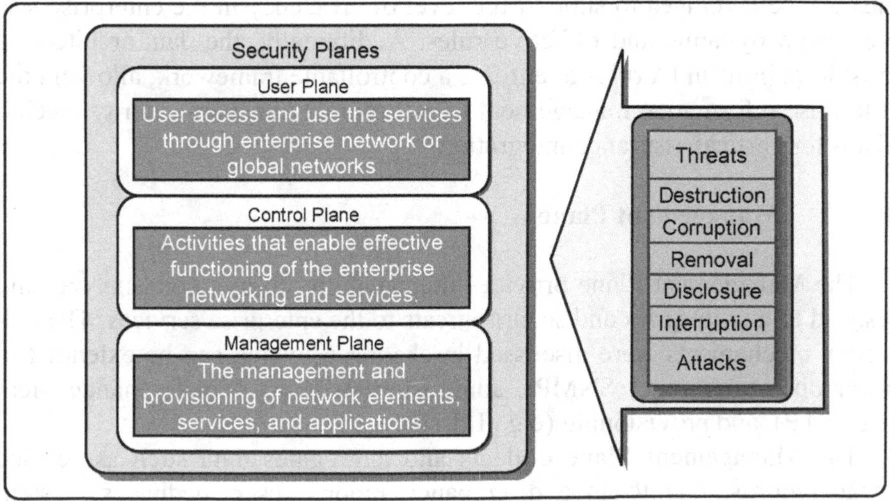

Figure 8.17. Three Security Planes.

8.5.1 User Plane

The User Plane is responsible for the end user data transfer and end-user application interaction, which may involve many communication protocols such as HTTP, RTP, POP, IMAP, TCP, UDP, FTP, IPsec, and TLS. Authentication and Authorization are two major areas in this plane. Authorization means consumers must possess certain privileges while accessing to a service. The authentication function demands information consumers to be authenticated by the provider before a service request is granted. Access control policies dictate the rules for who can access what services and under what conditions. Access policy can be mandatory or role-based associated with domain- or CoI-specific requirements. On the other hand, information consumers must authenticate service providers when a response is received. Authentication mechanisms can be configurable in accordance with service-specific requirements.

8.5.2 Control Plane

The Control Plane concerns the application and networking controls which includes update of database and life-cycle management of services such as initiation, control, and teardown.

The functionality of the Control Plane is to execute the rules and models defined in the data and assurance strategy in order to overcome any potential integrity and security risks posted to the data, software, and hardware architectures. The goal is to achieve full potential of the enterprise's parallel and distributed service offerings. It is very critical that the systems and technologies can be leveraged to support the level of efficiency in the enterprise services with dynamic and effective rules. Additionally, the data architecture must have built-in IA rules to enforce a controllable framework, allowing the enterprise information management to incorporate transport security mechanisms for vertical assurance integration.

8.5.3 Management Plane

The Management Plane provides the capability to monitor, analyze, and respond to any integrity and security treats to the enterprise services. The collection mechanisms were discussed in chapter 6, which can be extended to cover operations (e.g., SNMP), administration (e.g., Telnet), management (e.g., FTP), and provisioning (e.g., HTTP).

The Management Plane collects and aggregates data such as service usage records, maintenance discrepancy reports, user feedbacks, system failure reports, engineering plans, and assurance indicators for classifying attacks. A monitoring system incorporates detection, reporting, and response functions that enables rapid detection of and reaction to all sources of anomalous events. The analysis feature assists the enterprise to ascertain allowable deficiencies and discrepancies in a CoI environment or value-chain operations. Risk assessment mechanism determines any safety hazards and identifies the readiness and cost risks, which are associated with the identified problems or deficiencies. The analysis result can be a set of corrective actions sensible for strategic and tactical ramifications for the service offerings.

Figure 8.18 depicts four security layers which overlay upon the three security planes. These four security layers, from bottom–up, are transport layer, message layer, service layer, and application layer. They will be addressed in the following sections.

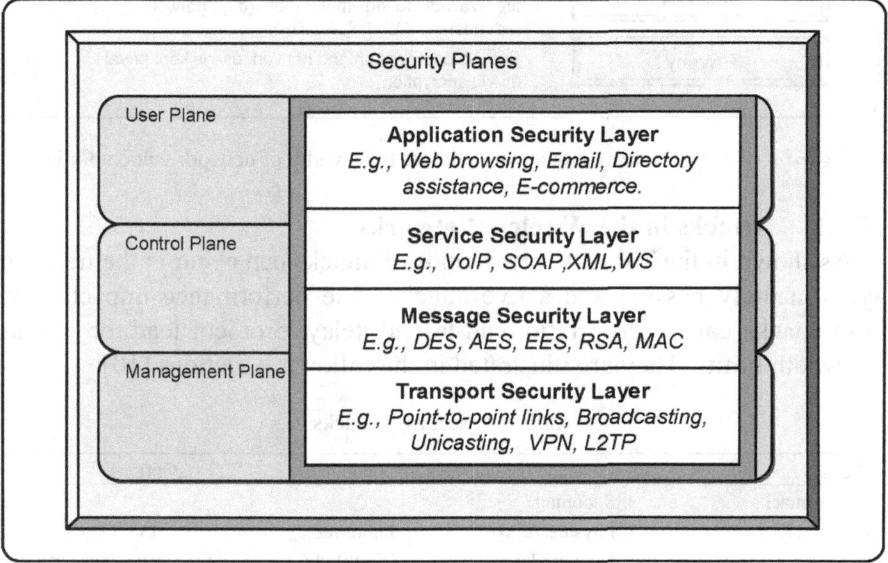

Figure 8.18. Four security layers.

8.5.4 Transport Layer Assurance

The sources of threats to the transport layer may be external or internal. For instance, the external attackers to the network may be caused by intruders trying to insert erroneous routing updates, replay old routing information, or even change routing updates. The internal attacker at the network can be caused by malicious node advertising incorrect routing information. The transport layer assurance is logically divided into eight layers as portrayed in Figure 8.19, ranging from the user control to information privacy. Each layer has different technological challenges and corresponding resolutions.

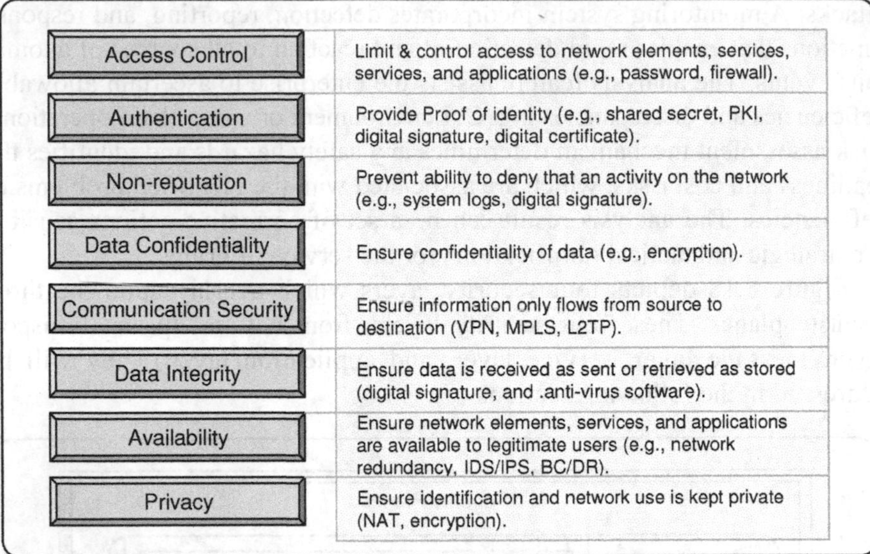

Figure 8.19. Eight security dimensions address the breadth of network vulnerabilities.

8.5.4.1 Attacks in the Wireless Networks

As shown in the Table 8.1, two kinds of attacks can occur at the transport layers, namely passive and active attacks. The performance impacts from these attacks can be drop ratio, end-to-end delay, protocol load, or exhaust bandwidth limits. They are illustrated in the following sections [10]:

Table 8.1. Security Attacks.

Attacks	Layers in the Network Protocol		Options
Passive attacks	Snooping		
Active attacks	Physical & MAC	Jamming	FHSS, DSSS
	Network layer	Wormhole	Packet Leashes
		Blackhole	
		Byzantine	
		Information disclosure	SMT
		Location disclosure	SRP, NDM
		Resource consumption	SEAD
		Routing attacks	SEAD, ARAN, ARIADNE
	Transport layer	Session hijacking	
	Application layer	Repudiation	ARAN
	Multiple layers	Denial of Service	SEAD, ARIADNE
		Impersonation	ARAN
		Manipulation of network traffic	
	Other	Device tampering	

Passive Attacks

In a passive attack, the attacker attempts to discover valuable information by listening to the routing traffic. For instance, the IP network is vulnerable because its (IP) address is presented with plaintext in headers, plus distributing symmetric keys to every node in the network is not feasible. Because this attack does not disrupt operations of a routing protocol, the attack is usually impossible to detect and defend in a wireless environment. Potential information of interest for the attacker includes the topology of adjacent nodes and the identification of the busiest node(s) in the network. Attackers attempting to disable important nodes can potentially bring the entire network down.

Active Attacks

Active attacks involve actions such as replication, modification, and deletion of data in order to route them to the attacker for analysis or just to disable the network. Different from passive attacks, an active attack is sometimes detectable. Active attacks include:

- *Black hole*: In a flooding-based protocol such as AODV, the attacker detects a request for a route message and creates a reply with an extremely short route. If the malicious reply reaches the requesting node before the expected reply from the actual node, a forged route will be created. As the result, the malicious device can insert itself between the communicating nodes and perform attacks such as denial-of-service to drop the packets or to perform a man-in-the-middle attack.
- *Jamming*: This is the attack at the physical or MAC level. It is about the transmission of radio signals that disrupt communications in order to decrease the signal to noise ratio and eventually disrupt control of the attacked network. The attacker's transmitter is tuned to the same frequency as the target receiving equipment and uses the same type of modulation. With enough power the malicious node can then override any signal at the receiver. The purpose of this attack is to block out reception of transmitted signals and to cause a nuisance to the receiving operator.
- *Location disclosure*: This attack can be as simple as using an equivalent of the *traceroute* command on UNIX systems or sending routing messages with inadequate hop-limit values. The malicious device can then analyze the addresses of the devices which reply with ICMP error messages. Such information can reveal the locations of nodes or the structure of the network.
- *Routing table overflow*: This attack intends to send excessive route advertisements to nonexistent nodes in order to prevent new routes from being created or to overwhelm the protocol implementation. Proactive

routing algorithms attempt to discover routing information before needed, thus making them more vulnerable to this attack. For example in AODV, two or more malicious nodes can cooperate to create false data efficiently. Then one node requests routes and the other replies with forged addresses.

- *Rushing attack*: This attack targets on-demand routing protocols (e.g., AODV) with duplicate suppression at each node. An attacker's node disseminates *Route Requests* quickly throughout the network and suppresses any legitimate requests. The receiving nodes will drop the legitimate messages due to the duplicate suppression. This attack can prevent the node from setting up a route to the desirable destination and cause failure of route discovery.
- *Sleep deprivation*: For a power sensitive network, this attack attempts to consume batteries by requesting routes, or by forwarding unnecessary packets to the node using, for example, a black hole attack.
- *Spoofing*: The malicious node misrepresents its identity in the attacked network by altering its MAC or IP address in outgoing packets. This attack can potentially launch many other attacks such as data interception, modification, or disruption of data transition.
- *Wormhole*: This attack uses a pair of attacker nodes. An attacker records packets (or bits) at one location in the network, tunnels them through the wormhole to another location, and retransmits them back to the first node. By creating a routing loop, this attack discards rather than forwards all data packets. It can disrupt routing by short circuiting the normal flow of routing packets to create a permanent *denial-of-service (DoS)* attack.

8.5.4.2 Securing Wireless Networks

Attacks at network level create different security threats to the enterprise services. This section describes some commonly used techniques to detect or prevent the attacks.

- *Self-stabilization*: Automatically injects a small number of malformed packets to trigger the network to recover from any problem in a finite amount of time without human intervention. This can defend against a black hole attack.
- *Isolation*: Identify misbehaving nodes and make them unable to interfere with routing. This can defend against worm hole and black hole attacks.
- *Spread spectrum modulation*: Resist the deleterious effects of jamming.
- *Location privacy*: Protect information about the location of nodes and the network structure. This can be used to defend against location disclosure attack.
- *Certain discovery*: Make the network always possible to identify the available route. This can defend against routing table overflow and a rushing attack.

- *Lightweight computations*: Confine heavy computing task to the least possible number of nodes (battery power protection). This can defend against sleep deprivation attack.
- *Authentication among hosts*: Prevent impersonation to defend against spoofing attack.
- *Byzantine robustness*: Function correctly even if some of the nodes participating in routing are intentionally disrupting its operation. This can defend against impersonation attack.
- *Trusted route discovery*: Send packets via trusted routes to defend against internal attacks.
- *Redundant paths*: Increase route robustness by providing more route choices.
- *Non-disclosure method*: Avoid the location disclosure by using distributed independent security agents.
- *Hierarchical structure or zone-based routing*: This approach provides foundation for authentication and local link state routing.
- *Attack traffic pattern detection*: This approach validates destination sequence and improves awareness of attacks.
- *Intrusion detection*: This application-level approach monitors behavior of suspected hosts for intrusion detection.

8.5.5 Message Layer Assurance

Message layer security services are generally implemented in infrastructure components responsible for receiving and routing messages to an internal endpoint. Such services allow the SoS to protect a message to a finer degree than transport layer security. In general, due to the cost of fine-grained message layer security implementations, message layer security tends to focus on end-to-end protection.

8.5.5.1 Attacks in the Message Layer

Cryptography ("secret writing" in Greek) also referred to as encryption, is a process of converting plaintext information into an unreadable cipher-text. Decryption is the reverse process, recovering a plaintext from an incomprehensible cipher-text version. Cryptanalysis, a.k.a. code-breaking, is the study to discover weakness or insecurity in a cryptographic scheme and circumvent cryptography. If the cryptanalyst accesses only to a cipher-text, it is called "ciphertext-only attack". This can usually be effectively immune by modern cryptosystems. If the cryptanalyst accesses to a cipher-text and its corresponding plaintext, it is called Known-plaintext attack. If the cryptanalyst chooses a plaintext and learns its corresponding ciphertext, it is called

Chosen-plaintext attack. If the cryptanalyst chooses cipher-texts and learns their corresponding plaintexts, it is called Chosen-ciphertext attack.

In addition to attacking the weaknesses of the algorithms, the traffic analysis attack studies the pattern and length of messages to reverse-engineering the algorithm. The timing attack uses the amount of time the attacked algorithm took to encrypt a number of plaintexts and report errors (e.g., password or PIN) to break a cipher.

8.5.5.2 Crypto Keys for Message Layer Security

A *cipher (*or *cypher)* is a single or pair of algorithms for encryption and decryption. The terms encipher and decipher are used to delineate cipher algorithm operations. The operation of a cipher algorithm is controlled by a key or secret parameter. The entire process of encryption and decryption involves cryptosystems, algorithms, protocols, and operating procedures. From service fulfillment perspective, key creation, key distribution, key protection, and key management are important part of the assurance process.

Symmetric-Key Cryptography

As aforementioned in section 5.2.7, symmetric-key cryptography uses the same key for both the sender and receiver. The applications of symmetric-key ciphers can be broken down to block ciphers and stream ciphers.

A block cipher takes a block of plaintext and a key, and converts them into a block of cipher-text of the same size. *Data Encryption Standard (DES)*, *Advanced Encryption Standard (AES)*, *Triple-DES*, and *Skipjack* are three common block ciphers.

- *Data Encryption Standard (DES)* and the migration from DES to *Triple-DES* are specified in *National Institute of Standards and Technology (NIST)* FIPS 46-3. The specification of Triple-DES is defined in ANSI X9.52-1998 X9. DES is now considered insecure and superseded by AES [11].
- *Advanced Encryption Standard (AES)* is specified in NIST FIPS 197, and is one of the most popular algorithms used in symmetric key cryptography. The implementation of the AES is relatively easy yet its execution speed is fast. Key sizes of AES are 128, 192, and 256 bits and with block size of 128 bits. A variation of AES is *Rijndael*, which is based on a *substitution-permutation network* instead of *Feistel network.* Rijndael can be specified with key and block sizes in any multiple of 32 bits, with a minimum of 128 bits and a maximum of 256 bits. In practical implementation, they are limited with key sizes of 128, 160, 192, 224, and 256 bits and block sizes of 128, 160, 192, 224, and 256 bits [12].

- *Skipjack algorithm* or *Escrowed Encryption Standard (EES)* is specified in NIST FIPS 185. Designed with rather old fashion building blocks and techniques, it represents a family of encryption algorithms as part of the NSA suite of "Type I" algorithms [13, 14].

Stream ciphers process a continuous stream of plaintext and produce the corresponding encrypted output stream based upon changing internal state. The internal state change is controlled by either the key or the plaintext stream. A typical example of is Stream ciphers is RC4.

The major disadvantage of symmetric ciphers is the effort involved for secure key management. Because the number of keys required increases very rapidly and each communicating parties must hold different keys, the management of these keys can become an administrative nightmare in large CoIs.

Public-Key Cryptography

Public-key or *asymmetric-key cryptosystems* use the "same" key for encryption and decryption. They are a pair of mathematically related keys, the encryption key is a public key, and the decryption key is a private or secret key. Possession of one key does not permit calculation of the other key, thus the public key can be freely distributed while its paired private key must be kept secret. There are two popular implantations, the *Diffie-Hellman* [15] key exchange protocol and *revised statues annotated (RSA)*. RSA is based on a problem related to factoring and is widely used in encryption and digital signature applications.

Public-key algorithms are based on the computational complexity of various "hard" problems, often from number theory. Therefore they are more computationally expensive than the approaches for block ciphers.

8.5.5.3 Cryptographic Hash Functions

Cryptographic hash functions are also known as message digest functions, are a related class of cryptographic algorithms that do not need keys. These functions perform one-way process and convert input data (often an entire message) into a short, fixed length, and hash output. The output is typically 160-bits long. A variation called *message authentication codes (MACs)* is similar to cryptographic hash functions, except it requires a secret key to generate and authenticate the hash value.

8.5.5.4 Digital Signature

A *digital signature* is implemented based on public-key cryptography. Similar to an ordinary signature, digital signatures are permanently attached to the content of the message and cannot be removed. There are two parts to these schemes; a signing algorithm uses a secret key to process the message, and a matched public key for verification of the signature. RSA and DSA are two of the most popular digital signature techniques. Digital signatures are used in public-key infrastructures and many network security mechanisms such as SSL/TLS and VPNs.

8.5.6 Service Layer Assurance

In a NCBO environment, perimeter-based security such as firewalls and intrusion detection are no longer satisfactory to a dynamic service environment. For instance, perimeter-based security requires an explicit user account creation on the application and machine to obtain access to functions of the application. In contrast, network-centric information sharing and collaboration demand the business functionality to be service-enabled and exposed to external consumers via standard Web Service protocols. Furthermore, any information consumers may act as service providers offering business functionalities to their downstream applications. Here, service consumers and providers can belong to different physical networks or even different companies. As the result, the application identities and network addresses published in a service registry cannot possibility be location dependent thus the perimeter-based security is far from satisfactory. Therefore, the emphasis of NCBO assurance is placed upon the service identities, trust, and authorized access instead of physical ownership and control.

8.5.6.1 Attacks in the Service Layer

The security challenges in a service environment come from different angles because the service-oriented application architecture is essentially a software-based solution comprising many interrelated technologies. Resolution to one technology may not necessarily enforce the others. An appropriate solution must possess enterprise-wide and cross-enterprise strategies. To appreciate potential security risks and weaknesses at the service layer, the threats can be profiled as the following five types:

- HTTP-based attacks to Web services. This attack may not be detectable by conventional firewall products.
- Lack of standard profiling at the service interface level may prevent the enterprise service security from reaching beyond the needed boundaries and open opportunity for attacks.
- The security semantic at the service-level may not offer comprehensive authentication and authorization features to ensure preinformation or transaction security.
- In the face of increasing joint business process or workflow, weakness in end-to-end composition and orchestration may risk a SOAP message

to be replayed by unintended third parties bearing the same operation signature.

- In an enterprise environment where multiple security-domain and classification-level are required, the cross-domain SoS may not feature connection-oriented function to support XML and SOAP message security as needed.

8.5.6.2 Web Services Security Standards

Web services security standards extend standard mechanisms like encryption, digital signature, and public-key infrastructure to handle XML and Web services specific problems. A hierarchy of the Web services standards is depicted in Figure 8.20. The relevant standards are shown in Table 8.2 [16].

A shown in Figure 8.20, conventional network security protocols are at the bottom-most layer. SSL, the predominant standard for Web security, provides only a point-to-point confidentiality thus cannot address intermediaries.

XML Signature and XML Encryption are two key solution mechanisms for security in online systems attempting to remap the existing concepts in Web-based security to the XML message-level security. By this definition, these protocols stress message-level security in contrast to session-level protocols. Leveraging the XML-Signature and XML-Encryption specifications, XKMS attempts to extend PKI for XML-based Web services in order to promote widespread acceptability of XML-based security mechanisms.

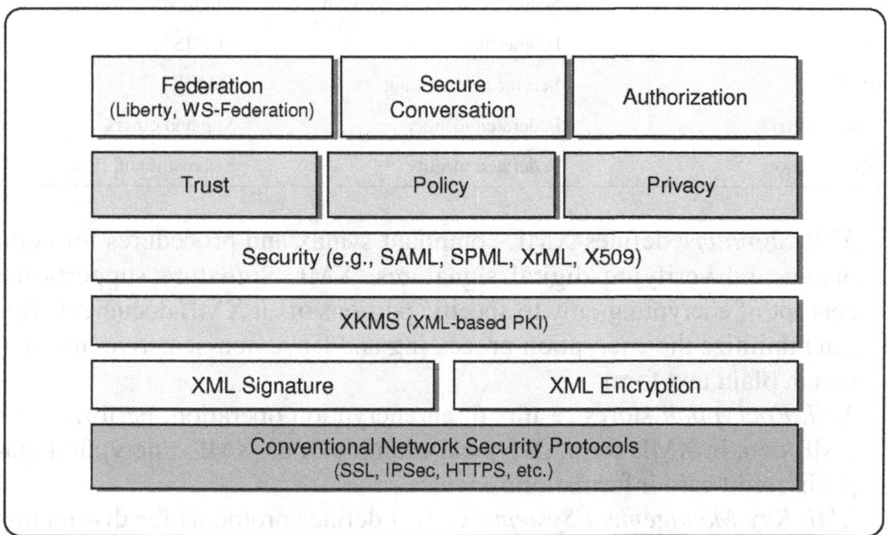

Figure 8.20. Web services security standards stack.

Above this layer are the Web services security standards. SAML and WS-Security are poised to become the most popular Web services security standards with wide acceptance, others have not seen widespread acceptance. Table 8.2 lists the standards, areas of interest, and originators of the most popular Web service security standards.

Table 8.2. Key Web Service Security Standards.

Web Service Standard	Security Requirements Addressed	Proposed by
XML encryption	Message-level confidentiality	W3C
XML signature	Message-level integrity, non-repudiation	W3C
XML key management system	XML-based PKI	W3C
Security assertions markup language (SAML)	Single sign-on, authentication, and authorization interoperability	OASIS
WS-security	SOAP message security, security credentials interoperability	OASIS
Extensible access control markup language (XACML)	Access control and policy management	OASIS
WS-trust	Trust management	Microsoft
WS-policy	Policy management	Microsoft
WS-SecureConversation	Secure session management	Microsoft
XBCF	Biometrics	OASIS
SPML	Service provisioning	OASIS
Project liberty	Federated identity	Sun and others
WS-federation	Federated identity	Microsoft and IBM

- *XML Signature* defines XML-compliant syntax and procedures for computing and verifying digital signatures. XML Signature supports the concept of encrypting only to specific portions of an XML document. This can minimize the encryption processing and leave non-sensitive information in plain text form.
- *XML Encryption* stores results of an encryption operation, performed on XML data in XML form. A typical example of an XML-Encryption output is credit card information.
- *XML Key Management System (XKMS)* defines protocols for distributing and registering public keys (PKI) suitable for use in conjunction with an XML Signature. It supports the key management functionalities including registrations, trust, and delegation.

- *Security Assertions Markup Language (SAML)* specifies the information on authentication or authorization for exchanging security credentials (assertions) among online business partners. The assertions can be authentication assertions (identity), attribute assertions (user limits and so forth), or authorization decision assertions (access control like read/write permission and so forth). SAML assertions can be signed using XML Signature. SAML is the base of the federated identity system developed by Project Liberty. It also specifies the protocols and the governing structure of SAML requests, responses, and mode of retrieval of assertions.
- *WS-Security (WSS)* is a framework of security for Web services. WS-Security allows interoperation of different existing security mechanisms with generic security tokens (public certificate, X.509 certificate and so forth) in SOAP messages.
- *Web Services Federation* includes mechanisms for different security realms to federate. They allow and broker trust of identities, attributes, authentication between participating Web services [17].
- *Project Liberty* is a simplified standard of federated identity allowing consumers to share credentials and enabling single sign-on to disparate applications and Web sites. Project Liberty bases its federated identity implementation on SAML combined features from XACML, XKMS, and XML Signature.
- *eXtensible Access Control Markup Language (XACML)* is a declarative access control policy language implemented in XML. It is a processing model, describing he generic attribute categories and the evaluation policies [18].
- *WS-Policy* specifies the policy requirements with respect to security or QoS in XML. The *Web Services Security Policy Language (WS-SecurityPolicy)* specifies the policy assertions that apply to SOAP Message Security, WS-Trust, and WS-SecureConversation [19,20].
- The *Web Services Secure Conversation Language (WS-SecureConversation)* builds on top of the WS-Security and WS-Trust models to provide secure communication between services. This modular SOAP-based specification defines mechanisms for establishing and sharing security contexts, and deriving keys from security contexts to enable a secure conversation. WS-SecureConversation by itself does not provide a complete security solution. It is a building block used in conjunction with other Web service and application-specific protocols (e.g., WS-Security) to accommodate security models and technologies [21].
- *Web Services Trust Language (WS-Trust)* uses the secure messaging mechanisms of WS-Security to define additional primitives and extensions for the exchange and validation of security tokens. WS-Trust also

enables the issuance and dissemination of credentials within different trust domains [22].

- *Service Provisioning Markup Language (SPML)* is an XML-based framework for exchanging user, resource, and service provisioning information between cooperating organizations. SPML defines how resources should be allocated between systems and organizations and is a major component of the identity management stack. It also handles provisioning – managing user accounts and access rights. SPML adapts some WS-Provisioning functionality [23].
- *XML Common Biometric Format (XCBF)* defines a common XML markup representation of the patron formats specified in NIST Common Biometric Exchange File Format. The XML values are presented in the ASN.1 schema with cryptographic message types defined in the X9.84 Biometrics Information Management and Security standard. The values may also contain X.509 certificates and other digitally signed or encrypted information [24,25].

8.5.7 Application Layer Assurance

Figure 8.21 depicts a sample relationship between the enterprise users and two major sources of information, namely the enterprise circle of trust and the consumer circle of trust. These two circles of trust link the users functional

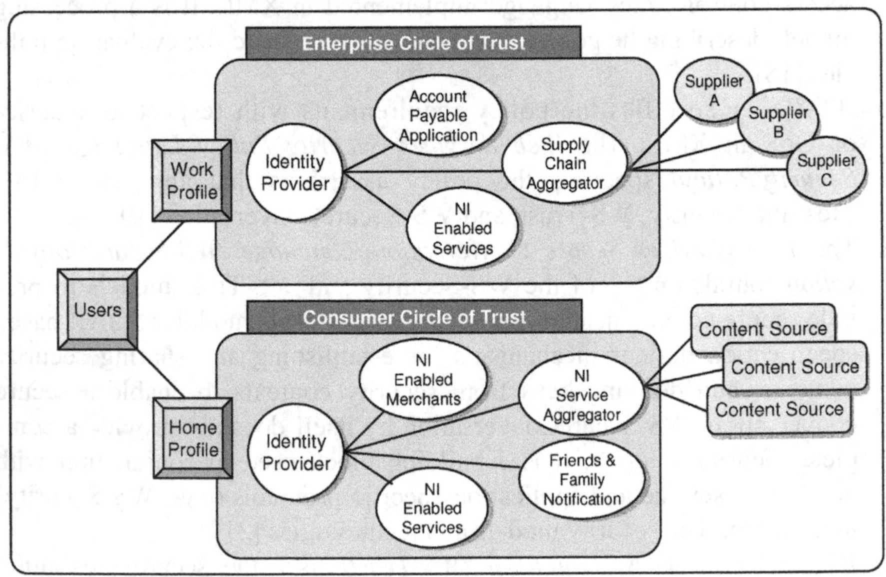

Figure 8.21. Two circles of trust.

block through different profiles with distinguished identity providers in order to set a secure separation of information flows [26].

8.5.7.1 Attacks in the Application Layer

In a NCBO environment, the access management may be implemented as a distributed service or a federation of coordinated services, potentially improving performance and avoiding single points of failure. Such design may increase vulnerability and thus requires more comprehensive considerations. Security threats at the application layer can come from the following several forms.

- *Data interception*: An unauthorized user monitors and captures any plaintext across the network.
- *Denial of service*: The intruder floods a service with requests that consume enterprise networking or computing resources.
- *Identity interception*: The intruder discovers a valid user name and password.
- *Macro viruses*: Application viruses exploit the macro language of sophisticated documents and spreadsheets.
- *Malicious mobile code*: Auto-executed ActiveX control or Java applet downloaded from the Internet can destroy or damage enterprise data. It is also referred to as Trojan Horse.
- *Masquerade*: An unauthorized user pretends to be a valid user with assumed identifier or address of a trusted system to gain the access rights.
- *Misuse of privileges*: An administrator of a trusted system uses privileges over the regular rules to obtain private data.
- *Repudiation*: Network-based transaction service may compromise the security if the recipient cannot identify the sender of the transaction.

8.5.7.2 Cross-Classification/Domain Information Flow

The cross-classification connectivity services, such as *cross-domain mediators (CDMs)*, provide enterprise capabilities of the selective sharing of information across security boundaries. This capability permits information to be shared in the domains with higher sensitivity and can be provided in both directions.

Mediation is a middle layer of processing between producers of information and consumers of information. Mediation provides automated capabilities for assured delivery, translation, conversion, fusion and routing of information between participants. Operational services on the enterprise network can be created by service providers in a mediated or unmediated form. Unmediated services do not use CDM and allow direct connection from the consumer to the service provider. As depicted in Figure 8.22, systems use mediated services which provides a range of additional capabilities including secured, guaranteed, completed, once-and-only-once delivery, scalability and fail-over of interactions, and standardized IA capabilities.

Users can leverage web portals to directly enter business rules to define new rules or roles against the various sources to create new services.

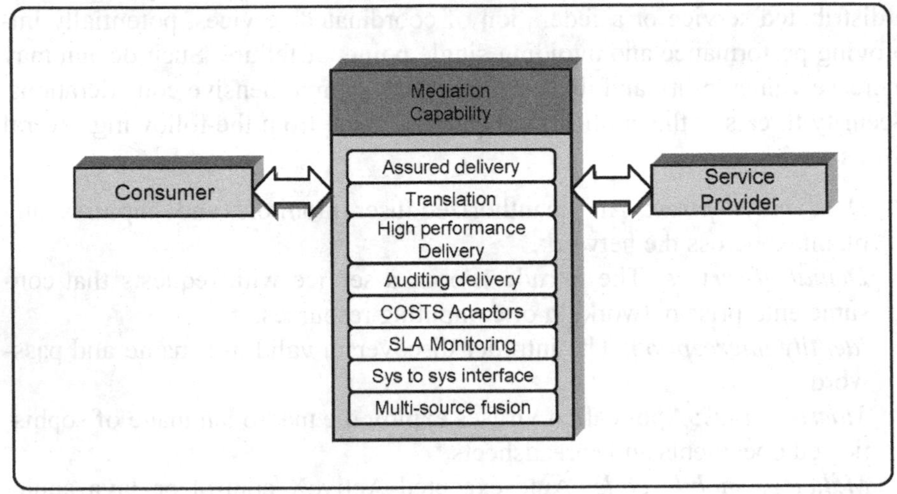

Figure 8.22. Mediation capability for cross-classification or domain interface.

8.5.7.3 Security Logging and Audit

Logging services provide the enterprise the ability to record security events for the determination of whether systems' usage are being abused or violated, and for holding individuals accountable for their actions. However, if an intruder gains administrator rights and permission, or if an administrator abuses the rights and permissions, the security log can potentially be removed and leave a trail of their actions. In this case, security services and tools can be configured to automatically scan logs to detect user or service use anomalies and notify the system and security manager. For example, an automated analysis tool may correlate seemingly diverse, disparate events that are in reality the product of a coordinated attack. Through authentication, audit, and time stamping services, the enterprise can increase effectiveness of its IA goals.

8.5.7.4 Digital Policy

Digital rights management (DRM) manages the confidentiality of sensitive information by restricting access to and use of digital content. In a NCBO environment, applications may likely become the predominant information customer rather than human.

A properly implemented Digital Policy Management infrastructure can facilitate the widest possible use of digital content, supporting the interests of information users, CoI coordinators, and content providers.

Policies may derive from internally determined data strategy practice, from the IA framework, or the service provider's SLA.

The Enterprise Policy Group coordinates the secure distribution of corporate digital media content across the entire CoI or across CoIs.

8.6 Data and Assurance Control

Enterprise data and assurance are typically employed through four interconnected drivers: business, technology, environment, and customers (see Figure 8.23). These drivers function within the relationships of objectives named dimensions, and respond to each other in dimensional, and interwoven networks. They are all interrelated and very often elements of one dimension can directly influence another dimension [27].

The Business dimension concerns the *return of investment (ROI)*, business cycle, market conditions, and legal considerations which could potentially have an effect on data architecture and management. It is possible that certain data architecture and management, while optimal, may not be potential candidates due to their cost. The fiscal motivators and ramifications must be under constant evaluation against the business goals. The business policies and rules describe the manner in which the enterprise wishes to process their data. The organizational policies, rules of regulatory bodies, industry standards, and applicable governmental laws (e.g., SOX and HIPAA) must be incorporated into this dimension.

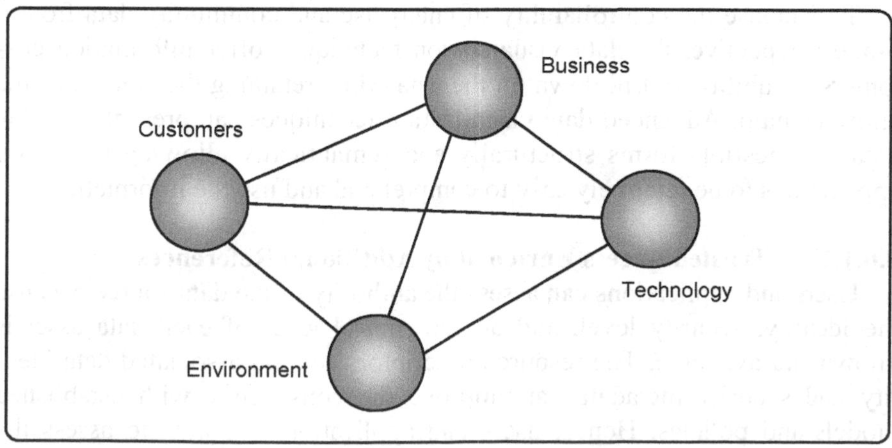

Figure 8.23. The drivers of data and assurance control.

Technology dimensions usually influences the life-cycle management of data architecture, database architecture, and data management. The technology driver focuses on the most feasible and effective means to implement the enterprise data strategy thus will ultimately control the functionality of the data infrastructure and management. Therefore, it must consider the existing organizational integration frameworks and standards, organizational economics, and existing resources. The administrative or operational aspects of this dimension pertinent to the policy's enforcement and maintenance must take into account of the hierarchical structure of information security.

The environment dimension revolves around the physical, social, legal, administrative, and spatiotemporal factors which potentially affect data or information entity. The cognitive feature analyzes the reaction of data quality and availability to these factors, and directly influences the success and functionality of the enterprise's policies. The physical time and space factors are important to enterprise service operations especially when data objects are accessed online; this implies that the information policing mechanism must be adoptive to mobility and service dynamics.

The customer dimension includes information customers who have interactions, either direct or indirect, with the data or information objects in or among CoIs. This dimension takes into consideration the experience, attitude, and acceptance of data from those who use the enterprise data or information. The expectations between the information suppliers and customers are typically captured in SLA. A comprehensive SLA can render acceptable and necessary or unacceptable and unnecessary access criteria with financial implications associated.

8.6.1 Increase Controllability of Enterprise and Community Data

To increase the controllability of enterprise and community data from a usage perspective, the data visualization techniques offer information customers the ability to drill down on the data while retaining the context of the entire domain. Advanced data visualization techniques can present complex data in digestible forms structurally and semantically allowing users and applications to be relatively easy to comprehend and use the information.

8.6.1.1 Trusted Access Enriched by Additional References

Users and applications can assess the authority of the data source because the identity, security level, and access control level of each data asset is known and available. The resource descriptors contain associated data identity and security metadata can improve the consistency with established models and policies. Hence, users and applications are able to assess the derivation of the data from known sources (by providing identification of the author, publisher, and sources) to enhance the reliability and quality of the access process.

Enterprise service provider may provide different level of protection rules, e.g., X.509 certificate based versus username/password authentication. Security policies must be expressive and flexible enough to be tailored according to a variety of parameters (e.g., principal attributes) to enhance the controllability. Furthermore, authoritative sources for key data assets available in the enterprise network can assist the CoI users and applications to evaluate and understand proper level of implications.

8.6.1.2 Interoperability Improved with Complement Metadata

Metadata can also be used for mediation or translation of data between interfaces allowing data to be exchanged between systems through predefined or unanticipated interfaces. To facilitate interoperability within a community, CoIs can determine the appropriate focus and level of data standardization within their community. A decentralized and distributed approach can improve the controllability of the service interfaces and data structures. Additionally, metadata can be expanded to increase interoperability with the following additions:

- Community-specific ontology to improve semantic and syntactic understanding of data set. It can include data categorization schemes, thesauruses, vocabularies, key word lists, and taxonomies.
- Associate content-related metadata to improve information search based on specific topics. Content metadata can include topics, keywords, context, and other content-related information.
- Associate format-related metadata to improve information searches by selecting objects that meet particular operating constraints or physical manifestation. It can include the type of digital file, such as file size, type, and dimensions.
- Community-specific content-related metadata to improve information search based on domain-specific or CoI-specific criteria. It can include particular domain area subjects or contents.

8.6.2 Rules and Governance

Rules can be classified in different aspects depending upon the service types and their functionalities. Some scopes of rules can apply at a very general level, others can be more specific. Each of these rules assists the right enterprise users to access the right information at the right time. In the enterprise data sharing paradigm, data posted by authoritative sources can support high degree of visibility, availability, and usability to accelerate decision-making with the concept of *only handle information once (OHIO)*. A simplified classification can be addressed as following:

- Language rules specify what languages will be used in the service environment.
- Dependency rules specify the conditions that regulate business policy such as information dependency.
- Conditional rules specify the state or event that can satisfy the expected criteria.
- Event rules specify the actions should be carried out when certain condition satisfied. Event can be direct or indirect. A direct event occurs as a result of an actual activity. An indirect event occur as a result of a state, e.g., specified time.
- Derivations rules specify how information can be derived from others.
- Role and Authentication rules specify who and how to establish service provider and service consumer identities, how to assign accountability to SLA, how to allocate service components in the service life cycle, and who should manage business processes and align service with business requirements.
- Data Encryption Rules specify edge-to-edge encryption for secure and available communications.

From an implementation perspective, Identity Management provides identity credential for service providers and service consumers, offers a centralized service to locate other attributes about enterprise resources (name, presence information, organization, role, privileges, and so forth), and a centralized service to verify these credentials. A sample application of identity management is white pages services.

A governance process ensures the providers and consumers can establish and maintain appropriate dependencies and trust based on agreed policies, standards, or common practices. The process should hold the right performance levels of discoverability, interoperability, and predictability even deal with rogue information and services. The goal is to abstract the actions and concerns of different stakeholders by improving situation understanding (see chapter 9) in order to avoid conflict of actions.

8.7 SoS Views of Information Assurance

In principle, the SoS level of IA should hold the basic features such that essential service activities are protected independently (e.g., compromise of security at the User Plane does not affect functions associated with the Management Plane). Additionally, it should be able to identify potential vulnerabilities that may occur based on the collected security measures.

Figure 8.24 demonstrates a sample security architecture which provides end-to-end communications. As shown, the external portal (point of contact or PoC) can access domain separated data through three distinguished channels with different protocols. The external portal accepts SOAP requests over HTTP protocol, this approach enables the SOA architecture to reuse large parts of the pre-SOA architecture, including the HTTP (transport layer) components.

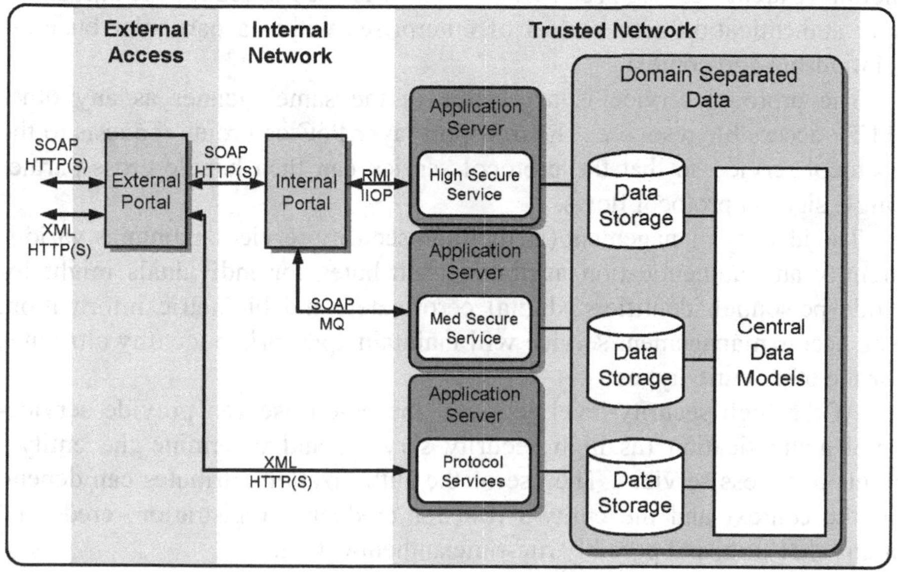

Figure 8.24. ITU-T X.805: Security architecture for systems providing end-to-end communications.

In the internal network, contact service (PoC) includes *XML firewalls and gateways*, *Web services gateways*, and other security services implementations. The internal portal (a Web services PoC) leverages trust services from within the trusted network and uses the RMI/IIOP protocol to communicate with the trust service. It also transforms the incoming SOAP/HTTP request into a SOAP/JMS request. Security services are often included within an XML/Web services gateway, with the standardization of the (SOAP-based) WSSecurity. Functionally, it performs authentication of requests and requestors, establishment and terminate a requestor's session. This internal network PoC includes routing as part of its service offering and is able to route a Web services request to the appropriate backend resource. More advanced PoCs might also be capable of transforming protocols that can expose, for example, a JMS-bound Web service internally to the external world with an HTTP binding.

The trust network is based on the validation of the incoming message, including the authentication of identities asserted in the message, and the mapping of identities and roles as established in existing business agreements with the partners.

Federation Service comprises trust and protocol services. The trust service includes logical security token services allowing the customers and providers to exchange tokens and providing detailed identity mapping on incoming identities (e.g., security tokens). It is used to reduce the amount of user authentication across a set of enterprises within a particular business relationship and context.

The protocol service is accessible in the same manner as any other HTTP-accessible resource. The transport layer PoC can route requests to the protocol service so that the protocol service can then handle cross-partner single sign-on protocol flows.

The identity management (as medium security service) maintains various identity and authentication attributes. Attributes for individuals might include personnel identifiers, digital certificates, and biometric information. The access management service will maintain appropriate identity attributes for the other entity types.

At the high security-level services, the enterprise can provide service-level authentication (as high security service) and determine the entity's rights to access services. The use of the authorization attributes can depend on the context and the entity's role for credential registration, credential status checking, and possibly run-time authentication.

These three security related services can establish appropriate IA-enforced sessions to the corresponding data storages, which contain a preapproved data image defined in the central data models.

8.8 Conclusion

An enterprise wide data and assurance management facilitates the communication of product data through the whole organization as well as links to other corporate systems such as ERM, CRM, and SCM. NCBO, by securely interconnecting people and systems independent of time or location, can support a substantially improved operational awareness, better access to business information, and dramatically shorten decision cycles. One of the challenges in developing a workable enterprise data strategy is the fragmented nature of data in today's corporate environment. The aim of Customer Data Integration is a 'single view of all aspects related to the customer' including sales, contact details, and service history. Data management includes metadata products, data warehouse DBMS, data mart DBMS, offline storage, user tools (application-building query environments, OLAP tools, ad-hoc query tools, report writers), and ETL tools.

A network-centric data management can make sharable data visible, accessible, understandable, and interoperable by capturing and registering the associated metadata and posting all data to shared spaces to provide access to all users except when constrained by security, policy, or regulations. Collaborative mechanisms allow any interoperable platform to collaborate and interoperate with authorized users. Advertising data assets requires that descriptive information (discovery metadata) be created for each asset, and that the discovery metadata be provided to a metadata cataloging capability. Enterprises are empowered to better protect assets, more effectively exploit information, more efficiently use resources, and create extended, collaborative communities to focus on the mission. Effective information security is an ongoing process requiring continual risk assessment and monitoring. It is also a very complex discipline requiring a high degree of training to become proficient. In essence, security architecture involves many computation-intensive tasks such as message signing, encryption, and certificate validation. Sending a properly signed message may be many times slower than a less secure version, and there is usually a direct inverse relationship between performance and security. Cautious planning and effective optimization techniques are necessary to ensure that a secured SOA environment will meet operational requirements.

The remainder of the chapter provided a detailed discussion of the information assurance challenges and resolution at different management layers. The discussion primarily focuses on types of attacks that highlight the situations and obstacles that might arise. The solutions also indicate potential benefits that result from applying a robust quality improvement and process management methodology.

Chapter 9

SERVICE KNOWLEDGE MANAGEMENT

The *detect-monitor-action (DMA)* model delineated in chapter 1 previewed the various business and organizational requirements. The coalescence of all pertinent technical knowledge in the previous chapters has provided supporting foundation to make the service information understandable and actionable. With an effective DMA infrastructure, policies and business mission plans are not limited to their initial specifications, but can be continuously enhanced in the fabric of the business process. In a broader definition, this capability permits organizations to bridge the knowledge gap, realizes the critical cost, time, and benefits of the offering services and can achieve the economies of scale. The center piece of realizing the claimed values comes from service knowledge management. In a heterogeneous service operation where a value chain is established upon interdependency of many different organizations, collaborated service agreements can be very sophisticated. Decision-making in a knowledge sharing environment will be heavily influenced by dynamic patterns of collaboration and associated with different levels of accountability. This requires the SOS level integration of the management processes, operational processes, and supporting processes.

This chapter illustrates the contents of service knowledge and introduces the concept of the service model and process. The objective of the modeling process is to offer integration within operational and supporting processes for managing enterprise service entities in such a way that the service knowledge can optimize the yields from the service providers' existing and future investments. The analysis and reporting sections profile available techniques to establish relationships and associations between many objects of different types, deduce valuable business knowledge, and create understandable reports. The control and enhancement section aligns the business knowledge reports as event triggers, performs futures studies, and conducts executions for continuous service and business enhancement. The SOS approach section concludes this chapter by introducing the enhanced SLM and service quality related processes and mechanisms.

9.1 Overview

In a dynamic enterprise environment where data flows are fluid, the enterprise information management has to maintain the accuracy and integrity of the base of assets, services, users, environment, and situation changes. While many platform-centric solutions can be used to evaluate and monitor the changes, their ability to address the analysis and enhancement needs at the enterprise level is limited [1].

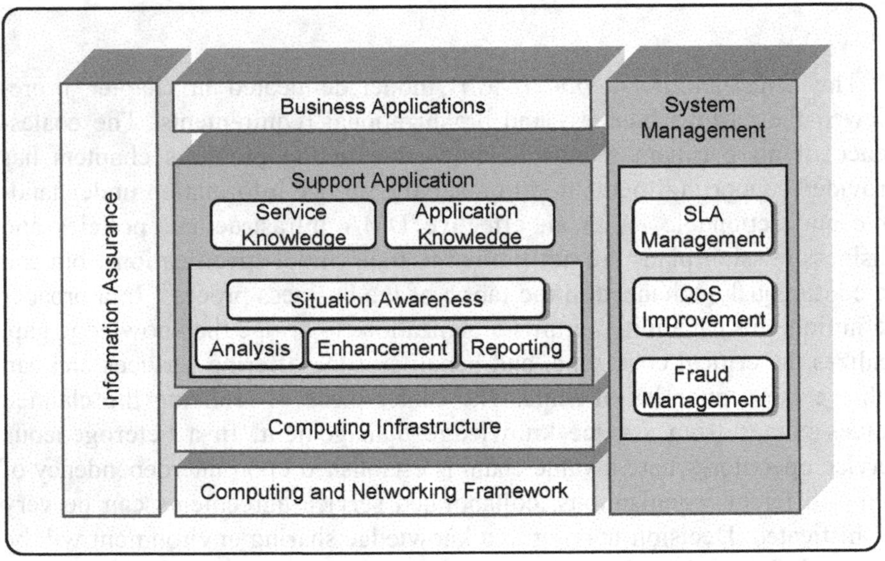

Figure 9.1. System architecture of enterprise services.

The information management in a typical enterprise is equipped with the process that can automatically organize information for pattern analysis such as classification, association rule mining, clustering, and so forth. Knowledge management identifies patterns and trends within data that go beyond simple analysis. Quality and usefulness of a network-based service in a knowledge sharing environment are heavily influenced by dynamic, self-defining patterns of information processing and collaboration. Through the use of event-based analytical algorithms, the enterprise can have the ability to identify key attributes of business processes and target opportunities.

As depicted in Figure 9.1, knowledge management is situated at the Support Application and System Management layers and offers a new form of reflexivity in relation to better service quality and decision-making. The Support Application layer encompasses service knowledge and application knowledge and are supported by the situation awareness function, which is built upon the analysis, enhancement, and reporting functions. Parts of service knowledge management are located in the System Management layer; they are SLM, QoS management, and fraud management systems. These three systems contribute essential functions in the enterprise's service assurance operations. These management functions are implemented as distributed systems and usually used by businesses and organizations to analyze market and operational results. However, they are increasingly used in the enterprise to extract knowledge and wisdom for forward looking decision-making by the enterprise customers [2].

Some strategic focus, for example, could be a narrative about what its objectives and objects are and what kinds of efforts should be put in place.

9.1.1 From Data to Knowledge, to Wisdom

In the terminology of knowledge management, the terms "data", "information", and "knowledge" are not generally interchangeable because they refer to different categories:

- *Data* is a representation of facts, concepts, or instructions in a formalized manner. Because it lacks context, data has no meaning and therefore requires further interpretation.
- *Information* is data placed in context, giving the perspective of *what*, who, when, and where. Information relates to description, definition, or perspective; it is an understanding of the relationships between data elements. Information is relatively static in time and linear in nature.
- *Knowledge* comprises strategy, practice, method, or approach (*how*), it is information with implications. Pattern embodies both a consistency and completeness of relations thereby creating its own context. Because pattern implies repeatability and predictability, knowledge has to realize their implications and to understand how the pattern will evolve over time. Patterns are seldom static.
- *Wisdom* embodies principle, insight, moral, or archetype (*why*). Wisdom arises when the foundational principles responsible for the patterns are understood. Wisdom tends to create its own context more than knowledge.

Knowledge management (KM) is a systematic process of discovering, filtering, organizing, distilling, sharing, developing, and using enterprise data to generate knowledge for the improvement of an enterprise's operational effectiveness.

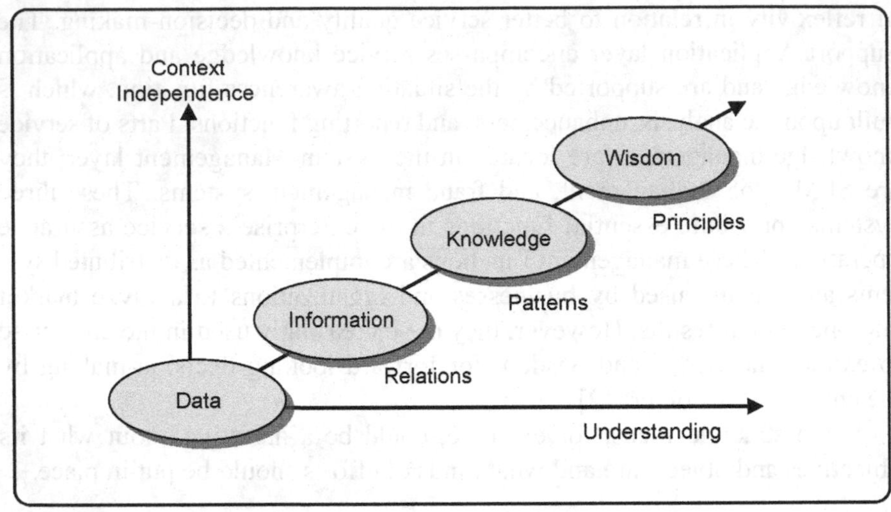

Figure 9.2. Data, information, knowledge, and wisdom.

Figure 9.2 portrays the understanding improvement based upon progressing relations, patterns, and principles analysis. This context cannot be simplified based on collections. Rather, the whole represents more than the sum of its parts and has its own synergy. To simplify future discussion, knowledge and wisdom will be exchangeable in this and the following chapter.

9.1.2 Two Orders of Knowledge Management

The basic idea of *knowledge management (KM)* refers to the ways in which organizations capture, process, share, and use information. In contrast to simply managing the flow of information, the goal of knowledge management is to leverage and disseminate information, insights, and knowledge that already exist in an organization so the stockholders (or even the service customers) will be able to seek out, utilize, and enhance their activities and processes. Furthermore, based on that experience, the stockholders and users can create new knowledge that ultimately improves organizational or service performance [3].

First-order knowledge management concerns defining, disseminating, and storing knowledge. It is a set of efforts to ensure a successful creation and sharing of knowledge. The second-order KM technology focuses on the logic and process of knowledge and the creation of strategy for knowledge accomplishment and associated knowledge indicators. The indicators introduce a new vehicle of reflexivity for strategic and tactical actions. Both of these two orders apply to the application knowledge and the service knowledge.

The application knowledge emphasis is more on the first-order knowledge management allowing knowledge sharing among experts to integrate their perspectives to better interpret and react to business conditions and problems. This can be coordinated through video-conferencing, e-mail, and other means with subject-matter experts (SMEs) to conduct analysis, recommendations, and execution.

Service knowledge focuses more on the SLO and SLA implications to the enterprise, thus they are keen on the metrics and indicator. Operations at each layer require specific knowledge to facilitate business missions. The orientation of horizontal domains represents that the needed knowledge has to come through the contributions of cross-departmental or cross-functional disciplines or rules of the business. The vertical orientation represents levels of responsibility or accountability for the totality of operations up through a given level. For instance, service trending indicators can assist service managers to predict potential service degradation. The implication for the service managers is to prevent penalties of SLA violation from happening. By measuring and tracking the services and applications, and using that set of metrics, the enterprise can align itself more closely with the business.

Figure 9.3 illustrates the knowledge model as a component of the overall assessment-decision-action loop and demonstrates how numerous individual and environmental factors interact. Among these factors, attention and working memory are considered the critical factors limiting effective situational awareness. Formulation of service models and goal-directed behavior compensated with the SME's recommendations serve as important mechanisms for overcoming these limits [4, 5].

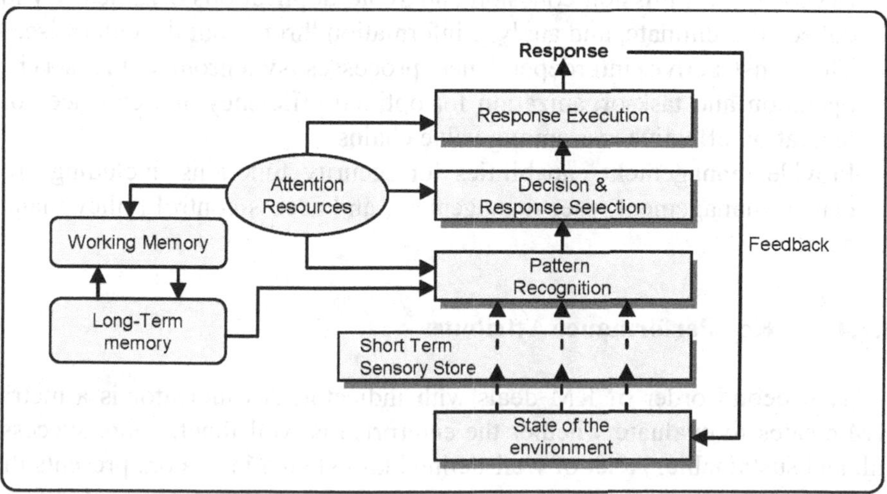

Figure 9.3. Basic information processing model.

9.1.3 Knowledge Management in NCBO

The value of KM relates directly to the effectiveness with which the knowledge can enable the decision makers to effectively envision the corresponding actions. With the network-centric, on-demand access feature in KM, every situation is addressable with the collected knowledge in a CoI. Qualitative methods which are appropriate for organizing knowledge assets can be classified as service-oriented, functional, or conceptual. The main features of KM in NCBO can be concluded as follows.

- Quickly appreciate complex information from diversified sources with near real-time data processing.
- Visibility makes the right information available from the right entities at the right place, at the right time, and in the right form. The KM can facilitate the effective analysis against this information to assess actionable conditions.
- The decision makers can promote a higher degree of business awareness by reducing information uncertainties and risks.
- Enable the creation of a common operational picture by supporting joint business plans, techniques, and procedures.
- Facilitated by the sharing power, cross-domain common framework, and hierarchy of knowledge, decision makers at all levels can "drill-down" to desirable aspects of the tactical or operational pictures regarding mission rules and the relevant status.
- Reduce errors among business silos caused by misaligned reference and misunderstanding with the cross-functional synergy.
- Leverage joint mission cohesion and avoid duplications organically with collect, disseminate, and analyze information throughout the enterprise.
- The constructive interdependence processes synchronize the service operation and task-organization for optimal efficiency and enhance collaboration effectiveness among value chains.
- Provide management capabilities for security functions, including credential management, user management, and access control policy management.

9.1.4 Key Performance Attributes

The second order of KM deals with indicator. An indicator is a metric KM creates to evaluate whether the enterprise is well functioning, successful, and sustainable. A set of well-defined knowledge indicators presents the purpose of intellectual capital as an appreciation of the service value from certain knowledge resources. Enterprise processes can be visualized by a series of indicators that reflect the actions, such as "customer profiles," "market development," and "quality assurance." The translations show how these ideas are actualized and the various elements help to refine and redefine each other [3].

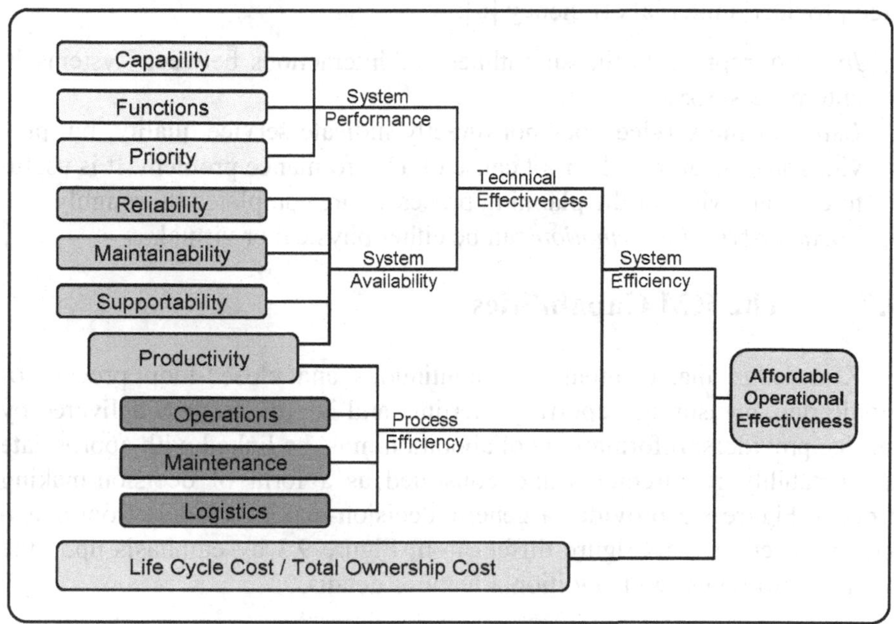

Figure 9.4. Affordable operational effectiveness.

As a service sample illustrated in Figure 9.4, *productivity* is a metric which incorporates customers' feedback, revenues, and expenditures to reflect ROI, customer satisfaction, or new customer increasing rate that can be represented for service monitoring; *performance* can be classified in the following levels: severely degraded, degraded, or normal. Performance degradations are usually related to traffic load and network resource balance and are not fault situations. The system performance, system availability, and process efficiency can be further concluded into system efficiency metric. Correlated with the inputs from life cycle cost and total ownership cost, this metric becomes an indicator to determine affable operational effectiveness indicator. A typical process of creating a useful knowledge indicator can start by

- establishing the commonality of information and functionality that is important for identifying services, especially commodity services,
- carefully controlling complexity and managing scale by dividing a business into sub-domains that focus on particular fields of interest,
- examining sub-domain dependencies in preparation for creating a set of indicators that is not constrained by existing organizational structures, and

- applying a strategic view that helps to derive tactical incremental understanding of the service behaviors that can be applicable in other contexts.

Other than the previous indicators, these are from the perspective of service provider's internal efficiency [6]:

1. *Integrity* represents the smoothness of interactions between systems in enterprise's SoS.
2. *Usage* of the service does not directly indicate service quality, but provides an indicator to the root cause of a performance problem. It is useful to evaluate whether the planning processes are completed thoroughly.
3. *Location-based information* can be either physical or virtual.

9.2 The KM Capabilities

Knowledge management is a continuous and closed-loop process of monitoring, measuring, reporting, alerting, and improving QoS delivered by service providers. Information collaboration must be linked with appropriate accountability requirements and construed as a form of decision-making process. Figure 9.5 provides a generic decision-making models from a system perspective. This figure differs from Figure 9.3 by emphasis upon the situation awareness with additional features details.

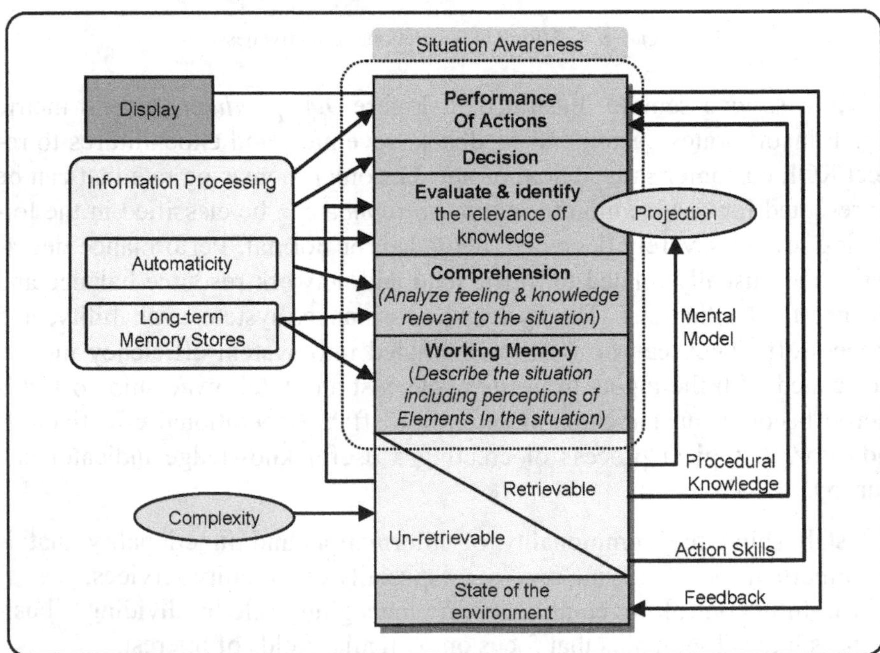

Figure 9.5. Generic decision-making model centered on the situation awareness process.

9.2.1 Define and Align Business Goals

To create an effective KM system, the first step is to define formal organizational, executive relationships, and operational responsibilities in accordance with mission requirements. This includes the definition of the operational environment, or *area of operations (AO)* in the military term. An AO is the area where a decision maker has authority to conduct operations in.

The enterprise's strategic goals and purposes must be fully appreciated and these targets must be in the alignment with the enterprise data model, *lines of business (LOB)*, processes, and strategies. Additionally, the AO also includes the enterprise's customers and stakeholders, as well as the relationships with value-chain partners. A strategic information assurance policy can include multilevel authorization rules for collaboration and information sharing. Such rules can help the enterprise to establish a sound collaborative foundation to reflect organizational structure and community vocabulary. To allow future expansion be more effective, knowledge dissemination strategy should support a dynamic mechanism for the enterprise to update collaboration patterns and adjust procedures or organization.

9.2.2 Establish Collaborative Data Sharing Mechanisms

Collaboration mechanism includes human- and machine-interactions. Human-interaction relies on collaboration tools and visualization techniques to conduct remote meetings in a virtual space. The machine-interaction is a flow-through system that automatically incorporates KM capabilities for information analysis. Collaborative data sharing can enhance the decision-making but the process must be continuous. It should include networking capability to link all separated participants.

In a NCBO environment, the data sharing capability must be a role based, adaptable, and tailorable. The networking feature must embed the capability for distributed, collaborative, systematic, on-demand, and flexibility for the creation and revision of executable plans. In order to develop a common understanding of problems and goals, the collaboration mechanism must provide access, collation, and display of information including indication of contextual relevance. The human-interaction mechanism must allow the users to schedule recurring meetings, notify participants of a meeting, as well as de-conflict schedules to support joint tasks.

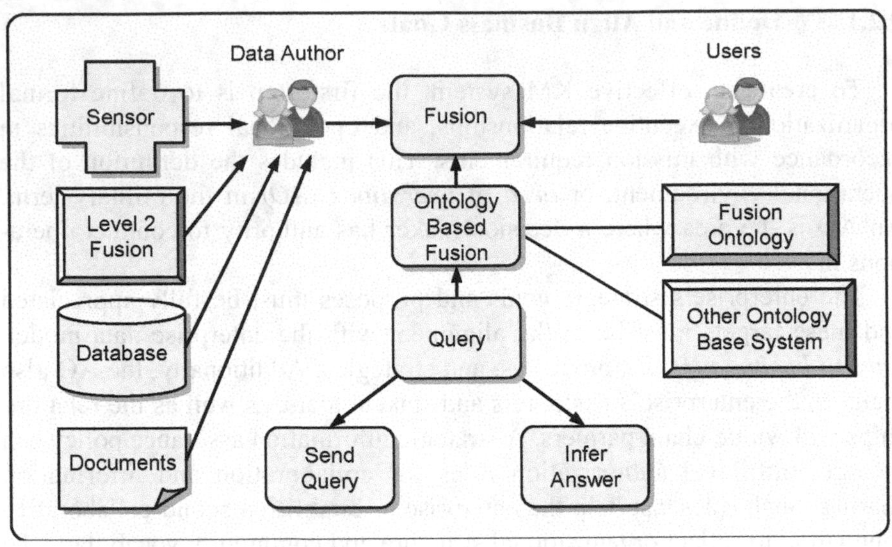

Figure 9.6. Fuse use case.

Figure 9.6 depicts a sample use case that comprises data fusion with human-interaction and information flow through. The approach to both situation awareness and data fusion requires the use of formal ontology to describe the fundamental events, objects, and relations between the situation's domain and logical rules. These rules should define ways of fusing information and identifying higher-order relations relevant to the situation.

9.2.3 Monitor and Identify the Environment Effects

Upon the establishment of the collaborative data sharing function, the enterprise can measure progress toward the business goals and establish a problem-solving framework. The monitoring function can be seen from either the service or human perspective. From a service perspective, this function should specify selection criteria and assess alternatives in order to decisively control operational situations. The details should include automation in exchange, fusion, and understanding of information. Additionally, the monitoring capability should interact effectively with collaborative tools to track and measure progress toward results. Any computing or networking resources directly or indirectly involve with the enterprise services should be monitored in accordance with the SLA and SLO with the techniques discussed in chapter 6. Log, audit, and generates report about the service health must be periodically reviewed. With the detection and alerting features, the service operators can either reinforce service activities or intervene to improve progress where needed. From human-interaction perspective, the collaborative tools provide synchronization between multiple applications allowing simultaneous user interaction. The traceability of using collaborative process are maintained and monitored for accountability. Typically, a combined service overlay is created as the action references. With description of crucial tactical significance, such reference can be used by the next phase of the process.

Sample situation awareness ontology is shown in Figure 9.7. This simplified relationship chart signify the objects located in a particular region or physical units where the attributes possessed by the objects are in a particular aggregate and grouping fashion. While objects may have location information, the aggregations of them do not directly have locations; such information must be inferred from the relationship between the objects and the aggregate [7].

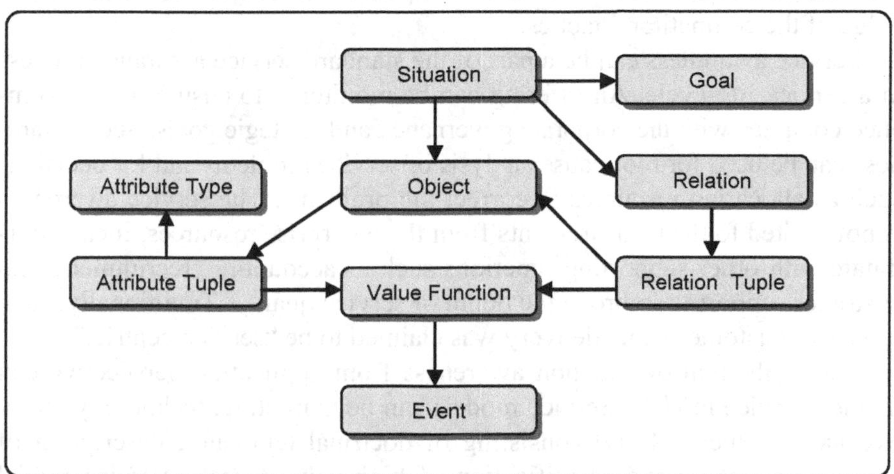

Figure 9.7. Sample core ontology.

9.2.4 Share Situational Understanding

Situation awareness is about a real-time process of event-based information from evolving situations and an attempt to understand this information. The awareness implies the ability to identify relations involving multiple objects within a situation which may have particular relevance to the phenomena or activity matched to predefined conditions or objectives. The analytical processes for establishing situation awareness necessarily involves data fusion. As data fusion is the process by which data from multiple sources are combined to produce new enhanced information [8].

Sharing understanding with an array of participants can lead to better collective understanding for higher quality decision-making. The process may involve the usage of geospatial and real-time displays of data from multiple sources in a fused format. For instance, key service performance metrics of critical service components can be made visible to the service operator. A notification feature is useful for any unusual signs or threshold violations in order to respond to threats or problems.

9.2.5 Evaluate the Situations and Behaviors

The situation awareness information from the managed resources can help the service operator to evaluate whether the offering is useful, worthwhile to continue, or additional features are needed. On the other hand, the service user can use similar but different situation awareness information to evaluate business threats from their competitors in conjunction with knowledge of the competitors' tactics.

Service awareness can be a part of the standard service assurance process in a service life-cycle. An offering can be monitored to ensure the performance complies with the corporate governance and strategic goals. Such awareness can be used for root-cause analysis of service problems and for decisions such as allocating resources to correct the problems. The service awareness is not limited to the measurements from the enterprise resources; it can coordinate with other supporting functions such as accounting, recruitment, and customer support to improve the depth of service quality. Traditionally, such proactive customer value delivery was claimed to be "service-centric."

The evaluation of situation awareness from application perspective can include service models. Service models can be marketing, technology, process, and products (R&D) consisting of doctrinal templates, description of competitor tactics, and identification of high-value targets. Service model templates are graphical representations of the product behaviors and performance patterns and dispositions that are undergoing by a service operator. It is important to note that the service model templates representation may not have physical limitations because this is for service analysis and reproduction, as will be discussed in section 9.3.2.

9.2.6 Course of Action for Control and Enhancement

Modern technologies permit the enterprise to configure, monitor, reconfigure, and manage distributed services remotely through a centralized interface. The integration of service knowledge and application knowledge opens the door for the decision makers to increase the controllability by offering real-time resource assignment and adjustment in any business missions. By increasing the situation awareness of the enterprise operations, knowledge, skills, and abilities, individuals and teams can be empowered through effective collaborative command and control tools.

A *course of action (COA)* is a detailed plan for the accomplishment of a mission, including the arrangement and deployment of service resources both spatially and temporally. The input to the COA generation process is hypothesized procedures sufficient to support the needed scenarios most effectively. After performing situation evaluation using the reports from the previous phases, the decision makers can combine these reports with information from other hypothesized COAs, to select appropriate/alternative COAs. The COA can be used for live or virtual constructive simulations and training. Ongoing feedback exchanged among the participants (see section 9.6) can assist the enterprise to improve procedures and schedules as needs. The potential refinements of objective, situation, threat, and process will surely offer the dynamic nature of future situation management.

9.3 Service Model Framework

Service models can facilitate the automation of data collection and process for analysis. A service model provides an intelligent structure to organize the enterprise information and distribute them to support other service management applications. The advantage of a modeling approach is its ability to incorporate enterprise rules, policies, procedures, and experiences from SMEs to tailor service assurance requirements. Different from the traditional modeling, the NCBO service models equip with actionable functions collaborating relevant information from different parts of CoI resources to make sensible recommendations to the service customers and service operators.

9.3.1 Service Modeling

The service model can be seen as a set of hierarchical service components and relationships between these service components. The graph structure facilitates the implementation of KM algorithms which are built into the service components. In the hierarchical graph, the service component is specified in a systematic manner and denoted as a graphical node, a directed arc represents a relationship between two components. The advantages of a NCBO service model are:

1. Business objectives dictate the content of the service and its operations. The service model possesses the flexibility to reflect any (e.g., market or value-chain member's) changes which come across as a result of new opportunity or situation changes.

2. Technologies revolution constantly adds new elements to competitive enterprise and influences the products, processes, or procedures of CoI operations. The service model can dynamically adopt changes from supporting technologies or integration technologies.
3. Service model can bridge physical resources to a logical (service) representation. Often time services exist as functions in an abstract form; the translation of such features into physical components allows the service operators and customers to aggregate their physical assets into higher level features to make cross-functional collaboration feasible.
4. Logical presentation of the service model detaches physical limitation thus allows the same or similar service to create "service templates" for reusability. The proliferation of wireless services has created a need for the enterprises to create similar configuration in different missions. Duplicating services from a template and focusing only on the customization of feature discrepancies can effectively reduce labor intensive efforts in the fulfillment process and achieve high ROI.
5. The NCBO service model offers a versatile framework with embedded actionable functions. It provides a valuable presentation combing knowledge and process that can easily integrate into all life cycle of both SoS and FoS solutions.

There are two fundamental relationships in the service model. They are dependence and containment. Containment relationship comes from the concept of the traditional configuration and inventory management. It delineates the relationship between two physical components or between a physical and a logical component, but not between two logical components. To avoid computational dead-lock the models should be acyclic, for instance, if A depends on B and B depends on C, then C cannot depend on A. A similar acyclic restriction also applies to the containment relationship.

In complex knowledge calculation, temporal factor is always a key element for situation awareness gathering. However, the connotation of temporal significance can be carefully addressed with event-driven models without involving specific temporal conditions.

As shown in Figure 9.8, a solid arrow indicates a dependence relationship or impact relationship. The containment relationship is represented by dotted arrow. For instance, component A is the parent of C and D, thus "depends" on component C and D. Operational states or performances of C or D influence the operational state or performance of A. The notation is $A \rightarrow C$ and $A \rightarrow D$. The reverse dependency relationship is the impact relationship, as shown in the figure, A depends on C, implies that C impacts A.

Additionally, physical component D, contains a physical component E and a logical component F. An example of the containment relationship is a host computer that contains (has) an Ethernet interface card. A use of the containment relationship is in root-cause analysis for identification of the exact location of a resource.

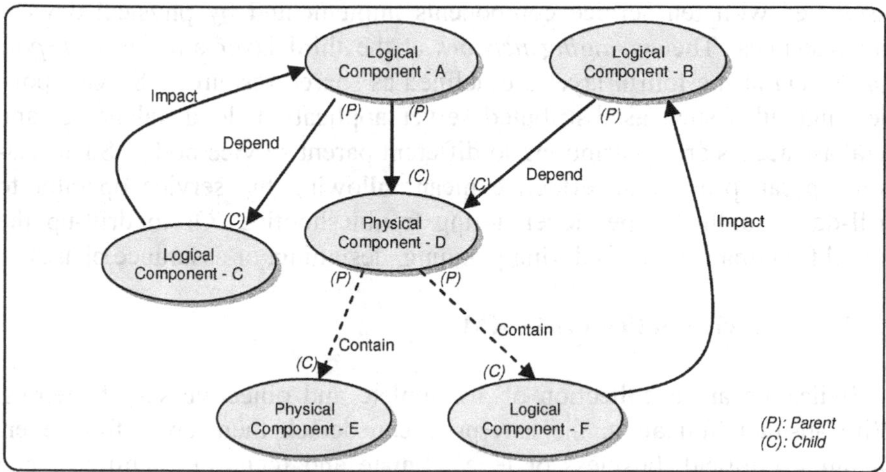

Figure 9.8. Anatomy of a component.

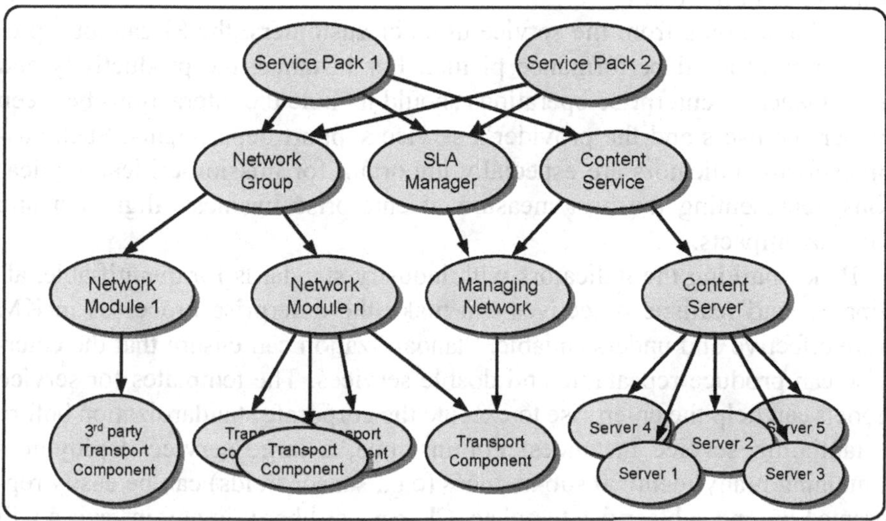

Figure 9.9. Sample service model containing managed network, managing network, and contents.

A service graph is not limited to a tree structure. Whereas a tree only allows a one-to-many relationship, the service model allows many-to-many, many-to-one, and one-to-many relationships. Figure 9.9 demonstrates a sample service model with two composite service packs, where the first one encompasses three services, and the second pack contains two services. These three services are further decomposed into four subsystems that are associated with ten service components implemented by physical devices and resources. The *managing network* at the third layer and the *transport component* at the fourth layer are defined as shared resources. Service policies and rules such as distributed server application, load balancing, and database access are contributing to different parent service nodes. Such relationship can provide an effective means allowing the service operator to drill-down to the proper level during troubleshooting. Or to drill-up the model for impact analysis during planning, designing, or assurance phases.

9.3.2 Service Indicators in KM

Indicators are a collection of a complete and objective set of metrics. With abstract indicators, the enterprise can detach themselves from ever-changing political, business or legal climate and focus on significant and achievable business measures. A *service indicator (SI)* is organized around outcomes, instead of the specific tasks required to reach the outcome. Well defined SI can eliminate bleary responsibility and avoid unnecessary finger-pointing and mistrust.

Without inputs from the service users or customers, the SI cannot represent an end-to-end performance picture. For instance, the productivity and performance of enterprise operations should include the interactions between the service users and the provider's service support departments. Such customer-focus indicators are especially important for mission-critical applications, representing the best measure of enterprise business alignment and potential impacts.

Benchmarking the indicators with industry standards for quantifiable, attainable, and realistic objectives can make the enterprise processes in KM more effective and understandable. Standardization can ensure that the enterprise can produce repeatable and doable services. The templates for service models can help the enterprise to execute the corporate standardization before instantiating service instances. For instance, a large service deployment containing many identical sub-services (e.g., sensor fields) can be easily represented by one sub-service template. Changes at liberty in any instances will eventually prevent the template from holding the representative relationship.

Additionally, the SI must be designed to hold appropriate levels of accountability in accordance with the organizational hierarchy. The indicator should by itself contain actionable metrics or a pointer to actionable metric(s). Although automated process is a key driver of service modeling, actionable indicators have to be process-focus instead of automation-focus. This is because automation has no direct relationship with efficiency factor that can satisfying bottom-line requirements.

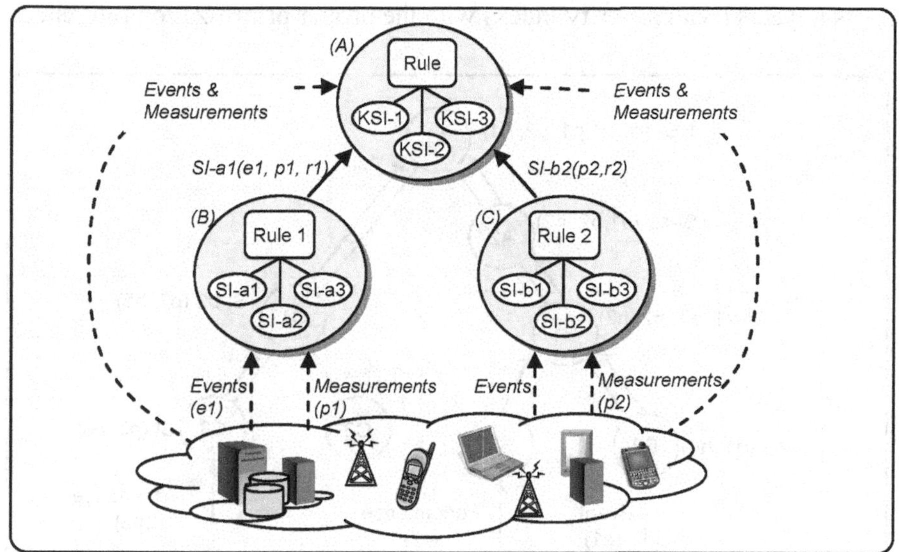

Figure 9.10. Anatomy of a service instance.

Fundamentally, an SI group provides a summary of the state, condition, and process encompassed by a service component. Every group has a relationship with their upstream and downstream counter-parties making scalability and suitability critical to a large service deployment. Figure 9.10 depicts a simplified anatomy of wireless service components where events and measurements generated from the managed networks are used to create SI's by the service elements. The SI's are further aggregated into *key service indicators (KSIs)* and used by service operators or customers' management at the top level of the model.

As shown in Figure 9.10, each component is responsible for their decision-making by gathering information from the subtending children components and producing indicators to the upper level elements. In this example, component B receives an event (e.g., alarm, e1) and a performance measurement (e.g., bandwidth, p1). It then triggers the rule engine (with rule r1) to produce a service indicator SI-a1 (e1, p1, r1) and propagates the indicator to the next level. In the same instance, a performance related indicator form service elements C is also propagated to element A, SI-b2 (p2, r2). Based on the two incoming indicators, the service element A produces a collaborated KSI in the form of KSI-1(e1, p1, p2, r3). Note that p1 and p2 are performance measurements thus they are periodically collected by the service elements (in this case, element B and C respectively). The rules can be defined for mathematical calculation, conditional checking, or hybrid with or without weight metrics. The service situation awareness can then be derived from assess impacts (with severity index) with the proper prioritization references.

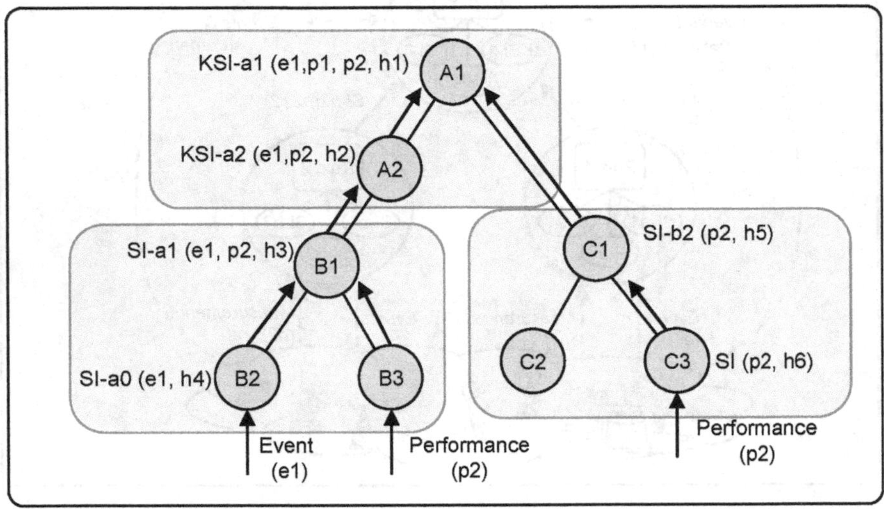

Figure 9.11. CSI propagation.

The SI process in each service element can involve complex calculations. The service instance in Figure 9.10 is redrawn with the form of service model in Figure 9.11. The service component A has two logical service objects, A1 and A2, each is responsible for a KSI calculation via a predetermined handler (a rule-based computing process, h1 and h2). Similarly, service element B has three service objects, B1, B2, and B3; service element C has three service objects C1, C2, and C3. With the indexes and weights are computed, a collaborated indicator KSI-a1 is obtained.

For instance, failure, error, hang, latency, delay, volume, availability from computing, and networking resources can provide an objective set of SIs. The model-based knowledge processing uses historical analysis as well as event instances to benchmark and alert the operator when the managed resource behaves abnormally. The final representations can be collaborated among all concern stakeholders, and preferably presented with *common operational pictures (COP)*. The following section will address the analytical methodologies in service knowledge management.

9.4 Service Data Analysis

To accomplish enterprise level knowledge management, the networks and systems have to be capable of sharing information across multiple geographical, operational, and organizational boundaries. In time of mission sensitive situations the awareness information must be prioritized and relevant.

The transformation of information into knowledge is a critical aspect of the collaborating and sharing process [10]. Cross-impact analysis intends to reveal perceptions of how current events may interact with each other to be used in forecasting. It provides an analytical approach for the operator to assess probabilities in view of judgments about potential interactions among assets and customers. This feature helps the provider to establish a relevant set of metrics to perform business alignment for the best practice.

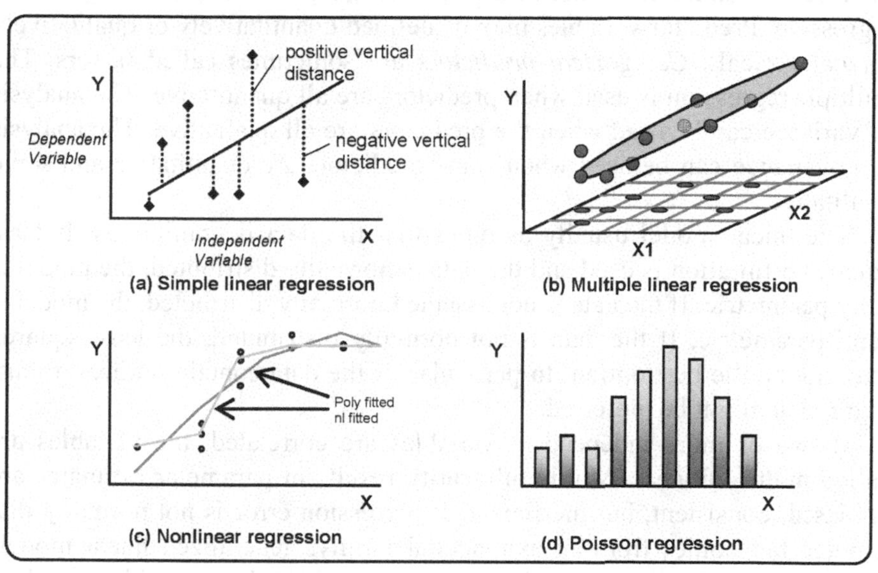

Figure 9.12. Four sample regression charts.

The following sections portray some popular techniques in analyzing information from the network-centric service environment.

9.4.1 Regression

In statistics, regression analysis is used to model relationships between random variables, determine the magnitude of the relationships between variables, and can be used to make predictions based on the models. Regression analysis models the relationship between one or more response variables (also called dependent variables, explained variables, predicted variables, or *regressands*) (usually named Y), and the *predictors* (also called *independent variables*, explanatory variables, control variables, or *regressors*) usually named X1, X2, and Xp. If there is more than one response variable, it is then called multivariate regression.

Figure 9.12 shows four sample regress charts. Figure 9.12(a) and (b) display the Simple linear regression and multiple linear regressions, where Simple linear regression refers to a regression on two variables and multiple regressions refers to a regression on more than two variables. Linear regression assumes the best estimate of the response is a linear function of some parameters (though not necessarily linear on the predictors). If the relationship between the variables being analyzed is not linear in parameters, as shown in Figure 9.12(c), a number of non-linear regression techniques may be used to obtain a more accurate regression. Figure 9.12(d) shows Poisson regression. Predictor variables may be defined quantitatively or qualitatively (or categorical). *Categorical predictors* are sometimes called factors. The multiple regression is used when predictors are all quantitative. The analysis of variance can be used when the predictors are all qualitative. The analysis of covariance can be used when some predictors are quantitative and some qualitative.

The linear model usually assumes that the data is continuous. If least squares estimation is used and the data is normally distributed, the model is fully parametric. If the data is not assumed normally distributed, the model is semi-parametric. If the data is not normally distributed, the least squares may not be the best option. In particular, if the data contain outliers, robust regression might be preferred.

If two or more independent variables are correlated, the variables are called multi-collinear. Multi-collinearity results in parameter estimates are unbiased, consistent, but inefficient. If regression error is not normally distributed but comes from an exponential family, generalized linear models can be used. For example, if the response variable takes only binary values (e.g., a Boolean or Yes/No variable), logistic regression is preferred. The outcome of such regression is a function that describes how the probability of a given event (e.g., probability of getting "yes") varies with the predictors.

"Maximum likelihood" can estimate the parameters of a regression model rather well for large samples. For small amounts of data when the estimates can have high variance or bias, Bayesian methods can be used to estimate regression models. This is because the *Bayesian methods* have the advantages of using all available information, thus they are exact, not asymptotic.

9.4.2 Correlation

Correlation is also called correlation coefficient which indicates the strength and direction of a linear relationship between two random variables. It refers to the departure of two variables from independence, although correlation does not imply causality. In this broad sense there are several coefficients, measuring the degree of correlation that is adapted to the nature of data. The best known is the Pearson product-moment correlation coefficient, which is obtained by dividing the covariance of the two variables by the product of their standard deviations. First introduced by Francis Galton, positive linear correlations between 1000 pairs of numbers and are graphed on the lower left, and their correlation coefficients listed on the upper right of Figure 9.13(a). Each square in the upper right corresponds to its mirror-image square in the lower left, the "mirror" being the diagonal of the whole array. Each set of points correlates maximally with itself, as shown on the diagonal (all correlations = +1).

While *Pearson correlation* indicates the strength of a linear relationship between two variables, the value may not be sufficient to evaluate this relationship, especially in the case where the assumption of normality is incorrect. Figure 9.13(b) shows four sets of data [11] where four y variables have the same mean (7.5), standard deviation (4.12), correlation (0.81) and regression line (y = 3 + 0.5x). Figure (i) seems to be distributed normally. Figure (ii) displays a non-linear relationship between the two variables thus

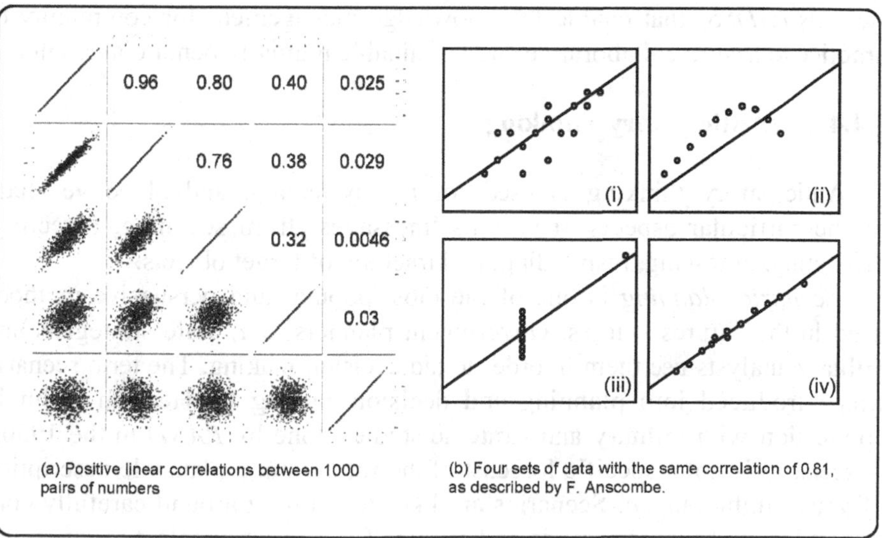

Figure 9.13. Correlation.

Pearson correlation coefficient is not relevant. Figure (iii) shows one outlier is enough to produce a high correlation coefficient; even the relationship is not linear. Figure (iv) displays a perfect linear relationship with one except outlier that exerts enough to lower the correlation coefficient. These samples reveal the fact that the correlation coefficient can serve as a summary statistic but in many cases not sufficient to replace an individual examination of the data.

9.4.3 Trend Analysis

Trend analysis observes and registers the past performance of a certain factor and forecast it into the future. It involves analysis of two groups of trends: quantitative, mainly based on statistical data, and qualitative, these are at large concerned with social, institutional, organizational, and political patterns.

In the quantitative trend analysis data is plotted along a time axis. Short term forecasting is normally quite simple; a more elaborated curve that uses times series analysis can often reveal surprising data patterns. It is one of the most demanding and creative methods in futures studies.

The game theory studies decisions is another popular trend analysis tool. It is made in an environment where various players interact, therefore is also called adaptive role-playing. Game theory studies choice of optimal behavior when costs and benefits of each option are not fixed, but depend upon the choices of other individuals. The efforts require *group decision support systems (GDSS)* that enable the knowledge management for community of practice to assure collaborative and sustainable mutually beneficial results.

9.4.4 Anticipatory Thinking

Anticipatory thinking is used for the systematic and objective study of the particular aspects of various 'messages' from scanning, detecting, projecting, assessing, responding, and tracking of target objects.

Scenario planning is one of the most popular and persuasive methods used in the futures studies. Government planners, corporate strategists and military analysts use them in order to aid decision-making. The term scenario was introduced into planning and decision-making by Herman Kahn in connection with military and strategic studies done by *RAND* in the 1950s. A scenario is not a specific forecast of the future, but a plausible description of what might happen. Scenarios are like stories built around carefully constructed plots based on trends and events. They assist in selection of strategies, identification of possible futures, making decision makers aware of uncertainties and opening up their imagination and initiating learning processes. One of the key strengths of the scenario process is its influence on the way of thinking of its participants.

Causal layered analysis (CLA), developed by Sohail Inayatullah, focuses on "opening up" the present and past to create alternative futures rather than on developing a picture of particular future. It is concerned with the vertical dimension of futures studies, with the layers of analysis. CLA assumes the problem, solution, and actors (see section 10.4) are correlated in multilayer relationships. The key principle of the method is using and integrating different ways of knowing. There are a number of benefits arising from the application of this method. Causal layered analysis increases the range and richness of scenarios; leads to inclusion of different ways of knowing among participants in workshops; appeals to wider range of individuals through incorporation of non-textual and artistic elements.

Morphological analysis (MA) is a technique developed by Fritz Zwicky. It was designed for multidimensional, non-quantifiable problems where causal modeling and simulation do not function well or at all. This approach addresses seemingly non-reducible complexity. Using the technique of *cross-consistency assessment (CCA)*, the system allows the reduction of possible solutions through the elimination of the illogical solution combinations in a grid box. MA has been employed for the identification of new product opportunities. The technique involves mapping options in order to attain an overall perspective of possible solutions [12].

9.4.5 General Linear Model

The *general linear model (GLM)* is a statistical linear model. The *basic analysis of variance (ANOVA)* model assumes that every observation is comprised of a deterministic model for its mean (expectation) and one or more error components. The mean model is a decomposition of the experimentally controlled variables into factors and their levels. It is a collection of statistical models and their associated procedures which compare means by splitting the overall observed variance into different parts. The models can be classified as fixed, random-effects, and mixed:

1. *Fixed-effects model* assumes that the data come from normal populations which differ in their means.
2. *Random-effects model* assumes that the data delineate a hierarchy of different populations whose differences are constrained by the hierarchy.
3. *Mixed model* describes situations where both fixed and random effects are present.

And depending on the number of treatments and the way they are applied to the subjects, ANOVA can be divided into the following types:

- One-Way ANOVA is used to test for differences among three or more independent groups where a separate random sample is taken from each population (one population per treatment level).
- One-Way ANOVA for repeated measures is used when the subjects are dependent groups.
- *2×2 (read: two by two) ANOVA*, the most common type of Factorial Analysis of Variance, is used when the experimenter wants to study the effects of two or more treatment variables. The advantage of this design is that multiple variables and their interaction effects can be tested at the same time.

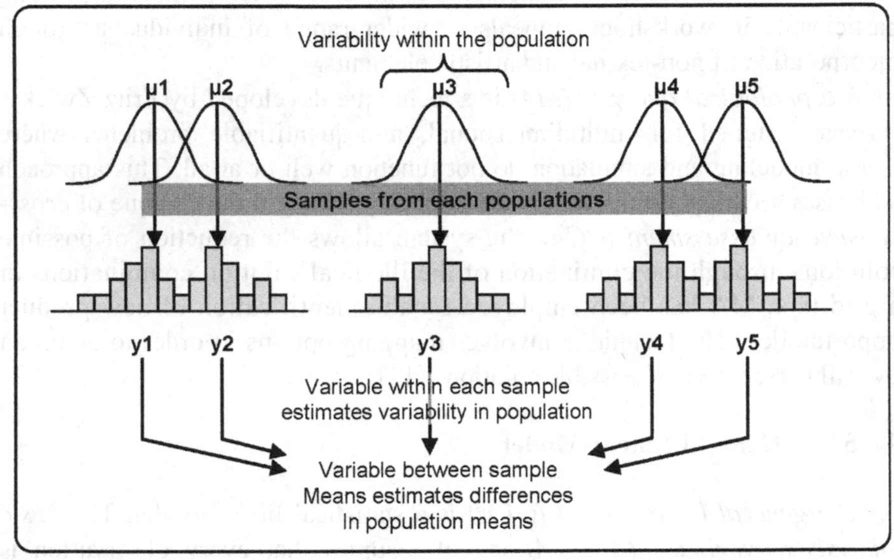

Figure 9.14. Variabilitys.

Multivariate analysis of variance (MANOVA) is simply an ANOVA with several dependent variables. Hypothesis tests with the general linear model can be made in two ways: multivariate and mass-univariate. Variability is illustrated in Figure 9.14 where samples are collected from each managed pointes and variations are derived from the means of measurements.

9.4.6 ANOVA Gage Repeatability and Reproducibility

ANOVA gage repeatability and reproducibility (ANOVA Gage R&R) uses *ANOVA* to assess a measurement system. A measurement system comprises measurement devices (machine) and operators (people). It measures the variability induced in measurements from the measurement system and compares it with the observed variability to determine the viability of the measurement system.

Repeatability is the ability of the device to provide consistent results from the same operator to measure the same object. Reproducibility is a measure of the variability induced by different operators to measure the same object with the same device. ANOVA Gage R&R is an important tool within the Six Sigma methodology (see section 9.6.2.1).

9.4.7 Chi-Square Test of Independence and Fits

Any statistical hypothesis test can be satisfied as chi-square test whereas the test statistic has a chi-square distribution and the null hypothesis. The probability distribution of the test statistic can be made to approximate a chi-square distribution as closely as desired by making the sample size large enough.

The chi-square distribution is a special case of the gamma distribution with one integer parameter to specify the number of degrees of freedom. In probability theory and statistics, the chi-square distribution is one of the theoretical probability distributions most widely used in inferential statistics. This is because under reasonable assumptions, easily calculated quantities can be proven to have distributions which approximate to the chi-square distribution if the null hypothesis is true.

The best-known situations in which the chi-square distribution is used are the common chi-square tests for goodness of fit of an observed distribution to a theoretical one, and of the independence of two criteria of classification of qualitative data.

9.5 Mission Data Fusions

Mission data fusions impose an intelligent structure on knowledge content, to locate and increase the accuracy and utility of the overall enterprise missions or services.

9.5.1 Level Two Fusion

Level two fusion aggregates individual entities or elements, analyze those aggregations, and resolve conflicts. This fusion level captures or derives events or actions from the information and interprets them in context with other information.

For instance, in an outdoor sports event such as bicycle race, terrain information supplies an important context for the service providers to deploy proper health care and security surveillance systems. The layout of terrain is a determining factor in the arraying of service points and the structuring of *courses of action (COAs)* in emergency situations. Combining information about terrain features with hypotheses about traffic conditions can lead to inferences of the most optimized routes and the least vulnerable path to the competitors [13].

9.5.1.1 Bayesian Decision Theory

The use of multiple sensors in data fusion applications can produce conflicting data. *Bayesian decision theory* is one of the most common techniques employed in level two data fusion to support the synthesis of meaningful information for guiding human decision-making. By consolidating and interpreting overlapping data provided by several data collectors, the approach adopts a probabilistic model of uncertain system states to determine conditional probabilities from a priori evidence. These revised probabilities are called "a posteriori probabilities." Without a probabilistic means of fusing data, data collectors are likely to produce only a binary "yes–no" response on the basis of the isolated, internal classification processes, this is known as "hard decision." Probabilistic data fusion generates can generate "soft decisions" with a greater measure of confidence by quantifying the uncertainty behind each sensor decision. Figure 9.15 shows the increased confidence level by soft-decision sensors.

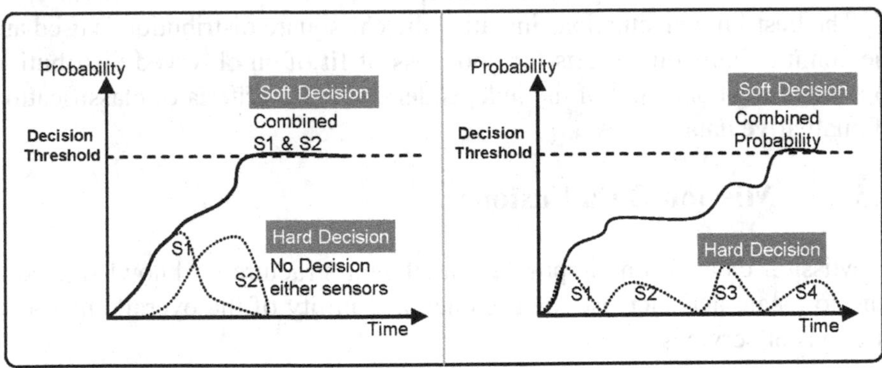

Figure 9.15. Increased confidence level made possible by soft-decision sensors.

Bayesian theorem implementation in data fusion is limited by its inability to depict the level of uncertainty in a particular sensor state. Uncertainty can come in many forms, including incompleteness, imprecision, inconsistency, and ambiguity (indistinguishable) to prevent the system to ensure consistency in a collection of interrelated propositions. The other drawback is its heavy computer processing and memory requirements [9].

9.5.1.2 Dempster–Shafer Evidential Reasoning

Dempster–Shafer evidential reasoning (DSER) is explored to deal with data uncertainty. DSER employs a confidence interval-of-certainty to replace the single-point probability of the Bayesian method. One major advantage of DSER is that sensor data can contain varying levels of abstraction; each sensor is allowed to contribute information at its own level of detail. Additionally, hypotheses do not have to be mutually exclusive, and the probabilities involved can be either empirical or subjective.

Because DSER sensor data can be reported at varying levels of abstraction, a priori knowledge can be presented in varying formats. It is also possible to use any relevant data that may exist as long as the distribution is parametric. Applications of the Dempster–Shafer method demands more computational capabilities than the Bayesian single-point probability method. Additional drawback includes its reliance on the basic assumption that two pieces of evidence must have the same population universe.

9.5.1.3 Neural Networks

An artificial neural network can be perceived as a web-like, information processing structure that emulates the human brain's own learning and decision-making processes. Neural networks require a "learning" period to establish and test the patterns or rules that will guide the system. The learning process in a typical multilayer neural network is a simple error feedback. One major advantage over Bayesian and DSER methods is in the neural network's capability to process incoming data streams simultaneously rather than sequentially. It uses many simple elements called neurons (or processing nodes) to collect and correlate information. They are connected by synapses that ascribe a weight to each neuron's output and then forward it, in a unidirectional path, to the next set of neurons. This is shown in Figure 9.16, the multilayer architecture of the perception incorporates four main functions: input/output (data transfer in and out of the computer), processing (executing specific information-handling tasks), memory (storing information), and the connections between the neurons (providing for information flow and control). A neuron may have many inputs, but it has only a single output. The three defining elements of a neural network are the following:

- The neuron's characteristics – the equations that define what a neuron will do.
- The learning rule – the guide as to how the weights between various neurons will change according to the stimuli they receive.
- The network topology – the manner in which the neurons are connected.

A neural network can be used to improve computerized traffic surveillance and automatic incident detection. Some most modern neural networks employ a topology that is capable of self-learning through a preprogrammed learning algorithm.

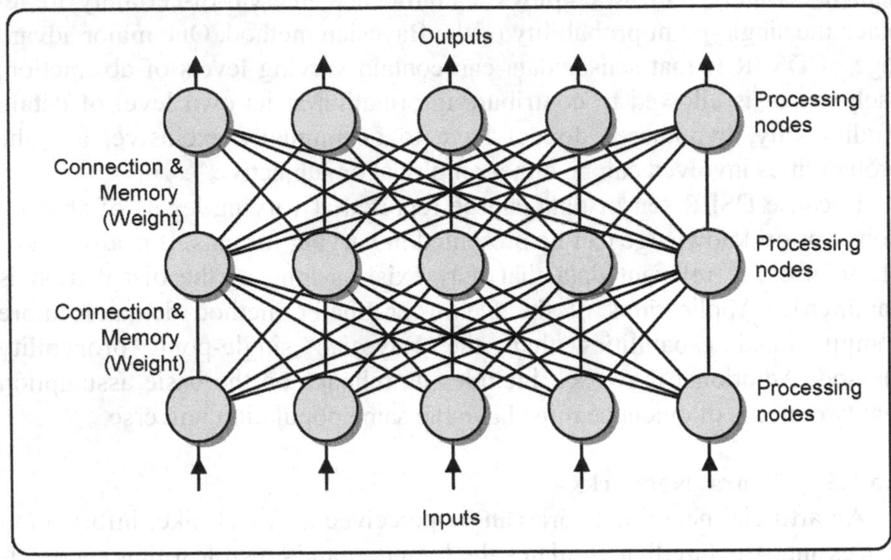

Figure 9.16. Original neural network system architecture.

9.5.2 Level Three Data Fusion

The role of level three data fusion processes is to transform high-volume, raw sensor data into low-volume, high-level information. Knowledge-based expert systems predominate in these instances because they can emulate the behavior of a human expert working in a well defined domain of knowledge. However, before any high-level information can be generated, the raw data from level one fusion must be preprocessed or association. The meaning of these sensor data can be derived with probabilistic methods, such as Bayesian decision theory, Dempster–Shafer evidential reasoning, or Neural networks.

Level three fusion interprets events and actions gathered from the managed environment by the predefined rules to determine the objectives of the monitored object, their pattern, and predict future actions and affects.

9.5.2.1 Complex Event Processing

Complex event processing (CEP) is a foundational technology for detecting and managing events that happen in event driven enterprises. CEP can assist the service operators to understand the events in the enterprise revealing what is happening, or going to happen, and provide techniques to help in taking action [14, 15].

Events can be organized into hierarchies, called event hierarchies. "Event hierarchy" is an application concept. Part of CEP is about the technology to organize event clouds into hierarchies in real time. This technology involves precisely defining patterns of events, detecting instances of patterns, and modeling causal, timing, and aggregation relationships between events.

Classifying events into levels in a hierarchy can assist the service operators to achieve understanding of what's happening in the enterprise. Figure 9.17 shows an example in which the event layers are: 1) subsystem events, such as messages from local service module; 2) system events resulting from use of individual system, such as database activities; 3) SoS events from across-application actions, such as transactions analysis for the managed enterprise; and 4) business process events, value-chain impact analysis, or over-arching collaborative analysis. Event patterns are used to create higher level events from the cloud of new events that is continuously appearing on the managing infrastructure.

The metrics can be low-level physical-oriented data or high-level logical intelligence, depending upon the role and viewpoint in the information hierarchy. It can be changed from moment to moment while the target system is in operation. CEP is used to create new events, like transaction views, that infer information from other events.

Event analysis can be conducted either *top–down* or *bottom–up*. The high-level events are closest to decision-making and their significance is most

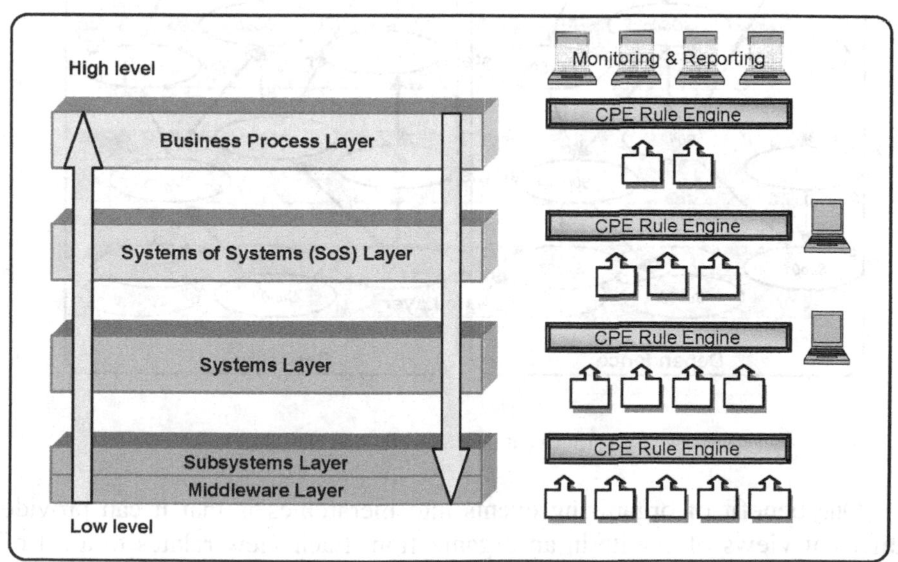

Figure 9.17. Anatomy of a component.

easily understood. The low level events can be most obvious for the service operators or engineering for troubleshooting or system analysis. The transformation of the low level events to higher level events requires techniques such as causal event histories, event patterns, event filtering, and event aggregation. Figure 9.17 signifies two important relationships that were discussed in section 9.3.3, namely dependence and causality. Event relationships are also used to reduce the search space in drill-down explanations of how high-level events happen, and why other events did not happen.

The left event hierarchy in the Figure 9.18 illustrates the high-level business process events depend upon various events happening at the lower levels to complete business transactions. These events can be created either by a business workflow engine or created manually. Showing on the right event hierarchy in Figure 9.18, the lower level events cause the higher level event to occur. A higher level event is called complex because it is caused by a pattern of many lower level events. It is an aggregation process that abstracts essential data from its lower level events over a time period.

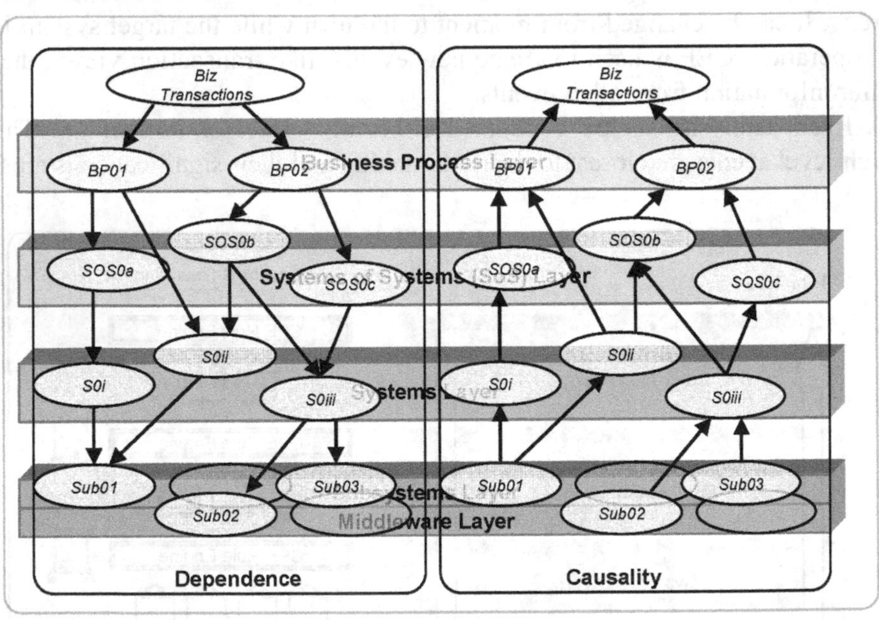

Figure 9.18. Event dependencies and causalities.

One benefit of organizing events into hierarchies is that it can provide different views of events in an organization. Each view relates to a set of roles or functionalities. Event processing can be implemented by a system of *event processing agents (*EPAs*)*, distributed over the infrastructure containing event pattern recognition and processing rules. Some EPAs filter events, some aggregate patterns of lower level events into higher level events, and the others process higher level events.

9.5.2.2 Expert Systems

An expert system can simulate the judgment and behavior of a human or an organization that has expert knowledge and experience in a particular field. For instance, a real-time expert system can guide autonomous vehicles on highways by coordinating road geometry, road conditions, velocity, and levels of safety, and provide appropriate driver commands [16–18].

As depicted in Figure 9.19, an expert system contains three major components: the knowledge base, the inference engine, the dialog subsystem, and the blackboard subsystem. The knowledge base is the set of facts and rules (heuristics) which apply to specific situations. The expert systems can be enhanced by adding or improving the knowledge base. These rules are usually constructed but not limited to the form of "IF-THEN" statements. The inference engine computes strategies and can derive conclusions either by forward chaining or backward chaining. The forward chaining is driven by the data. The backward chaining moves backward from the goal to the steps that need to be taken to accomplish that goal. Based on the rules, the outputs can be used to feed the dialog subsystem or directly to system control. The dialog subsystem provides the system interface to users and is capable of explaining reasoning for the conclusion is much like a

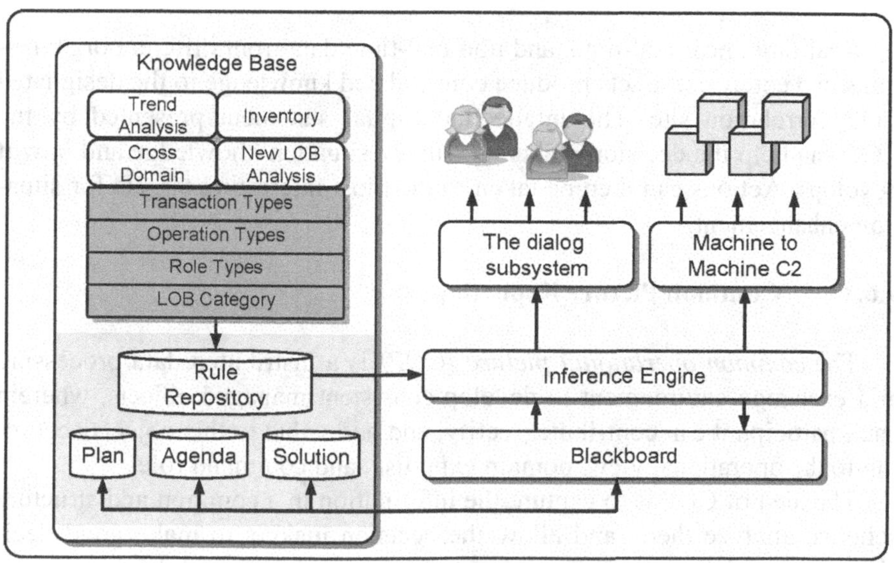

Figure 9.19. Expert system architecture.

human expert. The blackboard subsystem is a global database used for temporarily recording any intermediate decisions made by the system. The blackboard can keep three types of decisions, namely the plan, the agenda, and the solution. Where the plan specifies the overall strategy for problem resolution such as data fusion sequence, the agenda maintains a record of the upcoming actions, and the solution represents the hypotheses the system has generated thus far. Blackboard can be used to merge reports from different sources and enables system developers to partition the domain knowledge of the expert system into cooperating modules. It is important that domain knowledge is separated from control knowledge in a blackboard system.

Not shown in the figure are the data collection and the data fusion functions which collect, incorporate, and correlate data from the managed fields. The data is provided to the knowledge base and the inference engine to assist the system to make decision in real time.

Fuzzy logic is a popular mathematical method used to describe objects or processes that cannot be categorized into "0–1" binary code. The concept of fuzzy logic is similar to Dempster–Shafer evidential reasoning in dealing with data uncertainties with ambiguous descriptions [19, 20]. The concept of partial set membership includes *concentration*, which is used to delineate a sharp boundary for a fuzzy set, and *dilation*, which provides a more flexible boundary.

9.6 Reporting and Enhancements

Real-time, near real-time, and non-real-time data from different organizations and enterprise assets produce consolidated knowledge to the designated COP correlation site. The intellectual capital statement presented by the COP can help the decision makers to survey situation knowledge and how it develops. Actions can then be taken to the most interesting targets for situation enhancement.

9.6.1 Common Picture Reporting

The *common operational picture (COP)* is a distributed data processing and exchange environment to develop consistent managed objects, wherein each participant can contribute, rectify, and add value to this objects according to the operational view, domain expertise, and command role.

The idea of COP is to capture the information in a common and structure schema, analyze them, and allow the decision makers to make good decisions. The update of this picture has to be near real time and the updates are distributed to all subscribed users immediately. By tracking and associating the data and target goals, all contributing organizations can transfer their expertise from a tactical toward strategic-oriented operations. It can effectively stimulate the investigation of knowledge-based technology for interpretation and diagnosis problems. Additionally, a COP can work with real-world applications focusing the growing interest of data mining, information retrieval and digital libraries.

As shown in Figure 9.20, the COP allows the networked decision-making to occur and flow to the appropriate actors (user, system, or application) available. The efficiency of the COP process transfer knowledge so rapidly the enterprise can now capitalize the knowledge and wisdom assets on the dimension of time or on the speed of processing.

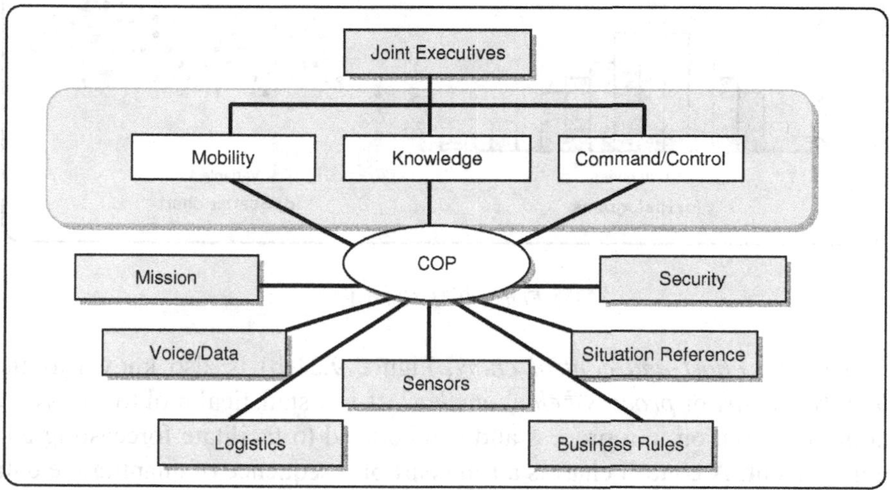

Figure 9.20. Common operational picture.

There are seven basic tools for quality control, which include the histogram, Pareto chart, check sheet, control chart, cause-and-effect diagram, flowchart, and scatter diagram. These are commonly used in a COP to display enterprise performance measurements.

Figure 9.21(a) depicts the *Pareto chart* where the values are plotted in descending order. It is named for *Vilfredo Pareto*. Typically, the left vertical axis represents the frequency of occurrence, it can alternatively represent cost or other important unit of measure. The right vertical axis represents the cumulative percentage of the total number of occurrences, total cost, or total of the particular unit of measure. The purpose of the chart is to highlight the most important among a (typically large) set of factors. In quality control applications, the Pareto chart is often used to analyze the most common sources of defects, the highest occurring type of defect, or the most frequent reasons for customer complaints, and so forth.

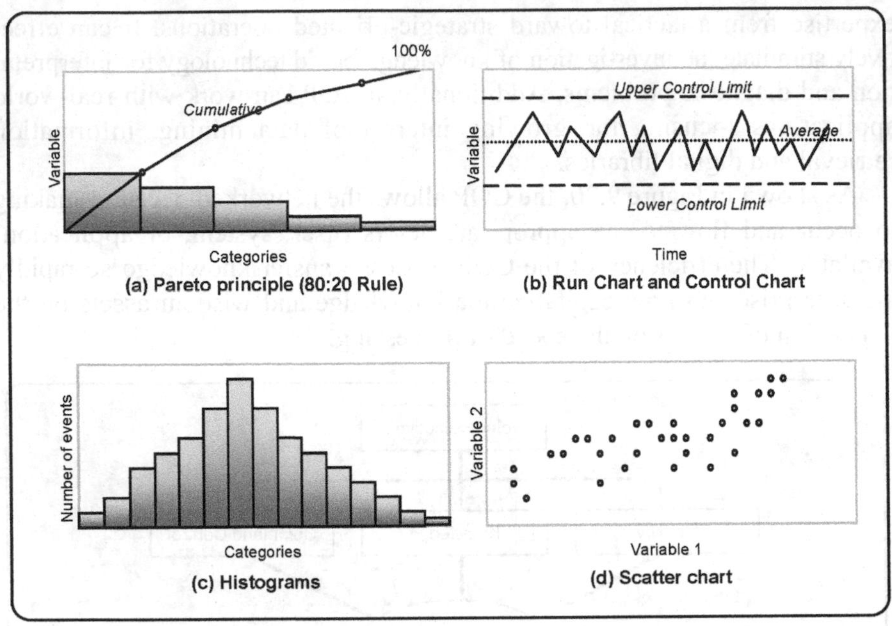

Figure 9.21. Chart 1.

The *run chart and control chart*, Figure 9.21(b) is also known as the *Shewhart chart* or *process-behavior chart*. It is a statistical tool to assess the nature of variation in a process and can be used to facilitate forecasting and management. A control chart is a run chart of a sequence of quantitative data with three horizontal lines drawn on the chart: 1) a center line, drawn at the process mean; 2) an upper control limit also called an upper natural process limit; and 3) a lower control limit also called a lower natural process limit.

This chart is the most commonly applied statistical quality control method to distinguish the variation due to special causes, from the variation due to common causes. The principle of the control chart is based on the assumption that the natural variability in any manufacturing process can be quantified with a set of control limits; variation exceeding the limits signals a change in the process.

Figure 9.21(c) shows *Histogram*, a graphical display of a table which shows proportion of cases fall into each of several or many specified categories. It is ideal for an overview of absolute numbers. The categories (bars) are usually specified as adjacent but non-overlapping intervals of some variable. Histogram shows the number of cases per unit interval so that the height of each bar is equal to the proportion of total number into that category. The area under the curve represents the total number of cases.

Figure 9.21(d) depicts the scatter plot chart, or scatter graph. It represents the association (not causation) between two variables. The data is plotted finitely; each datum has a coordinate on a horizontal and a vertical axis. The relationship between interval variables can be identified from the graph. A dot in the body of the chart represents the intersection of the data on the x and y axis. A scatter plot does not require specifications of dependent or independent variables, either type of variable can be plotted on either axis.

Figure 9.22(a) demonstrates a *cause and effects diagram*, as known as *Fishbone* or *Ishikawa Diagram*. This diagram is a graphical method for root-cause analysis by identifying the most likely causes for an undesired effect. An alternative use of the fishbone diagram is to identify desirable factors leading to an overall effect. The *main bones* include aspects such as *touch* and *braking* with the smaller bones including highly granular factors. Every factor identified in the diagram can be included in the final formula. The diagram starts by filling the short diagonal lines with causes; they are drawn with arrows and pointing toward the main bones of the diagram, and identifying the most likely causes for the effect.

Figure 9.22(b) depicts a sample of *flowchart*. A flowchart is a schematic representation of a process, commonly used in business presentations to visualize the content better, or to find flaws in the process. The start point, end points, inputs, outputs, possible paths and the decisions that lead to these possible paths are included.

Taguchi methods, shown in Figure 9.22(c) plays an important role in popularizing *design of experiments (DOE)*. A quality product is a product that causes a minimal loss (expressed in money!) to society during its entire

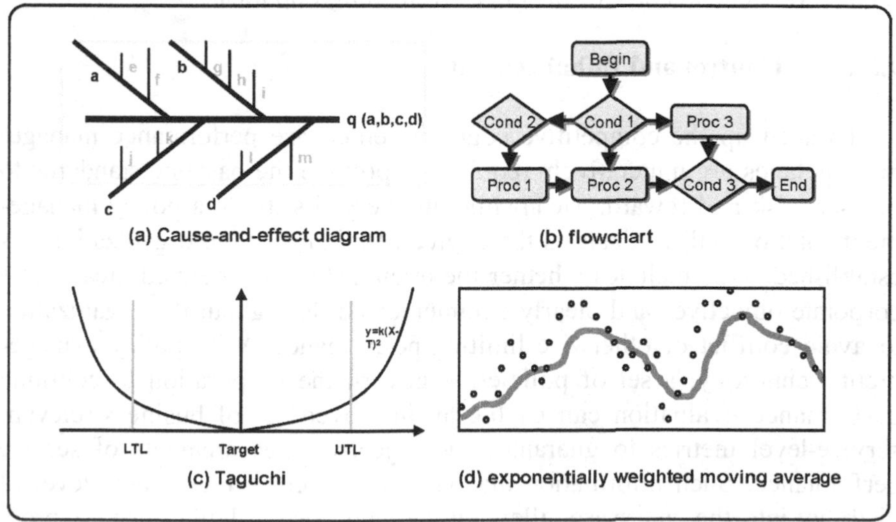

Figure 9.22. Chart2.

life. The relation between this loss and the technical characteristics is expressed by the loss function. The loss function establishes a financial measure of the user dissatisfaction with a product's performance as it deviates from a target value. Thus, both average performance and variation are critical measures of quality. Selecting a product design or a manufacturing process that is insensitive to uncontrolled sources of variation (called noise factor) improves quality. In dynamic applications, a signal factor moves the performance to some value and an adjustment factor can modify the sensitivity to this factor. With the horizontal axis as the signal factor and the vertical axis as the response, the adjustment factor can change the slope of the line. Being able to reduce a product's sensitivity to changes in the signal is useful. The Taguchi Loss Function describes the effects of variation in manufacturing defects based on the distance from the target value.

Moving average charts, Figure 9.22(d), can be used to decide whether a process is in control and to detect shifts in the process mean. In contrast to a Shewhart chart, where each point is based on information from a single subgroup, a moving average chart combines information from the current sample and past samples. As a result, moving average chart is more sensitive to small shifts in the process average. On the other hand, it is difficult to interpret patterns of points on a moving average chart, because consecutive moving averages are usually highly correlated. Each point on a uniformly weighted moving average chart (or *moving average chart*) represents the average of a specified number of the most recent subgroup means. Each point on an *exponentially weighted moving average (EWMA)* chart represents a weighted average of the most recent subgroup means.

9.6.2 Control and Enhancements

To keep up the competitive edge, the enterprise performance management policies are imperatively required to provide the baseline standards to measure risk and reward. Meanwhile, the very first thing a policy management solution will evaluate is the degree of alignment the organization has established. This includes whether the organization has defined measurable corporate objectives and clearly communicated throughout the organization to avoid conflict or otherwise limiting performance. With policy management technology, a set of policies to govern the corporation to continue performance evaluation can enable an improved set of business-relevant service-level metrics to guarantee the objective measurements of service performance. Such information management system brings a new level of visibility into the enterprise, allowing the enterprise to build business processes that capitalize on the strength of their fundamental corporate assets.

Some most popular control and enhancement processes are profiled in the following sections.

9.6.2.1 Six Sigma

The definition of Six Sigma is described as unacceptable deviation from the mean or target. Six Sigma is a methodology to manage process variations that cause defects, and to systematically work toward managing variation to eliminate those defects. The objective of Six Sigma is to achieve high performance, reliability, and value. Mathematically, it is targeted to improve quality in order to reduce defect levels below 3.4 *Defects per (one) million opportunities (DPMO)*. The relationship of Six Sigma and its relationships with corporate processes are illustrated in Figure 9.23 [21].

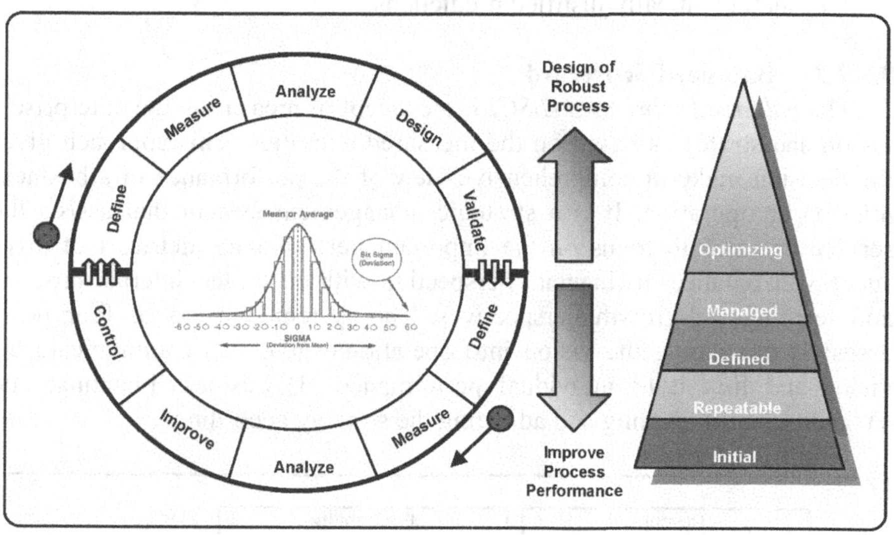

Figure 9.23. Six Sigma.

Six Sigma focuses on customer (beneficiary)-centricity, process orientation, metrics focus, and continuous improvement. The first methodology is used to improve an existing business process and consists of the following five phases:

- *Define* the process improvement goals.
- *Measure* baseline sigma on the current process for future comparison.
- *Analyze* relationship and causality of factors.
- *Improve* the process based upon the analysis using techniques like Design of Experiments.
- *Control* process capability, continuously measure the process, and institute control mechanisms to ensure that variances are corrected.

The second methodology is used to create new product designs or process designs in such a way that it results in a more predictable, mature and defect free performance. It consists of the following five phases:

- *Define* the goals of the design activity.
- *Measure* product capabilities, production process capability, risk assessment, and so forth.
- *Analyze* design capability to select the best design.
- *Design* and simulate the objective results, optimize the design if necessary.
- *Verify* design and handover to process owners.

The disadvantage of Six Sigma is that its calculations might not be robust enough to handle non-normal statistics. And the sample size can be too small to make mathematically justified predictions.

9.6.2.2 Balanced Scorecard

The *balanced scorecard (BSC)* is a concept of measuring the enterprise's vision and strategies based on the measured activities. This approach gives the decision maker a comprehensive view of the performance of a business mission or operation. It is a strategic management system that assists the service operator to focus on the important performance metrics that drive success. It balances a financial perspective with customer, internal process, and learning-and-growth perspectives. The system consists of four processes: 1) translating the vision into operational goals; 2) communicate the vision and link it to individual performance; 3) business planning; and 4) feedback and learning and adjusting the strategy accordingly.

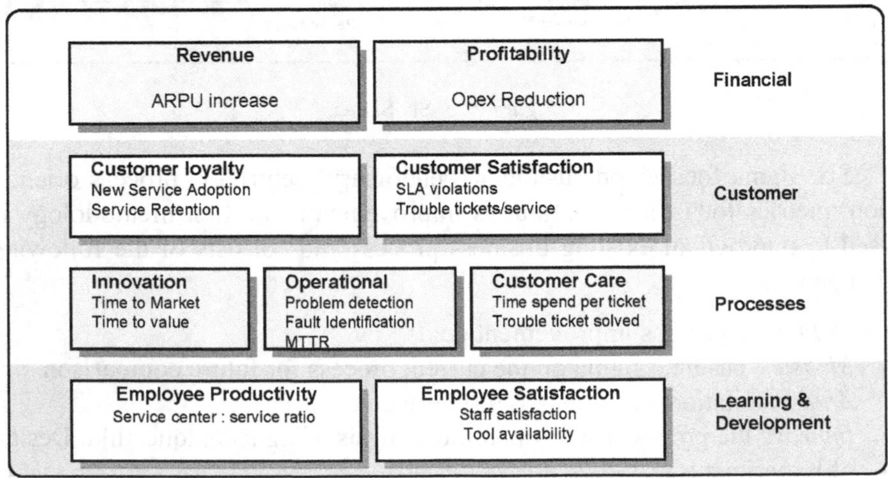

Figure 9.24. Balanced score card approach for service management perspectives.

The applications of BSC are to clarify and update strategy, communicate strategy throughout the enterprise, align unit and individual goals with strategy, link strategic objectives to long term targets and annual budgets, identify and align strategic initiatives, and conduct periodic performance reviews to learn about and improve strategy. A sample balanced score card for service management is depicted in Figure 9.24 [22].

9.7 SoS Views of KM

In general business process management or the emergence of business activity, service knowledge in quality management has shifted from the capability to monitor, analyze, and alert based on the data warehouse to a more real-time, event-driven fashion that enables business managers to track business data more dynamically. Enterprises have been using event-driven information to guide and affect key business processes.

An SLA is a key aspect of service management that underscores the service-driven aspect compared to the traditional network-focused performance management paradigm. Service customers include external customers, either wholesale or retail, and internal customers, who are administrative personnel from the same company but who have different responsibilities.

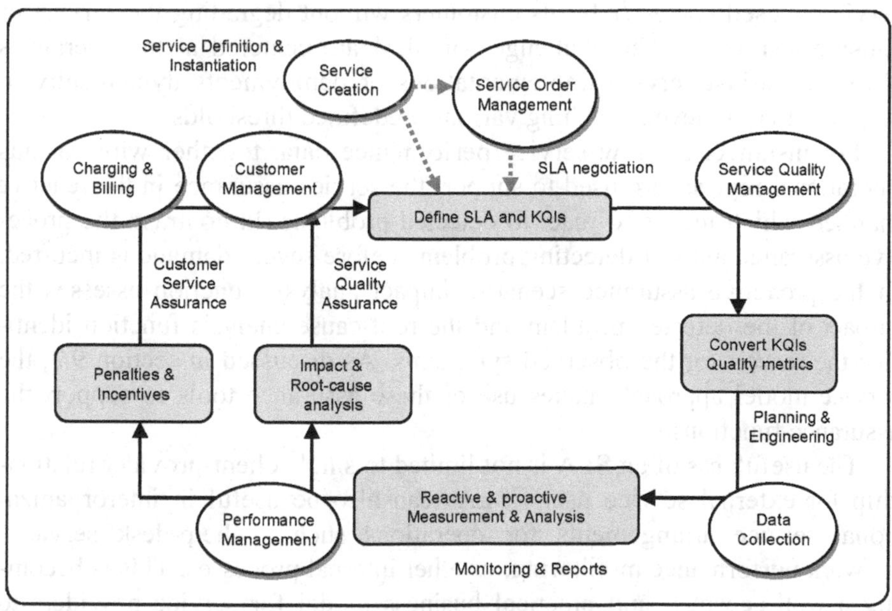

Figure 9.25. SLA management process.

Traditional SLM focuses on the operational aspects of applications within the enterprise rather than business interaction across business boundaries with the service objectives to cover capacity, availability, and security. Figure 9.25 represents a typical SLM process in a service enterprise; it can also be seen as a view-point of system flow.

The goal is to find a way to monitor effectively and efficiently the metrics defined in an SLA. If the increased revenue or performance gained by the SLA is completely offset by additional costs incurred to monitor compliance, then the SLA is not doing the company any good. Depending upon the terms of the SLA, QoS violations may result in a variety of actions, including compensation, future discounts, rebates, alternate service routing, and so forth. In a commercially competitive environment, customers will expect rebates if they are provided less than specified in the contract. The conditions under which these occur are a commercial issue between the service provider and the customer.

9.7.1 Enhanced SLA Management

An enhanced SLM is a two-way vehicle between the service customers and the service providers. The customers ideally demand the best service levels at an agreed price. On the other end, the provider requires the offered service is used *correctly* by its customers without degrading the service or causing disruption. The challenges of SLM are centered at the operator's ability to adjust service implementations or deployments dynamically in response to QoS levels reaching various predefined thresholds.

For instance, the raw service performance data, together with various operational reports, are used to support the service assurance in the reactive manner, which means to react to detected problems. In contrast, the proactive assurance aims at detecting problems before severe damage is incurred. In the proactive assurance scenario, impact analysis function assesses the impact of the detected problem and the root-cause analysis function identifies the reason for the observed symptoms. As discussed in section 9.3, the service model approach makes use of these assurance tools to support the assurance functions.

The usefulness of an SLA is not limited to single client-provider relationship for external service users. SLAs can also be useful in interorganizational service arrangements for operations such as help-desk services, network performance monitoring, or other internal processes. This is becoming a well-accepted and practical business model for service providers to establish responsibility assignments and goal setting that still allows different departments to operate in an independent, yet measurable, manner.

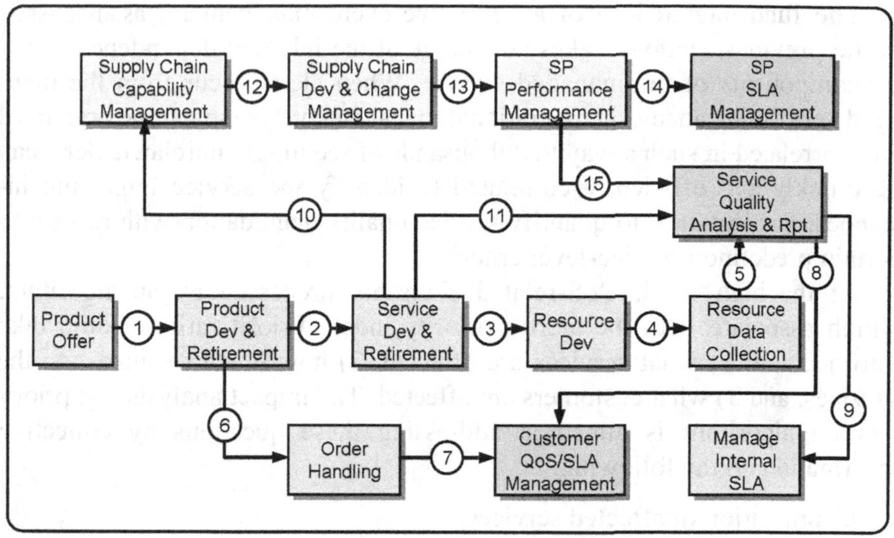

Figure 9.26. Service model–based assurance.

Furthermore, Figure 9.26 demonstrates a flow of knowledge management for an information-based service in a multiple provider scenario. SLAs presents in different ways to fulfill different types of business needs. While individual SLAs can be created to support any one-to-one service agreement, SLAs are increasingly becoming more oriented toward end-to-end and structured agreements. With a single SLA made up of internal, external, and third-party layers, it is seamlessly incorporated into the service models. The assurance functions which are supported by the service models can now have more in-depth service and customer knowledge to effectively support service capacity and traffic planning as well as problem identification and resolution.

9.7.2 Service Impact Analysis and Prioritization

In a large service deployment, thousands of alerts are generated by the bottom–up flow of the operational systems or subsystems. In platform-centric architecture, alerts are often handled without a well-thought-out process due to lack of collaboration and coordination. Both in theory and practice, processing enterprise service events are non-trivial because it requires the management systems to sort out which alerts are severe enough to warrant immediate attention from the operator. If the received events cannot be prefiltered, organized, related, and prioritized, the operator tends to ignore them. Such scenario normally results in false negatives and subsequently deferring the necessary actions until customers complain.

The fundamental idea of an effective event management, as discussed in the previous sections, takes advantage of the inherent dependence of the subcomponents of the managed service. When alerts occur from the managed service instances, the operational management system can be organized and correlated in such a way that thousands of seemingly unrelated alerts can be quickly and efficiently correlated to identify the service impacting instances. For instance, to quantify service-quality degradation with respect to certain predefined service-level criteria.

At the high level, QoS-related alerts are processed by an algorithm, which associate with the alert a priority index. Prioritization should take into account: 1) what services are affected; 2) how much of impact to the services; and 3) what customers are affected. The impact analysis and prioritization algorithm is aimed at addressing these questions by collecting information on the following:

- identification of affected services;
- service-quality impact based on service indicator, service index, severity of degradation (total interruption, duration of the interruption, performance degradation, data transfer accuracy);
- number of subscribers affected (percentage of premium and regular customers);
- usage impact.

The result of impact analysis can be used to support the following operations:

- prioritization of service and network alarms, QoS alerts, or other performance impacting events with respect to trouble ticket generation;
- prioritization for network and service resource expansion;
- adjustment of SLA for marketing.

As demonstrates in Figure 9.27, the alert flows are analyzed, prioritized, and sorted before delivering to the service center. The analysis and prioritization processes depend upon the rule sets to weigh the service indicators in order to create a final priority index. Identification of affected service depends upon how the service is implemented and how the service components are related (in the form of service topology and architecture), these information are available in the service models and service policies.

A comprehensive service model describes the steady component-level relationship is not sufficient to make effective rules. It is necessary that all models incorporate the dynamic nature of the supporting technologies in the managed services. For instance, there are levels of uncertainty as a result of the self-healing or fault-bypassing capabilities of IP networks, and many fault tolerant mechanisms that are built into the application layer. A simple example is that the failure of a router interface may be automatically bypassed by the routing algorithm, and subsequently, the router interface failure may manifest itself as just a reduction in capacity. This may or may not impact end-service, depending on the traffic load. Another example is if an application server is load-balanced among multiple computers, each running a copy of the application software. Requests for the service are served by multiple servers according to traffic-based *load balancing algorithm*, such as DNS round-robin or traffic-based allocation. Malfunction of one server can generate a severe alarm; however, all the application requests will now be directed to the remaining healthy servers without interruption. In both aforementioned scenarios, service impact may not be classified as severe if the load is light. These two samples illustrate why the filter process must be aware of the dynamic nature of the supporting services.

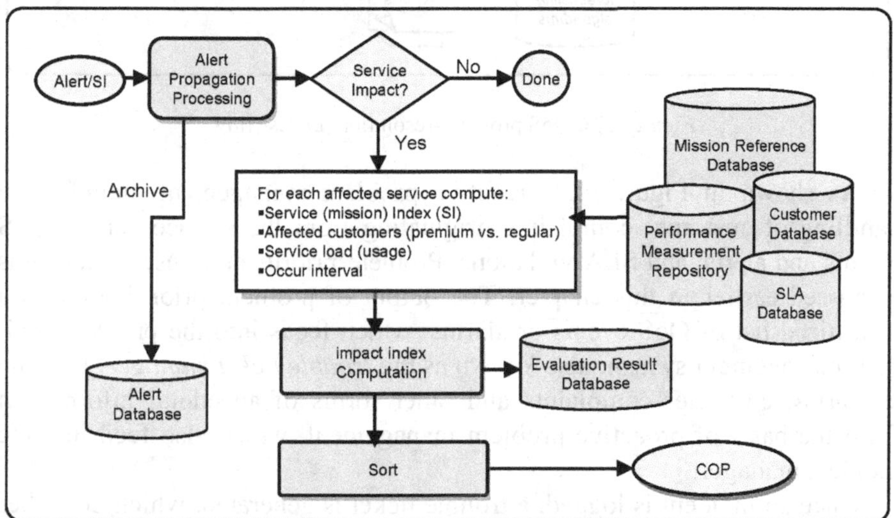

Figure 9.27. Alert prioritization flows.

9.7.3 Service Quality Problem Management

This section focuses on the problem detection and resolution functions of service assurance. In general, there are two types of problem handling: Reactive problem handling deals with existing indications of a problem. That is, some indications of the problem in the form of customer complaint, performance alarm, or SLA violation. The second type of problem handling is proactive problem handling, which deals with the process of actively searching for potential problems that are about to occur but have not surfaced obvious symptoms. The goal of the proactive problem process is to avoid the occurrence of problems.

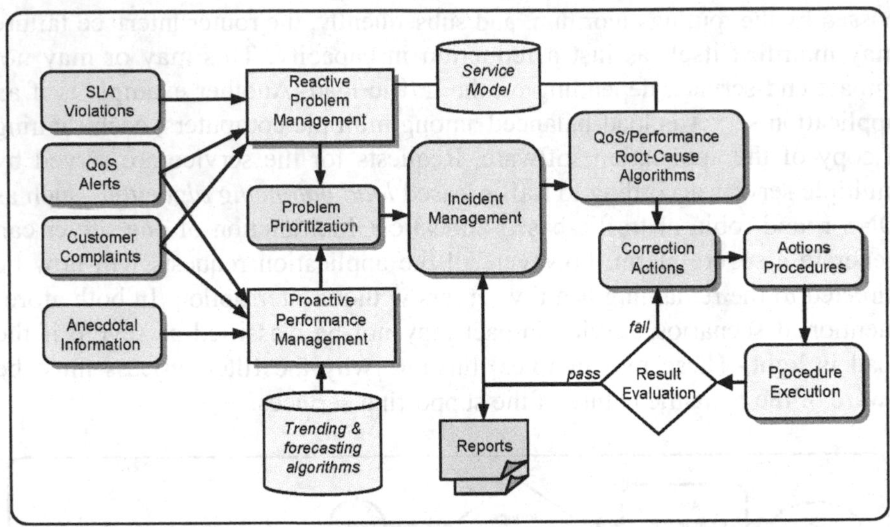

Figure 9.28. QoS problem-resolution process flow.

As shown in Figure 9.28, reactive problem management includes the handling of customer complaints originating from the service center, QoS alarms and alerts, and SLA violations. Problem prioritization uses algorithms discussed earlier in this chapter. The output of problem prioritization is a prioritized list of QoS events or alarms, which feeds into the problem incident management system, also known as the *trouble ticket manager*. In some scenarios, customer complaints and other forms of anecdotal information form the basis of proactive problem management, which also feed into the incident manager.

Once an incident is logged, a trouble ticket is generated, which describes the nature of the problem. The incident report or trouble ticket is assigned to an *issue owner*. This *owner* will use tools aforementioned to identify the *root cause* of the problem. The tools, including the service model, the KSIs, impact analysis, drill-down capability, access to customer and network configuration data, retrieval of statistics related to the problem, and viewing of past statistics, will all be used by the trouble owner for resolving the QoS problem.

When a potential problem is identified, the owner can evaluate or emulate different resolutions with the service models before applying to the real services.

9.7.4 Fraud Management Process

Fraud management is becoming an important business application in enterprises because a considerable amount of revenue can be lost due to service fraud. This is because technically the service provider does not know the location of the end of the wire, which would lead to the home of a fraudulent customer. In a mobile wireless application when roaming is required, a roaming visitor is not the service provider's customer; therefore, the service provider does not have complete information to assess fraud. As a result, fraud prevention is largely out of the control of the customer's home service provider, and end-to-end fraud protection has to rely on the service provider who is handling the call service [1].

Furthermore, fraud can happen in any operator's process flow. This characteristic also makes it difficult to represent fraud management easily. Typically, fraud management in wireless networks includes at least the following functions:

- Classify fraud-risk level on a per customer basis using demographic and credit information from the problem handling and rating and discounting processes.
- Update the fraud-risk level to the rating and discounting processes based on usage payment behaviors.
- Detect fraud patterns by accessing the current records in the rating and discounting, problem handling, customer QoS management, and invoicing and collection processes.
- Suspend the service of customers with a high fraud-risk level by reconfiguring the service and updating problem handling policies.
- Consult the home provider to assess fraud to determine if the visiting customers (i.e., roamers) should be suspended.

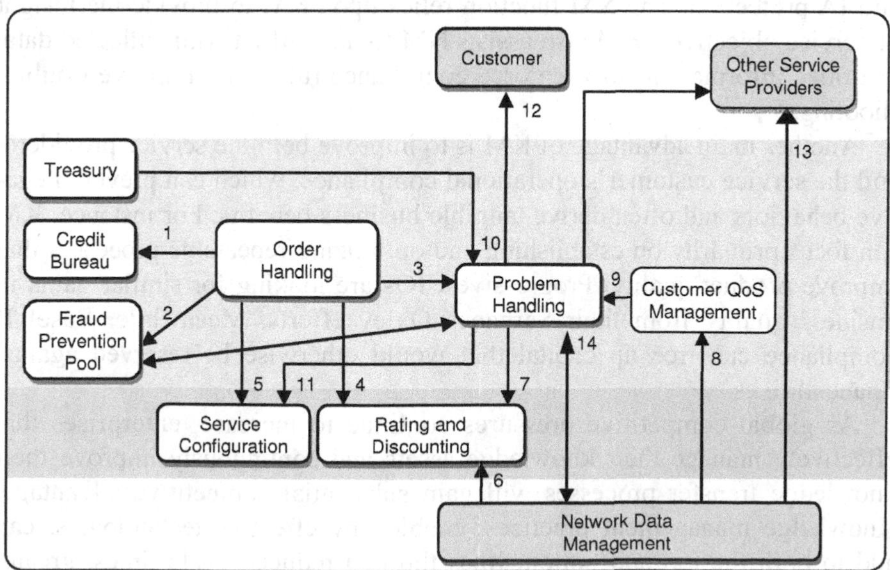

Figure 9.29. Fraud management flows.

Figure 9.29 shows the occurrence of fraud detection and prevention flows in a typical service operators processes.

9.8 Conclusions

Knowledge is a collection of identifiable objects. Knowledge management is a process which can aggregate individual objects, analyze these aggregations, resolve conflicts, and predict the future action or event of the objects. The KM function reduces information uncertainties and risks by promoting a higher level of business awareness for an enterprise. KM provides the synthesis of operational pictures and can be used for service knowledge processing and application knowledge communications. Such capability can help enterprises to make better use of all the available information for decision makers to make better judgment and for users and customers to obtain conclusive service results.

A knowledge management solution must include a knowledge directory of skills and expertise, so that service customers can quickly locate the experts they are looking for. An enterprise knowledge management system is defined as the group of information technologies used to facilitate the collection, organization, transfer, and distribution of knowledge among service customers. A knowledge management system must be open, distributed, customizable, measurable, and secure to effectively meet the organization's needs. For instance, the information that KM tools synthesize, collaborate, share, and display to KM customers relies upon the NM's transport service and IA protection. The NM function relies upon KM to provide the insight of service objectives. KM also assists NM to de-conflict with collected data, prioritize information flow, enforce compliance rules, and improve troubleshooting.

Another main advantage of KM is to improve both the service provider's and the service customer's operational compliance, which can prevent negative behaviors and often derive tangible business benefits. For instance, KM can focus primarily on establishing and optimizing repeatable processes that improve product quality. Progressive CIOs are looking for similar gains in business quality from their Sarbanes Oxley efforts. Meanwhile, Basel II compliance can free up capital that would otherwise be reserved against financial risks.

As global competitive pressures continue to increase, enterprises that effectively manage their knowledge assets and continuously improve their knowledge transfer processes will gain substantial competitive advantage. Knowledge management practices, enabled by effective technologies, can add to both the top and bottom lines through reduced cycle times, greater efficiency, and greater use of superior solutions across the enterprise.

Chapter 10

NETWORK-CENTRIC SERVICE-ORIENTED ENTERPRISES

Realizing the network-centric service-oriented architecture for an enterprise has both culture and technical challenges. While SOA is perceived as the ultimate framework of software technology that can accomplish complete service transformation in a diverse network environment, due to practical schedule and budget constraints, however, enterprises must deal with tremendous operational guidance that drive the IT forces to integrate legacy systems with the new services and applications. A typical IT approach to the comprised method is to layer some business-relevant services on top of existing applications and promote interoperability of data management through standardization of data elements. This minimizes their duplication across organizations. As a result, the abstraction process turning the service data into a flat and peer level reveals SOA's incapability to meet high-performance requirements and unexpected complexity to reproduce the legacy waterfall business process. Both drawbacks may make the enterprises owners doubt the true values of the transformation.

In support of network-centric SOE, the focus of this chapter aims to define a workable enterprise solution that makes business data visible, available, and usable when and where it is needed for accelerated decision-making. Building upon the methodologies and technologies discussed in the previous chapters, a conclusive blueprint presented here will transform these functional means into a real design plan. Chapter 10 sketches out the SoS solution from three perspectives – the operational view focuses on uses cases and service building-block identifications, the system view decomposes the building-blocks of the services and applications into the system or sub-system level, and the technical view addresses domain specific technologies to support the operational and system views as well as IT standards that can make this solution more open and adaptive for future enhancements.

10.1 NCBO Enables Enterprise Services

The concept of NCBO in the applications of enterprise services introduces an important aspect of business transition. It is to organize scattered business functionalities, consolidate information across enterprise, and conclude them into affiliated knowledge assets to support superior decision-making. Individual functional components and capabilities can be provided by separate service providers thus allowing investments from other stakeholders to be leveraged. Rather than creating systems that combine specific capabilities within a solution, orchestration mechanisms allow the enterprise to quickly select and arrange services to accomplish the same process [1].

The high-performance transport capability described in the previous chapters support a higher number of applications and users to effectively and dynamically access accurate and collaborated services in a relative shorter timeframe. As the enterprise transforms its process toward service orientation, it is affecting the culture of the enterprise. This is based on the fact that the operating organizations have to evolve and adapt the NCBO processes to fit their internal and external adjustments in order to maximum the investment.

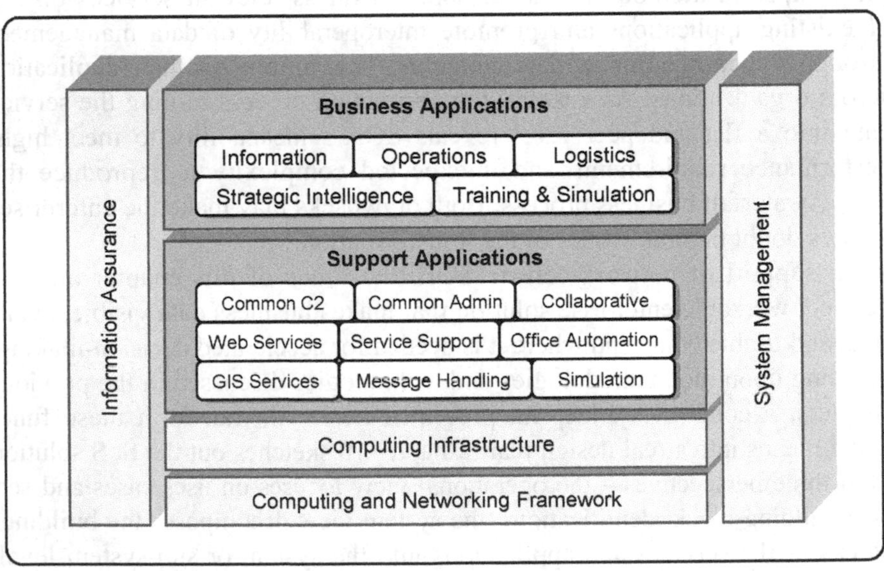

Figure 10.1. System architecture of enterprise services.

Figure 10.1 depicts the positions of the applications at the *Business Application* and the *Support Application* layers. This can be elaborated from the standpoints of operational and financial areas. The functional components in the *Support Applications* layer are part of the NCBO value-added features to enforce and enhance the network-centric capability from the networking and computing infrastructure at the lower layers. These value-added functions include *Common Control* and *Command interface*, *Common Administration interface*, *Collaboration*, *Web Services platform*, *Service Support interface*, *Office Automation engine*, *Global Information Services*, *Message Handling*, and *Simulation*. Note that many of these functions only serve as portals to the actual control or administration features from other building-blocks. For instance, *Common Administration* directly interfaces with *Information Assurance*, *System Management*, *Distributed Computing Infrastructure*, and *Computing and Network Framework*. The *Business Applications* layer can act as an independent service instance to support enterprise customers directly or be part of orchestrated resources to form complex service offerings.

In this chapter, a well-known SoS development methodology defined by DoD will be revealed with detailed design considerations and references for commercial applications.

10.1.1 Five Tiers of Enterprise Networks

Before proceeding to the details of service development, the networking hierarchy is reviewed again from the perspective of NCBO. This is because the discussions from previous chapters which paved the network foundation for service-oriented enterprise might not clearly uncover the true accent of network-centricity for the enterprise services from the business perspective. For instance, chapter 9 illustrated the NCBO service model and how a service template can be reused for different enterprise offering, but lacked the guidance for how to break-down the service elements into service objects. Even though there is no standard answer to the question. This section is intended to present a sample division for complex enterprise service offerings [2].

From the information management perspective, five tiers of networks can be qualified as the following. (Bear in mind, the connectivity described is logical, but supported directly or indirectly by physical enterprise resources).

- In *level 0 networking*, the information is essentially exchanged by physical access without any interoperable connection. These data models are private-based.

- In *level 1 networking*, agreeable interfaces (e.g., simple file with homogeneous format) with application-specific data model are used to conduct peer-to-peer connections. The access policy is either at local or site-level.
- In *level 2 networking*, structured (e.g., heterogeneous) or more complex date formats are used in local domain application communications. A Web interface can be used to increase openness of interactions.
- *Level 3 networking* has the capability to perform functional specific tasks across multiple networked systems. The data models are sharable across the enterprise but with "localized" views. Domain collaboration capability such as workflow management is a typical example of the level 3 applications.
- The *level 4 networking* achieves enterprise-level interoperability across functional and informational domains. Information and assurance (e.g., security or access control) models are shared globally. Multidimensional service hierarchies bridging logical and physical resources are accessible for all information consumers. A "virtual" workspace allows different applications to support either end users or service operators in an integrated manner.

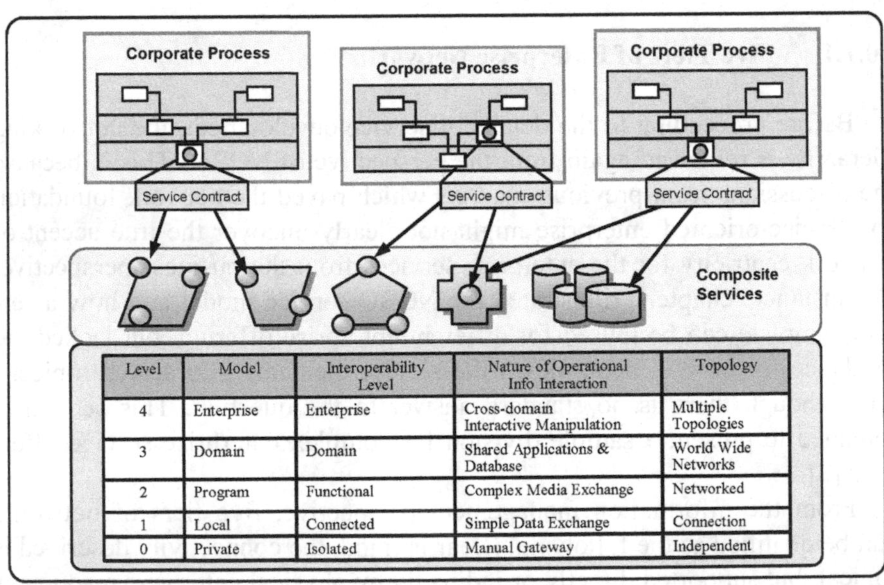

Level	Model	Interoperability Level	Nature of Operational Info Interaction	Topology
4	Enterprise	Enterprise	Cross-domain Interactive Manipulation	Multiple Topologies
3	Domain	Domain	Shared Applications & Database	World Wide Networks
2	Program	Functional	Complex Media Exchange	Networked
1	Local	Connected	Simple Data Exchange	Connection
0	Private	Isolated	Manual Gateway	Independent

Figure 10.2. Composite services offered to multiple processes over enterprise networks.

Figure 10.2 portrays a three-tier relation where corporate processes can access different composite service packs and perform information sharing with other enterprise identities. The composite services can be supported by any one of the five levels of networking in accordance with the business goals and objectives. As the cost and operational impacts to the enterprise rise when progressing to higher levels of networking, it is the enterprise challenge to balance the technology transformation and the long-term return of the new NCBO approach. The following sections will delineate the best practices of what directions to choose and how to define the strategic goals for a successful network-centric services which help the enterprises to evolve into a true service-oriented business model.

10.1.2 NCBO Service Integrations

The NCBO is an operational infrastructure that creates flexible, adaptable, and distributed computing environments. It includes a set of principles, patterns, and practices for creating service-oriented application functionality as shared, general-purpose, and network-centric. As seen in chapter 9, the service modeling and choreography mechanisms assist process modeling and management. In chapter 8, integrated service and workflows are created and stored in the registry for service reusability. In this chapter, a set of collaboration services is managed by the application server so that the participants within the CoI can collaborate with each other. The dissemination rule dynamically shifts works between similar services and routes the results. The network-centric resource management allows service operators and customers to dynamically select best-fit resources. The resource selections and other decisions making in the enterprise are governed by the policy management. Thus, unified polices throughout the enterprise can eliminate the likelihood of redundant and conflicting missions. Based on the service quality defined in chapter 7 and assurance rules define in chapter 8, the services can achieve secured load balance among value-chain service providers and to quickly deliver the right resources at the time of use. Service management discussed in chapters 6 and 9 aim to manage critical factors such as resources and processes involved in an enterprise service framework. This optimized process leverages services and capabilities to share work across providers for both preplanned and ah-hoc tasks. The flexibility of collaborated resource management results in decreasing in the number of stovepipe solutions, allows faster mergers and acquisitions. The capability of real-time command and control, for instance, offers optimal customer experiences and the ability to achieve effective resource utilization. It also improves operational controllability for the service provider to achieve with less cost and more efficiency [3].

Figure 10.3 depicts a sample logical framework of NCBO suitable for both information-driven service applications as well as typical service management applications. Through the service registry, business values of the enterprises and their value-chain partners can effectively exchange information to ensure optimized business practices.

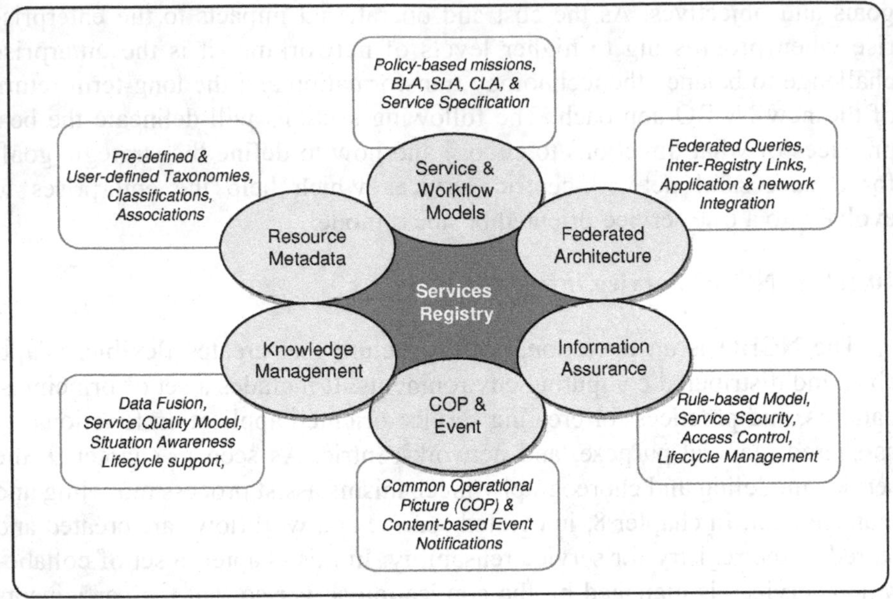

Figure 10.3. A logical framework of a service-oriented application.

10.1.3 Enterprise's Culture Impacts

By moving to service orientation, the enterprises may involve cultural changes when breaking down the traditional barriers between business and technology, and between systems and operations. Additionally, the community members that traditionally worked in domain specific environment, are finding the functional boundary eroded as enterprises are now opened to value-chain partners [4].

Service management is a key to improve both the services revenue stream through efficient management of services and the effective operations at all aspects of the service delivery business, including managing the customer life cycle from presales to in-life experience. Effective service orientation depends not only upon the supply–manage–consume model but also on how to create and use the knowledge created by the service framework. Business process execution carried out by the application resources which include the monitoring and management functionalities from the user and administrative tools must be closely linked with SLM.

As shown in Figure 10.4, the life cycle of a service starts from premission phase, service fulfillment, and enters into the service assurance phase. In the service assurance period, SLO is monitored and controlled from the provider's perspective, and SLAs are managed as contractual relationships with the service users. Policy specifications should work with other enterprise service management components such as IA management, SQM, and SLM to ensure service and process consistency [5].

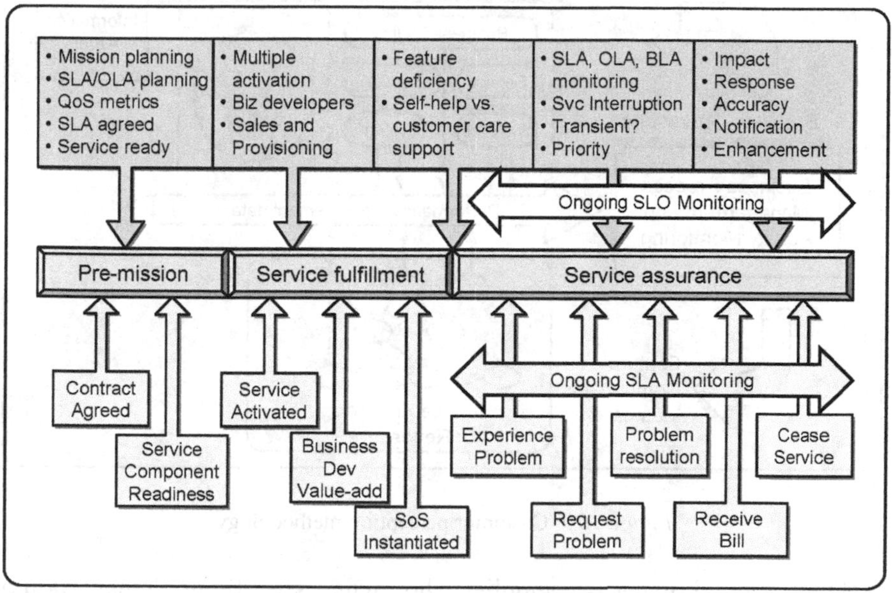

Figure 10.4. Life-cycle service management.

A customer-driven approach is predicated upon practical business cases for services to be part of the enterprise's business improvement plans. However, very broadly speaking, an enterprise may take a customer-driven approach to sourcing some services, a provider-driven approach to sourcing some other services, and a collaborative approach to sourcing the rest of services. In such complex configuration, every business owner owns the functionality specified in the SLAs. Customers buy the right to use the service, but not the service itself. A customer perception methodology in a horizontal provider relationship is illustrated in Figure 10.5 [6].

The chief officers and the line-of-business owners perceive the services as the business processes required to effectively operate the enterprise. The application and system users perceive the services as individual applications that enable their work within the enterprise. The information officers and the enterprise architects perceive the services as software packages that collectively support the enterprise business processes. The software developers perceive the services as the solution structure and the integration policy for one or more applications. Depending upon the roles and responsibilities, some of the perceptions may overlap with others or require to adapt new relationships where necessary.

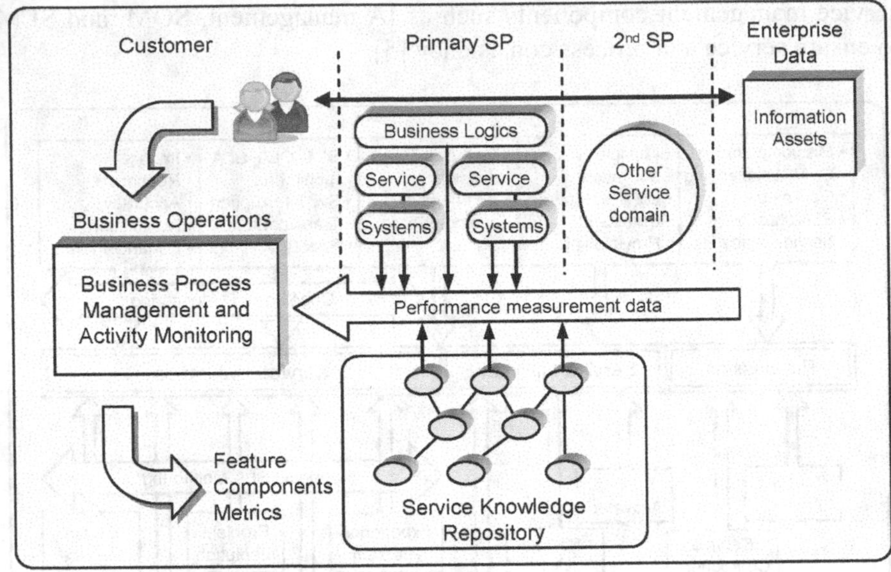

Figure 10.5. Customer perception methodology.

The technical owner is a supplier who owns a specific implementation of the service. A service may have a single business owner but different technical owners, one for each implementation of the service. Charging of services requires a clear charging model upon which charging is based. Regardless of whether it is flat-rate or usage-based, the details must be agreed between the customer and the provider, and documented in the billing section of the SLA. A service provider's SLA may contain a judgment section comparing the time and cost of acquiring the offered services from other third part vendors versus that of delivering services internally. If an aggregated service is determined then a plan is required for settlements – a way to share revenues with the provider's upstream or downstream service providers [7].

10.2 Creating Network-Centric Services

A set of loosely coupled services works together seamlessly and securely over a network can assist enterprises to establish a distributed, parallel information sharing and mobilized computing environment. Effective information gathering and collaborative operation in such an environment allows the enterprises to achieve information superiority. These services rely on well-defined interface contracts, and are managed by the service management tools at the enterprise level to ensure that the services can be published, discovered, mediated, and consumed in an orderly fashion [8].

10.2.1 Operational Procedures and Products

The determination of procedures and products requires the enterprise to thoroughly evaluate its end-to-end value-chain operations and follow up with service governance. It typically begins with high-level requirements that specify the processes and roles associated with given service objectives in a consistent fashion at varying levels of detail. Figure 10.6 depicts an operational procedure and process cycle for NCBO services [9].

This cycle has six stages each represents an important phase in creating an enterprise service offering.

1. A new service project starts from a clear and sensible mission and objectives definition. A set of profiles include the technology (IT profiles) and business (mission profiles) establishes a roadmap to guide the strategy for future implementation and adaptation. This strategic direction can ensure the alignment of business and IT will follow industry and enterprise standards (identified in *Technical View*). The business and technical stakeholders from contributing organizations should be part of the *Tech & Biz team* as they are jointly defining the common business service model, core processes, core business components, enterprise data strategy, and the set of assets for the project.

2. *The SME teams* are expanded from the *Tech team* to detail the rules, processes, metrics, data architecture, and information models needed for effective planning, steering, and controlling the service instances for better decision-making. Integration with the existing applications or legacy functions should be closely examined in order to avoid making radical changes to the existing business strategies (with *Operational View*). The business, information, and assurance model templates are specified in this phase to support modular processes.

3. *The information products* are developed and deployed in accordance with the systems, data, and processes requirements. All service-oriented analysis, design, and development should follow high- and low-level design abstractions defined in the project's *System View*. Various test efforts such as unit, integration, system, and acceptance tests are exercised in both the target and the existing environments.

4. *The service administration* phase addresses services insanitation and service assurance including but not limited to the functionalities such as managing QoS, enforcing BLAs and SLAs, managing IA requirements, charging-back services, and assuring revenue. This phase is in the *premission* phase of Figure 10.4.

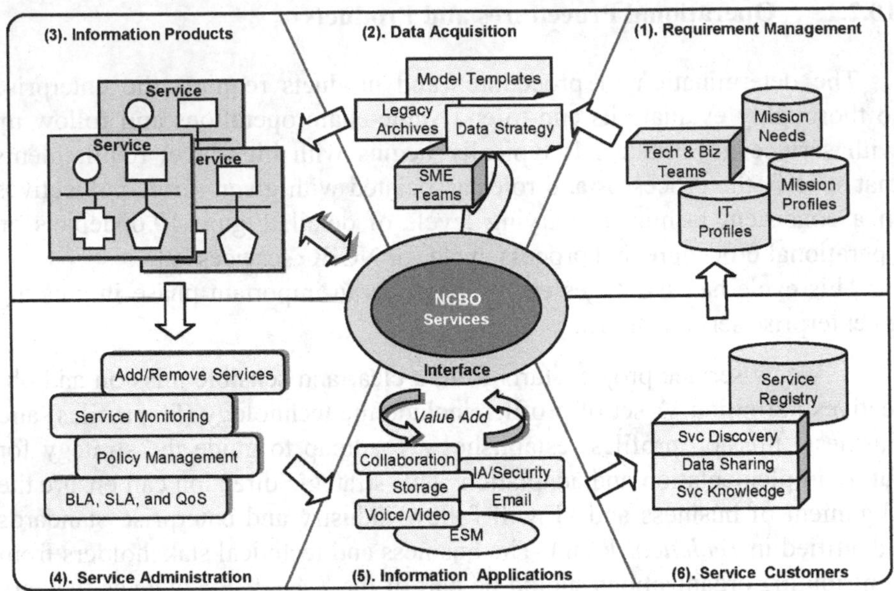

Figure 10.6. Operational procedures and process cycle.

5. The deployed service components serve as autonomous building-blocks allowing the business developers to orchestrate business process by assembling these blocks. Through composing and recomposing these components, the business developers can continue to grow values and features to the enterprise's business operations without additional system development effort. Hence, the enterprise can leverage the service features and respond rapidly to changing business conditions. This phase is in *service fulfillment* and early part of the *service assurance* phase in Figure 10.4.

6. Based on the actual data and information that information *customers* entered into the services (for instance via service registry or share space), the service analysts can adjust the service scope and focus on enhanced service quality accordingly. To complete a full cycle of continuing improvement, modest recommendations or studies will feed back to the *requirement management* phase for future process or organizational evolution. Adoption of lesson-learns from the service assurance aspect is essential for improving the development processes. These inputs are derived from the service knowledge management described in chapter 9. This phase is known as *service assurance*.

Depending upon scales of the enterprise operations and complexity of the CoI relationships with other value-chain partners, emphasis and duration in these six phases can vary.

10.2.2 Service Offering Life Cycle

Enterprise services must consist of the capability to access all the enterprise information from the networked resources and the capability to collaborate the community process and related activities to improve the timeliness, relevance, and accuracy of information or intelligence. The life cycle of service offering covers the Service Administration (4), Information Applications (5), and Service Customers (6) phases depicted in Figure 10.6. It provides an operational environment enabling rapid development and deployment of services, as well as supporting service enhancements and capacity with agreed cost and quality.

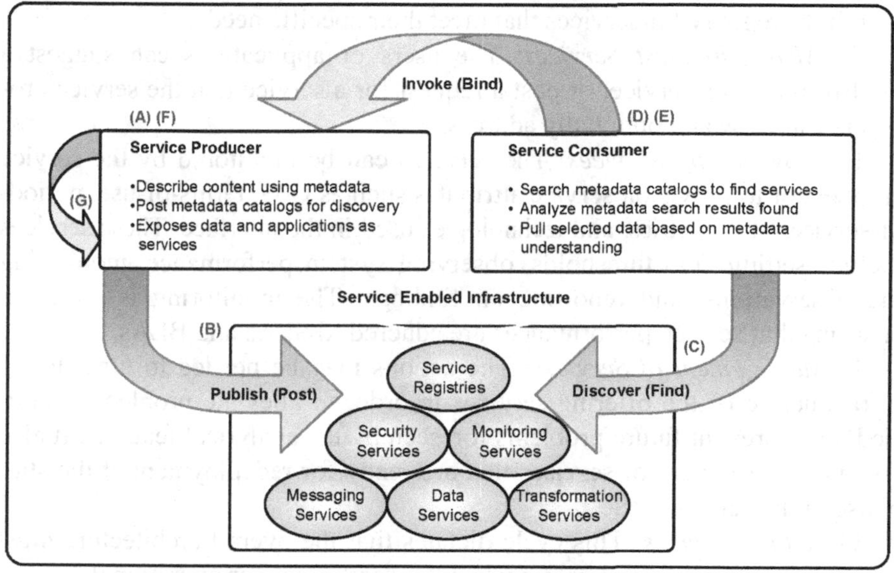

Figure 10.7. Life cycle of service offering.

The service-oriented approach is inherently dynamic. It allows fast formation of CoI to handle highly volatile situations and change mission requirements as necessary. It also supports stable operations of longstanding or institutional CoIs. As discussed in chapter 1, SOA is more about a mindset than it is about technology. The system developers in the enterprise must adopt an attitude to reuse than to build services. In the situation when no existing services are available for reuse, implementation of a new service must be designed reusable in the future. In a SOA environment, the service offering life cycle are illustrated in Figure 10.7.

A. *Create Service*: As services become available, federated registries allow them to be advertised in a reliable and secured location. The use of service models in the registry increases service reuse and scalability by allowing similar services to be easily interchanged. When a service model is selected, the corresponding service will not be activated until it is actually used. The routing registry provides a resource for storing services that will be used per model.

B. *Publish Service*: The registration capability allows a service producer to define services of a system in a registry. The service provider provides information to the registry about the service interface including: points of contact for the managing organization, interface specification, service metadata, optional SLA, optional QoS data, and optional IA specifications.

C. *Discovery*: Service discovery is for end-user consumption and *business-to-business (B2B)* integration. The users and applications can browse or search the registry for services that meet their specific needs.

D. *Modify/Request Services*: The users or applications can suggest a modification to a service, or post a request for a service that the service providers can view and optionally address.

E. *Provisioning Services*: The services can be monitored by the service an operator to provision service attributes such as QoS, terms-of-use, period-of-service, SLA metrics, and technologies used in the interface. These services include setting QoS thresholds, observing system performance, monitoring the observations, and reporting on findings. The monitoring is aimed at ensuring that service performances are adhered to SLAs and BLAs.

F. *Management of Services*: The actions may be needed to tune the IT infrastructure of the offering services in order to alleviate problems identified, or to prevent future problems foreseen by the analytical features. It also covers the discovery of services that are ready for redeployment at the start phase of the service cycle.

G. *Retire Services*: This cycle dictates that the overall architecture must accommodate service retirement when they are no longer operational.

10.3 Design Principles of NCBO Services

NCBO is a software-based SoS with models, rules, policies, and processes defined by the enterprise and its partners, and this set of solutions is capable of working with other applications and management solutions within a CoI or across CoIs. As discussed in chapter 1, either SoS or FoS has the capability to collaborate with other value-chain partners electronically to accomplish join missions.

10.3.1 Architecture and Integration

A key characteristic of the network-centric service architecture is that the SoS is knowledge-driven. Enterprise processes are essentially a set of well-defined rules and policies that respond to the knowledge provided by the situation-awareness function. To integrate the enterprise CoI processes, the NCBO architecture should include the following considerations.

- Adopt open and loosely coupled architecture to support a modular and layered hierarchy. This feature can encapsulate the underlying implementations and improve scalability.
- Use network-centric and open infrastructure to introduce and adapt changes to the process or organization. Increased flexibility allows greater possibility for collaborating information and functionalities to improve information quality and decision cycle.
- Emphasize existing and emerging standards, technologies, and processes to maximize the enterprise's values and the core competencies, meanwhile, to minimize any customization of generic features.
- Provide an enterprise-wide and *situation-aware COP* to increase information visibility. The concept of COP offers a valuable portal for CoI users to control and manage value-chain (physical or logical) assets.
- Raise the controllability of enterprise resources (e.g., frequency or computing unit) management and operations with on-demand computing. An autonomic computing system can reduce dependency of human interaction and realize "*Grid computing*" as many computers can coordinate tasks triggered by the situation awareness [10].
- Enforce community-based information visibility with effective data strategy and high availability. Data and service models closely associated with the enterprise's values, strategies, and operations can eliminate knowledge barriers between value-chain participants.
- Accommodate full spectrum of IA services with layered security in the assurance models. It should include authentication, authorization, integrity, confidentiality, and accountability defined in the integrated assurance policies.

10.3.2 Service Design

With the aforementioned principle, the scopes of service application can be expanded from the end-user information acquisition to the service management supporting the marketing, order, fulfillment, assurance, billing, and inventory synchronization. A success measure for designing enterprise services is based on the degree of adaptation of the network-centric, which delivers zero-latency and optimized knowledge to/from the domains of interest. Main design principles can be concluded as follows:

- Support flexible and dynamic services with service model approach, use thin clients or browser-based customer-facing devices, and reduce the tight coupling between service providers and consumers to support reusability.
- Design with minimal dependence on specific technologies or vendor proprietary implementations.
- Use consistent and accurate information within and between interacting community members.
- Provide high degree of interoperability both internally and externally. The external interoperability includes coalition business partners, and value-chain service providers.
- Use rule-based paradigm to describe the service in terms of functions, information, goals, and rules.
- Design the service to be as self-contained and autonomous as possible, ideally, whether there is dependency of other service or not.
- Integrate information assurance with prioritized data structure.

10.3.3 Service Operations

When implemented, the services should result in well-defined and realizable capabilities which can support either internal or external processes and provide a range of simple and complex functions. These services should allow decentralized operations and management to support federation and interaction among different parts of value chain in an end-to-end offering, and to support the integration and operation of business processes over the networks. The operational principles can be concluded as the following:

- Use the services model that can accommodate heterogeneity development models, languages, components, and so forth, and must support operations over a wide range of transport services.
- Increase operational effectiveness in all stages of decision loops by improving information quality and synergizing a wide range of individuals, units, and functions to improve better situation information and situation understanding.
- Provide decentralized knowledge indicators or service indicators with protection against impersonations or denial of service attacks conducted by either individual or colluding peers.
- Provide a full range of performance capabilities, in real time, near real time, and best effort to be tailored to reflect the important service quality of transport or computing resources.

- Operate as a family unit offering business capability with various levels of management information.
- Accommodate continual asynchronous changes and enhancements in the CoI and domain services. Modifications to one service must not break the integration of other applications.
- Support the mobility requirements from the user and operator's perspectives.
- Align the holistic and synergistic orchestration, management, and execution of actions within and between CoIs.

The processes embodied in this new service architecture should not be viewed as ancillary to the operations of the enterprise but an enhancement to increase productivity and revenue.

10.3.4 Formulating an Enterprise Service Framework

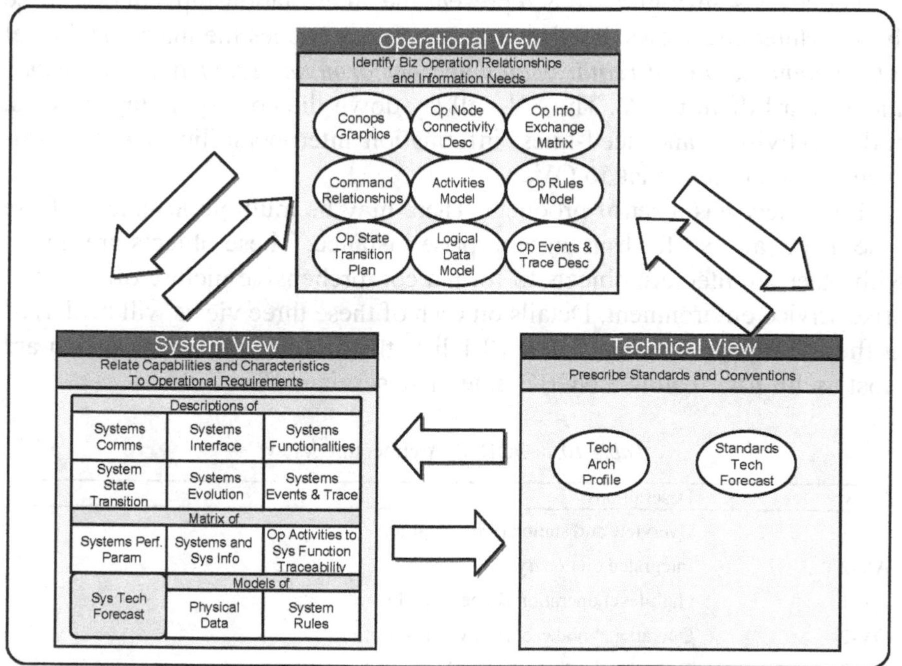

Figure 10.8. Linkages among the DODAF architecture views.

The enterprise NCBO is a collaborative environment that supports vertical and horizontal interoperability between enterprises business and operations. The DoD *Architecture Framework (DoDAF)* [11] provides a set of guiding principles for modeling and designing architectures in the DoD environment. These four architecture views include the *All View*, the *Operational*

View, the *System View*, and the *Technology View*. The operational, system, and technology views are shown in Figure 10.8 [12].

- The *All View* (*AV*) specifies the missions, objectives, scope, intended users, environment, resources, and terminology of the project (or program).
- The *Operational View* (*OV*) encompasses the specifications of tasks, activities, operational elements, and information exchanges required to accomplish the missions.
- The *System View (SV)* encompasses the specifications of systems, capabilities, and interconnection supporting operational requirements. In the case of integration, both current and postulated implementations are included.
- The *Technical View (TV)* articulates the technical standards, implementation conventions, rules, and criteria that guide the system implementation and operations.

The arrows in Figure 10.8 represent the interrelationships among these three architecture views. For instance, the OV produces the inter-nodal level *information exchange requirements* and *performance security requirements* and forward them to SV. The SV will lay-down the corresponding systems, nodes, activities, and need-lines, information interoperability and performance and send them back to OV.

Each view has a set of products. There may be multiple instances of use case, node, and so forth in an enterprise instance. These objects are linked with other architecture objects to form a comprehensive picture of an enterprise service environment. Details on each of these three views will be delved in the following sections. Table 10.1 lists the architecture views which are most useful for creating a NCBO enterprise service offer.

Table 10.1. DODAF Architecture View.

View	Descriptions
AV-1	Overview and summary information
AV-2	Integrated dictionary
OV-1	High-level operation concept graphic
OV-2	Operational node connectivity description
OV-3	Operational information exchange matrix
OV-4	Operational relationships chart
OV-5	Operational activity model
OV-6a	Operational rules model
OV-6c	Operational event/trace description
OV-7	Logical data model
SV-1	Systems interface description
SV-2	Systems communications description

View	Descriptions
SV-3	Systems–system matrix
SV-4	Systems functionality description
SV-5	Operational activity to systems function traceability matrix
SV-6	Systems data exchange matrix
SV-7	Systems performance parameters matrix
SV-10c	System event/trace description
SV-11	Physical data model
TV-1	Technology sStandards
TV-2	Technology standards forecast

10.4 DoDAF's Operational View

In formulating an NCBO service, the first step is to identify a set of high-level use cases based on the *concept of operation (CONOP)*, the scope of service, and the high-level requirements in accordance with the AV. The OV is intended to address how end users, systems, or applications use services. The use case can be presented in different forms. In the follow sample, the management case is a variation of the user case which focuses on the management scenarios of service operators [12].

Figure 10.9 shows a typical service operation involving service user and service operator (provider). The *use case*, *management case*, and *node* are the primary objects in describing the operational aspects of an enterprise service offering. The asterisks indicate multiple instances for an object and 1 means single instance [8].

The functions performed at the *Node* in the area A are supporting the user cases in the area C and the management cases in area B. An actor is a special type of node. The Actor in both B and C areas can be a user, system, or application using services or systems in the use cases (area C) or management cases (area B) to perform different activities. These nodes are roles, organizations, shared resources, or service nodes. If a node is a service consumer, then it is an actor in the use case for that service. A provider node contains information in the repository for consumer's access. The management actors are service and network *operational support systems* (OSS) discussed in the previous chapters; they allow the enterprise to manage the service throughout the entire life cycle of the offering. One key differentiator of NCBO that differs from the traditional paradigm is the situation awareness across these three areas in Figure 10.9. In a nut shell, the awareness of the user activities can assist the service operator to proactively monitor the user activities and provide adjustment on service performanceand security (e.g., roaming across multiple security domains) as necessary. The awareness of the management activities can assist the service users to conduct better decision in regard to resource allocation, trouble management, and mission execution.

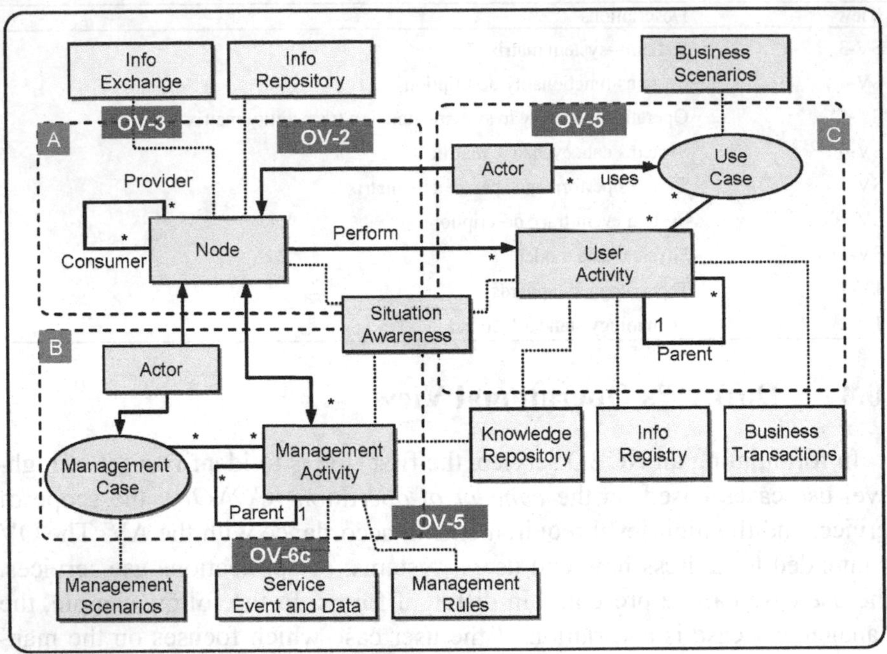

Figure 10.9. Architecture objects and their relations to the operational view.

In the OV specifications, high-level operational concept graphics are defined in OV-1. A use case contains a sequence of activities, which may be organized into hierarchical activities, to describe the external behavior of a service as seen or utilized by an actor. An example of elements in an activity model (OV-5) will be illustrated in section 10.4.2, it groups related activities into a hierarchy and defines the information exchange between nodes. The use-case diagrams often identify the nodes, the connections between the nodes form the operational node connectivity description (OV-2). The information exchange includes connections, provider nodes, consumer nodes, mode of exchange (e.g., synchronous), and security conditions are defined in OV-3. The rules for who should perform what roles are defined in OV-6a. The dynamic behaviors of such exchanges are described in a sequence diagram at the system and SoS level detailed in OV-6c.

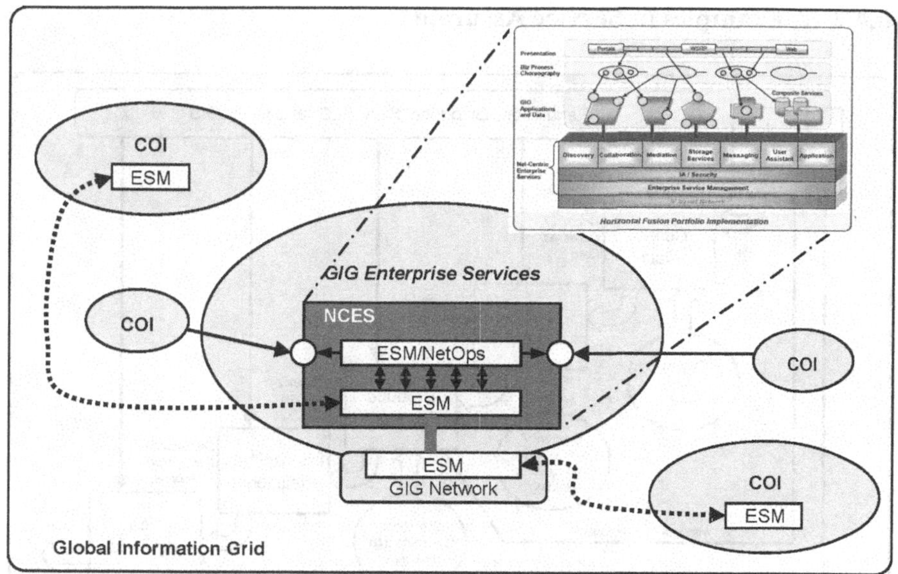

Figure 10.10. Operation node connectivity description (OV-2) of GIG enterprise services.

10.4.1 Enterprise Service Management

The DoD defined a set of management system functionalities named *Enterprise Service Management (ESM)*, to support the *Network-Centric Enterprise Services (NCES)* in the GIG environment. ESM provides infrastructure and service management, traffic management, cross-domain management for information exchange, cross-domain IT situational awareness and mission impact assessment, high service availability and assurance, and supporting the policies and procedures [13].

As depicted in Figure 10.10, CoI uses NCES to communicate with other CoI resources or processes. Two implementation options are available for a service operator to establish communication with other CoIs. In the first option, a networking module called ESM/NetOps provides communication services and proactively manages the services. In the second option, ESM enables a direct peer-to-peer data exchange with other CoIs.

As shown in the figure, ESM/NetOps provides a suite of operational processes, procedures, and technical capabilities to the remote CoIs. ESM/NetOps ensures services are accessible, available, protected, secure, operating, and performing as defined in SLA and OLA. Similar to ESM/NetOps, basic ESM usually offers the service provisioning, monitoring, reporting, problem anticipation, root cause analysis, life-cycle management, and regulations and governance functionalities.

10.4.2 Examples in Service Assurance

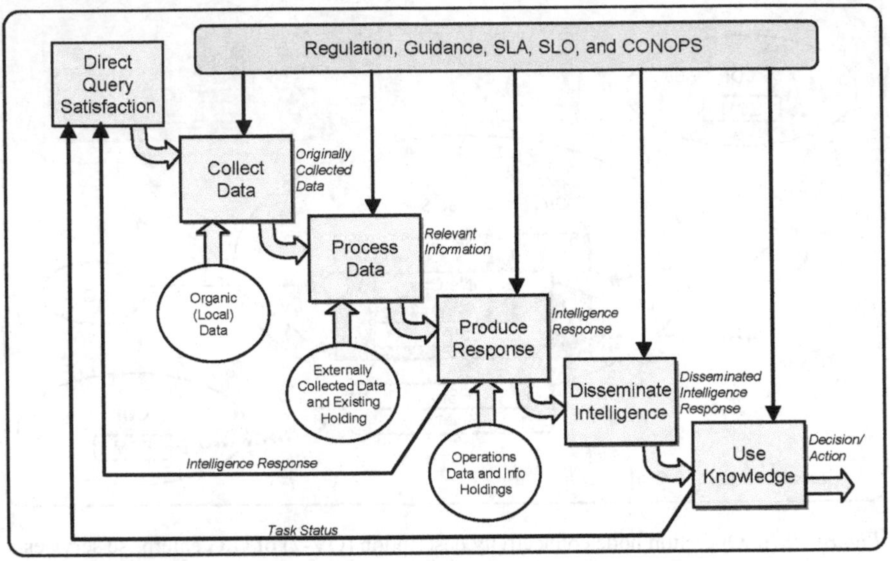

Figure 10.11. Activity model (OV-5) – service assurance operations.

The *activity model* (OV-5) specifies the applicable activities associated with the target architecture and the data exchanged among other activities. The model is hierarchical in nature. It describes the overall activities and decomposes the activity details. Figure 10.11 demonstrates the activity model of a typical service assurance operation [12].

The data collection function queries the management agents for measurements or event logs of organic assurance data in accordance with the CONOPS, SLA, and SLO specifications. The data is further processed with external reference or relevant information. The resulted service knowledge is disseminated to the actors that can make decisions or take actions. The service knowledge and task status are fed back to the query engine to make appropriate adjustment if necessary.

In Figure 10.12, the OV-6b specifies the *Operational State Transition* of a normal SLA management flow. Similar to the previous figure, service data is generated by the data collection function and navigate through three different threads based on the predefined service model and operational rules. Both two threads concerning trouble management threads are activated by alarms. The service information is then processed by the resource and service trouble managements respectively, and eventually arrives at the *resource support and readiness* and the *service support and readiness*. The third thread is a SLM thread, also triggered by service events. The service impacts reports are processed by the SQM and correlated with customer agreements from the *Retention and Loyalty* module to produce a service report for the *customer interface management* (e.g., CRM). The end customer receives this report either through scheduled statement or ad-hoc notifications.

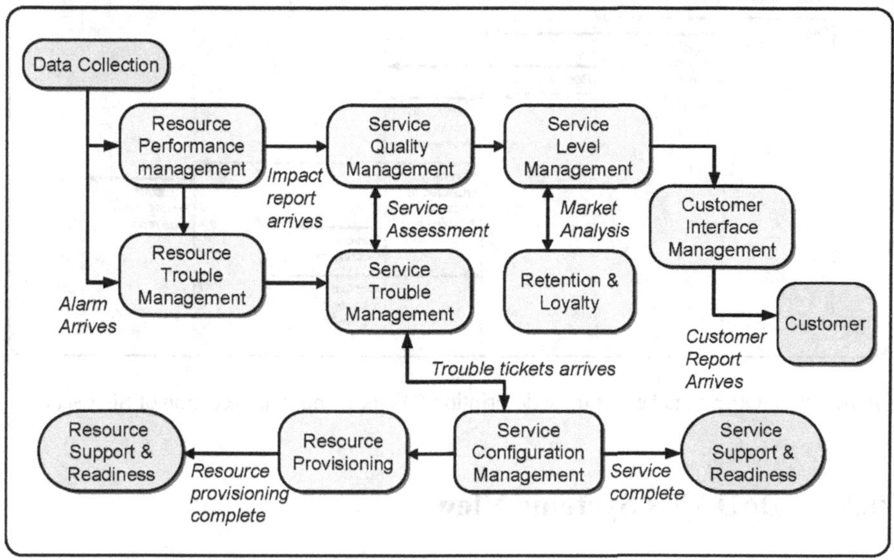

Figure 10.12. Operational state transition description (OV-6b) – normal execution of SLA service.

The *operational event and trace descriptions* are sometimes called *sequential diagrams*, *event scenarios*, and *timing diagrams*. It allows the service operators to trace actions in a scenario or a critical sequence of events in accordance with the service models defined. Figure 10.13 demonstrates the flow of a normal execution of SLM that was previously illustrated from the perspective of state transition and depicted in Figure 10.12. Three dimensions of the information flows are addressed. The *resource dimension* depicts the sequence of the service operator's performance in handling abnormal situation. The *service dimension* emphasizes service quality improvement and operational efficiency. The *market product and customer dimension* carries out the assurance operations to the marketing and financial level, typically called the business level. Because these flows often represent business processes, a flow representation is sometimes referred to as a *business process model*, or simply a *process model*.

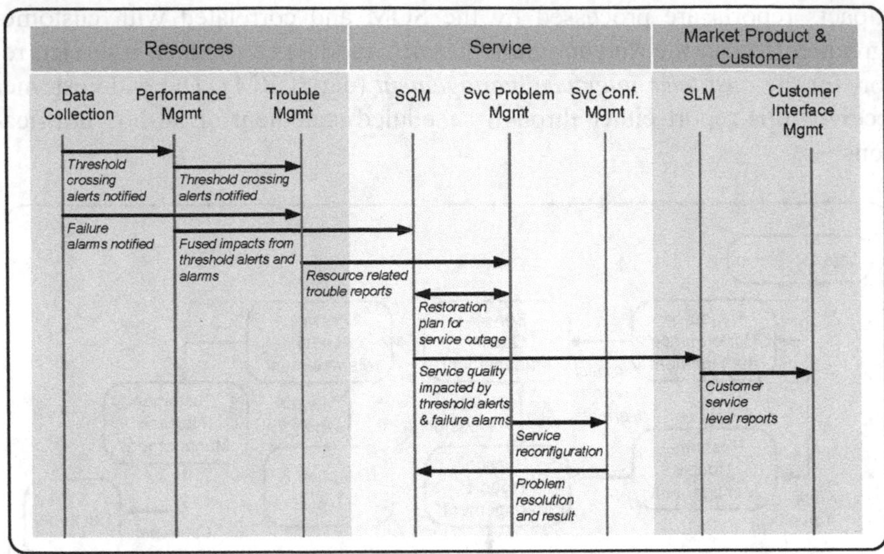

Figure 10.13. Operational event/trace description (OV-6c) – normal execution of SLA service.

10.5 DoDAF's Systems View

Once the operational aspects are identified, the next step is to identify the system view that can satisfy the operational requirements. In a service-oriented environment, an enterprise service typically encompasses a set of well-defined functions to its users or consumers. An application is presented as an integral set of logically connected services. A collection of applications and services forms the primary objects that describe the systems aspects of an enterprise service offering.

One important concept differs from the traditional system development view is that these services are application layer components whereas traditional system view is oriented toward resources such as middleware, operating system, hardware, and network elements. In a NCBO environment, the consumers are only exposed to the service endpoint other than the actual processes and components that implement the service. These supporting resources or systems are only accessible by the service provider or service operator [8,14].

The *SV* of a service-oriented offering that addresses the SoS and the interconnections is depicted in Figure 10.14. The asterisks indicate multiple instances for an object and 1 means single instance. In an enterprise service environment, as aforementioned, physical and static connection are less

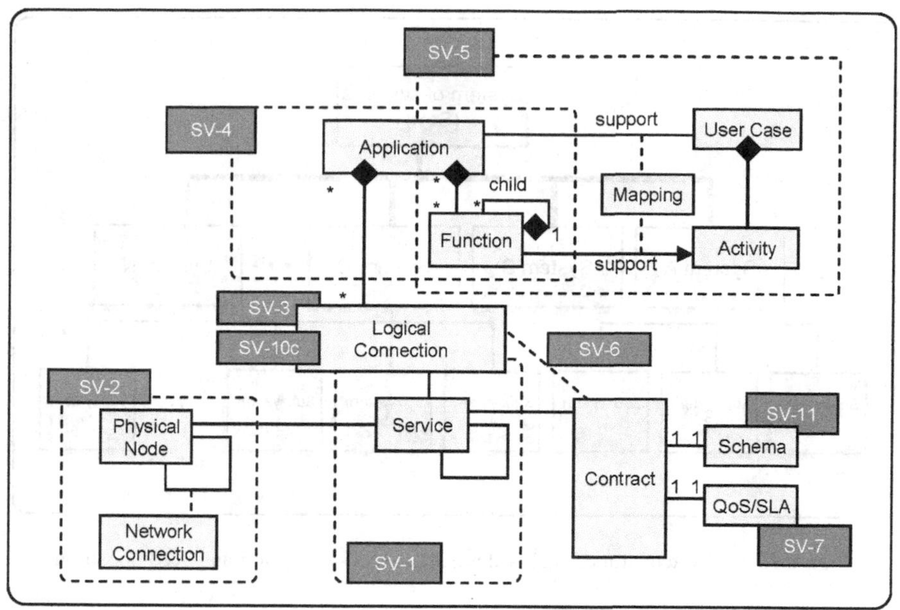

Figure 10.14. A Composite SV of the architectural objects and their relations.

significant than the logical interaction between service providers and consumers, thus a logical architecture diagrams for *system interface description (SV-1)* is normally satisfactory. *System communications description (SV-2)* reveals the connectivity and security criteria between service provider nodes (or components) and consumer nodes. The specification covers areas such as communication types, protocols, and assurance scenarios (e.g., network elements and computing nodes) and is therefore physical resource oriented. The *systems matrix (SV-3)* describes the relationships among systems in a given architecture. This can include system-type interfaces and planned versus existing (or legacy) interfaces. SV-4 captures the functional breakdown and the logical or physical structures that support these system functions. Figure 10.15 demonstrates a template of a SoS level system breakdown. Each application supports one or more use cases and may have a corresponding logical architecture diagram as defined in SV-1. Figure 10.16 shows a template of service data flow in SV-4.

Services connect to each other logically to provide functions via an application where the application satisfies the requirement by supporting the use cases. The *operational activity to systems function traceability matrix (SV-5)* contains mappings between applications and use cases and between functions and activities.

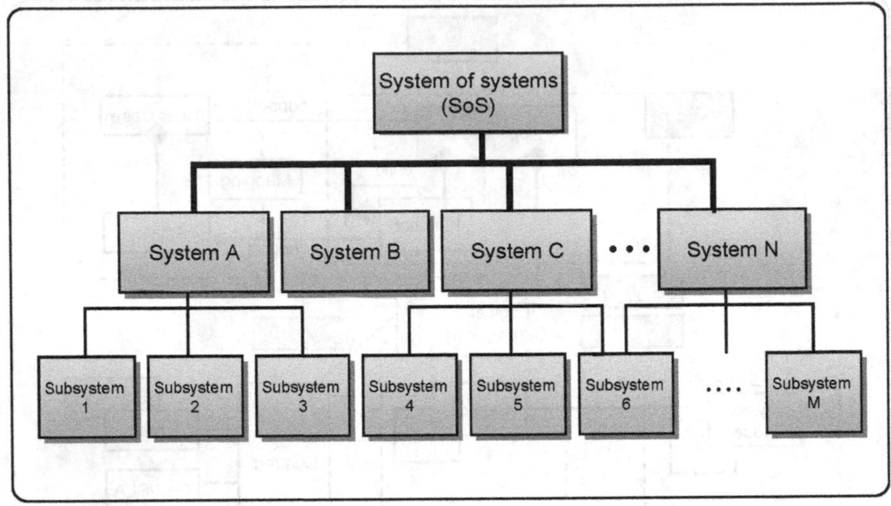

Figure 10.15. Systems functionality description (SV-4) – functional decomposition.

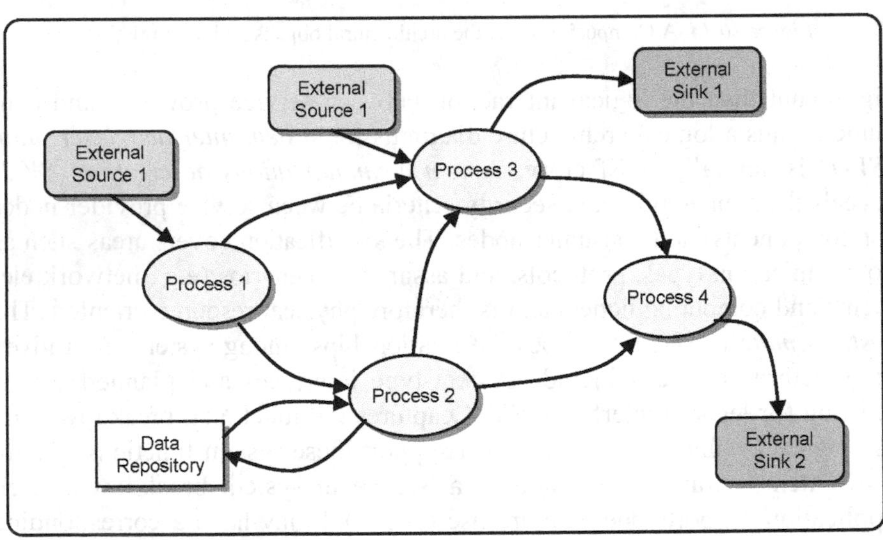

Figure 10.16. Systems functionality description (SV-4) – data flow.

Each logical connection provides detailed service contracts and a list of consumers of the services in the *system data exchange matrix (SV-6)*. SV-6, in essence, describes how the service provider can publish their services and how consumers can discover, subscribe, and consume the services. This specification may also capture other supplementary properties of a service, for instance, services from third party providers. The dynamic behavior of the data exchange can be captured by an *event trace* or *UML sequence diagram* in SV-10c.

The service contract dictates formats of the data exchanged between the providers and the customers. The *physical data model (SV-11)* specifies the data schemas in the service contract such as UML class diagrams, XML schemas, and so forth. The *systems performance parameters matrix (SV-7)* specifies the enterprise QoS or SLA performance requirements.

In an event trigger service, *UML state* diagrams *(SV-10b)* can assist the information customer to capture system or object state changes. As these changes are typically triggered by an event associated with a use case, it is vital for the enterprise to establish hierarchical process flows to compensate for the weakness of flat-based SOA applications.

Closely related use cases for similar services is a practical approach the enterprise can adopt to reuse valuable business assets for supporting different applications. In mission critical applications when loss of any part of the system may deprive the overall QoS or capability commitments, grouping the assets with appropriate assurance features can localize the impact to the operations.

10.5.1 SOA-Based Application Systems

As seen in section 10.1.1, the value-chain operations have evolved from sharing data and sharing applications into the realm of business process integration. The role of business operation architecture has shifted from system to SoS level and led the integration strategy of business processes beyond the enterprise boundary. This is also the driver behind the notion of the *Semantic Web*, for instance.

The business integration architecture is the design and implementation of methods and solutions to maximize efficiencies in enterprise-wide strategic business processes. Shown in Figure 10.17 as a SV-2 description, a SOA application has four functional blocks.

The Web Portal is based on Internet-standard protocols like HTTP, FTP, and SMTP providing ubiquity, unreliable, and native support for sophisticated message exchange.

The *Web business integration* block is composed of countless incompatible resources and processes such as platform selection, standards use, service sophistication, invocation pattern, skill-set, and so forth; all of which must be mitigated to enable seamless service sharing in the enterprise. Business integration architecture focuses on the life cycle of a given business function and the relationships, both internal and external to the enterprise [15].

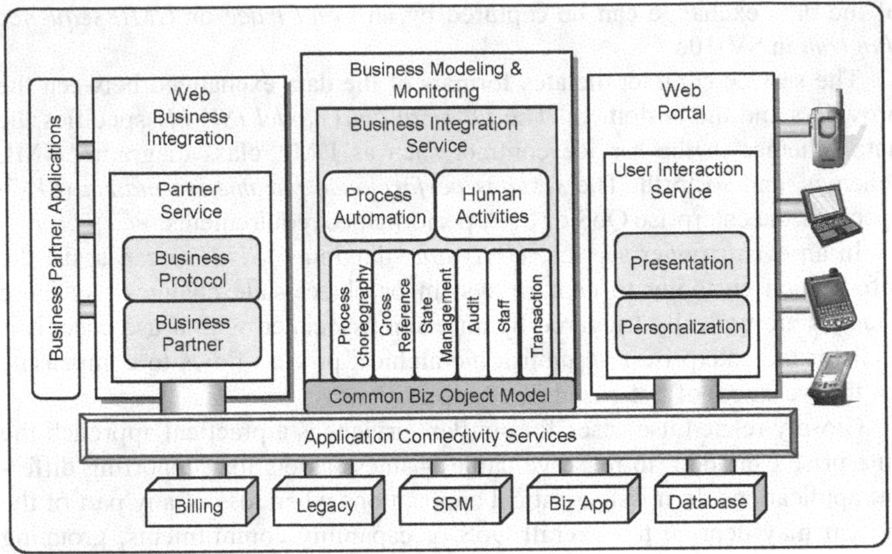

Figure 10.17. Systems communications descriptions (SV-2) – SOA applications.

The *Business modeling and monitoring block* is critical for operational efficiency because the enterprise has to eliminate inefficiencies by: 1) eradication of redundancies in processes and operations; 2) multilevel integration into common fulfillment processes; 3) leveraging process of partners, suppliers, and customers in B2B relationships; and 4) reallocation of corporate resources. This approach can bridge business knowledge to existing tightly coupled solutions and unlock their values for reuse by the enterprise. Deployed throughout the SOA, the distributed policy enforcement can guarantee business policies and govern enterprise-wide service sharing and reusability.

The *application connectivity services* handle dissimilar information representation. It is the concept of managing entities that are represented in the services environment offered by various domains and CoI. While the proprietary bus framework provides reliable messaging but lacks ubiquity, the NCBO methodology supports message reliability guarantees, combines ubiquity and reliability into a shared and uniform messaging backbone.

10.5.2 Network-Centric Enterprise Services

The NCBO solution is intended to solve incompatibilities and manage non-functional aspects problems. Based on requirement of service-oriented paradigm and network-centricity, NCBO is the best approach for the SOA governance framework because of its better efficiency, stability, and mobility than other alternative architectures [14].

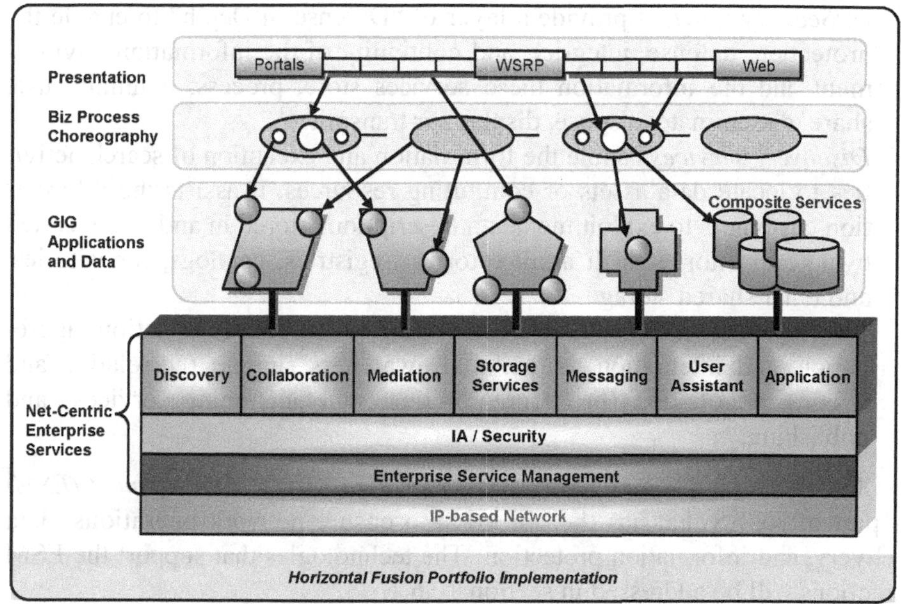

Figure 10.18. Systems communications descriptions (SV-2) – NCES components.

Supporting by the previous discussion, a NCBO solution can efficiently arbitrate services that have inherent incompatibilities, and guarantee message reliability in support of enterprise business that requires this level of sophistication. Additionally, NCBO provides a consistent and predictable communication between Web services deployed across a distributed SOA-based enterprise.

Figure 10.18 depicts the GIG NCES and their relationships with other GIG elements as well as the upper level applications. The enterprise services are built upon the GIG's IP-based network and composed of the following key functional services:

- *Application services* provision, host, operate, and manage the computing environment.
- *User Assistant services* automatically learn and apply user preferences and patterns in performing service tasks. This knowledge can assist users to more efficiently and effectively utilize GIG resources.
- *Storage services* provide on demand posting, storage, and retrieval of data, information, and knowledge.
- *Messaging services* support synchronous and asynchronous information exchange. It includes intermediation-based, networking-centric approaches to support enterprise SOA applications.
- *Collaboration services* allow users to work together and jointly use selected capabilities such as chat and online meetings on the network.

- *IA/Security services* provide a layer of "Defense in Depth" to enable the protection, defense, integrity, and continuity of the information environment and the information these services store, process, maintain, use, share, disseminate, dispose, display, or transmit.
- *Discovery services* enable the formulation and execution of search activities to locate data assets or computing resources. It assists the information customers to exploit metadata descriptions stored in and or generated by IT repositories such as directories, registries, catalogs, repositories, and other shared storage.
- *Mediation services* enable transformation processing (translation, aggregation, and integration), situational awareness support (correlation and fusion), negotiation (brokering, trading, and auctioning services) and publishing.

The underlying component called *Enterprise Service Management (ESM)* is part of NCES that has the objective to ensure network operations, data delivery, and information protection. The technologies that support the ESM functions will be addressed in section 10.6.1.

10.5.3 Examples of Business Integration Technology

Services are often organized into layers, with the lowest layer containing the core services to perform specific functions, and the upper layers containing the value-added or composite services. Service consumers may dynamically connect to one or many servers to access enterprise assets. The synchronous messaging services, reliable and integrated data storage, and enterprise-wide security in the core services are the key challenges to the service providers. Additionally, similar services or solutions can coexist simultaneously on the CoI network thus complicate the integration attempt. The following sections profile some popular approaches for the business integration technologies [16].

10.5.3.1 Business Integration Architecture

The "traditional" *Enterprise Application Integration (EAI)* technology focuses on message brokers, transformation engines, and accessing reusable software services. To satisfy service-oriented enterprise's new business requirement for multiple domain integration, the EAI technology has evolved into new scope which focuses on improving the accuracy and consistency of information within and between the participant-service entities. This updated technology provides a flexible environment enabling the enterprise to effectively support expansion of their current business and gain new competitive values. This transformation may influence the enterprise's internal or external interaction capabilities in the areas such as information integrity, process alignment, and visibility throughout the community [17].

The integration can occur at three points: the presentation integration is easy but the value-add is limited, the functional integration is the most effective but also the most complicated, and finally the data integration has a broader impact to other systems and may require software development.

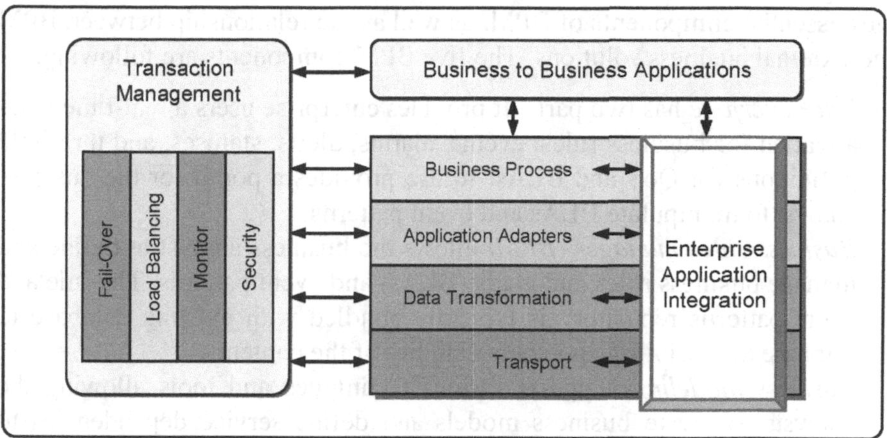

Figure 10.19. Systems communications descriptions (SV-2) – enterprise application integration.

The transformation can help the enterprise to obtain improved customer and supply-chain relationships, streamlined internal processes, and reduced time to market. Figure 10.19 demonstrates an example EAI solution in an enterprise application environment. In the figure, the EAI module integrates the business process, application adapters, data transformation, and transport services and supports the upper level business-to-business applications.

The goals of EAI are to reduce coupling as well as to improve automation, refinement, and integration of the enterprise operational processes. For instance, data visibility for important actionable conditions can improve the efficiency of identification and action awareness. Additionally, the overall process refinement is achievable when the cross-organization information visibility can be presented as a single cohesive unit in a value chain. As the result, the refinement can greatly enhance vendor-managed inventory, collaborative planning, forecast, and replenishment, evaluated receipt settlement, and so forth [18].

10.5.3.2 Business Process Management

The *business process management (BPM)* offers enterprises the ability to orchestrate business among people and system to achieve consistency and efficiency in complex and networked processes. It allows the business analyst to describe and modify the business process model, to execute business processes, and to coordinate activities of enterprise users or software applications. BPM can sometimes encompass other process applications, for instance, Six Sigma solution, *Sarbanes-Oxley Act* Solution, *Total Quality Management (TQM)*, and *business activities monitoring (BAM)* applications [19, 20].

Figure 10.20 demonstrates the relationship between BAM and the other four essential components of BPM, as well as the relationship between BPM and external business solutions. The five BPM components are following.

- *User interface* has two parts. It provides enterprise users a real-time visualization for business rules, events, alarms, alerts, statuses, and threshold definitions for QoS and BLAs. It also provides a portal for the business analyst to manipulate BLAs and event patterns.
- *Business rules manager (BRM)* allows the business analyst to define and manage business rules and goals (BLAs) and event patterns. The rule and event patterns repository is typically bundled with existing database to improve accessibility and controllability of the contents.
- *Business modeling* supports various techniques and tools allowing the analysts to create business models and define service dependencies to support software or non-software services, whether it is hierarchical or peer-to-peer structure. The basic tools may include swim-lane diagrams or service dependency diagrams.
- *Service realization* provides mechanisms to realize the software services defined in the modeling component. The outcomes are often offered in the form of service buses in the case of Web services. XML business process languages such as BPEL4WS can assist the enterprise to automate the choreography of Web services.
- *Process engine* executes the applications generated from the business process model and choreographs the services from the service realization component. It is the integration point that contacts with external business assets through the enterprise's Internet or Intranet. Although the figure shows the connections are WS-based, it can also be proprietary or other open interfaces.

BPM is increasingly becoming one of the major business integration platforms because of its capability to support the full life cycle of process design, deployment, execution, analysis, and optimization with the Web services technologies (e.g., ebXML, WSDL, WSFL, SOAP). Because of its open nature, BPM can enable the creation of collaborative business services and provide easy integration with packaged, legacy or custom-built applications with appropriate level of security and reliability [21].

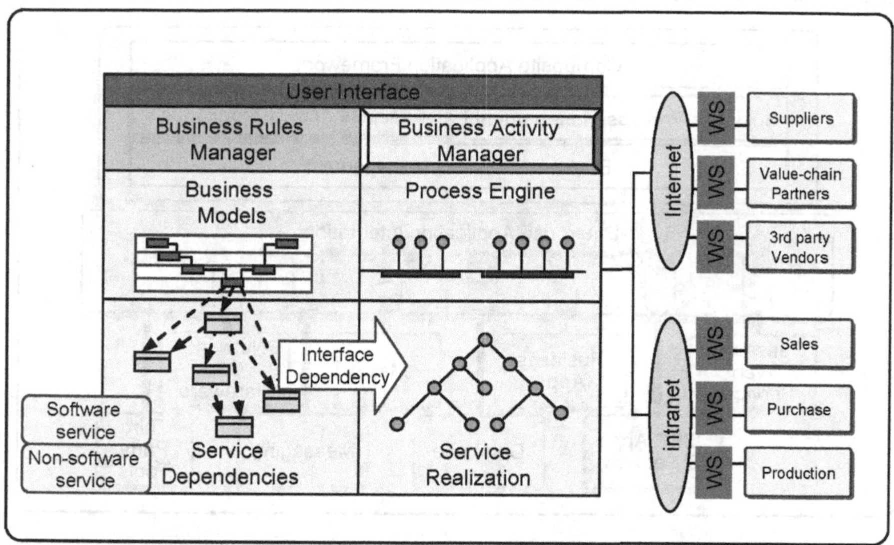

Figure 10.20. Systems communications descriptions (SV-2) – business process management.

10.5.3.3 Business Activity Monitoring

The *business activity monitoring (BAM)* refers to as the real-time monitoring, measuring, aggregation, analysis, and reporting on the execution of business transactions, operations, and processes. The feature goal of BAM is to ensure business problems can be informed thus sensible business decisions can be reached quickly.

BAM can be offered as an independent system or a building-block of a larger business management solution. In Figure 10.21, BAM situates as a peer component of BPM in part of the composite application framework, which is different from the presentation in Figure 10.20. Regardless of the relationship with other business applications, BAM captures data from ongoing business operations through the EAI layer. The sources of the monitored data can come from database, e-mail, messaging, transaction Web services, network, operating system, and business application. In addition to the real-time reporting, BAM is capable of correlating heterogeneous events against the business policy and models, identifying patterns, or performing causalities, aggregates, and thresholds analysis. The dependency of the BPM knowledge with respect to QoS attributes, BLAs, and business models becomes essential. That is why BAM and BPM are coupled in most solution offerings.

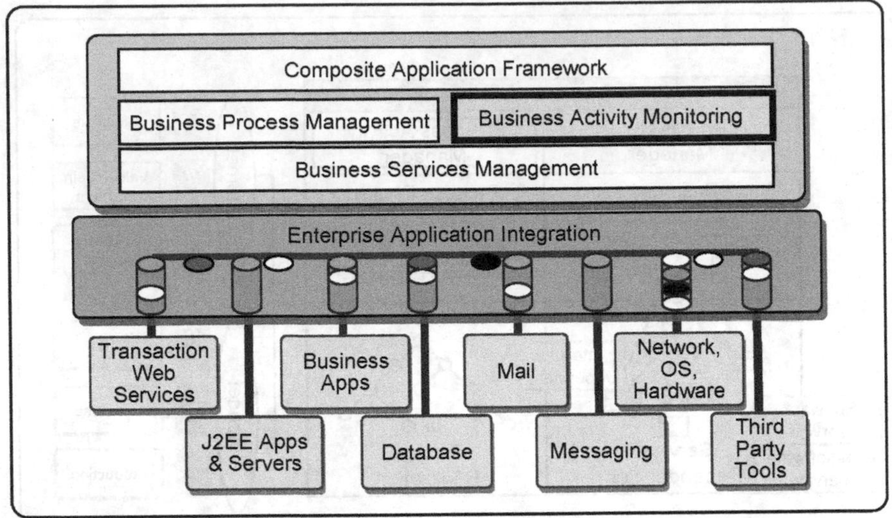

Figure 10.21. Systems communications descriptions (SV-2) – business activity monitoring.

Referencing the rules defined during process instrumentation, BAM can produce business knowledge reports on the progress of individual processes, and aggregate process execution audit information to describe the overall behavior of processes for a particular business domain. Although BAM usually uses dashboard technology to display business knowledge, it is distinct from the *business intelligence (BI)* dashboard. The BI dashboard is referred as a user driven reporting scheme which requires the users to determine the query scheduler for accessing historical database. BI helps enterprises to analyze large amounts of historical data, identify patterns, and understand trends that might affect the business. In contrast, BAM is driven by business events and process-oriented data. Combining the benefits from both BI and BAM as discussed in the Complex Event Processing section of chapter 9 can offer a comprehensive business intelligence solution.

In the event when the business knowledge requires direct interactions with the underlying enterprise resources for lower level information. The situation-awareness function described in chapter 9 can be treated as an independent data source of BAM or an integral part of BAM depending upon the design philosophy and the complexity of the business requirements.

10.6 DoDAF's Technical View

The TV includes technical standards, implementation conventions, rules, and criteria that guide the implementation of enterprise services. As shown in Figure 10.22, there are two major areas in TV. The *technical standards profile (TV-1)* references the key technical standards and technologies employed by the service offering. The *technical standards forecast (TV-2)* describes the forward looking standards that can support future technologies, methods, and procedures. The scope of TV addresses the technologies covering the enterprise operations, software, hardware, information, information system (application), governance, and other general technology infrastructure used in the service implementation and operations.

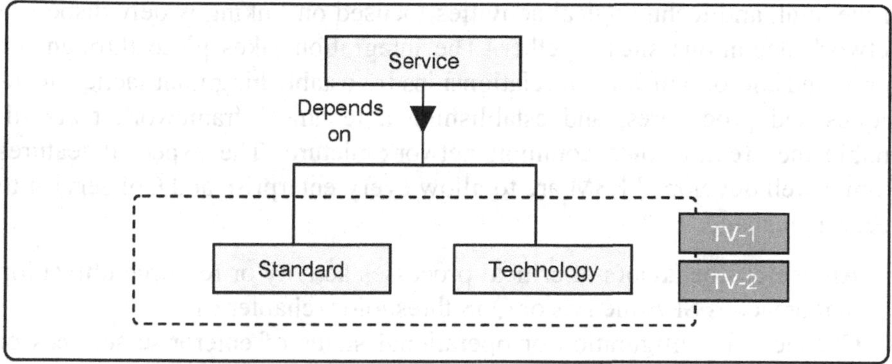

Figure 10.22. Technical view supports the enterprise service.

10.6.1 Enterprise Service Management

As seen in Figure 10.18, ESM is a service operational management portal which interacts with the low-level management systems to warrant end-to-end service availability, information protection, information delivery, and network operation. This management should be interoperable across traditional organizational management and security enclave boundaries. The basic capabilities include infrastructure/service management, traffic management, cross-domain management information exchange, cross-domain IT situational awareness and mission impact assessment, high service availability and assurance, and supporting the policies and procedures.

ESM is not restricted to a single management, organizational, or geographical dependent domains. In fact, it should be designed and deployed with SoS or FoS in mind whether large or small. Service operators from different management domains should share a common understanding of the service situations. As aforementioned, a COP can assist the management teams to align the processes with synergetic policies and procedures to optimize their business practices. Creating a cross-domain situational awareness capability via COP requires an infrastructure instrumented with monitoring and reporting capabilities, an in-depth knowledge regarding critical mission processes, an understanding of the relationships between the two, and the ability to present relevant status and associated mission impact assessments to the decision makers at all levels [22].

The supporting features for service and network operations have been discussed in chapter 2. The cope of network operations encompass the coordinated and comprehensive set of operational procedures and organizational structure that provide the needed fusion by the collection of systems and network management, information assurance, *information dissemination management (IDM)* into a single integrated operational construct. *Network operations concepts (NetOps)* are based on a combination of organizational, procedural, and technological activities focused on linking widely dispersed network operations sites together. The integration takes place through the command and organizational relationships by establishing joint tactics, techniques and procedures, and establishing a technical framework that will enable the creation of a common network picture. The expected features from a well developed ESM are to allow every enterprise and CoI service to securely manage:

- Anomalous behaviors of critical processes activity or resource utilization that breaches SLA metrics or QoS thresholds (chapter 6)
- Changes in configuration or operational status of enterprise services or networks (chapter 5)
- Aggregated or individual operational performance measurement which failure to meet SLA (chapter 6)
- Violations of security policy which could be indicative of a cyber-attack against the service (chapter 8)
- Adequate and timely service desk support (chapters 8 and 9)
- Trouble identification, reporting, escalation, resolution and notification processes and procedures (chapters 6 and 8)

10.6.2 Messaging Technology

The messaging technology for enterprise service includes hybrid architecture and Web-based messaging. The goal is to integrate data and voice messaging with the contact management hence cross-enterprise business processes, applications, rules, and databases can be fully communicated. In a more sophisticate situation, translingual feature may be included.

As depicted in Figure 10.23, through the contact management the enterprise users can access *instant messaging (IM)*, *notification services*, *awareness services*, *unified messaging* which are established upon mobile technologies such as SMS, EMS, MMS, IM, E-mail/PIM, and 3G or 4G wireless technologies.

IM offers text conversation for the conference attendees, presence detection and status, and secure synchronous messaging; even with mobile devices. This feature provides a convenient media for service users to contact mobile hosts as well as other information users. The IM standard is specified in the *Internet Engineering Task Force (IETF) IM and Presence Protocol (IMPP) (SIMPLE CPIM)* [23].

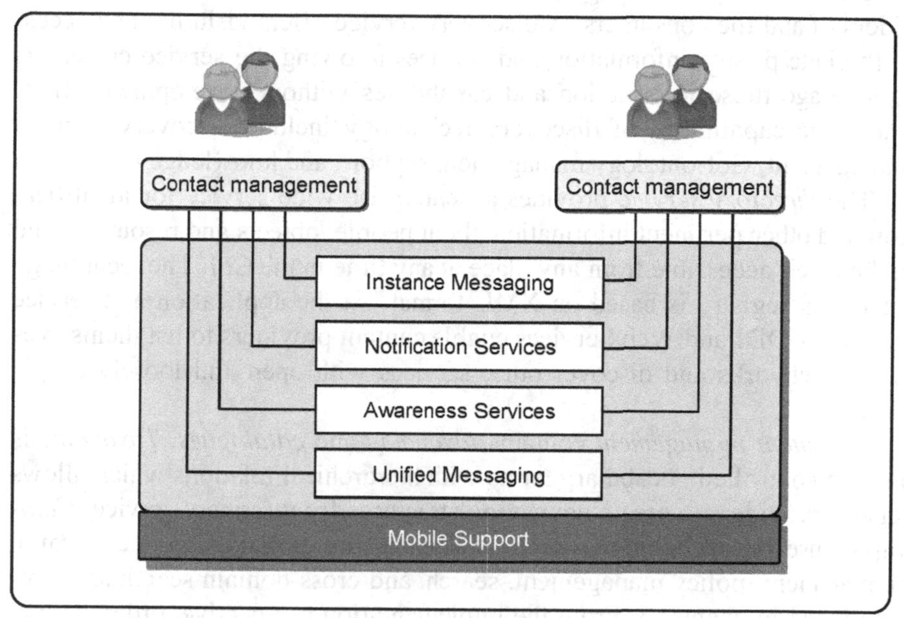

Figure 10.23. Messaging technology supports CoI users.

Enterprise services can facilitate the messaging technology to integrate with third party services via Web portals and take advantage of HTML and XML to support browser-based access to E-mail, instant messaging, light-weight wireless support, unified Fax, paging, voice, and video service, and interoperable global communications. These are expected to be operated efficiently on wide range of devices from high-powered desktop computers to thinly featured cell-phones and other short messaging devices using WAF, WAP, and so forth. To offer needed information assurance, this service can integrate with *Information Assurance and Security (IAS*; section 10.6.8*)* to ensure rigid information safety.

Notification service can be used by the users to notify or alert selected devices by using the *push and pull* technologies. *Shared white board* technology as an *awareness service* allows the users to publish or subscribe information that are available in the knowledge database or from other information participants. The standard for Shared White Board technology is specified in the ITU-T's *Multipoint still image and annotation protocol* (T.126) and *Non-Destructive overlays.*

10.6.3 Discovery Technology

The *discovery technology* provides service link between the service providers of and the consumers. A discovery service offers visibility and access to the enterprise's information and services allowing the service customers to leverage these information and capabilities without development effort. The basic capabilities of discovery technology include discovery, content management, CoI-ontology management support, and knowledge bases.

The *directory service* provides an enterprise-wide service for identification and other pertinent information about people, objects and resources, and makes their accessible from any place at any time in the CoI. The technology for object registry is based on XML format. At the application and service side, the UDDI and Web Services enable content providers to list themselves on the networks and discover other services with open and loosely-couple manner.

A *content management* contains *taxonomy* and *catalogues*. *Taxonomy* is a set of controlled vocabulary terms with hierarchical relations which allows service providers to create navigation structures for discovery service. *Catalogues* use the technologies such as domain and global catalogues, profile management, policy management, search, and cross-domain search as aforementioned in chapter 8. From the implementation perspective, ordered-ness, consistency, and completeness are three challenges of the registry service especially in a mobile environment. The challenges on the search aspect are reliability, resilience, and security. These are typically managed at the application level instead of standard level.

The CoI-ontology management support has been discussed in chapter 8. The knowledge base was addressed in chapter 9.

10.6.4 Collaboration Technology

As shows in Figure 10.24, collaboration services were historically handled manually via meetings, conference calls, e-mail and newsgroups. New generation synchronous collaboration services embraces browser-based, ad-hoc, and virtual shared workspaces offering service-oriented synchronous environment for peer-to-peer communication [24].

The basic capabilities of collaboration technology should support audio, video, and chat among conference attendees. The IP Telephony standards are defined in the *ITU Telecommunication Standardization Sector (ITU-T)* H.323 and the more recent technology in *Session Initiation Protocol (SIP)*. In addition, IM, shared workspaces, and whiteboard applications can be added to enrich the quality of information exchanges. The associated standards have aforementioned in section 10.6.2.

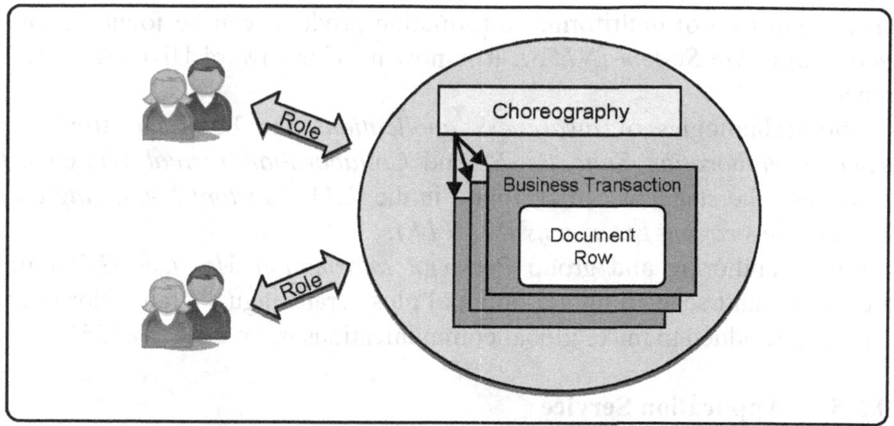

Figure 10.24. Binary collaboration among CoI communities.

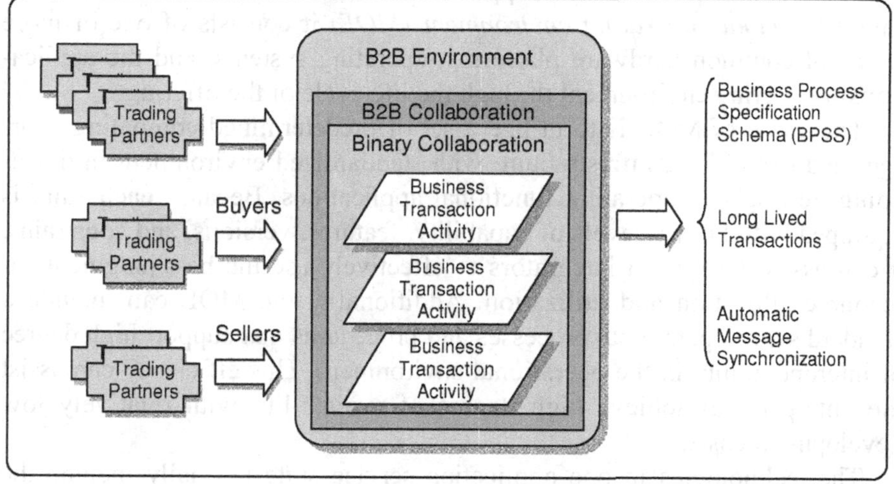

Figure 10.25. Multiple function and multiple parties collaboration.

Interoperability of multipoint conferencing sites has to consider across-domain, organization, and coalition security policy. Policy-based collaboration interoperability should address access controls over heterogeneous infrastructures across multilevel security and networks. Security services can be included to add a robust end-to-end encryption, digital signature, archiving, and other key security features.

For Web Conferencing Applications such as Webcast and WebEx, service users can share applications running on a networked machine without requiring the attendees to possess the applications. The standard of this technology can be found at *ITU-T's multipoint application sharing* (T.128 also know as T-share). The technology standard for *file sharing and virtual workspace repository* of multiformat information products can be found at *New Technology File System (NTFS)*, it is now moving toward URL-based reference.

The technologies of *awareness applications* can be found from the *Oracle Collaboration Suite (OCS)* and *Collaboration Virtual Workspace (CVW)* and the standard can be found in the IETF's *Instant Messaging and Presence Leveraging Extensions (SIMPLE)*.

Group authoring and group *Personal Information Manager (PIM)* for calendaring and scheduling are optional plus. Translingual (translation) services can be added to make global communications more effective [25].

10.6.5 Application Service

The Application service technology is about hosting core services and applications for providers to support networked services. The concept is called the *model operating environment (MOE)* it consists of one or more suites of common hardware platforms, operating systems, and the applications for hosting environment through the life cycle of the offering.

The value of MOE is to utilize a set of predetermined computing, storage, and networking infrastructure with standardized environment in developing, testing and operating functional applications. Because each suite is equipped with known levels of capability, features, versions, and constrains, it can assist the system integrators to effectively use the best judgment for resource allocation and utilization. Additionally, the MOE can include a standard set of operational processes and procedures that support high degree of interoperability in the operational environment. This efficiency can assist the enterprise to achieve high degree of availability with relatively low development costs.

The technologies in one application service suite normally include the physical elements, security requirements and definition, load balancing, GRID computing architecture, and content delivery architecture.

From an operational perspective, a suite can include service configuration managements and software distribution services to ensure consistent upgrades and changes procedures across geographically dispersed sites. The FCAPS should also include standardized operations and support levels, quality assurance, CERT security, disaster recovery, and event correlation for monitoring, managing, controlling, and load balancing of the hosted applications and services. Security levels for hosting environments are also typically on the MOE-basis.

Additionally, the *security technical implementation guides (STIGS)* can be added to a suite with the consideration of technology insertion updates. A service offering can use the *commodity service concept* to ensure its capacity processing is following the *on-demand paradigm.* The resources management should include system administration standard, DBA standard, certification process, and *Information Systems Security Manager (ISSM)* and *Information Systems Security Officer (ISSO)* guidance.

10.6.6 Mediation

Mediation is an optional service between the information provider and consumers. It provides a value-add middle layer with automated capabilities for assured delivery, translation, conversion, fusion, and routing of information between CoI members. A mediation function can be synchronous or asynchronous and its processing location can be distributed or central.

- A *central synchronous configuration* requires redundant network locations and fail-over procedures to guarantee a fair level of availability.
- A *distributed synchronous configuration* manages the execution of mediation processing across network thus can improve availability and performance.
- A *central asynchronous configuration* uses queues to transform and route message traffic in near real-time or in batch mode. It also requires redundant systems to ensure the service availability.
- A *distributed asynchronous configuration* is a true network-centric configuration. It uses the network as the queue to distribute message traffic.

The technologies for mediation services can be implemented in a staged approach. In earlier phases, the strategy for B2B integration can focus on the flexibility for adopting the new service model, e.g., asynchronous or synchronous. The subsequent phases should consider the accessibility and availability of logical (data and service) and physical assets in association with appropriate redundancy, survivability, performance, delivery, auditing, management, and security considerations. The implementation focusing on the assured delivery and service monitoring must be sensible to the SLA specifications.

If the enterprise has complex information assets, the near real-time nature of the data interactions from EAI should be included. As data traffic becomes a key feature of enterprise business, the mediation services should consider distribution, propagation, availability, load balancing, and networking issues at the physical level. Hardware and software placement and configuration should be optimized in accordance with the physical service positions and relations with other services. In this case, BPM can be used to improve the visibility of role, capabilities, and information for CoI members. BAM can bring the feature values such as translation, fusion, or aggregation of the service knowledge and metrics to enrich the depth of BLA and SLA for the improvement of the provider's competitive edge. As aforementioned, coupling BPM and BAM can improve the customer experience in managing B2B and/or B2C integration (see Figure 10.25).

In advanced services, features for the mediation technology can be extended to include content translation, additional application layer services measures, enhanced service model with refined performance expectations and auditing, automatic fusion opportunities identification, automatic business rules associated with data fusion process, automatic fused data posting, as well as mobility requirements.

10.6.7 Storage

The basic capabilities of a storage service includes shared storage capacity, enterprise storage architecture, storage capacity on demand, and storage management. To make data and information more widely and easily accessible by different community applications and information customers, the technical strategy of the storage service should satisfy the *task-post-process-use (TPPU)* paradigm. The storage service with this paradigm should achieve zero latency allowing information to be exchanged across technical and organizational boundaries quickly and securely.

Network attached storage (NAS) devices and *storage area networks (SAN)* are two essential technologies to support the network-centric operations.

A SAN is architected to attach remote computer storage devices such as disk array controllers, tape libraries and CD arrays to servers as if they are locally connected to these servers. This architecture is normally used to networking large disk arrays to high-bandwidth servers which can stand for heavy traffic. In the mean time many client computers access these servers for the needed data.

NAS is a data storage technology which allows storage devices to be connected directly to the network and provides centralized data access and storage to heterogeneous network clients. Because data access is not dependent upon any server, the server can be down while the users still have access to their data. Hence, the availability and performance of data can potentially be increased. However, if a NAS is occupied by high demanding I/O or CPU processing power, the performance of NAS can be very limited. In this case, the *direct-attached storage (DAS)* may be a better alternative.

From the assurance perspective, commodity based storage environment allows the enterprise to enforce closer monitoring, controlling, and protective access to the data with standardized mechanisms. With *storage on-demand* technology, the enterprise can add additional storage at a rate compatible to the projected growths. As the operational budget and the performance considerations for both data storage approaches become adjustable, the enterprise can foster a more dynamic and controllable environment. Finally, *persistent storage management* is a key technology to ensure the availability of data accessibility.

10.6.8 Information Assurance and Security

The *information assurance and security (IAS)* technologies provide a foundation for the enterprise to implement uniform, consistent, and effective security. IAS features should be invoked as needed by service providers and users to satisfy business and policy requirements. The basic capabilities of IAS include authentication infrastructure, access management, guards, access management, identity management, authentication, authorization, access-enforcement, cross-classification connectivity, and logging and auditing. Figure 10.26 portrays the service-oriented application layer and standard networking layer with corresponding security standards and protocols. Many of the technologies addressed in chapter 8 are integrated toward a unified communications and the *Real-Time Enterprise (RTE)*.

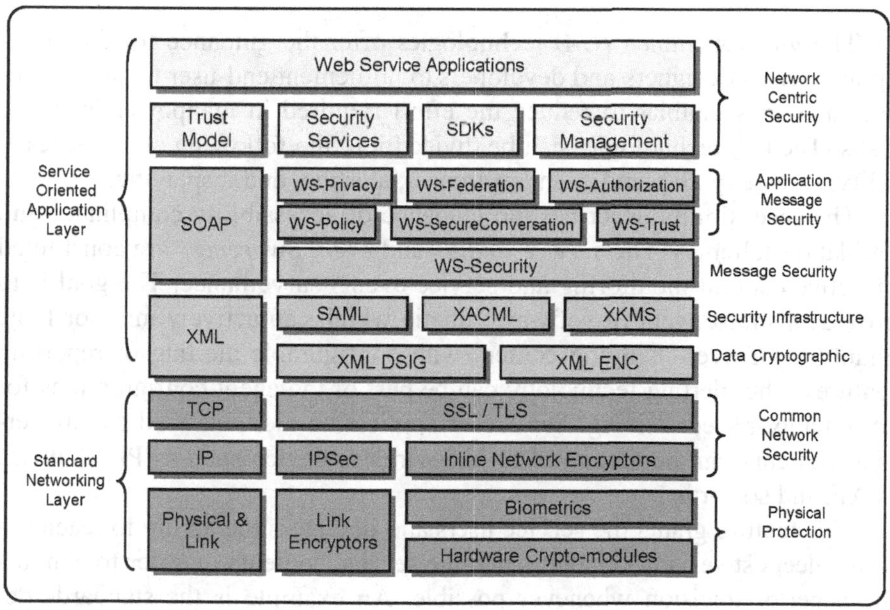

Figure 10.26. Service-oriented application layer and standard networking layer.

Among these different security technologies, one of the most popular and useful technologies is the *public key infrastructure (PKI)*. As mentioned in chapter 8, public key coupled with message-level confidentiality can offer relative secure messages at the application layer. Advanced features such as hardware tokens for higher domains (e.g., biometric technologies) can offer enterprise-level authentication and credential capabilities.

The *access management* technology maintains and uses identity, roles, privilege, and policy information to enforce access authorization decisions. The *cross-classification connectivity and control* can guarantee selective sharing of information across security boundaries in either or both directions. Critical messages shared across multilevel security can be managed by cross-domain gateways with general security tools such as anti-virus, anti-SPAM, and IDS.

The *logging function* provides the enterprise the ability to track and trace security events when the utilization of information or services are abused or violated. Proactive tracking technique automatically scans logs, provides a monitoring function to detect anomalies usages, and notifies the security manager in real time. This can provide an effective deterrent from insider and outsider attacks.

10.6.9 User Assistance

The *user assistance (UA)* technologies offer the guidance for the enterprise services designers and developers to implement end-user facing or end-user activities enabler to reduce the effort required in manpower intensive tasks. The UA technologies can be divided into the following areas: accessibility, service quality and event awareness, alerting, and displaying.

The accessibility describes the guidance of accessibility compliance and validation schemes. The *service quality* and *event awareness* are constituted of active content monitoring and service events surveillance. The goal is to provide a smart agent or software robotic which can actively monitor large quantities of ever-changing content with configurable alerting or reporting features. The alerting technology can be part of the agent configurations for community-based alerting. Service or application alerts as well as any service contents can be displayed on the wireless device such as PDA, WAP, WAF, and so forth.

This feature grants the service users and operators the ability to reach out to the deepest service behaviors and the service contents in order to conduct the superior decision whenever possible. An example is the standards defined by the *Web Content Accessibility Guidelines (WCAG)* 2.0 in dealing with new technologies and plug-ins.

10.7 Applications of NCBO

This focus of this chapter is to offer guidance on the design and implement considerations required for the enterprises to achieve higher standards in service-orientation operations with the network-centric paradigm. Many deployments have created success stories in different market contexts that may be applicable to even boarder applications which demand information-based strategies to create a competitive advantage in their respective domains [26].

- Implementation is more important than theory
- Competitive awareness
- Virtual organizations
- Cost and risk suppression
- Precision manufacturing
- Focused logistics
- Precision retailing
- The network is the market

10.7.1 Enterprise Operations

The main business driver in the area of enterprise operations concerns business agility. *Operational agility* describes the requisite levels of speed, cost-effectiveness, accuracy, and flexibility for organizational prosperity. Managing this array of functions requires appropriate processes that connect consumers and providers of services in a cohesive fashion. To maximize *Return of Investment (ROI)* for enterprise, multiple perspectives and factors need to be considered.

Process Improvement

- *Adaptation*: The ability to adapt the process gracefully to marketplace changes.
- *Optimization*: The ability to offer services in real time at high-performance levels.
- *Distribution of Labor*: Appropriate infrastructure to accommodate diverse demands. For example, Accounts Receivable will prioritize based on credit history, whereas the Shipping Department commits its focus to immediate, prescheduled destinations.
- *Foresight and Planning*: Considerations of outbound logistics and related decisions (e.g., what to do when demand for product exceeds supply).

Customer Awareness

- *Transparency*: The ease of customer experience in using a service; this includes consistency of information.
- *Customer Fit*: The use of core competencies to provide excellent products and experiences to customers; a crucial element of this is the ability to tailor offerings according to customer variation.

- *Customer History*: The context of a customer's relationship with the service provided is valuable in assessing both priority and urgency of needs regarding that customer.
- *Customer Projection*: Awareness of possible forthcoming trends contributes to the adaptation value-creation processes over time to maintain and increase value.
- *Needs Awareness*: Knowledge of, and sensitivity to, customer needs contributes to improvement in production, capacity, and logistics planning that can, in turn, improve product availability and reduce business risk. For example, when allocating finite resources against competing needs, the net profitability of a given customer is a key factor influencing those allocation decisions.

There are many applications can take advantages of wireless networks' mobility and openness features. In the following table, Table 10.2, sample front-end and back-end applications are provided for reference [27].

Table 10.2. Front-End and Back-End Applications.

Consumer	Business
Safety such as medical alerts, amber alerts, and public events.	Safety such as employee safety (e.g., safe-zone monitoring), business asset "Geo-fences", "ethics" monitoring.
Family security in the areas of family locator, after-school monitor, teen tracker (e.g., truancy monitor), child finder, pet tracking. For special zone tracking can include shopping malls, public events, zoos, and so on).	Business functions or processes include field sales force management, field technician dispatch; map forwarding, routing, fleet management; pickup/ delivery routing; vehicle management, office presence (location plus state, enabling new forms of business instant messaging), and facility finder; office finder Wi-Fi/location).
Mobile or interactive online games. End user services such as social enablers (singles), date finder, mobile personals, buddy finder, city guide, mobile concierge, and cyber wallet.	Vertical industries can include medical (Wi-Fi/location), railroad utilities (rail car locations), shopping malls (Wi-Fi/location), trucking (vehicle tracking, car tracking – shipping), insurance (adjustor routing), construction (contractor management), legal (ambulance chasing), security services (guard locator), and vending (consumer products).
"Viral" communities applications include social general, community specific and one-time "specials" (sports events, concerts, and so forth).	Education applications include campus location sensitive Wi-Fi partitioning, campus navigation, and community connectivity (location).
Professionals telemetry for navigation Assistance, "Lo-Jack" equivalents, and near-miss alerts.	Telemetry (businesses) for asset security and tracking, and geo-fences.
Driving directions, navigation aids, weather alerts, road assist (e.g., find gas).	Travel assistance, weather alerts, navigational aids.
Yellow pages (many permutations, such as ATM finder, restaurant finder, All the various shopping scenarios, and so forth).	(Business) yellow pages (many permutations possible, including specialized YP per verticals above).

Business Intelligence

NCBO is able to use information in order to suppress costs and reduce prices. This is enabled by information sharing across functional areas where resource-allocation decisions are made that maximize value from an overall enterprise perspective.

Increased awareness contributes to leveraging technology as a means of optimizing all value-chain activities in terms of effectiveness and efficiency; thus, costs and risks are minimized.

NCBO illustrates awareness in both developing strategy and boosting efficacy at the operational level. Awareness of one's customers, competitors, and the environment is essential to allow organizations to better understand what the characteristics or attributes of their products or services are or need to be for optimal value. In value-chain terms, partner connectivity allows enterprises the use of third parties in performing commodity services. Here, opportunities are created to streamline business process, improve professional relationships, and/or to generate revenue. At once, risk translates directly into increased cost and reduced value. Hence, the reduction of risk and its proper management are intrinsic to value creation, and have a truly significant impact on competitive advantage. The set of processes for exploiting this awareness result in an improved "bottom line".

Business process frameworks are particularly useful where adaptation is important. There are models of processes common to specific industry sectors and developed by industry groups. One such industry consortium is the TeleManagement Forum. eTOM defines all of the processes that are essential to a telecom company. The Supply Chain Council's Supply Chain Operations Reference (SCOR) provides another example of a business process framework that gives supply-chain teams a quick way to define a supply-chain process using a common vocabulary [28, 29].

10.7.2 Financial Services

Trading applications in the financial sector process an extremely large volume of transactions in near real time. Typically, a transaction is a single unit of information to be executed. However, differences in trading systems mean that it can comprise many subunits, all of which must activate in exact sequence. If any portion of a distributed transaction cannot commit as required, then the entire transaction must be rolled back. All of the information residing on different systems must be networked and consistently updated to complete a service order.

Trading systems should also be capable of simultaneously performing transactions while not affect one another, this is known as transaction isolation. In the event that transaction takes too long to complete – for instance, when a customer requests several purchase orders in a specific timeframe –

IA creates transaction durability to ensure completeness of the orders. This requires a network-centric operation. Financial companies are using the concept of NCBO to provide near real-time price awareness and enable near real-time transactions to achieve time compression and cost suppression.

Because traders can exploit their position of power by using information and information technologies to influence prices and delivery speed in trading objects, financial companies have instituted general operational requirements to avoid fraud by monitoring traders' trading patterns. Monitoring trading patterns from high-volume and inter-related transaction information is a challenge to all financial companies, requiring several networked analytic engines that, essentially, perform the functions of correlation and synchronization. The network-centric SOE can fulfill the need of transaction surveillances.

10.7.3 E-Commerce

Two essential competencies for a successful e-commerce business are obtaining loyal customers and acquiring commodity services at the lowest-possible cost.

Companies like Amazon recognized this need, launching an SOA-based technology (their "Apparel & Accessories Store") in November, 2002. This service allowed retailers to use the service provider (in this case, Amazon) as a major sales channel. Such "portal technology" caters to different customer needs through one set of services, typically offered through one channel at one time. As it continues to increase opportunities for aggregate services in "shop windows", the portal offers customers vast product selections from networked third parties on Amazon's product pages. The acumen of the e-commerce business model is realized in a one-stop experience that involves partner-service capabilities to be "plugged in" for a collaborated context-and-transition process.

Equally important is the underlying movement toward service orientation in the form of multichannel processes. Multichannel capability refers to end-to-end customer support throughout the process, using different channels to achieve continuity. For example, a customer can visit different vendors to complete a holiday shopping list. Across these domain processes involves a number of fundamental acquisition and completion among the commodity services vendors which is coalesced to enable a seamless network-centric operations. As the result, businesses (such as supermarkets) that once concentrated on retail domestic goods now offer pharmacies, gasoline stations, and insurance. This "info-structure" enables vastly improved competitive space awareness and shares this awareness through the e-commerce enterprise.

10.7.4 Retailing

Service-oriented enterprise offers business processes an agility solution for dynamic configuration when enterprises are codified into inflexible monolithic applications with choreography capability – the ability to respond easily to changes in business and technology.

Network-centricity additions can include both sensory capability and semi-automated transaction capabilities. In the transaction-intensive retail sector, information superiority can be accomplished by combining information with retailing data to achieve precision retailing. For instance, a sensor can scan, collect, and share product information with suppliers in near real time, enabling suppliers to optimize and control production and distribution, while appropriately managing their individual supply chains. The result is a significantly reduction of distribution costs, and high profitability.

The knowledge-management features delineated in chapter 9 can assist retailers to obtain high-level awareness by fusing real-time information with historical and environmental information. Combining their business knowledge with real-time transaction information allows retailers to develop a high degree of localized awareness. Upon choosing to share information directly with suppliers, operations become leaner, reducing costs and increasing performance. With the IA detailed in chapter 8, business processes collaborate smoothly through virtual value chains at infrastructural levels. The standards for choreography of Web services across multiple partners can rapidly affect business process across organizational boundaries.

Such business awareness can empower sectional managers to react to the market situation for pricing or stocking strategies to increase sales and revenues in near real time. Another advantage of such knowledge is more temporal. In a complex business environment, even the same entity can switch between customer and competitor, depending upon the business context and conditions. The enterprise must be able to comprehend appropriate role-playing to reflect changes in the market and hone adaptive organizational strategy. To succeed in a competitive market, existing and future business process models must be configured to adopt the NCBO into a corporate framework, allowing value-add services to be layered atop the model.

10.7.5 Military

As mentioned in earlier chapters, network-centric operations were devised by the military for the purpose of managing its battle power from a strong networking of a well-informed but geographically dispersed force. Based on a high-performance information grid, the network-centric warfare concept aims to provide applicability to all levels of warfare, contributing to the coalescence of strategy, operations, and tactics [30].

Increasing battle-space awareness yields increased combat power. Effective commanders continually acquire more and better information to improve quality of decisions that affect missions and operations. Any newly collected or derived knowledge can alter a competitive situation to the commander's unique advantage. This information-based warfare enables a shift from attrition-style warfare to a much faster and more effective war-fighting style. The applications of network-centric warfare can be categorized into speed-of-command and self-synchronization:

Implementation of speed-of-command requires a knowledge infrastructure to access to all appropriate information sources: weapons attributes, maneuver plans, organization, and mission specifications. More importantly, it has to integrate with command and control (C2) processes to include automated assignment of resources, sensor grids, and shooters. The uniqueness of speed-of-command is its ability to recognize environment changes in operating situation, achieving profound effect with closely coupled responses. As a result, forces can act effectively with speed and precision – using knowledge to achieve massing of effects rather than massing of forces. The shock of closely coupled events potentially disrupts the enemy's strategy; decisive altering early in engagement can even prevent loss of operations.

Conventional military-command structure centers upon top–down synchronization. The top–down mechanism is based on step function; thus, combat power can be discounted when discrepancies arise between a local element's operating rhythm or force movement and the commander's intent. The effect of self-synchronization is enabled by a high level of knowledge of the force, to organize and synchronize complex warfare activities from the bottom up. The organizing principle is unity of effort wherein the step function becomes a highly motivated and self-sufficient combat flow. Here, the quality of combat effectiveness can move to a high-speed continuum.

Strategically speaking, all elements in the battle-space and battle-time develop informed appreciation of competitive space. Close linkage among actors can improve unit integrity and enhance interactions among units and the operating environment. Tactically, sensors with fast and powerful networks, common display capability, and sophisticated *modeling and simulation* (M&S) capabilities can offset a disadvantage in numbers, technology, or position. With this new technology, network-centric warfare can achieve IS, evolving in concert with operational concepts, doctrine, and organization.

For instance, the Swedish Armed Forces in parallel to SWECCIS to establish a project called FM Ledsyst. The most current big project for command and control systems is *Armed Forces command and control system 2010 (FMLS 2010, Swe. FörsvarsMaktens LedningsSystem 2010)*. The objective of FMLS 2010 is to develop systems and concepts that can be incorporated into an operational system by the year 2010. The work is mainly carried out through four different projects. The goals for the Ledsyst project are:

- Evolve the ability to observe, orient, decide and act (the OODA-loop).
- Create possibilities to in a flexible way be able to join, deploy and adjust deployment forces to be able to deliver the necessary abilities in operations.
- Evolve the ability to gain efficiency in operations by increased precision and synergy effects between different functions.
- Create prerequisite for a quick, cost efficient and evolutionary development process for all function's development within the Armed Forces.
- Create the requisite security in handling of resources of the Armed Forces.

10.7.6 Manufacturing

In today's manufacture industry, business processes are becoming increasingly externalized in linking customers, partners, and third-party providers. Business partners or functional stakeholders face a growing need to share knowledge and work together to create effective products and services. Business functions such as logistics, marketing, customer relations, HR, and accounting are connected by the enterprise framework. NCBO support of process participants, be they integrated customers of the value-chain or service partners, to streamline a process has becomes a key characteristics of successful manufacturing business.

The ability to share information in near real time among all relevant departments can enable manufacturers to substitute information for inventory, simultaneously increasing flexibility and responsiveness. A direct benefit from speed of information sharing is a reduced cost of goods sold, because of lean inventory for parts and finished products. Network-centric process provides a consistent and standardized view of production to avoid risk from large inventories (e.g., excess finished product, or obsolete/overpriced components. An improved ability to sense the product attributes that consumers want can contribute to the design of more-attractive products while serving to trim project-delivery timelines.

Because the value-chain links with CRM and other customer-facing applications, manufacturers can have first-hand intelligence about customer expectations, and are thus more likely to provide what customers want. This effect can reduce both operational risk and end-product costs. Only by aligning NCBO with manufacturers' business processes such that product life cycle becomes reusable and renewable (in step with change) is it possible to reduce churn and provide long-term balance.

10.7.7 Transportation

In the transportation sector, traditional models have focused on moving objects from one place to another with best effort. The nature of such service had been rather restricted and not easily changed. Now, availability of status information in-transit has given service providers as well as customers the visibility of in-depth, real-time service information. Network-centric information transforms the transportation service into an innovative practice and introduces two new business differentiators, namely on-time delivery and increased in-transit traceability.

Improving on-time delivery relies upon two aspects: 1) a federated business model that involves dealing with smooth processes for customers, suppliers, providers, partners, operators, and drivers; and 2) the transport company's ability to reroute objects when original plans for timely delivery become infeasible. Routing management must configure an optimum path for delivery and ensure that the objects can be handled smoothly, hub by hub. When workload is increases, every transport hub should manage the equipment (trains, trucks, tracks, and so on) at whatever level is necessary to fulfill committed SLAs.

To increase in-transit traceability, an enterprise can integrate both sensing and transaction capabilities in supporting information networks. The sensing capabilities delineated in chapter 4 can generate near-real-time awareness on the precise status and locations of shipments. Such a high level of awareness can improve QoS, provide proactive status altering, identify sources of operational problems, and improve operational performance.

Furthermore, applying NCBO to the transportation sector opens a door for customers to perform online transactions (such as placing an order, monitoring an order, or modifying an order) and have almost real-time impact on the business process. This capability not only reduces corporate efforts to support new or altered service orders but also empowers customers with visibility about their in-transit orders. Both scenarios result in lower operational cost and higher profit from happy customers.

10.7.8 Information Technology Outsourcing

The motivator of IT outsourcing is both a focus upon an enterprise's core activities or competencies, and a corresponding diversification for areas in which they do not possess a competitive advantage. The goal of outsourcing is to reduce the costs and efforts needed to operate the business as a whole, organizing the enterprise to deal only with differentiating products or services in response to customer needs. The firm can then concentrate its internal resources on value-add services that are perceived as critical for customer retention and attraction. Customers are retained through company activity that differentiates it from competitors, and a company's consistent investment toward core services that are subject to change is essential.

The large-grain nature of many outsourcing arrangements has taken many an IT manager by surprise upon discovery that, after long periods of negotiation and renegotiation, an agreement fails to meet their post-transition expectations. Service-oriented models have helped enterprises to provide increasingly attractive options for dividing outsourced functionality into more-manageable, reusable chunks. Enterprise can use NCBO to relieve the stress of running and maintaining its commodity components by mixing and matching a range of provisioning options. Such network-centricity creates virtual organizations that convenes the resources and processes necessary to accomplish a particular task.

Virtual collaboration allows individual collaboration in virtual domains. Facilitated by networking, virtual organizations allow an enterprise to take advantage of potential gains in productivity that is associated with virtual collaboration, virtual integration, and outsourcing. Virtual integration enables companies to work in concert as if they were a single, vertically integrated, company. Product- or operation-specific virtual entities can then be formed as needed to manage timelines, reduce costs, and boost responsiveness.

A major payoff of collaboration its improved product-design process – one that not only is faster and less costly, but also produces better designs. Once a task has been executed, resources that had been related to its completion are freed for other purposes. Because networking reduces the structural significance of location, opportunities for collaboration, integration, and outsourcing are increased.

10.8 Conclusions

This book introduces a new breed of enterprise information management concept that collaborate its processes and operations around pervasive and dynamic business environment in order to create and exploit information superiority. NCBO brings together high-capacity, networked data collection, application systems and decision tools, merging operational and global functional capabilities with the most effective and assured information-handling capabilities. It allows the enterprise to leverage both technology trends and new value-chain relationships therefore supports the enterprise to accelerate its transformation to expand access to competitive knowledge and eliminate unnecessary development efforts. When fully realized, this SoS will optimize the enterprise's performance, return on investment, and maximizing the enhancement to overall business performance.

With many useful technology and methodology coverage throughout the book, the author wish to break the boundaries of commercial and defense industries in the information management arena and bring together a common understanding and approach to realize service-oriented practices for the best possible returns.

References

Chapter 1

1. The Open Group Conference, Architecting to the Edge, *Network Centric Operations Industry Consortium, Status Update*, April 24–26, 2006, https://www.opengroup.org/conference-live/uploads/40/10317/Wed_-_am_-_2_-_Thomas.pdf
2. Elena Macevičiūtė and T.D. Wilson, *The Development of the Information Management Research Area*, Borås, Sweden, http://informationr.net/ir/7-3/paper133.html
3. Curtis L. Blais, Niki C. Goerger, Paul Richmond, Burhman Gates, and John B. Willis, *Global Information Grid Services and Generation of the Mobility Common Operational Picture*, http://ms.ie.org/SIW_LOG/05F/05F-SIW-107.pdf
4. Alex Bordetsky and Daniel Dolk, *Knowledge Management for Wireless Grid Operation Centers*, Naval Postgraduate School, Hawaii International Conference on System Sciences, 2002
5. Mike Ferguson, *Let The Data Flow*, Intelligent Enterprise, March 1, 2006, http://www.intelligententerprise.com/showArticle.jhtml?articleID=179101909&pgno=1
6. David S. Alberts, John J. Garstka, and Frederick P. Stein, *Network Centric Warfare: Developing and Leveraging Information Superiority*, 2nd Edition, DoD C4ISR Cooperative Research Program (CCRP), February 2000, http://www.dodccrp.org/publications/pdf/Alberts_NCW.pdf
7. Arthur K. Cebrowski, U.S. Navy, and John J. Garstka, *Network-Centric Warfare: Its Origin and Future*, January 1998, http://www.usni.org/Proceedings/Articles98/PROcebrowski.htm
8. Grace A. Lewis, Edwin J. Morris, and Lutz Wrage, *Promising Technologies for Future Systems*, Integration of Software-Intensive Systems (ISIS), December 2004, http://www.sei.cmu.edu/pub/documents/04.reports/pdf/04tn043.pdf

9. Bill Kerr, *Software Development Guidance to the Department of the Navy Project Manager, Fleet Numerical Meteorology and Oceanography Center, Science and Technology Advancement Team*, 5 August 2004
10. Richard Lau, Ram Khare, and William Y. Chang, *Service Assurance for Voice over WiFi and 3G Networks*, Artech House, 2005
11. *SLA Management Handbook: Concepts and Principles, Vol. 2,* TMG GB 917-2, April 2004
12. Jonathan M. Tisch, Karl Weber, *The Power of We, Succeeding Through Partnerships*, John Wiley & Sons, Inc., 2004
13. Paul Allen, *Service Orientation: Winning Strategies and Best Practices,* Cambridge University Press, 2006
14. Zoran Stojanovic and Ajantha Dahanayake, *Service-Oriented Software System Engineering: Challenges and Practices*, Idea Group Publishing, 2005
15. *The Service Oriented Enterprise (SOE)*, ServiceOriented.Org, http://www.serviceoriented.org/service_oriented_enterprise.html
16. Ali Arsanjani, *Service-Oriented Modeling and Architecture*, IBM, 09 November 2004, http://www-128.ibm.com/developerworks/webservices/library/ws-soa-design1/
17. Association for Enterprise Integration, *Net-Centric Operations Industry Forum (NCOIF)*, Data Sharing and Services Strategy Working Group, April 22, 2005, http://www.afei.org/news/documents/IndustryBestPracticesforAchievingSOA_000.pdf
18. http://www.w3.org/
19. Jim Gabriel, *Best Practices in Integrating Data Models for SOA – Integrating Underlying Data Models Is an Essential Precursor to SOA*, SOA World Magazine, http://soa.sys-con.com/read/48031.htm
20. *DEFENSE ACQUISITIONS, The Global Information Grid and Challenges Facing Its Implementation*, United States Government Accountability Office, July 2004, http://www.gao.gov/cgi-bin/getrpt?GAO-04-858
21. Clay Wilson, *Network Centric Warfare: Background and Oversight Issues for Congress*, Foreign Affairs, Defense, and Trade Division, CRS Report for Congress, June 2, 2004, http://www.fas.org/man/crs/RL32411.pdf
22. *NET-CENTRIC OPERATIONAL ENVIRONMENT JOINT INTEGRATING CONCEPT, Version 1.0*, Join Staff, October 31, 2005, http://www.dtic.mil/futurejointwarfare/concepts/netcentric_jic.pdf
23. DAU, *Systems Engineering, Defense Acquisition Guidebook*, Chapter 4, Defense Acquisition University, July 24, 2006, http://akss.dau.mil/dag/GuideBook/PDFs/Chapter_4.pdf

24. *NATO C3 Technical Architecture (NC3TA)* Vols. 1–5, http://194.7.80.153/website/book.asp?menuid=15&vs=0&page=volume1%2Fch01%2Ehtml
25. Annette J. Krygiel, "Behind the Wizard.s Curtain: An Integration Environment for a System of Systems", DOD CCRP, 1999
26. John, *NEC Social and Organizational Factors*, HVR Consultation Service Ltd., Journal of Defense Science, Vol. 8, No. 3, September 2003, http://www.dodccrp.org/files/journal_defence_science_web.pdf
27. Andrew P. Sage, *Systems of Systems: Architecture Based Systems Design and Integration*, George Mason University, October 2005, http://ieeesmc2005.unm.edu/smc_keynote_sage.pdf
28. *Network Centric Operations Conceptual Framework, Version 1.0*, Office of Force Transformation, November 2003

Chapter 2

1. Geoffrey Fox, *A Grid-of-Grids Service Architecture for Net-Centric Operations*, Ground System Architectures Workshop GSAW, March 28 2006, http://grids.ucs.indiana.edu/ptliupages/presentations/gsawmar28-06_FOX.ppt
2. Rob Walker, *Common Operating Environment (COE) and Global Information Grid (GIG) Enterprise Services (GES)*, COE/GES Technical Exchange, September 24, 2003
3. A.K. Cebrowski, *The Implementation of Network-Centric Warfare*, Office of Force Transformation, Office of the Secretary of Defense, January 2005
4. *GLOBAL INFORMATION GRID (GIG),* JROCM 134-01, CRD Executive Agent, Commander in Chief, U.S. Joint Forces Command, August 30, 2001
5. Paul W. Phister, Jr. and John D. Cherry., *Command and Control Implications of Network-Centric Warfare*, Air Force Research Laboratory, http://www.afrlhorizons.com/Briefs/Feb05/IF0409.html
6. Clay Wilson, *Network Centric Warfare: Background and Oversight Issues for Congress,* CRS Report for Congress, June 2, 2004
7. David S. Alberts, John J. Garstka, and Frederick P. Stein, *Network Centric Warfare: Developing and Leveraging Information Superiority*, 2nd Edition, DoD C4ISR Cooperative Research Program (CCRP), February 2000
8. *NET-CENTRIC OPERATIONAL ENVIRONMENT JOINT INTEGRATING CONCEPT, Version 1.0*, Join Staff, October 31, 2005, http://www.dtic.mil/futurejointwarfare/concepts/netcentric_jic.pdf

9. Robert Vietmeyer, *Net-Centric Enterprise Services*, NCES Engineering DISA, http://www.opengroup.org/gesforum/uploads/40/5530/NCES_Update.ppt
10. *Network Centric Operations Conceptual Framework, Version 1.0*, Evidence Based Research, Inc., November 2003
11. *DEFENSE ACQUISITIONS, The Global Information Grid and Challenges Facing Its Implementation*, United States Government Accountability Office, July 2004, http://www.gao.gov/cgi-bin/getrpt?GAO-04-858
12. *Force Management Joint Functional Concept, Version 1.0,* 2 June 2005
13. DEFENSIVE INFORMATION OPERATIONS, *Protecting the Homeland, Report of the Defense Science Board Task Force,* 2000 Summer Study, Vol. II , March 2001, http://cryptome.sabotage.org/dio/dio.htm
14. *Net-Centric Enterprise Services (NCES) Metadata Management Capability*, Open Forum 2003 Metadata Registries, January 23 2003, http://metadata-standards.org/OpenForum2003/Presentations/Defense-final-version/2003_Jan_OpenForum_Defense_Walker.ppt
15. Grace A. Lewis, Edwin J. Morris, and Lutz Wrage, Promising Technologies for Future Systems, Integration of Software-Intensive Systems (ISIS), December 2004, http://www.sei.cmu.edu/pub/documents/04.reports/pdf/04tn043.pdf
16. W. Scott Harrison, Nadine Hanebutte, Paul W. Oman, and Jim Alves-Foss, *The MILS Architecture for a Secure Global Information Grid*, The Journal of Defense Software Engineering, October 2005, http://www.csds.uidaho.edu/papers/Harrison05a.pdf
17. Jeremy M. Kaplan, *Flow of Information in Modern Warfare*, Industrial College of the Armed Forces, April 3, 2005
18. *Transformational Communications Architecture,* Boeing, Satellite 2003, 26 February 2003
19. Robert W. McGraw, *Securing Content in the Department of Defense's Global Information Grid*, National Security Agency, September 23–24, 2004, http://www.cse.buffalo.edu/caeiae/skm2004/presentation_slides/B-Sessions/3B-1%20McGraw/3B-1%20McGrawC010305.ppt
20. Tony Montemarano, *Information Assurance & NETOPS*, Defense Information Systems Agent, May 2, 2006
21. C.L. Blais, N.C. Goerger, P. Richmond, B. Gates, and J.B. Willis, *Global Information Grid Services and Generation of the Mobility Common Operational Picture*, Paper 05F-SIW-107, Simulation Interoperability Standards Organization, 2005 Fall Simulation Interoperability Workshop, Orlando, FL, September 2005
22. Daniel Gonzales, Michael Johnson, Jimmie McEver, Dennis Leedom, Gina Kingston, and Michael Tseng, *Network-Centric Operations, Case Study: The Stryker Brigade Combat Team*, RAND Corporation, 2005

23. *OSS Solutions for Network Operators – white paper,* 2002
24. *Enhanced Telecom Operations Map (eTOM) The Business Process Framework For The Information and Communications. An eTOM Primer, Release 4.5,* TMF GB921P, November 2005
25. *Enhanced Telecom Operations Map (eTOM) The Business Process Framework, Release 6.0,* TMF GB921, November 2005
26. *Enhanced Telecom Operations Map (eTOM) The Business Process Framework For The Information and Communications Service Industry, Process Decompositions and Descriptions, Release 6.0,* TMF GB921V, November 2005
27. *Enhanced Telecom Operations Map (eTOM) The Business Process Framework for the Information and Communications Service Industry, An Interim View of an Interpreter's Guide for eTOM and ITIL Practitioners, Release 6.0,* TMF GB921V, November 2005
28. *DoD Architecture Framework Working Group: DoD Architecture Framework, Version 1.0 Volume II: Product Descriptions, DOD,* February 9, 2004, http://www.defenselink.mil/cio-nii/docs/DoDAF_v1_Volume_II.pdf
29. *Federal Enterprise Architecture,* FEA Program Management Office, February 2004, http://www.whitehouse.gov/omb/egov/documents/FEA_Overview.pdf
30. Bob Haycock, *Federal Enterprise Architecture (FEA): XML and Web Services across the Federal Government,* FEA-PMO, December 2002, http://web-services.gov/FEA-PMO%20Briefing%20for%20Open%20Source%20e-Gov%20Conference%20March%2017%20Rev0.ppt
31. *Federal Enterprise Architecture Records Management Profile, Version 1.3,* Architecture and Infrastructure Committee, Federal Chief Information Officers Council, July 12, 2005, http://colab.cim3.net/file/work/geocop/20050804_Posting/RM%20Profile.071205.v1.3.pdf
32. *The NGOSS Approach to Business Solutions, Release 1.0,* TMF GB930, November 2005
33. *NGOSS Architecture Technology Neutral Specification. Contract Description: Business and System Views, Release 4.0,* TMF 053B, August 2004
34. *The NGOSS Technology – Neutral Architecture. Release 6.0, TMF* 053, November 2005

Chapter 3

1. Ram Ramanathan and Jason Redi, *A Brief Overview of Ad-hoc Networks: Challenges and Directions,* BBN Technologies, http://www.comsoc.org/livepubs/ci1/public/anniv/ramana.html

2. Vern A. Dubendorf, *A History of Wireless Technologies*, John Wiley & Sons, 2003
3. Ramiro Jordan and Chaouki T. Abdallah, *Wireless Communications and Networking: An Overview*, IEEE Antenna's and Propagation Magazine, Vol. 44, No. 1, February 2002
4. Troy Meink, *Transformational Communications Systems for DoD Net-Centric Operations*, STSC, July 2006, http://www.stsc.hill.af.mil/crossTalk/2006/07/0607Meink.html
5. *Special Report: The USA's Transformational Communications Satellite System (TSAT)*, Defense Industry Daily, July 19, 2005, http://www.defenseindustrydaily.com/2005/07/special-report-the-usas-transformational-communications-satellite-system-tsat/index.php
6. *Joint Program Executive Office, Joint Tactical Radio System*, http://enterprise.spawar.navy.mil/body.cfm?type=c&category=27&subcat=60
7. Richard Lau, Ram Khare, and William Y. Chang, *Service Assurance for Voice over WiFi and 3G Networks*, Artech House, 2005
8. S.L. Tsao, *The Development of Application Services with IPV6 and 3B/B3G*, National Chiao Tung University, http://www.ipv6.org.tw/seminar/930317/930317-5.pdf#search=%22B3G%20architecture%22
9. Sanjiv Rai, *Crossroads & Convergence, The World of Anytime Anywhere Computing*, (ARE) Technologies, http://www.newhaven.edu/unh/pdf/eng/Wireless_Computing_and_Convergence.pdf
10. George Dimitrakopoulos, *Selection of Reconfigurations in the Context of B3G, Cognitive Infrastructures,* Wireless World Research Forum, April 27, 2006
11. Paal E. Engelstad, *Issues in Mobility Management in 4G Networks*, Computer, Vol. 34, No. 6, June 2001, http://folk.uio.no/paalee/referencing_publications/ref-mob-4gissues.pdf
12. Sandra G. Dykes, Ronnie L. Killough, Arthur N. Rasmussen, and Victoria Zhou, *An Adaptive Ad Hoc Routing Network for Mobile Wireless Devices, 10-9373*, November 2003, http://www.swri.edu/3pubs/IRD2003/Synopses/109373.htm
13. Katia Obraczka and Gene Tsudik, *Multicast Routing Issues in Ad Hoc Networks*, The University of Southern California's Information Sciences Institute (ISI), http://www.isi.edu/div7/publication_files/multicast_routing_issues.pdf
14. http://www.sdrforum.org/
15. John B. Stephensen, *Software-Defined Hardware for Software-Defined Radios, Using Programmable Logic in Amateur Radio applications,* ARRL. October 2002, http://www.arrl.org/tis/info/pdf/020910qex041.pdf
16. Ram Khare, *Mobile Broadband Service*, Sprint, 2006

17. Sami Tabbane, *Mobile Next Generation Network, Evolution towards 4G*, ITU/BDT Regional Seminar on Mobile and Fixed Wireless Access for Broadband Applications for the Arab Region, June 2006, http://www.itu.int/ITU-D/imt-2000/documents/Algiers2006/Additional%20contributions/Algiers_Presentation_AddContrib_STabbane.pdf
18. Ram Khare, *Overview of A-IMS Initiative*, SAIC, October 11, 2006
19. Next Generation Mobile Network (NGMN), http://www.ngmn.org/

Chapter 4

1. Lawrence A. Bush, Christopher D. Carothers, and Boleslaw K. Szymanski, *Sensor Networks, Balancing Energy Use and Quality of Service,* Rensselaer Polytechnic Institute, July 30, 2003, http://www.cs.rpi.edu/~chrisc/publications/bush-infocom-2004.pdf
2. Wolfgang Schröder-Preikschat, *Network-Centric Operating Systems for Control Grids*, Friedrich-Alexander University Erlangen-Nuremberg, http://www.cetic.be/coregrid/NCOS/presentations/Wolfgang_Schroeder.pdf
3. Edgar H. Callaway, *Wireless Sensor Networks: Architectures and Protocols,* Auerbach Publications, 2004
4. G.M.P. O'Hare, David Marsh, Antonio Ruzzell, and Richard Tynan, *Agents for Wireless Sensor Network Power Management*, University College Dublin, May 20, 2005, http://www.cs.ucd.ie/students/ARuzzelli/home/Publications/WSNET05.pdf
5. Yong Yao, J.E. Gehrke. *The Cougar Approach to In-Network Query Processing in Sensor Networks*, Sigmod Record, Vol. 31, No. 3, September 2002
6. Muneeb Ali and ZartashAfzalUzmi, *Energy-Efficient Node Address Naming for Wireless Sensor Networks*, IEEE INCC 2004 Lahore, June 11, 2004, http://www.dritte.org/muneeb/files/talks/muneeb_INCC-04.pdf
7. Curt Schurgers, Gautam Kulkarni, and Mani B. Srivastava, *Distributed Assignment of Encoded MAC Addresses in Sensor Networks*, ACM, 2001, http://delivery.acm.org/10.1145/510000/501463/p295-schurgers.pdf?key1=501463&key2=0969891611&coll=&dl=ACM&CFID=15151515&CFTOKEN=6184618
8. Wolfgang Schröder-Preikschat, *Network-Centric Operating Systems for Control Grids*, Friedrich-Alexander University, http://www.cetic.be/coregrid/NCOS/papers/PP_Wolfgang_Schroeder.pdf
9. *IEEE 802.15 WPAN™ Task Group 4 (TG4)*, http://www.ieee802.org/15/pub/TG4.html
10. *The ZigBee Alliance*, http://www.zigbee.org/en/index.asp

11. Mark Hachman, *Will Low-Power Wibree Spec Replace Bluetooth?* PCMag.com, October 3, 2006, http://www.pcmag.com/article2/0, 1895, 2023870,00.asp
12. http://www.wibree.com/
13. Daniel Robinson, *New Wireless Standard for Small Devices*, IT Week, October 4, 2006, http://www.itweek.co.uk/itweek/news/2165593/wireless-standard-small-devices
14. *IEEE 1451 Standards*, http://ieee1451.nist.gov/
15. Group: IEEE p1451.0, *Common Functions and Protocols, and TEDS Formats Working Group,* http://grouper.ieee.org/groups/1451/0/
16. Sasa Slijepcevic and Miodrag Potkonjak, *Power Efficient Organization of Wireless Sensor Networks*, UCLA, 2001, http://www.cs.ucla.edu/~miodrag/papers/ICC2001.pdf
17. Vijay Raghunathan and Pai H. Chou, *Design and Power Management of Energy Harvesting Embedded Systems*, 2006 ACM, http://delivery.acm.org/10.1145/1170000/1165663/p369-raghunathan.pdf?key1=1165663&key2=0462541611&coll=ACM&dl=ACM&CFID=15151515&CFTOKEN=6184618
18. Hyewon Jun, Mostafa H. Ammar, Mark D. Corner, and Ellen W. Zegura, *Hierarchical Power Management in Disruption Tolerant Networks with Traffic Aware Optimization*, ACM Press, 2006 SIGCOMM, http://prisms.cs.umass.edu/mcorner/papers/chants06.pdf
19. Barbara Hohlt, Lance Doherty, and Eric Brewer, *Flexible Power Scheduling for Sensor Networks,* UC Berkeley, 2004 ACM, http://barbara.stattenfield.org/papers/ipsn_hohlt.pdf
20. Andrew Howard, Maja J. Matarić, and Gaurav S. Sukhatme, *An Incremental Self-Deployment Algorithm for Mobile Sensor Networks*, Intelligent Embedded Systems, 2001, http://www-robotics.usc.edu/~ahoward/pubs/howard_ar01.pdf
21. Lakshminarayanan Subramanian and Randy H. Katz, *An Architecture for Building Self-Configurable Systems*, IEEE, 2000, http://www.cs.berkeley.edu/~lakme/sensor.pdf
22. Nirupama Bulusu, John Heidemann, Deborah Estrin, and Tommy Tran, *Self-Configuring Localization Systems: Design and Experimental Evaluation*, USC/Information Sciences Institute, 2002 ACM, http://lecs.cs.ucla.edu/Publications/papers/Bulusu02b.pdf
23. H. Wang, L. Yip, Maniezzo, J.C. Chen, R.E. Hudson, J. Elsony, and K. Yao, *A Wireless Time-Synchronized Cots Sensor Platform: Applications to Beamforming*, Computer Science Department and Electrical Engineering Department, UCLA, http://lecs.cs.ucla.edu/Publications/papers/Wang02CAS.pdf
24. *Technical Overview of Time Synchronized Mesh Protocol (TSMP),* Dust Networks, http://www.dustnetworks.com/docs/TSMP_Whitepaper.pdf

25. Kemal Akkaya and Mohamed Younis, *A Survey on Routing Protocols for Wireless Sensor Networks*, University of Maryland, MD, February 8, 2005
26. John Heidemann, Fabio Silva, Chalermek Intanagonwiwat, Ramesh Govindan, Deborah Estrin, and Deepak Ganesan, *Building Efficient Wireless Sensor Networks with Low-Level Naming*, ACM Press, 2001, http://www.isi.edu/~johnh/PAPERS/Heidemann01c.pdf
27. A.S. Chhetri, D. Morrell, A. Papandreou-Suppappola, C. Chakrabarti, A. Spanias, J. Zhang, "A Unified Bayesian Decision Theory Perspective to Sensor Networks", Proceedings of the 2005 IEEE International Symposium on, Mediterrean Conference on Control and Automation, 2005

Chapter 5

1. Randy H. Katz, *Towards a Bay Area Research Wireless Access Network (BARWAN)*, University of California, Berkeley, http://bnrg.eecs.berkeley.edu/~randy/Daedalus/BARWAN/BARWAN_layers.html
2. K. Chandran, S. Raghunathan, S. Venkatesan, and R. Prakash, *A Feedback Based Scheme for Improving TCP Performance in Ad-Hoc Wireless Networks*, in Proc. of the International Conference on Distributed Computing Systems (ICDCS'98), Amsterdam, Netherlands, May 1998
3. G. Holland and N. Vaidya, *Analysis of TCP Performance over Mobile Ad Hoc Networks*, ACM Wireless Networks, Vol. 8, No. 2, pp. 275–288, March 2002
4. D. Kim, C. Toh, and Y. Choi, *TCP-BuS: Improving TCP Performance in Wireless Ad Hoc Networks*, Journal of Communications and Networks, Vol. 3, No. 2, pp. 175–186, June 2001
5. J. Liu and S. Singh, *ATCP: TCP for Mobile ad hoc Networks*, IEEE JSAC, Vol. 19, No. 7, pp. 1300–1315, July 2001
6. Swastik Kopparty, Srikanth V. Krishnamurthy, Michalis Faloutsos, and Satish K. Tripathi, *Split TCP for Mobile Ad Hoc Networks*, IEEE GLOBECOM, 2002, http://www.cs.ucr.edu/~krish/splittcp.pdf
7. K. Fall and S. Floyd, *Simulation Based Comparisons of Tahoe, Reno, and Sack TCP*, in Computer Communications review, July 1996
8. *RFC 0791 Internet Protocol DARPA Internet Program Protocol Specification,* IETF, September 1981
9. *RFC 3168, The Addition of Explicit Congestion Notification (ECN) to IP,* IETF, September 2001
10. *RFC 2460 Internet Protocol, Version 6 (IPv6) Specification,* IETF, December 1998
11. John H. Shipp III, *IPv6 Army Transition Planning, NAIPv6 Summit,* Army Architecture Integration Cell, CIO/G6, Office of the Secretary of the Army, June 17, 2004

12. *RFC 3315, Dynamic Host Configuration Protocol for IPv6 (DHCPv6),* IETF, July 2003
13. *RFC2893, Transition Mechanisms for IPv6 Hosts and Routers,* IETF, August 2000
14. *RFC-3056, Connection of IPv6 Domains via IPv4 Clouds,* IETF, February 2001
15. R. Després, *The 4to6 Unified IPv4-to-IPv6 Transition Model*, 2004, http://perso.orange.fr/remi.despres/I-D_project_4to6_2004-11-01.txt
16. *RFC-3053, IPv6 Tunnel Broker,* IETF, January 2001
17. *RFC 2461, Neighbor Discovery for IP Version 6 (IPv6),* IETF, December 1998
18. *RFC 4311, IPv6 Host-to-Router Load Sharing,* IETF, November 2005
19. *RFC 2462, IPv6 Stateless Address Autoconfiguration,* IETF, December 1998
20. *RFC 4443, Internet Control Message Protocol (ICMPv6) for the Internet Protocol Version 6 (IPv6) Specification,* IETF, March 2006
21. *RFC 4291, IP Version 6 Addressing Architecture,* IETF, February 2006
22. *RFC 3041, Privacy Extensions for Stateless Address Autoconfiguration in IPv6, IETF,* January 2001
23. RFC 3587, RFC 3587, IPv6 Global Unicast Address Format, IETF, August 2003
24. *RFC 3344, IP Mobility Support for IPv4,* IETF, August 2002
25. Kan Zhigang, Ma Jian, LuoJun, Hu Jianping. *Mobile IPv6 and some issues for QoS.* The 11th Annual Internet Society Conference (INET2001), Stockholm, Sweden, 5–8 June 2001, http://www.isoc.org/isoc/conferences/inet/01/CD_proceedings/T28/T28.htm
26. Charles E. Perkins, *Mobile IPv6 and Cellular Telephony*, International Conference on Communication Technology Proceedings, 2000
27. Linton Wells II, *IPv6: A Key to Net-Centric Combat Operations*, Assistant Secretary of Defense Networks and Information Integration/DoD Chief Information Officer, May 24, 2005
28. *RFC 792, Internet Control Message Protocol,* IETF, September 1981
29. *RFC 1122, Requirements for Internet Hosts, Communication Layers,* IETF, October 1989
30. *RFC 2131, Dynamic Host Configuration Protocol,* IETF, March 1997
31. *RFC 2136, Dynamic Updates in the Domain Name System (DNS UPDATE),* IETF, April 1997, http://www.ietf.org/rfc/rfc2136.txt
32. RFC 2401, *Security Architecture for the Internet Protocol*, IETF, November 1998
33. *RFC 2409, The Internet Key Exchange (IKE),* IETF, November 1998
34. *RFC 2406, IP Encapsulating Security Payload (ESP),* IETF, November 1998

35. Peter Sholander, Glenn Frank, Sean Swank, Joseph Loyall, and Gary Duzan, *Multi-Layer, Mission-Aware QoS Management Techniques for IP Applications in a Joint Battlespace Infosphere*, Military Communications Conference (MILCOM), October 31–November 3, 2004, http://www. dist-systems. bbn.com/papers/2004/MILCOM-JBI/682.pdf
36. *RFC 2474, Definition of the Differentiated Services Field (DS Field) in the IPv4 and IPv6 Headers,* IETF, December 1998
37. *RFC 791, Internet Protocol, Protocol Specification,* IETF, September 1981
38. *RFC 2205, Resource ReSerVation Protocol (RSVP),* IETF, September 1997
39. *RFC 3376, Internet Group Management Protocol, Version 3,* IETF, October 2002
40. *RFC 1034, Domain Names, Concepts and Facilities,* IETF, November 1987
41. *RFC 1035, Domain Names, Implementation and Specification,* IETF, November 1987
42. *RFC 1305, Network Time Protocol (Version 3) Specification, Implementation and Analysis,* IETF, March 1992
43. *RFC 2453, RIP Version 2,* IETF, November 1998
44. *RFC 1771, A Border Gateway Protocol 4 (BGP-4),* IETF, March 1995
45. *RFC 2796, BGP Route Reflection, An Alternative to Full Mesh IBGP,* IETF, April 2000
46. *RFC 3065, Autonomous System Confederations for BGP,* IETF, February 2001
47. *Public key cryptography*, http://www.answers.com/topic/public-key-cryptography
48. J. Christopher Ramming, *Toward New and Better Protocols for Wireless Networking*, Software Defined Radio Forum Meeting, DARPA, April 11, 2006
49. Jon M. Peha, Spectrum Management Policy Options, IEEE Communications Surveys, Fourth Quarter, Vol. 1, No. 1, 1998, http://www. comsoc.org/livepubs/surveys/public/4q98issue/pdf/Peha.pdf
50. S.M. Radicella, *ICTP Lecture Notes:* Introduction to International Radio Regulations, ICTP, 3–21 February 2003, http://users.ictp.it/~pub_off/ lectures/lns016/Vol_16.pdf
51. Kimmo Kalliola, *Spectrum Sharing and Flexible Spectrum Use*, FUTURA Workshop, August 16, 2004
52. *NSF 06-516 – Networking Technology and Systems (NeTS),* National Science Foundation, http://www.nsf.gov/pubs/2006/nsf06516/nsf06516.htm

53. Joseph B. Evans, *The NeTS Program*, National Science Foundation, 5 February 2004, Arlington, Virginia, http://www.cra.org/Activities/workshops/nsf.wireless/Evans_ProWiN_NeTS_Program2.pdf
54. *General Spectrum Policy and Information*, DISA, http://www.disa.mil/jsc/gen_policy_info.html
55. *Spectrum and Electromagnetics 101*, Defense Acquisition University, https://acc.dau.mil/CommunityBrowser.aspx?id=21857
56. *JOINT TRANSITION COURSE PLANNING PRIMER*, Joint Forces Staff College, June 2005, http://www.jfsc.ndu.edu/schools_programs/jtc/JTC_Planning_Primer.pdf
57. B.G. Jeffrey W. Foley, *Update on Army Activities in Spectrum Management,* Annual Defense Spectrum Summit – 2006

Chapter 6

1. W. Chan Kim, Renée Mauborgne, *Blue Ocean Strategy: How to Create Uncontested Market Space and Make Competition Irrelevant,* Harvard Business School Publishing Corp., 2005
2. *Wireless Service Measurements Handbook Version 3.0,* TMF GB923, March 2004
3. *Internet End-to-end Performance Monitoring: Network Monitoring Tools,* IEPM, http://www.slac.stanford.edu/xorg/nmtf/nmtf-tools.html#com
4. Arthur K. Cebrowski, U.S. Navy, and John J. Garstka, *Network-Centric Warfare: Its Origin and Future*, January 1998, http://www.usni.org/Proceedings/Articles98/PROcebrowski.htm
5. Federal Standard 1037C *Telecommunications: Glossary of Telecommunication Terms*, http://www.its.bldrdoc.gov/fs-1037/
6. *ATIS Telecom Glossary 2000: ATIS Committee T1A1Performance and Signal Processing,* T1.523-2001, http://www.atis.org/tg2k/
7. *Wireless Service Measurement: Key Quality Indicators Version 1.5,* TMF GB923A, March 2004
8. *NCES Management Information and Data Models*, 33403/2006, FMV, September 2006, http://www.fmv.se/upload/Bilder%20och%20dokument/Vad%20gor%20FMV/Uppdrag/LedsystT/FMLS/FMLS_Generic%20Design/LT1K%20P06-0095%20NCES%20Management%20Information%20and%20Data%20models%201.0%20-%20c.pdf
9. *The PingER Project*, DOE MICS, http://www-iepm.slac.stanford.edu/pinger/
10. Tom Artell, *Management Protocols: TMN CMIP TINA WAP*, Advanced course in Network Based Automation, June 10, 2003, http://www.ac.tut.fi/aci/courses/7601010/2003/esitykset/3.1-3.3.ppt

11. J. Won-Ki Hong, *OSI Management Framework: Overview*, POSTECH, http://dpnm.postech.ac.kr/cs637/lecture/osi-overview.ppt
12. *RFC 1065, Structure and Identification of Management Information for TCP/IP-based internets,* IETF, August 1988
13. *RFC 1066, Management Information Base for Network Management of TCP/IP-based Internets,* IETF, August 1988
14. *RFC 1067, A Simple Network Management Protocol,* IETF, August 1988
15. *RFC 1441, Introduction to Version 2 of the Internet-standard Network Management Framework,* IETF, April 1993
16. *RFC 1442, Structure of Management Information for Version 2 of the Simple Network Management Protocol (SNMPv2),* IETF, April 1993
17. *RFC 1443, Textual Conventions for Version 2 of the Simple Network Management Protocol (SNMPv2),* IETF, April 1993
18. *RFC 1444, Conformance Statements for Version 2 of the Simple Network Management Protocol (SNMPv2),* IETF, April 1993
19. *RFC 1445, Administrative Model for Version 2 of the Simple Network Management Protocol (SNMPv2),* IETF, April 1993
20. *RFC 1446, Security Protocols for Version 2 of the Simple Network Management Protocol (SNMPv2),* IETF, April 1993
21. *RFC 1447, Party MIB for Version 2 of the Simple Network Management Protocol (SNMPv2),* IETF, April 1993
22. *RFC 1448, Protocol Operations for Version 2 of the Simple Network Management Protocol (SNMPv2),* IETF, April 1993
23. *RFC 1449, Transport Mappings for Version 2 of the Simple Network Management Protocol (SNMPv2),* IETF, April 1993
24. *RFC 1450, Management Information Base for Version 2 of the Simple Network Management Protocol (SNMPv2),* IETF, April 1993
25. *RFC 1451, Manager-to-Manager Management Information Base,* IETF, April 1993
26. *RFC 1452, Coexistence between Version 1 and Version 2 of the Internet-standard Network Management Framework,* IETF, April 1993
27. *RFC 1155, Structure and Identification of Management Information for TCP/IP-based Internets,* IETF, May 1990
28. *RFC 1901, Introduction to Community-based SNMPv2,* IETF, January 1996
29. *RFC 1902, Structure of Management Information for Version 2 of the Simple Network Management Protocol (SNMPv2),* IETF, January 1996
30. *RFC 1903, Textual Conventions for Version 2 of the Simple Network Management Protocol (SNMPv2),* IETF, January 1996
31. *RFC 1904, Conformance Statements for Version 2 of the Simple Network Management Protocol (SNMPv2),* IETF, January 1996

32. *RFC 1905, Protocol Operations for Version 2 of the Simple Network Management Protocol (SNMPv2),* IETF, January 1996
33. *RFC 1906, Transport Mappings for Version 2 of the Simple Network Management Protocol (SNMPv2),* IETF, January 1996
34. *RFC 1907, Management Information Base for Version 2 of the Simple Network Management Protocol (SNMPv2),* IETF, January 1996
35. *RFC 1908, Coexistence between Version 1 and Version 2 of the Internet-standard Network Management Framework,* IETF, January 1996
36. *RFC 1909, An Administrative Infrastructure for SNMPv2,* IETF, February 1996
37. *RFC 1910, User-based Security Model for SNMPv2,* IETF, February 1996
38. *RFC 3411, An Architecture for Describing Simple Network Management Protocol (SNMP) Management Frameworks,* IETF, December 2002
39. *RFC 3412, Message Processing and Dispatching for the Simple Network Management Protocol (SNMP),* IETF, December 2002
40. *RFC 3413, Simple Network Management Protocol (SNMP) Applications,* IETF, December 2002
41. *RFC 3414, User-based Security Model (USM) for Version 3 of the Simple Network Management Protocol (SNMPv3),* IETF, December 2002
42. *RFC 3415, View-based Access Control Model (VACM) for the Simple Network Management Protocol (SNMP),* IETF, December 2002
43. *RFC 3416, Version 2 of the Protocol Operations for the Simple Network Management Protocol (SNMP),* IETF, December 2002
44. *RFC 3417, Transport Mappings for the Simple Network Management Protocol (SNMP),* IETF, December 2002
45. *RFC 3418, Management Information Base (MIB) for the Simple Network Management Protocol (SNMP),* IETF, December 2002
46. *RFC 3584, Coexistence between Version 1, Version 2, and Version 3 of the Internet-standard Network Management Framework,* IETF, August 2003
47. http://www.jcp.org

Chapter 7

1. *EA & Services Oriented Enterprise (SOE)/Service Oriented Architecture (SOA) and Service Oriented Computing (SOC),* Institute for Enterprise Architecture Developments, http://www.enterprise-architecture.info/EA_Services-Oriented-Enterprise.htm
2. *SLA Management Handbook: Service and Technology Examples, Vol. 3, Version 2.0* TMG GB 917-3, July 2004

3. Paulo Rogrio Pereira, Elionildo Menezes, Djamel Sadok, and Centro De Informtica, *Management of Differentiated Services with Active Policies,* The Pennsylvania State University CiteSeer Archives, 2000, http://www.inesc-id.pt/pt/indicadores/Ficheiros/1031.pdf
4. Geoff Huston, *The ISP Column: Faster*, Internet Society, http://ispcolumn.isoc.org/2005-06/faster.html
5. *QOS Section 6, Weighted Random Early Detection (WRED),* CISCO Press, http://www.ciscopress.com/content/images/1587201283/samplechapter/1587201283content.pdf
6. Sally Floyd, *ECN and Defenses against Evil Applications*, January 1998, http://www.icir.org/floyd/ecn/ecn_congestion.txt
7. *The Addition of Explicit Congestion Notification (ECN) to IP,* The Internet Society, September 2001
8. P. Hovell, R. Briscoe and G. Corliano, *Guaranteed QoS Synthesis – An Example of a Scalable Core IP Quality of Service Solution*, BT Technology Journal, Vol. 23, No. 2, April 2005, http://www.cs.ucl.ac.uk/staff/bbriscoe/projects/ipe2eqos/gqs/papers/gqs_bttj05.pdf
9. *RFC 1889, RTP: A Transport Protocol for Real-Time Applications,* The Internet Society, January 1996
10. Geoff Huston, *Internet Performance Survival Series*, John Wiley & Sons, Inc., 2000
11. *Hierarchical Token Bucket (HTB) Homepage by Martin Devera, Includes Theory and Implementation,* http://luxik.cdi.cz/~devik/qos/htb/
12. P. Ferguson and G. Huston, *Quality of Service: Delivering QoS on the Internet and in Corporate Networks,* John Wiley & Sons, Inc., 1998
13. *RFC 1633, Integrated Services in the Internet Architecture: An Overview,* The Internet Society, June 1994
14. *RFC 2205, Resource ReSerVation Protocol (RSVP), The Internet Society,* September 1997
15. *RFC 2210, The Use of RSVP with IETF Integrated Services,* The Internet Society, September 1997
16. S. Blake, *An Architecture for Differentiated Services,* IETF RFC2475, December 1998
17. Xipeng Xiao and Lionel M. Ni, *Internet QoS: A Big Picture*, IEEE Network Magazine, March 1999
18. *RFC 0791, Internet Protocol DARPA Internet Program Protocol Specification,* The Internet Society, September 1981
19. Paresh Shah, Utpal Mukhopadhyaya, and Arun Sathiamurthi, *Overview of QoS in Packet-based IP and MPLS Networks*, NANOG, http://www.nanog.org/mtg-0602/pdf/sathiamurthi.pdf
20. *RFC 2474, Definition of the Differentiated Services Field (DS Field) in the IPv4 and IPv6 Headers,* The Internet Society, December 1998

21. *RFC 2597, Assured Forwarding PHB Group,* The Internet Society, June 1999
22. *RFC 2598, An Expedited Forwarding PHB,* The Internet Society, June 1999
23. Venkatesh Prabhakar, Srinivas R. Avasarala, and Sonia Fahmy, *Security in Differentiated Services Networks*, CERIAS, 2001, http://www.cerias.purdue.edu/symposium/2001/posters/post_16.pdf
24. RFC 2697, A Single Rate Three Color Marker, The Internet Society, September 1999
25. [ANSI.MLPP.Spec] American National Standards Institute, Telecommunications – Integrated Services Digital Network (ISDN), Multi-Level Precedence and Preemption (MLPP) Service Capability, ANSI T1.619-1992 (R1999), 1992
26. [ANSI.MLPP.Supplement] American National Standards Institute, *MLPP Service Domain Cause Value Changes*, ANSI T1.619a-1994 (R1999), 1990
27. [ITU.MLPP.1990] International Telecommunications Union, *Multilevel Precedence and Preemption Service (MLPP),* ITU-T Recommendation I.255.3, 1990
28. V. Fineberg, *Specification of the Military Precedence and Preemption in the DS-TE Networks*, Military Communications Conference, 2004. IEEE MILCOM 2004, October-3 November 2004
29. Kan Zhigang, Jian MA, Luo Jun, and Hu Jianping, *Mobile IPv6 and Some Issues for QoS*, INET 2001, http://www.isoc.org/isoc/conferences/inet/01/CD_proceedings/T28/T28.htm

Chapter 8

1. *Department of Defense Net-Centric Data Strategy*, Department of Defense Chief Information Officer (CIO), May 9, 2003, http://www.dod.mil/cio-nii/docs/Network-Centric-Data-Strategy-2003-05-092.pdf
2. *Net-Centric Environment Joint Functional Concept, Version 1.0*, Defense Technical Information Center (DTIC), April 7, 2005, http://www.dtic.mil/futurejointwarfare/concepts/netcentric_jfc.pdf
3. Craig Mindrum and Anderson Consulting. *NetCentric and Client/Server Computing: A Practical Guide*, AUERBACH, December 18, 1998
4. Anthony J. Simon, *Overview of the Department of Defense Network-Centric Data Strategy*, The Journal of Defense Software Engineering, July 2006

5. Andre Yee, *Building Resiliency into Your Enterprise Integration System*, ebizq.net, February 16, 2004, http://www.ebizq.net/topics/dev_tools/features/3783.html
6. Norbert Bieberstein, Sanjay Bose, Marc Fiammante, Keith Jones, and Rawn Shah, *Service-Oriented Architecture Compass: Business Value, Planning, and Enterprise Roadmap,* IBM Press, 2006
7. Nancy Mullen, *Information for Innovation: Developing an Enterprise Data Strategy*, Column published in DM Review Magazine, October 2001, http://www.dmreview.com/article_sub.cfm?articleId=4110
8. *NCES Management Information and Data Models*, Swedish Defence Materiel Administration (FMV) Document, 2006
9. Fredrik Landberg, *Flexible Role-handling in Command and Control Systems*, Tekniska Högskolan Linköpings Universitet, December 4, 2006, www.diva-portal.org/diva/getDocument?urn_nbn_se_liu_diva-7880-1__fulltext.pdf
10. Baruch Awerbuch, Reza Curtmola, David Holmer, Cristina Nita-Rotaru, and Herbert Rubens, *Mitigating Byzantine Attacks in Ad Hoc Wireless Networks: Technical Report Version 1*, Johns Hopkins University, March 2004, http://wireless.cs.jhu.edu/publications/Awerbuch-MitigatingByzantine-TechReport1-March2004.pdf
11. *DATA ENCRYPTION STANDARD (DES)*, U.S. DEPARTMENT OF COMMERCE/National Institute of Standards and Technology, FEDERAL INFORMATION PROCESSING STANDARDS PUBLICATION, FIPS PUB 46-3, Reaffirmed October 25, 1999, http://csrc.nist.gov/publications/fips/fips46-3/fips46-3.pdf
12. *ADVANCED ENCRYPTION STANDARD (AES)*, Federal Information Processing Standards Publication 197, November 26, 2001, http://csrc.nist.gov/publications/fips/fips197/fips-197.pdf
13. *Escrowed Encryption Standard (EES)*, Federal Information Processing Standards Publication 185, February 9, 1994, http://www.itl.nist.gov/fipspubs/fip185.htm
14. *SKIPJACK and KEA Algorithm Specifications*, May 29, 1998, http://csrc.nist.gov/CryptoToolkit/skipjack/skipjack.pdf
15. Keith Palmgren, *Diffie-Hellman Key Exchange – A Non-Mathematician's Explanation*, NetIP Security, August 2006, http://www.netip.com/articles/keith/diffie-helman.htm
16. Zoran Stojanovic and Ajantha Dahanayake, *Service-Oriented Software System Engineering: Challenges and Practices*, Idea Group Publishing, 2005
17. *Web Services Federation Language (WS-Federation) Version 1.1,* BAE, BMC, IBM, Microsoft, RSA, etc., December 2006, http://download.boulder.ibm.com/ibmdl/pub/software/dw/specs/ws-fed/WS-Federation-V1-1B.pdf

18. *OASIS eXtensible Access Control Markup Language (XACML) TC 2.0*, OASIS, February 2005, http://www.oasis-open.org/committees/tc_home.php?wg_abbrev=xacml
19. *Web Services Security Policy Language (WS-SecurityPolicy) Version 1.1*, Microsoft, VeriSign, IBM, and RSA Security, July 2005, ftp://www6.software.ibm.com/software/developer/library/ws-secpol.pdf
20. *Web Services Security Policy Language (WS-SecurityPolicy) Version 1.1*, Microsoft, VeriSign, IBM, RSA Security, July 2005, ftp://www6.software.ibm.com/software/developer/library/ws-secpol.pdf
21. *Web Services Secure Conversation Language (WS-SecureConversation)*, OpenNetwork, Layer 7, Computer Associates, Microsoft, IBM, VeriSign, BEA, Oblix, Reactivity, etc., February 2005, ftp://www6.software.ibm.com/software/developer/library/ws-secureconversation.pdf
22. *Web Services Trust Language (WS-Trust)*, OpenNetwork, layer 7, Microsoft, VeriSign, IBM, RSA Security, etc., February 2005, ftp://www6.software.ibm.com/software/developer/library/ws-trust.pdf
23. *Service Provisioning Markup Language (SPML) V2.0*, OASIS, April 2006, http://www.oasis-open.org/specs/index.php#spmlv2.0
24. *XML Common Biometric Format (XCBF) Version 1.1 [OASIS 200305]*, OASIS, August 2003, http://www.oasis-open.org/committees/wss/documents/WSS-XCBF.doc
25. *Public-Key Infrastructure (X.509)*, IETF, April 02, 2007, http://www.ietf.org/html.charters/pkix-charter.html
26. *Types of Attacks That Pose Security Risks in an Organization*, Microsoft TechNet, http://www.microsoft.com/technet/prodtechnol/windows2000serv/reskit/prork/prdd_sec_glkj.mspx?mfr=true
27. Newton Howard and Ammar Qusaibaty, *Network-Centric Information Policy*, The George Washington University, Université Paris-1 Sorbonne, March 2004, http://www.c4ads.org/papers/nip_draft.pdf?PHPSESSID=58a0b58b9bc16f2d1ffd916f4962c48b

Chapter 9

1. Mark Nissen and Raymond Levitt, *Dynamic Models of Knowledge-Flow Dynamics*, CIFE Working Paper #76, Stanford University, November 2002, http://www.stanford.edu/group/CIFE/online.publications/WP076.pdf
2. Howard Markson, VP Product Marketing, Reflectent Software, *Aligning the Business With the End User Experience*, eBiz, June 26, 2005, http://www.ebizq.net/topics/crm_int/features/6061.html
3. Anthony F. Buono and Flemming Poulfelt (eds), *Challenges and Issues in Knowledge Management*, Information Age Publishing, 2005

4. Troy Thomas, Sam Grable, and Jim Stratton, *Expeditionary Air Force Leaders, Cognitive Skills for the Naturalistic Battlespace*, USAF, February 26, 2001, http://www.airpower.au.af.mil/airchronicles/cc/stratton.html
5. Richard W. Pew and Anne S. Mavor, *Modeling Human and Organizational Behavior: Application to Military Simulations*, Commission on Behavioral and Social Sciences and Education (CBASSE), 1998, http://www.nap.edu/books/0309060966/html
6. *SLA Management Handbook: Service and Technology Examples, Vol. 3, Version 2.0* TMG GB 917-3, July 2004
7. Mieczyslaw M. Kokar, Christopher J. Matheus, Kenneth Baclawski, Jerzy A. Letkowski, Michael Hinman, and John Salerno, *Use Cases for Ontologies in Information Fusion*, Northeastern University, http://www.ece.neu.edu/groups/scs/kokar/publications/KokarUseCases.pdf
8. Christopher J. Matheus, *Position Paper: Using Ontology-based Rules for Situation Awareness and Information Fusion*, Versatile Information Systems, December 2004, http://www.w3.org/2004/12/rules-ws/paper/74/
9. Subhash Challa and Don Koks, *Bayesian and Dempster–Shafer fusion*, Sadhana Vol. 29, Part 2, April 2004, pp. 145–174, http://www.ias.ac.in/sadhana/Pdf2004Apr/Pe1158.pdf
10. *Multi-Sensor Integration within a Common Operating, Technology Demonstration Project*, Dedence R&D Canada-Ottawa, 2005, http://www.ottawa.drdc-rddc.gc.ca/html/RAST-218-cop_e.html
11. Anscombe, Francis J. (1973) *Graphs in Statistical Analysis. American Statistician,* 27, pp. 17–21
12. Tom Ritchey, *Modeling Complex Socio-Technical Systems using Morphological Analysis,* Swedish Parliamentary IT Commission, December 2002, http://www.swemorph.com/it-art.html
13. Robin Glinton, Sean Owens, Joe Giampapa, Katia Sycara, Chuck Grindle, and Mike Lewis, *Terrain-Based Information Fusion and Inference*, Proceedings of the Seventh International Conference on Information Fusion, July, 2004, http://www.cs.cmu.edu/~softagents/papers/GlintonFusionFinal.pdf
14. David Luckham (Stanford University), *Taking the Fear out of Complex Event Processing*, eBiz, February 6, 2005, http://www.ebizq.net/topics/cep/features/5580.html?page=4
15. James R. Borck, InfoWorld: *Coral8 Engine 4.6 presents a sea of CEP opportunity*, Complex Event Processing, April 2007, http://www.infoworld.com/article/07/04/02/14TCcoral_1.html
16. Mary Shaw, *Mobile Robot – Solution 4: Blackboard Architecture*, Composable Systems Group at Carnegie Mellon, 1995, http://www.cs.cmu.edu/People/ModProb/MRsol4.html

17. Ezhilan Narasimhan and Sujeet Vasudevan, and Marina Sum, *Integrating Blackboard Learning System with Sun Java System Identity Server 6.0, SP1:A Case Study,* Sun Developer Network (SDN), February 26, 2004, http://developers.sun.com/prodtech/identserver/reference/techart/blackboard.html
18. Murray Shanahan, Andreas Fidjeland, and Tim Guhl, *Robot Perception Using a Global Workspace Architecture, A Working Example*, 2006, http://www.doc.ic.ac.uk/~tpg99/vs.html
19. Dan. Snell, *Fuzzy logic systems*, Bournemouth University, December 3, 1997, http://www.ecfc.u-net.com/cost/fuzzy.htm
20. Hans-Jürgen Zimmermann, *Fuzzy Set Theory and its Applications*, Springer, December 7, 2005
21. Thomas Pyzdek, *The Six Sigma Handbook: The Complete Guide for Greenbelts, Blackbelts, and Managers at All Levels, Revised and Expanded Edition,* McGraw-Hill, March 20, 2003
22. *Wireless Service Measurements Handbook Version 3.0,* TMF GB923, March 2004

Chapter 10

1. *Industry Best Practices in Achieving Service Oriented Architecture (SOA): A Report of the Net-Centric Operations Industry Forum (NCOIF) Data Sharing and Services Strategy Working Group,* NCOIF, April 22, 2005, http://www.afei.org/news/documents/IndustryBestPracticesforAchievingSOA_000.pdf
2. Frank Martinez, *Reliable Messaging in a Services Network- Intermediation-Based, Networking-Centric Approaches Enable Your SOA to Support the Most Sophisticated Enterprise Applications,* Enterprise Architect, June 2, 2005, http://www.ftponline.com/ea/magazine/summer2005/columns/soainsights/
3. Amine Chigani and James D. Arthur, *The Implications of Network-Centric Software Systems on Software Architecture: A Critical Evaluation*, ACM Press, 2007, http://arxiv.org/ftp/cs/papers/0611/0611110.pdf
4. Norbert Bieberstein, Sanjay Bose, Marc Fiammante, Keith Jones, and Rawn Shah, *Service-Oriented Architecture (SOA) Compass: Business Value, Planning, and Enterprise Roadmap*, IBM Press, October 2005, http://www.ibmpressbooks.com/articles/article.asp?p=422305&rl=1
5. *Wireless Service Measurement: Key Quality Indicators Version 1.5,* TMF GB923A, March 2004
6. *Wireless Service Measurements Handbook Version 3.0,* TMF GB923, March 2004

7. Jonathan M. Tisch, Karl Weber, *The Power of We, Succeeding Through Partnerships*, John Wiley & Sons, Inc., 2004
8. Yun-Tung Lau, *Service-Oriented Architecture and the C4ISR Framework*, Cross Talk-The Journal of Defense Software Engineering, September 2004, http://www.stsc.hill.af.mil/crosstalk/2004/09/0409Lau.html
9. Dave Shaffer, *Best Practices for Building SOA Applications*, AJAX World Magazine, September 21, 2006, http://ajax.sys-con.com/read/275111_1.htm
10. R. Cherinka, R. Miller, and C. Smith, *Beyond Web Services: Towards On-Demand Complex Adaptive Environments*, MITRE, 2005, http://www.mitre.org/work/tech_papers/tech_papers_05/05_0683/05_0683.pdf
11. *DoD Architecture Framework Working Group: DoD Architecture Framework, Version 1.0 Volume II: Product Descriptions,* DOD, February 9, 2004, http://www.defenselink.mil/cio-nii/docs/DoDAF_v1_Volume_II.pdf
12. *C4ISR Architecture Framework Version 2.0*, AFCEA C4ISR Architecture Working Group (AWG), December 18, 1997, http://www.afcea.org/education/courses/archfwk2.pdf
13. *Access GIG Services*, Portal to the Global Information Grid, http://ges.dod.mil/pilotservices.htm
14. *NATO C3 Technical Architecture, (NC3TA),* http://nc3ta.nc3a.nato.int/website/book.asp?menuid=15&vs=3&page=vol5%2Dsup2%2Fch02%2Ehtml or http://194.7.80.153/website/book.asp?menuid=15&vs=3&page=about%2Ehtml
15. *INFORMATION SHARING ON NETWORKS*, A Cryptek Technical White Paper, April 05, 2005, http://uk.builder.com/whitepapers/0,39026692, 60145911p-39001550q,00.htm
16. Mike Ferguson, *Let The Data Flow*, Intelligent Enterprise, March 1, 2006, http://www.intelligententerprise.com/showArticle.jhtml?articleID=179101909&pgno=1
17. John Stelzer, *Moving Beyond EAI and B2Bi*, ebizq.net, December 11, 2005, http://www.ebizq.net/topics/tech_in_biz/features/6557.html?related
18. William A. Ruh, Francis X. Maginnis and William J. Brown, *Enterprise Application Integration: A Wiley Tech Brief*, John Wiley & Sons, 2001
19. Keith Harrison-Broninski, *The Future of BPM*, Role Modellers Ltd., May 11, 2006, http://www.ebizq.net/topics/bpm/features/6860.html?related
20. Paul Allen, *Service Orientation: Winning Strategies and Best Practices,* Cambridge University Press, 2006
21. James McGovern, Sameer Tyagi, Michael Stevens, and Sunil Mathew, *Java Web Services Architecture*, Sun Developer Network (SDN) , July 2003, http://java.sun.com/developer/Books/j2ee/jwsa/

22. Curtis L. Blais, Niki C. Goerger, Paul Richmond, Burhman Gates, MAJ John B. Willis, *Global Information Grid Services and Generation of the Mobility Common Operational Picture*, Proc. of the Simulation Interoperability Work-shop, Orlando, FL: March 2005
23. *Instant Messaging and Presence Protocol (IMPP) – SIMPLE CPIM, IETF*, January 2003, http://tools.ietf.org/html/draft-ietf-impp-cpimmsgfmt-08
24. *Enhanced Telecom Operations Map (eTOM) The Business Process Framework For The Information and Communications. eTOM-B2B Integration: Using B2B Inter-Enterprise Integration with eTOM,* TMF GB921B, March 2004
25. Norbert Bieberstein, Sanjay Bose, Marc Fiammante, Keith Jones, and Rawn Shah, *Service-Oriented Architecture Compass: Business Value, ness Value, Planning, and Enterprise Roadmap,* IBM Press, 2006
26. *Business Transformation Guidance, Version 1.0*, DoD, June 21, 2006, http://www.defenselink.mil/dbt/products/BTG/Business_Transformation_Guidance_(v1.0)_2006-21-06.pdf
27. Sanjiv Rai, *Crossroads & Convergence, The World of Anytime Anywhere Computing*, (ARE) Technologies, http://www.newhaven.edu/unh/pdf/eng/Wireless_Computing_and_Convergence.pdf
28. http://www.tmforum.org
29. http://www.supply-chain.org
30. A.K. Cebrowski, *The Implementation of Network-Centric Warfare*, Office of Force Transformation, Office of the Secretary of Defense, January 2005, http://www.oft.osd.mil/library/library_files/document_387_NCW_Book_LowRes.pdf

Index